D0549128

Ethics in Counseling and Psychotherapy

Standards, Research, and Emerging Issues

Ethics in Counseling and Psychotherapy

Standards, Research, and Emerging Issues

Elizabeth Reynolds Welfel

Cleveland State University

Brooks/Cole Publishing Company

I(T)P® An International Thomson Publishing Company

Pacific Grove ■ Albany ■ Belmont ■ Bonn ■ Boston ■ Cincinnati ■ Detroit ■ Johannesburg ■ London
Madrid ■ Melbourne ■ Mexico City ■ New York ■ Paris ■ Singapore ■ Tokyo ■ Toronto ■ Washington

Sponsoring Editor: *Eileen Murphy*	Manuscript Editor: *Linda Purrington*
Marketing Team: *Jean Thompson, Christine Davis*	Permissions Editor: *Fiorella Ljunggren*
Editorial Assistant: *Susan Carlson*	Interior Design: *Anne Draus, Scratchgravel Publishing Services*
Production Editor: *Nancy Velthaus*	
Production Service and Typesetting: *Scratchgravel Publishing Services*	Cover Design: *Laurie Albrecht*
	Printing and Binding: *Malloy Lithographing, Inc.*

For more information, contact:

BROOKS/COLE PUBLISHING COMPANY
511 Forest Lodge Road
Pacific Grove, CA 93950
USA

International Thomson Publishing Europe
Berkshire House 168-173
High Holborn
London WC1V 7AA
England

Thomas Nelson Australia
102 Dodds Street
South Melbourne, 3205
Victoria, Australia

Nelson Canada
1120 Birchmount Road
Scarborough, Ontario
Canada M1K 5G4

International Thomson Editores
Seneca 53
Col. Polanco
11560 México, D. F., México

International Thomson Publishing GmbH
Königswinterer Strasse 418
53227 Bonn
Germany

International Thomson Publishing Asia
221 Henderson Road
#05-10 Henderson Building
Singapore 0315

International Thomson Publishing Japan
Hirakawacho Kyowa Building, 3F
2-2-1 Hirakawacho
Chiyoda-ku, Tokyo 102
Japan

Printed in the United States of America

10 9 8 7 6 5 4 3 2 1

Acknowledgment: On page 155, "Exploitation Index" from "The Exploitation Index: An Early Warning Indicator of Boundary Violations in Psychotherapy," by Richard S. Epstein and Robert I. Simon, 1990, *Bulletin of the Menninger Clinic, 54,* 450–465. Copyright © 1990 by the Menninger Foundation. Reprinted by permission of the author.

Library of Congress Cataloging-in-Publication Data
Welfel, Elizabeth Reynolds, [date]–
    Ethics in counseling and psychotherapy : standards, research, and
  emerging issues / Elizabeth Reynolds Welfel.
      p. cm.
    Includes bibliographical references and index.
    ISBN 0-534-34302-3 (alk. paper)
    1. Counseling—Moral and ethical aspects.   2. Psychotherapy—
  Moral and ethical aspects.   I. Title
  BF637.C6W42   1998
  174'.91583—dc21
                                 97-41217
                                    CIP

To F. M.W. — 25 years is not enough.

About the Author

Elizabeth Reynolds Welfel is professor and coordinator of the graduate programs in counseling at Cleveland State University. She has also served on the counseling faculty at Boston College and was a teaching fellow at the University of Minnesota prior to receiving her doctorate there in 1979. In addition to this book, Dr. Welfel has co-authored *The Counseling Process* and has been publishing in the field of professional ethical issues in counseling for nearly 20 years. Her special interests are the process of ethical decision making and the design of ethics education to promote responsible practice. Dr. Welfel's involvement in these topics began when she was a graduate student at the University of Minnesota, doing research on moral and intellectual development in adulthood. Her fascination with the process by which adults sort through moral and intellectual dilemmas in their lives eventually focused on the unique moral dilemmas that the counseling profession presents to its practitioners.

Ethics is in origin the art of recommending to others the sacrifices required for cooperation with oneself.

—Bertrand Russell

 Contents

PART TWO Major Ethical Issues for Counselors 61

4 Competence to Practice: The Foundation for Doing Good and Avoiding Harm 63

5 Confidentiality: Supporting the Client's Right to Privacy 82

6 Informed Consent: Affirming the Client's Freedom of Choice 118

 **Preface**

The goal of this book is to sensitize readers to a wide range of ethical issues in the practice of counseling and psychotherapy and to provide them with resources upon which they can rely to help them deal responsibly with such issues. The book uses the codes of ethics and guidelines of the major professional associations (American Counseling Association, American Psychological Association, National Association of Social Workers, and American Association of Marriage and Family Therapists) to familiarize readers with the fundamental standards for responsible practice, and also includes analysis of the writings of ethics scholars and citations of relevant research. Ethics codes alone do not answer many ethical questions practitioners face, but the writings of scholars and the relevant research can help them respond appropriately to complex and confusing ethical issues not directly discussed in the code. For example, Chapter 7 includes analysis of the ethical considerations in nonerotic touch in counseling and psychotherapy.

The book also presents a new model of ethical decision making and shows its application to a variety of ethical dilemmas. The aim of this model is to guide readers through complex dilemmas in a systematic way. Coping with ethical issues in practice can be an intense emotional experience. The availability of a systematic model for analyzing ethical issues helps practitioners make decisions that are reasoned and client centered even when they feel strong emotions. Numerous cases for discussion are also offered, many of which include extensive analysis using the codes and related literature. Cases for independent analysis are available both in the text and in the supplemental casebook, *Casebook for Ethics in Counseling and Psychotherapy* (Brooks/Cole, 1998). The cases used in this book tend not to have simple answers. Instead, they have been designed to present realistic, complex, and sometimes confusing scenarios that mirror the types of situations counselors may encounter.

Another major goal of the book is to devote comprehensive attention to major ethical issues that confront practitioners—such as confidentiality, informed consent, dual relationships, and competence to practice—and the ethical issues that practitioners experience in special settings. Thus the book addresses the unique concerns of school counselors, community counselors, group and family counselors, researchers, and counselor educators. In addition, the content of the book includes material on emerging ethical issues in counseling and psychotherapy, such as ethics in managed mental health care, forensic practice, and consultation. Because sensitivity to multicultural issues is so crucial in responsible practice, that topic is interwoven throughout many chapters and is discussed in more depth in its own chapter.

Lastly, the book aims to help readers understand the philosophical and historical underpinnings of current ethical standards and to tie ethical standards to important legal rulings and statutes. Such knowledge is especially valuable in situations at the cutting edge of practice. I do not shy away from addressing controversies in the profession, and in these discussions I attempt to provide insight into each side of the argument. My approach to the text is not relativistic, however. The standards of the profession were not arbitrarily determined, and I show readers the reasoning and values underlying those standards.

The Intended Audience

The book has several potential audiences. Masters and doctoral students in counseling and psychotherapy are likely to be the primary audience, but the book will also be useful to professionals seeking to extend their knowledge about ethical decision making, to advanced undergraduate students, and to graduate students in related professions such as pastoral counseling and educational psychology. Consumers of psychotherapeutic services may also find its contents helpful in their search for a responsible professional. Its comprehensive approach to the subject matter and its inclusion of codes of ethics as appendixes make it appropriate for use as the main text in courses in professional ethics or professional issues courses. The book contains an extensive reference list and recommended readings for each chapter, so readers who want to explore the ethics scholarship in greater depth are directed to the proper resources.

The Structure of the Book

The book contains four parts. Part One provides a framework for understanding ethical decision making and gives readers a grasp of the process and procedures for redressing ethical violations by mental health professionals. In this section I describe the relationship of professional ethics in counseling to the broader discipline of ethics, integrate relevant literature from developmental psychology, and present a new model of ethical decision making. Part Two reviews the fundamental ethical issues for counselors and therapists, including the ethics of competence to practice, confidentiality, informed consent, dual relationships, responsible assessment, and multiple-person therapies. It ends with an extended discussion of the ethical issues in counseling in a multicultural society. Ethical issues in special settings are the focus of Part Three. Its topics include the ethics of supervision, teaching, research, community practice, forensic activities, consultation, and school counseling. This portion of the book deals most extensively with the emerging ethical dilemmas in the profession, such as the ethical dimensions of managed care and therapy mandated by the courts. Part Four, the final section, deals with an often neglected topic—the ethical responsibilities of those who recognize that they have violated the ethical standards of their profession. Because self-monitoring and personal accountability are at the core of the profession's values, the book discusses the steps professionals can take to redress their own misconduct and to reduce the likelihood that mistakes will recur. In that way, it is unique among the professional ethics books currently published. Each of the 16 chapters also includes a set of questions for further discussion and a list of recommended readings.

The chapters are presented in a logical order, but readers who choose to follow a different sequence will not be at a disadvantage. Also, those who find particular chapters irrelevant to their purposes may omit that material without compromising their comprehension of other parts of the book.

Because I refer repeatedly to the current codes of ethics of the American Counseling Association and the American Psychological Association, I have omitted the dates of their publication in all but their first citations. Continuous use of the publication dates would serve no useful purpose. I do, however, place dates with any other version of the ethics codes that I mention in the book.

Acknowledgments

I wish to thank the many individuals who assisted me in this project. My students and colleagues at Cleveland State have encouraged me, offered valuable insights into the content, and often taken on extra work to free me to make a full commitment to this book. Carl Rak deserves special recognition for his support, as does Lew Patterson, without whose mentoring I would not have had the courage or the skill to embark on so ambitious a task. My graduate assistants, Paula Danzinger and Marcia Lara, have done yeoman service well beyond their official requirements. Their long hours in the library and surfing the Web for relevant literature were crucial to the successful completion of the project. The following reviewers offered perceptive and extensive feedback on the chapters: Linda Forrest, Michigan State University; Rodney Goodyear, University of Southern California; Peter Maynard, University of Rhode Island; Maggie Miller, Boise State University; Richard S. Sharf, University of Delaware; and Rita Sommers-Flanagan, University of Montana. Their careful attention to the manuscript has significantly improved the book.

The editorial staff at Brooks/Cole provided just the right combination of support and challenge for the project. I owe a special debt to Eileen Murphy, counseling editor, and Nancy Velthaus, production editor, who were delightful to work with. I also thank Anne Draus of Scratchgravel Publishing Services and Linda Purrington, copy editor, for their attention to the many last-minute details in production.

Most of all I extend my thanks to my family—to my spouse, who always provided a calm and thoughtful response to my frequent worries about the progress of the book, and to my son, who sacrificed countless hours of computer games at the machine we shared and who always knew the right moments to say, "Keep writing, Mom; this book will be worth it in the end." He was right.

Elizabeth Reynolds Welfel

PART ONE

A Framework for Understanding Professional Ethical Standards

1

Introduction to Professional Ethics
The Need for Standards and Personal Accountability

Counselors, psychologists, social workers, and other therapists make some audacious claims. They assert that they are so skilled at helping people with their personal problems that they deserve to be licensed or certified by the state and that they have the right to fair payment for their helping services. Moreover, they claim that the state should prevent other individuals without their training or credentials from offering the same services for pay. Apparently, this argument has been quite convincing because currently, all 50 states license psychologists and social workers, and 40 states license professional counselors for independent practice. With this public pronouncement of special competence to help people in need, counselors and psychotherapists offer hope to those confused, distressed, or traumatized. They advertise counseling as a process wherein people can learn to think more clearly, act in more self-enhancing ways, and feel better.

This hope cannot be a false hope. Otherwise, counselors are little different than the "snake oil" salespeople who sold false cures to desperate, gullible people without sufficient education to understand the nature of their ailments or the absurdity of the claims they were hearing. Counselors' claims of relief from pain must be based on scientific evidence of effective therapeutic methods and on the skill, judgment, and compassion of the counselor to carry out those methods to a good result for the client. Thankfully, mental health professionals can point to a large body of research that demonstrates the effectiveness of counseling and psychotherapy if conducted properly (for example, see Bergin & Garfield, 1994; Seligman, 1995; Sexton, Whiston, Bleuer, & Walz, 1997). That audacious claim, then, is based in fact, and under the right circumstances, counselors can deliver on their pledge.

In essence, then, professional ethics is about being confident one has the correct combination of attributes to alleviate human distress as promised. Specifically, ethics encompasses four dimensions:

1. having sufficient knowledge, skill, and judgment to use efficacious interventions
2. respecting the human dignity and freedom of the client

3. using the power inherent in the counselor's role responsibly
4. acting in ways that promote public confidence in the profession of counseling

Pared down to those four essentials, acting ethically sounds simple. The first necessary ingredient seems to be a quality graduate and continuing education so that one is knowledgeable. Most states require counselors and therapists to pass a licensing examination and to have supervised work experience as an extra assurance of their knowledge. The other components of ethical counseling are consideration of the client's needs and rights as the highest priority, avoidance of the temptation to advance oneself at the cost of the client, and transaction of one's business in a way that peers and the public cannot disparage. In practice, however, determining the combination of factors that will render counseling most effective, most respectful of the client, and most in keeping with the good reputation of the profession is much more complicated. Sometimes little is known about which interventions will really be helpful, and at other times, even interventions with demonstrable effectiveness fail with a given person. In a rapidly changing profession such as counseling, keeping knowledge and skills current is a difficult task. If the counselor has neglected to keep up with the literature or lacks thorough training in a given population, is effective service being provided? How current does one's knowledge need to be to do effective counseling?

Similarly, when counselors honor the dignity of the individual by giving clients free choices about their lives, clients sometimes make choices that are not in their own best interest. Naturally, when the client introduces a counterproductive choice into the conversation, the counselor discusses it with the client and works to help the client see the likely consequences. Sometimes this review of the impact of the choice changes the client's mind. At other times, the counselor's perspective has no effect. Is the counselor really respecting the client's dignity if she limits her intervention to a discussion of the alternatives or a recommendation to take another route? Is it preferable for the counselor to use his power to limit a client's freedom by preventing the client from making a choice that will probably be regretted later? Is that an abuse of power or an appropriate extension of counselor influence? How do cultural factors influence the determination of which choices are in a client's best interest and which are not?

Finally, sometimes the very actions that help individual clients are actions that the public does not understand and that cause ordinary citizens to view professional helpers with a skeptical eye. For example, counselors are legally and ethically bound to maintain the confidentiality of the disclosures of an accused criminal (if that person is in an ongoing counseling relationship) unless the client releases them from their obligation or a court orders them to reveal this information. This refusal to betray the client's trust often dismays the public. People feel bewilderment and frustration with the professional's behavior. Does this loyalty to the client result in greater or lesser public confidence in the profession? This, too, is not a simple matter. Thus, living one's professional life in accordance with these principles is more complicated than it seems. Fortunately, there are a number of resources to help counselors wrestle with these issues.

Literature from Developmental Psychology

The first resource is the abundant literature on morality and moral reasoning. This literature helps counselors understand professional ethics and ethical decision making as a subset of the broader category of morality and moral decision making. It places professional rules for conduct into a context of fair, decent, and responsible human behavior and provides a framework for explaining what has gone wrong in the ethical decision-making process when ethical violations occur. Unlike other resources that focus on the content a person should consider to deal with an ethical question, the literature from developmental psychology gives a framework for conceptualizing the internal process of ethical decision making. It gives a view of the psychology of ethics. From this information, counselors derive methods to improve the quality of their own ethical decision making and find better ways to teach ethics to students and practitioners.

Components of Moral Behavior

When a person faces a moral or ethical decision, what provokes him or her to behave morally or immorally? Counselors often raise this question when they hear of a courageous or outrageous act by another human service professional. Rest (1983) has provided a useful framework for understanding that process. First, he defines a moral action as any behavior that can affect the welfare of another. For instance, if a person observes someone attempting to break into a neighbor's home, what he or she does when watching this attempted burglary is defined in moral terms because it affects the neighbor's well-being. (Of course, the would-be robber's actions also have a moral dimension, for the same reason.) If the person engages in an action that may benefit the neighbor, such as calling the police or yelling out the window to scare the burglar away, then that action is moral. Clearly, any action may backfire and the police may not arrive or the robber may ignore the call, but that is not the criterion for determining morality. What makes the action moral is that one makes a good-faith effort to help the neighbor. Conversely, if one did nothing and ignored a neighbor's welfare, that action could not be labeled *moral* unless the individual were endangered in some way by this burglar. We are not required by morality to risk our own welfare for another. That's why we label as heroes people who risk their own safety to help others; they have gone beyond their moral duty to ensure another's well-being.

Rest identifies four components of moral behavior that must take place if a moral action is to result—that is, before anyone can engage in an act intended to benefit the neighbor. The first of these is called *moral sensitivity,* the process of recognizing the situation as one with implications for the welfare of another. In the situation just described, it's possible that a person could see this intruder trying to break the lock on the neighbor's front door and think about the burglar's expertise, or lack thereof, with the crowbar. In these thoughts, one might even criticize or applaud the burglar's approach while silently watching the spectacle unfold. Or a person could feel pity for this neighbor who just lost her job, but then feel grateful that the burglar did not choose one's own home. Such a reaction suggests an assumption of no responsibility to intervene on behalf of the neighbor and exclusive concern with one's own welfare. If these responses occurred, Rest would say that the person lacks moral sensitivity, because he or she failed to recognize a moral responsibility to act to help the neighbor. In other words, the person is not sensitive to the moral meaning of what is occurring. Similarly, some people cheat on their income tax returns and brush it off as a common practice with no moral dimension. They also lack moral sensitivity, according to Rest.

Translated into professional ethics, moral sensitivity means realizing the implications of one's behaviors on clients, colleagues, and the public. If a counselor at a social gathering repeats a funny story about a client, perhaps she just did not consider the welfare of the client before she spoke. This person has missed the moral meaning of her action. She did not need to have a malicious *intent* to act immorally. Immoral actions frequently result from distraction from the moral implications of actions, too.

To illustrate in another way, consider the case of Mitchell, the counselor, and Maria, his teenage client:

Mitchell decides not to explain the limits of confidentiality at the start of counseling because he considers that material bureaucratic and distracting from the client's real purpose for coming. He does not intend to cause any harm to his clients and actually intends to serve a good purpose by immediately focusing on the "issue at hand." One day at the beginning of a session, Maria tells Mitchell that she has suicidal thoughts, mistakenly assuming that *everything* she says to a counselor is confidential. In reality, if a counselor believes a client to be at significant risk for suicide, he or she is obligated by the ethics code and (and usually the law) *not* to keep this material confidential. Maria's status as a minor obligates the counselor to consider her parents' rights too. When Mitchell explains the limits of confidentiality to Maria after she has already blurted out her secret, she now feels even more alone and betrayed, outcomes that are clearly detrimental to her already compromised welfare. She feels her lack of knowledge about the parameters of confidentiality robbed her of the choice of whether or when to disclose this private material.

Thus, Mitchell's notion that explaining the limits of confidentiality to a client is merely "bureaucratic" shows his moral insensitivity and resulted in unethical behavior. Obviously, sharing suicidal thoughts with a counselor can ultimately benefit a client. Counselors have an ethical duty to encourage clients to express such thoughts. However, when the client does not understand the implications of this disclosure, feelings of betrayal occur and can extinguish trust. The suicidal impulse may escalate. No such negative consequences ensue when the client discloses such information after building trust in the counselor and gaining some understanding of what may happen after such a revelation. A skillful and compassionate counselor can help a client build trust and elicit the issues of greatest concern.

Rest's second component of moral behavior is *moral reasoning*. Moral reasoning is the process of thinking through the alternatives, once a situation has been recognized as having moral dimensions. At first glance, this component sounds like a methodical, logical process, but it typically takes place rapidly and without great deliberation. It has an emotional as well as a cognitive aspect. When a person sees a burglar at a neighbor's door, one must act quickly so the process of thinking about what action would really benefit the neighbor is completed in seconds. Sometimes only one alternative comes to mind: Perhaps—call the police. At other times, the person weighs the merits of two or more alternatives such as going outside, calling another neighbor, or getting the gun kept for protection in the bedroom. Moral reasoning is the process of evaluating the choices and deciding which is best.

The research by Kohlberg (1984), Gilligan (1982), and others suggests that not all people reason about moral issues in the same way or with the same moral maturity. In fact, these researchers posit stage models of moral development based partly on biological maturity and partly on social experience. How people determine what is the most moral action differs according to their level of moral development, age, culture, and life experience. Some research suggests that counselors at higher stages of moral development make ethical decisions more in keeping with the standards of the profession (Welfel & Lipsitz, 1983), but other studies contradict this finding (Doromal & Creamer, 1988; Royer, 1985).

According to Rest, the third component of morality is *deciding to carry out the moral alternative*. Once a person has evaluated the options and determined which is most moral, then that person must decide whether to go forward. For example, a counselor may have observed a colleague whose behavior with clients is inappropriate. The colleague may be missing appointments, forgetting necessary paperwork, and showing signs of intoxication at work. The counselor recognizes this as a moral dilemma for herself because the welfare of clients, the practice, and the counseling service are at stake. The ethics codes also identify this as her ethical responsibility (American Counseling Association [ACA], 1995, Section H.2; American Psychological Association [APA], 1992, Sections 8.04, 8.05). She has weighed the moral alternatives and has concluded that the best course of action is confronting the colleague and insisting that he get help for his problems and improve his behavior with clients.

Essentially, the counselor asks herself, "Will I *choose* to do that which I now *know* is the right thing to do?" If she answers affirmatively, the counselor is one step closer to a moral action, but if not, then no moral action will take place. At this point competing values may interfere. Moral values are not the only values operating in a person, and values that compete with ethics may take priority. Self-interest is one such value. The counselor may realize that if the dysfunctional colleague deteriorates even further, he may leave the practice, resulting in more clients and more income for her. Or the counselor may value harmony in the workplace more than ethics and may decide not to risk internal conflict among the staff. Or the counselor may regard financial security higher than morality and decide to leave things as they are, for fear of losing a job. In short, this is the point in the process where the power of the counselor's moral values are tested against other values. If the moral values win, then the counselor decides to act responsibly. Research has found that when presented with hypothetical ethical situations, graduate students in psychology indicate that they *would* do what they know they *should* do approximately 50% of the time (Bernard & Jara, 1986). Practicing psychologists do somewhat better. In a related study, Bernard, Murphy, and Little (1987) found that at least two-thirds of the psychologists chose the ethical value. Two other studies (Smith, McGuire, Abbott, & Blau, 1991; Wilkins, McGuire, Abbott, & Blau, 1990) reported a similar pattern. These statistics show how strong competing values can be.

Of course, ethical decision making is not always fully conscious. Counselors often experience cognitive dissonance when choosing not to carry out the most responsible choice. Because counselors like to view themselves as ethical, their dilemma becomes how to remain good and ethical if they are rejecting the ethical choice. To reduce their mental discomfort, they sometimes redefine the problem. In the case of the intoxicated colleague, the counselor might reinterpret the behaviors she sees and hypothesize that the colleague is not really drunk or that the missed appointments are not as frequent as they seem. She may even convince herself that this colleague is on medication that affects his behavior. Of course, that may be true, but when the counselor's goal is to extricate herself from the ethical responsibility, the hypothesis is not tested and the facts of the case are not explored. Instead, she rationalizes, and thus her definition of her ethical responsibility has changed and her need to act declines. With this distortion of the facts, the counselor gets to avoid painful confrontation with the colleague and still view herself as ethical. This kind of self-deception is probably fairly common. The research of Wilkins et al. (1990) also shows that mental health professionals deviate from the ethical value more frequently when the law or code governing the issue is not clear.

If the counselor works in an environment that places a high priority on ethics and professionalism, the risk of self-deception is reduced. Counselors in supervisory positions facilitate responsible behaviors when they make it known to their subordinates that ethics truly matter and that employees will be rewarded and not punished for taking an ethical path. In business, such leadership is called "creating an ethical culture in the organization." The competing values have less pull then, and the person who pursues the ethical action is likely to be supported and not isolated.

Social and political factors also affect a person's capacity to make an ethical choice. Social norms sometimes render ethical action more difficult. A college student may believe that he or she ought to intervene to assist a gay student who is being harassed, but may not do so because of fear of social alienation. For the same reason, a citizen in a small, homogeneous community may vote for legislation he or she thinks is morally wrong.

Cultural definitions of what is ethical also vary (Pedersen, 1995). The high priority given to individual autonomy in Western cultures is not universally endorsed by other societies. Thus, culture affects not just the values that compete with ethical values but the very definition of what is ethical to some extent. (A later chapter will discuss the dilemma of a client whose parents have arranged a marriage that he does not want but which his cultural and religious tradition makes it difficult for him to refuse.)

Implementing the moral action is the final component of the process in Rest's model. One must actually carry out the moral action. Doing so typically requires virtues such as character, integrity, and moral courage. People who lack these characteristics may change their minds or withdraw before implementing the action or when they encounter resistance. In the case described in the last section, the counselor may express her concerns about the colleague's behavior, but if she receives an angry response or a revelation about personal troubles, she may back down and not ask him to stop drinking at work. A moral action cannot take place if it is not implemented. Sometimes, persevering with the moral plan is uncomfortable and has personal costs. That's where integrity and character are critical. Keeping one's eyes on the goal and on the welfare of clients in spite of other pressures is often a difficult task. Again, working with other professionals who are committed to the ethical ideals of the profession eases the difficulty of implementing the moral action.

Codes of Ethics

The second resource for ethical decision making is the code of ethics of the professional association. These codes have a variety of names, but they all specify the rules of conduct for members. Licensed professional counselors and school counselors can rely on the *Code of Ethics and Standards of Practice* of the American Counseling Association (1995), psychologists on the *Ethical Principles* of the American Psychological Association (1992), and social workers on the *Code of Ethics* of the National Association of Social Workers (1993). Because many counselors are members of more than one professional association, they often can refer to two or more of these codes of ethics to give them guidance through ethical dilemmas. In addition, professional associations supplement the codes with casebooks (Herlihy & Corey, 1996), commentary (Canter, Bennett, Jones, & Nagy, 1994), and guidelines for practice related to specific populations that have come to their attention. For example, the American Psychological Association has published ethical guidelines for providing services to culturally diverse populations (APA, 1993b) and for conducting telephone therapy (APA Ethics Committee, 1995a). Similarly, one division of the American Counseling Association, the American School Counselors Association (ASCA), has endorsed a code of ethics for school counselors (ASCA, 1992) that focuses exclusively on that work setting. Other divisions have similar specialized codes, and a sampling of these is contained in Appendix D. In addition to the national societies for these professions, state organizations also exist. These state organizations almost always adopt the national organization's code, but they tend to have their own ethics committees. In this way, professionals who join the state organization, but not the national one, are still subject to the national standards for practice.

These codes represent the official statements of the professions about what is expected of members, and all members are held accountable for actions that violate the code. Each professional association has established an ethics committee and empowered it to enforce its code. The American Counseling Association first published its code of ethics in 1961 and has revised it four times since (most recently in 1995). The American Psychological Association produced its first code in 1953 and published revisions in 1959, 1981, and 1992. The three most recent revisions of the NASW code took place in 1990, 1993 and 1996. The task of revising a code is onerous, and ethics committees usually begin compiling information for the next revision almost as soon as the latest version is adopted.

The intent of the code is to guide the professional through the most common pitfalls in practice and to identify the ethical goals of the profession. Thus, codes of ethics define prescribed (required) activities of counselors, such as explaining the benefits and risks of counseling to clients, as well as prohibited activities, such as having a sexual relationship with a current client. Codes also define the conditions under which certain other behaviors are permissible. For example, the ACA and APA codes both elaborate on the circumstances under which a professional can accept barter rather than money for services (ACA, 1995, Section A.10.c; APA, 1992, Section 1.18). Moreover, codes include "aspirational statements" that clarify the fundamental ethical values of the profession. For example, ACA's code (1995) states in its Preamble, "Association members recognize diversity in our society and embrace a cross-cultural approach to support the worth, dignity, potential and uniqueness of each individual" (p. 1). Codes of ethics are frequently included in regulations governing the practice of counseling and psychotherapy practice in the states. Thus, a licensed counselor is accountable not only to the professional association but also to the state licensing board. In other words, acting unethically automatically violates the laws in a number of states. All members of a professional association are thereby obligated to be familiar with the published codes and guidelines and to act accordingly. Ignorance of the codes does not excuse problematic behavior. The professions assert that if practitioners are benefiting from their professional identity, they have a duty to know and respect ethical standards.

Advantages and Limitations of Codes of Ethics

For the individual practitioner, the major contribution of a code is the support it gives the professional faced with a potential ethical dilemma. A prudent counselor always asks what the code states about an issue. Often a review of the code shows the counselor the responsible action, and no further deliberation is necessary. No code of ethics provides a blueprint for resolving all ethical issues, but codes represent the best judgment of one's peers about common problems. The existence and enforcement of codes of ethics also demonstrate that counselors take seriously their responsibility to protect the public welfare, thus enhancing the reputation of the profession and minimizing the damage done by irresponsible practitioners. The lengthy process of obtaining input from members about new revisions of the code and educating them about those changes keeps the code in the limelight so that members are frequently reminded of its importance. The inclusion of statements of aspirational ethics also furnishes members with a definition of what their colleagues consider the ethical ideal.

Codes also have limitations. First, the members of a professional organization typically work in diverse settings and engage in different activities. Some are primarily therapists, others are teachers, and still others are researchers or consultants. The populations served also differ dramatically. This diversity means that the code must be written broadly. Its application to any one setting is necessarily limited. Second, because the profession changes rapidly, with new forms of practice and new populations emerging constantly, codes are outdated as soon as they are published, despite the best efforts of their writers. Codes, therefore, do not address cutting-edge issues (Mabe & Rollin, 1986) such as human immunodeficiency virus (HIV) infection, and counselors wrestling with dilemmas related to new forms of practice must find other support. In addition, codes are developed within organizations that also have other values and priorities, so that the resulting documents sometimes represent what the board of directors can agree to, rather an ethical ideal. For example, the first 15 drafts of the 1992 APA code banned all sexual intimacies with former clients, but the version that the governing body approved allowed sexual contact with former clients after two years under certain conditions. Gabbard (1994) regards this change as a result of compromise and self-interest rather than concern about the public welfare. The self-interest of professional associations also dilutes to some degree the firmness of other statements in the codes. Bersoff (1994), for example, has criticized the 1992 APA code as a document of "moral compromise" that "at best builds an ethical floor but hardly urges us to reach for the ceiling" (p. 385). Payton's (1994) critique is even harsher: "All previous codes seemed to have been formulated from a perspective of protecting consumers. The new code appears to be driven by a need to protect psychologists" (p. 317).

Most important, though, codes of ethics are not cookbooks for responsible behavior. Largely because of the limitations already mentioned, they provide unmistakably clear guidance for only a few problems. For example, there is no doubt about the prohibition of a sexual relationship with a current client. The codes state that it is *never* appropriate. To quote section A.7 of the ACA code, "Counselors do not have any type of sexual intimacies with clients" (p. 1). In parallel fashion, the requirement for all counselors to do some work without payment (pro bono) is just as clear (see Section A.10.d. of the ACA code). For many other issues, though, the guidance is not so clear. The following situation illustrates the help a code typically provides:

Ms. Harks serves on a civic committee with Dr. Remmard, a licensed mental health counselor, and approaches him for help with depressive feelings. She says that she feels comfortable with him now that she's gotten to know him on this committee and hears that Dr. R. has a good reputation in the community. May the counselor accept her into counseling while they are serving together on the committee?

The codes address this matter but do not make the decision clear cut. (Note that the term *dual relationship* means having a second kind of relationship with a client in addition to the counselor–client relationship). The ACA code states in section A.6,

> Counselors make every effort to avoid dual relationships with clients that could impair their professional judgment or increase the risk of harm to clients. (Examples of such relationships include, but are not limited to, familial, social, financial, business, or close personal relationships with clients.) When a dual relationship cannot be avoided, counselors take appropriate professional precautions such as informed consent, consultation, supervision, and documentation to ensure that judgment is not impaired and no exploitation occurs. (p. 1)

The APA code similarly urges avoiding relationships that compromise objectivity and risk harm to the client (Section 1.17). The counselor must interpret the relevant code and apply its provisions. The code does supply the questions the counselor must ask, such as, Is this a social or close personal relationship? Can I avoid it? If I cannot, how do I ascertain that I will be objective with a client whom I see periodically in another setting? The code even gives recommendations for responding to the last point. However, in the end, Dr. Remmard must sort out the ethical considerations and use his best judgment. The counselor must deliberate about the nature of the connection with this woman and the degree to which objectivity may be compromised and the client's best interests served. The client's access to other qualified counselors is also a factor to consider. To adapt a phrase from Harry Truman, the buck always stops with the counselor.

On other ethical issues, the code provides even less guidance. Consider a counselor who works primarily with children and adolescents. This professional needs support in determining how much material from counseling must be shared with parents and guardians and what the disclosure of that material means to the progress of the counseling relationship with the child. Here is what the ACA code includes on this topic:

> When counseling clients who are minors or individuals who are unable to give voluntary, informed consent, parents or guardians may be included in the counseling process as appropriate. Counselors act in the best interests of clients and take measures to safeguard confidentiality. (Section B.3)

These statements are very general and say only that inclusion of parents or guardians is not prohibited and that the criterion for determining when to disclose is the broad principle of acting in the client's best interest. This is a broad-brush approach and provides relatively little help to a counselor struggling with an adolescent client who feels alienated from his parents and wants the counselor to keep his violation of curfew and experimentation with alcohol secret from his parents. The APA code makes even less reference to this topic in Section 5.01: "Psychologists discuss with persons and organizations with whom they establish a scientific or professional relationship (including, to the extent feasible, minors and their legal representatives) (1) the relevant limitations on confidentiality" and in Section 5.05 "(a) Psychologists disclose confidential information without the consent of the individual only as mandated by law or where permitted by law for a valid purpose." Here, the burden of analyzing ethical issues falls squarely on the professional and requires careful reasoning to ferret out the best solution. The counselor must turn to other resources to guide this decision-making process.

In short, ethics codes do not always simplify ethical decision making and cannot provide easy answers to complex questions. They serve instead as the critical starting point for developing independent judgment. Counselors who ignore them do so at their own peril; counselors who view them as the prescription for all ethical issues are equally at risk.

Literature from Philosophy

The third resource for making responsible ethical judgments is the growing body of literature that ties professional ethics to philosophers' writings on ethics and explains the philosophical underpinnings of the ethics codes adopted by the professions. This scholarship defines the ethical principles and theories that form the rationale for the specific statements in the codes. In essence, these writings connect the standards for professional conduct to the wisdom of the ages and are most frequently of use in coping with the most thorny and confusing ethical dilemmas.

Consider the following situation of Annette, the counselor, and Archie, her client:

Archie, a 17-year-old, tells his high school counselor in a counseling session that the claim he made of recent sexual abuse by his stepfather is not true. He now says that he fabricated the story because he wanted his mother to throw his stepfather, who has punched her many times, out of the house. Archie made the statements about abuse to his coach, who reported them to authorities.

Should Annette maintain confidentiality if the client does not agree to release this information? The counselor here is in a true ethical dilemma because there are potentially harmful consequences no matter what she does. The welfare of the boy, his mother, and his stepfather are all at stake. Reference to the ethics codes does not resolve the question, although it does provide some relevant information. The codes stress the importance of confidentiality as a protection of the client's right to privacy and indicate an exception to that right when laws demand and in situations of clear and imminent danger to the client or others. The codes first inform the counselor that the decision to violate confidentiality should not be taken lightly and then broadly define the exceptions. Does the law require disclosure? Consultation with an attorney may be necessary to answer that question. Is there a clear and imminent danger? There would be if the boy were talking of shooting the stepfather or committing suicide because he felt so hopeless. But is subjecting the stepfather to an investigation by children's services, and possibly causing the stepfather to leave the home, the same kind of danger? If criminal charges were brought against the stepfather and he faced incarceration, would that be clear and imminent danger? Is it Annette's responsibility to bring this information to the investigators from children's services, or is it their responsibility to ascertain the facts of the case? Is disclosing the confidential information ethical if it results in the boy terminating the counseling relationship at a time when he is in real psychological distress and feels alienated from his family? Should the boy's age influence in any way the counselor's decision? Does the fact that he is nearing the age of maturity make a difference?

In this situation, the counselor needs more information than the codes provide. An understanding of how philosophers conceptualize and prioritize ethical obligations can shed light on the problem and provide more structure to the decision-making process. (We will return to this case in the next chapter.) As Chapter 2 also describes in detail, the ethics codes spring from several ethical principles. By thinking through these ethical principles, counselors can better evaluate their options in such complex situations. For example, Beauchamp and Childress (1989) and Kitchener (1984) suggest that five ethical principles underlie professional codes of conduct in human service and medical professions. These principles include respect for autonomy, beneficence (the obligation to do good), nonmaleficence (the avoidance of harm), fidelity to promises made, and justice. In confusing dilemmas, counselors should weigh the alternatives according to these broader ethical principles.

Philosophers go on to describe another level of ethical reasoning that they term *ethical theories* (Kitchener, 1984). Consideration of ethical theories is needed when the ethical principles do not resolve the problem. As noted above, the next chapter elaborates on both ethical principles and ethical theories in the context of professional practice.

Other philosophers offer an alternative way to think about ethics. They talk not about ethical principles or rules or about ethical problem solving, but about an ethics of virtue. They are not interested so much in how professionals behave as in who they ought to be (May, 1984). This scholarship centers on the qualities professionals should develop and the habits of character they need to reach the profession's goals. Reference to such scholarship keeps the profession's attention not just on the rules of behavior and the criteria for applying those rules, but also on the moral ideals of the profession (Jordan & Meara, 1990; Meara, Schmidt, & Day, 1996).

Research on Professional Ethics

Another important source of information is the counseling literature that examines specific ethical issues in great detail, such as the limits of confidentiality with children and the ethical considerations in advertising counseling services. Over the past 20 years, published materials on ethics have increased dramatically. The authors of this literature are mental health professionals with special expertise in applied ethics. These books and articles are particularly helpful in new and emerging areas of practice where the codes of ethics are less likely to offer specific guidelines for professional conduct. In controversial areas, such as sexual contact with former clients or the limits of confidentiality with HIV-positive clients, these writings give practitioners a sense of the dimensions of the debate and the critical factors that influence experts' views on the issue. These writings are also free from the political and organizational pressures that often influence the content of the ethics codes. They usually encourage professionals to practice in the most responsible way possible.

In the case of Archie, the boy who tells his counselor he lied about sexual abuse, this literature can assist the counselor in several ways. It more fully defines the meaning of "clear and imminent danger" from the code (for example, Swenson, 1997), clarifies the limits of confidentiality with adolescents (Gustafson & McNamara, 1987), and hypothesizes about the likely effects of breaking confidentiality on the future of the counseling relationship (Nowell & Spruill, 1993). Used in conjunction with the codes and ethical principles, these resources can guide the counselor to resolutions of ethical problems in keeping with professional standards. In essence, this literature offers the counselor an opportunity to consult with the best thinkers in the profession on a given ethical issue.

The Scope of Unethical Practice

Ethics scholars have also researched the most common types of ethics offenses and the practitioner characteristics associated with them. This material warns counselors about "red flag" issues and the circumstances under which others have fallen short. Specifically, researchers have studied the pattern of complaints to licensing boards and professional associations, the nature of malpractice suits filed against counselors and psychologists, and the self-reports of professionals in national surveys. In addition, ethics committees publish annual accounts of their activities and the outcomes of the cases they handle (see, for example, APA Ethics Committee, 1996a; Garcia, Salo, & Hamilton, 1995). Moreover, when APA and ACA terminate members for unethical behavior, the committees send notice of the termination to all members along with their dues statements. APA also lists all individuals who have been found guilty of less serious offenses and the punishment that resulted.

From all these data, several important findings emerge. First, although some variation occurs depending on the source of the data, generally the same problems appear across different studies—sexual misconduct, improper practices, and dual relationships. Ethics complaints about psychologists are related primarily to sexual misconduct and other dual relationships, insurance or fee problems, and inappropriate professional practice. Inappropriate practice means working in areas where one is not competent, violating confidentiality, or making fraudulent or misleading public statements (APA Ethics Committee, 1994, 1995b, 1996a). A large percentage of these complaints come to APA after a state licensing board has ruled that the professional violated state regulations. The APA Ethics Committee then investigates and makes a separate ruling on the case.

The complaints to ACA's Ethics Committee also center on sexual misconduct, dual relationships, violations of confidentiality, and inappropriate professional practice (Garcia, Glosoff, & Smith, 1994; Garcia, Salo, & Hamilton, 1995; Smith, 1993). In the early 1990s there was a brief flurry of complaints against supervisors and counselor educators, but this pattern was not sustained in the 1995 data.

The total number of complaints filed each year is small when compared to the number of members of each organization. APA has 87,000 members but opens an average of 90 cases per year, and ACA, with membership of almost 60,000, averages approximately 30 cases annually. Most authors suggest that the actual number of ethical violations is much higher (Pope & Vasquez, 1991; Welfel & Lipsitz, 1984) and that few are reported because clients do not know their rights or do not feel empowered enough to complain, or colleagues knowledgeable about the infraction do not want to get involved.

Malpractice insurers also report sexual misconduct as the major reason for claims against psychologists but cite failure to prevent client suicide and incorrect treatment as ranking close behind. ACA (personal communication, Paul Nelson, October 16, 1995) also finds sexual misconduct and harassment to be the modal type of malpractice claim, representing 26.4% of all claims filed through 1992. Other forms of dual relationships rank next, at 17% of all claims. Following in rank order are breach of confidentiality (15.1%), client suicide (15.1%), and harmful counseling treatment (11.3%). All other reasons amounted to no more than 7% each.

State licensing boards for counselors (Neukrug, Healy, & Herlihy, 1992) indicate that the most common complaint they receive is practicing without a license. Of all complaints, 27% fall into that category. Complaints about sexual misconduct rank second, representing 20% of all complaints.

The 20-year pattern of malpractice claims against social workers shows a significant proportion of claims in two areas: incorrect treatment (18.6% of all claims) and sexual misconduct (18.5% of all claims) (Reamer, 1995). The largest settlements were focused on sexual misconduct, accumulating 41% of the total money paid in claims. The only other category that accounted for more than 10% of the dollars paid was patient suicide (11%). Following the pattern in psychology and counseling, only a small percentage of social workers have malpractice claims filed against them. There are 155,000 members of the National Association of Social Workers, but in the past 20 years only 634 malpractice claims have been filed (Reamer, 1995).

Because ethics complaints and malpractice claims do not provide data about ethical violations that never get reported, researchers have surveyed psychologists and social workers about violations they have engaged in or observed. The most common intentional violation of ethical standards shown by this research involves confidentiality. In one major study of psychologists (Pope, Tabachnick, & Keith-Spiegel, 1987), 8% of the sample indicated that they had discussed a client by name with a friend. More than half admitted that they had also unintentionally violated confidentiality in other ways.

Researchers have tried to determine which professionals are most vulnerable to such misconduct. The goal is to find predictors of unethical behavior so that preventive strategies can be devised. However, studies that examine demographic characteristics of ethics violators have found only one significant correlate: Male therapists and educators are more likely to engage in sexual misconduct than are female therapists (Pope, 1994; Tabachnick, Keith-Spiegel, & Pope, 1991; Thoreson, Shaughnessy, Heppner, & Cook, 1993). In addition, those who engage in sexual misconduct are likely to have done so more than once. No other clear pattern links other forms of unethical practice to demographic or educational characteristics.

Psychologists and counselors have been asked what kinds of ethical dilemmas they face in their work. The focus in this research is not on violations but on the frequency with which practitioners must cope with various ethics issues in the ordinary course of events. They report that the most frequent dilemma is confidentiality and its limits and application in various settings. Specifically, Pope and Vetter (1992) found that 18% of their sample listed this topic more than any other. The other highly ranked categories were blurred, dual, or conflictual relationships (17%); concerns about payment plans, settings, and methods (14%); and problems in academic settings, including teaching dilemmas and concerns about training (8%).

Unfortunately, a national survey of ethical practices of counselors has not yet been published (although a national survey of counselor beliefs about the ethics of a wide range of behaviors has been published; see Gibson and Pope, 1993). Only the most notorious of ethical violations, sexual misconduct, has been studied with a sample of counselors. Thoreson et al. (1993) reported that 1.7% of the male counselors responding admitted sexual misconduct with clients during a professional relationship. However, when sexual intimacies with supervisees and former clients were included, the prevalence rate increased to 17%. In a parallel study, Thoreson, Shaughnessy, and Frazier (1995) found that less than 1% of female counselors reported a sexual relationship with a current client or supervisee, but 4.6% reported engaging in a sexual relationship with a former client or supervisee after the professional relationship ended. Obviously, more research is needed to understand the other kinds of counselor misconduct and the types of ethical issues they face regularly.

The Impact of Unethical Practice

Thirty years ago, scholars characterized counseling and therapy as a benign enterprise; at best it helped, and at worst, it had no effect (Bergin & Garfield, 1994). History has proved that notion wrong. Inadequate, incompetent, or inappropriate counseling and psychotherapy are demonstrably harmful to clients. Doing the wrong things as counselors deepens clients' distress to a degree greater than might have occurred had they not sought professional help (Lambert & Bergin, 1994; Sexton et al., 1997)

As any member of an ethics committee can confirm, unthinking or unscrupulous practitioners can wreak havoc in clients' lives. Although client suicides because of counselor negligence are not frequent, their impact is enormous. Clients who lose their money in unnecessary or unhelpful sessions, or have their reputations damaged by disclosures of confidential information, would also have been better off had they never entered the counselor's office.

Because it is the most prominent violation, much empirical evidence on the negative effects of specific violations is concentrated on sexual contact with clients. Clients of counselors who have sexually exploited them show significant negative effects

(Bouhoutsos, Holroyd, Lerman, Forer, & Greenberg, 1983; Brown, 1988; Williams, 1992). Some have committed suicide or undergone hospitalization related to the therapist's actions, and most others suffer additional psychological distress in addition to their preexisting problem. Research demonstrates that these problems are not simply acute reactions that abate with time. Instead, they tend to be long-lasting and can become chronic. Bates and Brodsky (1989) present a detailed case example of the devastating effects of sexual abuse. Moreover, an experience with one exploitive counselor tends to make clients wary of all mental health professionals and reluctant to seek professional help for mounting problems. Pope (1990a) compares the effects of sexual exploitation by a therapist to the effects of rape or incest.

Unethical behavior causes harm in several ways. It has powerful harmful effects on clients and undermines the willingness of others who could benefit from counseling to seek professional help. Its legal ramifications are substantial: Some counselors end up in civil court in malpractice suits or in criminal court for libel, slander, or abuse (Crawford, 1994). The true frequency of violations is unknown, but it is probably a rare counselor who practices an entire career without a single minor ethical misstep. Ignorance of ethical standards or distraction from the ethical dimensions of practice is likely to cause harm more frequently than can be seen from ethics committee reports or licensing board sanctions. Some professionals appear to make a regular habit of such behavior (Pope et al., 1987).

The incentive for states to license counselors is tied to the evidence that counselors can harm clients. Without licensing, the only body to which counselors are accountable is the professional association to which they belong. Because membership in a professional association is entirely voluntary, those who do not elect to join are not accountable to anyone unless they are regulated by the states. State legislatures (often when encouraged by consumers or professional groups) thus exercise control over mental health professionals that is separate from the professional societies and that has the power of law. Providing this double safeguard of the client confirms and supports the importance of ethical counseling.

Ethics and the Law

Ethics deals with the actions professionals ought to take in relation to each other, to those who seek their services, and to the public. Ethics codes are the standards adopted by national professional associations to govern the definitions of ethical behavior for their members and lay out the penalties for misbehavior. As noted, they also include comments about the profession's ethical ideals and central values. Except in states that include codes of ethics as part of the regulations governing licensing of a professional, codes have power only over those who voluntarily join a professional association. The most severe penalty a professional association can inflict is expulsion from membership.

In contrast, statutes that govern professional practice are enacted by state legislatures, and case law is handed down by the courts of each state. Moreover, laws vary from state to state, but codes apply to the whole membership of a national association. Even when all states have laws governing the same issue, such as child abuse, variations in the exact wording of the laws result in varying interpretations in different jurisdictions. Thus a behavior considered legal in one state may be illegal in another. Violations of the law carry much stiffer penalties than codes, of course, ranging from limitations placed on one's license to practice and vulnerability to being sued, to criminal liability for the most egregious actions.

Ethical standards tend to cover a wider range of behaviors than do laws and generally are written partly to inspire professionals to do their best. Laws deal only with the "do's and don'ts" of practice and tend to describe a threshold level of behavior for professionals. State regulations governing counseling or psychology and the codes of ethics generally show similar content. For instance, most state regulations indicate a duty to avoid discrimination, and codes contain similar wording. However, areas of conflict appear between the guidelines of the code and any given state's regulations. The ethics code of APA comments on this matter as follows:

APA Ethical Principles 1.02   Relationship of Ethics and Law

If psychologists' ethical responsibilities conflict with law, psychologists make known their commitment to the Ethics Code and take steps to resolve the conflict in a responsible manner.

Counselors, then, are encouraged by the professional association to abide by the laws governing their profession. Usually, this guideline is easy to follow, but sometimes counselors believe that what is truly in their client's best interest conflicts with the law. For example, Pope and Bajt (1988) found that 57% of psychologists intentionally violated a law or rule because they believed compliance would injure more than help their clients. The failure to comply with the law can be merely a part of the self-deception that takes place when other values compete with ethics, but, on occasion, the practitioner may feel compelled to act according to a higher standard. Defying the law and/or code is an act of civil disobedience and is a serious matter. Counselors taking this path are still accountable to the state and the profession. One cannot claim immunity from laws and codes even if one considers an action to be a matter of conscience. Thus, any counselor entertaining such an option should consider it carefully and be willing to suffer the full penalty of the law if discovered.

In recent years counselors have expressed increasing concern about being disciplined by licensing boards or being sued by clients. Presentations at professional conferences on avoiding malpractice claims are well attended. Special seminars on legal issues in counseling and psychotherapy have attracted thousands of participants eager to learn the path to a lawsuit-free work life. Between 1993 and 1995 more than 2000 counselors registered for a seminar on legal aspects of counseling (personal communication, Paul Nelson of ACA, October 16, 1995). In other words, attention has been focused on knowing the law as a way to avoid malpractice. Although such knowledge is important, scholars repeatedly tell attendees that the single best way to avoid a malpractice suit or discipline by a licensing board is to know and follow the profession's code of conduct. Acting ethically offers counselors the best protection from legal problems. In this book, the focus is on the ethical guidelines of the profession. Legal issues are also addressed, but starting with legal issues implies more self-interest than devotion to client welfare. By aiming higher to understand the contents of the code and the reasons for the guidelines therein, counselors and the general public gain both ethically and legally.

SUMMARY

Because counselors, psychologists, and social workers boldly claim to be professional helpers, they have a duty to fulfill their promise of help and to protect the public from unscrupulous or unthinking mental health professionals. Acting ethically means being as competent as professed, considering the client's welfare as predominant, using power responsibly, and conducting oneself so as to enhance the reputation of the profession. When faced with an ethical dilemma, a counselor has four primary resources. The first is the literature from developmental psychology, which provides a framework for understanding the components of moral behavior. The second is the code of ethics of the professional association, which includes the standards one's colleagues have set for the profession. Next is the philosophical literature, which can help counselors understand the ethical principles and theories that underlie professional codes of conduct. Finally, counselors can rely on books and articles by their colleagues who are experts in professional ethics. These scholars discuss ethical dimensions of emerging types of practice and debate the critical controversial ethics topics. These resources can guide the professional through many agonizing dilemmas. Ultimately, however, individual counselors must take responsibility for their own actions.

The documentation of unethical behavior shows that sexual contact with clients is a frequent violation for which counselors are brought to ethics committees and court. Other kinds of dual relationships that compromise objectivity also occur repeatedly. Incompetent practice, including violations of confidentiality, negligence in responses to suicidal clients, and inappropriate fees are also recurrent problems. There is little correlation between types of unethical practice and the characteristics of mental health professionals with one exception. Male therapists are more likely than female therapists to engage in sexual misconduct with clients, former clients, students, and supervisees.

Codes of ethics and laws related to counseling and psychotherapy overlap substantially, but some conflicts arise. Moreover, laws seek to eliminate problematic behaviors, whereas codes also define good and desirable behaviors. Sometimes practitioners disregard state laws because they feel compliance would harm their clients. Such civil disobedience should be carried out only after serious deliberation and comprehension of the possible consequences. The best insurance for avoiding legal problems is understanding the codes of ethics and their underlying principles and acting in accordance with them.

DISCUSSION QUESTIONS

1. Only a tiny proportion of unethical practices gets reported. Why do you think this occurs? Does this low level of reporting hurt or benefit the professions?
2. What competing values may be operating when professionals decide to do less than they know they ought to do?
3. The reports of practitioners about the ethical dilemmas they most commonly face in their work do not match the ethical violations reported to ethics boards or used in civil suits. What do you think accounts for this discrepancy?
4. One alternative to the general ethics codes currently published by the mental health professions is a lengthier document that addresses ethics for specific kinds of practice. Should the professions retain the current form of the codes, or change to another format to make them more relevant to specific settings? What advantages or disadvantages would accompany such a change?
5. When ethics codes conflict with laws, the codes indicate that the professional may follow the law. Do you agree with that position? Why or why not?
6. How do you think the professions should deal with professionals who violate codes and laws because they have a different personal morality?

RECOMMENDED READINGS

Canter, M. B., Bennett, B. E., Jones, S. E., & Nagy, T. F. (1994). *Ethics for psychologists: A commentary on the APA Ethics Code.* Washington, DC: American Psychological Association.

Herlihy, B., & Corey, G. (1996). *ACA ethical standards casebook* (5th ed.). Alexandria, VA: American Counseling Association.

Pope, K. S., Tabachnick, B. G., & Keith-Spiegel, P. (1987). Ethics of practice: The beliefs and behaviors of psychologists as therapists. *American Psychologist, 42,* 993–1006.

2

A Model for Ethical Decision Making
Using Resources to Enhance Individual Judgment

The first chapter explained the importance of ethical standards in counseling and psychotherapy, identified a group of resources to guide counselors to responsible ethical decisions, and described ethical pitfalls counselors typically encounter. This chapter presents a systematic model of ethical decision making. The model itself contains nine steps designed to provide a systematic approach to resolving ethical questions. The most complex dilemmas will require completing each step, but the more obvious questions can be dealt with in an abbreviated approach. The model integrates the writings of ethics scholars along with the standards in the professional codes. The chapter begins by clarifying the varying forms of ethical reasoning.

Forms of Ethical Reasoning

Kitchener (1984) has suggested that there are two distinct forms of moral reasoning: intuitive and critical-evaluative. The following sections define these terms and illustrate their roles in ethical decision making.

Intuitive Ethical Judgments

When people make moral judgments, they commonly do so at an intuitive level (Kitchener, 1984). Moral judgments tend to be fairly spontaneous and motivated by factors not clearly in conscious awareness. Either the judgment is based on emotion rather than reason, or the moral rationale is implicit rather than explicit. For example, when reporters interview people who risked their lives to save others, these heroes are notably inarticulate about what made them decide to act so courageously. Many say that the thought of doing anything else never entered their minds. Others say they were not aware of any thoughts at all; they just acted. If pressed, they may generally refer to their upbringing or spiritual beliefs as a fundamental motivation for their behavior. Virtually no one provides a philosophical justification for his or her extraordinary behavior, even after the fact. To apply Rest's model of morality (1983), these heroes had immediate moral sensitivity, used good intuitive moral reasoning, and acted on their commitment to do what they sensed was right.

Needless to say, not all people have such admirable moral intuitions. Those who walk away from people in trouble also tend to be inarticulate about their motivation. The people who failed to respond to Kitty Genovese's cries for help in the famous case from the 1950s just said they did not want to get involved (Cunningham, 1984). Twenty-seven neighbors in her apartment building ignored her repeated pleas for help. No one came outside or even picked up the phone to call the police. She was stabbed to death in the alley outside the building. Similar callousness to others' pain is recorded daily by the media. Moral insensitivity is not limited to the general citizenry, however. The history of the helping professions offers ample testimony to the problematic nature of some professionals' ethical intuitions. For example, in the 1960s and 1970s some mental health professionals (for example, McCartney, 1966) argued that sexual intimacies with clients were good and desirable actions for therapists and that sex with clients constituted a legitimate *treatment* for some disorders! Similarly, in the mid nineteenth century a new medical diagnosis was added to the psychiatric nomenclature, called "drapetomania." It meant running-away-from-home disease and was used to diagnose slaves who tried to run from their masters (Weisskopf-Joelson, 1980). By this definition, any slave who chose freedom over enslavement was considered mentally ill. In these and other cases, professionals either lacked ethical sensitivity or rationalized an unethical act as ethical. Some of this lack of ethical sensitivity related to cultural norms and political pressures at the time. Thus, relying on the intuitions of counselors to guide them to the responsible ethical choice has proved an unwise approach to protecting the public welfare. People's ethical intuitions are uneven and unpredictable at best. Consequently, our profession demands that we be able to *justify* the ethical decisions according to ethical principles we make and show how they fit with accepted standards for moral behavior.

Critical-Evaluative Ethical Judgments

To make adequate ethical decisions on a reliable basis, Kitchener (1984) recommends consciously and deliberately analyzing the ethical issue. This analysis should include considering professional standards, examining the knowledge of ethics scholars, and intensive problem solving based on ethical principles. The analysis must also be grounded in a commitment to virtues that the profession values (Jordan & Meara, 1990). Otherwise, this analysis degenerates into an empty intellectual exercise. Stated another way, analyzing principles centers one's attention on ethical obligations but gives insufficient recognition to the role of ethical ideals (Meara, Schmidt, & Day, 1996).

Kitchener (1984) named this method the *critical-evaluative* level of justifying an ethical decision. When ethical issues are critically analyzed in this way, the public is less vulnerable to the idiosyncratic intuitions of a given counselor. The following model of ethical decision making builds upon the work of Kitchener (1984) and provides a step-by-step method of deliberating about ethical issues. Figure 2.1 graphically represents the model.

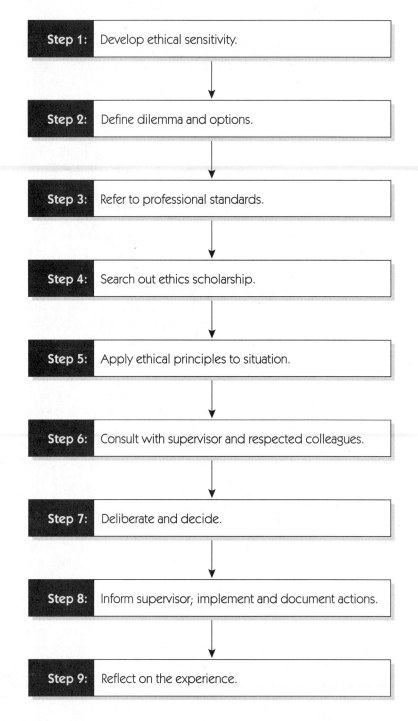

Step 1:   Develop ethical sensitivity.

Step 2:   Define dilemma and options.

Step 3:   Refer to professional standards.

Step 4:   Search out ethics scholarship.

Step 5:   Apply ethical principles to situation.

Step 6:   Consult with supervisor and respected colleagues.

Step 7:   Deliberate and decide.

Step 8:   Inform supervisor; implement and document actions.

Step 9:   Reflect on the experience.

Figure 2.1   A Model for Ethical Decision Making

A Model for Ethical Decision Making

At first glance, this model seems to suggest that ethical decision making is necessarily time consuming and that at the first sign of an ethical issue counselors must immediately go through all steps of this elaborate process. A model that required so much time would be neither realistic nor practical. Counselors do not always have extended periods of time in which to deliberate about ethical problems. Sometimes they must act immediately. For example, a school counselor who sees a teacher supplying correct answers to students during a standardized test must act quickly, or the test results will be invalidated. Even when a counselor need not make an instantaneous decision, there is still pressure to act expeditiously. How do counselors apply the decision-making model in such situations? Quite simply, they comply by having done their ethics homework. Time pressures do not relieve counselors of their responsibility to act ethically. Counselors must have enough background to come to a decision based on more than intuition. Counselors advance the process by being well studied in the ethics codes. Either they already know the contents of the codes, or they remember the relevant section of the code. Similarly, counselors who work in specific settings, such as school counseling, expedite decision making by keeping up with the ethics literature for their setting. Practitioners with this kind of preparation are more likely to act responsibly despite the time pressure. Experience in using the model with hypothetical cases also hastens the process.

There is a second benefit to this preparation and experience. Confronting an ethical dilemma is a highly stressful experience for a counselor. For example, Holland and Kilpatrick (1991) found that their sample of social workers experienced "a poignant sense of loneliness or isolation in their struggle with moral questions" (p. 140). Figuring out how to respond to the dilemma of a teenager who now asserts he was lying about prior disclosures of sexual abuse, for example, is both intellectually challenging and emotionally agonizing. The potential harm from a wrong choice is obvious, and counselors feel tremendous anxiety about their responsibility in such situations. Comprehension of ethics standards, familiarity with the literature, and background in sorting out other complicated dilemmas all help to keep the stress manageable and let the decision making proceed with a clearer head.

Step 1: Become Sensitive to the Moral Dimensions of Counseling

In this era of declining budgets, managed care pressures, and multiple role demands, counselors have many crucial issues to think about—ethics is only one of many concerns. Clients do not always come to counseling willingly, and their problems seem more complex than time, budget, or insurance reimbursement allow for. Much energy is expended to establish rapport with clients and help relieve their distress. Defining potential ethical dilemmas is often the last thing on a counselor's mind during a counseling session. Rest (1984) comments that graduate education often encourages this focus on the technical aspects of the profession and provides little encouragement to see its ethical dimensions. Research confirms that mental health professionals get caught up in the clinical aspects of their work and often disregard even well-publicized ethical problems. Lindsey (1985) and Volker (1983) found that more than one-third of the counselors and psychologists they studied failed to recognize ethical issues in taped simulations of counseling sessions. Instead, the professionals attended to the potential diagnosis of the client, the counselor's skills, and what kinds of interventions would be appropriate with such a client. In fact, a quarter of their samples failed to recognize the ethical issues even when prompted by the researcher in follow-up questions. Using the same measure, Podbelski and Weisgerber (1988) reported that 25% of counseling students failed to recognize the ethical issues. Obviously, three studies do not constitute a definitive body of research, but they do suggest a vulnerability to ethical insensitivity that is important to examine. Combined with the documentation of unethical practices and beliefs discussed in Chapter 1 (see, for example, Gibson & Pope, 1993; Neukrug, Healy, & Herlihy, 1992; Pope et al., 1987; Reamer, 1995), these studies point to a substantial lack of ethical sensitivity among some practitioners.

How can a counselor improve ethical awareness? Ethics scholars have several recommendations. One approach is best summarized by the guideline, "Preparation is everything." The best form of preparation is formal education in ethics. Enrollment in courses that deal with both the content of professional standards and processes for moral decision making heightens the likelihood that counselors will be aware of the ethical dimensions of their practice (Eberlein, 1987; Wilson & Ranft, 1993). Educators obviously endorse this view; the number of ethics courses available over the past 20 years has increased dramatically (Vanek, 1990; Welfel & Hannigan-Farley, 1996; Wilson & Ranft, 1993). After completing graduate school, counselors can foster ethical sensitivity through continuing education and dialogue with colleagues. Especially in complex cases, counselors can benefit from the objective, informed, outside feedback from colleagues. The perspectives of fellow professionals can counterbalance the counselor's sometimes one-sided view. Next, as noted, prior experience in dealing with ethical dilemmas seems to make a counselor more alert when a new ethical issue arises. Therefore, much ethics training focuses heavily on case analysis and class discussion.

Counselors also need insight into their own values and motivation for entering the mental health field. Ethical sensitivity assumes not only knowledge and background in professional ethics but also personal principles and philosophy consistent with the profession. A person motivated exclusively by narrow self-interest has little likelihood of achieving ethical sensitivity. Consistently doing the right thing demands altruistic motives. As Jordan and Meara (1990) suggest, an ethical professional is first a person of virtue. People at the start of their careers ought to frankly assess their reasons for choosing this profession, and people in the midst of their careers should periodically conduct the same kind of self-analysis. Real compassion for human problems and an unwavering commitment to be of service are essential for ethical sensitivity.

Finally, a shift in one's mental set about ethics is needed. Because so much of what is presented about ethical violations deals with sensational cases, many professionals may mistakenly conclude that only those who are unscrupulous or outrageously naive act unethically. A corollary misperception is that ethical dilemmas occur rarely and loudly announce their arrival. Both of these conclusions are mistaken. Instead, counselors need to recognize the commonness, complexity, and subtleties of ethical dilemmas. Without vigilance, even well-intentioned counselors can sometimes end up significantly harming clients. As a practical step to heighten ethical sensitivity, counselors need to establish a protocol for examining the ethical dimensions of every intake and ongoing session. This protocol can prevent the distraction from ethics to which busy practitioners may be vulnerable. The simple step of adding a question about potential ethical issues to the intake form or the outline for case notes may be sufficient to alert the counselor to issues he or she might otherwise miss.

Step 2: Identify the Type of Dilemma and the Alternative Courses of Action

Once a counselor knows that a situation with ethical dimensions exists, he or she needs to organize all relevant case information and identify the broad category of ethical issue this situation represents. Consider Archie's case from Chapter 1:

The Case of Archie

Archie, a 17-year-old, tells his high school counselor, Annette, in a counseling session that the claim he made of recent sexual abuse by his stepfather is not true. He now states that he fabricated the story because he wanted his mother to throw his stepfather, who had punched her many times, out of the house.

Annette's initial task here is to ask herself if all relevant information is available. When the facts of the case are clear, then the counselor attempts to classify the type of ethical issue involved. In this case the main issue deals with the degree of confidentiality a counselor owes a child when the welfare of other family members is also involved. Some situations may present two or more ethical issues. Defining the broad type of problem allows one to utilize the ethics codes and the literature more effectively and helps one access prior training on the topic. Next, the counselor needs to list the potential courses of action that come to mind. Essentially, the counselor brainstorms about the possible ways to approach this situation—naming options without censorship. Evaluating and eliminating options comes later. This brainstorming is important to ensure that the counselor's analysis goes beyond the one or two choices that might emerge from his or her ordinary moral intuition about the situation. In this process, counselors should acknowledge which options are intuitively appealing to them and recognize the ways in which their personal moral values are influencing their professional decision making.

In this case, Annette's alternatives are:

- Tell no one and maintain confidentiality, letting the client the decide what to do next.

- Tell Archie that she needs to break confidentiality to tell his parents, even if he is uncomfortable with this option.
- Call the investigator from children's services in the case, and tell him or her about Archie's disclosure, even if Archie is uncomfortable with this action.
- Encourage Archie to tell someone himself, but do not disclose without Archie's consent.
- Tell Archie that continued counseling is contingent upon his disclosing this information himself or allowing her to do so.

Thus, at the end of Step 2 the counselor has broadly defined the type of ethical dilemma and listed potential responses available. Further reading and consultation may produce additional alternatives, of course, but at least a workable list now exists. In Archie's case, Annette also acknowledges that her moral intuition and ordinary moral values lead her to want to disclose this information to Archie's mother or the social worker investigating the case. She consciously decides not to act on this intuition until she has studied the issue further. Evaluating the merits of each alternative takes place through the next several steps in the process.

Step 3: Refer to the Code of Ethics and Professional Guidelines

Once a counselor identifies an ethical issue and his or her options, the next step is to refer to the code of ethics to determine how it applies. As Chapter 1 discusses, the code indicates that confidentiality is important but is limited by laws, by Archie's status as a minor, and by situations of clear and imminent danger. For many other problems, the dilemma can be resolved at this step, as the following case illustrates:

The Case of Yolanda

Yolanda, a supervisor of counseling interns, has been supervising Justine, an exceptionally skilled and mature intern, for several months. In various friendly conversations during internship meetings, Yolanda has discovered that she and Justine share a number of mutual interests. Both play stringed instruments and ride horses in their free time. Yolanda wants to ask this intern to audition for the open cello seat in the community orchestra to which she belongs and to join her in horseback riding one weekend soon. She wonders if it would be ethical to offer Justine these invitations.

Yolanda shows ethical sensitivity insofar as she recognizes that the behavior she is entertaining may have an ethical dimension (Step 1). Usually such ethical sensitivity comes from ethics education and experience rather than from inherently good intuitions. Organizing the facts of the case is fairly simple because this dilemma came from Yolanda, not from an interaction with a client or colleague. The three facts are clear. First, Justine is under her supervision and will be so until the end of the academic year. Second, Justine may need reference letters from Yolanda from time to time after this year. Third, Yolanda is unlikely to supervise this intern again or be in any other evaluative role with her. Yolanda then identifies the category of ethical issue involved. Yolanda thinks these outside contacts might represent an inappropriate relationship with her intern, a kind of dual relationship, and has identified three possible courses of action (Step 2). The first is to go ahead with the invitations. The second option is to withhold the invitations until Justine's internship is completed, and the last is to ask Justine to do just one of the two activities with her.

The third step in the process is for Yolanda to refer to the ethics code to weigh the merits of her options. The ACA code states:

> Counselors clearly define and maintain ethical professional and social relationship boundaries with their students and supervisees. They are aware of the differential in power that exists and the student's or supervisee's possible incomprehension of the power differential. Counselors explain to students and supervisees the potential for the relationship to become exploitive. (Section F.1.b)

This section of the code has no unmistakable directive but suggests that if Yolanda were to extend the invitations, she would be acting as though she were a colleague or casual acquaintance of Justine's rather than her supervisor. Thus Yolanda would be failing to acknowledge her power over the supervisee. On this basis, Yolanda also reasons that riding together would be the more problematic of the two situations because it would set up a personal relationship that blurs the boundaries in their supervisory relationship. Inviting this intern to audition for the orchestra is a less obvious violation because there is no guarantee that the supervisee would pass the audition, and no one-on-one relationship would necessarily follow if Justine were accepted. However, belonging to the same orchestra could be uncomfortable for Justine, and if the invitation to audition came from Yolanda, Justine might feel she had to impress her supervisor. Justine might also feel that to refuse her supervisor's invitation could negatively impact her professional evaluation. If Justine learned of the orchestra opening in some other way and decided on her own to try out, there would probably be no inherent ethical problem with belonging to the same arts organization, provided Yolanda did not develop a separate personal relationship with her intern during the year of supervision. The final sentence in this section of the code reminds Yolanda that discussing power differences between supervisees and supervisors is her responsibility. So she concludes that she should also initiate discussion of this topic in the next supervision meeting.

Because Yolanda is also an associate member of APA, she consults that ethics code and finds the following statement:

> A psychologist refrains from entering into or promising another personal, scientific, professional, financial or other relationship with such persons [previously defined in the code to include supervisees] if it appears that such a relationship reasonably might impair the psychologist's objectivity or otherwise interfere with the psychologist's effectively performing his or her functions as a psychologist, or might harm or exploit the other party. (Section 1.17)

Here Yolanda finds an even clearer statement of standards. She must not begin a friendship with an intern if it would affect her objectivity about supervision, interfere with her ability to supervise Justine or the other interns in the group, or otherwise take advantage of the supervisee.

Having reviewed both codes, Yolanda decides to refrain from inviting Justine to join her in either social activity, because doing so might make it harder for her to objectively evaluate the student's work and it might send confusing messages to other interns. Moreover, Justine might misunderstand the invitations and may feel awkward in future supervision meetings. The risk of negative effects of outside socialization at a supervisor's initiative seem too great. Yolanda then chooses her third alternative: She will consider a social relationship with this (or any other) intern only after the supervision is completed and she no longer has an evaluative role in the intern's professional development. This point would most likely occur when the intern has graduated from the program.

This case illustrates how carefully interpreting the code of ethics and consulting related codes as necessary can help a counselor resolve an ethical question. When a professional is so familiar with the codes that he or she can immediately locate the appropriate section, a decision can be made quickly. Then the counselor need not complete steps 4 and 5 of the model and can move directly to the last three steps.

The codes of ACA, APA, and NASW differ somewhat. This divergence is a particular problem to those belonging to more than one organization. For example, the ACA code requires counselors to engage in some pro bono work (professional service rendered without fee), whereas the APA and NASW codes only encourage but do not mandate such work. Counselors motivated by narrow self-interest might decide to follow the least restrictive directive. Such a rationale is shortsighted and ignores the aspirational parts of the codes. The wisest course is to abide by the strictest mandate. Doing pro bono work on a regular basis is appropriate within the frame of reference of all three professional associations. Moreover, it is more consistent with the aspirational statements in all three codes.

Counselors also need to be aware of other official statements of ethics committees. From time to time ethics committees publish special guidelines to inform members about emerging ethical issues or to respond to an issue brought to the committee by many members. In 1995, for example, the APA Ethics Committee, in response to reports of increasing use of telephone and Internet conversations as therapeutic interventions, published a statement about telephone therapy (APA Ethics Committee, 1995a). The committee's statement did not represent new ethical standards, but rather an application of current ethical standards to this emerging form of practice. The list of special guidelines and statements, especially from APA, is long and is included in Appendix D of this book. Reference to these resources ties the decision making of practitioners to that of their most knowledgeable colleagues.

Finally, all codes direct counselors to act in accordance with existing laws. This means that the counselor needs to refer to relevant federal and state statutes and regulations governing an issue. Case law, the rulings of courts in cases that come to trial, may also apply. The laws in Yolanda's state may make no special reference to a social relationship between a supervisor and an intern. However, the state's regulations governing licensed counselors may specify that all should abide by the ACA code. Thus, the law too recommends restraining the impulse to extend the boundaries of the relationship with Justine.

Returning to the case of Archie and Annette, the laws about confidentiality with minors differ from state to state. Moreover, even within the same state, statutes and court opinions about confidentiality with minors may be conflicting. So Annette would be well advised to get information about the state's laws. In a number of other situations, both the law and the codes will not be definitive or will be mute on a subject. When that happens, the counselor should move to the fourth step in the process.

Step 4: Search Out the Relevant Ethics Literature

This step involves consulting books and articles by other mental health professionals who have grappled with the same ethical issues. Researching this literature gives the counselor the perspectives of experts and helps the counselor become aware of previously unconsidered aspects of the situation.

In the case of Archie, Annette can locate literature that suggests how to determine the circumstances under which a child's disclosures should be kept confidential (for example, see Gustafson & McNamara, 1987; Melton, 1983). This literature, which is less general than the ethics codes, suggests that the degree of confidentiality that must be maintained is related to the child's maturity (and gives criteria for maturity) and more fully defines the child's best interests (Koocher & Keith-Spiegel, 1990). From this literature, Annette concludes that Archie's age (17) is relevant and that his right to decide to keep disclosures private from his parents is greater than if he were five or six years younger. Other writers provide suggestions for dealing with parents to get them to affirm the privacy of the interactions between counselor and client (for example, see Taylor & Adelman, 1989). Annette decides that immediately communicating his disclosure to parents or investigators would probably fail to acknowledge his age and maturity. Annette concludes that the options that involve breaking confidentiality immediately must be reworded to allow disclosure perhaps after additional discussion with Archie. She is still unsure about whether her other options are ethical. The literature has reminded her about attending to Archie's feelings and has affirmed that her primary responsibility is to him, not his parents. However, she cannot completely disregard his parents' rights and their responsibility for Archie.

The literature on a wide variety of common ethical issues has mushroomed in the past 20 years. The following chapters introduce counselors to the extensive scholarship on issues such as confidentiality, informed consent, dual relationships, diagnosis and testing, group and family counseling, and special ethical concerns for counselors employed in school and agencies. This body of work is a rich resource for counselors who tend to feel vulnerable and isolated in ethical decision making. When they are familiar with this literature, counselors can better justify their decision to superiors, clients or their relatives, or legal bodies and can trace their own reasoning to that of the experts. One can also argue that knowledge of this literature is a necessity, not a luxury, for a competent counselor, especially when dealing with an ethical issue that is common to a population or setting. To function without knowledge of this literature could be seen as acting incompetently, especially now that electronic communication makes published works so easily accessible. Many key writings from this literature are discussed later in this book.

Of course, review of the literature is no panacea for all ethical issues. It will not always be definitive and does not reduce the responsibility of the individual counselor for the choice taken. More often than not, counselors will need to deliberate further about the issue. They will then go to Step 5 in the process.

Step 5: Apply Fundamental Ethical Principles and Theories to the Situation

At this point the counselor grapples with the fundamental philosophical principles in the situation. The professional literature may narrow and clarify the options, but it rarely points to a single path. The counselor who reaches Step 5 without clearly resolving his or her ethical dilemma must now conduct a more intensive analysis of the issues and rely on the philosophical literature and then on consultations with trusted colleagues. These are the same philosophical principles that underlie the codes of ethics. By thinking in terms of basic ethical principles, counselors can bring "order and coherence" to the discussion of particular cases (Beauchamp & Childress, 1989, p. 1). In addition, by understanding ethical principles, counselors can better see the patterns among different cases and seemingly unconnected situations. Building on the work of Beauchamp and Childress (1983) and Drane (1982), Kitchener (1984) has identified five primary ethical principles governing human service professions. None of these principles is absolutely binding. For example, counselors may commit a person to a hospital if that person is endangering him- or herself or others. Involuntary commitment violates autonomy but serves a greater good of protecting human life. Most philosophers describe ethical principles as *prima facie binding,* which means that they are binding in all situations except when in conflict with equal or greater duties (Beauchamp & Childress, 1989). Ethicists argue that principles must always be reckoned with: "Principles count even when they don't win" (Beauchamp & Childress, 1989, p. 47). In the next section, each principle is defined and applied to the case of Archie.

Respect for Autonomy.   Respect for autonomy means respect for the inherent freedom and dignity of each person. In other words, because they are people, all individuals should be free to make choices for themselves. A person without freedom is a person without dignity. This principle derives from philosopher Immanuel Kant's notion that people are ends in themselves and should not be treated only as a means to another end (Kant, 1785/1964). Implicit in autonomy is the concept that the person is responsible for him- or herself. To respect autonomy means that "a person's choices should not be constrained by others" (Beauchamp & Childress, 1989, p. 62). Paternalism, the opposite of autonomy, means acting as a parent to another, determining that person's best interest.

Respect for autonomy does have limits, of course. One's actions cannot interfere with the freedom of another, and autonomy must be based on an understanding of the meaning and implications of one's choices. The actions do not need to be rational in the sense that they need not seem sensible to others. Autonomy does require that the person be able to understand the consequences of the decision. So a person can be free to act foolishly, even in ways that harm him- or herself, if that person is capable of understanding the implications of the choice and if others are not hurt by those actions. Children, people with profound mental retardation, or people in a psychotic state do not have autonomy of actions because they are (at least at the moment) unable to understand the implications of their choices for themselves or others. In these circumstances, others act paternalistically on behalf of the individual.

The right to privacy is coupled with freedom of choice as a part of respect for autonomy. A person should have the power to decide what information about self to share, a right to control what others know about his or her private life. As with autonomy, without privacy there is no dignity.

The connection between respect for autonomy and the codes of ethics is easy to see. The duties for counselors to obtain informed consent to counseling and to maintain confidentiality of disclosures made in session derive directly from this principle. Similarly, many aspects of research ethics relate to respect for autonomy.

Counselors trying to resolve an ethical dilemma use the principle of respect for autonomy by asking which of the alternatives under consideration is most consistent with this principle. In Archie's case, respect for autonomy is crucial. If he can be granted the same measure of autonomy as an adult, then the counselor must honor his wishes for confidentiality to the extent that those wishes do not substantially harm others. Immediately, two questions arise. Can he be granted the same measure of autonomy as an adult? How much harm does his action cause others? (The counselor at this point is probably wishing that Archie had waited until his next birthday to share this information with her.) Most children have limited competence, and as they mature, the limits on their competence decrease. The ethics literature explains the relationship between competence and maturity and suggests that an adolescent at 17 probably is mature enough to act autonomously (for example, Gustafson & McNamara, 1987). It suggests that a counselor with a client so near adulthood should start by assuming maturity and autonomy, unless there is evidence to the contrary. Given her knowledge of Archie, Annette decides that he can be granted a full measure of autonomy. Her analysis of the potential harm inflicted is another important consideration. An allegation of sexual abuse may affect his stepfather's work, his emotional stability, his marriage, his ability to parent his stepson, and perhaps his personal freedom. His mother may also suffer psychological distress and be affected by the harm her husband experiences.

If Archie is now telling the truth, then his refusal to admit his prior lie to anyone else violates the stepfather's rights. Of course, Archie may be lying *now,* feeling uncomfortable with his earlier revelation. Young people sometimes deny real abuse because they fear the consequences. This later denial may be an effort to reduce the present distress. If so, disclosing his denial would clearly not be in his best interests. The stepfather might even be free to abuse him again. The process of applying the principle of respect for autonomy to this case reveals the importance of the facts of the case. The counselor's ethical analysis depends on her assessment of the boy and his family. Her knowledge about the client is crucial in helping her evaluate which is the real lie and what the consequences of disclosure (or nondisclosure) are likely to be. The principle of respect for autonomy requires that Archie's wishes must figure prominently in Annette's decision, and that if doubt exists about the harm to others, the client's right to make his own choice about what is revealed should weigh heavily in the counselor's decision.

Nonmaleficence. The second ethical principle has its roots in medical ethics and is often associated with the Hippocratic oath, which physicians take. This oath admonishes physicians to heal the sick and never injure or harm them. This is derived from the principle called nonmaleficence and is often seen in its Latin form, *primum non nocere*. Its specific translation is "First, do no harm," and it has been called the most fundamental ethical principle for medical and human service professionals. This principle also includes avoiding preventable risks. Counselors have a duty to use only those interventions that they know are not likely to harm clients. This duty means that counselors must know and evaluate the risks of counseling for their clients and act accordingly. The duty to avoid harm also applies to the other roles of mental health professionals. For example, researchers are prohibited from conducting research that will hurt participants, and educators may not use teaching methodologies that damage students. Counselors cannot always foresee all consequences of their services because unexpected events happen. The duty to nonmaleficence does not require omniscience, just knowledge and careful, prudent judgment.

The concept of avoiding harm must be put in a context because many aspects of counseling can be uncomfortable and clients may temporarily feel worse before they feel better. A person trying to cope with a history of physical abuse in childhood may be more distraught after counseling sessions that examine the impact of those experiences on current functioning than he or she was at the start of the sessions. For a while, the person may have trouble sleeping, may cry often, and may be less productive at work. This would constitute harm if the intervention used had no evidence of benefit in the long run, or if the client had not consented to a treatment including temporary negative effects. If a counselor is competent in the use of a treatment that is known to typically have positive effects, and the counselor has evaluated the effectiveness of this approach with this client, the counselor is complying with the principle of nonmaleficence. The counselor's only additional duty is to monitor the client's progress to identify and handle unanticipated negative effects of counseling.

Another aspect to the principle of nonmaleficence implies that doing nothing is preferable to engaging in an action that could be reasonably anticipated to cause harm. For example, a family physician untrained in cardiac surgery would never attempt a cardiac bypass operation—even if a patient needed it and refused to see another physician. If all efforts to persuade the patient to see a cardiac specialist failed, the family physician still would not do the surgery, even if the patient's condition worsened, even if the patient risked death. The ethical rationale is clear. A family physician is likely to do great harm engaging in a procedure in which he or she is untrained. That harm is avoidable because other doctors with that training are available. Consequently, the only ethical stance is for the physician to refuse the patient's request. The risk of death from surgery by an untrained physician is greater than the risk of death by no treatment, or at least death is a more immediate risk with an unskilled surgeon. Similarly, counselors cannot engage in actions that they know or should know are likely to do harm—even if they are asked to by clients or colleagues, even if it means counselors do nothing instead. The harm they would cause is probably not as visible and dramatic as in the medical example just given, but the psychological injury can be just as real. Nonmaleficence demands that counselors untrained in powerful counseling interventions do nothing rather than engage in procedures that are likely to do harm in inept hands.

The principle of nonmaleficence is the basis for the ethical standards concerning competence to practice, informed consent to counseling and research, dual relationships, and public statements. It also is the foundation for the sections of the code dealing with appropriate use of psychological tests and research methods with animals.

When we apply the principle of nonmaleficence to the case of Archie, we realize that we must consider the harm that can come from each alternative, beginning with the harm to Archie if the counselor discloses the information without his consent. Because the counselor's primary duty is to the client, the analysis starts with Archie. So the counselor must carefully weigh Archie's mental state, emotional stability, and tendency to impulsive or destructive behavior along with the effect disclosure would have on each of these facets of functioning. She also needs to acknowledge that revealing the confidence may cause Archie to drop out of counseling or, at the very least, lose trust in her and refuse to reveal any other personal information. She must consider the harm the loss of a trusting counseling relationship could cause her client. Then she should evaluate the harm that comes to Archie's family members from each of her options. In different ways both the mother and stepfather are harmed if the allegation goes forward but is not really true. Finally, the counselor needs to weigh the injury her client would suffer against the injuries his family members would suffer. If Archie is likely to experience minor, brief discomfort, but his stepfather is likely to have a criminal conviction or his mother to file for divorce, that information should be part of Annette's deliberation. The principle of nonmaleficence asks counselors to use their power wisely so that the client, student, or research participant leaves the experience at least no worse off than he or she began.

Beneficence. The third ethical principle is beneficence, which is defined as the responsibility to do good. Because counselors advertise themselves as professional helpers, they have a duty to be of real help to those who enlist their services. Beneficence also includes a duty to help society in general and people who are potential clients. This duty is not imposed on all workers who sell their services to the public. People who manufacture shoelaces, copiers, or potato chips do not market themselves as helpers, and so ethically they have no obligation to help, only to produce the goods without causing harm to the public. Of course, it is *desirable* for such workers to help others. The distinction is that helping others is not a *duty* imposed by the nature of their work.

The principle of beneficence also underlies the provisions in the code requiring counselors to work within the limits of their competence and to promote the public welfare. Acting in an incompetent way means that the counselor will not be able to give the help that has been promised and that a client has the right to expect.

Of course, not all counseling ends up having a positive benefit for the client. Sometimes counseling is ineffective, and less often, it may inadvertently leave the client feeling worse. Moreover, counseling can help only those who agree to actively participate in the process. The ethical obligation of beneficence is not to a guaranteed positive outcome; rather, the obligation is to do one's best to be of help and to offer alternatives when counseling does not appear to be succeeding. When counselors consistently leave clients no better off at the end of counseling than at the beginning, they are violating the principle of beneficence.

Beneficence also requires counselors to engage in professional activities that provide general benefit to the public. Thus, determining the benefits in each possible course of action is important in resolving an ethical dilemma. Beneficence adds a responsibility to the duty to avoid harm. It asserts that it is insufficient for counselors simply to avoid injuring their clients. A counselor's interventions should be based on avoiding harm as a first requirement and on doing good as a second requirement.

Applied to Archie's case, beneficence means being committed to a resolution that not only avoids preventable harm to Archie, but also leaves him better off after counseling. Moreover, beneficence means the counselor should consider what is good for Archie's family and her other potential clients. Annette ought to evaluate what course of action could really help the whole family the most. She also must examine the impact of breaking confidentiality on her role as a secondary school counselor. If other students learn that she disclosed Archie's statements outside the counseling office, perhaps they would refrain from using the counseling service, even when they might benefit. In other words, she should seek a solution that increases her likelihood of continuing to help all those she serves. Again, her responsibility to do good for Archie takes precedence over other considerations, but all aspects of beneficence need to be explored.

Justice. Justice is the obligation to act fairly. This principle calls for counselors to recognize the dignity of all people and avoid bias in professional action. This principle is best expressed in a statement attributed to Aristotle: "Justice means treating equals equally and unequals unequally, in proportion to their inequality" (cited in Kitchener, 1984). Justice means being fair and nondiscriminatory. When Oscar Wilde defined morality as "the attitude we adopt towards people we personally dislike," he was emphasizing the justice component of morality. The risk of violating this principle is greatest when one stereotypes a group. Counselors should not show bias on the basis of race, age, gender, culture, and any other variable irrelevant to the real matter at hand, because doing so is inherently unfair.

Justice is more than avoiding prejudice, however. It also means offering additional services to those whose difference is relevant. For example, a counselor who teaches has an obligation to evaluate all students' performances using the same criteria. However, if one student has a hearing impairment, the educator would be unfair to treat that student exactly the same as the others. Instead, justice dictates that the student's hearing problem be recognized and adaptations to the teaching environment be made so that the student can understand what is being communicated. Once those adaptations are in place, however, fairness also demands that equal performance standards be used. A faculty member would be unethical to grade that student's work more leniently because of the impairment.

The principle of justice also obliges counselors to be sure their professional services are accessible to the public. For instance, it is unethical to deny those who are poor access to counseling and psychotherapy because they cannot pay or to deny people who do not speak English because their language is different. Justice does not require that counselors accept so many poor clients that they cannot support themselves or that they become multilingual, but it does require counselors to make accommodations so that factors that are really irrelevant to a person's ability to profit from therapy do not determine that person's access to therapy.

This principle is at the root of statements in the codes against discrimination and sexual harassment and supporting pro bono work and public service. It is also the foundation for the obligations to protect the public welfare and to actively combat discrimination whenever found.

Applying this principle to Archie's case suggests that Annette should deal with Archie as she would with any other adolescent client of hers, insofar as she should not let extraneous variables enter into her ethical reasoning. Archie's parents' position in the community, for example, should have no bearing on her actions because their social status is irrelevant. Similarly, if Annette dislikes the stepfather or sees parallels between Archie's mother and her own mother, justice demands that she give these personal feelings no weight in the decisions she makes about confidentiality with Archie. If Annette is unable to treat Archie and his family fairly, she should arrange for Archie to see a counselor who can.

Fidelity. The fifth ethical principle is fidelity, and it deals with faithfulness to promises made and to the truth. Fidelity is loyalty. Counselors must place clients' interests ahead of their own and be loyal to clients even when such loyalty is inconvenient or uncomfortable. Fidelity derives from the central role of trust between counselor and client. Trust becomes impossible if a counselor's words or actions are unreliable. In addition, fidelity is necessary because clients are vulnerable and the role of the counselor holds inherent power. Truthfulness is an essential aspect of fidelity in counseling and psychotherapy because the primary medium of the service is verbal communication. Clients expect to be able to believe what counselors say—the whole enterprise would likely crumble without trustworthy counselors. The emphasis is on avoiding deception and on trust, however, not on brutal honesty. Obviously, a counselor who finds a client's style of communication boring or who disagrees with a client's political views has no obligation to share all these reactions with a client. Honesty must be tempered with consideration for the effects of such information on clients. Still, the prima facie duty is to truthfulness, unless overruled by another principle.

The principle of fidelity also implies loyalty to colleagues and the profession. It obliges us to do what we have agreed to do. Because counselors have a contract with their employers to give professional service in exchange for compensation, they should be loyal to that agreement as long as they are collecting a paycheck. Counselors have a similar contract with the profession. In exchange for the benefits of their professional status, they have agreed to act according to the rules of the profession and to respect other professionals. These agreements sometimes take the form of written contracts, but at other times they are informal or implied.

Fidelity is the principle underlying the statements in the codes regarding the structure of the counseling relationship and relationships with colleagues, employers, and professional associations. Fidelity is also the foundation for the caution about the use of deception in research designs. Counselors wrestling with an ethical dilemma need to ask themselves which of the courses of action under consideration is most faithful to the promises that have been made.

In Archie's case, fidelity demands that Annette remain loyal to Archie and to promises made to him. If promises have been made or implied to Archie's parents, then she also has a duty to be loyal to those promises. If the loyalties conflict, then her first obligation is to her client. Annette cannot desert her client, making excuses to refer him elsewhere just because the situation is now so difficult for her. Fidelity means keeping commitments.

When Ethical Principles Conflict. Applying ethical principles to a particular dilemma can reveal internal conflicts between different principles. In Archie's case, different principles lead to incompatible conclusions. The principle of respect for autonomy emphasizes Archie's freedom and responsibility for his decision, whereas the principle of nonmaleficence uses harm to Archie and others as the measure of what is right. The principle of fidelity implies loyalty to the promise made to keep disclosures private, whereas the principle of beneficence suggests that disclosure may be best for the whole family.

How are these conflicting recommendations reconciled? As noted earlier, some philosophers argue that nonmaleficence is the most important ethical principle and that its requirements take priority over the claims of other ethical principles (Beauchamp & Childress, 1989). The central issue is the nature and intensity of harm to the client if disclosure is made without his or her consent. The principles of autonomy, beneficence, fidelity, and justice play secondary roles. The counselor's ultimate goal is to find a way to abide by all the ethical principles, but his or her first task is to ascertain as best as possible the probable injury to the client.

Returning to Archie, the crux of the issue then becomes whether Archie is telling the truth now or when he made the initial disclosure about abuse. If the client is acting out of fear or worry now and the abuse actually happened, then the harm from disclosing this current denial could be significant for the boy. If he was really fabricating the abuse in a desperate attempt to help his mother, then the harm to Archie from disclosure may be of a different nature and severity. In any case, Annette should consider the potential injury to Archie if he abandons counseling after she breaks confidentiality. Clearly, others are at risk for injury here. If the abuse never happened, then the parents are also being unnecessarily harmed.

The principle of nonmaleficence suggests that the counselor has a duty to be as sure as possible about what the real truth is. That probably means that Annette needs more discussion with Archie to get a better sense of his motivation for retracting his prior claim of abuse. Annette needs as fully informed a judgment as possible about what really happened in order to decide on the least harmful alternative. Caution in proceeding also fits with the other three principles. If the abuse did not occur, respect for autonomy, in conjunction with nonmaleficence, might lead Annette to help Archie disclose the lie himself, either to his family or to the investigator from children's services. By exploring the implications of his behavior with Archie, Annette may assist Archie to gain enough insight for him to decide to undo the harm he is causing. Such an approach is consistent with the duty to beneficence. Helping Archie take responsibility for his actions helps him behave in a more mature and self-sufficient way— clearly a desirable outcome. Supporting Archie in communicating about the frustrations and fears that led him to lie might be an outcome that benefits the whole family and gets them intervention for the real domestic violence. Obviously, if Archie chose to disclose the fabrication himself, then Annette would not be breaking any promises to Archie or to his family.

Ethical Theories.   There are even thornier dilemmas than the one Archie presents. For instance, a client whose medical condition is terminal and who is experiencing overwhelming pain may seriously consider suicide. Is suicide under such circumstances always wrong, or is there such a thing as rational suicide? Does the counselor have a duty to prevent suicide for this kind of client, too? This is an agonizing problem. In such situations, the principles conflict, and the harm seems equal no matter which alternative is chosen. Under those circumstances, counselors can turn to ethical theories that are broader than ethical principles. Ethical theories are at the very foundation of Western societies' beliefs about morality. Ethical theories represent the perspectives of great ethicists throughout history. A full discussion of ethical theories is beyond the scope of this book, but the following material gives a sense of the scholarly thinking.

In Western culture, several ethical theories have been proposed by philosophers. These theories are at the core of our religious, social, and political institutions. One is the moral law theory, which argues that there are universal moral values that must be absolutely followed. A similar theory is what Newton (1989) describes as biblical theory, encompassing absolute laws for human behavior expressed in the holy writings of the great religions of the world. In either case, the rules are treated as moral laws and are held to be universally binding. At the other end of the continuum is utilitarianism, a theory that defines morality in terms of the benefits an action provides for society. In the simplest terms, utilitarianism defines morality as the action that brings the greatest happiness to the greatest number. No action is inherently good or bad in utilitarianism; an action's effects on the happiness of the larger group determine its morality.

Ethical theories describe different assumptions about the central essence of moral behavior. For the most complex dilemmas, in which a counselor agonizes about the process and in which each alternative seems to have negative consequences, thinking about how he or she defines morality at the most basic level may help in resolving the dilemma. Counselors are well advised to consult with ethicists when analyzing the relationship between moral theory and the facts of a particular case.

Step 6: Consult with Colleagues About the Dilemma

An ethical dilemma can be intellectually overwhelming and emotional distressing for both the client and the counselor. Objective feedback from trusted colleagues can provide a wider view of the problem, opening new options, a new focus on unconsidered facts, or additional relevant literature. Consultation also offers comfort and reduces the moral and emotional isolation that counselors often feel. Colleagues do not often have easy answers, but they do have insight, experience, and compassion to share. Consultation with colleagues can take place at any point in the decision-making process and need not be limited to this step. For instance, one might seek input from a colleague about interpreting a confusing section of an ethics code or clarifying the relevant facts of the case. Research suggests that psychologists underutilize consultation to assist them with the dilemmas of practice, and this failure sometimes diminishes the quality of the care clients receive (Clayton & Bongar, 1994). Counselors are more likely to use consultation with colleagues when they fear a malpractice suit (Wilbert & Fulero, 1988).

Whether a colleague can be approached with information that identifies a specific client depends on the consent to consultation a counselor has obtained from the client. Identifying information can be released to colleagues or supervisors with client consent or, in the absence of consent, with legal authority. Counselors who have not received such consent may discuss the case only in a way that protects the client's identity. Usually that means disguising not only the name but also other information that might make the client's identity obvious to other professionals.

When consulting with colleagues, counselors should describe the facts of the situation, their own understanding of the relevant ethical standards, their interpretation of how the ethics literature and ethical principles apply to the case, and their current assessment of which alternatives are most responsible. In other words, the counselor should summarize the decision-making process thus far and ask the colleague the following questions:

- What facts of the case seem most important to you in determining the ethical alternatives?
- What have I not considered?
- Is my interpretation of the ethics code accurate?
- What other parts of the code are applicable that I have not identified?
- What other books and articles do you know of that are relevant to my decision?
- Does my analysis of the ethical principles appear sound?
- Is my evaluation of the most responsible options consistent with your judgment?
- How would you resolve this dilemma? Why would you make that choice?

The number of colleagues one consults will vary with the nature of the dilemma and the experience and circumstances. Some consultation is always advised. Of course, not all the feedback received will be useful. Some colleagues may even advise an unethical route, and conflicting advice is not uncommon. Even when the feedback is disappointing, the endeavor is worthwhile. The process of articulating one's dilemma and the steps one has taken to resolve it forces a counselor to put his or her thinking into words and in that way clarifies the thinking and makes fully conscious ideas that may have been at the periphery of awareness. Just as the process of self-disclosure helps clients to see their problems more clearly, so too, discussing ethical dilemmas with colleagues aids counselors to gain a fuller vision of the issues.

If a counselor is under supervision to obtain a professional license or as part of a training experience, consultation with supervisors is not optional. Discussion with one's supervisor should take place at the first opportunity and the feedback from one's supervisor should be weighed more heavily than any from colleagues in making the final decision. In practice, supervisors usually advocate for the counselor in training, supporting him or her and providing practical advice. Of course, even those not yet licensed for independent practice are still obligated to act in accordance with the standards of the profession, so that any advice contradictory to the standards may not be followed, even if it originates with a supervisor. The counselor is responsible for his or her actions with a client and is still accountable. No one can claim that "a supervisor made me do it." More explanation about responding to such dilemmas in supervision follows in Chapter 12.

Consultation with colleagues can include discussion with members of professional ethics committees to get advice about the problem. National associations are accessible to members through a toll-free phone call. Many state organizations also have ethics committees who can discuss dilemmas with members. Moreover, state licensing boards typically provide access for licensed professionals seeking ethics advice. Because none of these committees will have the full facts of the case, they do not provide members with recommendations guaranteed to comply with their standards. Rather, they help members understand the codes and related publications more fully and assist them in raising all the relevant questions. In other words, they do not take the responsibility for the decision, but they can offer considerable guidance about how other professionals have dealt with similar situations.

Step 7: Deliberate Alone

At this step the data collection process has ended, and the private, individual process of sorting out the information begins in earnest. Through this personal deliberation, the counselor decides which alternative is most ethical and develops a plan for implementing that action. For example, in Archie's case Annette's deliberations might result in calling Archie back for another session later that same day to explore his new disclosure more fully, to ascertain, as well as possible, what the real events were. She decides that if Archie was fabricating the story of the abuse, the counseling must focus on helping him understand the implications of his action and how he can undo some of the damage already done. She will not threaten or coerce him into disclosing his lie, but she will engage in a respectful process of helping him face the meaning of his actions and take responsibility for making things right. She will maintain confidentiality for the immediate future. If Archie refuses to change his position after additional counseling, she will need to reconsider her decision. She may still need to honor the confidentiality but will want to go through the decision-making process again at that time. If Annette believes Archie is now lying for fear of the consequences of admitting abuse, she has a duty to maintain confidentiality but will work with him to find alternative ways to cope with his obvious distress.

Essential to this personal deliberation is an examination of the competing values that may make implementing the ethical choice more difficult. As noted in Chapter 1, competing values are other personal values that influence a person's behavior. A counselor may value the good opinion of a supervisor so much that that value takes priority over ethical values. All people have other values, and there is nothing inherently problematic about them. In themselves, many competing values have ethical merit. A professional's commitment to provide financial support for his or her family and to have an harmonious relationship with co-workers are good values to have. These values become problematic only when they override a counselor's ability to choose the professional ethical value. What tempts individual counselors not to implement ethical choices differs somewhat in each case, but worry about negative consequences to self, lack of support from colleagues or supervisors, or fears that doing the right thing will complicate one's life are frequent competing values. When counselors become aware of the factors that pull them in another direction, they can devise a plan to counteract these pressures and increase the likelihood of acting responsibly.

Counselors should also acknowledge the costs of the ethical choices. Sometimes complying with ethical standards results in more work, pressure, and anxiety. For instance, Annette will need to schedule extra sessions with Archie to ascertain the truth, and if she maintains confidentiality, she risks angering the parents, investigators, and even school administrators. Acting ethically may sometimes mean defying supervisors or even risking one's employment or income. By frankly confronting these possible costs, the counselor may discover ethical ways to minimize or eliminate them or, at least, to protect him- or herself from an unexpected cost. In addition, the counselor can muster strength for uncomfortable consequences of the ethical choice.

Of course, not all choices are painful or difficult. Counselors who believe they have come to an informed decision about the problem often feel a sense of professionalism and allegiance to the highest values of the profession. They take pride in their moral courage and gain confidence to face future problems. The ethical climate of the profession and the workplace also influences the feelings about implementing an ethical action. The past 20 years have spawned greater awareness of the major ethical issues in the profession, and counselors trained in recent years have more formal education in ethics (Welfel, 1992). When a counselor knows colleagues are committed to ethical practice, the temptation of competing values lessens, and support from those co-workers increases. Counselors gain the respect of their colleagues and also have the satisfaction of knowing that they are modeling ethical behavior for others in the workplace. Most important, they have the satisfaction of knowing that even under pressure, they considered the welfare of the client above their own needs.

Step 8: Inform Appropriate People and Implement the Decision

When a counselor is ready to carry out an ethical decision, he or she needs to inform supervisors. Supervisors have a right to hear the choice and the rationale for it. Then the counselor needs to communicate with other people. Who else may be relevant? Needless to say, the client is the first person to consider. If Annette decided to break confidentiality with Archie, then Archie should be told about her decision. He should also hear her rationale and be given time to discuss the issue with her. Informing the client is necessary because of the principle of autonomy and must be done unless a greater ethical good is at stake. For example, sometimes when clients are homicidal, counselors may break confidentiality to warn the intended victim. Under these circumstances, the client should be told only if the disclosure does not put the victim at greater risk for harm. If the client is a child, parents or guardians may need to be informed. In each case, only people who truly have claim to the information should get it. The client's right to privacy must still be honored to the fullest extent possible.

In implementing the ethical choice, the counselor should remember to engage the supports outlined in the last step when resistance is encountered. One may benefit from another consultation with a trusted colleague or from rereading the ethical standards or literature to help one shore up resolve to stick with the choice. Ethical courage has several sources. One's moral character is one piece of it, and structuring the environment to minimize temptation is another. A third aspect is habit—people are more likely to act morally in major issues if they have made a habit of acting responsibly in the less important matters.

Formal documentation of one's decision in records, case notes, or other files is the final portion of this step. Written information about the choice taken and the rationale for that decision offers a counselor the best available protection from later challenges to that decision. Process notes ought to begin at Step 2 with the list of options to consider and then include the outcomes of each step of the decision-making process. Additional discussion of the ethics of documentation follows in Chapter 14.

Step 9: Reflect on the Actions

Experience without reflection is wasted. Experience alone teaches little, but coupled with reflection it can provide real insight. Ethical decision making is not complete without a time for contemplating the experience. Such reflection gives counselors an opportunity to acknowledge the responsible way in which they acted and a chance to evaluate the flaws in their thinking and actions that may be avoided when the next dilemma comes along. Now that the pressure is at least temporarily lessened, the mind may be able to see what the emotions had clouded. Reflection also increases ethical sensitivity so that the next ethical issue that arises will be noticed more quickly and addressed more effectively. Specifically, at this step the counselor should ask him- or herself the following questions:

- Did I attend to the ethical dimensions of the situation as soon as they arose?
- Did I know enough about the ethics codes to use them effectively?
- What ethical literature do I need to keep in my personal library for easier access the next time it is needed?
- How effectively did I consult? What could I have improved?
- How well did I identify the competing values and other pressures affecting my decision making? What could I have done better?
- What else could I have done differently?
- What am I proud of doing?
- How can I use this experience to assist other counselors faced with similar problems?

This period of reflection begins after the decision is fully implemented and its consequences are known. Thus there may be some delay between the last two steps. Counselors must take care to engage in this step so that the full benefit of the experience is gained.

SUMMARY

When counselors make ethical decisions that impact others' lives, these decisions should not be intuitive, but instead should be made after careful deliberation about the ethical justification of various potential actions. A nine-step model for justifying ethical decisions begins with (Step 1) recognizing the ethical dimensions of the situation and moves to (Step 2) examining all the relevant facts and categorizing the type of ethical dilemma involved. In Step 3, counselors consult the codes of ethics of their profession and laws of their jurisdiction for applicable standards for practice. In Step 4, counselors examine the relevant ethics literature to learn the views of experts in applied ethics. Step 5 involves analyzing the five ethical principles that govern human service professions: respect for autonomy, nonmaleficence (avoiding harm), beneficence (doing good), justice or fairness, and fidelity to promises made. If analysis of these principles does not resolve the dilemma, a counselor may need to move to a deeper level of ethical justification—ethical theories. At Step 6, consultation with supervisors and respected colleagues obtains alternative perspectives. In Step 7, once all the data are obtained, the counselor must deliberate and decide on his or her own. Deliberation entails acknowledging pressures and practicalities that may make implementing the decision more difficult. Step 8 involves informing supervisors and other relevant individuals, usually including the client, and then implementing the chosen action. The final step is a period for reflection on the experience that allows one to take pride in one's honest effort to act responsibly and to identify ways in which the process could be improved when the next similar dilemma occurs.

Not all ethical issues require progressing through all nine steps. Some are resolved expeditiously. When ethics codes are definitive, a counselor can move immediately to the final three steps of the model. In addition, although the process appears time consuming, it can be shortened by familiarity with the ethics codes and the relevant ethics literature and by ensuring ready access to a set of knowledgeable colleagues with whom to consult. Up-to-date ethics knowledge and prior experience with ethical problems also speeds up decision making.

DISCUSSION QUESTIONS

1. Do you agree with the view that nonmaleficence should be the primary ethical principle governing the human service professions? Why or why not?
2. Which aspect of the codes of ethics seem most definitive to you? Why?
3. How would you determine which colleagues to consult about an ethical problem?
4. How would you define your own implicit theory of morality? What fundamental assumptions do you make?
5. Do you agree with the way Annette and Yolanda resolved their ethical dilemmas? Why or why not?

RECOMMENDED READINGS

Beauchamp, T. L., & Childress, J. F. (1989). *Principles of biomedical ethics* (3rd ed). Oxford, England: Oxford University Press.

Gibson, W. T., & Pope, K. S. (1993). The ethics of counseling: A national survey of certified counselors. *Journal of Counseling and Development, 71,* 330–336.

Jordan, A. E., & Meara, N. M. (1990). Ethics and the professional practice of psychologists: The role of virtues and principles. *Professional Psychology: Research and Practice, 21,* 107–114.

Kitchener, K. S. (1984). Intuition, critical evaluation and ethical principles: The foundation for ethical decisions in counseling psychology *The Counseling Psychologist, 12,* 43–55.

Pedersen, P. B. (1995). Cross cultural ethical guidelines. In J. B. Ponterotto, J. M. Casas, L. A. Suzuki, & C. M. Alexander (Eds.), *Handbook of multicultural counseling* (pp. 34–50). Thousand Oaks, CA: Sage.

3

Ethics Complaints
Policies and Procedures

Consider the following situation:

A 20-year-old college junior named Martina makes an appointment at the university counseling center. Martina tells her counselor, Dominic, that she has been feeling anxious and depressed for a long time, but that lately these feelings have worsened. She goes on to say that she tried counseling a few months ago but had "a bad experience" and did not want to see that counselor again. She says the other counselor (Jack) kept suggesting that she ought to have a more active social life, and repeatedly volunteered to take her to the movies to distract her from her anxiety. She refused Jack's offers and kept attending sessions until he suggested that maybe they could start dating once counseling was over. At this session he also commented on her attractiveness. Martina's friends told her that Jack was acting unprofessionally, that most counselors did not do such things. Martina now wants to take some action against Jack so that "he cannot keep using his practice as a dating service." She asks Dominic for guidance in figuring out how to report Jack's behavior.

Although the particular facts presented in this case are fictional, research suggests that clients frequently tell their counselors about unethical behaviors by other mental health professionals. According to Pope (1994), approximately half of all therapists have had at least one client who revealed sexual involvement with a prior therapist. Sometimes clients are not as aware as Martina of the inherent problems in sexual exploitation and other ethical violations, but they do mention them in subsequent counseling experiences with sufficient frequency to require that counselors be prepared for such eventualities. When this happens, the new counselors have an opportunity to model ethical behavior and to counteract some of the damage done to the client and the profession by the prior counselor.

Information about ethics violations also may come from co-workers and from one's own observations of others' behavior in the workplace. A colleague may describe changing a diagnostic code to get additional sessions for a client, or mention a failure to report child neglect. At times, colleagues or supervisors will even ask for complicity in a violation. These data suggest that counselors should be aware of the practical aspects of ethics complaints in order to help clients like Martina and to prepare themselves to handle a violation by another counselor.

This chapter reviews the procedures for responding to ethical problems and filing ethics complaints with professional associations and licensing boards. Its aim is to identify criteria for filing a complaint and to clarify the complaint process and its rationale. Finally, this chapter discusses counseling interventions to help the client who wants to take action against an unethical mental health professional.

Accountability of Counselors and Therapists

When counselors act unethically, they are held accountable to a variety of organizations. They may be disciplined by their employers, the state licensing board, the national professional association, and the state professional association. A counselor who belongs to more than one professional association may be charged for the misconduct by each association. Conceivably, complaints for the same set of actions may be filed in each organization. Professional associations commonly forward complaints against their members to licensing boards in the states where the member holds a license. Interstate communication among licensing boards and professional associations also occurs. Consequently, a professional licensed in two states may find that disciplinary action by one state board is communicated to the other board. Former clients may take civil action and sue their counselors for negligence or malpractice. For very serious matters, there may also be criminal accountability. In some states, sexual contact with a client carries criminal penalties (Strasburger, Jorgenson, & Randles, 1991). In other words, one unethical action may have consequences for a counselor in several different arenas. Multiple accountability also means multiple choices for those who wish to pursue ethics complaints. Clients often profit by assistance from their new counselors in sorting through their options.

Procedures for Filing Complaints

There are a variety of options for people who want to respond to the behavior of a professional that may be unethical. The following section presents approaches that involve the filing of formal complaints and others that attempt to resolve the problem informally.

Informal Remedies Through Professional Associations

The ethics codes of APA and ACA both recommend informal remedies as a first step in addressing misconduct. Their rationale for this strategy is not explicitly stated, but it is reasonable to surmise that it is based on loyalty to colleagues, an interest in a speedy, nonbureaucratic resolution of problems, and minimization of negative publicity damaging to the reputation of the mental health professions. Specifically, the professions advise that when a professional learns of an ethics violation by another member, that professional should confront the colleague to see if the problem can be resolved without a formal complaint.

ACA *Code of Ethics,* Sections H.1.d and H.1.e

When counselors have reasonable cause to believe that another counselor is violating an ethical standard, they attempt to first resolve the issue informally with the other counselor, if feasible, providing that such action does not violate confidentiality rights that may be involved.

When an informal resolution is not appropriate or feasible, counselors, upon reasonable cause, take action such as reporting the suspected ethics violation to the state or national ethics committees, unless this action conflicts with confidentiality rights that cannot be resolved.

APA *Ethical Principles,* Sections 8.04 and 8.05

When psychologists believe that there may have been an ethical violation by another psychologist, they attempt to resolve the issue by bringing it to the attention of that individual if an informal resolution appears appropriate and the intervention does not violate any confidentiality rights that may be involved.

If an apparent ethical violation is not appropriate for informal resolutions under Standard 8.04, or is not resolved properly in that fashion, psychologists take further action appropriate to the situation, unless such action conflicts with confidentiality rights in a way that cannot be resolved. Such action might include referral to state or national committees on professional ethics or to state licensing boards.

A careful reading shows that both codes qualify their standards to indicate that informal resolutions should be attempted only where "feasible" or "appropriate," but unfortunately, neither explains what circumstances might be defined as feasible or appropriate. Moreover, neither mandates that an ethics complaint be made; they say only *some action* must be taken if the informal approach is unsuccessful. But neither code gives any clue about what types of action are desirable. Why not? The most plausible explanation lies in the range of types of ethical violations that occur, and their varying degrees of seriousness. Any code of ethics succinct enough to be usable could not possibly cover such a wide territory in a definitive way. Unfortunately, though, the current language gives professionals almost no guidance.

The older versions of the codes, ironically, made more specific recommendations for handling ethical violations. For example, the 1981 APA code indicated that informal resolutions were less appropriate for serious ethical offenses (APA, 1981a) than for minor infractions. Similarly, the 1988 ACA code explained that taking action against a violator meant using the avenues available in the person's place of employment as a first step and using the association procedures as a second step against the violator (AACD, 1988). The second step was initiated only if the first failed to fix the problem. These old standards still are useful in determining how to respond to a violation.

In particular, counselors should use the seriousness of the offense as the major criterion for deciding what kind of action is appropriate. Minor violations seem more amenable to private interventions such as a one-on-one conversation between the offending and the concerned counselor. Consider the counselor who does not obtain a complete informed consent to counseling as advised in the ethics code. Instead, she discusses only the limits of confidentiality very briefly. If there is no known harm to clients thus far and she seems to be acting from ignorance of the codes rather than disdain for them, informal confrontation seems a prudent choice. In this conversation, she can be educated about the ethics of informed consent and be placed on notice that further noncompliance will be taken more seriously. This approach lets the colleague retain some dignity and probably achieves as much behavior change as would be gained from a full ethics committee investigation. In addition, there is a practical argument in favor of an informal approach—it's speedier. A formal complaint can take months, even years, to resolve. An intervention for a minor infraction can take place immediately and the harm can be remedied almost as quickly.

ACA's old recommendation to use the employing institution to rehabilitate a practitioner before moving into association channels also makes sense, especially in minor or moderate offenses. An employer with policies for adjudicating ethics complaints can probably deal with the problem in a reasonable time frame and with consideration for the rights of all involved. The employer has clout over the counselor and is in the position to monitor future behavior. The disadvantages of complaining to employers are variability in enforcement procedures, inexperience in processing ethics complaints, and lack of influence over the counselor if he or she takes employment elsewhere. In addition, friendships among employees often hinder objective processing of a complaint. Consequently, reporting a problem to an employer is more likely to be beneficial if it is mildly or moderately serious and needs an objective investigation, if monitoring the counselor's future behavior is desirable, and if the employee is not likely to change jobs in the immediate future.

Using the seriousness of the offense as a criterion to determine the level of intervention, let us return to Martina's case. Clearly, her former counselor (Jack) did not comply with the ethical standards of either ACA or APA. Initiating a social relationship with a current client is a serious matter that violates Sections A.6.a and A.7.b of the ACA code and Sections 1.17, 1.19, and 4.07 of the APA code. In addition, Jack's invitation to begin dating immediately after counseling was terminated showed he was probably interested in a physical relationship with Martina. The latter is even more emphatically prohibited by the codes. The codes state that dating former clients is usually unethical and can be ethical only in some circumstances after two years have passed. So the codes take this counselor's unprofessional interest in Martina very seriously.

The harm from such behavior is also important to examine, to ascertain whether this offense was serious enough for a formal complaint. Research evidence suggests significant harm to clients whose counselors engage in sexual contact with them (for example, Bouhoutsos et al., 1983). Martina herself reports feeling even worse after her encounter with Jack. Even though no sexual contact took place, Martina's functioning deteriorated further after Jack expressed romantic interest in her. That is probably sufficient to constitute psychological injury to Martina. Is there also harm that extends beyond Martina? The research evidence also suggests that counselors who engage in sexual contact with one client are more likely to have had sex with other clients (Pope, 1994). The possibility exists, then, that Martina is not the first client who has suffered Jack's advances. In any case, unless something changes Jack's behavior, Martina is unlikely to be the last client injured by this man's irresponsibility. Taken together, then, the evidence suggests a formal complaint to the licensing board and the professional association, in addition to a complaint to his employer. This man hurt Martina, may have hurt other clients in the past, and may do so again.

The ability of Dominic, the current counselor, to help rehabilitate Jack comes into play in the decision about using a formal resolution in serious cases such as Martina's. Let us assume the Dominic does not work at the same agency and has no supervisory relationship or regular contact with the offender. Thus Dominic has no effective ways to monitor Jack's behavior on an ongoing basis. Moreover, Dominic probably does not have time to fully investigate the incident and objectively evaluate the evidence presented by both parties. If no wrongdoing occurred, a counselor accused of a serious violation by a client also deserves the opportunity to have his or her name cleared. An informal resolution does not really allow such an outcome. Thus, from several perspectives, it is wiser to report a potentially serious violation to a body empowered to carefully investigate and to assert authority over future behavior, than to use a private intervention (Canter et al., 1994). It offers better protection both to the professional who may be falsely accused and to the client who may have been victimized.

Another option that has been recommended and used with clients who have been sexually exploited by their therapists is mediation. Its primary advantage is its speed and moderate structure. It works less quickly than an informal approach, but is speedier than a formal complaint. It also has more structure than a one-on-one intervention. Its disadvantage is that a formal complaint to an association or licensing board may not be forthcoming, a substantial limitation for a serious offense. Mediation may also function to favor the counselor, who is usually the more powerful party in the dispute. See Bouhoutsos and Brodsky (1985) for a more detailed examination of the use of mediation for professional misconduct.

One caution is in order about reporting violations. The language in the codes about resolving ethical violations also establishes the priority of the client's right to confidentiality over the counselor's duty to intervene when another professional acts irresponsibly (Canter et al., 1994). One can approach a colleague or file a complaint to a board or committee that involves a client only if the client has consented and waived his or her preexisting right to confidentiality. The only exceptions are situations in which there may be a legal mandate to act otherwise. (For example, a few states mandate reporting of sexual misconduct by therapists regardless of client consent.) So if Martina wanted to do nothing about her former therapist and wanted no information disclosed, professional ethics demands honoring her decision. When an adult client makes this choice, counselors may worry about future clients of this man, but the duty to the current client takes precedence. Of course, with time and good counseling the client may change her mind about making a complaint against the former counselor.

American Counseling Association Complaint Procedures

The functions and goals of the ACA Ethics Committee are to educate members about ethical standards and deal with ethics questions and complaints (ACA, 1995). The committee has six members, all of whom are professional counselors who serve three-year terms. This body aims at protecting the rights of the person who originated the action and the rights of the counselor to a fair hearing.

Complaints against ACA members can come from the public, other members, or the committee itself, acting *sua sponte*. A *sua sponte* action means that if the Ethics Committee has information suggesting a member violated the standards, the committee itself can initiate the complaint.

The Ethics Office's first contact with a person considering an ethics complaint usually comes by telephone. If after that conversation the person decides to proceed with the complaint, he or she is instructed to send the Ethics Office a signed letter documenting the events as specifically as possible. Once that letter is received at ACA, a preliminary investigation ascertains whether the person complained against is a member of the organization and whether there is good reason to suspect that an ethics violation has occurred. Many cases against counselors do not meet these criteria and are not pursued. The person initiating the complaint is informed of the outcome and its rationale, and the case is closed.

If sufficient reason exists to explore the matter further, the person named in the complaint is notified of the charges being made and is given copies of the complaint and all related materials. He or she is asked to respond in writing within 60 days. Accused members have the option of asking for a face-to-face hearing before the committee. When all material has been obtained within the stated time limits, the committee deliberates about the case. The committee has several options in its ruling. It can determine that no ethics violation took place, that there isn't enough information to determine whether a violation took place, or that the person accused is guilty of the ethics violation. If misconduct is found, the committee then determines the appropriate sanction. The sanctions can range from remedial requirements to permanent expulsion from the organization. Needless to say, detailed procedures are outlined so that members can appeal unfavorable decisions. The appeal committee is composed of two former chairs of the Ethics Committee and the president of the person's primary division within ACA.

American Psychological Association Complaint Procedures

The APA Ethics Committee also has both educational and enforcement mandates from the association (APA, Ethics Committee, 1996a). Currently eight people serve on the committee, for three-year terms. One is a public, nonpsychologist member, and the rest are psychologists. There are also four associate members, who do not vote and who act as fact finders. APA also hires professional and support staff to assist the committee. All procedures for handling ethics complaints are designed to balance the rights of the person complaining against the rights of the psychologist, respecting the dignity of each party in the process. Their goal is to prevent harm to the public and to prevent harm to members from malicious or frivolous claims. The approach typically taken by both APA's and ACA's ethics committees is rehabilitative, with as much emphasis on interventions that can rehabilitate the counselor as on sanctions against him or her. In contrast to ACA's procedures, APA's procedures are more structured and elaborate.

A complaint may come before the APA committee in one of three ways. A consumer or other ordinary person in the society can file a complaint; another mental health professional can complain; or the Ethics Committee can initiate action against a member, *sua sponte*. Usually the initial inquiry about a potential violation comes by telephone to the Ethics Office. In this contact the person learns that all complaints must be written and is sent an official complaint form. This form requests identifying information from the person accusing as well as the accused, along with a detailed description of the situation. When the APA Ethics Committee receives a complaint, it conducts a preliminary review focused on three areas. The first review determines whether the complaint is within the committee's jurisdiction, which usually means whether the person named in the complaint is an APA member. If the person named is not a member, the case is immediately closed and that information is forwarded to the person who originated the complaint. Information is usually provided so that the person can file a complaint with a state licensing board or other professional association if appropriate. The second review examines whether the complaint has been filed within the appropriate time limits. If the time limit is exceeded, the person who complains is given an opportunity to ask for a waiver of the time limit. The third focus is on the sufficiency of the information furnished. In other words, the committee assesses whether there is adequate evidence to warrant further investigation. APA Ethics Committee reports (1994, 1995b, 1996a) indicate that relatively few complaints move beyond the preliminary investigation. Most cases are closed for one of these three reasons.

When a claim remains open, the next step is an evaluation by the chair of the Ethics Committee and the director of the Ethics Office. This involves a determination of whether a *cause for action* exists. According to APA, a "cause for action shall exist when the complainee's alleged actions and/or omissions, if proved, would in the judgment of the decision maker constitute a breach of ethics" (APA, Ethics Committee, 1996b, Rules and Procedure, Section 5.1). If a cause for action has been found, the person named in the complaint is notified of the filing and that person receives copies of the complaint. The member is required to respond in writing to the complaint within 30 days and may submit additional information about the matter for the committee to consider. The committee may also seek out information from other sources that it deems potentially relevant. Once this information is gathered the committee decides if there is enough information to show a cause for action. If there is not, the case is closed at this point, but if there is reason to suspect an ethics violation, a formal case is opened.

The psychologist involved is then formally charged with an ethics violation. The member receives written notification of the nature of the charges and the section(s) of the ethics code he or she is alleged to have violated. As in the preliminary step, the psychologist is now required to respond in writing within 30 days. In some cases, the psychologist is asked to appear in person before the committee. The person filing the claim is also notified of the formal charge and can submit additional information relevant to the charges in the allotted time period. When the investigation is complete, the committee deliberates and issues its ruling. It may dismiss the charges, recommend a sanction less than formal charges, or issue formal charges against the member. A lesser sanction is recommended when the committee believes that the violation occurred, but would be better resolved without formal charges. In this respect, the committee is given a good deal of discretion. Formal charges are issued when the misconduct represented a substantial harm to another person or the profession. In this event, the committee recommends to the board of directors that the individual be dropped from membership in the organization. Here, too, the committee has a good measure of flexibility because it can let a member resign instead of being dropped if it believes the severity of the misconduct does not warrant the full action. The board of directors may accept or reject the recommendations of the ethics committee. Of course, a member may appeal a decision of the Ethics Committee, and a rather elaborate description of the appeal process is presented in the published rules.

Licensing Board Procedures

The procedures for complaining about the activities of a licensed professional vary from state to state and profession to profession. Generally, licensing boards are authorized to discipline professionals who violate the written regulations. The type of discipline ranges from reprimands and limitations placed on one's practice to loss of license. For some offenses, criminal sanctions may also exist, and the board will turn evidence over to the legal system. A person seeking to give information about an ethics violation to a licensing board begins the process with a telephone call or letter to the appropriate state agency. Because licensing boards have more authority and power to regulate the future actions of a professional, some scholars advocate that aggrieved clients should file first with a licensing board (for example, Siegel, 1991). Interstate reporting has also begun so that a licensing board in one state can know if an applicant has been judged guilty of an offense in another state. Such reporting is also an argument for including a state board in any ethics complaint.

Complaints to Employers

As already mentioned, people who believe counselors have acted inappropriately may also notify employers or supervisors about the problem. If a counselor has partners in a group practice, any or all partners can be contacted. Large employers, such as community mental health centers and psychiatric hospitals, are more likely to have procedures in place for investigating such complaints. Smaller employers and colleagues in a practice are more prone to handle matters on a case-by-case basis. Again, people who complain need to identify themselves and provide specific information and documentation, if possible, about the events they believe are problematic. Employers who know that such information is also being forwarded to the licensing board or professional association may give the matter more serious attention, even though they may postpone a decision about the matter until the other bodies have ruled. Obviously, counselors in individual private practices are self-employed, so complaints against them must be referred to a professional association and/or licensing board.

Supporting the Client Through the Complaint Process

When a client such as Martina wants to complain to an authority about a mental health professional, the current counselor can play an important role in helping a client clarify his or her thinking and understand the practical aspects of the process. Most clients have very little knowledge of professional rules and regulations, and counselors provide a valuable service when they give clients such information. Counselors can also help clients sort out their emotions about the prior experience and about the complaint process. Clients should understand that their identity will be known to the committee and that the person they are accusing will have access to all written materials they provide to the committee. (However, other people will not have access to these materials.) The client is also likely to feel victimized by the former counselor and may not easily understand the committee's responsibility to protect the rights of the accused as well as the victim's. It may reduce the client's frustration to explain that the principle of "innocent until proven guilty" holds in this arena.

Clients need full autonomy in deciding whether to proceed with the complaint, especially because only a minority of complaints submitted to professional associations result in formal charges against the member. So far, there is very limited empirical evidence that complaining will help the person heal from the wound (Vinson, 1987). The most realistic benefit for the client is the knowledge that if the action is successful, other future clients are at less risk for this misconduct. Counselors can sometimes be so outraged by the unethical behaviors of colleagues described by a client that they mistakenly advocate for the filing of the complaint. They act like crusaders for justice rather than therapists for their client's pain. In this environment, the counselor's emotion can carry the client forward to an action the client never freely chose. In such an event, a client may end up feeling taken advantage of by both counselors, even though the intention of the new counselor was noble.

In contrast, sometimes counselors have difficulty acknowledging that fellow professionals behave irresponsibly. They may take a "head in the sand" approach and minimize client accounts of counselor misconduct or attribute such accounts to negative transference or psychopathology. Because all counselors probably have been tempted to engage in some kind of ethical offense at least at one point in their careers, they may feel uncomfortable helping a client take action against a colleague. Their empathy for the colleague may cloud their judgment and interfere with their responsibility to the client and the public. Sometimes counselors worry about reprisals from other professionals and feel disloyal to colleagues (Levenson, 1986). This view acts as a kind of professional jingoism that implies that loyalty to colleagues is the highest value. When clients mention actions of prior counselors that seem unethical, counselors have a responsibility to explore this matter further with their clients. If additional discussion clarifies a potentially serious unethical practice, the new counselor has a duty to inform the client about ethical standards for professionals and his or her options for action. The counselor's goal in such discussion is to keep an open mind, respect the dignity of all involved, and help the client determine his or her next step.

False claims against counselors are relatively rate. Pope and Vetter (1992) report that about 4% of claims of sexual contact between therapists and clients were not true. The elaborate, time-consuming, and often uncomfortable process of filing a complaint militates against the filing of large numbers of false complaints. A counselor who believes a client is falsely accusing a prior therapist of misconduct should explore the matter extensively in counseling. Counselors who worry about such false claims can also take comfort in the careful analysis by the committees and boards involved that also militates against a false finding against an innocent professional.

The client will need extra support at several other crucial points in the counseling process. First, putting the information in writing to the committee may cause the client to revisit the pain of the experience itself. Counseling time devoted to those feelings is wisely spent, focusing on the reality of the pain and attributing responsibility to the mental health professional (not the client) for the misconduct. The second point is when the committee decides whether to pursue the complaint and issue formal charges. Most complaints do not advance beyond this point, and the client may now need support if the complaint is dropped for insufficient evidence. Angry and sad feelings are to be expected. Counselors should be prepared to help clients brainstorm about other avenues to pursue. For example, a state licensing board or internal employment committee may take a different view of the evidence from a professional association. A third crucial point comes if the committee issues a ruling against the member. The outcome may be less than the client hoped for and may evoke feelings of betrayal. However, if the outcome seems to fit the offense, the client may feel guilty about the negative consequences for the violator. Again, the client may take on the responsibility for the professional's behavior, blaming him- or herself for the outcome. Clarifying the professional's duty to honor the profession's standards in all situations may help the client think more accurately about whose behavior was problematic. Finally, no matter what the outcome of the complaint, the counselor must help the client find ways to bring closure to this episode.

Responding If an Ethics Complaint Is Filed Against You

The risk of an ethics complaint happening to an individual counselor is not high. As described in Chapter 1, the proportion of claims to members in counseling, psychology, and social work is extremely low. Counselors who worry excessively about a complaint are misdirecting their energies. However, realistic concern is appropriate. If you are informed that an ethics complaint has been leveled against you, the ethics codes contain guidelines for your response. For example, Section H.3 of ACA's code states,

> Counselors cooperate with investigations, proceedings and requirements of the ACA Ethics Committee or ethics committees of other duly constituted associations having jurisdiction over those charged with a violation. (ACA, 1994, p. 19)

APA's code is even more specific:

> Psychologists cooperate with ethics investigations, proceedings and resulting requirements of the APA or any affiliated state psychological association to which they belong. In doing so, they make reasonable efforts to resolve any issues as to confidentiality. Failing to cooperate is itself an ethical violation. (APA, 1992, Section 8.07)

The central message is the need to cooperate. Ignoring an inquiry by an ethics committee or licensing board is the worst possible response, because failing to cooperate is an ethics violation in itself. The counselor may be especially tempted to ignore a inquiry that appears groundless, but even frivolous and false claims require a response (Anderson & Swanson, 1994). Cooperation entails providing all relevant information in a timely fashion. Each professional organization has somewhat different timelines, so it is important to refer to the rules governing the process in the organization in which the claim is made. Cooperation also means that you do not try to resign from the organization to avoid an ethics inquiry. Once a proceeding has begun, a member is not allowed to resign until the investigation is complete (ACA, 1995; APA, Ethics Committee 1996a). Even then, a resignation may be accepted only under certain conditions. Many people hire attorneys to assist them in this process and ensure that their rights are protected. This option is available to any counselor throughout the process.

Learning of an ethics claim against oneself arouses strong emotions. A wise counselor gets appropriate emotional support in this situation (Chauvin & Remley, 1996). When counselors believe that they have been falsely accused, these emotions can be truly overwhelming. In that situation, some reality testing is in order. History shows that most claims are dismissed before formal charges are issued, so that there is no need to panic about a preliminary investigation.

If you have committed the unethical action with which you are charged, but believe there are relevant extenuating circumstances, you should document the particulars to the committee or licensing board. Extenuating circumstances do not excuse such behaviors (and members who try to make excuses hardly ever win the favor of the committee), but they can put the misconduct in context. If you have subsequently taken steps on your own to prevent such actions in the future, your case may be strengthened by providing such information to the committee. Such an approach is consistent with the committee's interest in rehabilitating professionals rather than punishing them. Counselors who take responsibility for their mistakes and demonstrate a sincere commitment to rehabilitation go a long way in helping to save their careers.

SUMMARY

Counselors learn of ethics violations by other professionals in several ways—from clients, from colleagues, and through their own experience. Hearing of colleagues' misbehavior from clients is not uncommon. Counselors are obliged to address these violations themselves, or help clients who choose to address them to do so. However, when the desire to confront a colleague about an ethics violation conflicts with a client's right to confidentiality, confidentiality takes precedence.

The ethics codes recommend beginning with an attempt at an informal resolution of the problem. Usually, this starts with a conversation between the concerned and the offending counselor. If the concerned counselor is convinced that the offense did not occur or that rehabilitation efforts will be effective, no further action is necessary. If the counselor doubts whether the public will be protected from further misconduct, a formal complaint is the next step.

Individuals may submit ethics complaints to a variety of bodies, including licensing boards, professional associations, and employers. Procedures for handling such complaints are laid out in state regulations, ethics committee rules and procedures, or employee policy manuals. The central issue for the committees hearing such complaints is balancing the rights of the person making the complaint against the rights of the person accused. As in all other aspects of U.S. society, a professional is assumed innocent until proven guilty.

If a client has experienced unethical behavior by a former counselor, the current counselor should explain the client's options about reporting and help the client deal with the emotions during the process. The client should be free to decide autonomously about pursuing a complaint, because the complaint process is long and demanding, and can result in some reexperiencing of the initial pain. If the client decides to proceed, he or she needs to recognize that its primary benefit will be to future clients of that therapist, although it's possible the client will find the experience a healing one.

If an ethics complaint is filed against you, the ethics codes demand that you cooperate with the investigation and produce written responses to the complaint within the specified time limits. If a licensing board or ethics committee rules against you, you have the option to appeal that ruling. The goal of a professional ethics committee is rehabilitation rather than punishment, and whenever possible, sanctions short of losing one's professional membership are chosen. The deciding factor is the protection of the public welfare.

DISCUSSION QUESTIONS

1. Do you agree with the author's resolution of the case of Martina? Would you argue for an informal resolution? Why or why not?
2. Reporting an unethical behavior to an employer has both benefits and disadvantages. Discuss the strengths and weaknesses of this strategy.
3. What feelings may affect a counselor trying to support a client who is filing an ethics complaint against another counselor?
4. Do you think the findings of ethics committees should be made known to the public? Currently, many organizations provide information about members who have been disciplined for ethics breaches. What might be gained or lost by more widespread communication of such findings?

RECOMMENDED READINGS

American Counseling Association. (1994). *Policies and procedures for processing complaints of ethical violations.* Alexandria, VA: Author.

American Psychological Association of the Ethics Committee. (1996). *Rules and procedures.* Washington, DC: Author.

Chauvin, J. C., & Remley, T. P., Jr. (1996). Responding to allegations of unethical conduct. *Journal of Counseling and Development, 74,* 563–568.

Levenson, J. L. (1986). When a colleague acts unethically: Guidelines for intervention. *Journal of Counseling and Development, 64,* 315–317.

PART TWO

Major Ethical Issues
for Counselors

4

Competence to Practice
The Foundation for Doing Good and Avoiding Harm

Professional competence defies easy definition, but three major components capture the typical use of the term in the profession. These are *knowledge, skill,* and *diligence.* This chapter begins by defining each term, reviews the statements in the ethics codes on this topic, and discusses guidelines for determining the limits of competence and for expanding areas of competency. It ends by analyzing the impact of counselor distress and impairment on competent functioning.

Components of Professional Competence

Knowledge

To be knowledgeable means being schooled in the history, theory, and research of one's field and cognizant of the limits of current understanding. Knowledge implies having both a body of information that has been absorbed and a set of objective criteria for evaluating new theory and research. (The latter is especially important in counseling because theory and research are always evolving.) In mental health professions, knowledge is first achieved by completing a credible graduate-degree program in a given discipline. The most direct measure of a quality program is accreditation by the discipline, although that is not the only measure used. Degree programs accredited by a professional association have been reviewed by the discipline and judged to meet the discipline's standards for an adequate knowledge base. ACA (through its branch the Council for Accreditation of Counseling and Related Educational Programs), APA, and NASW all set high standards for graduate programs that seek accreditation. For counseling and social work, the entry-level degree is the master's, but psychologists have defined the entry-level degree as the doctorate. However, because knowledge is not static and research on human behavior is always revealing new information, a graduate degree, even from an accredited program, is only a starting point for competence. Without continued study after graduation, one's knowledge base soon erodes. In fact, some scholars suggest that approximately half of what a mental health professional learns in graduate school is obsolete within a decade of graduation (Dubin, 1972; Jensen, 1979). For this reason, many professional associations and state licensing boards mandate continuing education for their members. To be knowledgeable, one must stay current with developments in knowledge relevant to one's practice. Unfortunately, research evidence suggests that many practitioners fail to stay current with the published literature (Morrow-Bradley & Elliott, 1986) and thereby hasten the erosion of their knowledge.

Skill

The second component of competence is skill, not just in understanding therapeutic procedures, but also in successfully applying interventions with actual clients. Norman (1985) and Overholser and Fine (1990) divide this component into two kinds of skills: *Clinical skill* is the counselor's appropriate use of basic interviewing skills, and *technical skill* concerns effective use of specific therapeutic interventions. Clinical skills include the capacity to ask open-ended questions and to sensitively explore uncomfortable aspects of a client's problem. Technical skills include, for example, the ability to conduct desensitization for a client with test anxiety or to administer an individual intelligence test. Implicit in the general concept of skill is the capacity to make judgments about which interventions are appropriate in which situations. To help students develop these skills, all mental health training programs require field experiences such as practica and internships as major parts of their degree requirements. Applying knowledge with a client is a higher-order process than comprehending that information, and no one is competent until he or she has mastered both. For example, graduate students typically learn about treating phobias in their classes, becoming familiar with both the theory and the research on such treatments. They may read transcripts of sessions and view videotapes showing how counselors treat phobic clients. Students may even practice these approaches in role-plays with each other. Then students are tested on their grasp of the theory, research, and procedures. However, even students who pass such tests are not competent unless they can skillfully apply all this knowledge to clients who can benefit from such interventions. Typically, students using such interventions are closely supervised by experienced professionals who assess their skills, recommend improvements in the intern's behaviors, and ensure that the clients are benefiting. Because of the complexity of skill building in counseling, many hours of field experience are necessary to achieve success in applying counseling interventions. Additional supervised experience after the awarding of a degree is also typically required before states will license mental health professionals for independent practice. Some states require as much as three years of full-time work experience before granting a license.

The complexity of counseling also means that no single professional will be skillful in all interventions, either at graduation or at any point in his or her career. The staggering range of human problems people bring to counseling, coupled with the diversity of counseling interventions, renders universal competence impossible. Counselors must limit their work to some subsample of problems and populations. Some counselors focus on particular problems such as anxiety and depression or career indecision, whereas others focus on particular age groups, such as college students or the aging. Still others limit their practice to a particular cultural group or to group or family counseling. Counselors who limit their practices thus have a better chance of providing effective service by keeping their knowledge and skills current. Beware the counselor who claims to do everything well: Either some of those skills are underdeveloped, or that person is a fraud.

Diligence

Diligence, the third component of competence, is a consistent attentiveness to the client's needs that takes priority over other concerns. A diligent counselor gives deliberate care to appropriate assessment and intervention for a client's problem and maintains that care until counseling is completed. Diligence means that the professional is willing to work hard to help a client and is ready to refer the client elsewhere if the counselor feels unable to give competent help. This attentiveness is grounded in self-knowledge—only counselors who understand their strengths and limitations can be truly diligent. Diligent counselors honestly evaluate their own skills and seek additional training when necessary. Evidence of a diligent attitude emerges in several ways. It is present in the thoroughness of counseling. A diligent counselor wants to be as sure as reasonably possible about the problem and the treatment. (Note the words *reasonably* and *sure*; diligence does not require obsessive concern with detail.) Diligence is also present in the counselor's willingness to engage in additional reading and research about the problem and to consult with colleagues about the case. A diligent counselor is interested in following up clients who stop counseling, to check the long-term effectiveness of interventions. Such information can help both the former client and future clients. In short, diligence means that the counselor is willing to "go the extra mile" to help each client and to improve professional skills.

Thus competence takes much intellectual and emotional energy and is as much a goal as a reality. The competence continuum runs from incompetent to exceptionally competent (Koocher, 1979). A competent professional is always seeking to enhance current skills and knowledge. Competence is not perfection. Instead, competence implies adequacy in skills and is operationally measured in a comparative fashion. One is competent when one's knowledge and skills are as well developed as those of other competent mental health professionals previously demonstrated to be effective in the specified area. One is deemed competent if, after education and supervised practice, one can carry out an intervention at least as well as supervisors or colleagues. A comparative criterion has its perils, however—one might settle for being as incompetent as one's colleagues. A more valid and objective criterion for competence is one's effectiveness in helping clients. Counseling that benefits the client and avoids unnecessary risk to him or her is the more fundamental measure of competence. Sometimes a third criterion exists—attainment of the standards established by a professional association for a particular type of practice. For example, the American Psychological Association has produced specialty guidelines for providing services in clinical, counseling, school, and organizational psychology (1981b) that identify skills essential for competence in these areas. Similarly, the American Association of Marriage and Family Therapists (AAMFT) has established criteria for competence in that discipline (Everett, 1990).

Competence as Performance, Not Capacity

Competence refers to a person's professional performance, not to abilities. One may have the *ability* to perform a task competently, but competence is judged in the *performance* of the task itself (Jensen, 1979). Many factors can interfere with a capable person's performance. These factors range from environmental circumstances (such as impossible work demands) to unpredictable events (such as a sudden illness in the middle of a session) to mental health problems in the therapist (such as burnout). Ability is a prerequisite for competence, but is not identical with it.

Competent performance probably also varies somewhat from client to client or day to day. No mental health professional performs at exactly the same level of skill and diligence with every client. Fatigue, distraction, and stress are just a few problems that can compromise competent performance. No counselor should expect completely uniform performance in all situations. A more realistic standard is for counselors to set a threshold level, which they do not cross, for competent work with clients. This threshold level should be defined as adequate service that provides the client with benefit. If counselors give service less competent than that, they need to make diligent efforts to rectify the problems created by their actions. For instance, a counselor may invite a client back for another session without charge to compensate for a prior meeting, or may consult a colleague or supervisor to deal with the stress that caused the lapse. (A later section of this chapter discusses service made persistently inadequate by impairment or distress.)

Professional Standards for Practice

All the major codes of ethics governing mental health professions contain statements about competence. Both the ACA and APA codes make lengthy comments on the topic, underscoring its importance. These standards derive from the ethical principles of beneficence and nonmaleficence, the duty to do good and to avoid harm. As mentioned in Chapter 1, genuine skill at helping people in distress is essential for professions that publicly proclaim their expertise in this area. Offering anything less constitutes dishonest advertising.

ACA *Code of Ethics,* Section C: Professional Responsibility

C.2.a Counselors practice only within the boundaries of their competence, based on their education, training, supervised experience, state and national professional credentials, and appropriate professional experience. . . .

C.2.b Counselors practice in specialty areas new to them only after appropriate education, training and supervised experience. While developing skills in new specialty areas, counselors take steps to ensure the competence of their work and to protect others from possible harm.

C.2.c Counselors accept employment only for positions for which they are qualified. . . .

C.2.d Counselors continually monitor their effectiveness as professionals and take steps to improve when necessary. . . .

C.2.f Counselors recognize the need for continuing education to maintain a reasonable level of awareness of current scientific and professional information in their fields of activity. They take steps to maintain competence in the skills they use.

APA *Ethical Principles,* Section 1.04: Boundaries of Competence

(a) Psychologists provide services, teach, and conduct research only within the boundaries of their competence, based on their education, training, supervised experience, or appropriate professional experience.

(b) Psychologists provide services, teach, or conduct research in new areas or involving new techniques only after first undertaking appropriate study, training, supervision, and/or consultation from persons who are competent in their areas or techniques.

(c) In those emerging areas in which generally recognized standards for preparatory training do not yet exist, psychologists nevertheless take reasonable steps to ensure the competence of their work and to protect patients, clients, students, research participants, and others from harm.

APA *Ethical Principles,* Section 1.05: Maintaining Expertise

Psychologists who engage in assessment, therapy, teaching, research, organizational consulting, or other professional activities maintain a reasonable level of awareness of current scientific and professional information in their fields of activity, and undertake efforts to maintain competence in the skills they use.

Both codes acknowledge the impossibility of universal competence in every aspect of counseling and thus emphasize the importance of working within the limits of one's knowledge and skill. They place the duty to monitor one's competence directly in the hands of the individual professional. That professional is obligated to evaluate current skills and seek to improve them whenever skills begin to erode. Finally, the codes indicate that competence typically results from formal education, supervised practice under supervision, and continuing education. They imply that informal, unstructured approaches to developing new competencies are likely to be insufficient. Professionals seeking to extend their competence to a new area should have a plan consistent with existing standards and committed to a comprehensive understanding of the new area. APA's code also attends to the difficult issue of establishing competence in new and emerging areas of practice for which widely accepted standards of competence do not yet exist. The codes' guidance in such situations is rather vague, but the section imposes a duty to do as much as reasonably possible to become competent and to protect clients and other consumers of such untested approaches.

The Relationship Between Competence and Professional Credentials

Licenses and certificates are designed to protect the public from frauds and charlatans pretending to provide professional services. Procidano, Busch-Rossnagel, Reznikoff & Geisinger (1995) capture the function of licenses well: "What the states license is the absence of deficiencies, rather than the presence of competencies" (p. 427). Certifying bodies review only the knowledge component of competence. They can weed out the least knowledgeable because they prevent people who lack appropriate graduate degrees from becoming licensed or certified A graduate degree is, after all, the primary credential for professional competence; licenses and certificates are secondary (Koocher, 1979). Because counselors typically need to pass a state examination to get a license, individuals who managed to receive a degree without benefit of much learning to accompany it are not likely to pass the examination.

Credentialing bodies evaluate the skills component rather indirectly, through the requirement that candidates for licensing amass a substantial number of hours of supervised experience in the field. These bodies tend not to measure diligence at all, except as they inquire about prior ethics violations or personal impairments that may compromise practice. When the other requirements are met, diligence is assumed. The continuing education requirements built into most mental health licenses aim to protect the public from practitioners whose knowledge and skills are obsolete. Unfortunately, in most cases these continuing education requirements are too minimal to serve the purpose. Finally, licensing boards usually require applicants to specify their areas of competence. Many credentialing bodies also request this information at each subsequent renewal of the license. In a small way, this process forces practitioners to identify the boundaries of their competence and reminds them that the limits they specify are a matter of public record. Working outside those boundaries carries a risk to their license.

Professional organizations that branch off from the national associations have been formed to provide more stringent measures of competence. One such organization is the American Board of Professional Psychology. Practitioners may apply to this body to be certified as "diplomats" in their field. If applicants pass the rigorous review process for this status, they have demonstrated a well-recognized level of professional accomplishment. The National Board of Certified Counselors provides the same service for counselors. These certifications go a step beyond a professional license to practice, although they are also categorized as secondary credentials. However, even such status does not guarantee competence, because of the inherent weaknesses in the procedures used to evaluate candidates. True measures of therapeutic effectiveness are difficult to find. Moreover, possessing such certificates does not imply future competence. Without continued effort to maintain knowledge and skill, competence still erodes, no matter how firmly established it has been at any prior point.

Challenges in Defining the Limits of Competence

How do counselors determine the areas in which they are competent, and how do they develop new areas of competence after completing graduate school? The codes give reasonable direction in this area:

> **ACA *Code of Ethics,* Section C.2.b: Professional Competence**
> Counselors practice in specialty areas new to them only after appropriate education, training, and supervised experience. While developing skills in new areas, counselors take steps to ensure the competence of their work and to protect others from possible harm.

> **APA *Ethical Principles,* Section 1.04.b Boundaries of Competence**
> Psychologists provide services, teach, or conduct research in new areas or involving new techniques only after undertaking appropriate study, training, supervision, and/or consultation from persons who are competent in these areas or techniques.

Before one can claim competence in any given procedure, population, or assessment tool, formal training is necessary. Formal training typically entails classroom learning, reading, and discussion with experts. The length and depth of the instruction depends on the complexity of the new competence, its potential to help or harm clients, and the prior background of the counselor. For example, a counselor well trained in play therapy with school-age children, who wants to become competent in a new form of play therapy, may need less classroom time than another child therapist unfamiliar with any play therapy methods. The latter person would require in-depth instruction in the history, theory, and procedures of play therapy, along with supervised practice in established interventions, before he or she could advance to the new technique. Both would require supervised experience in the new technique. The amount of supervised experience will also differ with each practitioner; the criterion for success is the capacity to judge when the technique is appropriate and to apply the knowledge in a skillful way with a number of children. If the new play therapy technique has been demonstrated to be a powerful counseling intervention (one that can offer substantial help when used properly or cause substantial harm when used improperly), the standard for competence with the intervention should be set very high. Practically, this translates into longer and more intensive training and practice with the technique. It is important to remember that the requirements for competence are not different for those who are already competent in other forms of counseling. What may be different is the speed with which counselors can proceed through the requirements because of their history and background.

Some weekend workshops and brief seminars are advertised as training professionals in new interventions. Because they seldom offer time for reading, research, and supervised practice in the technique with actual clients, however, they are unlikely to produce counselors truly competent in the technique. When these interventions have the potential to be powerful therapeutic tools, lack of time for reading, reflection, and supervised practice can be particularly problematic. Only professionals who take extra time to read, reflect, and seek out competent supervision will probably gain real competence. Moreover, the definition of competence implies scientific value. In other words, one can really claim competence only for interventions that have provided scientific evidence of their effectiveness in helping clients. Independent research demonstrating the efficacy of the approach is the cornerstone of such evidence. Without such evidence, new interventions are experimental, and claiming competence in such situations seems premature. No certainty about their therapeutic value exists. Thus, when counselors are looking for continuing education to expand their competencies, they need to ascertain whether the proposed training (a) is based on scientific evidence, objectively obtained; (b) includes sufficient classroom time to absorb the new material; and (c) and provides opportunities for supervised practice and recommendations for obtaining additional supervised experience at one's workplace. Sometimes direct inquiries to the workshop organizers are necessary to obtain this information. The wording of the APA code in the following section supports this interpretation:

> **APA *Ethical Principles*, Section 1.06: Basis for Scientific and Professional Judgments**
> Psychologists rely on scientifically and professionally derived knowledge when making scientific or professional judgments or when engaging in scholarly or professional endeavors.

Limits of Competence with New Populations of Clients

The boundaries of competence extend not just to intervention strategies such as play therapy or career counseling, but also to new populations, cultures, and age groups. A person may be skilled in career counseling for one cultural group or age group but may be incompetent to use that intervention with other age groups or cultural groups. This happens because these contexts can affect the way the intervention is received and its effectiveness. Competent work with particular populations also assumes knowledge of the group and demonstrated skill in working with clients from that group. A college counselor who applies without modification the career counseling approaches he uses with university students, to middle school students is unlikely to help those children. He has failed to adapt his intervention to their developmental level, and he may thereby have inflicted unintended negative effects on the children. Very few counseling interventions have universal effectiveness. The evidence supporting most interventions usually comes from one or two subpopulations.

Similarly, helping a Cambodian immigrant to the United States deal with depressed feelings may demand competencies different from those needed to treat someone raised in the United States. In this situation, knowledge of the impact of culture and immigration status on the etiology and symptoms of depression is important. Counselors competent in treating depression in America have a duty to recognize the unique parameters of this case and to seek additional training to help the client or refer him to another counselor already competent with these issues.

The professional associations recognize the need for knowledge and skill in working with different populations in two major ways. First, APA has published special guidelines for conducting therapy with women (APA, Task Force, 1978) and for providing services to ethnic and culturally diverse populations (APA, 1993b). These documents are a resource for practitioners seeking to evaluate their competence with clients from these populations. Second, ACA has addressed the topic in its ethics code. Section C.2.a reads, "Counselors will demonstrate a commitment to gain knowledge, personal awareness, sensitivity, and skills pertinent to working with a culturally diverse population" (ACA, 1994). In addition, Section C.2.g of that code emphasizes that continuing education is necessary to maintain competency with culturally diverse populations.

Limits of Competence in Rural Environments

One challenge in identifying and working within the boundaries of competence arises from the geographical location of a given counseling practice. Professionals in urban and suburban settings tend to have many referral sources for clients to whom they do not feel competent to offer services. These referral sources are usually located in the same community, and a referral presents no real hardship to the client. Thus, urban and suburban practitioners have relatively little difficulty setting clear boundaries to their practices, and have the luxury of focusing on areas in which they have developed significant expertise. In contrast, practitioners in rural areas and small towns do not have many referral sources nearby. Seeing another professional frequently entails a real inconvenience for a client because it means traveling some distance. The inconvenience escalates to hardship if a client does not have access to a car or other supports to ease the problem of going many miles to get counseling. Sometimes the local mental health professional is the only available source of services. If he or she cannot provide counseling, clients will try to cope on their own. Consequently, out of necessity professionals in rural areas usually practice as generalists. If they became highly specialized, they probably would not have enough clients, and would need to turn away clients with problems outside their specialty who truly need mental health services.

The ethical challenge for rural counselors is to provide competent service across a wide range of issues, age groups, and populations, while acknowledging that they are not supercounselors who can do everything (Hargrove, 1986). What criteria should rural counselors use when trying to decide whether a given client request is beyond the limits of their competence? The major determination evolves from the principle of nonmaleficence—avoiding harm to clients. Clients who are at risk for harm from an incompetent counseling intervention are better served by a referral, no matter how impractical. Second, counselors should evaluate the opportunity to do good and should compare the risk of harm to the opportunity to help. If the risk of harm is high and the chance to help is less high, then one should refrain from intervention. If the risk of harm is low and the opportunity to do good is significantly greater, then the intervention can be considered. In this case, rural counselors should use inventive strategies to enhance their knowledge and gain access to appropriate supervision. Finally, rural counselors should monitor client progress and aggressively intervene when the client seems not to be benefiting from counseling. If rural counselors see a pattern of client problems at the boundaries of their competence, they have a duty to gain additional education to become more competent in serving this community need. (Needless to say, informed consent takes on even greater importance when the intervention approaches the boundaries of a counselor's competence. Clients should be informed about the level of their counselor's competence and give written consent to counseling.)

Additional Criteria for Evaluating Competence

Haas and Malouf (1995) recommend that mental health professionals ask themselves two other questions when they are unsure about their competence with a particular client. The first question is "Are you emotionally able to help the client?" (p. 23) They suggest that counselors ask themselves whether they can maintain objectivity in the situation. Perhaps the nature of the client's problem is too close to the counselor's own experience for the counselor to avoid countertransference. To maintain objectivity, counselors need to have insight into their behavior and have a professional support system available to double-check the accuracy of their own interpretations of the client. Even then, some client issues are strong triggers for some counselors, and those safeguards are insufficient. Referral is then the safest choice. The second question Haas and Malouf suggest is "Could you justify your decision to a group of your peers? (1995, p. 24)." They also refer to this as the "clean, well-lit room standard," which means that any action that a counselor would feel comfortable describing in an open discussion with his or her peers is likely to be appropriate. Conversely, any counseling activity that a professional would like to hide or be ashamed to admit to peers is probably not a responsible action. This standard applies not only to questions of competence to treat but also to other ethical issues in practice, especially dual relationships.

The Limits of Competence: Case Examples

Consider the following cases, both of which illustrate the challenges of defining the limits of one's competence as a counselor.

The Case of Mrs. Varos

A couple makes an appointment with Mrs. Varos, a licensed professional counselor with 10 years of experience in private practice. This couple is requesting sex therapy, and the initial assessment suggests that they have accurately identified the major difficulty in their relationship. In fact, the sexual dysfunction they describe is very common, and is typically responsive to therapy. Mrs. Varos had no formal courses in sex therapy in graduate school, but has read several books on the topic and attended a two-day workshop in the subject nine months ago. Mrs. Varos also has a colleague with extensive training and experience in this area who is willing to supervise her for this case. In this situation, can Mrs. Varos consider herself competent to offer professional services to this couple?

The first step in determining whether Mrs. Varos should accept this couple as clients is to ascertain whether she has the requisite knowledge of sex therapy. Knowledge usually means formal education, which she lacks. However, if Mrs. Varos can demonstrate that her independent reading and the workshop she attended are equivalent to what others receive in formal courses, then it is conceivable that she could meet the knowledge requirement, although not likely. The second issue is whether she has enough appropriate supervised experience in sex therapy to be skillful in its application. She has no such experience, a significant obstacle to demonstrating competence in sex therapy. If her experience as a professional counselor includes marriage and family therapy, and she is competent in this related field, she may not need extensive hours of supervised experience in sex therapy to become competent. However, her complete lack of such supervised experience probably renders her incompetent to serve as sex therapist to this couple at this time, even though their problem usually responds to therapy. Her colleague's offer to supervise her work with this couple is a factor to consider, but it is not sufficient to make her competent. The availability of a colleague with expertise to help this couple actually constitutes a strong argument for referral. Why risk harming or simply not helping this couple when another professional with proven skill is easily accessible? For all these reasons, the welfare of the clients requires a referral.

The clean, well-lit room standard also leads to a recommendation for referral. Mrs. Varos probably would not be comfortable reporting to respected colleagues that she treated this couple without supervision or additional knowledge.

One way in which Mrs. Varos could accept these clients would be for them to consent to treatment by a novice under supervision in sex therapy. If they understood the limits of Mrs. Varos's competence and the implications of supervision by another therapist, and they wanted to continue with Mrs. Varos, then she could work with this couple. She would have the responsibility to fill gaps in her knowledge as soon as possible, to monitor their progress closely, and to use supervision wisely.

The Case of Dr. Marcello

Dr. Marcello is a licensed psychologist who has worked in a community mental health agency for five years. He specializes in family therapy, an area in which he has had considerable academic training and supervised experience. Dr. Marcello views himself as competent as a family therapist. Mr. and Mrs. Turner make an appointment to see him because they are concerned about their teenage son, who has been truant from school often and has been ignoring curfews and other family rules. The Turners are African-Americans and Dr. Marcello has little experience in counseling African-American families. He did have formal courses in multicultural issues in graduate school and has kept up with the literature in this area. His own cultural background does not match that of the Turners. In fact, the population served by the mental health center has very few African-Americans, and no other staff member at the agency has such experience. Does Dr. Marcello's experience in family therapy make him competent to work with the Turners?

The case of Dr. Marcello is more complicated than the first case. There is no doubt of his competence in family therapy. His knowledge base on multicultural issues may also be adequate. The cultural difference between the therapist and the potential clients here, coupled with Dr. Marcello's lack of experience in family therapy with African-American families, is the central issue. Should his lack of experience with African-American families prevent him from accepting this family as clients? To resolve this question, several other questions must be addressed:

1. To what degree does the literature suggest that family dynamics in African-American families differ significantly from those in other cultures?
2. To what degree have the approaches to family therapy in which Dr. Marcello has been trained been shown to be effective to African-American families?
3. What evidence exists that these approaches have harmed or failed to benefit African-American families?
4. What is the attitude of this family to this psychologist, and what are their views about whether the cultural differences between them will inhibit effective therapy?
5. Exactly how much prior experience has Dr. Marcello had with African-American families? Can he arrange for competent supervision for this case?
6. Are there other competent professionals in the community to whom Dr. Marcello can refer this family?

By reviewing the requirements for competence, knowledge, experience, and diligence to resolve this dilemma, we can surmise that Dr. Marcello's knowledge is probably adequate, given his education and continued reading. His commitment to stay current in the literature on multicultural issues and his demonstrated competence as a family therapist also are positive signs of diligence and sensitivity. His limited supervised experience is the problem, a problem complicated by the unavailability of an appropriately trained professional at his agency. At the very least, because of this deficit Dr. Marcello cannot proceed in this case as he has in others. He has two ethical alternatives. He may refer the family to a competent professional at another agency, or he may make special arrangements for supervision from a professional outside the agency, and then obtain the Turners' consent to such supervision. In the latter case, the Turners would understand Dr. Marcello's strengths and weaknesses as their family therapist, and would agree to the supervisor's involvement in the case.

Of course, referral to a professional competent in this area is not always practical, be-cause relatively few African-American family therapists with this competency are prac-ticing, and many non-African-American therapists have insufficient knowledge or ex-perience in family therapy with this cultural group. If obtaining a competent referral is problematic, and the Turners are likely to benefit from intervention, the argument in fa-vor of Dr. Marcello's taking on this case is stronger. As in the case of Mrs. Varos, the family's progress must be carefully monitored so that any negative effects of counseling can be identified and counteracted. In the end, the central consideration is doing good for the clients and avoiding harm to them.

These cases also demonstrate the responsibility of the individual practitioner to in-terpret the meaning of the ethical mandates for each situation and to use the ethical principles to complement the codes.

Distress and Impairment Among Professionals

The jobs of counselors are inherently stressful. They repeatedly see the pain and destruc-tiveness of people, and although they can usually offer help and hope to those in need, they have no magic wand to quickly make things right for their suffering clients. The cumulative effects of witnessing so much suffering can wear down even the most dili-gent professionals. Counselors also have the increasingly burdensome responsibility of dealing with institutions, and governmental agencies indifferent or hostile to counseling, or with managed care providers whose demands for short-term counseling for lifelong problems often seem cruel and absurd. Counselors are being asked to do more with less, and there is no end to that trend in sight. It's no wonder that in the face of these exter-nal pressures counselors often become emotionally exhausted by their work. In its most extreme form, this emotional exhaustion becomes burnout, a syndrome that significantly compromises the competent performance of mental health professionals. A true burnout syndrome consists of emotional exhaustion, the loss of a sense of accomplishment in one's work, and a depersonalization of those served (Maslach & Jackson, 1986). Research shows that burnout affects a small but significant number of mental health professionals (for example, see Ackerly, Burnell, Holder, & Kurdek, 1988; Raquepaw & Miller, 1989) and school counselors (for example, see Welfel, O'Dell, & Schuttenberg, 1991). Findings indicate that 1% to 5% of those sampled suffer from a full syndrome of burnout, but ap-proximately one-third of the counselors scored high in emotional exhaustion in a num-ber of these studies. A recent study of psychologists also found about one-third admitting "episodes of emotional exhaustion and fatigue" (Mahoney, 1997).

Counselors who work in crisis situations with those traumatized by violence, war, and natural disasters often experience a form of trauma themselves. They can suffer from the very symptoms of posttraumatic stress that they are treating, a phenomenon labeled in the literature as *compassion fatigue* or *secondary posttraumatic stress disorder* (Fig-ley, 1995). Mental health services for those who help victims of crises such as the

Oklahoma City bombing of 1995 are being recognized as a necessary component of crisis intervention services.

Of course, counselors have their share of stress in their personal lives, too. They juggle careers, family responsibilities, relationships, and civic duties simultaneously and sometimes get hit broadside by unexpected catastrophes. From time to time these stresses become overwhelming for all counselors. If the distress is temporary, the usual coping mechanisms of taking time off, restructuring responsibilities, or getting support from colleagues and loved ones usually prevent any lengthy compromise in competent performance (Coster & Schwebel, 1997). Occasionally, however, the stress becomes so unmanageable that the usual coping strategies are inadequate and job performance is impaired. According to Stadler (1990), "impaired counselors have lost the ability to transcend stressful events" (p. 178). Research has documented that this phenomenon is not uncommon. Pope et al. (1987) found that 62% of the psychologists responding to their survey had reported working when overwhelmed by stress, and most of these (85%) recognized that it was unethical to do so. In another study, Guy, Poelstra, and Stark (1989) found that more than one-third of their sample of mental health providers admitted giving substandard care while distressed, although only 5% of those thought the care was poor enough to be defined as incompetent. Psychologists have called such impairment a serious problem for the mental health professions (Laliotis & Grayson, 1985; Wood, Klein, Cross, Lammers, & Elliott, 1985). Unfortunately, few data exist regarding the incidence of impairment in licensed counselors (Stadler, Willing, Eberhage, & Ward, 1988).

Other researchers have reported that substance abuse problems occur frequently among psychologists and psychiatrists. Thoreson, Nathan, Skorina, and Kilburg (1983) estimated that approximately 6,000 psychologists suffer from alcohol and drug abuse. In a more recent study, 9% of the psychologists sampled by Thoreson, Miller, and Krauskopf (1989) indicated that drinking was a problem for them. Substance abuse has been cited as the most frequent cause of impairment in physicians (Bissell & Haberman, 1984). In a rare study that included master's-level counselors along with other therapists, Deutsch (1985) found that 10% of her sample reported substance abuse difficulties.

Of course, mental health professionals are not immune from other psychological disorders. In fact, some studies show a higher rate of suicide among psychiatrists (Knutsen, 1977) and female psychologists (Roeske, 1986) than in the general population. The rates of depression and other emotional problems do not appear different from rates in the general population, with about 10% of psychologists reporting depression (Thoreson et al., 1989) and about 15% of psychiatrists showing evidence of emotional problems (Herrington, 1979). The only study that showed a significantly higher report of depression among therapists than in the general population was that of Deutsch (1985), in which about half of the therapists reported difficulties with depression.

Another common cause of distress among counselors is dissatisfaction with their intimate relationships. Deutsch (1985) found this the most common problem cited by her sample, and Guy et al. (1989) reported this difficulty as the second most frequent one identified by psychologists.

The codes of ethics comment directly on the phenomenon of impairment:

ACA *Code of Ethics,* **Section C.2.g: Impairment**

Counselors refrain from offering or accepting professional services when their physical, mental or emotional problems are likely to harm a client or others. They are alert to the signs of impairment, seek assistance for their problems, and if necessary, limit, suspend or terminate their professional responsibilities.

APA *Ethical Principles,* **Section, 1.13: Personal Problems and Conflicts**

(a) Psychologists recognize that their personal problems and conflicts may interfere with their effectiveness. Accordingly, they refrain from undertaking an activity when they know or should know that their personal problems are likely to lead to harm to a patient, client, colleague, student, research participant, or other person to whom they may owe a professional or scientific obligation.

(b) In addition, psychologists have an obligation to be alert to signs of, and obtain assistance for, their personal problems at an early stage, in order to prevent impaired performance.

(c) When psychologists become aware of personal problems that may interfere with their performing work-related duties adequately, they take appropriate measures, such as obtaining professional consultation or assistance, and determine whether they should limit, suspend, or terminate their work-related duties.

These codes place the responsibility for avoiding incompetent practice on the individual professional. (This responsibility is discussed in greater detail Chapter 16.) The professional has the duty to self-monitor and to take steps to amend or interrupt practice, if necessary, to prevent harm to clients. Both codes imply that professionals ought to seek counseling and psychotherapy as appropriate or to engage in other activities that will help the professional regain his or her prior level of professional functioning. The ethical principle underlying the comments in the codes is nonmaleficence.

Research shows that compliance with this standard is far from universal. Guy et al. (1989) found that 70% of their sample took steps to help themselves, including getting therapy, but Deutsch (1984) reported that the majority of therapists in her sample showed reluctance to seek therapy for personal problems. Results from Pope et al. (1987) also suggest that this duty is breached fairly often.

Avoiding Harm to Clients from Burnout and Impairment

In addition to monitoring their own emotional status and stress levels, counselors can take additional actions to prevent burnout and impairment (Welfel et al., 1991):

1. In the face of external stresses such as managed care, budget cuts, and unsympathetic administrators, counselors need to work with other professionals to fight changes

that harm clients and to get support from colleagues who share their experiences. Isolation from colleagues enhances the risk of burnout.

2. Counselors, who define themselves as professional helpers, need to set clear limits about how much help they can humanly give. Out of misguided good intentions, members of this profession sometimes take on more than they can handle. Learning to set boundaries increases effectiveness and decreases the risk of burnout and failure.

3. Counselors should take their own advice about self-care. All too often counselors fail to take time for themselves even as they admonish client after client about the importance of self-care. Without time to nourish him- or herself, a counselor soon becomes overstressed and ineffective.

4. Counselors need to recognize their own vulnerability and seek help and support when overwhelmed. The combination of work stress and life's complexity often leads to emotional difficulties. Acknowledging these difficulties is a strength, not a weakness. A self-help network for psychologists has been available for more than a decade (Kilburg, Nathan, & Thoreson, 1986; Schwebel, Schoener, & Skorina, 1994). Through this network, psychologists can find colleagues who volunteer their time to help other psychologists with drug and alcohol problems. The earlier that intervention is sought, the more quickly the distress will diminish. Besides, counselors who cannot accept the value of therapy for their own problems are either denying the value of their work or suggesting that they are superior to their clients. Such a position, dehumanizes clients and places mental health professionals in a different class.

5. Following the lead of Stadler et al. (1988), counselors should encourage ACA and state associations to become more active in defining, remediating, and preventing impairment among counselors.

6. Counselors in training should consider counseling for their personal problems, even if not overwhelmed by them. Counseling provides greater insight, better tools for managing problems that may become overwhelming in the future, and empathy for the experiences of their clients who are often awkward and afraid about coming to therapy. In some training programs, personal counseling is required (Patrick, 1989).

7. Counselors who work in crisis settings should be prepared for symptoms of secondary posttraumatic stress and take full advantage of support services available to crisis workers.

Legal Ramifications of Incompetent Practice

Counselors who perform incompetently are potentially subject to legal action as well as discipline by their professional association. Incompetent service is often negligent service, and counselors can be sued for negligence in civil court. If the facts of the case merit a judgment against a mental health professional, damages can be awarded to the person(s) who have brought the suit (the plaintiff). The thought of being sued frightens most counselors, and with some justification. Litigation against mental health professionals has increased in recent years. As Voltaire once wrote, " I was never ruined but twice: once when I lost a lawsuit and once when I won one." The process is indeed uncomfortable regardless of the outcome. However, counselors should not be immobilized by such fears. They ought to take comfort in the relative infrequency of civil suits for practicing outside of the boundaries of one's competence.

Many responsible counselors who worry about lawsuits fail to understand the distinction between ordinary mistakes, to which every professional is sometimes vulnerable, and negligence for which one can be held liable. Four criteria must be met for a court to rule in favor of the plaintiff. (For a fuller explanation of these concepts, see Bednar, Bednar, Lambert, and Waite, 1991, or Swenson, 1997.) The first criterion is that the professional's duty to the client must be established. To establish a duty to a client, a counselor needs to be in a professional relationship with that client. When a client enters into a professional relationship with a counselor, that client implicitly cedes to the counselor some control over his or her concerns, and the counselor's duty to the client is thus created. A counselor does not have a duty to the person sitting next to her on the bus, or to a person he or she meets at a social event. No professional relationship exists in these situations, and hence no potential control over the person's actions is present. Thus, a counselor cannot be found negligent for any harm that comes to the person sitting next to her on the bus or for any harm that person may inflict on other riders. The next logical question is, How long does it take to establish a relationship so that a duty can be defined? Courts have varied somewhat in their judgments, but in some jurisdictions as little as a single counseling session has been found sufficient.

The second criterion for negligence is that the counselor must have breached a duty to the client. Specifically, this means that the care the counselor provided fell below the accepted standard of care for the profession. The standard of care is defined as the quality of care that other competent professionals would provide in this kind of situation. The standard of care is *not* the best possible care, but rather, adequate care. Formerly, the standard of care was judged largely according to local standards, but since the onset of electronic communication and easy access to professional literature, the standard of care has become more nationally uniform, with counselors in Pocatello, Idaho, for example, held to a very similar standard as those in Miami. It is important to emphasize that this standard allows for mistakes and errors in judgment. Competence does not imply perfection. Rather, the errors one makes constitute negligence only if they are errors that other professionals, acting competently, would be unlikely to make. For example, a mental health professional, exasperated with a client's frequent threats of suicide, suggests that a client "put up or shut up" about suicide. Later that day, after taking an overdose of sleeping pills, the client is rushed to the hospital. If a suit is brought against that counselor, the central issues would be whether the suggestion made by the counselor is an error, and whether this error was one that other competent professionals would not make under the same circumstances. To answer these questions, the attorneys would look to the professional literature and the experts in suicide. If both evidence of error and substandard practice exist, then the counselor's behavior would have met the second criterion for negligence. However, the suit can be successful only if two additional criteria are met.

To meet the third criterion, an injury or damage to the client must be established. A counselor's mistake, no matter how wrongheaded or incompetent, is not legally meaningful unless some injury results. (By the way, this criterion need not apply for an ethics complaint to be upheld.) If the suicidal client just described ignored the counselor's advice and immediately sought assistance from another more competent professional, that client would have difficulty demonstrating injury. Even an irresponsible mistake does not result in legal liability if it has no negative effect on the client.

Finally, if injury or damage does happen to the client, the client's attorney must prove the harm was caused by the therapist's mistake. If the harm would have happened to the client regardless of the therapist's action, then negligence cannot be proved.

In short, the standard for liability for negligence is a rigorous one, and its very rigor should reassure counselors about the risks of frivolous or unjustified lawsuits. However, the best protection against lawsuits is, in accordance with the codes of ethics, practicing within the boundaries of one's competence. Civil suits for practice beyond the limits of one's competence are unlikely to decrease in the decade ahead.

SUMMARY

Competence has three primary components: knowledge, skill, and diligence. Competence means that one performs effective counseling techniques as well as other skilled professionals and according to accepted criteria. Competence is distinguished from perfection, because universal competence is unattainable. Rather, competence should be thought of as spanning a continuum from incompetent to exceptionally competent. A counselor should always aim for higher levels of competence. Because of the evolving nature of knowledge and practice, competencies must be maintained through continuing education and consultation, or they will erode.

The ethics codes demand that to avoid harm to clients, professionals must practice within the limits of their competence. When seeking to develop new competencies or to determine whether a particular activity is within their existing skills, counselors must evaluate their level of formal training and supervised practice in the area. Both formal training and supervised practice are prerequisites for competence. Counselors who judge their skills inadequate for a client's needs should refer the client to a competent colleague. Counselors in rural areas have special concerns about the limits of competence, because referral sources are scarce and the pressures on them to act as generalists are great. The central ethical issue is the capacity to assist the client and avoid risk of harm. Counselors need to take developmental and cultural issues into account when evaluating their competencies, because no counseling intervention has been demonstrated effective across all ages or cultures.

At times the stress of this occupation becomes overwhelming. When this happens, competent performance is threatened and a formerly competent counselor may provide inadequate service. The codes place the responsibility for self-monitoring stress on the individual counselor, and they mandate that counselors limit or interrupt their practices if necessary to avoid harm to clients. Burnout caused by occupational stress, and impairment caused by emotional, relationship, or substance abuse problems, are the most common reasons for this kind of incompetent service.

When counselors practice outside the boundaries of their competence or provide incompetent service, they are at risk for a civil suit against them in addition to an ethics complaint. Lawsuits are still relatively uncommon and no diligent counselor needs to worry excessively about this eventuality. Counselors need to understand that negligence is not identical with professional error, and that a lawsuit against a counselor for negligence can be won only if (a) the counselor has a demonstrable professional relationship with the client, (b) if the counselor made a mistake that showed substandard care, (c) if the client suffered an injury, and (d) the injury was directly caused by the counselor's actions.

DISCUSSION QUESTIONS

1. There is debate in the mental health professions about the value of professional credentials such as licenses and certifications. Some argue such credentials do more to protect the professions than to protect the public. What is your view on this issue?

2. Some say that the standards for practicing within the limits of one's competence are unfair to rural practitioners, who must try to help an extraordinarily wide range of people if they are to have any practice at all. They contend that the standard has a bias in favor of urban and suburban practitioners. What do you think of this argument?

3. The advent of managed care presents new dilemmas for mental health professionals, who see competence as a combination of knowledge, skill, and diligence. What do you see as the dilemmas in managed care (as they relate to competence)?

4. How well do the workshops and continuing education programs you have seen advertised meet the criteria set forth here for evidence of scientific value?

5. A number of people enter the mental health professions because of their own histories of recovery from emotional pain. They want to help others live full lives, as they have learned to do. How might this history affect their risk for impairment? Is such a history an advantage or a disadvantage in this regard?

RECOMMENDED READINGS

Bradley, F. O. (1991). *Credentialing in counseling.* Alexandria, VA: American Association for Counseling and Development.

Figley, C. R. (Ed.). (1995). *Compassion fatigue: Coping with secondary traumatic stress disorder in those who treat the traumatized.* New York: Brunner/Mazel.

Kilburg, R. R., Nathan, P. E., & Thoreson, R. W. (Eds.). (1986). *Professionals in distress: Issues, syndromes and solutions in psychology.* Washington, DC: American Psychological Association.

Neufield, V., & Norman, G. (Eds.). (1985). *Assessing clinical competence.* New York: Springer.

Pines, A., & Aronson, E. (1988). *Career burnout: Causes and cures.* New York: Free Press.

5

Confidentiality
Supporting the Client's Right to Privacy

This chapter discusses the roots and meanings of confidentiality, the distinction between its legal and ethical dimensions, the ways in which the law has limited confidentiality in counseling, and the need to balance confidentiality against the professional's legitimate need to consult with colleagues. The next sections of the chapter deal with the special considerations regarding confidentiality when counseling minors, clients who are HIV positive, and clients in group and family counseling. The final section analyzes emerging issues in confidentiality, including dilemmas in managed care, and computer communications between counselors and the public.

"Can I tell you something in confidence?" is a question most people have been asked in the course of their personal relationships. The person is typically seeking reassurance that the disclosure will not be shared with others without permission. The questioner wants both to communicate something, in order to gain support, understanding, or advice, and to control the spread of this private information. If the respondent says no, or seems ambivalent, nothing important will be disclosed. But if the respondent says yes, the person almost always shares a disclosure. Thereafter, if the receiver of the confidence fails to honor the promise of confidentiality, the other party feels betrayed and usually places no further trust in that individual.

There are parallels between this ordinary experience and the expectations clients have when they approach counseling. Typically, they assume that the private material they disclose will not be shared elsewhere without their consent. If clients discover that their trust has been misplaced, they feel betrayed and their capacity to trust other counselors diminishes. Clients also have conflicting feelings about revealing personal information to counselors. On the one hand, they feel they need support, and on the other hand, they worry about whether they will be judged negatively for private thoughts and feelings about which they themselves feel uncomfortable. In addition, they sometimes fear that counselors will behave dishonorably, as friends occasionally do. Thus, both clients and friends reveal secrets only when they believe the receiver is worthy of their confidence and will not berate them for their imperfections.

There are also contrasts between the confidentiality of the professional relationship and that of ordinary friendship. First, with a few exceptions to be discussed later, every portion of the conversations between counselors and their clients is confidential, no matter how mundane. Clients may mention that they dislike Chinese food, play the harmonica, or lift weights. This information is not especially private or embarrassing, and it is probably easily shared with friends and acquaintances without any expectation of confidentiality. However, if that communication takes place within a counseling relationship, it must be kept confidential. Second, much of the material clients disclose to counselors is sensitive information to which no one else in their lives is privy. Clients often tell counselors things they consider too private even to share with friends or loved ones. They often feel ashamed of their feelings and behavior and are troubled about its implications for their mental stability. For example, a college student may admit that she has abused alcohol and cocaine to a counselor before she tells anyone else, or a professional dancer may reveal that he uses self-induced vomiting to control his weight, even though he hides this information from all his friends. These clients are anxious about their ability to cope with the stresses in their lives and worry about admitting such behaviors, even to a counselor. The stigma associated with mental illness in our society renders admissions about psychological dysfunction difficult and risky.

The next distinction between confidences in friendships and in counseling relates to the assumptions clients bring to the counseling process. Clients usually assume they can trust mental health professionals, so they omit the step of asking for reassurance of confidentiality. They tend to have greater confidence in counselors' capacity to keep things secret than in that of their friends. In fact, research suggests that most clients expect that *everything* disclosed in counseling will be held in strict confidence (Miller & Thelen, 1986). This frame of mind, coupled with the sensitive nature of the material revealed, heightens the sense of betrayal a client may experience if confidentiality is violated. Of course, not all clients assume their counselors are trustworthy, but most do give them the benefit of the doubt.

The fourth contrast deals with the difference in consequences for the violator of the confidence. If friends violate a confidence, they risk only a loss or change of that relationship; there are no professional or legal sanctions against them. However, if a counselor violates a confidence, both legal and professional consequences accompany the negative effect on the counseling relationship. The counselor's professional reputation, jobs, and licenses may be at stake, and he or she is vulnerable to civil action.

The last major distinction is in the scope of confidentiality. Confidentiality in counseling encompasses not only the words spoken between counselors and their clients, but also all records related to those interactions, and the identity of the clients. A counselor is obligated not even to disclose the identities of any of his or her clients without the client's permission. Scholars have named this form of confidentiality *contact confidentiality* (Ahia & Martin, 1993). Counselors are expected to provide a therapeutic environment in which client words cannot be overheard, client records cannot be accessed by unauthorized people, and even client presence at the counseling center is protected as much as possible. Contact confidentiality implies that clients seeing college or school counselors should not be expected to wait in a heavily trafficked hallway for their appointment, nor should clients in a community agency share a large waiting room with many other people seeking other kinds of public services. In such circumstances, clients could obtain counseling only if they were willing to let random citizens from their community know about their private decision to seek counseling—a disclosure they should not be forced to make against their will. Thus, confidentiality demands that even the presence of a person in a counseling office is protected as much as possible. Moreover, the ethical obligation to confidentiality extends past death. In other words, the death of a client does not release a counselor from his or her obligation to maintain confidentiality (Burke, 1995). For example, when, after the murder of Nicole Brown Simpson (ex-wife of O. J. Simpson), her therapist spoke with the press about matters her client had revealed to her in therapy, the Board of Behavioral Science Examiners of California took disciplinary action (Simpson case, 1994). Similarly, when the therapist who treated Anne Sexton, a critically acclaimed American poet who had died by her own hand some years before, released hundreds of tapes of her therapy sessions to Sexton's biographer, there was a public outcry, and many called it a betrayal of Sexton (Burke, 1995).

In short, even though confidentiality in counseling is built on the same foundation as other kinds of confidentiality, it has unique characteristics and carries important obligations for the mental health professional. Driscoll (1992) calls the profession's obligation to confidentiality a "sacred covenant." This term aptly reflects the deeply important role confidentiality plays in the counseling process. Research also supports the prominence of confidentiality in the ethical dilemmas practitioners face. For example, when psychologists were surveyed about the ethical dilemmas they encounter in the course of their work, dilemmas involving confidentiality were most commonly named (Pope & Vetter, 1992). Most of these dilemmas involved the management of confidentiality when clients appeared to endanger others, but others dealt with the relationship between confidentiality and child abuse reporting and with HIV-positive clients. A study of college counselors revealed the same pattern, with nearly two-thirds of all dilemmas cited by the sample relating to confidentiality (Hayman & Covert, 1986). In recent years, confidentiality complaints constituted 10% of the caseload of APA's Ethics Committee and were the fourth most common topic brought before licensing boards for investigation (Peterson, 1996).

Ethical Principles Underlying Confidentiality

The importance of confidentiality derives first from the ethical principles of autonomy and fidelity, and second from the principles of beneficence and nonmaleficence. Respect for autonomy includes an acknowledgment that each person has the power to decide who may have access to private information about him- or herself. Newton (1989) argues that privacy is an essential component of individuality and selfhood. If the individual loses the power to make these decisions, then in many respects no true self remains. Violations of confidentiality are automatically disrespectful to the dignity of the person and constitute invasions of privacy. Confidentiality is also based on the principle of fidelity, because counselors implicitly and explicitly promise not to disclose what clients reveal to them. When we disclose information without a client's consent, we are unfaithful to our promise.

Confidentiality is also related to the principles of beneficence and nonmaleficence. Because trust is so crucial to effective helping, breaches of confidentiality jeopardize counselors' capacity to do good and can harm clients whose feelings of betrayal reduce or destroy their engagement in the counseling process. Violations of confidentiality can do visible harm and place clients at psychological and physical risk. For example, clients whose disclosures about their sexual orientation are betrayed can be ostracized from their families, victimized by gay bashing, and discriminated against at work. In a less dramatic example, a client who hears an embarrassing anecdote he shared with a mental health professional repeated at a social gathering can feel stripped of dignity and may remove himself both from counseling and from a circle of friends important for his emotional stability. Moreover, violations of confidentiality undermine the public trust in the profession, diminishing the profession's capacity to help people who may benefit from counseling, but who have come to distrust counselors.

Codes of Ethics

The ethics codes of both ACA and APA refer extensively to confidentiality, emphasizing its place at the foundation of professional behavior. The codes discuss the broad obligation to honor confidentiality as follows:

ACA *Code of Ethics*
Section B.1.a: Respect for Privacy
Counselors respect their clients' right to privacy and avoid illegal and unwarranted disclosures of confidential information.

Section B.1.h: Subordinates
Counselors make every effort to ensure that privacy and confidentiality of clients are maintained by subordinates including employees, clerical assistants, and volunteers.

Section B.1.i: Treatment Teams
If client treatment will involve a continued review by a treatment team, the client will be informed of the team's existence and composition.

Section B.4.b: Confidentiality of Records
Counselors are responsible for securing the safety and confidentiality of any counseling records they create, maintain, transfer, or destroy, whether the records are written, tapes, computerized, or stored in any other medium.

Section B.4.c: Permission to Record or Observe
Counselors obtain permission from clients prior to electronically recording or observing sessions.

Section B.6.a: Respect for Privacy in Consultation
Information obtained in a counseling relationship is discussed for professional purposes only with persons clearly concerned with the case. Written and oral reports present data germane to the purposes of the consultations, and every effort is made to protect client identity and avoid undue invasion of privacy.

Section B.6.b: Cooperating Agencies
Before sharing information, counselors make efforts to ensure that there are defined policies in other agencies serving the counselor's clients that effectively protect the confidentiality of information.

APA *Ethical Principles*

Section 5.02: Maintaining Confidentiality
Psychologists have a primary obligation and take reasonable precautions to respect the confidentiality rights of those with whom they work, or consult, recognizing that confidentiality may be established by law, institutional rules, or professional or scientific relationships.

Section 5.03: Minimizing Intrusions on Privacy
(a) In order to minimize intrusions on privacy, psychologists include in written and oral reports, consultations and the like, only information germane to the purpose for which the communication is made.
(b) Psychologists discuss confidential information obtained in clinical or consulting relationships, or evaluative data concerning patients, individual or organizational clients, students, research participants, supervisees, and employees, only for appropriate scientific or professional purposes and only with persons clearly concerned with such matters.

Section 5.04: Maintenance of Records
Psychologists maintain appropriate confidentiality in creating, storing, accessing, transferring, and disposing of records under their control, whether these are written, automated, or in any other medium. Psychologists maintain and dispose of records in accordance with law and in a manner that permits compliance with the requirements of this Ethics Code.

Section 5.06: Consultations
When consulting with colleagues, (1) psychologists do not share confidential information that reasonably could lead to the identification of a patient, client, research participant, or other person or organization with whom they have a confidential relationship unless they have obtained the prior consent of the person or organization or the disclosure cannot be avoided, and (2) they share information only to the extent necessary to achieve the purposes of the consultation.

Of these two codes, the ACA code offers the most specific guidance for the counseling process and has the benefit of being less general and legalistic in tone. The ACA code clearly delineates some behaviors that are necessary, such as obtaining permission to use electronic recording devices in counseling, and the circumstances under which other behaviors, such as use of a treatment team, are permissible. Unfortunately, a person reading the APA code on this topic might surmise that it was written with the goal of protecting the psychologist from ethics claims rather than protecting the public from unwarranted disclosures (Bersoff, 1994).

Confidentiality and Communication with Other Mental Health Professionals

Both the APA and the ACA ethics codes allow counselors to share confidential information in order to consult with other professionals when they believe they need guidance about a case. The presumption is that the other mental health professionals understand the need for confidentiality and carry the same obligation not to disclose elsewhere the information obtained in discussions with colleagues. Often other mental health professionals can be consulted without revealing client-identifying information. The anonymity of the client is thus maintained, and the counselor's need for input to provide competent treatment is met. In some clinical settings, counselors work in treatment teams and consultations cannot be conducted anonymously. When this happens, the codes recommend that the client be informed that team discussions will occur and that the client consent to that arrangement. Clients who feel confident that the treatment team is working in their best interest are usually quite willing to give consent.

As discussed in greater detail in Chapter 12, when a counselor is not yet licensed or is still in training, his or her supervisor also has access to confidential information from counseling. In fact, a counselor in training may not take on a client unless that client is willing to have the supervisor know about the progress of counseling.

Consultation to maximize counseling services must be distinguished from idle discussion of counseling material among mental health professionals. Counselors have a normal impulse to share events from their workday with co-workers or loved ones. Communicating such anecdotes can add a little humor to a stressful day, or elicit support or compassion over a particular work stress. How do counselors ethically meet this need? The first consideration must be for the dignity and welfare of the client. The best standard for determining whether to share information with colleagues is whether one would make the comment in the client's presence. Almost always, the answer is no. First, the counselor probably does not have consent to release information that does not fit the criterion of professional consultation. Second, even if the identity of the particular client is not revealed, the client would probably feel uncomfortable with the disclosure. The client would be less willing to disclose personal information in future sessions and would feel misused. For example, if the funny anecdote were discussed in the client's presence, the client would probably feel embarrassed or insulted. Similarly, clients who share pain expect that their privacy will be guarded, not violated. Clients who learn about violations of their privacy may be more guarded in future sessions at best, and at worst, may prematurely leave counseling. Thus, counselors cannot ethically meet their needs for stress reduction by discussing client disclosures outside formal consultation sessions. Embarrassing or painful information should be shared only within a formal consultation environment, and all sharing should respect the dignity of the individual. Counselors who are unsure of whether a particular situation fits that criterion should use a variation of Kant's universalization principle (Newton, 1989): If the roles were reversed, and the counselor were the client, would the counselor feel the disclosure was necessary and appropriate? If one can answer yes, the disclosure is probably acceptable.

Counselors in school, university, and business settings are working in cultures that are unaccustomed to the level of confidentiality necessary in counseling. Teachers, administrators, and other school personnel often share student information and tend to expect counselors to do the same. Managers are accustomed to discussing employee performance with human resource personnel and other managers and are unlikely to understand the reluctance of counselors to do likewise. In these environments counselors have a responsibility to educate their co-workers about their unique professional responsibilities and to resist the ever-present temptation to trade client confidentiality for a perception of being a team player.

Confidentiality and Communication Within the Counselor's Family

Counselors are rarely social isolates. They are often part of families, either traditional or nontraditional, and tend to have committed relationships with other adults. The norms of families suggest that adult partners share details of their daily lives with each other. This sharing not only helps each partner feel supported and revitalized for the next day, it also is a symbol of closeness between them (Baker & Patterson, 1990). These norms conflict with the rules on professional confidentiality. Nowhere in those rules is an exception written for families of counselors. Professionals are expected to keep clients' secrets even from their life partners. Baker and Patterson (1990) suggest that this standard is routinely violated, that mental health professionals frequently share with their partners information about client sessions. Evidence from Pope et al. (1987) and Dudley (1988) offers some support for this suggestion; more research is needed on the scope of the problem. Baker and Patterson speculate that professionals are torn between their need for intimacy and connection with their partners and their responsibility to those they serve. Moreover, counselors may feel they owe their families some explanation for their long hours at work, or for their interruptions of a family activity to respond to a client crisis. The degree to which professionals experience guilt about this practice is not known. The frequency with which this behavior results in further breaches of client confidentiality is also unknown, but it is not inconceivable that partners inadvertently divulge information to others that counselors have shared with them. When family tension is high, partners may also disclose such information as a way to hurt the counselor or get revenge for a counselor's behavior.

Is there an alternative way to resolve this conflict between family loyalty and professional responsibilities? Baker and Patterson (1990) offer a reasonable suggestion, sharing information with a partner in such a way that no identifying information is communicated. Under this guideline, a professional would be able to say, for example, "I'm working with a 35-year-old woman with two small children who has just been diagnosed HIV positive, may have to leave her job because she's too sick to work, and has no health insurance. Her ex-husband is a professional with a good income, but he plays games with child support payment and she gets no alimony. I'm so saddened and angry about what's happened to her." Using this rubric, the identity of the client is protected, but the professional still has an opportunity to "decompress" about struggles or successes at work.

Such an approach seems consistent with the profession's ethical standards. However, this solution has its perils—the partner may correctly guess the client's identity, or the counselor may inadvertently disclose it. It may also lead to a "slippery slope" phenomenon—first the counselor makes disclosures to life partners, then to other family members, then to close friends, and so forth. Each disclosure represents a greater level of risk to client privacy. Nor does this practice fit comfortably with the expectations that clients bring when they seek professional help. They neither expect or desire the counselor to have dinnertime discussions about their cases, even if their names are not revealed. It insults their dignity. If we use Kant's universalization principle (Newton, 1989)—that the principles we would wish others to use in interacting with us should be the principles we use in interacting with them—we can hypothesize that most counselors would not want their secrets to be the subject of another's dinner conversation, however carefully disguised. Why should they expect clients to react otherwise? Finally, the practice is somewhat disingenuous. Counselors who talk about specific clients at home are promising a level of confidentiality they do not intend to honor.

For these reasons, a better solution is for counselors to develop a regular supervision or consultation relationship with other professionals to deal with their own emotional reactions to client cases. In that way, the professional gets the benefit needed to continue effective work without compromising confidentiality to a nonprofessional. Some counselors also keep a private journal about their own feelings about counseling. This journal is not a record of counseling, but rather a reflection of the counselor's experience of their profession. Such personal journals can serve as a vehicle for reflection and an outlet for emotion. Next, counselors should explain to their partners the standards governing confidentiality and the ethical principles underlying this rule, and should establish clear limits about the material that can be disclosed at home. An acceptable boundary allows a counselor to discuss broad outlines of problems he or she is experiencing at work. In this way, counselors can still feel connected to a partner by discussing important aspects of their work, but not breach professional standards. Using the same HIV-positive client as an example, this guideline means the following statement would be acceptable: "I'm saddened by news of a client's life-threatening illness that is adding further pain to an already difficult situation." (Notice that this omits age, occupation, gender, and details of the client's individual experience of the problem. It does not even identify the disease.) A partner who has been informed about the professional's obligations in advance will likely understand the counselor's stress or the sense of accomplishment and offer support without seeking further disclosure. In any case, the burden of maintaining confidentiality always rests with the professional.

Confidentiality and Privileged Communication

The terms *confidentiality* and *privileged communication* both deal with the client's right to keep private all material disclosed in counseling. These terms are often used almost interchangeably, but there are important differences in their meanings. Confidentiality primarily concerns the ethical obligation to keep client identity and disclosures secret. It is a moral obligation rooted in the ethics code, the ethical principles, and the virtues that the profession attempts to foster. The legal term *privileged communication* refers to the client's right to prevent a court from demanding that a mental health professional reveal counseling material (Swenson, 1997). Whereas the term *confidentiality* deals with the prevention of voluntary disclosure of inappropriate material by mental health professionals, the term *privilege* refers to the rules for preventing involuntary disclosures requested by parties in a legal action (Roback, Ochoa, Bloch, & Purdon, 1992). In other words, confidentiality reminds the counselor that client information should not be revealed even if the counselor feels inclined to do so, and privilege protects client information from inappropriate disclosure pressed for by others, rather than entertained by the counselor. Privilege is established by law. Because common law requires all citizens to testify when called by the court, exceptions must be established by statute (Knapp & VandeCreek, 1986). Federal courts interpret privilege differently from state courts. If counseling records are requested by a federal court, a counselor should seek legal advice about the status of privilege in that circumstance (Haas & Malouf, 1995).

It is important to emphasize that the privilege is the client's, not the counselor's; it is the client's right to refuse to reveal counseling information to the court. Thus, a counselor asserts privilege on behalf of a client and the counselor does not have the option to disclose client information even if so inclined. In other words, in states where privilege exists counselors are legally bound not to reveal client information, and the personal inclinations of counselors about disclosure are irrelevant. The mental health disciplines whose clients can assert privilege vary considerably from state to state. Clients of psychiatrists and psychologists are usually included; licensed social workers and mental health counselors are also sometimes named. In a few states, the clients of school counselors are also covered by privileged communications statutes, and privilege sometimes extends to paraprofessionals and office assistants of mental health professionals. Privilege deals with situations in which a court or officer of the court seeks to learn about communications from a client to a counselor.

Officers of the court can make demands in three ways. First, they can issue a *subpoena,* a legal demand to appear to produce testimony. Second, they can issue a *subpoenas duces tecum,* a command to appear in court and bring along specific documents. Finally, a court can establish a *court order* for a mental health professional to provide either documents or testimony, or both. In states where privilege is established, counselors may not disclose material even if subpoenaed by an attorney. However, this does not mean that mental health professionals may ignore subpoenas! Instead, they should inform the court about the obligation to keep communication privileged and seek further guidance from a judge. Counselors would be well advised to seek legal counsel for themselves during this process. (Section B.1.e of the ACA ethics code takes the same position on requests from the court to obtain confidential material.) The judge typically holds a hearing and then rules on the applicability of privilege in the case. If the judge rules that privilege is not applicable, he or she is likely to order the counselor to testify. In that event, the counselor may testify and/or produce records from the counseling interaction. Counselors who relinquish records and content without first seeking a judge's ruling about privilege are violating ACA's ethical standards. Huber and Baruth (1987) make an important point about subpoenas: "Subpoenas should be viewed as the formal commencement, not the conclusion, of any disclosure controversy" (p. 20). Mental health professionals practicing in states that grant privilege to their clients are also at risk for legal action against them if they disclose counseling information to a court without first seeking client consent or asserting privilege. Counselors are ethically and legally protected, however, if a court refuses to acknowledge the client's right to confidentiality. The counselor's only other alternatives are to file an appeal of the ruling to a higher court or to endure the legal penalties imposed for refusing to testify or produce documents. Often this means being found in contempt of court.

The Limits of Confidentiality

Newton (1989) notes that our society is ambivalent about confidentiality. On the one hand, we value it and admire those who are loyal to their friends. Children ridicule tattletales, and nations reserve their most severe punishments for traitors. Most democracies have enacted laws to ensure that those accused of crimes can trust their lawyers with their confidences, their physicians with their illnesses, and their priests with their confessions. As indicated earlier, state laws also govern confidentiality between mental health professionals and their clients, requiring psychologists, counselors, and social workers to keep counseling disclosures private. It is important to note, however, that therapists and counselors are relative latecomers to this protection, and the laws are generally less complete and more weakly supported for these professions than for lawyers, physicians, or priests. This unwillingness to grant mental health professions the same degree of confidentiality as other professionals is a reflection of our society's ambivalence about confidentiality. These reactions emerge from the antisocial nature of confidentiality, according to Newton (1989), because confidentiality frequently acts in opposition to some other public interest. To return to an earlier example, even though there is no public interest in a client's preferences for Chinese food or harmonica skills, there is a strong public interest in a client who tells a counselor about fantasies of violence against a boss. In the latter situation, the antisocial nature of confidentiality is clear because maintaining the confidence is in direct opposition to the society's desire to protect a citizen against harm. The stronger the likelihood this client will act on the fantasy, the greater is the public interest in disclosure. Prosecutors in criminal cases have also claimed a public interest in obtaining evidence from mental health professionals who have been seeing the accused person in counseling. Society's discomfort with confidentiality has led to increasing the limits on professional confidentiality. Some ethical and legal scholars argue that the ways in which the courts have eroded confidentiality are counterproductive to the client, the profession, and the public's need for access to the mental health system (for example, see Baumoel, 1992; Bollas & Sundelson, 1995). These scholars wonder if people will seek counseling if they are not assured of confidentiality.

However, the public also has an interest in the continuation of professional confidentiality insofar as professionals can help those who have antisocial tendencies, to change their behavior. If no confidentiality existed, people would probably be unwilling to disclose such tendencies and feelings. Without disclosure, the counselor's opportunity to prevent antisocial acts would be lost. People who want help to stop themselves from taking harmful actions would look elsewhere for assistance, or would despair of getting help. The whole society would be worse off. For these reasons, the legal system and professional organizations have sought to limit exceptions to confidentiality. Both systems have affirmed the fundamental value of confidentiality even as exceptions and limitations are codified. The tension between the public interest in the content of counseling sessions and its acceptance of confidentiality as a client's right has not been resolved. Thus, counselors should keep current with changes in statutes, case law, and ethical mandates.

Currently there are seven major types of exceptions to confidentiality in counseling, described as follows.

1. Client Request for Release of Information

The first limit to confidentiality is based on the client's autonomy. Because clients have control over personal information, any client who wishes material disclosed or releases information for communication elsewhere has the right to have that disclosure made. The ACA *Code of Ethics* addresses this as follows: "The right to privacy may be waived by the client or their legally assigned representative" (Section B.1.b); and the APA *Ethical Principles* (5.05.b) states, "Psychologists may also disclose confidential information with the appropriate consent of the patient or the individual or organizational client (or other legally authorized person on behalf of the patient or client), unless prohibited by law." Clients frequently waive their right to confidentiality when moving to a new community or when they are obtaining a consultation about a specific issue and wish the new counselor to see their records and speak with their regular counselor. Similarly, sometimes clients want their physicians to have access to counseling records and waive their rights so that copies of their records can be sent to those professionals. Many people waive the right to confidentiality in order to have insurers cover the costs of their mental health services. Insurers only pay for services that they have determined are appropriate. Thus, in order to make that determination insurers routinely ask clients to waive confidentiality.

A release from a client does not give a counselor blanket approval to release confidential information to any party the client has named on the release form. On the contrary, the counselor has two responsibilities: to determine, as much as possible, that the receiving professional will continue to treat the materials received as confidential and to ascertain that that person is qualified to understand the material. When both questions can be answered affirmatively, the counselor is expected to comply with the request. The rationale behind these stipulations is the best interest of the client. People who are unqualified to responsibly evaluate counseling information are at significant risk of harming the client by misusing those data. If the counselor determines that these conditions cannot be met, the counselor ought to work with the client to identify a qualified person to whom the data can be released, a professional who can be trusted to respect its confidentiality.

The ACA code also mandates that clients be allowed access to their own counseling records, unless such access would not be in their best interests. The mandate also derives from the principles of autonomy and beneficence.

> **ACA** *Code of Ethics,* **Section B.4.d: Client Access**
> Counselors recognize that counseling records are kept for the benefit of clients, and therefore provide access to records and copies of records when requested by competent clients, unless the records contain information that may be misleading and detrimental to the client.

The APA code makes a more general comment on records, again focusing on the relationship between access and the best interests of the client.

> **APA** *Ethical Principles,* **Section 5.10: Ownership of Records and Data**
> Recognizing that the ownership of records and data is governed by legal principles, psychologists take reasonable and lawful steps so that records and data remain available to the extent needed to serve the best interests of patients, individual or organizational clients, research participants, or appropriate others.

As will be discussed in Chapter 14, this right to access means that counseling records should be written with the assumption that the client may be reading them.

2. Court Orders for Confidential Information

The second major limitation to confidentiality occurs when the courts demand access to records and counselor testimony. There are several circumstances under which this may occur and under which privileged communication statutes usually do not apply. Confidentiality is not protected when a counselor acts as an expert witness or as a consultant for the court to evaluate a person involved in a legal proceeding. Mental health professionals may be used to assess whether a person is mentally competent to stand trial, is a fit parent, was mentally ill at the time of a crime, or has suffered psychological distress subsequent to an injury or accident. Mental health professionals have been increasingly involved in such activities over the last several decades. The person being evaluated has either waived his or her right to confidentiality, or the court never recognized any such right in the first place. In these circumstances, the entire professional relationship is based on the assumption that all information disclosed may be shared with the court.

Sometimes attorneys seek to obtain counseling records from mental health professionals who have a preexisting counseling relationship with someone accused of a crime or whose fitness as a custodial parent is being challenged. Attorneys have also sought this information in civil suits and in federal courts adjudicating civil rights cases. In criminal courts prosecutors often want to use, as evidence of guilt, the material the accused has revealed in counseling. In one federal case recently decided by the U.S. Supreme Court (*Jaffee v. Redmond,* 1996), the family of a person killed by a police officer filed a wrongful death action and then sought counseling information from the licensed social worker who counseled the officer after the shooting. The state courts considered that information privileged, but no such privilege for social workers had been established in federal courts. The federal district court ruled that the social worker should testify (thereby refusing to recognize the privilege), but the federal appeals court overturned that ruling. In its holding, the Supreme Court determined that the privilege should be honored and the social worker could not be forced to testify about her client's disclosures. Professional mental health organizations were relieved that the Court took such a strong stance in favor of the value of confidentiality in psychotherapy. Whether a mental health professional has a legal right to refuse to give testimony in a particular court is not fully resolved, however. The Supreme Court ruling in *Jaffee v. Redmond* applies most directly to social workers, psychologists, and psychiatrists and does not address the privilege of other kinds of mental health professionals. (Some authors, however, believe that in the future federal courts will honor the privilege of clients of mental health counselors licensed to conduct psychotherapy in their states. Remley, Herlihy, and Herlihy, 1997, discuss in detail the application of this holding to counseling.) Thus counselors need to be informed about the regulations governing privileged communication in their states and how those regulations apply to their profession. The guidelines published by the Committee on Legal Issues of the American Psychological Association (1996) are valuable resources for professionals attempting to make responsible decisions about legal demands for client information. (Also see the previous section of this chapter on privileged communication.)

3. Client Complaints and Litigation Against Counselors

The third limit to confidentiality occurs when clients bring a legal action against their counselors (Swenson, (1997). If a client sues a counselor for negligence or breach of contract, by virtue of initiating a legal action the client is waiving the right to confidentiality. Therefore, the counselor may discuss the counseling interaction in court without threat of legal or ethical sanction. In other words, counselors have a right to defend themselves against claims of malpractice brought by clients. Similarly, if a client files an ethics complaint against a mental health professional, the client must waive the right to confidentiality if the claim is to be pursued. Thus, the counselor accused of misconduct can respond with case information and counseling records to an ethics committee without worry about an unethical or illegal release of private information.

4. Other Client Litigation

The fourth limit comes into play when clients initiate against another party a civil legal action that includes claims of psychological harm, and in building their case they refer to counseling services used to diagnose or alleviate that distress (Swenson, 1997). The claim of psychological injury makes any relevant counseling material potentially available to the court. For example, when a person sues an employer for sexual harassment and alleges psychological injury as part of the harm from the harassment, that plaintiff also waives the right to confidentiality of any counseling in which the issue arose if he or she has referred to the need for counseling in the complaint filed with the court. Access to that information is important for a fair hearing of the complaint and can be made available if the defendant seeks it. If the client reasserts a right to confidentiality of that information, the case may not be able to go forward. Let us take another example: When someone alleges that her anxiety disorder originated in the car accident for which another driver was responsible (if the client connects the need for counseling to the accident), the counselor can release to the court information about the extent and etiology of the disorder. In either case, because the client is voluntarily revealing psychological information in order to pursue the claim, the client is waiving the right to have other relevant psychological information kept confidential. In essence, in order to build an adequate defense the person against whom the claim is being made has the right to all relevant data. It is important to note that confidentiality in such situations does not hold precisely because the client is voluntarily bringing legal or professional action against someone else and has the freedom not to go forward with these claims if he or she does not wish to do so. A defendant in a criminal case is not there voluntarily; hence the legal system more scrupulously guards his or her confidentiality.

5. Limitations Based in State and Federal Statutes

Some material has been excluded from professional confidentiality by statute. Every state has statutes mandating that counselors and other mental health professionals (along with many professionals in other fields) report child abuse and neglect to the proper authorities. The Federal Child Abuse Prevention and Treatment Act (1987) also requires such reporting. The details of the statutes vary somewhat by state, but the central message is consistent. Counselors who learn of child abuse or neglect are legally obligated to report this information to social service or police agencies, usually within a day or so. The penalties for failing to report also vary, but often include criminal sanctions. The reporting of abuse and neglect takes precedence over any legal privilege or ethical obligation to confidentiality. The APA Committee on Professional Practice has published a helpful article on the legal and professional issues in child abuse (1995). This article summarizes the professional's role in assessing, reporting, and intervening when abuse occurs, and lists national resources available to assist mental health professionals in these processes.

The legislatures have reasoned that the public interest in protecting those who cannot protect themselves from abuse outweighs the obligation to confidentiality. However, even in mandated reporting situations, the law typically limits disclosure of confidential information to what is relevant to the abuse or neglect. Other aspects of counseling disclosures that have no bearing on this matter can and should be kept confidential. Because the statutes vary from state to state, counselors must be aware of changes to and wording of statutes in their states.

Research shows that mandated reporting of child abuse occurs commonly in mental health practice. According to Melton et al. (1995), 90% of child psychiatrists, 63% of clinical psychologists, and 70% of social workers have filed one or more reports of child abuse. Only a few studies have examined the impact of a report on the therapeutic relationship, and they have found mixed results (Steinberg, 1994; Watson & Levine, 1989). The most negative result seems to occur when the client is reported as the perpetrator (Levine & Doueck, 1995).

Brosig and Kalichman (1992) also describe a substantial amount of noncompliance with the reporting law. Their analysis of the literature concludes that almost one-third of clinicians have declined to report suspected child abuse. Research suggests professionals experience a conflict between the desire to keep the client involved in counseling and maintain confidentiality, on one hand, and a recognition of legal mandates and potential harm to the child, on the other. Kennel and Agresti (1995) contend that "many professionals appear to place child abuse on a continuum of severity that separates *suspected* abuse from *reportable* abuse" (p. 612). The vagueness of some states' reporting laws also contributes to this noncompliance (Melton et al., 1995). Counselors who sometimes decline to report seem to want to be more sure about the existence of abuse, given the implications of a breach of confidentiality. This reluctance to report suspected abuse can cause legal and ethical problems for the counselor. Many statutes mandate reporting *suspicions* of abuse, not *incidences* of abuse. Thus the counselor bears the burden of determining if the suspicion is reasonable. This determination can be difficult, just as is ascertaining when a client is dangerous. The ultimate criteria for decision making are avoiding harm to the child and protecting of the child's best interests.

A number of other variables seem to influence this reluctance to report. When mental health professionals fail to report, they often believe that reporting will not be in their client's best interest (Kalichman, 1993). Counselors who fail to report abuse are more likely to view child protective services as ineffective (Levine et al., 1991) and to worry that reporting will sever the counseling relationship or otherwise irreparably damage therapeutic progress (Haas, Malouf, & Mayerson, 1988).

Some mental health professionals attribute their failure to report to a personal conviction that confidentiality in counseling is absolute and should not be violated even in cases of suspected abuse. In essence, they are engaging in civil disobedience and opposition to the ethical standards of the profession that encourage compliance with legal requirements. Such counselors should understand that they are at risk for ethical and legal sanctions against them. Moreover, if their failure to report results in greater harm to a child, they must bear moral and legal responsibility for that harm. In other words, refusing to report child abuse has serious and long-lasting consequences for all involved and should not done lightly. Counselors who find themselves declining to report should examine their motivation and reasoning and seek out consultation with peers about this issue. Failing to report abuse may stem from counselor bias or countertransference, rather than from moral values or concerns about client welfare. Counselors should apply the "well-lit room standard," and should ask themselves whether they would be proud to communicate such a decision to a group of professional peers and could expect that audience to respect their position. If not, failing to report is not really a matter of principles or civil disobedience; it is a matter of personal needs or lack of objectivity.

A number of states also have statutes mandating that counselors report neglect or abuse of dependent elders by those responsible for their care (Veldick, 1995). In states that have such statutes, counselors are mandated to report elder abuse or neglect to human service agencies if clients disclose this information in counseling. As with child abuse, state legislatures have reasoned that the duty to protect a dependent elder from harm he or she cannot probably otherwise stop is stronger than the counselor's obligation to confidentiality. Because the wording of these statutes varies somewhat by state, counselors need to be familiar with the law in states where they practice.

6. Dangerous Clients and the Duty to Warn and Protect

Communications from clients who are dangerous to themselves or other people are not protected by the same level of confidentiality as other material. When the mental health professional judges a client to pose an immediate threat to others or to the client him- or herself, the ACA and APA ethics codes allow disclosure of confidential information. The wording in the codes is as follows:

> **ACA *Code of Ethics*, Section B.1.c**
> The general requirement to keep information confidential does not apply when disclosure is required to prevent clear and imminent danger to the client or others or when legal requirements demand that confidential information be revealed. Counselors consult with other professionals when in doubt about the validity of an exception.

APA *Ethical Principles,* Section 5.05

Psychologists disclose confidential information without the consent of the individual only as mandated by law or where permitted by law for a valid purpose, such as (1) to provide needed professional services to the patient or the individual or organizational client, (2) to obtain appropriate professional consultations, (3) to protect the patient or others from harm, or (4) to obtain payment for services, in which instance, disclosure is limited to the minimum that is necessary for that purpose.

The current codes are written to allow counselors and psychologists to breach confidentiality when they believe clients are dangerous, but courts in many states have tended to view this breach as an obligation, not an option. They have mandated disclosure if it seems necessary to prevent harm to an intended victim. The legal requirement to disclose imminent danger stems from a 1974 California case in which the family of a woman sued her killer's psychologist (and the University of California) because he failed to tell about the client's threat to kill her. The rulings of the lower state courts on this now famous *Tarasoff* case were appealed to the California Supreme Court, which ruled twice on the issue (*Tarasoff v. Regents of the University of California,* 1974, 1976). The result of these rulings imposed on mental health professionals a "duty to warn and protect" victims of violent clients. This duty soon came to be endorsed not just by California, but by courts in a number of other states. Soon thereafter, professional associations revised their ethical standards to better reflect the legal position on this issue. Before the *Tarasoff* case, ethical guidelines suggested *notifying* the authorities about dangerous clients, but contained no recommendation to breach confidentiality otherwise. In essence, *Tarasoff* means that if a counselor evaluates a person to be in imminent danger from the actions of a client, the counselor must now act to *protect* the intended victim from that danger. The court envisioned mental health professionals as having a duty to the public as well as duty to their clients (Smith & Meyer, 1987). The court reasoned that if someone's life or health is at risk from a client, the benefit from a breach of confidentiality significantly outweighs the cost of that breach and should be undertaken. The court ruled that "the privilege ends where the public peril begins" (*Tarasoff,* 1976, p. 347). The profession has interpreted that duty as an obligation to break confidentiality to inform the intended victim of the danger.

Many mental health professionals refer to this obligation as "the duty to warn." That designation is misleading because the crucial obligation identified by the courts is to use reasonable care to protect the one at risk (Givelber, Bowers, & Blitch, 1984). A breach of confidentiality to the victim is frequently a means to that end, but it is not an end in itself. Moreover, if a mental health professional deals with this duty by breaching confidentiality to an intended victim, the responsibility does not end with the action of warning the victim. If it did, a telephone conversation with an intended victim might go something like this:

Counselor: Are you Mr. X?
Mr. X: Yes.

Counselor: I am the counselor for Ms. Y, who has made a threat to kill you that I
  strongly believe she intends to carry out as soon as she can. I do not know of Ms.
  Y's whereabouts since she left my office one hour ago. The police have been
  informed as well. Ms. Y stated that she had access to a gun. I believe she was going
  to get that gun when she left my office. Do you understand what I have told you?
Mr. X: Yes, I understand.
Counselor: Goodbye, then.

Such a scenario is ludicrous. The counselor in this situation has technically warned the
intended victim but has done little to protect the victim or to intervene to prevent the
client from acting on her threat. Needless to say, the person receiving the phone call
might disbelieve the counselor and do nothing to protect himself, might be traumatized
by the phone call and be immobilized from the stress so that he does not take steps to
protect himself, or he may get angry and decide to get his own gun and kill Ms. Y. before she kills him. And these are only the obvious possibilities. The point is that the
California court's initial rulings did not limit the responsibility to warning, and they focused more on protection than on warning. In the *Tarasoff* case, warning the victim was
viewed as a necessary part of protection, but the court did not see warning as essential
in every situation.

If the counselor does warn a victim, the counselor is expected to help that person
get protection from the client. That assistance may take the form of helping the person
connect with loved ones who can offer protection or obtain police protection. A frequent way of protecting the victim is to restrain the freedom of the client so that access
to the victim is not possible. One common way to restrain the client is involuntary
commitment to a psychiatric unit. That option is not always available because most
states require that a person be diagnosed as *both* mentally ill and dangerous in order to
authorize involuntary commitment. People who are dangerous but not mentally ill cannot be committed to a psychiatric unit.

If all this sounds as if counselors must put themselves in jeopardy to protect victims,
that impression is wrong. The counselors are not expected to risk their personal safety,
but rather to intervene with the client and/or the victim to prevent the violence as
fully as reasonable. Counselors must do as much as other competent counselors would
do in the same situation.

Subsequent court cases have clarified and extended the *Tarasoff* ruling to limit the
duty to situations of *imminent* danger, usually interpreted to mean situations in which a
threat of immediate action has been made or implied. If this threat is judged by the
counselor as significant and likely to be carried out in the near future, the duty is imposed (Ahia & Martin, 1993; Anderson, 1996). The duty does not extend to every situation in which a client may express a violent feeling toward another person. When
people are angry, they often use violent language to express their anger. Many people in
the midst of divorce have threatened to kill their partners, and many people have said
they would rather commit suicide than get cancer or AIDS. Few clients who utter these

words will carry out a homicide or suicide. The counselor must often sift through these angry and desperate words and identify those whose intent is truly violent.

This process is called *risk assessment*. Unfortunately, the literature indicates that mental health professionals cannot predict dangerousness with a high degree of accuracy (for example, see Bednar et al., 1991; Otto, 1992). Otto concludes that recent evidence indicates that their predictions are better than chance, however, especially in the short term. Generally, though, mental health professionals tend to overpredict violence. In other words, they tend to predict danger in cases where no violent action actually occurs (Smith & Meyer, 1987). Many people who seem serious about harming someone never act on the impulse, and others who express limited frustration and anger do indeed take violent action. The courts, nevertheless, impose this duty on counselors and recommend that mental health professionals use the best evidence available to determine dangerousness. For this reason, counselors are well advised to become familiar with the literature on risk management with dangerous clients and to become as skilled as possible in assessing the risk of violence. The assessment always includes a history of the client's violent behavior, the current social conditions that may exacerbate or diminish the likelihood for violence, and the client's current psychological functioning (Ahia & Martin, 1993). Monahan (1981) specifies access to a means for committing violence as a crucial part of evaluating social and environmental conditions. A client who has easy access to a gun is more dangerous than a client without such access, all other factors being equal.

A methodical assessment of dangerousness is also important because of the emotion that having a violent client evokes in a counselor. Working with a client whom one thinks may cause injury is very stressful. Counselors can be overwhelmed by their sense of responsibility for the client's actions and may be concerned about their own safety under such circumstances. If not balanced by a careful evaluation of the real risk, these fears and worries can compromise clear thinking and ethical action. For a more detailed discussion of risk management, see Bednar et al. (1991), Costa and Altekruse (1994), and Monahan (1993). Borum (1996) also describes standardized instruments that have been developed to enhance the accuracy of risk assessment.

Recent court rulings in California (Leong, Eth, & Silva, 1992) suggest another reason for careful risk assessment before breaching confidentiality. In three recent cases, once a warning was issued to a third party, psychotherapists were required to give testimony that went well beyond the *Tarasoff* warning. This testimony was used in all three cases to help establish the guilt of the defendants (clients) in criminal trails. According to Meyers (1991)

> There is no way to tell whether psychotherapists, following *Tarasoff*, have ever saved a potential victim from injury, but it is clear that at least two psychotherapists, ordered to testify over objections and claims of privilege, helped prosecutors convict an ex-patient of first-degree murder and contributed to sentencing him to the penalty of death. (p. 27)

It is too early to determine whether other state courts will follow California's lead in this matter, but these events offer counselors another reason to be prudent and reasoned in their decision to warn third parties.

When attempting to determine the predictability of danger, a counselor should consult with colleagues and possibly an attorney, both because of the risk of injury and because the exception to confidentiality applies to imminent danger, not potential danger. In other words, breaching confidentiality without immediate danger can result in legal and ethical complaints against the counselor by the person whose privacy was not protected (Schultz, 1982). Even though some states, such as California, have offered mental health professionals protection from liability claims stemming from good-faith breaches of confidentiality under this duty, not every state has addressed this matter either in case law or in statutes.

The courts have also clarified who should be told about violent clients. Typically, law enforcement officers should be informed about the dangerous client, and the potential victims should be told of his or her violent intent. Counselors should disclose to the police only information relevant to the danger, not other counseling communications. Counselors should also warn victims whom the counselor can reasonably identify and those so close to the possible victim that they too are in danger. For example, a dependent child of a custodial parent who is the object of the threat also is seen by the legal system as a person whom the counselor has a duty to protect. Most state courts have rejected the notion that counselors have a duty to warn in situations in which clients make broad or vague threats, or situations in which the counselor has no information to identify the victim. In that situation, the duty of the counselor shifts somewhat. If the risk assessment leads the counselor to believe the client is truly dangerous, but the counselor has no way to identify a victim to prevent the injury, the counselor should consider intensifying treatment and possibly initiating involuntary commitment proceedings against the client. (In a number of states, counselors do not have the authority to initiate such proceedings on their own and must enlist the assistance of other qualified mental health professionals.) If a client is detained in a hospital setting as an emergency procedure, he or she endangers no one during the period of hospitalization.

The states vary in their interpretation of the duty to warn and protect. For example, a few states have rejected the *Tarasoff* doctrine (Maryland is most notable), and some others have extended it to include nonidentifiable victims (Bednar et al., 1991; Monahan, 1993). In a few states, a *history* of violent action coupled with a reasonably identifiable victim may be enough to require a breach of confidentiality, even in the absence of any specific threat (Ahia & Martin, 1993). In other words, in those states a *threat* of harm is not a necessary component for the duty to be imposed. These wide variations in state statutes are confusing for counselors and show that counselors need to become informed about their own state's laws. Complicating matters even further is the rapid rate at which case law and statutory law on this subject change. Counselors who fail to keep up to date on legal developments in their state may find that their professional practice varies from current laws.

One final note about the duty to warn and protect is in order. Courts interpret this duty to apply not only to situations in which a counselor knows about a dangerous person making an imminent threat, but also to situations in which the counselor *should have known* about the danger. This means that if the counselor's ignorance about a danger stems from incompetent or negligent practice, or from a refusal to explore issues for fear of what the client might say, then that counselor has also violated this duty. The courts simply do not view incompetence or negligence as an adequate defense against a claim of failure to protect.

Given this history of legal challenges to the confidentiality of client communications, a counselor could mistakenly conclude that confidentiality does not apply to violent clients. Such an interpretation is not only wrong, it is also inconsistent with court rulings that tend to support the need for confidentiality as a general principle in counseling and psychotherapy. Even in situations of imminent danger, confidentiality is not entirely eliminated. Any communications about the client to victims or to police must be limited to information relevant to the threat that may help prevent harm to the victim. A counselor does not disclose all counseling notes or conversations, even if a duty to warn and protect applies. The client's privacy should still be protected as much as possible. No relevant information to prevent the harm should be withheld, but no peripheral information unrelated to the threat should be disclosed.

When clients are at immediate risk of suicide, the primary obligation of the counselor is to protect the client from the self-destructive impulse. Whether there is a legal duty to breach confidentiality to inform significant others in the client's life is uncertain (Bongar, 1991). The legal and ethical responsibility to protect the client from harm is unequivocal, however. To achieve this goal, counselors have a number of options. They may intensify treatment, notify law enforcement authorities and/or significant others who can offer the client support and protection from the suicidal impulses, or hospitalize the client. Counselors who choose to breach confidentiality should act prudently in communications with family members and should reveal only material necessary for the significant others to help the client. In an ideal situation, such disclosures are made with the client's consent and involvement, so that they are not truly breaches of confidentiality, but rather the result of a joint decision to act toward a therapeutic goal. If a counselor judges that the client would not be safe with significant others or that intensifying the current treatment would be insufficient, then hospitalization may be wise. Careful risk assessment is as important in determining self-endangerment as in assessing danger to others. Working with suicidal clients has been termed the most stressful aspect of clinical work (Deutsch, 1984), so counselors need to be sure that they are making decisions on the basis of reason, not emotion. Bongar (1991) and Maris, Berman, Maltsberger, and Yufit (1992) are excellent sources of information on assessing suicidal risk.

7. Counseling HIV-Positive Clients

Counseling people with HIV spectrum disorders raises a number of ethical issues. Manuel et al. (1990) identify eight broad categories of such issues for health care and mental health professionals. Of greatest concern for counselors are the confidentiality of client disclosures in counseling and the risk of discrimination against HIV-positive clients. The first issue has sparked the most debate. The controversy centers on the confidentiality of a client's disclosures of activities that put others at risk for infection (Harding, Gray, & Neal, 1993). The highest-risk behaviors commonly known are the sharing of needles in intravenous drug use and unprotected sexual contact. (Of course, not all forms of unprotected sexual contact carry exactly the same degree of risk, but unprotected sex is the category under which some very-high-risk behaviors fall.) The ethical dilemma for counselors lies in balancing their responsibility to an HIV-positive client and to people whom that client places at risk for getting the disease. Given the trend toward limiting confidentiality when clients make threats of imminent homicide or suicide, scholars have vigorously debated whether the same ethical responsibility to warn and protect applies in this circumstance (for example, see Harding et al., 1993; Hughes & Friedman, 1995; Stanard & Hazler, 1995).

Only the ACA *Code of Ethics* makes special reference to the limits of confidentiality with people with fatal contagious diseases:

Section B.1.d: Contagious Fatal Diseases

A counselor who receives information confirming that a client has a disease that is commonly known to be both communicable and fatal is justified in disclosing confidential information to an identifiable third party, who by his or her relationship with the client is at a high risk of contracting the disease. Prior to making a disclosure the counselor should ascertain that the client has not already informed the third party about his or her disease and that the client is not intending to inform the third party in the immediate future.

Neither the American Psychological Association code nor that of the National Association of Social Workers specifically mentions exceptions to confidentiality regarding contagious diseases. However, both organizations have issued documents on the topic. In 1991, APA published a resolution on applying duty-to-warn issues to people with HIV disorders. In this document APA opposed the establishment of a legal duty-to-warn provision for HIV-positive clients whose behavior increases the risk of transmitting the virus. (As of this writing, no legal duty to warn and protect people at risk for HIV exposure has been imposed on mental health professionals.) The APA resolution goes on to describe the wording the association would find acceptable if such laws were written. These words closely parallel the contents of the ACA code:

If, however, specific legislation is considered, then it should permit disclosure only when (a) the provider knows of an identifiable third party who the provider has a compelling reason to believe is at significant risk for infection; (b) the provider has a reasonable belief that the third party has no reason to suspect that he or she is at risk; and (c) the client/patient has been urged to inform the third party and has either refused or is considered unreliable in his/her willingness to notify the third party. (APA, 1991)

Moreover, APA's *Ethical Principles* allow disclosure of confidential information to third parties in situations where the law permits (see Sections 5.02 and 5.03).

In 1990, the National Association of Social Workers issued a policy statement dealing with third parties at risk from HIV-positive individuals (NASW, 1997). After stating that social workers should develop guidelines for such situations, based on the NASW ethics code, the duty-to-protect principle, and existing laws, the policy goes on to say,

> Practitioners should use the strength of the client-worker relationship to encourage clients with HIV/AIDS to inform their sexual or needle-sharing partners of their status. Social workers should be familiar with applicable state law regarding duty to warn. Agencies have a clear responsibility to establish clear guidelines for social workers whose clients place others at risk of infection. (p. 161)

The American Psychiatric Association position also emphasizes the importance of confidentiality with HIV clients, recommending that confidentiality be breached only after "scrupulous attention has been given to all other alternatives" (American Psychiatric Association, Ad Hoc Committee on AIDS Policy, 1988, p. 541).

A central theme in each of these documents is that confidentiality should be protected to the greatest degree possible. Hasty breaches of confidentiality based on emotion or intuition, rather than on careful reasoning, are inherently problematic. This message is underscored by research suggesting that the ability of mental health professionals to make objective decisions about breaches of confidentiality in this circumstance is compromised by their attitudes toward homosexuality (McGuire, Nieri, Abbott, Sheridan, & Fisher, 1995). McGuire et al. found that psychotherapists who scored higher on a measure of homophobia were more likely to breach confidentiality in hypothetical cases than those who scored lower in homophobic attitudes. In their sample of mental health professionals Crawford, Humfleet, Ribordy, Ho, and Vickers (1991) also found evidence of prejudiced attitudes toward people with HIV disorders. Thus counselors need to be especially careful that any decision to warn a third party is based on a rational consideration of the facts and on a balanced assessment of the rights of the client and of the person at risk. Counselors who decide to breach confidentiality because of their own fear of HIV diseases, or of their bias against people who engage in high-risk behaviors, are acting unethically.

As mentioned, the legal questions are largely unresolved about whether confidentiality may be breached with a client with HIV who is risking transmission of the infection. Evidence of discrimination and violation of privacy laws in cases of HIV-infected people has led some states to initiate laws to protect such clients (Hughes & Friedman, 1995). In these jurisdictions, breaches of confidentiality could lead the client to bring a civil suit against the counselor. As mentioned, no duty-to-protect statutes for HIV disorders have yet passed, but counselors may still be vulnerable to civil action for malpractice if they decide not to warn a third party. How pronounced is that risk? Burris, as quoted in Barret (in press), suggests that the counselor's vulnerability to such legal action is not especially high and is almost nil if the partner is unidentifiable. Thus counselors should direct their energies toward resolving the ethical dilemma that emerges when HIV-positive clients persistently engage in high-risk behaviors. On the one hand, the practical realities that influence the risk of a malpractice suit have no bearing on the counselors' ethical duty to act responsibly. On the other hand, counselors cannot afford to approach the legal dimensions of the dilemma cavalierly, because other state laws may exist for which the counselor can be held accountable. Familiarity with the state's laws about the rights of people with HIV disorders and the obligations of mental health professionals who interact with those clients is prudent. Burris (in Barret, in press) and others (such as Harding et al., 1993) point out that state laws on this issue are constantly evolving.

The emergence of new medications to treat the HIV virus (Clay, 1997) may have some bearing on the interpretation of the ACA code. Protease inhibitors are reducing the amount of the virus in patients' bodies to an almost undetectable level. At the time of this book's publication, medical science was uncertain about the meaning of this reduction, either for transmitting the virus or for long-term survival (Clay, 1997). Obviously, the answers to these questions will affect counselors' considerations about breaching confidentiality to warn others about their risk to contract the virus.

Confidentiality with Special Populations

Much of the prior discussion assumes that counseling is a one-on-one activity with a competent adult client. When counseling varies from that framework, different considerations regarding the ethics of confidentiality emerge. The following will discuss the interpretation of confidentiality when counseling children, groups, families, and people with diminished capacity.

Children and Adolescents

A counselor working with minors is required to honor confidentiality in most of the same ways as with adults. No counselor may gossip about a client just because that client is underage, nor may the counselor share client information with people other than the parents without proper consent. The counseling records of a minor must be kept secure from unauthorized people, and the identity of minor clients should also be protected. The rationale for this position is the same as for adult confidentiality: Without it, client autonomy is diminished and the trusting counseling relationship is jeopardized. In short, respect for the client's dignity and welfare is not a concept limited to any age group. (Of course, the limits on confidentiality with adults described in the last section of this chapter also apply to minors.)

The distinction in applying confidentiality to young clients stems from their legal status as minors. Minors are not granted the same privacy rights as adults. In fact, until 1967, U.S. law did not recognize that minors were "persons" with any privacy rights in constitutional terms. In that year a U.S. Supreme Court ruling concluded, "neither the Fourteenth Amendment nor the Bill of Rights is for adults alone" (In re Gault, 1967, p. 28). Since 1967 some foothold has been gained to view children and adolescents as persons; however, minors are generally not allowed to have secrets from their parents or guardians (Koocher & Keith-Spiegel, 1990). Thus, in the absence of state or federal statutes to the contrary, parents have a legal right to information disclosed in counseling unless they give permission for it to be kept from them.

As mentioned in Chapter 2, the ethics codes give only broad-brush attention to confidentiality with children and adolescents. The ACA code states,

> When counseling clients who are minors or individuals who are unable to give voluntary informed consent, parents or guardians may be included in the counseling process as appropriate. Counselors act in the best interests of clients and take measures to safeguard confidentiality. (Section B.3)

These statements mean that counselors have permission to include parents or guardians in the counseling process, using "the best interests of the child" as their criterion. The APA code is even less specific in Sections 5.01 and 5.05. Thus, the codes leave to the judgment of the individual professional the burden of deciding when to involve or exclude parents or guardians.

Fortunately, a number of ethics scholars have examined the issue of confidentiality in counseling minors and have suggested guidelines for determining how much confidentiality a child can be granted. A common thread is that the degree to which confidentiality can be honored is directly related to the age and maturity of the minor. The closer the young person is to the age of maturity, the greater the likelihood that he or she can be granted a fuller measure of confidentiality. This judgment is based on research that has found that adolescents of 14 or more seem capable of making judgments about counseling as competently as adults. In other words, they seem to understand the nature, risks, and benefits of counseling sufficiently to give informed consent (Gustafson & McNamara, 1987). In contrast, children under 11 have not been able to show the necessary level of understanding to give informed consent. Moreover, younger children tend to be less assertive and to defer to authority rather than express their own wishes.

The capacity of children between 11 and 14 to understand counseling varies according to their level of cognitive development, particularly their attainment of formal operations thinking (Weithorn, 1983). When children have attained this level of thinking, they can conceptualize about abstract possibilities and reason hypothetically, capacities that seem crucial for effective participation in counseling. Thus, when working with youngsters in this age range, scholars suggest assessing the client's cognitive maturity to determine his or her capacity to participate independently in counseling. Of course, not all children over 14 have attained the level of formal operations. Thus a careful judgment about intellectual maturity is appropriate whenever counseling a minor.

The law has also defined four general exceptions to parental consent for counseling minors (Gustafson & McNamara, 1987). The first exception is for the mature minor, a minor capable of understanding treatment and its consequences. The second exception is for a minor who is "legally emancipated" from parents and guardians. These adolescents operate with independence in virtually all aspects of their daily lives. The third exception is for emergencies. Any minor can be treated if immediate treatment is urgently needed. Finally, parental consent can be waived by a court order.

A number of states have allowed minors to receive medical and psychological treatment without parental consent when the requirement for parental consent would interfere with a youngster's willingness to seek treatment. For example, teenagers may often seek care for substance abuse, pregnancy, sexually transmitted diseases, and contraception without parental knowledge or consent. Other states, such as Ohio, allow adolescents to seek mental health services without parental consent for a limited number of sessions, after which parents must be informed or treatment ended.

Other authors suggest that focusing on ways to keep counseling information from parents and guardians is misguided. Instead, they maintain that because parents have so much power in their children's lives, they should be welcomed into the process rather than excluded from it (Taylor & Adelman, 1989). These authors argue that at times, keeping information confidential from parents "can seriously hamper an intervener's efforts to help a client" (Taylor & Adelman, 1989, p. 80). Enlisting parents' cooperation as an initial phase in the counseling process not only encourages them to cooperate with the counselor, but also provides an opportunity to educate them about the appropriateness of confidentiality with minors. Experts suggest a preliminary session in which parents are given information about the counseling process, are reassured that vital information that affects their child's well-being will be shared, and are instructed about the importance of trust and privacy for any person who enters counseling. After such an orientation, parents are not only more likely to give consent to counseling, but they are also more willing to support rather than sabotage the counselor's efforts and to respect their child's right to privacy about counseling sessions.

Needless to say, not all parents are willing to engage in such a process, and frequently a child's difficulties stem from the parents' problems. Adolescents caught in an alcoholic family may have parents who deny their substance abuse. Such parents often object to the teenagers' attempts to get counseling, but the adolescents still need a forum in which they can discuss their concerns and learn coping skills. Similarly, a adolescent struggling with sexual identity issues often cannot broach these matters with family. Many adolescents who do so are turned away from their homes. Gay youth are also at risk for violence, even from family members, according to Hetrick and Martin (1987). In their study, 49% of the gay and lesbian adolescents who sought services to help them deal with violence against them indicated that they were assaulted by family members.

In such situations, the counselor needs to weigh the legal rights of the parents against the child's emotional well-being and decide on a course of action that serves the child's best interests. The ultimate goal of the counselor should be to find a way to get the family involved, because the best resolution to the youngster's difficulty may be family treatment.

Group and Family Counseling

The fundamental ethical responsibility to respect the client's right to confidentiality does not change in group or family counseling. The counselor must not disclose to those who do not have a right to it, the identity of clients or information revealed in counseling. The presence of other people in the room when an individual client reveals personal information complicates confidentiality from both an ethical and legal perspective. First, as the codes indicate, the counselor cannot guarantee that the other people hearing these disclosures will also respect the client's privacy. Of course, the counselor emphasizes the importance of confidentiality in any multiple-client situation and asks all participants to honor confidentiality, but the counselor has no real power to enforce that request. Thus, all participants in group and family counseling need to understand this as another "limit" on confidentiality.

ACA *Code of Ethics,* **Section B.2.a: Group Work**

In group work, counselors clearly define confidentiality and the parameters for the specific group being entered, its importance, and discuss the difficulties related to confidentiality in group work. The fact that confidentiality cannot be guaranteed is clearly communicated to group members.

ACA *Code of Ethics,* **Section B.2.b: Family Counseling**

In family counseling information about one family member cannot be disclosed to another member without permission. Counselors protect the privacy rights of each member.

APA *Ethical Principles,* **Section 4.03: Couples and Family Relationships**

(a) When a psychologist agrees to provide services to several persons who have a relationship (such as a husband or wife or parents and children), the psychologist attempts to clarify at the onset (1) which of the individuals are patients or clients and (2) the relationship the psychologist will have with each person. This clarification includes the role of the psychologist and the probable uses of the services provided or the information obtained.

(b) As soon as it becomes apparent that the psychologist may be called on to perform potentially conflicting roles (such as marriage counselor to husband and wife and then witnesses for one of the parties in a divorce proceeding), the psychologist attempts to clarify and adjust, or withdraw from, roles appropriately.

Second, whether information disclosed in group or family counseling can be regarded as privileged information in a courtroom is an open question. The privilege concept is based on one individual communicating privately to a lawyer, physician, or priest. When a person communicates information to a mental health professional in front of third parties, the claim that that information is privileged has not been universally honored in the legal system. This is called the *third-party rule:* Any information disclosed in front of third parties is generally ruled by the courts not to be privileged (Swenson, 1997). Thus, clients in multiple-person counseling also need to understand the uncertainty of whether privilege really applies even in states that may grant the mental health professional privilege for individual counseling (Corey, Williams, & Moline, 1995). Some states have privilege statutes protecting communications in group and family therapy, but most do not (Freed & Walker, 1988; Myers, 1991).

Emerging Challenges to Confidentiality

When counseling originated nearly a hundred years ago, the only people involved were clients and their counselors (Heppner, 1990; Whiteley, 1984). All counseling took place in a face-to-face meeting, and all financial aspects were handled directly by the individuals involved. Records were kept on paper, and the counselor and the client were the ones who decided the length and nature of treatment. The advent of third-party reimbursement, computerization of records, and access to counselors through media, telephone, and the Internet have revolutionized the counseling process and compounded confidentiality dilemmas. For example, when insurers began to reimburse people for mental health expenses they sought information regarding the nature of the problem and its treatment. If they were to pay for services, insurers had a right to know that appropriate services were being rendered. So clients signed a release so that counselors could communicate with the insurers. When managed care came into being, the insurers' demands for information about the diagnosis intensified and their involvement in recommending both the length and type of treatment expanded. Currently, managed care providers also claim the right to audit counseling records to ascertain that the reimbursement was properly used and to be deeply involved in monitoring the progress of treatment. Counselors sometimes have to provide detailed information to justify additional counseling sessions. Each of these demands compromises the privacy of the client. Not only does the gatekeeper at the managed care organization have extensive information on clients, but others in the managed care organization and the client's workplace may gain access to that material. It is not unusual for almost a dozen people to have private information if a client submits counseling costs for reimbursement by a managed care provider. Managed care companies have sometimes failed to prevent people who have no involvement in a case from accessing confidential mental health records of that case (Scarf, 1996). Of course, because clients and their employers pay for mental health insurance, they have every right to use it to offset costs. Many clients might not have access to mental health care without insurance help. Yet clients often fail to understand how deeply their privacy can be invaded in this process. Counselors have an obligation to help them understand the implications of using insurance for the confidentiality of counseling.

The computerization of counseling records also can affect confidentiality. As Bongar (1988) points out, the computer's ability to store large amounts of data on small magnetic media make counseling records vulnerable to theft, duplication, or loss on a level unrivaled by old-fashioned paper records. Conceivably, a counselor's entire set of case records could be stored on one or two floppy disks, and thus easily stolen, lost, or ruined. In this era of the Internet and networks of computers, material stored on a counselor's hard drive may be equally vulnerable to loss. Counselors who use computers for client records must be alert to this potential for misuse and must make extra efforts to protect the client's confidentiality (Sampson, Kolodinsky, & Greeno, 1997). Research on psychologists' use of technology shows substantial reliance on computers (Rosen & Weil, 1996). In that study, 52% reported storing client financial records on computer and 15% reported keeping case notes on computer. Another 11% administered psychological tests by computer, and 6% gave "direct client assistance" by computer (Rosen & Weil, 1996, p. 636).

When using facsimile machines, caution should also be taken to transmit client materials and client release forms. Fax machines may be located in an open, public space to which access is not restricted. Transmissions may occur when the receiving office is not open, so the documents may be unprotected for many hours. Consequently, a telephone contact before transmitting of the facsimile is prudent. The call can ensure that a qualified person is available to retrieve the confidential material. In parallel fashion, a follow-up call is desirable, to ensure that all materials were received as transmitted. In addition, the cover sheet on the facsimile should include a clear and easily readable statement about the confidentiality of material on the following pages. Highly sensitive client records, such as data that reveal a client's HIV status or history of incest, may not be appropriate for facsimile transmission under any circumstances.

Most recently, as the Internet and the World Wide Web have become major avenues for interpersonal communication, enterprising mental health professionals and clients have begun to use this medium for therapeutic interaction. Questions about providing counseling through the Internet came to the American Psychological Association's Ethics Committee frequently enough for this group to issue a statement on the ethics of such communications (APA, Ethics Committee, 1995a). This statement cautioned psychologists about the appropriateness of Internet counseling, given the risks to confidentiality and the inaccessibility of nonverbal feedback. In short, APA says that counseling through the computer, in particular, is fraught with risks to both confidentiality and competence and therefore does not appear ethically justified. The National Board of Certified Counselors (NBCC) has also embarked on a study of counseling on the Internet and will present its recommendations on the subject shortly (Sampson et al., 1997).

CASE FOR DISCUSSION

Using the decision-making model presented in Chapter 2, consider the following case:

Raymond is an 18-year-old college freshman living in a residence hall. He is the eldest of five children, and his parents live in a nearby state. Raymond is HIV positive, as the result of an infected blood transfusion from six years ago. He has been asymptomatic since then. No one, except his parents, knows of his HIV status. In fact, his parents have not even informed his younger siblings or either set of grandparents. He comes to see a college counselor because he is confused and worried. He has met a young woman and has dated her a few times. He wants to become sexually intimate with her, but has not told her about his HIV status. Raymond is afraid that disclosure would end her interest in him or the interest of any young woman with whom he wants a serious relationship. He has some brochures about safer sex practices and believes if he did become intimate with this woman that he would use a condom and follow other guidelines for safer sex. He is currently resistant to the idea of disclosing his HIV status to anyone. After a lengthy counseling session, the counselor concludes that Raymond is likely to practice safe sex if he does become intimate with this woman. Moreover, intimacy is not imminent, because he does not even see her again for a week. The counselor determines that there is no ethical basis for breaching confidentiality to this woman in the near future. Do you agree with that professional judgment?

Step 1: Develop Ethical Sensitivity.

- Do you agree that there is an ethical dilemma here? Why or why not?
- Whose welfare is affected by the actions of the counselor, and how?
- What was your immediate emotional and intellectual response to reading this case?
- How would you feel if you were in this counselor's position?

Step 2: Define Dilemma and Options.

- Precisely how do you define the ethical dilemma(s) for Raymond's counselor?
- What facts of the case cause you to define it in this way?
- Are there any other facts you should be considering?
- When you brainstorm about this case, what options can you identify?

Step 3: Refer to Codes and Laws.

- What do the codes of ethics say about the dilemma and the options you have identified?
- Do other documents from the professional associations speak directly to this dilemma? (Describe.)
- Are there laws in your state that are relevant to this dilemma? (Describe.)

Step 4: Review Ethics Scholarship.

- What do scholars on this subject say about responsible resolutions of the dilemma?
- If scholars disagree, which arguments seem most compelling, and why?

Step 5: Apply Ethical Principles.

- What ethical principles underlie this dilemma?
- Does consideration of the principles lead to a single response or to different responses? If different, which principle do you think should take priority? Why?

Step 6: Consult with Other Professionals.

- What are the views of your supervisor and colleagues on ethical resolutions of this dilemma?

- Do those views coincide with the recommendations of the codes, the scholars, and the ethical principles? In what ways do they differ?

Step 7: Deliberate and Decide.
- Is your list of options still adequate? Should it be revised in any way? How?
- Now that you have accumulated all this information and heard others' perspectives, what have you decided?
- What is your rationale for that decision?

Step 8: Inform Supervisors.
- How should you go about informing your supervisor, implementing the actions, and documenting your decision?

Step 9: Reflect on the Experience.
- Now that you have been through this process, what has it meant to you?
- What have you learned?
- How will this experience change your response to similar ethical dilemmas?
- Do you have any knowledge that you ought to share with colleagues? If so, how can you do that most effectively?

Resolutions of Raymond's Dilemma

First, the choice the counselor makes is clearly a matter of ethics because the welfare of several people is at stake. Raymond may be harmed if his HIV status is disclosed to a third party. He may withdraw from counseling, or may suffer harm in the residence hall where he lives if that information becomes widely known, and it may be quickly communicated across the campus. After all, the third party to whom counseling information is disclosed has no legal or ethical obligation to keep that information secret. Raymond may drop out of college or feel the need to transfer elsewhere and lose credit for the term in the process. He may decide that his family's secretiveness about his health status is the best course and never reveal his HIV infection to anyone again, even to other sexual partners. Other students may assume that Raymond is gay and make him the victim of "gay bashing." Other negative consequences for Raymond are possible. He may even become suicidal, a common occurrence among those with HIV disorders. The disclosure of Raymond's HIV status at the college would also be painful for Raymond's family, whose capacity to cope with his illness seems already diminished even without this disclosure.

In addition, the welfare of the young woman Raymond is dating is at stake. If they become sexually active, and if the couple fails to take appropriate precautions, the sexual contact puts her at some risk for being infected with the virus. Currently there is no cure for HIV infection, and in most cases the infection leads to AIDS and, eventually, to an early death.

Given what's at stake here, the ethical dilemma can be defined as balancing Raymond's right to privacy and need for further counseling against the potential duty to warn and protect from HIV infection the young woman Raymond is dating.

The relevant facts of the case are that Raymond is an adult who is so concerned about how his HIV status will affect this emerging romantic relationship that he sought the assistance of a professional counselor. He is, at this point, resistant to revealing his medical condition to anyone else, but is not unwilling to consider precautions that reduce the risk of transmitting the virus. Several other facts are less clear than they first appear. First, the counselor does not have real confirmation of Raymond's HIV status. Even though it is unlikely that the client would be purposely deceiving the counselor, it is possible he is delusional or does not really understand the medical information he received six years ago. At that time, he was only 12 years old. Moreover, it appears that his family has not talked much to him about his infection and has reacted with secrecy and denial, which might leave unchallenged for all these years any misinformation Raymond had at age 12. A single session with Raymond may not be sufficient to judge his rationality, veracity, or sophistication of knowledge.

Second, the counselor has no verification that the young woman returns Raymond's affections, or that if she does, she is ready to advance the relationship to the level of sexual intimacy Raymond wants. In other words, she may have no serious interest in him and may view him as a friend rather than a lover. Raymond's lack of dating experience makes this even more likely than it might be for a college freshman with dating experience. Or her personal values may cause her to refrain from sexual intimacy until engaged or married.

Third, the counselor has no certain information about Raymond's commitment to using safer sex practices should he become sexually involved with this woman. He may act responsibly in this regard, or he may not. This fact is important because it has such important implications for the degree of danger to which the woman is exposed. Fourth, regardless of the use of safer sex practices, the exact risk of transmitting the virus in a single sexual encounter is unknown (Keeling, 1993). Many cases of repeated heterosexual intercourse have resulted in no transmission of the virus, but in some cases, transmission has occurred after a single contact. Fifth, the counselor has no knowledge of the woman's understanding of sexually transmitted diseases or her commitment to practices that minimize her risk of such infections. She may be fully prepared to insist on safe sex regardless of Raymond's inclinations on the matter. Sixth, the woman herself may be HIV positive. The rate of infection in heterosexual adolescents is rising, and she may have already contracted the virus. This is a statistically unlikely scenario, but not impossible. Taken together, these uncertainties show how little this counselor really knows about the degree of risk Raymond represents to this particular young woman.

The counselor's options are

- To inform the young woman immediately even if Raymond does not agree to disclose immediately himself
- To keep the information confidential for the duration of counseling and to educate the client about safe sex practices
- To set disclosure of his HIV status to the woman as a counseling goal for Raymond
- To postpone a decision until the facts of the case are clearer

The ACA *Code of Ethics* allows disclosure of information about clients' fatal contagious diseases to third parties if certain requirements are met. The counselor must have confirming information about the disease, the third party must be at high risk of contracting the disease, and the client must be unwilling to disclose to the third party in the immediate future. It is important to note that the code *permits* such disclosure; the code does not mandate nor even recommend disclosure. The exact wording is "A counselor . . . is justified in disclosing" (Section B.1.d). This wording means that the codes do not prescribe a certain behavior. Instead, they give permission for disclosing or for maintaining confidentiality. As in many other situations, then, the codes provide general guidelines, not specific mandates.

Applying these guidelines to this case, the first implication is that the counselor does not yet have confirmation that Raymond is HIV positive. Perhaps verification from Raymond's physician is needed. Nor can the counselor ascertain with any clarity the degree of infection risk to the young woman in whom Raymond is sexually interested. In addition, the potential for any sexual contact is probably delayed for a week or more. Thus, the criterion of immediacy is not clearly met either, for the counselor could schedule additional sessions with the client in the intervening time period. From this analysis, it seems that the code does not endorse disclosure at this juncture, but that future events may make it justifiable. The other professional documents on this topic also echo the message that counselors should carefully consider breaches of confidentiality in this situation and should avoid rushing to disclose because of the risk of harming the client and the uncertainty of how dangerous a single sexual encounter may be.

The state laws on the issue of disclosure vary considerably. For example, states such as Massachusetts forbid any disclosure of HIV status to third parties (Hughes & Friedman, 1995), whereas other states allow such breaches. Thus, depending on the jurisdiction, one would respond in very different ways to this dilemma.

Scholars' views generally echo the arguments in the documents of the professional associations. They suggest weighing the implications of disclosure for the client as carefully as weighing the risk to the third party. They also remind counselors that disclosure may rupture the counseling relationship, and thereby eliminate the counselor's potential to influence the client's behavior in the future. The opportunity to ever help a client learn how to disclose HIV status or use safer sex practices may be irretrievably lost. It is this argument that swayed the counselor in the case and that appears particularly compelling, given the young man's initial voluntary entry into counseling. After all, he could have continued developing the physical relationship with this young woman, never sought counseling, and never informed her of his medical condition. The counselor in this case has a valuable opportunity to help Raymond and to prevent his ever infecting anyone with the virus.

The ethical principles underlying this dilemma relate to respecting the autonomy of this man to make free decisions for himself and avoiding harm to him and those in contact with him. There is also the issue of fidelity to promises made, unless the counselor explicitly explained the limitations of confidentiality at the outset of counseling. The principle of nonmalficence is most important to consider, especially the potential harm to the client and the woman. There is little doubt that disclosure without his consent will harm this young man, although his injuries are likely to be psychological rather than physical. Her potential injury is physical, but the psychological ramifications of exposure to HIV infection are also crucially important. Still, the probability of infection for her is lower than the risk of harm to him from disclosure. How should one balance an improbable but potentially fatal harm against a fairly certain (but not life-threatening) harm?

Given this information and the results of consultations with colleagues and supervisors, the revised list of options is

- Focus on safer sex practices and on getting Raymond to agree to a "no sex" contract until the counselor has had several more meetings to discuss the issue further. If the client agrees to these conditions, then no immediate disclosure should be made.
- Review with Raymond the limits of confidentiality again, and then ask his permission to bring the young woman into a session to discuss the issue together. If he continues to refuse such an approach in the next session as well, reveal the client's information to her.
- Decide that if Raymond commits to practicing safer sex, then the danger is so low that there really is no justification for a breach of confidentiality

The option that seems most ethically sound at this point is the first one. Raymond needs counseling, is willing to participate in counseling now, and seems prepared to accept some responsibility for his behavior insofar as he is willing to practice safer sex. Moreover, the risk to the young woman is not imminent and the counselor has a week in which to continue to work with the client before sexual contact is even possible. Given all this information, disclosure seems premature at this point. As events unfold, that decision may change, depending on Raymond's attitude and behavior and the degree of risk to the woman.

SUMMARY

Confidentiality is the cornerstone of effective counseling and psychotherapy, because it allows the client to freely share experiences without fear of unwarranted disclosure to others. The ethics codes devote considerable attention to this topic, emphasizing its importance and the situations in which counselors may have permission to communicate client disclosures to others. Confidentiality in counseling covers both the content of disclosures and contact with clients, so the identity of those who seek services is also kept secret from public knowledge. This ethical standard is rooted in the principles of respect for client autonomy and fidelity to promises made.

Confidentiality of counseling disclosures is often also protected by legal statutes. In many states, the clients of mental health professionals can prevent those counselors from testifying in court about material revealed in counseling. Such material is called *privileged communication*.

There are seven major exceptions to confidentiality in counseling. These include (1) a client's request for release of confidential information to him- or herself or to a qualified professional; (2) a court order for confidential information; (3) an ethics complaint or lawsuit against a counselor; (4) other client litigation in which the client raises the issues of counseling treatment as part of the client's civil suit against another party; (5) limitations to confidentiality based on statutes, such as reporting child and elder abuse; (6) dangerous clients who are putting themselves or others at imminent risk for injury or death; and (7) clients with contagious fatal diseases, such as HIV disorders, whose behavior puts others at imminent risk of infection. When dealing with dangerous, suicidal, or HIV-positive individuals whose behaviors are irresponsible, counselors have an obligation to carefully assess the degree of risk involved and to honor the privacy rights of the client to the greatest degree possible.

Confidentiality issues also arise when counselors work with children, families, and groups. With children and adolescents, the issue is the degree to which the child client can keep counseling disclosures secret from parents and guardians. The law tends to give minors few rights to privacy; the ethical guidelines tend to see confidentiality for minors increasing with age and maturity. Generally, the more mature the minor, the greater the measure of confidentiality that young person is given in counseling. When working with groups and families, counselors need to be aware that they cannot guarantee clients the same degree of privacy as in individual counseling. When clients reveal personal information in front of third parties, the counselor cannot prevent those third parties from breaching confidentiality. The counselor should contract with all participants to honor confidentiality as a condition for inclusion in the group or family counseling, but clients need to understand that these contracts are voluntary, and counselors have little power to prevent other members from violating their promise if they decide to do so.

DISCUSSION QUESTIONS

1. Do you agree with the California court that "privilege should end where the public peril begins"? Why or why not?
2. Do you think that the fact that a child protection services agency is ineffective or overworked is a rationale for not reporting suspected child abuse? Why or why not?
3. Why do you think violations of confidentiality happen so frequently among practicing mental health professionals?
4. Do you think that "rational suicide" is possible? Should a duty to protect apply in this situation? (Explain.)
5. Some scholars are very concerned about the erosion of confidentiality in the courts and the managed care arena. How do you think counselors should approach the discussion of confidentiality with clients who want to submit claims to managed care companies or who may be facing court involvement?
6. Do you think children have the right to keep material confidential from their parents?

RECOMMENDED READINGS

American Psychological Association, Committee on Legal Issues. (1996). Strategies for private practitioners coping with subpoenas or compelled testimony for client records or test data. *Professional Psychology: Research and Practice, 27,* 245–251.

American Psychological Association, Committee on Professional Practice and Standards. (1995). Twenty-four questions (and answers) about professional practice in the area of child abuse. *Professional Psychology: Research and Practice, 26,* 377–383.

Bongar, B. (1991). *The suicidal patient: Clinical and legal standards of care.* Washington, DC: American Psychological Association.

Gustafson, K. E., & McNamara, J. R. (1987). Confidentiality with minor clients: Issues and guidelines for therapists. *Professional Psychology: Research and Practice, 18,* 503–508.

Harding, A., Gray, L., & Neal, M. (1993). Confidentiality limits with clients who have HIV: A review of ethical and legal guidelines and professional policies. *Journal of Counseling and Development, 71,* 297–305.

Kalichman, S. C. (1993). *Mandated reporting of suspected child abuse: Ethics, law and policy.* Washington, DC: American Psychological Association.

Koocher, G., & Keith-Spiegel, P. S. (1990). *Children, ethics and the law.* Lincoln: University of Nebraska Press.

Levine, M., & Doueck, H. J. (1995). *The impact of mandated reporting on the therapeutic process: Picking up the pieces.* Thousand Oaks, CA: Sage.

Monahan, J. (1993). Limiting therapist exposure to *Tarasoff* liability: Guidelines for risk management. *American Psychologist, 48,* 242–250.

Remley, T. P., Jr., Herlihy, B., & Herlihy, S. B. (1997). The U.S. Supreme Court decision in *Jaffee v. Redmond*: Implications for counselors. *Journal of Counseling and Development, 75,* 213–218.

Truscott, D., Evans, J., & Mansell, S. (1995). Outpatient psychotherapy with dangerous clients: A model for clinical decision making. *Professional Psychology: Research and Practice, 26,* 484–490.

VandeCreek, L., & Knapp, S. (1993). *Tarasoff and beyond: Legal and clinical considerations in the treatment of life-endangering patients* (Rev. ed.). Sarasota, FL: Professional Resource Exchange.

6

Informed Consent
Affirming the Client's Freedom of Choice

Counseling and psychotherapy clients buy counseling services (either directly or indirectly). As consumers, they have ethical and legal rights—consumer rights—to information about the nature and potential results of those services. Because most people have no other way to gain such "product information," counselors have an obligation to provide it. The need for information is heightened by the fact that the limited knowledge people believe they have is often erroneous. For example, people may believe counselors only dispense advice, or will trace their problems to poor toilet training, or similar absurdities. Also, counseling significantly affects the client's mental, emotional, and social functioning. Research shows that counseling is an effective intervention for many human problems (for example, see Bergin & Garfield, 1994; Seligman, 1995; Sexton, Whiston, Bleuer, & Walz, 1997)—but the client still may experience negative as well as positive results. Counseling does not come with a guarantee of success or ease of change. During the process, clients often experience interruptions in normal patterns, feelings, and social relationships. These interruptions may add up to positive changes over the long run, but meanwhile, clients may feel uncomfortable and should be made aware of these possibilities. Finally, the most fundamental reason for providing information about counseling is that it shows respect for the client as a person with rights and responsibilities in a democratic society. Even if they are not purchasing services, clients still deserve information on which to base consent, as a function of their human rights.

Informed consent has two central aspects. The first is *disclosure* by the counselor of all important information the client needs to decide whether to start counseling, and the second is *free consent*. Free consent means that the decision to engage in an activity is made without coercion or undue pressure. Providing full information empowers the client to determine his or her level of involvement in counseling. Underlying the requirement of informed consent is a view of the client as an autonomous human being capable of directing his or her own life and of collaborating with a counselor to make necessary changes. The call for informed consent rests on a model of counseling and psychotherapy as a partnership in which mental health professionals use their expertise to help clients achieve their own goals. Clients, in turn, use their understanding of themselves and their personal circumstances to help the counselor identify useful interventions and to inform the counselor about their progress. Thus, informed consent depends on the notion of the client as an active participant in counseling, with dignity and power to work toward achieving therapeutic goals.

This chapter seeks to provide a well-rounded overview of informed consent, beginning with a history of how this principle developed. This chapter dispels several myths about informed consent in counseling:

- That informed consent is easily dispensed with in the initial counseling session by having a client sign some forms
- That informed consent is restricted to discussion of the limits of confidentiality and little more
- That informed consent is a distraction from the real business of counseling
- That informed consent is undertaken primarily to protect the counselor from legal liability
- That clients understand and remember the information conveyed to them in the initial informed consent procedure

This chapter also describes the stance of the ethics codes on informed consent and the ethical principles undergirding those guidelines, the research on practitioners' interpretations of informed consent, and the interplay between ethical and clinical considerations. In its later sections, the chapter also explores the application of informed consent with minors, in emergencies, court situations, and with adults with diminished mental capacity. Finally, it concludes by discussing the empirical research on practitioners' beliefs and practices in regard to informed consent and with cases for analysis. (Informed consent in research discussed in Chapter 13.)

The History of Informed Consent

The requirement of informed consent for counseling and psychotherapy largely derives from medical case law. Although the first case can be traced to England in 1767 (Smith & Meyer, 1987), before the twentieth century physicians had little legal or ethical obligation to explain medical procedures to their patients or to obtain their express consent. The paternalistic attitude reigned supreme: "Doctor knows best" and "patient is too ignorant to understand or choose anyway." This attitude sprang from a society in which average citizens were poorly educated and ignorant about anatomy and physiology. Also, consumer rights in general were a little-known concept until the 1950s. Vestiges of such paternalism persist in the medical and human service professions. As Haas and Malouf (1995) point out, this attitude toward recipients of care is problematic for several reasons. First, it prevents people from coming actively involved in their own care. The opportunity for the client to assist with treatment in a deliberate way is lost. In a doctor-knows-best system, patients do not feel responsible for their own health and recovery. Second, it is vulnerable to abuse. Uninformed patients can be exploited more easily, and unethical practitioners can avoid accountability more readily.

The spark for change ignited when patients won medical malpractice suits showing that physicians harmed their patients by failing to communicate the nature and risks of medical treatment. Other factors also encouraged the trend away from paternalism. Outrageous violations of patient rights in Nazi Germany and in the infamous Tuskegee experiments in the United States were the most striking of these influences (Jones, 1981). (In the Tuskegee experiments, African-American men with syphilis were "studied" for 40 years to observe the progression of the disease. These men were told they were going to receive free medical care in exchange for their cooperation in the project. However, they were never informed of their diagnosis, were required to undergo painful procedures, and for many years were denied the penicillin that could cure them. Many died unnecessarily from this cruel and inhumane treatment.)

By the 1970s case law had unequivocally established that patients had the right to knowledge that would equip them to make informed decisions about their own treatment. Because physicians were typically the ones who possessed the requisite knowledge, the courts ruled that physicians had an affirmative duty to provide such information. The court in *Canterbury v. Spence* (1972, p. 783) concluded that "The duty to disclose is more than a call to speak merely on the patient's request, or merely to answer the patient's questions; it is the duty to volunteer, if necessary, information a patient needs for an intelligent decision." In 1980 a California court expanded the physician's duty to include informed refusal. The term *informed refusal* means that physicians have an obligation to explain the medical consequences if patients refuse a treatment. This reasoning is based on the notion that ordinary citizens are not likely to have sufficient medical knowledge to accurately evaluate the implications of rejecting treatment. Because physicians do understand, they are bound to communicate that information as well (*Truman v. Thomas,* 1980).

The specific requirements for the contents of informed consent procedures in medicine, and indirectly in mental health, also emerged from a medical malpractice case, *Natanson v. Kline* (1960). The court in that case specified that disclosure should include the nature of the illness, the treatment(s) available, their risks and the probability of their success, and alternatives to treatment and their risks. These types of information are still major components of informed consent in medicine and mental health today.

The mental health professions quickly applied these legal mandates to their work, and the ethics codes began to include requirements for practitioners to develop an informed consent process with their clients. The professions recognized the connection between these legal rulings and the client's inherent right to self-determination, and endorsed the precedent. Although some have cautioned against applying medical methods of developing informed consent to the counseling process wholesale, without considering of the needs of the individual client (for example, see Pope & Vasquez, 1991), many scholars agree with the general trend.

Underlying Ethical Principles

The fundamental ethical principle underlying the precepts of informed consent is that of respect for autonomy. The client should not be treated paternalistically or have his or her freedom to choose usurped by a mental health professional, regardless of the professional's rationale in doing so. As mentioned, the effects of counseling rest on the client, who thus ought to have all the data needed to freely choose whether to proceed. This precept is also based on the principles of nonmaleficence and justice. When clients understand the procedures, risks, and potential benefits of counseling, they are probably somewhat insulated from unanticipated unpleasant consequences of counseling. For example, clients who are instructed about the emotional pain that can accompany exploration of family issues may better cope with that pain. Justice demands informed consent because justice implies treating other competent adults as equals. By developing informed consent with each client, counselors confirm that all people have the right to manage their own lives and have the potential to assist in their own care. Obviously, some people do not have that capacity, but justice requires that counselors assume competence until contrary information is available. Justice also means that counselors should treat clients as they themselves would wish to be treated. Any person embarking on counseling would want be fully informed about the process. A failure to honor that right implies that we are treating our clients as unequal or less human than we are. Research also suggests that people want information about their prospective counselors (Hendrick, 1988) and that they may view counselors who provide information about informed consent as more expert and trustworthy (Walter & Handelsman, 1996).

Codes of Ethics

The ACA and APA ethics codes contain very similar standards for informed consent. The ACA code contains more detailed instructions about informed consent:

Section A.3.a: Disclosure to Clients

When counseling is initiated, and throughout the counseling process as necessary, counselors inform clients of the purposes, goals, techniques, procedures, limitations, potential risks and benefits of services to be performed, and other pertinent information. Counselors take steps to ensure that clients understand the implications of diagnosis, the intended use of tests and reports, fees, and billing arrangements. Clients have the right to expect confidentiality and to be provided with an explanation of its limitations, including supervision and/or treatment team professionals; to obtain clear information about their case records; to participate in the ongoing counseling plans; and to refuse any recommended services and be advised of the consequences of each refusal.

Section A.3.b: Freedom of Choice

Counselors offer clients the freedom to choose whether to enter into a counseling relationship and to determine which professional(s) will provide counseling. Restrictions that limit choices of clients are fully explained.

The APA code discusses the topic in several different sections, but most of the information is in Sections 4.01 and 4.02:

Section 4.01 Structuring the Relationship

(a) Psychologists discuss with clients or patients as early as is feasible in the therapeutic relationship appropriate issues, such as the nature and anticipated course of therapy, fees, and confidentiality. . . .

(b) When the psychologist's work with clients or patients will be supervised, the above discussion includes that fact and the name of the supervisor, when the supervisor has legal responsibility for the case.

(c) When the therapist is a student intern, the client or patient is informed of that fact.

(d) Psychologists make reasonable efforts to answer patients' questions and to avoid apparent misunderstandings about therapy. Whenever possible, psychologists provide oral and/or written materials, using language that is reasonably understandable to the patient or client.

Section 4.02: Informed Consent to Therapy

(a) Psychologists obtain appropriate informed consent to therapy or related procedures, using language that is reasonably understandable to participants. The content of the informed consent will vary depending on many circumstances; however, informed consent generally implies that the person (1) has the capacity to understand consent, (2) has been informed of significant information concerning the procedures, (3) has freely and without undue influence expressed consent, and (4) consent has been appropriately documented.

The language in the NASW code is broader and more general, but follows the same logic. It reads, ". . . social workers should use clear and understandable language to inform clients of the purpose of the services, risks related to the services, limits to services because of a third-party payer, relevant costs, reasonable alternatives, clients' rights to refuse or withdraw consent, and the time frame covered by the consent. Social workers should provide clients with an opportunity to ask questions" (NASW, 1996, 1.03a).

Taken together, these codes designate the following ingredients to an ethical approach to informed consent. For each aspect, the codes recommend a frank and clear communication of

- Goals, techniques, procedures, limitations, risks, and benefits of counseling
- Ways in which diagnoses, tests, and written reports will be used
- Billing and fees
- Confidentiality rights and limitations
- Involvement of supervisors or additional mental health professionals
- Counselor's training status
- Client's access to records
- Client's right to choose the counselor and to be active in treatment planning
- Client's right to refuse counseling, and the implications of that refusal
- Client's right to ask additional questions about counseling and to have questions answered in comprehensible language

Scholars further recommend that several other topics be added to this list. First, the scholars recommend that counselors give the client a description of their *credentials,* regardless of their training status (Haas & Malouf, 1995; Pope & Vasquez, 1991). In fact, many state licensing boards require mental health professionals to display public disclosure statements that list their training, credentials, and areas of specialization. In these states, failure to inform clients about such matters violates the law and puts the mental health professional at risk for discipline by the licensing board. Research suggests that clients are especially interested in information about the therapist (Braaten, Otto, & Handelsman, 1993). Second, the scholars suggest that many of the *logistics* of counseling be disclosed, not just the fees and billing procedures (Haas & Malouf, 1995). Clients should understand procedures for making and rescheduling appointments, for reaching the counselor in an emergency, and for handling interruptions in service such as counselor illness or vacation. If counselors have a standard length of appointment, such as the "50-minute hour," the client should be told about that practice. In addition, if counselors have an estimate of the number of sessions that may be necessary, that estimate should be shared. Third, for *insurance reimbursement,* clients who wish to submit the costs of service to insurers, and who thus must release records, need explicit information about the implications for the confidentiality of their counseling records. (Chapter 14 discusses in detail the ethical issues in managed care and independent practice.)

Hare-Mustin, Marecek, Kaplan, and Liss-Levinson (1979) advise that when discussing the benefits and risks of therapy, counselors should attend to the *indirect effects* of therapy: consequences that are secondary to the changes the client seeks and agrees to. For example, a client who seeks treatment for agoraphobia (fear of leaving familiar places) should understand that when his agoraphobia diminishes and he returns to his normal activities, this change may indirectly affect aspects of his life he did not expect to be affected. His aging parent may be uncomfortable with his son's absence from the home and may be angry or sad. Similarly, a spouse who is accustomed to always having her husband at home may have difficulty dealing with his mobility. Family members who prefer the client's old behavior may even sabotage the treatment. Of course, positive indirect effects of successful counseling are just as common. This client may experience new intimacy in his marriage, or a less strained relationship with his parent, that he never anticipated. Counselors who know from experience and the professional literature that a therapeutic intervention is likely to affect additional aspects of a client's functioning, need to tell the client so as a part of the informed consent process.

Fifth, counselors should disclose the *alternatives to counseling* that may be available for the client's problems (Bednar et al., 1991; Bray, Shepherd, & Hays, 1985). The range of potential alternatives is wide; some examples include joining Alcoholics Anonymous for substance abuse problems, family or group therapy instead of individual counseling, psychotropic drugs for mental and emotional disorders, and self-help groups and books for less severe life stresses. Underlying this recommendation is the belief that a choice to enter counseling can be freely made only if the client knows the other options. It is important to note here that if counselors' professional judgment leads them to believe that counseling is the most desirable of the available alternatives, they can share that view with the client if the communication is noncoercive and objective. In addition, counselors are free to recommend any of the alternatives to treatment as adjuncts to counseling.

Sixth, whenever counselors are planning to *use an experimental or untested counseling technique* or procedure, clients need to be told and consent for treatment must explicitly include an understanding of the nature of the proposed intervention (Witmer & Davis, 1996). How does one determine which interventions fall into this category? The most basic criterion is the absence of research and clinical evidence of the technique's effectiveness. New therapeutic approaches for which no objective evidence of efficacy yet exists would most likely be defined as experimental.

Finally, counselors should include in their informed consent procedures an indication of how the client can address *grievances* should any arise (Handelsman & Galvin, 1988). Some state licensing laws require similar disclosures about methods for filing ethics complaints. Counselors who work in agencies would be well advised to include grievance procedures internal to the agency as well as professional organization and licensing board procedures. The most practical way to communicate this information is in a form that the client may keep and refer to later.

An additional requirement for informed consent can be found in Section B.4.c of the ACA code, which states, "Counselors obtain permission from clients prior to electronically recording or observing sessions" and in Section 5.01c of the APA code. When counselors want to record sessions, they must disclose this intent to the client, explain the purposes of recording and the uses to which the recording will be put, and ask for the client's consent. A client who does not wish to be electronically recorded has the right to refuse. Similarly, a client should understand that he or she can withdraw consent to record at any time without penalty. If the counselor believes that electronic recording is essential for competent service, as may happen with an intern or novice, then the counselor must refer the client to a counselor who is competent to work without recording if the client so chooses. In some situations, training centers use a one-way mirror to observe trainees or have counseling rooms wired so that the conversation can be heard by supervisors in an adjoining room. Such methods are especially common in family counseling training centers. However, the codes make clear that this arrangement may not be used unless the client freely consents to it.

It is important to differentiate between *informed consent* and *notice* (Jacob & Hartshorne, 1991). Notice means informing people involved about impending events, but it does not assume a prior agreement to those events. Informed consent, therefore is quite distinct from the mere practice of telling people what will be happening to them in counseling or therapy. Notice alone is ethically insufficient.

Similarly, professionals who attempt to deal with informed consent through a "blanket consent" form are not complying with ethical or legal standards. In other words, counselors who use a single, general verbal or written consent procedure that is nonspecific and all-purpose are vulnerable to charges that they failed to develop proper consent (Jacob & Hartshorne, 1991).

Approaches to Informed Consent

Two primary methods are commonly used to obtain informed consent—a discussion of the issues with no written forms or a discussion accompanied by written documents. The codes of ethics do not specify any particular method, except to note that the completion of informed consent should also be documented in case notes (APA, *Ethical Principles,* Section 4.02). Research (Handelsman, Kemper, Kesson-Craig, McLain, & Johnsrud, 1986; Somberg, Stone, & Claiborn, 1993) suggests that most psychologists rely exclusively on oral discussion of informed consent. Verbal discussion has some advantages. It allows the professional to adapt the wording of the informed consent information to the unique needs of the individual and to humanize and personalize the process. In addition, a verbal format may provoke the client to ask more questions and become more involved in the discussion. However, verbal discussion has drawbacks. Most important, clients can be overwhelmed with all that information and may forget or not absorb much of what they hear. Research suggests that forgetfulness is a significant problem even when written materials are used (for example, see Cassileth, Zupkis, Sutton-Smith, & March, 1980). The risk of forgetfulness increases with the level of distress the client is experiencing. People think less well when under stress. The emotions that provoked a visit to a counselor may be so predominant that cognitive processing is compromised, but without a document to take home, clients have no way to review the information or to be sure that they really understood it. By the same token, the counselor who uses a verbal format must guess at how much the client understood and remembered or must quiz the client on his or her retention. Neither alternative is particularly appealing or professional. Also, specific information, such as options for addressing a grievance or procedures for contacting the therapist in an emergency, is most vulnerable to forgetfulness. Yet this kind of data may have the greatest practical usefulness to the client. A final disadvantage is that this practice is at odds with the recommendations of legal scholars and ethics experts, who urge professionals not to rely exclusively on conversation to conduct informed consent. For example, Bennett, Bryant, VanderBos, and Greenwood (1990) contend that written documents are rapidly becoming the "community standard," and they caution professionals that failing to use them may have adverse consequences for them in any legal challenge or ethics complaint.

The written materials used in informed consent take various forms, but they usually bear a title such as "Client Information Form" or "Patient Rights and Responsibilities Statement" and address the major components listed earlier. The strengths of these forms are that they become a permanent part of the record and are available for consultation at a later date by both parties. Some authors suggest giving clients a set of questions that they have a right to have their therapists answer (Handelsman & Galvin, 1988). Clients typically read and then sign these documents, and take copies home for future reference. These forms have other merits, too. When counselors need to discuss informed consent issues during counseling, they can use the document as a starting place. Client forms can also speed up a time-consuming process. Finally, they can hold the attention of the client to the topic and reduce the amount of material that is missed or forgotten. Even the most clear-thinking and motivated client may tune out some of a lengthy verbal description.

The problems with the written materials lie primarily in their vulnerability to misuse. The most obvious disadvantage of such forms is the tendency for counselors to rely too heavily on them. Counselors can (and often do) erroneously assume that a document in the hands of a client substitutes for a discussion of the topic. When this happens, informed consent becomes pro forma and the client's rights are not really protected (Pope & Vasquez, 1991). In some counseling settings, informed consent is (mis)handled by having a clerical staff member hand the document to a client and request a signature before an appointment. This approach violates both the spirit and the letter of the professional guidelines. The second major disadvantage is that the client may not have the necessary level of literacy. In fact, the research in mental health settings has found that the average informed consent form requires more than a 12th-grade reading ability (Handelsman et al., 1986; Handelsman & Martin, 1992). In fact, 63% of the forms used for informed consent in a study by Handelsman et al. (1995) were rated at the graduate school reading level, and the lowest rating was a seventh-grade reading level. Since the average reading level of a U.S. citizen is less than high school, (ninth grade), the average client cannot understand the vast majority of such forms. Particularly troublesome is that the reading levels of counseling consent forms are significantly higher than those used in medicine (for example, see Feldman, Vanarthos, & Fleisher, 1994). In other words, our medical colleagues have made complex medical information more accessible to patients than we have made less complex information accessible to our clients.

The final significant problem is that these forms can distance the client from the counselor in the crucial early moments of counseling, when trust needs to develop. This situation occurs when counselors misunderstand informed consent and treat the documents as bureaucratic procedures to be rushed through and handled identically with every client. They see the process as an empty ritual (Pope & Vasquez, 1991) rather than as a process of collaboration and open invitation for the client to actively participate in therapy. Such a misuse of forms can give clients the message that their individual needs are being ignored, that the paperwork of counseling is more important than their concerns, and that the counselor does not care whether they really understand what they are being asked to sign. Forms that are written in a style suggesting they are meant to protect the organization from lawsuits, rather than to inform the client also lend themselves to this negative interpretation. Pope and Vasquez remarks, "Nothing blocks a patient's access to help with such cruel efficiency as a bungled attempt at informed consent" (1991, p. 74).

A very small percentage of professionals (Somberg et al., 1993) rely on audiotapes or videotapes to inform clients about counseling. These tapes may be sent home with a client to view at leisure, or they may be viewed in a private area in the counseling office. These approaches seem underused and have good potential. They may help clients absorb a great deal of information in a efficient and familiar format. A rapidly growing percentage of households have tape players, so tapes are easy to use. Moreover, clients are becoming accustomed to videotapes and audiotapes as teaching tools as well as sources of entertainment. Many physicians use patient education tapes to help patients understand medical procedures, and home computer companies insert videotapes into packing boxes to help consumers install their equipment. Tapes can be replayed if the client wishes, and can be used regardless of the client's reading proficiency. They can even be made available in different languages, if necessary, and are a livelier and more human format than written materials. Tapes may be able to reduce the client's anxiety, because they can provide a preview of the counselor before sessions begin.

Undoubtedly, by this time some counselors have found ways to use e-mail and fax machines to develop informed consent and get immediate information to prospective clients. However, problems may arise with electronic formats, too. They are subject to the same misuse as written materials if counselors substitute them for real dialogue about treatment.

Any method of developing informed consent requires a counselor who can communicate a lot of information in an efficient and interesting way so that the process doesn't become tedious and overwhelming. Debunking the myth that informed consent is completed at the initial session lets the client comfortably accept all this information. Informed consent is a process, not an event. The process must be substantially accomplished at the first contact, but it is not really finished until counseling ends. For instance, as treatment options emerge during the course of counseling, professionals need to get the client's consent to each new treatment. When conducted skillfully and respectfully, informed consent is not an obstacle to trust and therapeutic progress, but rather a symbol of respect for the client's dignity and an invitation to actively collaborate with the counselor.

The Interplay of Ethical and Clinical Considerations

As with all other ethical dimensions of counseling, responsible development of informed consent requires good judgment. Counselor judgment about applying informed consent procedures is especially important when clients are in crisis or under very great stress. A client in crisis, for example, may be prepared to hear only about the nature and limits of confidentiality before getting to the crisis. A lengthy explanation of all aspects of informed consent could be counterproductive to a client whose mental health and well-being are at stake. (It is important to note, however, that the crisis may require postponing the full discussion, not eliminating it.)

In rare circumstances, no time is available for informed consent. Consider the following situation:

A 36-year-old man knocks on the counselor's door. When she opens it the man blurts out, "Please help me! I have a loaded shotgun in the trunk of my car outside and I think I'm going to kill myself." The man appears frightened, poorly groomed, sleep-deprived, and desperate for help. The car is only 30 feet away and the man still holds the keys in his hand. The counselor immediately invites the man inside and asks him to tell her more about his distress. Within 45 minutes the man has surrendered his car keys, agreed to be hospitalized, and wants to be saved from his own suicidal impulses. In another half-hour transportation to the hospital arrives and the man leaves in the ambulance. No informed consent procedure of any kind ever took place.

Was the counselor acting unethically by omitting discussion of informed consent? The answer is negative if the counselor's professional judgment told her that to delay attention to the man's suicidal impulse would heighten his already high risk for self-destruction. Her primary obligation is to protect his best interests and his life. If she believed she would be putting him at jeopardy by diverting his attention to any other matter, and if other competent professionals in a similar situation would make the same judgment, then her decision was fully justified and fully ethical. Legal scholars may suggest that the man gave *apparent consent* insofar as his behavior implied agreement to talk with the counselor (Bray et al., 1985). To abandon informed consent completely in less dire circumstances would be imprudent.

Judgment is also necessary in discussing the diagnosis, length of therapy, and potential benefits and risks. Learning that there is a psychiatric name for one's distress can be shocking sometimes, so the requirement to inform the client about this information needs to be balanced against the discomfort it may cause. For example, parents who learn that their child is being diagnosed with attention deficit disorder may be highly distressed by this information. Similarly, adults who are told that their mood swings fit the diagnosis of manic-depression may be overwhelmed by the diagnosis and its implications. Discomfort should be a signal to be tactful, compassionate, and cautious in disclosure. A client who appears overwhelmed by stress may benefit from a temporary delay in developing informed consent on this issue. Similarly, when providing information about the risks and benefits of counseling, mental health professionals need to take into account the client's need for hope of change and for optimism about the future, as well as available research evidence about therapeutic success rates. Clients often enter counseling feeling fearful and pessimistic, and a counselor who is overinsistent about explaining risks and negative outcomes can cause a client to give up hope that counseling can help before the process even begins. Because of their frame of mind, clients selectively attend more to negative possibilities. Counselors must gauge clients' interpretation of the material and help them see both sides of the equation. Counselors also need not paint rose-colored pictures of therapy. The goal is to provide accurate information to maximize client understanding without dimming the client interest in or commitment to counseling. An informed consent procedure, skillfully executed, typically fosters hope and reinforces the client's willingness to engage in counseling.

Another clinical consideration about informed consent is that some information required in developing informed consent simply cannot be determined accurately in the first session. A valid diagnosis may take several sessions to develop, and reliable estimates of the length and intensity of treatment can seldom be reached at intake. Similarly, the techniques and procedures that may address the presenting issues sometimes do not become clear for several sessions, and even then may change as counseling unfolds. As events emerge, the counselor has the responsibility to broach the topic. The ethics codes acknowledge this reality and encourage the mental health professional to use professional judgment in determining how intensively and how frequently to discuss informed consent.

A final clinical consideration that interacts with the ethics of informed consent is that some clients tend to be submissive, reluctant to ask questions, and unwilling to disagree with a counselor. Clients often view counselors as authorities and experts, to whom an ordinary person tends to defer. Moreover, clients often hope their therapists approve of them and fear the therapists will judge clients negatively. So it is not surprising that clients may not ask about aspects of informed consent that they do not understand and may censor their inclinations to refuse an intervention the counselor is recommending. Counselors must be alert to nonverbal signs of confusion or resistance and must establish trust and acceptance so that real agreement to counseling can be secured. Settling for anything less undermines the chance of clinical success and compromises truly informed consent.

Applications to Special Populations

As with the issue of confidentiality, informed consent becomes more complex in counseling certain populations. Children and teenagers, people with impaired cognitive capacity, and involuntary participants are the most obvious such populations.

Minors

By law, minors usually cannot give informed consent; their parents or guardians must give consent instead. Counselors should obtain consent of the custodial parent. (See Chapter 15 regarding exceptions for school counseling.) If custody is shared, consent of both parents is probably advisable. As discussed in Chapter 5, under some circumstances adolescents may be exempt from this law. Ethical requirements are somewhat more flexible because consent is based on the capacity of the client to understand the information presented and freely choose the course of action in response to that knowledge. The closer adolescents are to an age of maturity, the more likely they are to exhibit such comprehension and capacity to choose. Younger children are much less likely to have the cognitive maturity or ability to make a free choice. Given the interaction among these developmental factors, ethical guidelines, and legal requirements, most ethics scholars recommend that counselors obtain the *assent* of minors to counseling in all cases. As the adolescent matures, assent procedures should more closely approximate informed consent procedures. Assent to counseling means that counselors need to involve children in decisions about their own care and, to the greatest extent possible, obtain the child's agreement to engage in counseling (Koocher & Keith-Spiegel, 1990; Melton, 1981). The APA code specifies that psychologists should obtain assent from those incapable of giving consent (Section 4.02c), but the ACA and NASW codes do not speak to this matter. Thus, except for psychologists, acquiring assent is not mandatory, although scholars clearly argue that it is sound practice, with both clinical and ethical value. The ethical ideal embedded in this practice is the communication of respect for the inherent dignity of the person, regardless of age or circumstance. As a practical matter, clients who do not understand counseling, and whose commitment to the enterprise is unknown, are unlikely to be cooperative clients who can work toward therapeutic goals. Without assent, they have little ownership of the goals that have been established.

Research on counselor practices regarding consent with minors focuses primarily on adolescents and has found that a growing percentage of psychologists seek to secure an adolescent's agreement to participate in counseling (Beeman & Scott, 1991; Taylor, Adelman, & Kaser-Boyd, 1984). By 1991, 70% of child psychologists indicated that they regularly obtained the adolescent's agreement along with the parents' consent (Beeman & Scott, 1991).

If a child refuses to give assent, going forward with counseling anyway is not unethical, although its clinical value is highly questionable. In such a situation, a counselor would be well advised to work closely with the family to help them understand the importance of the child's willing involvement in counseling. In the meantime, the counselor should continue to attempt to build trust with the child so that assent can be gained as soon as possible. The ultimate criterion, of course, is the course of action most fitting with the best interests of the child. No therapist should keep a child in counseling if therapy is not helping that child.

People with Diminished Capacity

Generally, adults are assumed to be competent to consent until evidence exists to the contrary. At times counselors encounter clients who are clearly not competent. Examples include people with profound mental retardation, with advanced dementia, or with acute psychosis. Such clients are said to have "diminished capacity," meaning they can't currently comprehend events that affect them. Without comprehension, they cannot make an informed choice; others must make that choice for them. Usually a family member fills this role; or the court may appoint a guardian. Regardless of the specific person providing the substitute consent, the counselor must go through the consent procedure with the substitute as though he or she were the client. In addition, the counselor is responsible for giving the client as much involvement in the decision making as he or she can manage.

When a client's capacity to give consent is in question, a prudent practice is to give the client the benefit of the doubt and go forward to the greatest extent possible. In addition, counselors ought to consult with a colleague who is competent to objectively assess the client's capacity. The goal is to avoid treating clients paternalistically and to carefully evaluate the client's intellectual functioning. Taking away a client's freedom to choose is a serious step that should not be taken lightly.

In Court-Mandated Counseling

Over the last 50 years, mental health professionals have become more involved with the courts. Judges have learned of the value of counseling for citizens who come before them, and they frequently "mandate" counseling for people whose legal difficulties seem to stem from emotional, relationship, or substance abuse problems. Usually defendants are given a choice between a criminal penalty and counseling. Many defendants in juvenile and adult courts thus "choose" counseling. The histories and current predicaments of these people point to a strong need for intervention to help them cope with pain, learn alternative behaviors, and build healthier relationships. However, the circumstances under which they enter counseling raise questions about the degree to which their selection of counseling really represents a free choice. Consider the following questions:

- If jail is the only other alternative, is the selection of counseling really voluntary?
- If losing custody of children seems imminent, will a parent feel coerced into counseling?
- After an third or fourth arrest for driving under the influence, would anyone choose permanent loss of driving privileges over temporary loss of license and counseling? If not, is there really any choice?
- Can a client who opts for counseling over the alternatives in any of the preceding situations be considered a willing and motivated client ready to actively participate in the process?
- How does a counselor establish trust and measure therapeutic progress with a client who sees counseling as the "least worst" alternative?

These questions probe the contradiction between the usual definition of informed consent and its use in court settings. Ordinarily, informed consent is based on capacity (the ability to understand the information being presented), comprehension (the understanding of the specifics of the information), and voluntariness (a free, unforced choice). Voluntariness is at risk when the alternative is illusory, is an option no rational person would choose. This practice seems to fall within Warwick and Kelman's (1973) definition of manipulation: the "structuring of options in such a way that one is more likely to be selected than others while preserving the appearance of free choice" (p. 403). Thus, in this setting, the counselor has a dilemma: Should he or she accept the client regardless of the lack of voluntariness, or should the contradiction be pointed out immediately and the counseling delayed until the client is in a better position to decide his or her own fate?

There is no absolute rule for this situation. The ethics codes do not give much guidance, except for their general directive to promote the dignity and welfare of the client. Once again, the counselor's judgment comes into play. The task is to weigh the deficiency in consent against the possible good that counseling might do for a particular person. In essence, one engages in a kind of risk–benefit analysis, asking oneself, Would counseling without free consent be likely to do harm? Would the failure to provide counseling, even under these compromised circumstances, be likely to cause more harm than providing it? Do I have the skills, compassion, and attitude to help the client overcome the distrust inherent in mandated counseling? The answers to these questions should guide the decision. In any case, the counselor needs to proceed through an informed consent process with such clients, to disclose appropriate information about counseling, and to make sure the client understands it. The ultimate objective of the mental health professional is to find a way to facilitate the court's interest in counseling services for citizens who require them without violating the rights and dignity of those citizens.

Research Findings

Research on informed consent in psychotherapy is both encouraging and discouraging. On the one hand, researchers have found that informed consent can benefit clients and therapists. Clients who have experienced a responsible informed consent process seem to view self-disclosure more positively and have more optimistic expectations for counseling outcome (Goodyear, Coleman, & Brunson, 1986). Also, some evidence suggests that adult clients view therapists who carefully develop informed consent as more trustworthy and expert than those who do not (Sullivan, Martin, & Handelsman, 1993). Similarly, parents of children appreciate informed consent information (Jensen, McNamara, & Gustafson, 1991) and expect that mental health professionals will provide that information to them.

On the other hand, research also suggests that compliance with informed consent mandates, both ethical and legal, is inconsistent. Moreover, some of the informed consent procedures in use seem to meet only the letter and not the spirit of the guidelines. In one study of the practices and attitudes of psychologists toward informed consent, Somberg et al. (1993) found that virtually no one in their small national sample dealt with the whole topic. A majority omitted several required components with most clients. Only 59.5% indicated that they discuss the limits of confidentiality with every client, and less than a third of the sample discussed the risks of therapy, its length, or alternatives with every client. Moreover, 18% reported that they never discussed the risks of therapy with clients. The timing of informed consent discussions was also highly variable. Of those who discussed major components of informed consent, most tended to do so by the end of the first session. A disturbingly high percentage, however, indicated that they discussed informed consent matters only "as the issue arises" (Somberg et al., 1993, p. 156). That implies that these psychologists discuss duty-to-warn issues or mandated reporting of child abuse only when the client brings up the issue. Waiting until the client discloses something that cannot be held confidential is rather like closing the barn door after the horse has already escaped. Postponing informed consent in this way also violates the principle of fidelity. The point of the ethical mandates is that clients should understand the implications of such disclosures *before* they make them. Swenson (1997) describes the explanation of the limits of confidentiality as a "psychological *Miranda* warning" that clients must have in order to judge the consequences of their disclosures (p. 72). (A *Miranda* warning is the list of rights law enforcement personnel must disclose to a person accused of a crime before questioning.) Because in some circumstances courts can demand testimony from mental health professionals about clients, failing to develop properly informed consent can sometimes make clients incriminate themselves. Other researchers also have found the same variability and insufficiency in informed consent procedures and documents (for example, Claiborn, Berberoglu, Nerison, & Somberg, 1994; Sherry, Teschendorf, Anderson, & Guzman, 1991; Talbert & Pipes, 1988). For instance, Claiborn et al. (1994) found that only 6% of the clients surveyed indicated that their therapists had given them information on the limits of confidentiality. Research on informed consent procedures with adolescent clients reveals better compliance with ethical guidelines. For example, Beeman and Scott (1991) found that 93% of the psychologists in their sample secured the informed consent of parents for treating their teenagers. As mentioned earlier, 70% also obtain the adolescent's agreement to participate.

Surprisingly, almost no malpractice cases have arisen from claims of negligent informed consent (Bednar et al., 1991) despite evidence of inconsistent compliance with standards. Similarly, relatively few ethics complaints have dealt with this violation, although these claims have appeared more often than legal challenges. Whether this low level of complaints will continue in an increasingly consumer-oriented and litigious society is an open question.

In summary, despite client interest in informed consent information, and evidence that there may be both ethical and therapeutic value to communicating such information, the compliance of practitioners with this standard is incomplete at best, and nonexistent at worst.

CASES FOR DISCUSSION

The two cases that follow illustrate the ethical dilemmas embedded in informed consent.

The Case of Dr. Doolittle

Dr. Doolittle is a counselor who works with adults rehabilitating from spinal cord injuries. His clients have all their intellectual capacities intact but are often paralyzed or have other mobility problems. The informed consent materials he uses make no reference to the risks or alternatives to counseling. He contends that his clients have experienced enough trauma and do not need to worry about the negative effects counseling may have. Their lives are already completely disrupted by their injuries, he reasons, and they have little to lose and everything to gain by counseling. He also believes there are no good alternatives to counseling for people with spinal cord injuries because they need emotional support, vocational counseling, and guidance in practical living issues. Is Dr. Doolittle justified in omitting these topics?

The Case of Ms. Berens

Ms. Berens is a high school counselor. One of her clients is a 15-year-old sophomore who has been truant from school for the last nine weeks. Marianna has refused to attend school since she had a tonsillectomy. After her recovery from surgery, she told her mother she could not tolerate being in school. Now, she stays at home reading, watching television, and doing household chores. If Marianna does not return to school soon, legal action will be taken. Marianna is not a willing client in counseling. She has refused to assent to it, but her mother gave consent and insists that her daughter attend counseling anyway. Ms. Berens has outlined the aspects of informed consent with Marianna, and she believes the young woman understands the concepts. Marianna indicates that her problems are psychological and that she does not want to discuss her private life with a school counselor. How can Ms. Berens balance the girl's refusal to give assent against her mother's consent to counseling?

SUMMARY

Informed consent means that the client understands the counseling process and willingly agrees to it. Informed consent is required by the ethical codes and is based primarily in the ethical principle of respect for the client's human autonomy. Also, because counseling is a service that clients purchase and because that service has powerful effects on their lives, both during and after the process, clients have a right to understand its implications and to make a free choice about participating. The central ingredients in informed consent are understanding of the procedures, risks, benefits, and alternatives to counseling; the limits of confidentiality; the logistics of counseling; the counselor's qualifications; the use of counseling records and tests; and the indirect effects of counseling. In addition, clients have a right to know about any electronic recording, supervision of the counselor, or how to file grievances against their counselor. The need to discuss all aspects of informed consent as soon as feasible in the counseling process is superseded by considerations of the client's welfare. Particularly in a crisis, some aspects of informed consent may need to be deferred until the crisis is past.

In some situations, obtaining informed consent directly from the client is not always possible. Most notable among these are when the client is a minor or a person with diminished intellectual capacity. Scholars recommend securing the assent of a minor child to counseling, along with the informed consent of the parent or guardian. When a client does not seem to have the capacity to process information about informed consent in order to make a free choice about participating, then consent should be obtained from someone acting in the client's behalf. Usually that substitute is a family member or a person identified by the court.

Even though some practitioners believe informed consent is a bureaucratic procedure to be dispensed with as soon as possible at the onset of counseling, both research evidence and ethics scholarship show that proper informed consent does not hinder, but potentially enhances counseling. Moreover, developing informed consent is more appropriately thought of as a continuous process, not a finite procedure. This process symbolizes cooperation and collaboration between partners pursuing a common goal. The research highlights the need for greater attention to compliance with ethical guidelines by practitioners.

DISCUSSION QUESTIONS

1. What do you think accounts for the inconsistency in informed consent procedures used by practitioners?
2. Does a client have a right to be ignorant of risks of counseling if that person does not want to know? (Explain.)
3. What methods of structuring the review of informed consent information do you think are best? Why?
4. Can there ever be truly informed consent in court-mandated situations? If you think not, can a counselor ethically conduct such counseling? Explain.
5. In mental health settings, people with severe mental disorders, such as schizophrenia, have the legal right to refuse treatment, including medications. If their disorder is not in remission and it clouds their thinking, is their refusal really an informed refusal? How can their rights to control over their own body be balanced against their need for treatment?

RECOMMENDED READINGS

Bennett, B., Bryant, B., VanderBos, G., & Greenwood, A. (1990). *Professional liability and risk management*. Washington, DC: American Psychological Association.

Handelsman, M. M., & Galvin, M. D. (1988). Facilitating informed consent for outpatient psychotherapy: A suggested written format. *Professional Psychology: Research and Practice, 19,* 223–225.

Somberg, D. R., Stone, G. L., & Claiborn, C. D. (1993). Informed consent: Therapists' beliefs and practices. *Professional Psychology: Research and Practice, 24,* 153–159.

Sullivan, T., Martin, W. L., & Handelsman, M. M. (1993). Practical benefits of an informed-consent procedure: An empirical investigation. *Professional Psychology: Research and Practice, 24,* 160–163.

Weithorn, L. A. (1983). Involving children in decisions affecting their own welfare: Guidelines for professionals. In G. B. Melton, G. P. Koocher, & M. J. Saks (Eds.), *Children's competence to consent* (pp. 235–260). New York: Plenum.

7

Sexual Contact with Clients, Students, and Supervisees

Violations of Power and Trust

There are two unmistakable facts about sexual contact with clients. First, all mental health professions expressly prohibit such contact during a therapeutic relationship. The wording of the codes is unequivocal:

ACA *Code of Ethics* **(1995), Section A.7.a**

Counselors do not have any type of sexual intimacies with clients and do not counsel persons with whom they have had a sexual relationship.

APA *Ethics Principles* **(1992), Section 4.05**

Psychologists do not engage in sexual intimacies with current patients or clients.

NASW *Code of Ethics* **(1996), Section 1.09**

Social workers should under no circumstances engage in sexual activities or sexual contact with current clients, whether such contact is consensual or forced.

American Association for Marriage and Family Therapy (AAMFT)
Code of Ethics **(1991), Section 1.1.2**

Sexual activity with clients is prohibited.

American Psychiatric Association *Principles of Medical Ethics* **(1993), Section 2.1**

Sexual activity with a current or former client is unethical.

As the following pages amply demonstrate, the prohibition against sex with clients is grounded in empirical evidence of harm to clients, in philosophical argument, and in the theoretical foundations of counseling and psychotherapy. In short, the practice is inconsistent with every value of the professions.

The second fact that emerges from the evidence is that sexual misconduct by mental health professionals has not been eradicated despite the prohibition. Moreover, violators are not confined to those who are poorly trained, mentally unstable, and at the margins of the professions, but have included leaders in their fields (see, for example, documantation by Noel & Watterson, 1992; Pope, 1990a). Pope (1990a) cites examples of sexually exploitive therapists who have served as presidents of state professional associations, chairs of state licensing and ethics committees, and faculty in prestigious universities.

This chapter examines the rationale behind the absolute proscription against sexual activity, the scope of the problem, and the characteristics correlated with sexual misconduct. The stance of the ethics codes on sexual contact with former therapy clients is described, along with the debate about its wisdom. The next focus is the ethics of sexual contact between counselors and those they teach, supervise, employ, or consult with. The chapter presents strategies to help counselors deal responsibly with their own sexual feelings that emerge during counseling and discusses the place of nonerotic touch in counseling. Finally, it reviews guidelines for counselors working with clients who have been sexually exploited by former therapists.

Rationale for the Prohibition

The reasons for the prohibition against sex with a client derive from the client's vulnerability to exploitation during counseling and the implications of that exploitation for the client, the counselor, and the reputation of the profession. Even though it would be flattering to suggest that the professional associations have led the way in seeking to understand and eradicate this problem, the truth is that the professions' history on this issue is blemished. In the 1960s and 1970s some mental health professionals argued that sex with clients could be therapeutically valuable (for example, see McCartney, 1966; Shepard, 1972), and scholars who tried to publish evidence of sexual misconduct by mental health professionals had difficulty getting their research published in scholarly journals (Dahlberg, 1970; Gechtman, 1989). For many years, until the landmark case of *Roy v. Hartogs* (1975), the courts were not interested in malpractice cases claiming sexual misconduct, because the legal system accepted the claims that the accusations arose from the sexual fantasies of mentally unbalanced women (Pope, 1994). The initial response of the therapist and police to Barbara Noel's claim that her psychiatrist sexually exploited her was "You must be dreaming" (Noel & Watterson, 1992). However, the courage of many victims in pursuing claims despite the resistance, coupled with the perseverance of scholars researching this topic, has led the professions to endorse the explicit ban on sexual contact with clients by all mental health professionals.

Factors That Increase Client Vulnerability to Exploitation

Research suggests that consumers of mental health services are ignorant about the ethics of sexual contact between therapists and clients. Many do not know it is prohibited by the professions (Vinson, 1987). People typically enter counseling when their emotional distress is high, their interpersonal relationships are at risk, and their self-esteem is compromised. In this condition people are more vulnerable to harm from incompetent or irresponsible professionals than they would otherwise be. Clients whose world has suddenly been upended by a traumatic event are also at risk from inappropriate professional behavior. The trauma they have just experienced affects their judgment and emotional vulnerability. In addition, scholars suggest that a history of emotional and/or sexual abuse may increase vulnerability to sexual exploitation by a therapist and heighten the damage inflicted (Pope, 1994). In all cases, the defense mechanisms of clients are weakened by stress, so they may have difficulty refusing the overtures of an unscrupulous professional, especially if the professional labels such activity as "therapeutic"—a common ruse.

Further complicating this vulnerability is the social stigma often associated with seeking counseling. The dominant cultural myth is that "sane" people solve their own problems. People who seek counseling sometimes conclude that they are weak or crazy, and have diminished trust in their own judgments. When belief in the stereotypes about people who see "shrinks" interacts with the self-doubt inherent in emotional distress, the likelihood increases that clients will be overly deferential to a counselor's judgment about what is in their best interest. In this context, clients are more likely to ignore their own intuitions about appropriate and inappropriate behavior by counselors. Carolyn Bates captures her feelings thus: "I remember walking into Dr. X's office feeling absolutely humiliated that I needed psychological help and at the same time, feeling out of control emotionally" (Bates & Brodsky, 1989, p. 21).

The status of counselor as "expert helper" also encourages the client to accord the counselor's behaviors greater credibility than other people's. In other words, a client wants to give the counselor "the benefit of the doubt" about what may be therapeutic. When she researched his background at the library, Barbara Noel remembers being impressed by the list of accomplishments of the psychiatrist to whom she had been referred (Noel & Watterson, 1992). Her skepticism about the wisdom of his recommended therapeutic approach was outweighed by her confidence in the judgment of such a renowned professional. Thus, a client may take at face value a counselor's suggestions of an embrace at the end of a session or a candlelight dinner together after a session "to get a sense of your behavior in a social environment," and may not see these deceptions as the transparent overtures to start a social relationship that they actually are. Even clients who easily decode the real meaning of such suggestions in other settings may resist making that interpretation about their counselor. Sometimes clients lack the assertiveness to refuse a professional's request, even if they recognize its inappropriateness and want to decline. They may also worry about the effect of refusal on future treatment, wondering if the counselor will abandon or punish them if they fail to comply. Counselors intent on pursuing a sexual relationship have sometimes suggested that the client's resistance to sexual contact must stem from their emotional problems. Such a counselor then suggests that physical contact would be a sign of therapeutic progress. Carolyn Bates's therapist interpreted her denial of sexual interest in him as a sign of her problems relating to men in social settings (Bates & Brodsky, 1989). Clients agree to the social or physical contact because they trust the professional to have a therapeutic intention, or believe they have too much to lose if they fail to cooperate. Carolyn Bates describes the experience: "I could not doubt his interpretations of my resistance without doubting the doctor himself, and our entire therapeutic relationship. So I remained, unwilling to discount the trust I had spent 8 months building. I did not challenge him. I did not dare assert myself and state that I wasn't sexually attracted to him" (Bates & Brodsky, 1989, p. 32).

Sometimes clients *are* responsive to the idea of a sexual relationship with a counselor, but this responsiveness is rooted either in the problems that caused them to seek counseling, in misunderstandings of the counseling process, or in the mistaken belief that the feelings they have toward the counselor are indications of true romantic love. Occasionally clients' misinterpretation of the counseling relationship is so extreme that they attempt to encourage a counselor to be sexually interested. People who have been sexually exploited before by others in power may believe that sexual favors are the price they must pay for emotional closeness and help with their distress. For other clients, the responsiveness stems from a misperception of the counselor's professional concern and unfamiliarity with the normal roles and behaviors associated with the counseling relationship. From the start of counseling, mental health professionals show concern through attentive listening, expressions of empathy, and attitudes of respect and warmth toward a client. These counselor behaviors are grounded in a desire to promote the well-being of all clients and foster the development of trust. By interacting in this way, counselors establish rapport, get a clearer and fuller view into the client's world, and are better equipped to provide therapeutic assistance. Unless clients are informed about the nature of the counseling process, they can easily misinterpret these counselor behaviors as expressions of personal interest and be unaware that the counselor is in no way singling them out for special treatment. It is a small step from believing the counselor is treating one in a special way to speculating that the professional is interested in more than a professional relationship.

Two other factors sometimes lead clients to acquiesce to a sexual relationship at this point. First, in daily life most clients rarely experience such warm, attentive interest in their thoughts and feelings as they receive in counseling, and they are drawn toward people who provide such attention. Moreover, a client's past experience of such attention may have been limited to lovers or close friends. Frequently the counselor's behavior may represent exactly what the client has found desirable but often lacking in prior relationships. Thus the counselor may come to symbolize the kind of person the client is seeking for an intimate relationship. Second, the counselor's professional status adds further attractiveness to that fantasy because people are often flattered by the attention of a person they see as having high social status. None of these motivations is a solid foundation for a meaningful personal relationship, and it is the responsibility of the counselor to help the client understand the boundaries of the professional relationship. Consequently, if a counselor engages in sexual contact with a client who seems receptive to such contact, the counselor is still behaving irresponsibly. In terms of ethical principles, sexual contact is improper because it violates the autonomy of the client. The client's "choice" to enter into this sexual relationship is based at least in part on erroneous assumptions and dysfunctional experiences; hence, it is not a "informed" choice at all. For these reasons ethics committees, disciplinary boards and courts have dismissed claims that clients "consented" to sexual relationships with their counselors. These bodies have consistently judged that the consent of the client in this situation is neither informed or freely given. Whatever the client's behavior, the professional may never use that client's apparent willingness as an excuse to violate the codes. No client behavior, however provocative, justifies a counselor's misconduct.

Professionals who endorse the concept of transference see an even deeper problem with sexual intimacies with clients. They envision the therapeutic relationship as a transference relationship in which the client transfers onto the therapist feelings from prior significant relationships that have not been resolved. Often this means the therapist is seen, at least on an unconscious level, as a parent figure, not just as another adult. A sexual contact with a client in such a framework takes on an incestuous character (Gabbard, 1989). Bates saw her relationship with Dr. X from this perspective: "I have no doubt that much of the trust and love I had for my father was directed toward Dr. X, for I perceived him as having both wisdom and an unconditional concern for my well-being" (Bates & Brodsky, 1989, p. 24). Even if the nature of the transference is not parental, sexual contact with a client is still inappropriate, because any kind of transference means that the client is not really reacting to the counselor as a separate person but as a representation of someone significant from the past.

Still other dimensions of sexual contact make it inherently exploitive. For one thing, sexual contact is contradictory to the principle of beneficence, the responsibility of a professional to do good. Clients rarely understand that they are relinquishing the possibility of further progress in exchange for a sexual relationship. Many continue to seek out the counselor's advice and insight about their problems, in hopes that they can make therapeutic gains while sexually involved with the therapist. However, researchers point out that meaningful therapeutic progress stops when sexual contact begins (Kitchener, 1988). The counselor has lost objectivity about the client and now has a personal interest in the client's present and future. That interest inevitably affects the way the counselor functions. Objectivity is a crucial part of what clients need from their counselors (coupled with professional competence, of course). For example, a counselor who is sexually involved with a client may refrain from making a necessary confrontation because of worry about interfering with a romantic evening later. At a deeper level, the counselor may no longer be inclined to facilitate client exploration of issues that threaten the future of their relationship. In parallel fashion, once clients begin intimate contact with their counselor, they tend to censor their disclosures in counseling for fear of the counselor's reaction or the effect such comments may have on the personal relationship.

Sexual contact with clients not only stops therapeutic progress, but also inflicts significant psychological damage on the client (Bouhoutsos et al., 1983; Brown, 1988). Sexual contact thereby constitutes a flagrant violation of the ethical principle of non-maleficence, the duty of the counselor to avoid harming the client. Pope (1988) has postulated that the negative effects often form a pattern that he calls "the therapist–

patient sex syndrome." He and others (for example, Gabbard, 1989) liken the psychological devastation of the syndrome to rape or incest, and identify parallels to battered-spouse syndrome and posttraumatic stress disorder. The psychological damage may appear immediately, or it may remain latent for some time and then emerge, perhaps when the client is involved in a more appropriate intimate relationship. Specifically, Pope (1988, pp. 224–225) lists 10 features of this syndrome in clients:

- Ambivalent feelings toward the therapist including rage, disgust, and fear on one hand, and need for and worry about the therapist on the other
- Guilt for their own behavior, even though they bear absolutely no responsibility for the sexual contact
- A sense of emptiness and isolation and an incapacity for other future deep connections with other humans
- Sexual confusion about their own sexual identity subsequent to the contact
- Impaired ability to trust others, especially professionals, because of the betrayal they have experienced
- Identity, boundary, and role confusion between the self and other significant persons
- Emotional liability in which the changeability of emotions is overwhelming to clients
- Suppressed rage, which clients have difficulty acknowledging or dealing with because of the ambivalence toward the therapist and because of their own feelings of guilt
- Increased suicidal risk from feelings of guilt and hopelessness
- Cognitive dysfunction in the areas of concentration and attention because images from the trauma appear in the clients thoughts unpredictably

Pope is careful to caution that the syndrome is not experienced by all people in exactly the same way or to the same degree. Others point out that there is no convincing empirical evidence to support this group of symptoms as a distinct psychological disorder (Bisbing, Jorgenson, & Sutherland, 1995). It is clear, though, that the mental health problems that victims of sexual exploitation incur are neither mild nor transitory, and are widespread (Stake & Oliver, 1991). Through survey research and case studies, researchers have documented suicides, hospitalizations, and prolonged psychological and interpersonal difficulties traceable to the sexual contact with the therapist (Bates & Brodsky, 1989; Bouhoutsos et al., 1983; Feldman-Summers & Jones, 1984; Rutter, 1989; Sonne, Meyer, Borys, & Marshall, 1985). Another important negative effect is that clients feel reluctant to reenter therapy even though their presenting difficulty has not been resolved and the problems spawned by the therapist misconduct need attention. Carolyn Bates's eloquent words capture this pain: "Within 2 months [of ending therapy] the combined effects of the sexual abuse and the unresolved problems that had originally prompted me to enter psychotherapy made life seem unbearable. I was burdened with an unending depression, and my thoughts progressed from occasional ideas about suicide to a studied contemplation of it" (Bates & Brodsky, 1989, p. 40). Family and friends of those who have been sexually exploited also suffer negative effects (Schoener, Milgrom, & Gonsiorek, 1989) and become "secondary victims" of the abuse. Similarly, colleagues of a professional found guilty of such behavior are significantly disturbed by the event, according to Regehr and Glancy (1995).

Counselors who engage in sexual misconduct sometimes do not limit their misconduct to the sexual arena. As Simon (1991) points out, sexual contact seldom arises suddenly. Instead, it usually occurs in a context of numerous violations of responsible practice, such as omitting necessary treatments, including risky or counterproductive interventions, and diverting the sessions to focus on the therapist's problems. Besides their sexual contact with clients, the therapists cited by Bates and Brodsky (1989) and Noel and Watterson (1992), for example, also engaged in many other practices that were unethical and substandard.

Some offending counselors often continue to charge the client for the sessions, even if sex was the only activity. One psychologist who admitted sex with his client argued that his continuing charges to the client were for the therapeutic minutes, not for the sexual minutes during their sessions (Bates & Brodsky, 1989). Because there is absolutely no evidence that sex can be therapeutically useful, or that clients or therapists can make such artificial separations between sex minutes and therapy minutes, charging for that time may be considered fraudulent. This practice also puts clients in the untenable position of either ignoring the billing or asking their therapists about why they are having to pay for physical intimacy. If bills are submitted to third-party payors, they too are being deceived about the counselor's activities. Even if counselors separate the sexual contact from the therapeutic hour, continuing to charge for counseling may still qualify as fraudulent, because counselors are engaging in inherently harmful practices. The therapy time is just the deception that allows the sexual exploitation to continue.

Effects on the Counselor

The effects on the counselor judged guilty of the offense of sexual activity with a client are relatively minor compared to the harm caused to clients. First, in the last decade the professional taboo against sexual contact with clients has become quite strong, and fellow therapists are more likely than ever before to view this practice with serious concern. Most professionals recognize the harm this practice causes clients (see, for example, Pope et al., 1987; Stake & Oliver, 1991). They probably have counseled clients who have been victimized by former therapists (Stake & Oliver, 1991; Wincze, Richards, Parsons, & Bailey, 1996), and they have watched the cost of their liability premiums increase, due at least partly to substantial cash awards in sexual exploitation cases (Reaves & Ogloff, 1996; Smith, 1996). In addition, they may have read news reports about the problem (for example, see Zane, 1990). The professions have also taken an active role to educate counselors about the implications of sexual misconduct. In the mid-1990s, for example, ACA sponsored many continuing education workshops on this issue. Those who violate this standard in such a climate risk loss of referrals from colleagues and vulnerability, and complaints to ethics committees or licensing boards. Even colleagues who are reluctant to take active steps to report an irresponsible professional may stop referring clients to the offender and may end any collegial contact.

Statistics on the number of ethics complaints lodged annually suggest that many instances of sexual misconduct go undetected and that not all professional colleagues act with the level of professionalism just implied. Research suggests that only 5% of victims take formal action against the therapist (Bouhoutsos, 1984; Pope & Bouhoutsos, 1986). However, when a complaint does go forward, most adjudicating bodies tend to respond with careful consideration and treat proven violations with significant penalties. Because the professional standard is so unequivocal, counselors do not have the option of claiming that the specific situation did not fit the standard or of using extenuating circumstances to justify their behavior. If the counselor is found guilty, the probability of disciplinary action is substantial, as is the risk of a malpractice suit with damages amounting to the hundreds of thousands of dollars (Reaves & Ogloff, 1996). Counselors employed by agencies may lose their jobs. Licenses are often suspended, or conditions placed on future practice. The option to continue to practice without oversight is gone. Moreover, the professional liability insurers write policies to limit the amount they will cover for such claims, so that the burden of payment falls largely on the individual. Such an award is a financial disaster for most therapists. Even if they manage to stay in practice, they may find their liability insurance canceled and other insurers unwilling to offer coverage. In some states, criminal penalties have been added to the civil and professional liability so therapists may be charged with a crime (Strasburger, Jorgenson, & Randles, 1991). In Minnesota, Wisconsin, Colorado, North Dakota, California, and Maine, sexual misconduct is a felony (Bisbing et al., 1995). Similar laws exist in Florida, Georgia, Iowa, New Hampshire, South Dakota, New Mexico, Connecticut, Arizona, and Texas. Still other states are considering such legislation. Five states have determined that this is such an important public health issue that they have enacted reporting statutes that ask subsequent therapists to disclose clients reports of sexual exploitation by prior therapists. Minnesota has gone so far as to mandate reporting even when clients object, but the other states (Wisconsin, Rhode Island, California, and Texas) allow either for anonymous reporting or for reporting only when the client consents (Haspel, Jorgenson, Wincze, & Parsons, 1997; Strasburger, Jorgenson, & Randles, 1990). This kind of legislation is controversial and threatens client confidentiality, but its existence does highlight how seriously legislative and professional bodies have come to regard this problem.

Effects on the Reputation of the Profession in the Community

Data about the impact of sexual intimacies with clients on the reputation of the profession are more difficult to obtain. Publicity about such misconduct probably makes people less likely to seek out counseling, and the profession cannot easily gather data about people who never become clients. Nevertheless, it is reasonable to assume some impact exists, especially in a culture that already exhibits such deeply rooted skepticism about the wisdom of seeking professional help for mental health problems. In fact, the APA *Ethical Principles* (1992) acknowledges this effect in Section 4.07. Worry about this problem can even affect those who are brave enough to begin counseling. Clients who have learned of sexual exploitation through the media or through experiences of friends and family may have difficulty trusting their counselor, and may misunderstand legitimate inquiries into personal and sexual issues directly related to the presenting problem. Publicity about such unscrupulous behavior certainly does not simplify the task of convincing legislatures, government regulators, and insurers of the value of the professional services we provide.

Research on the Scope of the Problem

Who engages in sexual misconduct, and how frequently does it occur? This is the single most studied question in the area of ethical misconduct (Pope, 1994). Our knowledge about perpetrators comes largely from surveys of mental health professionals who have volunteered information about their sexual practices, along with data from ethics committees, licensing boards, and malpractice suits. A few studies have explored the reports of clients about sexual exploitation by former therapists (such as Brown, 1988), and some case studies have been published (Bates & Brodsky, 1989; Noel & Watterson, 1992). None of these sources of knowledge is an ideal gauge of the true scope of the problem. Disciplinary committees and the courts deal only with the accused; those not yet accused are not counted. Similarly, national surveys obtain data only from those willing to complete and return them to researchers—usually less than half of those to whom the form is mailed. Are those who have violated the codes as willing to complete the surveys as those who have not? There is no way to judge. Moreover, surveys rely on the willingness of respondents to tell the truth about their unethical practices. Researchers have no method for ascertaining the honesty of the responses they receive. Given the professional taboo against sex with clients, it is not unreasonable to wonder if all those who deny such misconduct are answering sincerely. Still other flaws in the research exist. Client reports of exploitation by former therapists tell us nothing about people who have been exploited but who have not sought counseling again. Case studies give us a sense of the depth of the injury to one client, but do not address the breadth of the problem. For these reasons, it is important to evaluate with some caution research about the scope of the problem. At the same time, the evidence can lead to some tentative conclusions:

- The overwhelming majority of offenders are male, and the overwhelming majority of victims are female (Pope, 1994). Male therapists have shown from 1.5 to 9 times the frequency of sexual misconduct of female therapists.
- Sexual contact is not limited to adult clients. Reported victims include girls as young as 3 and boys as young as 7. The mean age for female minors is 13, for male minors, 12 (Bajt & Pope, 1989).

- Sexual exploitation evidence has been accumulated in other parts of the world, not just North America (Bisbing et al., 1995).

- Therapists who violate this standard tend to be older than the clients they get involved with. The average age of psychiatrists was 43 and of clients, 33 (Gantrell, Herman, Olarte, Feldstein, & Localio, 1989). For psychologists, the mean age was 42 and their clients, 30 (Bouhoutsos et al., 1983).

- The percentage of mental health professionals who admitted sexual misconduct with clients in the 1970s and 1980s varied from study to study, but the aggregate average across all studies was 8.3% (Pope, 1988). Psychiatrists admitted this behavior more frequently than psychologists, and social workers had the lowest admitted rate (Pope, 1994). However, the admission rate does not necessarily correlate with the true incidence.

- Surveys conducted in the 1990s generally show smaller percentages, with studies of counselor misconduct showing rates ranging from 1.7% (Thoreson, Shaughnessy, Heppner, & Cook, 1993) to 0.7% (Thoreson, Shaughnessy, & Frazier, 1995) in all but one published study. Nerison (1992) reported rates from 3% for sexual contact with a current therapist. Recent social work data shows an average rate of 2% (Bernsen, Tabachnick, & Pope, 1994). One study of family therapists yielded zero admissions of sexual contact with clients (Nickell, Hecker, Ray, & Bercik, 1995). The change may represent a real decrease in incidence, a greater reluctance of professionals to admit such behavior even in anonymous surveys, an increased focus on mental health professionals other than psychiatrists or psychologists, or a combination of these factors.

- Therapist characteristics other than gender have not been reliable predictors of sexual dual relationships. Type of degree, experience, or theoretical orientation have not been consistently associated with this problem (Pope, 1994). Some evidence suggests that higher levels of education and higher levels of professional accomplishment are better predictors than more typical levels of professional achievement (Pope, 1990b), but neither of these variables is a strong predictor of sexual misconduct.

- Efforts to rehabilitate mental health professionals who have violated this standard have not shown much success (APA Insurance Trust, 1990; Pope, 1989). In fact, given the poor results of their research on this phenomenon, California licensing boards have concluded, "prospects for rehabilitation are minimal and it is doubtful that they [perpetrators] should be given the opportunity to ever practice psychotherapy again" (Callanan & O'Connor, 1988, p. 11, as cited in Pope, 1990b). Other authors are less pessimistic about rehabilitation, however (for example, see Schoener & Gonsiorek, 1988).

Data on Sexual Attraction of Therapists to Clients

Sexual attraction to clients is an almost universal phenomenon among therapists, but most do not act on that attraction and work to handle their reactions in a responsible manner. Research shows that 80 to 90% of the psychologists sampled admitted at least one experience of sexual attraction to a client, but only a small percentage acted on those feelings (Pope et al., 1987; Stake & Oliver, 1991). Data from social workers and family therapists reveal that sexual attraction to clients is a frequent occurrence in these professions also (Bernsen et al., 1994, Nickell et al., 1995).

Sexual Contact with Former Clients: A Controversial Issue

The incidence of therapist sex with former clients is very similar to the rate with current clients, although more recent studies do not necessarily report lower rates than earlier studies. In reports published between 1977 and 1996, the incidence has ranged from 3.9% to 11% (Akamatsu, 1988; Borys & Pope, 1989; Holroyd & Brodsky, 1977; Lamb et al., 1994; Salisbury & Kinnier, 1996; Thoreson et al., 1995; Thoreson et al., 1993). Akamatsu (1988) reported a mean interval of 15.6 months between the end of therapy and the beginning a sexual relationship. A majority of practitioners believe post-termination sexual relationships are unethical, but their disapproval of this practice is not as strong or unanimous as their condemnation of sex with current clients. Akamatsu found that 23% of his sample viewed this practice as "neither ethical or unethical" (1988, p. 455), and Lamb and his associates (1994) reported that the interval since termination affected psychologists' judgments of appropriateness. In other words, the longer the time elapsed since therapy, the fewer the number of respondents who condemned the practice. (When the time elapsed was a month or less, the practice was judged highly unethical.) In their survey of counselors, Salisbury and Kinnier (1996) indicated that a third of their sample viewed sexual contact with former clients as acceptable, at least under some circumstances, while Gibson and Pope (1993) found that 23% of counselors rated this behavior as ethical.

Some of this lack of consensus on the ethics of sexual contact with former clients stems partly from the history of silence of the ethics codes on this issue. The codes of APA, NASW, and ACA were mute on the subject until the 1990s. Only the code of the American Psychiatric Association explicitly prohibits sexual contact with former clients (1993). The current standards are as follows:

ACA *Code of Ethics,* **Section A.7.b**
Counselors do not engage in sexual intimacies with former clients within a minimum of two years after terminating a counseling relationship. Counselors who engage in such a relationship after two years following termination have the responsibility to thoroughly examine and document that all such relations did not have an exploitive nature, based on factors such as the duration of counseling, amount of time since counseling, termination circumstances, client's personal history and mental status, adverse impact on the client, and actions by the counselor suggesting a plan to initiate a sexual relationship after termination.

APA *Ethical Principles,* **Section 4.07**
(a) Psychologists do not engage in sexual intimacies with a former therapy patient or client for at least two years after cessation or termination of professional services.

(b) Because sexual intimacies with a former therapy patient or client are so frequently harmful to the patient or client, and because such intimacies undermine public confidence in the psychology profession, and thereby deter the public's use of needed services, psychologists do not engage in sexual intimacies with former therapy patients and clients even after a two-year interval except in the most unusual circumstances. The psychologist who engages in such activity after the two years following the cessation or termination of treatment bears the burden of demonstrating that there has been no exploitation, in light of all relevant factors, including (1) the amount of time that has passed since therapy terminated, (2) the nature and duration of therapy, (3) the circumstances of termination, (4) the patient's or client's personal history, (5) the patient's or client's current mental status, (6) the likelihood of adverse impact on the patient or client or others, (7) any statements or actions made by the therapist during the course of therapy suggesting or inviting the possibility of a posttermination sexual or romantic relationship with a patient or client.

The wording of these sections is meant to convey the message that sexual contact is usually unethical even after the two-year interval. They imply that only extraordinary circumstances allow such a practice to be acceptable. In their commentary on the APA code, Canter et al. (1994) refer to this standard as an "almost never rule" (p. 98). The codes attempt to place a heavy burden of proof on the mental health professional to demonstrate that the situation with a former client is sufficiently extraordinary to merit acceptance as the exception to the general rule. The professional bodies seem to want to allow for the circumstance in which the initial professional interaction between a client and a counselor was brief and uncomplicated by severe dysfunction, not deeply transferential, properly terminated, and entirely ethical while it endured.

The professions seem to be alluding to a scenario, for example, in which a client comes to a counselor to stop smoking, make a decision about a career change, or seek support during a normal grieving process. Strong emotional ties and deep transferences do not necessarily develop under such circumstances. The argument seems to be that if the professional relationship is truly terminated and the issues effectively resolved, then the rights of consenting adults to determine the people with whom they associate should take precedence over what they judge to be a low risk of harm to the former client. The professional associations seem to have wanted to protect the professional who completes a counseling relationship in good faith from being forever barred from a intimate relationship with all former clients. The codes also suggest that any professional who entertains the idea of a sexual relationship with a client at any point before termination does not meet the criterion for the exception The implication is that when professionals and former clients meet two years or more after therapy, their meeting must have been "accidental" and not plotted out by the therapist during their professional contact.

The two-year time period has also been recommended by Gonsiorek and Brown (1989) as the minimum interval before a sexual relationship with a former client. These authors have elaborated a set of rules for decision making about this matter that, when applied to the codes, make clearer the motive for the time limit in codes. Gonsiorek and Brown suggest that mental health professionals must differentiate between therapy in which transference is a central feature (Type A), and short-term therapy that gives limited opportunity for transference to become a major aspect of the interaction (Type B). These authors propose that sexual contact with Type A clients is never appropriate, regardless of the interval between the end of therapy and the subsequent contact. They also classify any therapy with severely disturbed clients as Type A, regardless of its duration. Posttermination contact with Type B clients is permitted only if the following conditions are met: (1) the initiation for the contact does not come from the therapist, (2) at least two years have elapsed since therapy, (3) no social contact has occurred in that two-year interval, and (4) therapy was completely terminated and no recommendation for follow-up treatment was given. They suggest that if there is any doubt about whether a therapy falls into Type B, then it ought to be considered as Type A and be prohibited. Herlihy and Corey (1992, 1997) also refer to the length and type of counseling as factors that influence the ethics of a posttermination relationship. They contend that contact should be allowable if the counseling has been brief and not deeply personal.

The work of Gottlieb (1993) is also helpful in clarifying the professions' reasoning on this issue. Gottlieb identifies three aspects of the therapist–client interaction that should be considered in evaluating the ethics of dual relationships. The first is the *power* of the therapist, and Gottlieb argues that in traditional psychotherapy relationships, the power of the therapist is high. The second dimension is *duration* of the relationship. Duration is really a subset of power. The longer the relationship endures, the greater the power the mental health professional has over the client. The third dimension is *clarity of termination,* referring to the likelihood that the client will ever contact the professional for additional services at a future point. He suggests that the professional must assume that the "professional relationship continues as long as the consumer assumes that it does, regardless of the amount of time elapsed or the contact in the interim" (p. 44). The higher the relationship is positioned on the continuum of power, duration, and clarity of termination, the more clearly prohibited the sexual contact.

As mentioned in Chapter 1, this provision was not originally proposed by the APA Ethics Committee when it was developing drafts of the revised code. (Earlier drafts had included a blanket prohibition against sexual contact with former clients.) Nor was it included in the first 15 drafts of the 1992 revision, many of which were published for member comment (Gabbard, 1994). In fact, it was added in the final debate by the APA governing body on the request of delegates who had not been part of the code-writing process. Many scholars believe this policy runs counter to the public interest and the profession's reputation. Gabbard (1994) summarizes these scholars' disagreement with the policy:

- The two-year designation is arbitrary and not based on any empirical evidence that transference is resolved in any particular time period. The suggestion that two years is sufficient is speculative, not scientific, and the profession should not place former clients at risk based on speculation alone.

- Professionals do not have good measures of a successful resolution of transference. Moreover, it seems imprudent to leave the judgment of whether a transference has been successfully resolved in the hands of a counselor who is now entertaining a sexual relationship with a former client (Hartlaub, Martin, & Rhine, 1986). That professional has little objectivity about the issue at that point. As Gottlieb (1993) points out, only the client can determine that the professional relationship has ended.

- The suggestion that one's professional responsibilities to a client are completed within two years after termination conflicts with other professional standards. For example, client records must be maintained for significantly longer than two years, and confidentiality must be maintained in perpetuity. If asked to testify in a legal proceeding, mental health professionals have no two-year limit on privilege. Thus, this standard conflicts with other guidelines that suggest that the professional relationship continues for substantially longer than two years.

- The unequal power relationship is never leveled off, and information obtained for therapeutic purposes can be misused in a later personal relationship. The counselor cannot simply "forget" all the information shared in counseling, and the client cannot ignore the unequal power levels that existed during their professional encounter. Moreover, if a former client later feels exploited by a therapist, he or she may be reluctant to file a complaint.

- Allowing posttermination relationships may change the nature of therapy. Patients who experience sexual feelings for a therapist may know that there is the possibility in the future that the therapist can have a sexual relationship with them. Clients with powerful attractions may resist delving into issues that must be explored for their recovery but that may interfere with acting on their attraction. In similar fashion, therapists may consciously or unconsciously shift the focus of therapy because of the potential, however distant, of after-therapy contact with the client. Therapists with the ability to delay gratification for two years can begin to view clients as future sexual partners.

- There is no evidence that sexual contact with clients after two years of therapy is free of risk to clients. In fact, some research suggests that posttermination relationships can cause harm (Brown, 1988; Pope & Vetter, 1991). Clients have filed claims of psychological damage for relationships that began as long as four years after termination (Gottlieb, Sell, & Schoenfeld, 1988).

- The codes should not include an exception to the rule for a highly atypical case. The criteria set forth for a sexual relationship with a former client disallow all but the most unusual situation from consideration for sexual contact. The professions' interest in protecting the autonomy rights of the professional in this rare instance seem to be overriding their commitment to protect the public from harm by an unscrupulous professional using this loophole to serve his or her own needs. Given the evidence of significant harm to clients exploited by therapists, the profession should not give the impression that this atypical case happens more commonly than it really does.

What is the other side of the argument? One statement that can be made in defense of the standard is that it addresses a gap in the former codes. Prior to 1992 practitioners, ethics committees, and licensing boards had no guidance from the professions about how to address complaints against therapists who engaged in posttermination sexual relationships. Sell, Gottlieb, and Schoenfeld (1986) found that these bodies held widely divergent opinions about whether such relationships were ethical and about the appropriate length of time between therapy and the personal relationship. (At the same time, they point out that not a single psychologist charged with sexual exploitation was exonerated on the grounds that the disciplinary body believed an appropriate interval had elapsed since termination.) Thus this part of the code is an improvement over past codes, and it provides some guidance about how to evaluate the claims of therapists who tried to defend themselves against ethics' charges by arguing that the sexual activity began after therapy ended.

Canter et al. (1994) contend that this provision is more practical than the broader prohibition and easier to defend from constitutional challenges. They seem to be referring here to legal claims that such a rule would violate a professional's right of free association. They also state that this standard is easier than a blanket prohibition to defend "socially," but unfortunately, they do not explain what they mean by this term.

Finally, some forms of therapeutic contact do involve minimal transference and are better characterized as a "consultation" than as counseling or psychotherapy. These consultations parallel what Gonsiorek and Brown (1989) refer to as Type B therapy. For example, a single parent may consult a mental health professional about her child's night terrors and receive the needed information and reassurance in a single session. The professional relationship between this parent and the counselor is of a different character from the interaction between a counselor and a client who has multiple visits to help him cope with a child's substance abuse problem. If the client in the first case has no intention of contacting the counselor again for professional assistance and her life proceeds smoothly for the next two years, and she then wishes to initiate a personal relationship with the counselor, this standard allows the professional to respond if the situation meets the other criteria laid out in the codes.

The debate on this issue will continue. Research and the experience of ethics committees in dealing with claims from former clients will help illuminate which perspective is wiser. Counselors who consider such a relationship with a former client should be extraordinarily cautious about acting on the idea. Careful consideration of all the aspects mentioned in the code, along with consultation with trusted colleagues, are essential to a truly ethical result in this situation.

It is important to note that individual state laws may differ from the ethics codes on this issue. For example, Florida views the therapist–client relationship as existing "in perpetuity" and thus allows clients to sue for damages regardless of time elapsed since termination (Lamb et al., 1994). A therapist in that state who uses the code to guide behavior may still be vulnerable to legal sanctions for sexual contact after termination. Thus, mental health professionals should understand the laws and regulations that may govern this issue in their states.

Consider the following case:

Manuel and Olga

Manuel, a 31-year-old librarian, sees Olga, a mental health counselor, for three sessions because he has been experiencing insomnia and loss of appetite. He is worried that he is depressed, because his family has a history of depression. Both his brother and his mother have been diagnosed with major depression. Manuel is experiencing no other depressive symptoms, and although he is stressed by his work and his financial obligations to his aging parents, he describes his mood as positive and his life satisfactory. In the sessions, the counselor assesses Manuel's suitability for a depressive diagnosis and the quality of his coping skills, deciding that no diagnosis of a mental or emotional disorder is warranted. Olga recommends that the client get a medical examination to rule out physiological causes for his symptoms. Then she focuses attention in the second counseling session on bolstering Manuel's coping skills. In the third session, the client reports that he believes his coping skills have improved and he is now able to deal with stress better. He also discloses that his physician changed his high blood pressure medication so that his sleep and appetite problems have eased considerably. After three sessions, counseling is terminated. The client expresses must relief that he does not have a depressive illness and seems very grateful for Olga's assistance. The file is put in the "closed cases" section.

For nearly three years, Manuel makes no effort to contact the counselor. At that point, they accidentally meet at an orchestra concert and have a wonderful conversation. Manuel has been promoted to director of his library, and he seems to be thriving. The next day he calls and asks Olga to dinner. The counselor is attracted to Manuel and would like to accept. Is it ethical for her to do so? Why or why not? (After you have analyzed the case and come to a decision, you may turn to the end of the chapter to read the author's analysis of the case.)

Sexual Contact in Educational, Consultation, and Employment Settings

The ACA and APA codes of ethics extend the prohibition of sexual intimacies with current clients to people in other kinds of professional relationships with counselors:

APA *Ethical Principles,* Section 1.19: Exploitive Relationships

(a) Psychologists do not exploit persons over whom they have supervisory, evaluative or other authority, such as students, supervisees, employees, research participants, and clients or patients.

(b) Psychologists do not engage in sexual relationships with students or supervisees in training over whom the psychologist has evaluative or direct authority, because such relationships are so likely to impair judgment or to be exploitive.

ACA *Code of Ethics,* **Section F.1.c**
Counselors do not engage in sexual relationships with students or supervisees and do not subject them to sexual harassment.

ACA *Code of Ethics,* **Section D.1.k**
Counselors do not engage in exploitive relationships with individuals over whom they have supervisory, evaluative, or instructional control or authority.

The rationale for this prohibition parallels the rationale for excluding sex with clients—the power of the professional, the extended nature of the professional contact, and the frequent lack of clarity in termination. Supervisors and faculty determine whether a student will be allowed to graduate and practice his or her chosen profession. Graduate training in counseling and psychotherapy often lasts for several years, and new graduates rely on faculty and supervisors for references for a number of additional years. Employers have similar influence and determine whether their employees can succeed at their jobs. Participants in research projects rely on the good faith of researchers to interact with them appropriately. A person in any of these subordinate roles has significantly less power and may feel vulnerable to the potential misuse of the power of the superior. He or she worries about the risks of refusing an overture and typically becomes uncomfortable in the professional relationship thereafter, even if the person in power imposes no penalty for the refusal. An anonymous article "Sexual Harassment" (1991) captures these strong feelings in the author's description of attempted sexual exploitation by a counseling faculty member. Even students and supervisees who agreed to a sexual relationship and believed they were making free and uncoerced choices about sexual contact with faculty and supervisors at the time, later come to label those relationships as coercive and a hindrance to their professional development (Glaser & Thorpe, 1986; Miller & Larrabee, 1995; Robinson & Reid, 1985). In other words, in retrospect they tend to view the relationship as one in which the faculty members took advantage of their higher status and power. Other students and supervisees who learn that one of their number is in a sexual relationship with a superior wonder whether they will receive fair consideration if they are competing with that person for professional rewards. When students and supervisees wish to end the sexual relationship before the superior, they may be anxious about the implications of terminating the affair. Conversely, if superiors end the sexual contact before the termination of the professional contact, students may feel uncomfortable for the duration of their interaction.

Incidence of Violation of This Standard

Researchers have gathered data on this topic from two sources—from surveys of professionals who admit engaging in this practice, and from surveys of mental health professionals who experienced sexual overtures from faculty or supervisors while they were in training. More psychologists have been canvassed on this issue than counselors, social workers, or psychiatrists, but some data are available about each profession. Most studies have found a higher rate of sexual contact with students than with clients. The prevalence rate for faculty–student sexual contact ranges from 0% for female counseling faculty describing their actions as professors (Thoreson et al., 1995) to 17% of female psychologists reporting on their own experiences during their student years (Glaser & Thorpe, 1986). The mean percentage for faculty–student sex across these studies is 8.8%. Fewer studies examined sexual contact between clinical supervisors and supervisees, but the range of finding is from 0.2% (Thoreson et al., 1995) to 4% (Pope, Levenson, & Schover, 1979) and the mean is 2.5%. Table 7.1 provides the specific findings for each study. Most of the contact has been reported to occur between male faculty in their forties and female students in their late twenties and early thirties. In addition, the majority of relationships began while the supervisory relationship was in place. For example, Hammel et al. (1996) reported that 86% of the contacts in their study happened either during or prior to the professional relationship.

This literature also identifies a related problem. In the studies that asked mental health professionals about their experiences of sexual exploitation in graduate school, respondents described an even larger number of incidents in which faculty and/or supervisors made unwanted sexual advances. Unwanted sexual advances constitute sexual harassment. For example, Miller and Larrabee (1995) found that 18.7% of their sample of counselors experienced unwanted sexual advances. Robinson and Reid (1985) and Glaser and Thorpe (1986) indicated even higher percentages for female psychology students; 48% and 33%, respectively. The percentages of female students reporting sexual

Table 7.1   Rates of Sexual Contact Among Faculty, Supervisors, and Students in the Published Literature

Researchers	Research Population	Rate for Faculty	Rate for Supervisors
Pope et al., 1979	Psychology educators	12%	4%
Robinson & Reid, 1985	Psychologists' remembrances of training	13.6%	NR
Glaser & Thorpe, 1986	Female psychologists' remembrances of training	17%	NR
Pope et al., 1987	Psychologists	NR	3.3%
Thoreson et al., 1993	Male counselors	1.7%	2.5%
Miller & Larrabee, 1995	Female counselor educators' remembrances of training	6%	2.5%
Thoreson et al., 1995	Female counselors	0%	0.2%
Hammel, Olkin, & Taube, 1996	Psychologists' remembrances of training	11%	

Note: NR = not reported.

harassment by faculty or supervisors fell slightly to 17.8% in a more recent study (Mintz, Rideout, & Bartells, 1994). In short, these studies suggest that sexual harassment is a continuing problem for substantial numbers of female students. The codes of ethics also clearly forbid sexual harassment:

> **APA** *Ethical Principles,* **Section 1.11: Sexual Harassment**
>
> (a) Psychologists do not engage in sexual harassment. Sexual harassment is sexual solicitation, physical advances, or verbal or nonverbal conduct that is sexual in nature, that occurs in connection with the psychologist's activities or roles as a psychologist, and that either (1) is unwelcome, is offensive, or creates a hostile work environment, and the psychologist knows or is told this; or (2) is sufficiently severe or intense to be abusive to a reasonable person in the context. Sexual harassment can consist of a single intense or severe act or of multiple persistent or pervasive acts.

The ACA code (Section C.5.b) uses very similar wording, save for the term *psychologist.* Its description of the behaviors that constitute sexual harassment come from the legal definition of the term.

Consider the following case:

Isabelle and Yoritomo

Isabelle, a graduate student in school counseling, enrolls in a course in substance abuse counseling as an elective. The course is taught by Yoritomo, adjunct faculty member with an active private practice in the community. About 10 weeks into the semester, Isabelle approaches Yoritomo after class, seeking additional readings on substance abuse educational programs for teenagers. They discuss the topic at length, and they meet a few times after that in Yoritomo's office to talk over the readings. When Isabelle is turning in her final examination, Yoritomo asks her to come to his office in a few minutes. At that time he suggests that they continue to meet to discuss this issue and get to know each other better. In an offhand way he suggests that perhaps they could have dinner together sometime. Isabelle hears in his comments an invitation to a dating relationship. If her assessment of the professor's interest is correct, did Yoritomo act unethically? (After you have analyzed the issue independently, turn to the case analysis at the end of the chapter.)

Distinguishing Between Sexual Feelings and Sexual Misconduct

As mentioned previously, research suggests that nearly all mental health professionals experience times when they have felt sexually attracted to a client and that they tend to feel guilty, confused, and anxious when this happens (Pope, Keith-Spiegel, & Tabachnick, 1986; Rodolfa et al., 1994; Stake & Oliver, 1991). Unfortunately, the literature also indicates that training programs give insufficient attention to this issue (Pope & Tabachnick, 1993). Pope, Sonne, and Holroyd (1993) refer to it as "the topic that isn't there" (p. 23). Given the gravity of the problem of sexual misconduct by counselors and therapists, how should sexual attraction to clients or others under our professional authority be viewed? Is attraction an ethical violation in itself? Occasional counselor experiences of sexual arousal toward a client are normal and need not produce guilt or worry. They do not constitute misconduct. After all, counselors cannot leave their sexuality outside the consulting room door. Such feelings can be stirred by events in the counselor's personal life or by comments that the client makes. If counselors handle these feelings responsibly, they can work effectively in the future with that client. An experience of sexual arousal must be distinguished from sexualizing of the therapy relationship. A momentary feeling that is not acted on nor disclosed to the client, and that does not prevent the counselor from attending to the issues the client wishes to discuss, is not ethically problematic (Pope et al., 1993). Naturally, the counselor has a duty to self-monitor effectiveness and carefully scrutinize the quality of his or her counseling in that session. If the arousal significantly compromised the competence of service, then the counselor should consider referring the client to another practitioner or, at a minimum, provide additional time to the client without charge, to compensate for the inadequate service.

Sexual feelings that occur more frequently or that are more prolonged must be dealt with more carefully. To help resolve the sexual attraction, a counselor in this situation should consult a colleague or supervisor about what is occurring. In the Rodolfa et al. (1994) study, 60% of the sample took this action when attracted to a client. These psychologists reported that they used consultation to ensure that they were objective, that they were attending to the welfare of the client, and that they understood the motivation behind their attraction. If such consultation fails to keep the counselor's attention on the client's needs, a referral to another counselor is in order. Whenever sexual arousal is frequent or persistent, a counselor is well advised to seek therapy to understand the source of this feeling. In the meantime, the counselor should accept only those clients with whom sexual arousal is unlikely to occur. Again, Rodolfa's findings highlight the importance of this recommendation: Of the psychologists sampled, 43% believed that their sexual attraction to a client had negatively affected therapy.

Epstein and Simon (1990) have published an exploitation index that can help mental health professionals identify early signals that they may be at risk for engaging in exploitive activities with clients. One section of this index asks the following questions:

- Do you find yourself comparing the gratifying qualities you observe in a patient with less gratifying qualities in your spouse or significant other?
- Do you feel that your patient's problem would be immeasurably helped if only he or she had a positive romantic involvement with you?
- Do you feel a sense of excitement or longing when you think of a patient or anticipate his or her visit?
- Do you take pleasure in romantic daydreams about a patient?
- When a patient has behaved seductively with you, do you experience this as a gratifying sign of your own sex appeal?
- Do you touch your patients? (Exclude handshakes.)
- Have you engaged in a personal relationship with a patient after treatment? (p. 459)

If sexual attraction prompts a counselor to seek consultation or therapy, or to refer a client to another counselor, that professional may wonder whether the attraction ought to be disclosed to the client. After all, the client may notice that something is wrong or may wonder about what motivated the recommendation to refer. The counselor in this situation must weigh the client's interest in disclosure against the potential for that information to cause harm or impede therapeutic progress. The nature of the transference, the client's distress, and the power of the professional make such a disclosure risky and potentially quite harmful. This revelation would probably draw attention away from the client's concerns and toward the counselor's problem. Pope et al. (1993) have published a very useful book to help counselors and therapists understand their sexual feelings and manage them appropriately in professional settings.

What should counselors who have experienced sexual feelings for a client do when that client discloses a sexual attraction to them? Generally, the literature cautions against revealing the feeling even if there is no intention to act on it (Pope et al., 1993) unless the revelation has a clear treatment rationale and would not risk harm to the client, but there are diverse opinions on this topic (for example, see Gorkin, 1987; Weiner, 1983). Almost 80% of psychologists view such a disclosure as unethical in itself (Pope et al., 1987). Some research supports this position. Using an analogue study with taped, scripted counseling simulations, Goodyear and Shumate (1996) found that mental health professionals judged counselors who disclosed their sexual attraction to a client as less therapeutic and less expert than those who held their reactions to themselves. This negative evaluation occurred even though the counselor in the simulation made it clear that he or she would not act on the felt attraction. Goodyear and Shumate seem to capture the sentiment of most professionals when they state that client expressions of attraction ought to be handled as manifestations of the client's distress rather than true romantic interest (p. 614). Of course, refraining from such disclosures does not mean that client's expression of attraction should be ignored; rather, it should be addressed as a representation of the problem that provoked them to enter counseling. Clients should also be told that such feelings happen to many clients in the course of an intense therapeutic relationship.

The Place of Nonerotic Touch in This Context

The issue of whether counselors should ever touch adult clients in counseling and therapy, even if the touch is meant to be nonerotic, has always been controversial. Nonerotic touch includes such things as a handshake, touch on the hand, arm, shoulder, a hug, or other brief physical contact. In most cultures a kiss does not seem to fit in this category (Stake & Oliver, 1991). On one side of the issue are those who view touch as a forbidden behavior that interferes with therapeutic progress, confuses clients, and risks the generation of overtly sexual feelings in both parties (Menninger, 1958; Wolberg, 1967). Wolberg called physical contact "an absolute taboo" (1967, p. 606). This strong rejection of touch has been based on the concepts of transference and clear boundaries between the roles of client and therapist. Touching a client, some argue, can blur the boundaries and encourage the participants to view the relationship more as a personal than a professional contact (for example, Guntheil & Gabbard, 1993). Other nonpsychoanalytic therapists have taken the opposite view, believing that touch is valuable in engaging clients in the therapeutic process and promoting therapeutic change (for example, see Levy, 1973; Satir, 1972). These professionals point to the evidence that human touch is essential to development in children (for example, see Bowlby, 1951; Harlow, 1971) and to the common belief that a judicious use of touch may reassure or console a client in a way that verbal communication cannot. In fact, most therapists do have nonerotic physical contact with clients at least on occasion, and few evaluate that practice as unethical or untherapeutic (Pope et al., 1987; Stake & Oliver, 1991). Unfortunately, the empirical evidence does little to clarify, because some studies suffer from methodological problems and others offer contradictory results. One consistent result is that the highest frequency of physical contact occurs between male professionals and female clients with the male professionals initiating the contact (Holub & Lee, 1990). This finding, coupled with the evidence of higher levels of sexual contact by male therapists, has led some writers to be concerned about a "slippery slope" phenomenon, in which nonerotic touch can be a first step toward sexual contact (Guntheil & Gabbard, 1993; Holroyd & Brodsky, 1980). Generally, however, therapists who use touch are not more vulnerable to sexual misconduct than those who do not use touch (Pope, 1990b). Whenever counselors feel sexually attracted toward their clients, they should at that time avoid even nonerotic touch (Kertay & Reviere, 1993).

What are the criteria for nonerotic contact with an adult client? (The codes of ethics do not speak directly to this issue except insofar as they prohibit exploitive actions and behaviors that do not serve the best interests of the client.) A definitive answer to this question awaits rigorous research on the subject, but several reasonable recommendations can be made. First, a counselor must be clear about his or her motivation to touch a client. Professionals who explain their approach to touch in counseling as a result of their personality, with comments such as "I'm just a touchy-feely sort of person" or "In my family everybody was always touching each other to show support and connection" have not sufficiently examined their motivation or the need to modify personal habits to fill client needs and achieve therapeutic goals. In making such comments, counselors are implying that their own need to touch is more important than their clients' needs. Bacorn and Dixon (1984) hypothesized that counselors may sometimes touch clients to relieve their own anxiety in the face of the emotions clients express. Psychoanalytic therapists wonder if the urge to touch is based in unresolved personal issues or a need to be seen as an expert or loved person by the client. When counselors are feeling strong countertransference, they ought to be especially cautious about touch, as those feelings may signal a risk of attending more to the counselors' personal needs than to the client's welfare. Strong countertransference feelings can blur professional boundaries even when touch does not occur. Touching may accelerate that process. Other authors, such as Corey et al. (1993), suggest that counselors should avoid touch if the behavior is not congruent with their feelings. A disingenuous touch risks harming the trusting relationship, in their view. Of course, genuineness of feeling is not the only criterion that should be used. After all, counselors can be sincerely wrong or misguided in their feelings.

Counselors who find they have a pattern of differentially touching male and female clients must also examine their motivation for touching. A differential pattern based on gender alone has been called sexist (Holroyd & Brodsky, 1980) and may signal that the counselor is not as attuned as required to the client's needs. Alyn (1988) argued that even if touch is not interpreted in sexual terms by females touched by male therapists, its use by these men can contribute to feelings of disempowerment in female clients.

The decision about whether to touch a client must also be grounded in an understanding of cultural and social issues. Touching has highly variable meanings in different cultures, and it is easy for an uninformed counselor to violate cultural norms. For example, Orthodox Jews would see any touch by a person of the opposite gender as highly inappropriate. Among other cultural groups, kissing on both cheeks is as universal and nonerotic a greeting as a handshake. Any decision to touch a client must therefore take into account the client's cultural definitions of touch. Social psychology also teaches us that the privilege of touching is based on socioeconomic status. A higher-status person has greater freedom to touch than does a person of lower status. Thus, a counselor has more liberty to touch a client than a client has to touch a counselor. Similarly, a professor has greater privilege than a student. Consequently, touching without regard for its roots in the counselor's power can be an abuse of that power.

Geib (1982) hypothesizes about the factors associated with a positive interpretation of touching. Geib identifies five factors:

- Clarity regarding touch, sexual feelings, and boundaries of therapy
- Client control in initiating and sustaining contact
- Congruence between the closeness in the relationship and the use of touch
- Client belief that the touch is for his or her benefit rather than the therapist's
- A match between the client's expectations for therapy and his or her experience of the therapist

In their research, Horton et al. (1995) also found that the strength of the therapeutic alliance is related to a positive interpretation of touch in therapy.

Client characteristics and experiences ought to weigh heavily in the decision about whether touch is therapeutically appropriate. Willison and Masson (1986) recommend avoiding touch if it creates discomfort in the client. Research shows that many clients have had prior experiences of sexual abuse and harassment, and these people may have difficulty with a therapist's use of touch. They may misinterpret it or be distracted from their therapeutic issues by it (Vasquez, 1988). Other clients dislike touch, either because of family history, individual experience, or the psychological issues that prompted them to enter counseling. For example, a client who has an obsessive-compulsive fear of germs may be overwhelmed by a counselor's touch. Physical contact early in counseling may even cause such a client to drop out rather than risk another touch. Kertay and Reviere (1993) recommend discussing with a client the role of nonerotic touch in counseling. As a general guideline, they suggest asking permission before physical contact occurs. This recommendation seems especially prudent before the first time a counselor believes that physical contact may be therapeutic.

In short, all these factors should lead a mental health professional to be cautious about the use of touch. Some writers suggest completely abstaining from touch except for handshakes, but most recommend a judicious use of touch. Under the right circumstances, touch can be reassuring and therapeutically useful. In their study, Horton et al. (1995) found that clients were very positive about nonerotic touch and many viewed the physical contact as especially important in resolving their problems. One study does not lead to any definitive conclusions, of course, but wisely and prudently used, touch may be therapeutic. At the same time, it is wise for counselors to learn a whole repertoire of behaviors for demonstrating emotional connections with clients so that they can adapt their response to the needs of the individual client. If counselors decide to touch clients, the burden is on them to demonstrate that the touch served the needs of the client, not their own.

Providing Effective Subsequent Therapy for Victims

Approximately half of those practicing counseling and psychotherapy will occasionally see clients whose former therapists sexually exploited them (Pope & Vetter, 1991; Stake & Oliver, 1991, Wincze et al., 1996). Effective treatment for such clients is difficult and requires expert and diligent treatment (Sonne, 1987). Therapists who seek to provide competent service to these clients should familiarize themselves with the growing body of literature on the topic, get qualified supervision, and be prepared to have an emotional reaction to the information the client is disclosing. Sonne and Pope (1991) caution therapists that when they first hear of this exploitation they may experience disbelief, denial, or minimization of the harm done. They may even be tempted to blame the victim or may experience sexual reactions to the material being revealed. It is difficult to hear that one's colleagues in a helping profession have behaved in such destructive, self-serving ways. These reactions are problematic if acted on because they can put the client at risk for a revictimization. The kind of open, compassionate, empathic response a mental health professional would give in any other highly personal disclosure is essential here too. If a counselor doubts that he or she is competent to provide this service, then a referral is appropriate. The article published by the APA Committee on Women in Psychology (1989) and entitled "If Sex Enters into the Psychotherapy Relationship" is an important document to share with clients who reveal such a history. It is written for consumers to help them understand why the profession regards sexual contact as unethical and provides them with options to address their reactions, including ways to file a claim against the offender. If clients wish to pursue an ethics complaint against a former counselor, the current counselor is obliged to provide information about the process and to give the client the option to discuss, in subsequent sessions, feelings and reactions to pursuing a complaint. This document also has obvious use as part of an informed consent process for all clients. Both consumers and therapists support its value in that application (Thorn, Shealy, & Briggs, 1993).

CASES REEXAMINED

The Case of Olga and Manuel

The first step in answering this question is to evaluate the facts of the situation as written. Manuel was not diagnosed with a mental or emotional disorder at the time of counseling, and the majority of his problems were attributable to medical rather than psychological issues. Three sessions were held in which the counselor first ruled out the existence of a depressive disorder, and then focused attention on bolstering the client's coping skills for work stress and responsibilities for aging parents. By the third session the client reported improvement in coping skills, happiness that his other problems were relieved by changes in his medical treatment, and gratitude to the counselor for her assistance. Counseling terminated, the counselor reported the case as closed, and no contact occurred for three years. The initial meeting after those three years was accidental, at a community event, and the client, not the counselor asked for the date. The client reports good functioning in the intervening period. The case description presents no information about the nature of the emotional ties or transference that occurred during the three sessions, nor does it indicate whether either party felt sexually attracted to the other while counseling was taking place.

When the standards in the ACA code are applied, the following conclusions seem valid:

- More than two years have elapsed since termination.
- Counseling was of short duration.
- Termination seemed to be desirable to both parties and appropriate insofar as the client did not again seek counseling from Olga or anyone else.
- The client did not suffer from significant psychological problems at the time of counseling and did not admit any current psychological issues in his accidental meeting with the counselor, although when he made the counseling appointment he was worried that he suffered from a serious mental illness.
- There is no evidence that the counselor initiated this personal contact with her former client.

Thus far, the contact seems to fit within the boundaries allowed by the rule. However, some important questions remain unanswered:

- What is the risk of an adverse impact of a dating relationship on the client?
- What was the nature of the emotional connection or transference between Manuel and Olga at the time of counseling?

- Did either party fantasize about a personal or sexual relationship while counseling was ongoing? If so, to what degree might this experience have affected the material disclosed by the client or the diagnosis assigned by the counselor?
- Does Olga practice in a state that has regulations that ban posttermination relationships under all circumstances?

In the absence of answers to these questions, one cannot conclude that this contact would be permissible. Moreover, even if these questions were resolved in the most positive way possible, a prudent counselor would agree to a social relationship only after clear and frank discussions of the possible problems that may arise in a posttermination relationship. The first such conversation should take place with a supervisor or trusted colleague who can more objectively evaluate Olga's motivation. If colleagues fail to agree that this contact fits the criteria, Olga would be wise to refuse the invitation, at least for some time. The counselor should also "consult" with experts in the field who have differing views about the advisability of posttermination contact, by reading their writings and judging the merit of their arguments in her case. If colleagues conclude that the situation meets the criteria set forth in the code and Olga believes she has satisfactory responses to criticisms of this kind of contact, she should give herself a little more time to be clear about her decision. After all, there is no time limit to decision making in this case. (Given the possibility of a messy ending to a personal relationship in this circumstance, Olga may want to consult her attorney as well.)

If at that point she still wishes to go forward, her second discussion should be with Manuel, before accepting or rejecting the invitation. At the end of that discussion, both the client and the counselor should understand that any future professional relationship between them would be completely ruled out. Even with this understanding, both should realize that their history will likely impose other complications on their personal relationship with which they will need to cope. Moreover, as the relationship continues, Olga should meet regularly with a colleague to discuss any issues that develop relative to her professional history with Manuel. Manuel may be well served by a referral to another mental health professional for the same kind of discussion if he wishes it.

This case highlights both the burden that is placed on a mental health professional when trying to decide what is ethical, and the crucial importance of continuing to place the welfare of the client over one's personal needs or desires.

The Case of Isabelle and Yoritomo

A review of the facts of the situation reveals that

- An adjunct faculty member has asked a counseling student enrolled in his course to have dinner with him sometime.
- The invitation comes as the student is submitting her final examination and subsequent to several professional conversations related to the content of the course.

■   The student's interest in pursuing a dating relationship with the instructor is unknown, as is her emotional reaction to his suggestion, but her interest in the subject matter he teaches is substantial.

The ACA ethics code prohibits sexual relationships with students, sexual harassment of students, and exploitive relationships with students. If Yoritomo was asking Isabelle for a date before completing his instructional control, then he was probably violating this standard. He had not yet graded that final exam, nor had he determined the course grade. Did he ask at this time because he knew (at least unconsciously) that he had more power and that Isabelle might be more agreeable to a dinner together while he was still her instructor? If so, that means he attempted to exploit his professional position to get what he wanted from this student. Even if he intended to keep the grading completely separate from her answer to his question, his objectivity in evaluating this student's work is also likely to be compromised. Is that fair to her or to the other students in the course?

From Isabelle's perspective, she may feel trapped, worrying about the implications of a refusal on her grade in the course. She also may have wished to continue her professional contacts with Yoritomo as she developed substance abuse programs in her school. She may wonder if the date is the "quid pro quo" for that continuing professional advice. If so, this behavior fits the definition of exploitation and sexual harassment. Similarly, she may have been considering asking him for a recommendation for doctoral programs if she did well on her final, an option that would be eliminated if she agreed to a date. She may also feel uncomfortable discussing a romantic relationship with a faculty member with friends who are also students in the program. In short, Isabelle is not in a position to make a free consent or refusal to his request.

Even if Yoritomo's intentions were entirely honorable, his request was unethical because he insensitively placed the student in an embarrassing and stressful position in which the lines between a professional and personal relationship were blurred. If he wanted to communicate to Isabelle a willingness to continue his assistance to her in her work at school, he had other options. He might have called her or sent her a note after course grades were submitted.

If Yoritomo had waited one month after the termination of the course to invite Isabelle to dinner, the ethics codes give less clear guidelines. They do not speak to the issue of posttermination sex with students. The judgment in this case is based on the likelihood that his evaluative role will continue in some way, so that Isabelle's freedom to consent or refuse is jeopardized. Full-time faculty are likely to continue in some sort of evaluative role, whether to teach other courses to the same students, to be involved in placement or scholarship decisions, or to decide whether students are admitted to advanced graduate study. Yoritomo's status as an adjunct faculty member makes it possible that he could have no further evaluative role with students after they finish his course. That may remove one aspect of the ethics problem. However, if Yoritomo uses his course as a way to fill his social calendar, then his intent is exploitive and waiting a short time until grades are submitted does not eliminate the ethics problem with dating former students. In this as in all cases, the welfare of the population served must be the first consideration.

SUMMARY

Sexual exploitation of clients by therapists is a blatantly unethical practice, as is sexual contact with students, employees, supervisees, research participants, and others for whom the professional has responsibility. Sexual contact with former clients is always prohibited for at least two years after the termination of therapy. Even after two years sexual contact is permitted only in the most unusual circumstances. The codes do not directly address the issue of sexual contact after teaching or supervision responsibilities have ended, but in these cases professionals must demonstrate that the supervisory responsibilities have truly ceased. Moreover, they must be able to show that the sexual contact is nonexploitive.

Sexual misconduct by mental health professionals has been widely studied, and the results show clear evidence of sexual exploitation by professionals. Up to 12% of therapists have admitted sexual contact with current and former clients, and some have acknowledged multiple contacts. Since this research relies on the willingness of professionals and clients to disclose such events in therapy, the reliability of that figure is probably not high. In any case, surveys of mental health professionals have found that approximately half of those sampled have seen at least one client who reports an experience of sexual exploitation by a former therapist. A similar percentage of faculty and supervisors have admitted the same misconduct. The only demographic variables associated with this violation are gender and, to a lesser degree, age. Older male therapists and faculty are more likely to engage in this behavior than younger or female therapists. Victims, on the other hand, are more likely to be female and younger than the therapist. Children as well as adults have become victims of sexual exploitation by therapists. Research has shown that sexual misconduct inflicts serious and long-lasting psychological damage on victims. In fact, that damage has been compared to the effects of rape or incest.

Sexual misconduct needs to be distinguished from experiences of sexual arousal. A great majority of counselors report having been sexually attracted to a client on occasion. The experience of attraction is not unethical in itself as long as it is handled responsibly. The counselor has the duty to monitor his or her behavior so that the attraction does not distract the client from the therapeutic focus of the session and does not prevent the counselor from providing competent service. Consultation and supervision are also advised when an attraction occurs.

Given this context, it is not surprising that the use of nonerotic touch as a therapeutic approach in mental health is controversial. Some call it taboo, and others view it as an appropriate counseling approach if used wisely. All professionals regard nonerotic touch as inappropriate if it serves the counselor's needs over the clients' or is insensitive to cultural, social, or gender considerations.

DISCUSSION QUESTIONS

1. Given the contents of the codes of ethics, how would you evaluate the ethics of a sexual relationship between a child counselor and the parent of one of her clients? Would sexual contact several months after termination be considered ethical?

2. What is your analysis of the debate on the two-year rule for posttermination sexual contact with clients? Does it seem prudent and sensible? Why or why not? If you sat on the committee assigned to write the next revision of the code, what position would you take?

3. Professional associations seem caught between their commitment to protect the public from sexually exploitive therapists and their obligation to promote the good image of the profession. Some criticize these organizations for being too passive about the dangers and too lenient with offenders, and others argue that so much attention to the problems of a small percentage of practitioners gives the misimpression that all members act exploitively. What do you think the proper role of the professional association is in dealing with a serious ethical problem such as sexual misconduct?

4. Do you think the codes of ethics ought to address the issue of sexual relationships with former students, supervisees, employees, or research participants? Why or why not?

RECOMMENDED READINGS

Anonymous. (1991). Sexual harassment: A female counseling student's experience. *Journal of Counseling and Development, 69,* 502–506.

Bartell, P. A., & Rubin, L. J. (1990). Dangerous liaisons: Sexual intimacies in supervision. *Professional Psychology: Research and Practice, 21,* 442–450.

Bates, C. M., & Brodsky, A. M. (1989). *Sex in the therapy hour: A case of professional incest.* New York: Guilford.

Gabbard, G. O. (Ed.). (1989). *Sexual exploitation in professional relationships.* Washington, DC: American Psychiatric Press.

Pope, K. S. (1994). *Sexual involvement with therapists: Patient assessment, subsequent therapy, forensics.* Washington, DC: American Psychological Association.

Pope, K. S., Sonne, J. L., & Holroyd, J. (1993). *Sexual feelings in psychotherapy: Explorations for therapists and therapists-in-training.* Washington, DC: American Psychological Association.

Vasquez, M. J. T. (1991). Sexual intimacies with clients after termination: Should a prohibition be explicit? *Ethics and Behavior, 1,* 45–61.

8

Nonsexual Dual Relationships
Risks to Objectivity and Client Welfare

Consider whether the counselor acted ethically in the following situations:

Roberta, a client of Dominique, comes to the final session of their counseling relationship with a gift for Dominique. Roberta says she wants to show her counselor just how much she appreciates all the help and support she provided while the doctor was coping with the sudden death of her child in a car accident. The gift—a subscription to the next season of the most prominent theater company in the region—is valued at several hundred dollars. Dominique decides to accept the gift, even though she usually refuses expensive gifts from her clients. Dominique has reasoned that for someone in Roberta's position, a gift of a few hundred dollars represents a token, such as a flower or paperback book may represent a token from a college student client.

Nicholas, a counselor for whom Marco acted as clinical supervisor during Nicholas's internship two years ago, has just moved into the home across the street from the doctor. Marco did not know this was occurring until the moving van pulled up. Within days, the children from the two families became friends. Marco's wife suggests that he invite Nicholas and his family over for a "welcome to the neighborhood" barbecue. Marco agrees and volunteers to telephone the man himself to issue the invitation.

Li Qing, who has been going to counseling for shyness and social withdrawal, decides to take action to become more social, so she attends a church service one morning. Soon thereafter, she decides to join the congregation. Because her counselor, Roxanne, was out of town the weekend her client attended the service, Li Qing does not know that Roxanne belongs to that church. When the client tells Roxanne that she has decided to join, the counselor discloses the coincidence of church membership and asks Li Qing to describe her feelings about it. The counselor decides to continue seeing the client, even though they will be members of the same church.

Olive's husband is considering opening a fast-food restaurant. As they discuss the business opportunity, she learns that the regional representative from the fast-food chain is a former client who terminated therapy eight months ago. If Olive's husband goes forward with this restaurant, he will have ongoing contact with this former client. Olive asks her husband to investigate other franchise opportunities, saying that her past professional connections with the representative could make the arrangement awkward for everyone. Reluctantly, her husband agrees.

Mr. K is attending an open house at his child's elementary school. The child's teacher, Mr. Goodheart, approaches Mr. K because he knows that Mr. K is a licensed mental health counselor. The teacher asks if Mr. K has room in his schedule for a good friend of his who is anxious and depressed. The counselor gives Mr. Goodheart his card and tells the teacher to have his friend call to arrange an appointment.

Wilma's former client operates a private college admissions advising service. This client works with high school students and their families to help them with the college application process and with securing financial aid. Wilma has twins who are beginning their senior year of high school. When the two accidentally meet one Saturday at the post office, Wilma wonders whether her former client could help her sort through the maze of college applications before her. The next day Wilma telephones the client and asks for an appointment for herself and the twins. In all, they have three meetings, for which Wilma pays the regular fee.

Dr. Z is a counselor educator with a small private practice. A professor in the history department calls Dr. Z's practice to ask if she could schedule a counseling appointment. Dr. Z knows this woman from campus and from serving together on the faculty senate. Dr. Z suggests that the history professor make an appointment with her partner instead. In spite of receiving an explanation of the reasons why Dr. Z would prefer to have the prospective client see her partner instead, the historian is angered by the action and refuses to make an appointment.

Alberto's wife's boss requests that Alberto see in therapy the boss's 16-year-old son, who has been suffering from panic attacks. Alberto is well known in the community for his skill in counseling people with anxiety disorders. Alberto telephones his wife's boss and suggests that the family come in for a consultation the next day.

Gerhard, a client who terminated therapy three years ago, calls Dr. P to ask if she is interested in an investment opportunity. Dr. P does some research on the investment and learns that it is a legitimate opportunity and that the potential exists for a substantial return. Dr. P also knows from her therapeutic contact with Gerhard that he is scrupulously honest and highly competent in his work. Dr. P contacts him and suggests a meeting to discuss specifics. After several more meetings, she invests $10,000 in the business.

Each week Dr. S goes to the same bakery for bread. He establishes a friendly relationship with the young person behind the counter. On various occasions this bakery clerk has seen Dr. S with his spouse, his children, and his parents. One day the clerk's name appears on Dr. S's appointment calendar for a counseling session for relationship problems. The doctor learns from the secretary that when she made the appointment, this woman asked to see him in particular. Dr. S is pleased that the person sought him out, and looks forward to a productive professional relationship.

Six months after Delini, a counselor, successfully terminated counseling with a musician client, this client sends her a ticket to the orchestra's next performance, indicating that he remembers his therapist is fond of the pieces the orchestra will be playing that night. Delini attends and approaches the musician after the concert to thank him for the ticket. He asks Delini to attend a postperformance party with him and his wife. Delini agrees. Within a few months the three become friends who frequently attend music events together.

A therapist in town with whom Robin has been acquainted for 10 years requests that Robin see him as a client. The client's sister was killed in a terrorist bombing and he believes he is now suffering from posttraumatic stress. He is adamant that he wants to see Robin and not another therapist because he trusts Robin's clinical judgment more than anyone else in the area. Robin schedules an initial appointment that afternoon.

What are your intuitions about the ethics of each situation? Do some seem more problematic than others? Do some seem perfectly acceptable with no real ethical dimensions at all? Are some difficult to evaluate without more information? In this chapter the focus is on the issue of nonsexual dual relationships with those with whom we have a professional role (sexual dual relationships were discussed in Chapter 7). The chapter begins by defining terms and proceeds to elaborate the ethical standards and the rationale for those standards, including research on practitioners' beliefs and practices about this topic. Next it presents a set of questions practitioners should ask themselves when considering whether to become involved in a dual relationship. The chapter concludes by discussing the ethics of receiving gifts from clients, the difficulties of managing dual relationships for rural practitioners, and bartering—the practice of trading goods and services instead of money for counseling.

Definition of Terms

Whenever counselors have other connections with a client in addition to the therapist–client relationship, a dual or multiple relationship exists. The counseling profession has retained the use of the term *dual relationship* for such overlapping roles, but psychology has begun to use the designation *multiple relationship* for such an occurrence. In each of the cases just described, some level of dual relationship has been established or has the potential to exist. Sonne (1994) clarifies that multiple relationships can be either concurrent with the professional relationship or consecutive. If consecutive, the therapeutic role may precede or follow the other role. Because counselors function in a variety of roles in their professional and personal lives, the possibility of a dual relationship is always present. The following list shows examples of dual relationships.

Concurrent	*Consecutive*
Professional and personal (researcher and friend)	Professional and personal (therapist, 1995–1996, and business partner, 1997-98)
Professional and professional (supervisor and therapist)	Professional and professional (professor, 1994–1995, and therapist, 1996)
Multiple professional (employer, clinical supervisor, and counselor)	Personal and professional (friend since college—15 years— then marriage counselor in 16th year)

Ethics scholars (such as Kitchener, 1988) and the codes of conduct concur on the risks inherent in many kinds of dual relationships, although neither imposes a blanket prohibition against all forms of them. Essentially, the major risk is that the existence of the nonprofessional relationship will compromise both the judgment of the professional and the response of the client to counseling. This can reduce counseling benefit for the client and perhaps inflict harm. Kitchener (1988) and Jennings (1992) refer to this problem as one of conflict in social roles and the often incompatible claims of each role on the professional. The greater the divergence between roles, the greater the risk of an unsatisfactory counseling outcome. Role differences entail different expectations for self, other, and the relationship, along with varying obligations for each party. Role differences exist along a continuum, and the risk of problems with role differences varies directly with the degree of disparity in expectations and obligations. For example, the role expectations and obligations of a spouse and a professor diverge significantly. A spouse is expected to support, assist, and be especially attentive to the partner's needs, but a professor is expected (and obliged) to be objective and fair to all students, singling no one out for special treatment. Moreover, the professor's duty is to evaluate students and to give negative evaluations to those whose performance is substandard. Thus, the roles of spouse and professor are so highly contrasting that the risk of misconduct rises significantly. The case of Alberto and the boss's son is another good illustration of the concept of diverging role expectations and obligations. Examining each person's role in the scenario reveals that the roles Alberto is considering are highly incompatible.

Other role expectations and obligations are more similar and involve less vulnerability to negative outcomes. Combining the roles of therapist and shopper in a supermarket in which a client works illustrates a situation with much less potential for harm. There is little conflict between the role obligations of shopper and therapist, except if knowledge of the therapist's purchasing habits and food choices poses a problem for the client's expectations of the therapist. Because this situation has a rather low risk of harm, the worker in the supermarket probably ought not to be denied the mental health service she seeks because of her outside contact with the therapist. Dual relationships at the low end of the role difference continuum carry very little chance that they will harm either party. This is the primary reason that the professions have not proscribed all dual relationships.

Three other factors weighed in forming the profession's position on dual relationships. First, in some forms of dual relationship the consumer stands to benefit substantially from the contact. The bakery clerk's personal life may be significantly improved if she enters counseling with Dr. S. She may gain the strength to end an abusive relationship or learn how to achieve the emotional intimacy with her partner that she has been seeking. Second, avoiding all dual relationships would place a great burden on mental health professionals and those with whom they associate. For example, in the second case in the chapter, a total prohibition of dual relationships would be unworkable for Marco. Requiring him to move would be unthinkable, demanding him to ignore his new neighbor would be uncomfortable for the whole family (and the neighborhood), and asking Nicholas to relocate would be just as impossible. Third, repudiating all dual relationships is inconsistent with the right to free association that citizens in a democratic society have. Nicholas has a right to live where he chooses and to be as friendly with his neighbors as he sees fit. Also, even though Marco's professional obligations take precedence over his right of free association with those with whom he has had a professional relationship, that right is not entirely eliminated when the professional contact is largely over.

How, then, should a counselor determine whether any given dual relationship is permissible? Analyzing the variance in role obligations and expectations between the different types of relationships is an important task. In addition, the professional standards advise cost–benefit analysis to determine the ethics of any particular dual relationship. The professional guidelines are founded on the assumption that the counselor's approach to dual relationships ought to be *risk preventive* (Sonne, 1994). This means that high-risk situations are to be avoided even if they carry with them the possibility of significant benefits.

ACA *Code of Ethics,* Section A.6: Dual Relationships

a. Avoid when possible

Counselors are aware of their influential positions with respect to clients, and avoid exploiting the trust and dependency of clients. Counselors make every effort to avoid dual relationships with clients that could impair their judgment or increase the risk of harm to clients. (Examples of such relationships include, but are not limited to, familial, social, financial, business, or close personal relationships with clients.) When a dual relationship cannot be avoided, counselors take appropriate professional precautions such as informed consent, consultation, supervision, and documentation to ensure that judgment is not impaired and no exploitation occurs.

b. Superior/subordinate relationships

Counselors do not accept as clients superiors or subordinates with whom they have had administrative, supervisory or evaluative experience.

ACA *Ethics Code,* Section E.1.e: Close Relatives

Counselors do not accept close relatives as students or supervisees.

ACA *Ethics Code,* Section F.2.h: Dual Relationships as Supervisors

Counselors avoid dual relationships such as performing the role of site supervisor and training program supervisor in the student's or supervisee's training program.

APA *Ethical Principles,* Section 1.17: Multiple Relationships

(a) In many communities and situations, it may not be feasible or reasonable for psychologists to avoid social or other nonprofessional contacts with persons such as patients, clients, students, supervisees, or research participants. Psychologists must always be sensitive to the potential harmful effects of other contacts on their work and on those persons with whom they deal. A psychologist refrains from entering into or promising another personal, scientific, professional, financial, or other relationship with such persons if it appears likely that such a relationship reasonably might impair the psychologist's objectivity or otherwise interfere with the psychologist's effectively performing his or her functions as a psychologist, or might harm or exploit the other party.

(b) Likewise, whenever feasible, a psychologist refrains from taking on professional or scientific obligations when preexisting relationships would create a risk of such harm.

(c) If a psychologist finds that, due to unforeseen factors, a potentially harmful multiple relationship has arisen, the psychologist attempts to resolve it with due regard for the best interests of the affected person and maximal compliance with the Ethics Code.

APA *Ethical Principles,* Section 1.19: Exploitative Relationships

(a) Psychologists to do not exploit persons over whom they have supervisory, evaluative, or other authority, such as students, supervisees, employees, research participants, and clients or patients.

Note: The recommendation to avoid dual relationships is not limited to the therapeutic setting. The caution applies to a significant degree to the other professional roles counselors take on—teacher, supervisor, consultant, researcher, or employer. Sections of the codes also specify that counselors should avoid multiple relationships in which the professional contact follows a personal connection.

A close reading of the codes shows that they are less than definitive in other ways. For example, the ACA code allows both concurrent and consecutive dual relationships. It implies that under certain circumstances, accepting a family member, business partner, or close friend as a client might be ethical if efforts to avoid the dual relationship are unsuccessful. It is interesting that the ACA code expressly forbids supervising or teaching a close relative, but does not explicitly prohibit providing counseling to a close relative. The spirit of the code obviously leads a prudent professional in that direction, but the wording is more equivocal than one might expect.

The APA code more strongly discourages such relationships, indicating that psychologists should "refrain from" such relationships if negative outcomes might reasonably be predicted. The codes require mental health professionals to evaluate whether the combination of roles being considered jeopardizes their professional judgment, the welfare of the client, or their capacity to perform their job competently. The ACA code specifies several steps counselors must take if they engage in a dual relationship to minimize the hazards from this undertaking, including exercising care about informed consent and recordkeeping, and obtaining supervision or consultation about the case. Still, the codes do not provide a blueprint for practice, so the burden of assessing the ethics of any given prospective dual relationship falls largely on the individual practitioner. Neither code addresses the issue of consecutive multiple relationships when the professional relationship precedes the personal. Their silence on the issue gives the practitioner even less guidance about this type of dual relationship.

Underlying Dynamics in Dual Relationships

Ethics scholars have identified three underlying dynamics of the counseling relationship that can help practitioners evaluate the risk of any potential dual relationship: The counselor has a fiduciary relationship to honor promises to the client, the counselor has more power than the client, and the client is emotionally vulnerable in counseling. These dynamics sharply reduce the chance of clients benefiting as they should in such relationships.

The Fiduciary Obligation

Sonne (1994) focuses on the first dynamic, the *fiduciary relationship* between a mental health professional and client. The term *fiduciary relationship* derives from legal sources, and means that the counselor's primary obligation is to promote the client's well-being. A counselor who fails in this responsibility is violating the most fundamental covenant with the client. Dual relationships imply that the counselor is vulnerable to other interests that compete with promoting the welfare of the client and thus are typically contradictory to the fiduciary responsibility. Using the case of Alberto again, he may have difficulty placing the well-being of the adolescent client above the wishes of the client's father, who is the boss of Alberto's wife. Or Alberto may wish so much to impress the boss with his therapeutic skill that the therapy becomes more of a display of Alberto's therapeutic talents than a treatment of the boy's panic attacks. In a particularly problematic scenario, Alberto's worry about his wife's future employment may cause him to neglect to report to authorities the father's physical abuse of the boy. In all three instances, the counselor is neglecting his fiduciary responsibility.

Simon (1992) describes this dynamic a little differently. He asserts that counselors have a *duty to abstinence* from gratifying self-interests in therapy. This duty means that the only acceptable profit from therapy is the fee paid and the satisfaction received from a client's therapeutic gains. This obligation to abstain is incompatible with many dual relationships. The duty to abstinence is very difficult to uphold when the temptations to serve self-interests are as strong as they are for Alberto if he takes on the son of his wife's boss as a client. More is at stake for Alberto than the income from the therapeutic time or the client's well-being. One could even wonder whether Alberto is accepting this case with the specific goal of enhancing his wife's career.

The fiduciary obligation to the client is also connected to another responsibility cited by Simon (1992), *the duty to neutrality.* He postulates that a therapist is ethically bound to enhance the client's autonomy and independence. Simon also asserts that because autonomy and independence are so fundamental to achieving of the client's therapeutic objectives, a counselor should have no other agenda. If Alberto is committed to his wife and her welfare, he has little neutrality about this adolescent client. He may even attempt to interfere with this adolescent's appropriate developmental separation from parents if that separation displeases the parents. Another way to frame the duty to neutrality is to describe it as a duty to objectivity and disinterest in any particular aspect of the client's life other than attaining therapeutic aims. Disinterest and objectivity should not be confused with a cold or uncaring attitude (Pope & Vasquez, 1991), but rather is highly compatible with a warm, empathic approach.

Note that Alberto is at risk for violating his fiduciary duty to this client even if he enters the relationship intending to honor that obligation. For this dual relationship to be problematic, he need not be self-interested or callous about his client. The intensity of his connection to his wife, and the ramifications to them both if counseling does not proceed as the boss intends, make objectivity and exclusive devotion to the client's goals almost impossible. In fact, counselors with good intentions to help people who need therapy are often especially vulnerable because they underestimate the limits their other role places on them and overestimate their capacity for objectivity in the face of strong personal interests. In other words, they do not recognize the conflict of interest inherent in the situation.

The Client's Emotional Involvement in Counseling

The second dynamic that makes dual relationships risky is the client's *emotional involvement with the therapist.* The therapist becomes an important person in the life of the client, at least during their professional contact. Research shows that a substantial part of what makes counseling therapeutic is the human relationship between the people involved (for example, see Bergin & Garfield, 1994; Luborsky et al., 1988; Sexton & Whiston, 1994). Client trust, confidence in the therapist's expertise, clarity about the rules and boundaries of the relationship, and mutuality of expectations are all crucial features of successful therapy. When a counselor has another role in a client's life, the client's emotional reaction is confused. Trust is endangered, the rules for interaction are less obvious, and expectations may diverge. Exposure to the therapist's foibles in other settings may erode the client's confidence. In addition, sharing a very painful or embarrassing secret may be more difficult for a client who has dual contacts with a counselor. For fear of repercussions, a business executive may avoid disclosing her experiences of mania to a counselor who has invested in that business. The executive may feel she would be jeopardizing the company's future if she disclosed.

In a more practical vein, dual roles may make the client unsure about when therapy begins and ends and what kinds of conversation are appropriate in which setting. A client who is also a neighbor may feel uncertain about when to bring up particular topics with the counselor, or may feel that *every* contact with the counselor is appropriate for therapeutic dialogue. In the latter situation, a client could develop feelings of dependence; a counselor, feelings of resentment. Therapists who view transference as a central feature of counseling are particularly troubled by this dynamic. They contend that a client cannot work through a transference with a counselor who plays another role in his or her life. Research shows that psychoanalytic therapists tend to view nonerotic dual relationships as significantly less ethical than their cognitive or humanistic counterparts (Baer & Murdock, 1995).

The Power Imbalance

The third dynamic, the *power differential* between counselor and client, was discussed at length as an important factor in sexual exploitation (Chapter 7). This imbalance may make clients acquiesce to the therapist's wishes even when doing so is at odds with their own desires. This can happen not only in session, but also in the second relationship. A supervisee who is also a supervisor's client may defer any disagreement with the therapist/supervisor because the risk of negative fallout is so great. Clients can also fear emotional abandonment (Sonne, 1994) if they offend the therapist in his or her other role. If clients refuse the therapist/friend's social invitation, they may wonder if the therapist will retaliate by missing a session or even terminating therapy. The client's autonomy is jeopardized by the dual relationship (Kitchener, 1988).

The power difference also contributes to what has been called *role slippage* (Smith & Fitzpatrick, 1995). Role slippage means that the more powerful therapist may loosen the boundaries between the therapeutic relationship and the other relationship. A therapist might end a session with a conversation about a committee issue with a client who also serves on that body. Then, the therapist may suggest that they go out for a cup of coffee after a committee meeting to follow up on an unresolved issue. In this conversation, the therapist may disclose other information about himself to which the client does not know how to respond. Finally, the therapist may take even more time for the committee agenda in later sessions. Under these circumstances, a client make feel reluctant to divert the discussion to more relevant matters. After counselors disclose extensive information about their personal lives, clients may even come to see themselves as caretakers for the counselor (Smith & Fitzpatrick, 1995). Eventually, both the client and the counselor lose sight of the boundaries between the professional and personal relationships, and the focus on the client's therapeutic goal becomes secondary.

Still another aspect of dual relationships is troublesome: The confidentiality of counseling is endangered. The chances that a counselor might inadvertently reveal information disclosed in counseling are increased by the outside contact. In the situation described in the last paragraph, the counselor might accidentally repeat to another committee member something the client said within session. Keeping track of what was said in which setting is burdensome. Intentional violations of confidentiality are also more likely when a counselor's self-interest in a dual relationship has not been met. The scenario of Wilma (the therapist who consulted a former client about her children's college applications) could easily lead to an intentional violation of confidentiality if Wilma were dissatisfied with the advice her former client gave her children. In anger she might disclose to her family something about the former client's reasons for seeking therapy.

The Views of Ethics Scholars

Given the potential for problems, many ethics scholars take a stronger stance than the codes do against dual relationships, especially those in which one role is therapeutic. Kitchener (1988) and Sonne (1994) argue that mental health professionals cannot accurately predict the degree to which their capacity to practice competently will be impaired, or the harm that may come to a client as their relationship progresses. In light of this reality, they contend that most dual relationships represent "undue risks" that should not be undertaken. Pope and Vasquez (1991) assert that mental health professionals who engage in many kinds of nonsexual dual relationships are frequently justifying their behavior with reasons that do not stand the test of logic or true commitment to the client's well-being. Using Simon's terms (1991, 1992), close examination of these counselors' motives usually reveals that they are acting without neutrality or abstinence. These practitioners seem to underestimate the conflict of interest or to overestimate their own skill. Simon also argues that a dual relationship places the therapist at significant risk for other boundary violations, in a slippery slope analogy. A therapist who takes on a former business partner as a client may then accept investment advice from another current client, suggest a business relationship with a supervisee, and so forth. When business relationships with clients become common and acceptable, the extension to social and romantic relationships is rather natural. Clear boundaries help the counselor stay focused on the client's welfare and help avert many other problems as well. Essentially, these writers are basing their arguments on the principle of nonmaleficence. Because preventing harm is such an important professional value and because that harm cannot always be foreseen, prudence and devotion to the client's welfare demand that counselors should almost always avoid dual relationships.

Other scholars take a more liberal stand (for example, see Corey et al., 1993; Herlihy & Corey, 1992, 1997), suggesting that the ethics of a dual relationship need to be examined on a case-by-case basis. They greatly emphasize that counselors can make reasonable assessments when they know about the facts of a particular situation. These scholars also view a rigid posture against nonsexual dual relationships as impractical, because counselors live in communities and are bound to have contacts with people who may at some point be clients. They also point out the importance of the principle of beneficence and argue that prohibiting dual relationships may diminish the counselor's opportunity to do good. Finally, they appropriately stress the role of community and cultural variables in determining whether a dual relationship is ethical. For instance, if at an agency with many Chinese immigrants, only one counselor speaks Chinese, that counselor's special skill should be taken into account. That counselor may be well advised to establish somewhat looser boundaries with those Chinese clients, because of the unique capacity to do good. Community variables also play a crucial role in a rural practitioner's decision making (see the fuller discussion later in this chapter).

All scholars seem to agree on at least one point. Regardless of the stance a professional takes on any given dual relationship, if he or she observes a pattern of involvement in dual relationships that is more frequent than colleagues working in similar communities, that person should step back and reevaluate the dynamics underlying the behavior. Along with that reassessment should come careful supervision and consultation to unearth the underlying dynamics of the practice.

Questions to Consider in Decision Making

Based on the codes, the literature, and the ethical standards, the following questions present important issues to address in determining whether a particular relationship is ethical:

- Are the role expectations and obligations so divergent as to be incompatible?
- Is promoting the client's welfare the exclusive motivation of the counselor in initiating the professional relationship?
- Can the professional attain the same degree of objectivity about this person as is achieved in other professional relationships?
- Is misuse of the professional's power a plausible occurrence?
- Is this dual relationship a low-risk and high-benefit situation for the other person?
- Is the counselor reasonably certain that the dual relationship will not negatively affect the client's emotional involvement in counseling or capacity to achieve the therapeutic goal?
- Is the dual relationship truly unavoidable? Have all other options really been considered?
- If a counselor is embarking on a dual relationship, has a fully informed consent procedure been undertaken so that the other party understands the situation, including its risks and the special arrangements that may be necessary?

- Have both parties evaluated the changes that may result in their other relationships because of the professional contact they are now considering, and are they both comfortable with these changes?
- If the decision were presented to the counselor's respected colleagues (using the clear-light-of-day standard), is it likely that they would support the decision to go forward with this dual relationship?
- Is the counselor willing to document the dual relationship in case notes?
- Has the counselor made provision for continuing consultation and/or supervision to monitor the risks and benefits to the client as the relationship develops?
- Have the client and counselor developed an alternative plan in the event that the relationship does not unfold as they expect?
- Is the counselor committed to diligently following up, so that if problems from the dual relationship arise after the professional contact has ended, the counselor will be able to provide assistance?

The length of this list of questions demonstrates the exceptional care a counselor must take when considering initiating a nonsexual dual relationship.

Research Findings: Practitioners' Views

The research on practitioners' attitudes toward nonsexual dual relationships is not as abundant as the literature on their views about sexual contact, but there is enough evidence to draw some reasonable conclusions. First, significant diversity appears in practitioners' opinion about the ethics of this practice. Some call it unquestionably unethical, but others show considerable tolerance for such multiple commitments. For example, in one study 26% of psychologists labeled accepting a client's invitation to a party as unquestionably unethical while 17.5% viewed the same practice as ethical under many circumstances (Pope et al., 1987). Second, most studies show a much greater tolerance for nonsexual dual relationships than for sexual ones among psychologists, social workers, counselors, and psychiatrists. More professionals view nonsexual contacts as ethical, at least under some circumstances, and even when viewing them as unethical, do not see them as such egregious violations as sexual misconduct. For example, three different surveys found that many therapists viewed the practice of becoming friends with a former client as ethical at least sometimes. The percentages endorsing this view ranged from 44% (Borys & Pope, 1989) to 59% (Gibson & Pope, 1993) to 70% (Salisbury & Kinnier, 1996). Moreover, 26% of those surveyed by Borys and Pope admitted to engaging in this practice at least once. Pope et al. (1987) found that a much larger percentage admitted to this practice, a full two-thirds (67%) of their sample. Practitioners responding to surveys have also admitted engaging in several other kinds of dual relationships. These include the following (Borys & Pope, 1989; Pope et al., 1987; Lamb et al., 1994):

- Accepting friends as clients
- Providing therapy to an employee

- Employing a client
- Going into business with current and former clients
- Providing therapy to students and/or supervisees
- Allowing a client to enroll in a course taught by the therapist
- Inviting clients to a party
- Selling goods to a client

The specific percentage acknowledging such activities varies from survey to survey, as does the form of the question asked, but each of the surveys that found at least 2% of those responding endorsed these behaviors. The most common dual relationship reported was providing therapy to a student or supervisee (29%, Pope et al., 1987) and the least frequent was going into business with a current client (2%, Pope et al., 1987).

Some of the behaviors just listed are clearly prohibited by the ethics codes (such as providing therapy to an employee—ACA, 1995, Section A.6.b), but most others fit the category of dual relationships to avoid or refrain from if possible. The available evidence does not reveal whether these activities met the criteria established by the codes or fell short of them. Nor does it reveal the outcomes of these relationships for the consumers or therapists involved, unfortunately. These data suggest that mental health professionals may not be acting as cautiously as they should when faced with a prospective dual relationship. To use a colloquial phrase—one need not be a rocket scientist to realize that providing therapy for a friend or employee has a high probability of clouding one's objectivity, impairing one's judgment, or impeding the progress of therapy—each of which harms the client.

Accepting Gifts from Clients

Clients sometimes bring presents to their counselors. The urge to give gifts can be motivated by a number of different factors. Some clients are driven by a belief that gifts may gain them special status in their counselors' eyes or otherwise help maintain good service. For others, the action is connected to the very problems that sparked their decision to enter counseling. For instance, clients with low self-esteem may perceive gifts as the path to keep the counselor interested in them, because they believe themselves to have little intrinsic value. A few clients may even attempt to use gifts as bribes for a positive report or a special favor. Still others wish to bestow a token of their appreciation for the gift that counseling has been to them or to ease the sadness of termination by leaving something from them with their counselor as they depart. Consequently, the ethics of accepting a gift from a client depends substantially on the circumstances under which it was offered. (It also depends on the attitude of and impact on its recipient.) Perhaps this explains why the professional codes are silent on the matter. Still, some guidelines for when to accept or reject a gift can be presented.

When gifts are a "quid pro quo" for better or special service, or are a manifestation of the client's dysfunction, the counselor probably should not accept them. Taking them implies, in the first case, that the counselor can be manipulated (and thus undermines trust and devotion to promoting client welfare), and in the second case, suggests that the counselor agrees with the client's distorted self-assessment or view of relationships (and thereby inhibits therapeutic progress). However, when a present represents a token of appreciation for a successful counseling experience or a common cultural ritual (such as sharing holiday cookies in December), it may not be unethical to receive it. Specifically, accepting a gift is more likely to be ethical if *all* the following criteria are met:

- It promotes rather than endangers the client's welfare.
- It does not compromise the therapist's objectivity or capacity to provide competent service in the future.
- It is a token of appreciation consistent with the client's cultural norms and with a small monetary value.
- It is a rare event in counseling rather than recurrent practice.

The definition of what is expensive varies from person to person and from decade to decade. Research seems to indicate some consistency in the way mental health professionals define a "token gift." Practicing psychologists, social workers, and counselors seem to believe that a value of approximately $10 is the limit for what is ethical (Borys & Pope, 1989; Gibson & Pope, 1993). When clients want to bestow more elaborate gifts on their therapists, that desire may be "grist for the therapeutic mill" that the two parties should discuss in session. When a client seems insistent on giving a valuable gift as a symbol of the tremendously positive impact that counseling has had on his or her life, a compromise can sometimes be reached by having the client make an anonymous contribution to a charity in the name of the agency. The latter option seems prudent to consider only at the point of a successful termination and only after a full airing of the impact of the gift on the professional relationship and on the profession if the gift becomes known. An expensive present should not be accepted by an individual counselor because it poses such a high risk of reducing the counselor's objectivity. To expect counselors to be totally unaffected by an elaborate gift is to deny their humanity. It is for this reason the counselor described in the opening section of this chapter should not accept Roberta's gift of a theater subscription. Even though a few hundred dollars represents little more than a token to this client, it probably carries more meaning to the counselor. The counselor would be unlikely to be able to work objectively with Roberta in the future because of the past largesse. Moreover, if another wealthy client came her way after Roberta, the counselor might be distracted by thoughts about the possibility of other such presents at termination. Instead of taking the tickets, Dominique could work with Roberta to donate the tickets to a charity or to a school for the arts as an incentive for drama students. The counselor should simultaneously express to the client that the therapeutic change in her client is all the reward she needs, and should make sure that before she leaves, Roberta fully understands Dominique's rationale for refusing the gift.

Even token gifts, such as a homemade loaf of bread or flowers from a client's garden, should not become a recurrent event. If it does, the practice ought to be discussed in counseling. Perhaps the client brings presents because it is the only way she knows to express emotional connection. If so, helping the client learn alternative ways to express closeness can become an explicit counseling goal. A recurrent gift is also a distraction for the counselor. A counselor might start to look forward to that loaf of fresh bread each week, and then be disappointed when the client did not produce one. Such a motivation to see a client is inconsistent with the principle of neutrality and objectivity.

Counselors who are tempted to conclude that the simplest path is to refuse all client gifts without exception, should be cautious in taking such a stance. In some cultural groups, gifts are important interpersonal rituals. For these clients, an absolute refusal of all gifts might well be counterproductive. Similarly, for clients who wish to present a small token at successful termination of an intense counseling relationship, the refusal to graciously receive a small present may interrupt a positive resolution of the relationship, especially if the client had no warning that gift giving might be inappropriate.

Herlihy and Corey (1992, 1997) recommend that the issue of gift giving be included in a professional disclosure statement or brought up during the informed consent process early in counseling so that no one ends up embarrassed, confused, or angry over an inappropriate present. They go on to suggest that a policy be written to discourage the practice. With such a policy clients will then understand both the counselor's interpretation of the practice and the rationale underlying it long before they are likely to want to bring the counselor a present. Moreover, if the counselor's policy to dissuade clients from gift giving conflicts with the client's cultural tradition, the two can then discuss this discrepancy at an early stage. In short, clarifying policy at an early stage can prevent later misunderstandings. If Roberta had known that Dominique might not accept her gift, she might have saved herself both the cost of the tickets and the distress of their refusal at what was otherwise a very positive final counseling session.

On the other hand, discussing gift giving early in therapy may present problems. Adding one more item to the already long list of topics to discuss early in the informed consent process may make that process even more burdensome. The client may misinterpret the policy and assume that token gifts *ought* to be given. In some cultural contexts in which gifts are an important aspect of interpersonal relationships, this policy would be vulnerable to misinterpretation. Thus, counselors ought to consider all the implications of such a policy before mandating it for all clients.

Dual Relationships and Rural Practice

Mental health practitioners who work in large metropolitan areas can rather easily avoid many forms of dual relationships. The pool of potential clients from whom they can build their practices is large, so that there is little economic incentive to engage in a dual relationship. They can work in a different part of the city from their home to prevent contacts with clients, students, or supervisees in civic, religious, or social settings. Counselors in large cities rarely encounter in other settings people with whom they have had professional obligations. In addition, urban practitioners have many referral sources for people whom they ought not to take on as clients because of the risk of a dual relationship. They can be confident that the clients they decline to accept will still receive competent professional service. By refusing to accept such clients, these counselors are not jeopardizing consumers' access to professional services. Using the words from the ACA code, it is almost always "possible" to make other arrangements. Urban counselors also have the benefit of the relative anonymity of the large city. Few people in the community know or care about their occupation. If they accidentally meet their clients in other settings, neither party has to worry that a brief conversation would reveal to the community their professional contact.

In contrast, rural counselors have dramatically different experiences because of both the demographics of their communities and their cultural norms. Their pool of potential clients is smaller, their referral sources more limited, and the chances of preexisting, concurrent, or subsequent connections with clients significantly greater. A smaller population base from which to draw clients can mean that turning away clients for dual-relationship reasons will be a financial hardship for counselors. Competent referral sources are often many miles away in an area with little public transportation, so clients' access to mental health care is more restricted when local practitioners decline to see them. Unless rural counselors refrain from joining any social, religious, or civic organizations and commute long distances to the workplace, they cannot easily avoid additional contacts with clients (Schank & Skovholt, 1997). Moreover, in a small community many people know the counselor's occupation and are acquainted with the people with whom the counselor may interact. As Jennings (1992) points out, "Life in the city is characterized by anonymity; whereas life in rural areas is characterized by an unusual degree of openness—one's behavior, and the behavior of one's family are not only open to public scrutiny, but become favorite topics of community discussion" (p. 94). Thus the avoidance of dual relationships is more complex for rural practitioners. Rural counselors often get requests to work with people with whom they are acquainted or whom they have seen at community, religious, or social functions. Even if the counselor is unfamiliar with a particular person, he or she may know a family member and may be privy to information about the client from those other people (Gates & Speare, 1990; Hargrove, 1982). Sobel (1992) points out that dual-relationship complications arise when the secretary or other staff of the counselor have connections with prospective clients. Rural practitioners also know that when professional contact ends, they are likely to have at least intermittent contact with the client afterward. Their children may have the same teacher, they may both volunteer for the United Way drive, or they may bump into each other waiting at the dentist's office. Since they drive the same streets all the time, they may even be involved in the same traffic accident at some point!

Research by Horst (1989) supports these claims. In her study of psychologists from urban and rural communities in Minnesota, she found significantly more overlapping relationships between rural practitioners and their clients. Rural psychologists had more out-of-session contact and experienced more after-termination contact. Most of the out-of-session contact was through involvement in joint large organizations or in meetings in stores or other community settings. Rural practitioners were not significantly more likely to engage in dual relationships that carried with them high risks of complications, however. For example, Horst found no difference between the rates at which urban and rural psychologists indicated they had accepted friends or employees as clients.

Public perception of dual relationships also differs in rural places. People in cities expect that the professionals who serve them will be strangers; they seem to prefer that arrangement. Rural dwellers tend to take the opposite stance, because they are so accustomed to interacting with familiar people. Thus they may be more likely to seek out a familiar counselor rather than a stranger and may be quite reluctant to establish a therapeutic relationship with an unknown counselor. The challenge for the rural practitioners, then, is to serve the mental health needs of the community without causing undue harm to clients with whom they have at least peripheral connections.

Of course, one must be careful not to characterize the contrasts among urban, suburban, and rural settings too extremely. Sometimes clients in suburbs and cities choose a particular therapist because he or she is part of a "shared community" with a client, participating in the same civic organization, social action group, or ethnic or cultural minority (Adelman & Barrett, 1990). So practitioners in these communities can be as familiar with the dilemma of overlapping connections as their rural counterparts. Still, counselors in larger population areas tend to have more referral sources and more opportunities for consultation and supervision than those in small towns.

Along with the case of the bakery clerk presented in the opening section of this chapter, the following examples of ethical dilemmas derive from the author's brief experience as the only psychologist in a small country town. In each instance, the author had to assess whether the problems that might accrue from the dual relationship might reasonably harm clients or otherwise prevent them from benefiting from therapy. At that time the nearest referral sources were at least 30 miles away and inaccessible by public transportation.

- A woman who seeks counseling because of grief over her father's death works in the same office as the psychologist's husband. The husband is not the direct supervisor, but he is CEO of the organization.
- A woman referred to the psychologist by her family physician for treatment of a panic disorder is the mother-in-law of the psychologist's neighbor. The psychologist sees this neighbor regularly, although they are acquaintances rather than friends.
- The psychologist is asked to give a deposition in a custody matter, and finds when she goes to the meeting that the attorney doing the deposing is the estranged husband of a current client.
- The children of the psychologist and of her client attend the same day care center. In fact, on the day of the client's weekly appointment, both people drive directly

from her office to pick up their children at the day care center. It is the only day care center in town.

■ The banker with whom the psychologist has done business is referred to her for counseling after his hospitalization for a brief psychotic break.

Jennings (1992) provides other vivid examples of recurring dual-relationship problems in rural areas. In one case, he was involved in a court case to give expert testimony and discovered when he entered the courtroom that the judge and three of the jurors had been clients in his private practice. In a second case, his teenage son had asked a girl to the prom whose parents were in therapy with Jennings. The boy, of course, had no knowledge of his father's connection to the family. All these cases highlight the close interconnections of people's lives in rural communities. They also illustrate the kind of harm an unscrupulous counselor might inflict on clients. Participants in other research studies identify similar problems in rural practice (for example, see Schank & Skovholt, 1997).

Jennings (1992) and Hargrove (1986) have argued that the professions have not pain enough attention to the special concerns of rural practitioners and that ethical standards derive too heavily from an urban culture. The most recent versions of the codes showed more responsiveness to this criticism. In fact, the wording of the ACA and APA codes on this topic was crafted with the situation of the rural practitioner in mind. Jennings offers additional guidelines to help the rural counselor act ethically. The first is to reject the notion that dual relationships are avoidable in a rural setting. The price of rejecting all such contacts would be eliminating mental health services for many consumers. Traveling long distances to referral sources whom the client is likely to distrust as "strangers" is not a viable option for most people. The decision about whether to accept a client must be made with the issue of accessibility of alternative services prominently in mind. Jennings recommends that those who work in rural settings make a real commitment to the fundamental ethical values of the profession and develop a generous capacity for tolerating ambiguity in their relationships. In his judgment, a mental health professional who is unequipped for such tolerance would be better suited to an urban climate.

Jennings also emphasizes the value of using extensive informed consent procedures when embarking on a therapeutic relationship with a client one knows from another interaction. Both parties should understand what the other expects when they meet in another setting. This aspect is especially important given the public awareness of the counselor's position. By merely addressing a person by name in the supermarket, a counselor could be perceived as signaling to other shoppers that the person is in counseling. Craig (quoted in Sleek, 1994) asserts that "When someone is parked in front of a psychologist's office, everybody in town knows it" (p. 27). Jennings also implies that ingenuity is an important asset for rural counselors in designing interventions to meet needs without putting clients at risk. His next recommendation is to use dual relationship issues as "grist for the therapeutic mill." The client's feelings after encountering the therapist at a social function should be openly discussed, as should the client's interest in aspects of the therapist's life that are known in the community.

When the prospective dual relationship is closer or more intense, Jennings suggests that "the psychological intervention is limited in direct proportion to the intensity of the interpersonal relationship" (p. 100). In other words, the mental health professional ought to offer only briefer, less intense services to those with stronger business, social, or community ties to the counselor and to reserve long-term counseling for people with whom outside connections are nonexistent or peripheral. A school psychologist in a rural community, for example, might go forward with an evaluation of a learning disorder in her physician's child, but would arrange for a referral for ongoing counseling services to help the child and the family cope with the disorder. Effant (quoted in Sleek, 1994) takes a different view of the problem of such multiple relationships, cautioning professionals about unanticipated complications. "Too many psychologists in smaller communities think they can handle multiple relationships, and that their clients can, too. It always complicates the relationship. The psychologist needs to be very humble about how different the process of therapy is going to be because of it" (p. 27).

In short, the rural practitioner should be especially sensitive to the ethics of dual relationships. Jennings calls this a more demanding standard than applies to urban professionals. Counselors need to continually balance the obligation to serve the public's mental health needs against the risk of harm and should seek out consultation to ensure that the difficult judgments necessitated by the environment are well founded.

The Ethics of Barter

Between 1988 (Ethics Committee of APA) and 1992, APA prohibited bartering, the exchange of goods and/or services instead of money in a business or professional transaction. The 1992 code reversed that prohibition and made bartering acceptable under certain conditions, described as follows:

> **APA *Ethical Principles,* Section 1.18: Bartering**
> Psychologists ordinarily refrain from accepting goods, services, or other nonmonetary remuneration from patients or clients in return for psychological services because such arrangements create inherent potential for conflicts, exploitation, and distortion of the professional relationship. A psychologist may participate in bartering *only* if (1) it is not clinically contraindicated and (2) the relationship is not exploitive.

For the first time, the 1995 ACA code deals directly with this issue, expressing a parallel view to APA, although it elaborates additional conditions to be met if bartering is to be permissible:

> **ACA *Ethics Code,* Section A.10.c: Bartering Discouraged**
> Counselors ordinarily refrain from accepting goods or services from clients in return for counseling services because such arrangements create inherent potential for conflicts,

exploitation, and distortion of the professional relationship. Counselors may participate in bartering only if the relationship is not exploitive, if the client requests it, if a clear written contract is established, and if such arrangements are an accepted practice among professionals in the community.

Why did the APA ever forbid bartering, and why do both organizations now restrict it? The practice is problematic because it can create a dual relationship. When bartering services, for example, the counselor becomes the client's employer for the duration of the service. The professional contact is jeopardized in many of the same ways as an ordinary dual relationship. The client's power to complain about working conditions or address problems in the service arrangement is limited. If the client voices discontent with the barter, will he or she then worry that the counselor will end counseling? In addition, the emotional connections between the people get confused when a client views a counselor as an employer. For clients with some kinds of emotional problems, this confusion can stop or reverse therapeutic gains. For this reason, the APA code specifies the absence of clinical contraindications as one precondition for bartering to be allowed. Moreover, the progress of therapy may be endangered if the counselor's neutrality is compromised by his or her investment in the service the client is providing. For instance, if a client is trading carpentry services for therapy and begins to recover from his depression before the counselor's deck is completed, the counselor may be tempted to prolong counseling to meet her own needs or simply fail to recognize the client's progress because it conflicts with her own agenda. The client may delay or hasten work on the deck, depending on his evaluation of therapeutic progress. Conversely, professional judgment may be impaired if the client has a major setback after the deck is completed. The counselor may provide less diligent care if no remuneration is possible or may be inclined to terminate therapy sooner than appropriate. One final problem is the difference in cost between the services. The services clients typically can provide have a lower monetary value than counseling, so that when counseling is lengthy, the client may become like an indentured servant to the therapist, working long hours to pay off the accumulated debt (Kitchener & Harding, 1990; Keith-Spiegel & Koocher, 1985). In most economies, the hourly wage for a typist or house painter is considerably less than for a mental health professional.

Bartering goods is somewhat less complicated, because a market value for a good can be independently established, but even such arrangements can be exploitive. A client trading a piece of sculpture for sessions may believe the art has been undervalued and then feel cheated and resentful. Or the counselor may get salmonella poisoning from farm eggs bartered for treatment, and feel poorly served by the arrangement. One final reason makes this practice risky. The legal recourse typically available to parties dissatisfied with a business transaction is not easily available to either client or counselor. A counselor who brought a client to small claims court would be violating confidentiality, and a client taking the same action would be risking disclosure of counseling information.

The issues just presented seem to lead to the conclusion that barter is simply not worth the trouble it can cause for both counselor and client. That generalization is mostly true. However, there are two important reasons not to eliminate the possibility of bartering altogether. Barter can have value in making professional services accessible to those whose financial resources are limited. Some people refuse to accept free services and see them as an affront to their dignity, but are willing to offer a barter arrangement. For clients who reject the argument that they have already paid for "free" services through their taxes, barter may be an important option (Canter et al., 1994). Others (Pope & Vasquez, 1991) argue that therapists should be careful about the frequency with which they claim that pro bono arrangements are not feasible as an alternative to barter, cautioning that self-interest and lack of ingenuity may be the real motivations for accepting barter in some situations. Second, in rural communities and some subcultures barter is a common practice and refusing to engage in it would run counter to cultural norms and restrict access to care (Canter et al., 1994).

Sonne (1994) presents a divergent view, arguing that there is little evidence that barter is a common practice. Sleek (1994) echoes this view, suggesting that its prevalence has faded considerably even in rural environments in recent years. Fewer than 10% of psychologists have accepted goods or services for payment more than rarely in their practice (Borys & Pope, 1989; Pope et al., 1987). Other research shows that psychologists tend to view the practice as rarely ethical (for example, see Baer & Murdock, 1995). Sonne questions the need to reverse APA's 1998 policy prohibiting barter for what does not appear to be a frequent problem or a source of significant professional disagreement about the ethics of the matter. Sonne also points out the contradiction between the code and some state regulations. California (California Department of Consumer Affairs, 1990) prohibits all forms of bartering in therapy, and some malpractice insurers exclude claims arising from a bartering arrangement (Sonne, 1994). She contends that these bodies are judging the problems more realistically. In any case, counselors who are considering barter with a client should assess not only their compliance with the code, but also the stance of their state licensing board and their liability insurer.

As with any other ethical issue, a counselor should consult with other professionals and carefully scrutinize one's own motivation before proceeding with a bartering arrangement. One should also scrupulously document that process, the informed consent procedures, and the progress of therapy. Although only the counseling code requires a written contract for bartering, using such a document would be prudent for other mental health professionals. That document should include the details of the barter and an alternative to the barter should either party become dissatisfied with the agreement at a later point. The designation of a mediator for any disputes should also be included in that document.

CASES REEXAMINED

Two of the cases from the opening section of the chapter are now analyzed using the codes and related literature.

Roxanne and Li Qing

In this case, the client, Li Qing, innocently began attending the same church that her counselor, Roxanne, frequents. When her counselor discovered the coincidence, she disclosed her membership to the client and initiated a discussion of the issue in a counseling session.

Because Li Qing is a current client, the remarks in the codes clearly apply. Roxanne has a responsibility to avoid exploiting the client's trust and misusing her influence, or otherwise risking harm to the client. Now Roxanne must decide whether their attendance at the same church is likely to result in any of those negative outcomes. Too little information is given to determine whether bringing the topic up for discussion in session is a wise idea. Its wisdom depends largely on the client's emotional stability and particular problems, about which the case description doesn't give enough information. It also depends on the capacity of the counselor to respond in an appropriate way immediately after being surprised by this revelation. After all, there is no urgency to deal with this topic at this juncture. As long as the counselor can hold another session before the next church service, or refrain from church attendance until she analyzes the problem and decides whether to discuss it with her client, the topic can be postponed.

Several other factors should be considered before the counselor makes a judgment about the appropriateness of continued mutual participation in the church. The size and sense of community in the congregation is important. In a large congregation with multiple services, the two people could arrange not to attend functions simultaneously. A small congregation with one weekly service and strong sense of community would present more complications for both parties. In the latter circumstance, one option for the counselor would be to temporarily suspend her churchgoing until counseling with this client was terminated. Another alternative would be to attend services at a different church for the same period. One alternative seems clearly unethical—to ask the client to choose another church. Li Qing's choice of this congregation seemed to be driven by her therapeutic goals and made without knowledge of the counselor's affiliation. Suggesting that the client select another church might impede future progress and be especially difficult for a shy client to resist.

If, in the end, both parties decided that this dual connection is appropriate and workable, they would need to follow the code to be sure the client's best interests were protected, including the practical management of times when they met at church functions. Even if the dual relationship is not judged problematic, Roxanne should avoid extensive personal contact with her client at church. For example, she ought not to co-chair a committee with her client, or spend every social hour after church in conversation with Li Qing. The interactions at church should be cordial, brief, and not too frequent, for the duration of the professional relationship at least. To answer questions from other church members who wonder how they became acquainted, they also should prepare a response that does not include divulging their professional relationship. These arrangements should be documented, and Roxanne should obtain ongoing case supervision to ensure the continuation of objective, competent care. The therapist has a responsibility to make a judgment about the advisability of this dual relationship independent of her client's current expressions about the matter. The client may not foresee the potential problems, may have motives for desiring personal contact that would be counterproductive to real change, or may simply be mouthing words she believes the counselor wants to hear. The client's expressed feelings should be taken into account, of course, but they should not be the only factor considered. The burden to analyze all the considerations falls on the shoulders of the counselor, not the client.

Mr. K and the Teacher's Request

Mr. K, the parent of an elementary school child, is approached by his son's teacher (Mr. Goodheart) to provide counseling for a depressed friend of his. Mr. K responds by giving the teacher his business card and suggesting he tell her friend to call to set up an appointment.

Does Mr. K's connection through this prospective client's friend make this a dual relationship to be avoided? Because the case deals with a prospective client, it undoubtedly falls within the purview of the codes. The crucial issue is whether his connection to the teacher will impair his judgment, impede the progress of therapy, or affect the client's capacity to relate to Mr. K or to otherwise benefit from therapy. There is a relatively little chance that this distant a connection will cause such problems, but more information is needed to make a definitive judgment. At a minimum, Mr. K ought to have asked Mr. Goodheart some questions about his relationship with this person and about his understanding of the rules of confidentiality should the friend accept a referral. The nature of the connection between the prospective client and the teacher is not clearly stated. The term *friend* has a wide range of meanings. This man could be someone the teacher is simply acquainted with, or it could be his life partner. The latter circumstance would make the dual relationship more problematic, as Mr. Goodheart would have a very big stake in the progress and outcome of counseling and may even need to be involved in joint counseling sessions to resolve relationship difficulties. In that case, the dual-relationship risks become much more likely. Even if the connection between the teacher and his friend is less intense, the counselor would have an obligation to clarify to all parties involved the boundaries between contacts and to reassure the client about the confidentiality of counseling material.

Next a responsible resolution of this case also requires more information about the child and the family's frequency of contact with the teacher. If Mr. K's son is an ordinary child whose parents need not be closely involved with his school, that circumstance would argue for the choice Mr. K made, but if the child's characteristics require the family to have intense, frequent, or conflictual contact with school personnel, that would argue for a more cautious approach. In the latter circumstance, Mr. K would be advised to go forward with the referral only if the relationship between the teacher and the prospective client is not especially close.

Finally, because of the potential complications, the prospective client may be reluctant to enter counseling with a person his friend knows or may simply wish to see a different counselor. Perhaps he knows he would wish to discuss counseling sessions with Mr. Goodheart, but would hesitate if he chose Mr. K as his counselor, or perhaps he would rather see a female counselor, or someone who is older. In other words, because Mr. K cannot anticipate the client's preferences and because his ultimate commitment should be to the client's welfare rather than his own financial gain, Mr. K's ideal action would be to give the teacher one or two other names of competent professionals, even if he also provides his own card.

Analysis of Other Cases

To promote independent ethical reasoning, the analysis of the other cases is left to the individual reader. Note that a number of the other cases do not have clear-cut answers, and it is quite possible for responsible professionals to come to somewhat different conclusions about the ethics of a given case. Referral to the ethical decision-making model presented in Chapter 2 and discussion with others about the issues involved may be particularly useful.

SUMMARY

Effective, beneficial counseling depends on the therapist's ability to provide objectivity and single-minded commitment to the client's welfare. It also depends on the client's ability to trust the counselor. Implicit in that trust is confidence in the counselor's selfless interest in the client and a sense of emotional closeness to the professional. When a counselor has an additional personal or professional relationship with a client, objectivity, selfless commitment to the client, and client trust are all endangered to some degree. In other words, when a counselor is both friend and researcher or therapist and teacher, the counselor is putting him- or herself in a conflict-of-interest situation. Both parties in the professional relationship may be hampered in reaching their therapeutic goals by the existence and demands of the other relationship. Having more than one relationship with a person with whom there is or has been a professional relationship is called a *dual relationship* in counseling, and a *multiple relationship* in psychology.

The ethical difficulties of dual relationships are most apparent in therapeutic relationships, but they are often inappropriate in other forms of professional contact as well. Nonsexual dual relationships with clients seem to occur more frequently than sexual relationships, according to researchers. The professions' ethics codes discourage most forms of dual relationships and prohibit some entirely. The criterion on which they base this judgment is the counselor's duty to promote the client's welfare without undue risk of harm. Multiple connections with clients impair counselor objectivity, interfere with therapeutic progress, and affect the client's emotional connection to the counselor. They also can intensify the power difference between counselor and client, and can result in exploitation of clients. Dual relationships have these effects partly because the obligations and expectations from different roles are often inherently incompatible. The more divergent the obligations of two roles, the more likely the dual relationship will be unethical.

Because not all dual relationships can be avoided, especially in rural settings, counselors need to examine carefully whether to start a particular dual relationship. Clients' access to alternative competent care ought to be considered, along with cultural variables and the potential for an individual to benefit from counseling despite the multiple connection. Generally, though, the attitude of the mental health professional should be to prevent risk (Sonne, 1994). High-risk relationships should not be initiated even if they have the potential to do good. If the relationship cannot be avoided, the counselor should discuss the implications and risks of the situation with the client, and then carefully document both that discussion and the subsequent progress of counseling. The counselor should seek expert supervision and develop an alternative plan in the event of unforeseen complications. If counselors find themselves frequently engaging in dual relationships, they need to examine their motivation and become more creative in finding alternative access to care for the clients involved.

Bartering—trading goods or services instead of money for counseling—is also a practice discouraged by the ethics codes, but not entirely forbidden. Bartering represents a form of a dual relationship in which the counselor becomes either the employer or customer of the client, and hence is ripe for abuse and dissatisfaction. A professional who is entertaining a bartering relationship with a mental health client should read the professions' codes carefully and should consult his or her state laws and regulations. Some states forbid the practice, and some professional liability insurers exclude claims resulting from a bartering arrangement.

DISCUSSION QUESTIONS

1. Why do you think the codes of ethics are silent on the issue of nonsexual dual relationships with former clients? Do you think they should take a stand on this topic, and if so, what position do you think best?

2. Research shows a great diversity in professionals' opinions about the ethics of nonsexual dual relationships, in contrast to their views of sexual contact with clients. What do you think accounts for this diversity? Do you think it is healthy?

3. Do you agree with the standards written into the codes of ethics about nonsexual dual relationships? Would you recommend stronger or more lenient wording? Why?

4. Friends, social acquaintances, and business associates frequently ask counselors to accept them as clients. Sometimes counselors do, taking the view that their preexisting knowledge of the client can facilitate therapeutic progress. They believe that in such relationships, trust occurs more easily and insight happens more quickly. Is their position justifiable? How would you respond to a colleague who made such an argument?

5. Should bartering of services be distinguished from bartering for goods in the ethics codes? Is this a real distinction or a semantic one? What would you describe as an ideal standard on this issue?

6. What stance do you think you will take on accepting gifts from clients? Do you agree that this topic should be included in informed consent? How would you feel if your counselor initiated this kind of discussion at that point in the process?

7. Given the literature on accepting gifts from clients, how would you evaluate the ethics of counselor gifts to clients, for example, at termination?

RECOMMENDED READINGS

Anderson, S. K., & Kitchener, K. S. (1996). Nonromantic, nonsexual posttherapy relationships between psychologists and former clients: An exploratory study of critical incidents. *Professional Psychology: Research and Practice, 27,* 59–66.

Borys, D. S., & Pope, K. S. (1989), Dual relationships between therapist and client: A national study of psychologists, psychiatrists and social workers. *Professional Psychology: Research and Practice, 20,* 283–293.

Gibson, W. T., & Pope, K. S. (1993). The ethics of counseling: A national survey of certified counselors. *Journal of Counseling and Development, 71,* 330–336.

Herlihy, B., & Corey, G. (1997). *Boundary issues in counseling.* Alexandria, VA: American Counseling Association.

Simon, R. I. (1992). Treatment of boundary violations: Clinical, ethical and legal considerations. *Bulletin of the American Academy of Psychiatry and the Law, 20,* 269–288.

9

Group and Family Counseling
Unique Ethical Responsibilities

The fundamental ethical values and standards that guide individual counseling are also at the core of group and family counseling. However, four distinct features of group and family practice are essential for counselors to understand if they wish to honor these standards. Some of these features are obvious to any observer, but others reveal themselves only after thoughtful reflection. First, in such therapy the client is encouraged to disclose personal information not only to a therapist, but also to others who are not licensed mental health professionals. Under these circumstances, admitting personal secrets feels (and is) riskier. The others to whom this personal information is revealed may not respond sympathetically, may be judgmental, or may use that information in ways that are counterproductive to the client. Because the only person in the room who can be held accountable for misusing the information is the mental health professional, a client must rely completely on the good intentions of others in the group to act responsibly. Both a high level of trust of others and a strong expectation of benefit from such disclosures are required for active participation in a group. In family therapy, the audience to whom a client discloses personal information is obviously quite familiar, but that familiarity does not necessarily reduce the risk for the participant. Indeed, family members have more opportunity to misuse that information than do strangers in a group.

Second, the very dynamics of therapeutic change are different in multiple-person therapies. In individual counseling, the relationship between the two parties, coupled with the interventions used, results in therapeutic change. In group and family counseling, effectiveness is based largely on the interdependence that develops among all participants (Lakin, 1994; Yalom, 1995). Growth stems from the help and support group members give each other as much as from the activities of the group leader (Morran, Stockton, & Bond, 1991). Typically, feedback from peers in a group has significant impact on members (Corey & Corey, 1997). Given this facet of therapy, group and family therapists have a duty to help clients develop an interdependence that empowers rather than weakens them. The skills and ethical sensitivities necessary for this task differ substantially from those required by individual counseling.

Third, a counselor leading a group or family counseling experience also has less control over events that take place during or between sessions. The counselor cannot always predict how participants will respond to other members, nor can he or she even be aware of all the interactions among members. The dynamics of this phenomenon are obvious in family therapy where clients have continuous contact with each other, but are no less real in group therapy. For example, a few group members may continue a discussion initiated in a session over coffee afterward or may telephone each other to offer additional support between sessions. Paradoxically, though, this lessening of control does not necessarily result in less power for the counselor. Clients in group therapy can also become excessively dependent on the leader if that counselor manipulates group process to foster such dependency. Family members may fall into the practice of deferring all decisions until the counseling session and may use the words and actions of the therapist as the sole influence in arriving at a decision.

Finally, research shows that group and family counseling are especially powerful interventions, with the capacity for greater good or greater harm than many forms of individual counseling, depending on the particulars of the situation (for example, see Lambert & Bergin, 1994; Yalom, 1995). Kottler (1994) maintains that the emotional intensity of group therapy in itself makes group treatment more powerful. Moreover, groups and families lend themselves to interventions that may be inherently riskier (Lakin, 1994) than the approaches that dominate individual work. For instance, families frequently delay so long before entering counseling that problematic patterns resist change and often require more forceful interventions if goals are to be achieved. Group and family therapists sometimes seek out innovative interventions that can break through the blocks to therapeutic gains. This drive to provide therapeutic benefit to these clients must be balanced against the inherent risk in newer, riskier, and less proven techniques. In such situations, the principle of nonmaleficence should take precedence over beneficence.

This chapter examines the implications of these distinct features of group and family counseling on the ethics of practice in these domains. It also explores the applicability of the concepts discussed in previous chapters—competence, informed consent, confidentiality, and dual relationships—to multiple-person therapies. First I discuss the ethics of group counseling. Next the focus turns to family and couples counseling. Finally, the chapter ends with a brief description of the legal issues affecting these modalities.

Group Counseling and Psychotherapy

The ACA and APA codes of ethics make relatively brief references to group counseling and psychotherapy. Specifically, the ACA code refers to three responsibilities. The first is to screen prospective members for compatibility with the group, the second is to avoid harm, and the third deals with confidentiality. (The standard for confidentiality in groups is presented later in the chapter.)

ACA *Code of Ethics,* **Section A.9: Group Work**

a. Screening

Counselors screen prospective group counseling/therapy participants. To the extent possible, counselors select members whose needs and goals are compatible with goals of the group, who will not impede the group process, and whose well-being will not be jeopardized by the group experience.

b. Protecting Clients

In a group setting, counselors take reasonable precautions to protect clients from physical or psychological trauma.

Ethics scholars have criticized the codes' failure to attend to the many other distinctive features of groups (for example, see Lakin, 1994), but there are other sources of guidance for the practitioner in this domain. First, there are the guidelines published by the Association for Specialists in Group Work, or ASGW (1989), a division of ACA. This document identifies 16 separate ethical responsibilities of group leaders. (See Appendix E for a copy of this code.) The precepts presented in this document provide extensive advice about specific procedures group counselors should use from the orientation and screening stage of a group to termination and follow-up. They also describe the practitioner's obligations regarding continuing education and referral of clients to other services. The ASGW document ends by elaborating on the counselor's responsibility regarding the reporting of unethical behavior. The American Psychological Association published standards for therapists of growth groups in 1973, and that document is still useful to those who lead such groups today.

The second resource is the body of literature by ethics scholars that comments on the codes (for example, see Corey, Williams, & Moline, 1995; Forrester-Miller & Rubenstein, 1992), gives in-depth analysis of particular ethical concepts (for example, Davis, 1980), and elaborates on the application of group ethics to certain kinds of groups (for example, see Aubrey & Dougher, 1990; Merta & Sisson, 1991). This growing body of research and theory offers the practitioner thoughtful analysis of some of the most thorny issues in group work. Taken together, these resources compensate for the omissions in the other codes and guide the practitioner to a solid understanding of his or her ethical duties in group settings.

Competence and Group Counseling

Obviously, competent group counseling requires a mental health professional with knowledge of group theory, process, and research, with successful experience in leading groups under supervision, and with a diligent attitude toward the work. Sometimes, though, counselors and therapists mistakenly conclude that their competence in individual counseling transfers directly to the group setting. Such a conclusion is unfounded. Effective leadership of a therapeutic group demands a background in this particular modality because of the power of the experience, the vulnerability of the client to harm from both leader and other participants, and the potential for negative outcomes inherent in group settings. The Association for Specialists in Group Work has published *Professional Standards for the Training of Group Workers* (1990) to assist mental health training programs and professionals interested in developing this competency. This document delineates the knowledge base and skills essential for professionals who wish to lead groups. It specifies both the content and skills required at a basic level of competence and the capacities required by the various kinds of therapeutic groups, ranging from task-oriented and psychoeducational groups to long-term psychotherapy groups. For example, this document defines the following information as essential knowledge for competent group counselors:

- Comprehension of the major kinds of groups and the criteria to be used in assigning clients to membership in each
- Knowledge of the fundamentals of group dynamics and the therapeutic aspects of a group
- Understanding of how the personal characteristics of group leaders affect the group and how professional ethics apply to group situations
- Familiarity with the research on group process and outcome
- Comprehension of group stages and the roles members take on
- Knowledge of the circumstances that make groups beneficial or contraindicated for clients, and the criteria for recruiting and screening potential members
- Mastery of current definitions of group work, its purposes, and four major forms
- Appreciation of the role of evaluation in group process

It proceeds to elaborate details of essential skills and minimum levels of supervised experience. The message of these standards is that brief and cursory exposure to group theory and practice is insufficient for competent practice.

Many counselors and therapists fail to monitor their own competence in this area. Lakin (1994) decries the casual attitude of many professionals toward the complexities of group process. He labels involvement in group leadership without appropriate competence a serious ethical violation and illustrates his reasoning with examples. For instance, Lakin argues that a group counselor needs a comprehensive understanding of the role of group cohesion in fostering therapeutic progress. Helping the members develop enough cohesion to be beneficial without transforming group cohesion into pressure to conformity is a difficult task. Inadequately trained professionals either fail to foster enough cohesion, or overemphasize it and make the group suffocating for some members. Lakin cites other unique aspects of groups, such as the encouragement of emotional expression or the formation of subgroups and scapegoating, which also require a skilled therapist with good judgment. Otherwise, genuine emotional expression becomes false emotionality pressured by the group and has little therapeutic value.

Corey and Corey (1997) stress that a professional's competence to lead a group depends partly on the particular kind of group involved. A person who is qualified to lead a substance abuse group may not be competent to lead a long-term psychotherapy group or an assertiveness group. In other words, no blanket statement of competence covers all group situations. Counselors must always evaluate the match between the type of group under consideration and their prior training and experience.

The literature also suggests that not all clients can benefit from groups. In fact, some can be harmed by participation (Yalom, 1995). Counselors need the knowledge to identify such people and direct them to other types of counseling, or to other kinds of groups. They must also be able to judge when a group is not profitable for a member and must take effective action to remedy the problem or refer the client to another source of assistance.

Finally, mental health professionals who lead groups are obligated to update their skills and knowledge lest they lose the competence they have established. The ASGW code mandates participation in professional development activities related to group leadership, echoing the standards presented in the ACA and APA codes on working to keep professional knowledge and skills current (ASGW, Executive Board, 1989, Section 16).

Informed Consent in Group Counseling

Because group counseling involves additional risks and responsibilities beyond those typically experienced in individual counseling, informed consent is crucially important. The informed consent process for groups begins with orienting the client to counseling, an activity that occurs before the beginning of the group sessions and that also involves screening prospective group members. As with individual counseling, developing informed consent in groups should include describing the goals, techniques, procedures, limitations, risks, and benefits of the group. Counselors should make a special effort to ensure that prospective clients understand the roles of the therapist and other group members in a successful group, as well as their personal responsibility to be active in helping other group members. Clients also need to know the characteristics of a typical group session and the expectations of members in those sessions. If the group is one in which emotional expression will be encouraged, clients should be told of this emphasis. Group sessions can be quite intense, and that intensity can be exhilarating or exhausting, or both. Clients who are prepared to expect an intense experience may not only make better choices about participation, but may also better tolerate and learn from that climate.

Corey and Corey (1997) list risks specific to group counseling that should be explained to prospective group members, including

- Scapegoating
- Group pressure to disclose private material
- Discomfort with confrontation or inappropriate use of this approach in the group
- Negative effects (even temporary) in the client's lives stemming from the group experience

Some groups that employ physical techniques have injured clients. Any group that involves such techniques must also disclose this potential risk.

The practical matters regarding fees, times and locations of meetings, duration of the group, and so forth, should be addressed. If insurance is to be billed for group sessions, all aspects of informed consent relevant to third-party payors as described in Chapter 6 should be reviewed. If a co-leader is to be used, as often happens, explaining this fact to clients is an obvious aspect of a fully informed consent to participate. The client ought to be given an opportunity to learn the co-leader's qualifications and to meet the co-leader before the group, to ask him or her questions. In addition, if a co-leading arrangement is used, clients should understand how leaders will communicate with each other about clients.

Because group cohesion is such an important feature of an effective group, clients should also appreciate the degree of commitment asked of them when they decide to join a group. In a group, clients, too, are therapeutic agents for others, and they need to understand that their regular attendance and active involvement are necessary for the group's success. The delicate issue of dropping out of the group should be openly discussed. This is a delicate issue because all clients have the right to refuse to continue counseling if they wish, but most group leaders want members to maintain membership at least until an individual has reached his or her goals for the group experience (Corey, 1995; Yalom, 1995). Part of what makes a group beneficial in the eyes of experts on this modality is its power to help clients work though difficult emotions and stick with commitments to others. When people drop out prematurely, they rob themselves of the opportunity for that important personal learning and they diminish group cohesiveness and the group's potential to be helpful to other members. Most leaders, therefore, ask members to attend at least one final session to tell the others of their decision to terminate (Corey et al., 1995). The goal of that session is to help the member reach some degree of closure to the group process, to limit the damage to group cohesiveness, and to improve the chances that the group will continue to have therapeutic value for those who remain. The not-so-hidden agenda in the final session is to encourage the person to change his or her mind and remain in the group (Kottler, 1982). When group leaders hold such a view about the importance of a "proper" termination process, they must inform prospective clients about it and help them understand its rationale. With that knowledge, clients are then empowered to accept or reject the conditions of membership the leader has set forth. The legal concept of informed refusal (the right to reject offered services without penalty) also operates in groups. No group leader can ethically or legally mandate participation if an individual wishes to withdraw. Thus the goal of this portion of informed consent is to enlighten without biasing, and to encourage without pressuring. Clients should feel free to act in ways they believe are in their best interest.

Confidentiality in Group Counseling

The counselor's duty to maintain the confidentiality of client communications is unchanged in group counseling. However, the fact that nearly all of what is disclosed is communicated before other group members complicates both the ethics of confidentiality and the legal interpretation of privilege. As already discussed, other group members cannot be held accountable as professionals are held accountable if they violate confidentiality. Group members who keep confidences may do so out of a personal moral standard, a commitment to the group process, and/or some fear of group censure.

Even though group counselors cannot guarantee confidentiality, they are still obligated to do their utmost to encourage it. That responsibility usually entails thoroughly explaining of the role of confidentiality to each prospective group member, describing the specifics of its operations, and asking for a commitment to honor confidentiality at all times in the group. The ACA standard on group confidentiality reads as follows:

> **ACA** *Code of Ethics,* **Section B.2.a: Group Work**
> In group work, counselors clearly define confidentiality and the parameters for the specific group being entered, explain its importance, and discuss the difficulties related to confidentiality involved in group work. The fact that confidentiality cannot be guaranteed is clearly communicated to group members.

Most group scholars also recommend that leaders remind group members about confidentiality both at the first group session and periodically throughout the group process (ASGW, Executive Board, 1989; Corey & Corey, 1997). Those intermittent reminders should be given immediately after particularly intense or risky sessions. Corey et al. (1995) emphasize that the issue of inadvertent disclosures should be addressed along with deliberate infractions, because even well-intentioned members may be vulnerable to accidental violations.

A practical approach to ensuring that members have the skills and judgment to avoid both kinds of disclosures involves role-playing situations that tempt members to violate confidentiality. In this simulation, one person might take the role of a friend who asks the group member about the identities of other group members and another person role-plays a response. Group members themselves might develop scenarios they think could happen in their lives and role-play them in group. Ideally, such role-playing would take place fairly early in the group process. Its result should be to give individual members confidence in their abilities to honor their promise to confidentiality and to increase trust in other members' commitment to secrecy. Group counselors may also opt to develop orientation videos that highlight confidentiality and show simulations of members coping with temptations to break confidence.

Some group counselors use contracts for confidentiality that members must sign to become part of the group. These written contracts clarify expectations and symbolize the importance of confidentiality to the therapeutic process. They are a visible representation of the value the leaders place on this facet of group behavior. The use of confidentiality contracts is supported by some ethics scholars (such as Arthur & Swanson, 1993; Corey et al., 1995), but preliminary research suggests that most practitioners do not favor them (Roback et al., 1992). These researchers found only 23% of group therapists in their survey actually used them. Such documents may be underused in practice, but the reasons for this problem are uncertain.

The limits of confidentiality that apply to individual counseling, elaborated in Chapter 5, are all transferable to group settings. The duty to warn and protect, to report child abuse and neglect, to respond to a court order for confidential information, and to answer charges of unethical or illegal behavior made by clients all hold for group counseling. Therefore, all prospective members need to be informed about these limits to confidentiality so that they freely choose what information to disclose to whom. Special care should be taken in explaining the fact that the counselor's duty to confidentiality does not extend to other members of the group. Counselors need to help clients understand the risks they are undertaking as well as the potential benefits of the group experience.

Unfortunately, there is a paucity of published research on compliance with this standard. The one published study that attended to this question found only 32% of group therapists who explicitly discussed the risks of disclosure of private information by other group members (Roback et al., 1992). What accounts for this reluctance? No empirically based answer can be given yet, but Roback and colleagues (1992) hypothesize that group leaders are concerned that such information would discourage people from entering groups or from revealing personal material during sessions. However well intentioned the motivation for such a stance, it is inconsistent with existing ethical standards. Disregard of this standard could also spell legal trouble. Roback et al. point out that consciously deciding not to discuss the limits to confidentiality could be interpreted as deliberately misrepresenting the risks of the process, for which a group counselor could be held liable in the courts.

There is still another reason for informing clients about this limit. When violations do occur, the group often experiences at least a temporary setback in cohesion and productivity (Roback et al., 1992). In addition, after such a breach some members permanently retreat from active involvement in group process. These negative outcomes argue strongly both for an emphasis on prevention by completely and explicitly discussing this issue with prospective group members, and for a backup plan for recovery from such harm if prevention fails. Logic also suggests that it would be difficult to avoid mentioning this aspect of confidentiality if a group leader had thoroughly oriented group members to the crucial importance of confidentiality.

Legal considerations also argue for comprehensively discussing confidentiality. The degree to which the material disclosed by any client in a group setting is considered privileged varies considerably by state. Generally, courts have held that any statement made in front of third parties is not covered by privilege (Paradise & Kirby, 1990; Swenson, 1997). A few states honor a therapist's privilege in group settings to the same level as in individual therapy, but others view a communication shared before other parties as sharing it in a public place. In such jurisdictions, a counselor has no defense against discussing it in a courtroom. In still other states, including Minnesota, a special kind of group privilege has been established (Gregory & McConnell, 1986). Because of the changing nature of state statutes, counselors are well advised to stay current with the laws and regulations in their state.

Of course, privilege typically applies only to the licensed professional in the session. There is rarely any privilege for other group members who heard the same information as the counselor, so they can be mandated to testify even if the mental health professional cannot. Explaining this reality to prospective members is essential. Failure to do so conflicts with their right to make autonomous decisions about activities that affect them. Lest clients become overly concerned about some legal risks, it is important to balance this explanation of risk against the low probability that it will occur. Clients need not be unduly frightened about a very-low-probability event. Court cases involving group counseling or therapy are relatively rare (Paradise & Kirby, 1990), and few counselors or participants have actually had to testify against a group member. That should not foster complacency, but if history is any guide, the level of that risk is very small.

The Ethics of Dual Relationships in Group Counseling

The prohibition against sexual contact with clients obviously extends to group counseling, as does the standard of avoiding other forms of dual relationships. Although the dynamics of therapeutic change differ in groups, the therapist's power is not significantly reduced. Social, personal, business, or other connections with current clients can compromise the leader's professional judgment and objectivity and can affect the client's emotional response to the group. In addition, dual relationships with group members can diminish group cohesion when other members suspect that one of their own has a special relationship with the leader. Such contacts can also engender more hostility toward the leader and distract the group from productive activities.

The Ethics of Concurrent Individual and Group Counseling

According to Taylor and Gazda (1991) and Lakin (1994), the practice of seeing the same clients in both group and individual counseling, or of gathering one's individual clients together into a group happens rather frequently. A client may also start out in group and then be seen individually, while the group continues. Professional codes do not address this behavior. Lakin (1994) reports that most practitioners see no ethical problems with it. However, Lakin (1994) has identified several important potential difficulties with concurrent individual and group counseling:

- Risks to confidentiality and privilege because of communications between co-leaders or difficulty remembering which disclosures were shared in which setting
- Interference with the client's emotional relationship with the counselor and with transference, including "sibling rivalry" among group members and an increased risk of countertransference from the leader
- The creation of an overpowerful therapist and an overdependent client, resulting in a higher probability of misuse of therapeutic power
- The financial gain for referring to oneself that blinds a counselor to the client's real needs (Lakin, 1994; Taylor & Gazda, 1991)

Taylor and Gazda list actions mental health professionals can take to minimize these risks, the most central of which are informed consent to concurrent counseling, careful monitoring of the counselor's power and the client's dependence, and scrupulous attention to the client's well-being. Supervision and consultation also seem crucial. Regardless of the precautions taken, the dangers of this practice should be acknowledged and prudent counselors would be well advised to consider it "as a last resort." If individual therapy is needed for a group member, a referral elsewhere should be considered. Similarly, when therapists are entertaining the idea of gathering their clients together into a group, especially an open-ended therapeutic group, those professionals ought to examine their motivation, get supervision or consultation, and be prepared to accept responsibility for problems that develop.

The Ethics of Involuntary Group Participation

Both the ASGW *Ethical Guidelines* (1989) and ethics scholars discuss the complicated ethics related to involuntary group participation. Courts, treatment facilities, and other agencies often mandate participation in a group. The person involved theoretically has a choice, but the alternative is so unappealing that the person sees no other realistic course of action. A neglectful parent may be required to attend a parenting group as a condition of maintaining custody of his children, or a woman arrested for driving while intoxicated can "choose" between an alcohol education group or a criminal record. A person who enters a hospital for treatment of bipolar disorder (manic depression) may learn that participation in daily group therapy sessions is a condition of treatment. Without the group involvement, the person cannot receive the individual counseling or medication management that he or she really seeks. In each instance the person agrees to group participation as the "least worst alternative." The fundamental question underlying this practice, as noted in Chapter 6, is whether informed consent is really possible in the absence of a completely free consent, and whether it is ethical for mental health professionals to make such demands on clients. Neither the major codes nor the ASGW guidelines address this basic issue for group counseling, implying (but not explicitly stating) that the benefit the person and the society can receive from the group outweighs the temporary loss of autonomy about this decision. The ASGW guidelines (1989), (Section 4) read as follows:

> Group counselors inform members whether participation is voluntary or involuntary.
>
> Group counselors take steps to ensure informed consent procedures in both voluntary and involuntary groups.
>
> With involuntary groups, every attempt is made to enlist the cooperation of the members and their continuance in the group on a voluntary basis.

The last statement indicates that even though the association seems to accept involuntary groups and does not deem them unethical, it is uncomfortable with the concept and encourages leaders to do all they can to help involuntary clients understand the benefits the group may have for them. Corey and Corey (1997) point out the practical benefits of that approach—the potential for the therapeutic work of the group to be advanced is severely limited if individuals do not have at least a basic level of commitment to the group. Involuntary clients who feel tricked and manipulated into group membership are unlikely to profit from the experience. Thus most writers on the subject highlight the importance of dealing with the clients' feelings about involuntary participation both in screening sessions and early in the life of the group. They should be allowed to express their frustration about the loss of autonomy and their fears or reservations about the group. Corey et al. (1993) suggest that the chance to openly discuss these feelings may reduce resistance and increase cooperation.

Developing informed consent is especially important with involuntary clients. Explicit attention to all aspects of the group is needed, along with a review of the rights the person retains. If the degree of a client's involvement in the group is to be reported to a court or public agency, the client should understand that fact and the implications of his or her behavior in the group for subsequent actions by those agencies. To return to the example of the parent who joins a group as a condition of retaining custody of his children, if the counselor must report to the child protective agency that the man has been silent and uninvolved in group sessions, the man should be informed of that fact. If the counselor knows from experience that such a report is likely to reduce the chances that the client will keep his children, the counselor should also tell the client that.

In short, the central message in acting consistently with the ethical values of the profession while accepting nonvoluntary clients into groups is that the counselor must zealously guard the client's remaining rights and work energetically to help the client make a free choice for participation. If that is not possible, at least the counselor should aim for fully informed consent about the ramifications of the client's reaction to the mandate. If a counselor believes that mandated group counseling is unlikely to benefit the client and may bring harm, the counselor then has an obligation to communicate that professional judgment to the parties demanding participation and to work toward an alternative therapeutic placement satisfactory to all involved.

Ethical Issues in Multicultural Groups

Few groups are truly homogeneous. Most include people of different religions, cultural background, ethnicities, gender, physical capabilities, sexual orientation, and age. Sometimes the personal problem they share is all they have in common. Heterogeneous groups make group cohesion more difficult to achieve and make the leader's skill even more crucial to its accomplishment. Ironically, in diverse groups sometimes there is greater pressure for cohesion, and counselors must be alert to pressures for cohesion that are insensitive to cultural values (Corey et al., 1995). Similarly, counselors need to recognize how their own cultural backgrounds affect their values and their approach to building a cohesive group. APA's *Guidelines for Providers of Psychological Services to Ethnic,*

Linguistic, and Culturally Diverse Populations (1993b) is an especially useful resource for the mental health professional who seeks to develop these skills.

Sensitivity to diversity issues also increases the likelihood that members will be treated fairly. Fairness implies that there is no conscious or unconscious discrimination against members because of differences. For example, a client whose cultural background discourages intense emotional expression or direct confrontation must be given flexibility in responding to the tasks of the group and must not be ridiculed or labeled as dysfunctional because of this cultural background. Because cultural differences are not always apparent to others, counselors must work to protect the rights of all clients to dignified and fair treatment in the group. If leaders see other members scapegoating one participant because of cultural issues or otherwise behaving in insensitive ways, the counselor has a responsibility to intervene to stop that behavior. Leaders whose own behavior models respect for each client go a long way toward achieving the goal of sensitivity. In addition to sensitive attitudes and knowledge of cultural differences, group counselors are obliged to learn strategies for leading multicultural groups that increase the likelihood of success. Resources such as DeLucia et al. (1992), Johnson et al. (1995), and Merta (1995) discuss such strategies.

Family and Couples Counseling

Family and couples counseling is a separate discipline that demands significant expertise to practice competently. Thus the first tenet of ethical family and couples counseling is sufficient training and supervised experience in the field to be competent. Counselors without special courses and supervision in this area would be well advised to remedy those deficiencies before involvement in this specialty, to eliminate risks of ethical charges or malpractice claims for working beyond the boundaries of their competence (Corey et al., 1993).

Case Illustrations of Special Issues

The following scenarios represent fairly typical occurrences in the work of the family counselor. The pages that follow examine the ethical issues embedded in each.

Scenario 1
One participant in couples counseling telephones and asks for an individual appointment to share some information he thinks the counselor should know but that he wishes to keep secret from his partner.

Scenario 2
A wife calls for an appointment for family counseling because of family conflict over a teenager's rebellious behavior, but she cautions that her husband refuses to attend counseling, although he has agreed to the attendance of the other four members of the family.

Scenario 3

A couple asks for marriage counseling to save their marriage at all costs to each partner personally. They say their individual happiness and emotional well-being are secondary to staying married.

Scenario 4

A couple whose child was killed in a car accident 18 months ago recently separated. They begin couples counseling to see if there is any hope for their relationship. After a number of sessions, the counselor concludes that continuing the relationship would probably be destructive for one partner, but ending the relationship would probably be destructive for the other.

Scenario 5

After six individual counseling sessions, a client asks to begin couple counseling because she has realized that the crux of her problems is relational. Her partner is willing, and the counselor agrees with her assessment about the need to attend to relationship issues at this point. She asks to continue seeing the same counselor with her partner.

Scenario 6

A family with two parents and three children is experiencing significant conflict. The wife/mother started her own business a year ago. It has been quite successful, and the demands on her time are extensive. Her efforts to get some household chores reassigned to her partner or teenage children have not been successful. Two weeks ago, she got so upset that she went "on strike" from those chores. The whole family is now angry at her and frustrated with the chaos that has developed in the house. The husband/father has requested the appointment "to get this mess straightened out and get back to normal."

Scenario 7

A family counselor recommends that the parents of a 10-year-old who has refused to leave the house even to attend school should not continue to press the child to do any of the feared activities. In fact, the counselor suggests that if the boy shows any interest in those activities, the parents should not encourage that interest, but should remain entirely neutral. The counselor's message to the boy is that he seems to need this time at home and should not worry too much about his behavior. In fact, he probably should not force himself to do things he does not feel ready for. The counselor's rationale for this recommendation is grounded in the literature on paradoxical approaches in family therapy. In the three weeks since that recommendation was implemented, the boy has not attended school or left his parents' side at any time. So far, the child has shown no signs of interest in school or other activities. The parents have complied with the therapist's directions.

Scenario 8

A lesbian couple makes an appointment with a heterosexual counselor. The partners are considering adopting a child and wish to discuss the implications of their decision on their relationship and the child. Their motivation is to ensure that the transition to parenthood goes as smoothly as possible for all members of the family.

Scenario 9
A minister refers a couple from his church to family counseling because of domestic violence. The man has shoved, kicked, and pushed the woman around on numerous occasions during their 10-year marriage. The most recent occurrence took place five days ago. The woman approached the minister because she is worried about the effects of the violence on the children. The minister believes he could persuade both people to agree to family counseling. The minister reveals that the man was defensive when queried about the violence and tended to place a good part of the blame on his wife.

Scenario 1: Confidentiality of Disclosures to Family Counselors in Individual Contacts

The ethical standards of the American Counseling Association directly address this question:

> **ACA** *Code of Ethics,* **Section B.2.b**
> In family counseling information about one family member cannot be disclosed to another member without permission. Counselors protect the privacy rights of each member.

The code of the American Association of Marriage and Family Therapists (AAMFT) is even more detailed. (See Appendix F for a copy of the AAMFT Code of Ethics.)

> **AAMFT** *Code of Ethics* **(1991), Sections 2 and 2.1**
> Marriage and family therapists have unique confidentiality concerns because the client in a therapeutic relationship may be more than one person. Therapists respect and guard confidences of each individual client.
>
> Marriage and family therapists may not disclose client confidences except (a) as mandated by law; (b) to prevent a clear and immediate danger to a person or persons; (c) where the therapist is a defendant in a civil, criminal, or disciplinary action arising from therapy . . . ; or (d) if there is a waiver previously obtained in writing. . . . In circumstances where more than one person in a family receives therapy, each such family member who is legally competent to execute a waiver must agree to the waiver. . . . Without such a waiver . . . a therapist cannot disclose information received from any family member.

In contrast, the APA code is rather vague:

> **APA** *Ethical Principles,* **Section 4.03**
> (a) When a psychologist agrees to provide services to several persons who have a relationship (such as a husband or wife or parents and children), the psychologist attempts to clarify at the onset (1) which of the individuals are patients or clients and (2) the relationship the psy-

chologist will have with each person. This clarification includes the role of the psychologist and the probable uses of the services provided or the information obtained.

The APA standard recommends that psychologists be clear about their roles and the ways they plan to use information, but does not explicitly prevent psychologists from sharing material divulged by one family member in an individual session to the other family members in therapy. In their commentary on the code, Canter et al. (1994) do not address the meaning of this section in relation to Scenario 1, but suggest that if a psychologist sees family members in both individual and family sessions, separate records may be required for each (p. 94). Separate records imply boundaries among disclosures in each setting, but unfortunately, their commentary does not clarify this point. Nevertheless, given recent trends, a prudent psychologist would be well advised to keep individual communications private unless the right to confidentiality was waived, or the psychologist's procedure for handling such individual communications was fully explained in the informed consent.

The ambiguity of the psychology code reflects a debate in the professional literature that was particularly strong in the 1980s about the proper use of such individual disclosures. According to Margolin (1982) one side argued that maintaining secrecy let the therapist get more honest and complete information from family members, increasing the likelihood of an accurate assessment of family dynamics, and thus an increased potential for positive change. The other side contended that a nonsecrecy policy was wiser, because it prevented subgrouping and complicated transference relationships with the family therapist. Therapists holding this view would explain their policy at the beginning of family therapy so that all participants knew there would be no guarantee of confidentiality of material from other family members. The criterion the therapist would use for determining whether to divulge a particular secret was its effect on therapeutic progress and family welfare. The wording of the 1992 APA code suggests that this organization saw merit in each argument, but by 1995 ACA had come down clearly on the first side of the argument.

When these codes are applied to the first scenario, the ACA and AAMFT standards indicate that if the counselor hears the "secret" from the individual family member in a one-to-one conversation, the counselor is obligated to keep that information confidential, even from other family members, unless the client waives that right. Needless to say, in this situation the counselor has no duty to hear the secret communication and should decide how to respond to this client's request on the basis of clinical considerations and an assessment of what would be in the best interests of the family.

It is important to note that the codes do *not* indicate that it is unethical to conduct concurrent individual and family counseling. But if a counselor chooses to do so, a heavy burden to maintain the confidentiality of individual communications falls to the professional. Whatever the course of action taken, ethics scholars in family therapy advise a comprehensive approach to informed consent on issues of confidentiality (for example, Lakin, 1994) and privilege (Swenson, 1997).

Scenario 2: The Problem of Nonattending Family Members

Many theories of family therapy are rooted in the view that real improvement in the functioning of a family is fundamentally tied to the treatment of the whole family system (see, for example, Becvar & Becvar, 1996), and research evidence suggests that for some relational problems, this claim has validity (Patten, Barnett, & Houlihan, 1991). According to this view, the individual problems of family members stem from a dysfunctional family system. Therefore, meaningful change requires the participation of all family members. If one member refuses to engage in therapy, the probability that counseling will be of real benefit declines, because changes in the system are thus made so difficult. Some even argue that change is thus made nearly impossible (Minuchin, 1974; Napier & Whitaker, 1978). For these reasons, some family therapists experience the refusal of one member to participate as both a clinical and an ethical dilemma. The codes of ethics are silent on this subject, but practitioners still wonder—should the members who want counseling be served because they have the desire, or should counseling be postponed until the reluctant member changes his or her view? How actively should the counselor work to involve the nonengaging person?

Scholars in family therapy have suggested a wide range of answers to these questions, but the recommendations of Teisman (1980); Wilcoxin and Fennel (1983); and Miller, Scott, and Searight (1990) are especially useful. All suggest efforts to remove the obstacles to the nonattender's participation without coercing involvement or interfering with that person's autonomy rights, which include the following:

- Taping a session with the other family members for the nonparticipating individual to review, with the goal of helping that person gain more knowledge of the process. (Consent of the other family members to taping is required, of course.) If misperceptions or fears are at the core of the refusal, this procedure might be effective (Teisman, 1980).
- Writing a letter to the nonattending person, explaining the family therapy process and describing the changes that may take place in the rest of the family as a consequence of counseling based on the research evidence. The letter acts as an invitation to reconsider the refusal, both as a gesture to help others in the family, and as a way of promoting his or her own interests. When a signed copy of this letter is returned, the therapist proceeds with family therapy even if the document is not persuasive to the nonattender (Wilcoxin & Fennell, 1983; Miller et al., 1990).
- Offering a single individual session with the nonattender to help that person understand the concerns and allay fears and misperceptions of counseling (Teisman, 1980).
- Referring other family members for individual therapy until the whole unit is available (Wilcoxin & Fennell, 1983).

The goal of each of these methods is to inform, demystify, and open the family counseling process to the reluctant person. Any of these methods can be misused to coerce participation, and such action would be clearly unethical. The counselor must approach this person with respect for his or her rights and with a recognition that the resistance to therapy may serve an important function both for that individual and for the family.

Scenarios 3 and 4: Conflicts Between Individual and Family Welfare

As the stigma of divorce has faded, counselors hear pleas to save a marriage at all costs less frequently than they probably did 20 years ago. Yet the words are still voiced often enough to be of concern to ethics scholars and practitioners in this field. This request asks the counselor to overlook the pain and dysfunction that maintaining the relationship causes the partners and focus exclusively on continuing the marriage. Sometimes this desire is grounded in religious convictions. At other times it occurs because of fears of change, worries about losing daily contact with children, or a dysfunctional mutual dependency. At still other times, the narrow focus on continuing the marriage is the agenda of a counselor who equates divorce with treatment failure (Margolin, 1982). In Scenario 4, the situation is somewhat different—the relationship is helping one partner and harming the other. Nevertheless, the ethical issue of how to respond to negative effects on the individuals involved is at the center of both cases.

Scholars in marriage and family counseling point out that the ideal interests of individuals are likely to conflict somewhat with the best interests of the family (Margolin, 1982; Patten et al., 1991). Promoting individual and family development simultaneously is not always possible. Still, coping with minor compromises in individual functioning for the good of the family is a different order of problem from that presented in these scenarios. The first section of the AAMFT code states,

> Marriage and family therapists advance the welfare of families and individuals. They respect the rights of those seeking their services, and make reasonable efforts to ensure that their services are used appropriately." (Section 1)

This section enjoins professionals to aim for increased well-being of all involved in therapy, despite the practical problems and minor deviations already noted. Engaging in family counseling to save or prolong a marriage that is inherently harmful to at least one participant (Scenario 3) does not appear to be an appropriate use of the service. That is not to suggest, however, that it is the role of the counselor to advise the couples to divorce. The AAMFT code is explicit on that point:

> Marriage and family therapists respect the rights of clients to make decisions and help them to understand the consequences of those decisions. Therapists clearly advise a client that a decision on marital status is the responsibility of the client. (Section 1.4)

Ethics scholars in family counseling generally concur on this point (for example, see Gurman, 1985). When caught in such dilemmas, counselors should carefully assess the degree of harm they believe will ensue from continuing the relationship. If it represents a serious and continuing harm for either member, counselors should discontinue work on that goal. Instead, counselors should frankly discuss their reservations with both members. No counselor should participate in an activity that seriously compromises a person's mental health even if that person wishes the activity to continue.

Scenario 5: The Ethics of Consecutive Individual and Family Counseling

Consecutive individual and family counseling is not unethical as long as several conditions are met. First, the counselor has judged that such a sequence would be beneficial to the client and has the competence to engage in both activities. Second, an appropriate informed consent procedure has been conducted so that the client understands the different risks, benefits, procedures, and confidentiality issues of relationship counseling, especially the professional obligation to keep confidential information shared during individual counseling, unless the client waives that right. Finally, a similarly careful informed consent procedure has been undertaken with the partner as well. As counseling progresses, the counselor must be alert for any issues that may arise because of the different histories of contact with the counselor. The partner needs time to develop the same level or trust as the original client, and the counselor should make a special effort to get a good independent assessment of the partner's functioning in the relationship. Communications from the original client about the partner are not likely to convey a fully accurate picture of that person. In addition, the counselor should be alert for signs that either partner views the counselor as "taking sides" or for negative feelings the original client may develop in "sharing" the counselor with the partner.

Scenario 6 and 7: The Influence of the Counselor's Beliefs and Values About Gender Role Socialization and Sexual Orientation on Diagnosis and Treatment

No counseling process is value free. Family counselors have definitions of good and poor functioning, healthy and unhealthy communication, and normal and abnormal ways of relating. In fact, without these definitions, no therapeutic work could take place. As long as one distinguishes between desirable and undesirable change, one is invoking values. Sometimes family counselors have beliefs about healthy families that are too rigid and narrow and that fail to allow for individual differences. Research by APA (APA, Task Force, 1975) has shown, for example, that family counselors tend to view behaviors that are nontraditional for women as less acceptable than traditional behavior. For example, they tend to assume that women will be better adjusted if they remain married than if they do not, and that a woman's extramarital affair is more serious than a man's. Guterman (1991) and Sekaran (1986) also suggest that counselors are frequently less sensitive to the demands of a woman's career than to those of her partner's. In other words, evidence suggests that family counselors have not been immune from the effects of gender bias and that in the way they work with families they have attempted to perpetuate existing norms. Some scholars have argued that family therapists have a responsibility to change sexist patterns in their clients (and themselves, of course) (Hare-Mustin, 1980), but others caution against a campaign to change client beliefs to those the therapist endorses (for example, see Wendorf & Wendorf, 1985).

The goal of the responsible counselor in dealing with family issues related to gender role is to respect the client's autonomy on the matter as much as possible, and to identify the ways in which the family's conceptualization of gender roles may be related to their dysfunction. In Scenario 6, the family therapist will need to help the family members communicate and renegotiate their mutual expectations. There are two pitfalls to be avoided—blaming the husband and children for not respecting the woman's right to change her responsibilities in the family, and assuming that the woman really should be taking responsibility for her household chores just because she's "the wife." The therapist should help the family develop a response to the changing family circumstances that respects each member's human rights and recognizes each person's responsibilities to the family. Counselors should consult the *Principles Concerning Counseling/Psychotherapy with Women* (Fitzgerald & Nutt, 1986) for a fuller discussion of these issues.

Counselor values clearly come into play in Scenario 7 as well. The codes of ethics of ACA, APA, NASW, and AAMFT all explicitly prohibit discrimination on the basis of sexual orientation:

ACA *Code of Ethics,* **Section A.2.a: Nondiscrimination**
Counselors do not condone or engage in discrimination based on age, color, culture, disability, ethnic group, gender, race, religion, sexual orientation, marital status, or socioeconomic status. [Similar statements are also found in Section C.5.a of this code.]

APA *Ethical Principles,* **Section 1.10: Nondiscrimination**
In their work-related activities, psychologists do not engage in unfair discrimination based on age, gender, race, ethnicity, national origin, religion, sexual orientation, disability, socioeconomic status, or any basis proscribed by law.

AAMFT *Code of Ethics,* **Section 1.1**
Marriage and family therapists do not discriminate against or refuse professional service to anyone on the basis of race, gender, religion, national origin, or sexual orientation.

NASW *Code of Ethics,* **Section 6.04d**
Social workers should act to prevent and eliminate domination of, exploitation of, and discrimination against any person, group, or class on the basis of race, ethnicity, national origin, color, sex, sexual orientation, age, marital status, political belief, religion, or physical or mental disability.

Thus, counselors should be prepared to respond to the request of this couple for preparenting counseling, as they would for any other couple. The decision to accept them as clients should be based on clinical considerations. The counselor should not use their sexual orientation as a basis for decision making. If the counselor had competence in the area and had knowledge about the literature relevant to this particular couple's concerns (for example, see Rohrbaugh, 1992), the couple should not be turned away simply because they are not heterosexual. If the counselor's personal beliefs about homosexuality prevent the counselor from providing objective professional service, then the counselor is responsible for locating competent referral sources to assist this couple with their request. A counselor who accepted this couple with the intention of "getting them to change their minds" because the counselor thinks lesbians should not be parents, would be violating these sections of the codes and the fundamental values of autonomy and respect for human dignity at the core of the values of counseling professions.

Scenario 8: The Ethics of Risky Interventions

In this situation, the therapist is using a variation of a paradoxical technique: It seems both illogical and inconsistent with the obvious therapeutic goals of the family, yet it is used for therapeutic gain. The therapist is seeking to dissipate the energy from the client's resistance to change and to remove the secondary gains the boy may be receiving for his school refusal. Therapists sometimes apply this technique when more traditional approaches seem unlikely to produce immediate results. Lakin (1994) points out that there is a deceptive element to its use because the therapist does not really want the child to be housebound, nor does he wish to eliminate the parents' concern for their son. He needs to persuade the family that such behaviors are desirable, but does not fully disclose to them that it matters little to the therapist whether the family complies with the recommendation or not. In a paradoxical approach, the theory is to set up a "win–win" situation in which some therapeutic gain is made regardless of the family's reaction to the intervention. If the family complies, the boy's behavior loses its attention-gaining value for the child and the boy's energy to resist his parents' wishes may be lessened. Both of these changes represent progress toward a therapeutic goal. If the boy does not comply with the suggestion to stay home and the parents react favorably to the child, the family still "wins" because they have achieved what they sought.

The use of such techniques has sparked a fierce debate in the professional literature. Some scholars have questioned their effectiveness (for example, see Sexton, Montgomery, Goff, & Nugent, 1993), their ethics (for example, see M. C. Henderson, 1987; Ridley & Tan, 1986) and their implications for the reputation of the profession (for example, Lakin, 1994). Stevens-Smith and Hughes (1993) also warn that the use of paradoxical techniques may foster an unhealthy dependence on the counselor. Others have defended their value, contending that they are important tools to systemic change (see Haley, 1976; Wendorf & Wendorf, 1985). The most provocative elements of the approach are its deceptiveness, its manipulative quality, and its risk of negative outcomes. Lakin (1994) asserts that the dishonesty in this intervention contradicts the honest, forthright communication that counselors seek to help clients develop. Haley (1976) referred to such methods as "benevolent lies," but others question whether such deceptions can ever be truly benevolent. Problems also arise with the significant risk of misuse by incompetent or overzealous professionals. Moreover, such interventions are inconsistent with informed consent and autonomy. Clients cannot consent to the object of a therapeutic deception, however well intentioned.

This scenario also underscores the risk of paradoxical approaches; they may be ineffective or even harmful. In this case, no apparent progress has made for several weeks and the boy has not developed the kind of impatience with his confined existence that the therapist hoped for. The parents may be waiting patiently for change or may be starting to question the competence of the therapist. People frequently stop counseling prematurely, and if the parents get discouraged enough they may even drop out of counseling and seek other methods to help their son. Even if they do continue in counseling, perhaps the ineffectiveness of this method will reduce their compliance with future interventions, as their confidence in the expertness of the counselor may be shaken.

When counselors use paradoxical approaches, they are deciding, at least temporarily, not to use other approaches. If a counselor chooses this nontraditional intervention over a method with more evidence of efficacy, then he or she may be violating the client's right to the best possible service at the lowest possible risk. Nontraditional approaches with limited evidence of effectiveness are justifiable only when more proven approaches are unsuccessful or unworkable.

For all these reasons, paradoxical techniques should be used with great caution. They are a method of last resort, at least until the evidence of therapeutic value is clearer. In addition, if a paradoxical intervention is ever used, it may be wise to "debrief" clients after the intervention, just as one debriefs participants in research projects that involve deception. For additional recommendations about responsible use of such approaches, consult Huber and Baruth (1987), Sexton et al. (1993), and Solovey and Duncan (1992).

Of course, paradoxical techniques are not the only powerful interventions used in family counseling. Family sculpting, a procedure in which the relations between members are acted out by creating live sculptures of the people in a session, can also have powerful—and sometimes unpredictable—effects (Lakin, 1994). Other interventions that evoke strong emotions or uncover feelings long held secret can also leave the client vulnerable to harm. Family counselors have a responsibility to carefully consider the ramifications of such approaches. Consultation with colleagues about the wisdom of using the method with a particular family is well advised, along with diligent monitoring of the intervention's effects on each participant.

Scenario 9: The Ethics of Family or Relationship Counseling Concurrent with Domestic Violence

Effective family therapy requires that participants feel free to share their ideas and feelings in session and to enact behavior change between sessions. Honest, direct communication between family members is the cornerstone of this modality. When one partner is being abused by the other, the foundation for successful therapy is gone. Fearing the consequences, the victim cannot express his or her true thoughts or feelings or risk behavior change. Victims who risk such disclosures in sessions may end up being re-victimized. In addition, one defense that victimizers frequently use—that the other partner provoked the abuse—is not really challenged when the problem is framed as a family issue. In such a context, it is harder to get abusers to take responsibility for their actions. Thus, most scholars recommend avoiding family therapy while there is ongoing abuse (for example, see Houskamp, 1994). Instead, family counselors should see partners individually so each can explore his or her own needs. Joint sessions can be initiated after the abuser takes responsibility for the abuse and begins to rehabilitate, and the victim begins to feel some power and control. Because not all families that are experiencing domestic violence freely disclose it, counselors should stay alert for signs of this problem in the assessment and screening phase of family counseling.

Legal Issues in Family Counseling

The most common legal issues for family counselors relate to divorce and custody. Many families and couples in counseling decide to divorce, so it is not surprising that family counselors get drawn into the legal battles. One partner's attorney commonly tries to get the counselor to testify about the other partner's mental health and stability or about what happened in counseling. Obviously, the ethical duty to confidentiality applies here as in other forms of counseling, and some states may even protect communications in family counseling as privileged. Nevertheless, counselors are advised to be explicit during informed consent about confidentiality and privilege. They should explain to clients, preferably in writing (Stevens–Smith & Hughes, 1993) that they regard the family unit as the client, not any individual members. They should elaborate further the implications of that view for any future legal actions. Needless to say, family counselors should consult with their attorneys about such requests for information or testimony about clients whenever they occur.

Divorcing couples in custody disagreements sometimes attempt to get the counselor to take one side or the other in those battles. Counselors should use extreme caution under such circumstances. Evaluations of child custody arrangements require special competencies that many professionals have not developed, and even if the prior counselor has such competencies, an independent evaluator may better serve the purpose. The psychological evaluation of the children and the fitness of the parents often significantly influence the court's decision. In addition, the role of influencing the court's decision about child custody is a very different role from that of therapist for the couple. The perspective obtained from doing the therapy may not give an especially clear view of the child's best interests. Consequently, counselors are well advised to discuss the counselor's role in any custody conflict when developing informed consent. The AAMFT code does not touch on this issue, but the ACA and APA codes use virtually identical wording in stating their standards:

APA *Ethical Principles,* **Section 4.03: Couple and Family Relationships**

(a) When a psychologist agrees to provide services to several persons who have a relationship (such as husband and wife or parents and children), the psychologist attempts to clarify at the onset (1) which of the individuals are patients or clients and (2) the relationship the psychologist will have with each person. This clarification includes the role of the psychologist and the probable uses of the services provided or the information obtained.

(b) As soon as it becomes apparent that the psychologist may be called upon to perform potentially conflicting roles (such as marriage counselor to husband and wife, and then witness for one party in a divorce proceeding), the psychologist attempts to clarify and adjust, or withdraw from, roles appropriately.

Increasingly, courts are also using family counselors to act as expert witnesses, and to assist in divorce mediation and child custody evaluations. Typically, these roles do not involve a preexisting relationship with any of the people involved. The obligation of the family counselor who provides such services is to give competent, honest, objective advice to the court, and to ensure that all people being evaluated understand that the counselor is assisting the court and is not in a therapeutic relationship with the client.

Recent years have seen an increase in the number of ethics complaints against psychologists serving in these roles (APA, Committee on Professional Practice and Standards, 1995), and much negative press has been written about mental health professionals who act as "hired guns" for attorneys. Professional associations have published guidelines to help professionals act ethically in such activities, and ethics scholars have written widely on the subject. Counselors asked to act in these roles should become familiar with this literature in order to make responsible decisions about such roles. Some of the most helpful materials are listed in the recommended readings at the end of this chapter.

SUMMARY

Group and family counseling entail special ethical and legal challenges for counselors. These challenges include the competent use of therapist power in modalities that have significant potential for good or harm depending on the counselor's professionalism and the wise management of confidentiality issues in a setting where client disclosures cannot be guaranteed privacy. The emotional intensity of the setting, the powerful interventions commonly used, and the pressure for group cohesion can all have negative effects on clients if the counselor does not manage these aspects of therapy skillfully and sensitively. Confidentiality is complicated because other clients may reveal material discussed in session, and not all courts recognize privilege for professionals when other people also hear client communications. These additional risks and benefits make a careful and thorough informed consent process even more imperative in group and family therapy than in individual therapy.

Counselor values and biases significantly influence group and family therapy. Counselors therefore need to recognize how their personal values may interfere with productive counseling and base their work on the principles of respect for human dignity and individual differences. Personal beliefs about what constitutes a family, about gender roles, and about sexual orientation play especially central roles in family counseling. Counselors using group and family therapy should consult the codes of ethics of the Association of Specialists in Group Work, Executive Board (1989) and the American Association for Marriage and Family Therapy (1991) for additional guidance on ethical practice in these modalities.

DISCUSSION QUESTIONS

1. Research has shown that many practitioners choose not to use confidentiality contracts in group counseling. What do you see as the advantages and disadvantages of such a choice?

2. What do you see as the dangers and values of the methods that have been recommended to encourage nonparticipating family members to attend counseling?

3. Should a counselor conduct individual and couples counseling simultaneously with the same clients? Why or why not?

4. Many counselors regularly seek out co-leaders for their groups, because of the therapeutic value of dual leadership. Does co-leadership also have ethical value? In what way?

5. If a member drops out of a group and is unwilling to attend even one more session to obtain "closure," should a leader try to persuade that member to change his or her mind? How far can the leader go in doing so before violating ethical standards?

6. Sometimes families have problems because members have differing ideas about social role expectations. For example, a man may believe that his wife should take care of the home, whereas she believes that responsibility is shared. How can a family counselor ethically assist a family with such a conflict?

RECOMMENDED READINGS

Association for Specialists in Group Work (ASGW). (1990). Professional standards for the training of group workers. Alexandria, VA: American Counseling Association.

American Psychological Association, Committee on Professional Practice and Standards. (1994). Guidelines for child custody evaluations in divorce proceedings. *American Psychologist, 49,* 677–680.

Huber, C. H., & Baruth, L. G. (1987). *Ethical, legal and professional issues in the practice of marriage and family therapy.* Columbus, OH: Merrill.

Remley, T. P., Jr. (1991). *Preparing for court appearances.* (ACA Legal Series, Vol. 1). Alexandria, VA: American Counseling Association.

Swenson, L. C. (1997). *Psychology and law for the helping professions* (2nd ed.). Pacific Grove, CA: Brooks/Cole.

10

The Ethics of Assessment
Using Fair Procedures in Responsible Ways

Clients seek the professional help of counselors and therapists with two major goals in mind—to gain a better understanding of problems they have and to find ways to overcome those difficulties. The procedures that clients and counselors use to achieve the first goal are collectively called *assessment*. There is a wide variety of such procedures, ranging from clinical interviews to standardized tests, behavioral observations, mental status exams, data collections from significant others, and analysis of case records. Once these data are collected and evaluated, the counselor makes a professional judgment about their meaning. Ideally, assessment is collaborative: Both counselors and clients contribute to the judgment, although the specific language usually derives from the expertise of the professional. Assessments can be expressed in a variety of ways, depending primarily on the counselor's theoretical orientation and use of formal classification systems for emotional difficulties. The more accurate the assessment of the problems, the more likely that they will be successfully resolved.

Assessment is not limited to individual and group counseling. For example, consultants assess the strengths and weaknesses of organizations, school counselors assess students for eligibility to enroll in classes for the gifted, and educational psychologists assess the characteristics of effective learning environments. Whatever the setting, accurate, fair, and responsible assessment is the cornerstone of successful intervention.

Two aspects of assessment are especially vulnerable to abuse—the use of diagnostic categories to define client problems in individual, group, and family counseling, and the use of psychological and educational tests. The ACA *Code of Ethics* discusses these topics in separate sections, but the APA *Ethical Principles* groups them together. In both documents, assessment receives extensive coverage, to help professionals avoid the numerous ethical pitfalls in this area. This chapter attends to these ethical problems, elaborating on relevant comments in the codes, the views of ethics scholars, and related research evidence. The chapter also considers guidelines for ethical assessment in a multicultural society (a topic that is also discussed in Chapter 11) and the responsible use of computerized test interpretations. Finally, special emphasis is given to the recent trend toward using psychological tests in employment settings.

The Ethics of Diagnosis

To diagnose means to define in professional terms the nature, limits, and intensity of a problem a client brings to counseling (Patterson & Welfel, 1994). The professional names used to designate problems are derived from scholarly research and practice and are frequently found in compilations such as the *Diagnostic and Statistical Manual-IV,* or DSM-IV (American Psychiatric Association, 1994). However, the term *diagnosis* encompasses more than the medical model expressed in that compilation. Diagnosis involves any organized system for defining client problems that other therapists with a similar theoretical orientation or specialty would also know and use. For example, family therapists sometimes diagnose family system problems using typologies different from the DSM-IV, but they are still classification systems because other family therapists give the same problems the same names (Sporakowski, 1995). Whatever the classification system, diagnostic names provide a common language for mental health professionals and can guide them to appropriate interventions that improve functioning. Using common classification systems makes the findings of researchers accessible to practitioners and allows counselors to better use research advances to help clients.

Because of its association with naming and specifying problems, diagnosis has been pejoratively called "labeling" by some professionals, a term that implies that diagnosis is inherently dehumanizing and harmful. Some counselors caution against allowing diagnosis to distract from the human needs of the individual (Gladding, 1992). Even counselors who acknowledge the potential value of diagnosis are somewhat ambivalent about its application (Hohenshil, 1996). When diagnosis is wrongly done, such characterizations of diagnosis are not far from the mark. The history of mental health is replete with examples that show harmful effects when diagnosis is misused, but evidence also shows that when appropriately done, diagnosis can and does serve a valid and beneficial function for clients. In fact, effective, ethical treatment *demands* careful definition of problems. One cannot treat what one has not identified. The relationship between diagnosis and treatment is like that of a map for a road trip. One is more likely to reach the destination by following a map than by randomly selecting roads to see where they lead. The diagnosis is a map, a picture of the terrain that leads to a goal (destination), and a plan for reaching that goal (a sequence of roads to be taken). Thus, diagnosis is not a hindrance but a prerequisite for beneficial care for clients. Nevertheless, it is important to acknowledge both the debate on the validity of diagnosis as currently conducted, and the evidence that mental health professionals have sometimes misused the diagnostic processes (for example, see Pope & Vasquez, 1991; Valliant, 1984; Wakefield, 1992). Practitioners who are philosophically opposed to the term *diagnosis,* either because of its association with the medical model of disease or because of its potential for misuse, are free to substitute another term. Central here is the recognition of the value of carefully defined client strengths, weaknesses, and problem areas, not the acceptance of any particular word used to describe that process.

A Rationale for Emphasizing Ethics in Diagnosis

Ethics should govern the diagnostic process for many reasons. The most important is that applying a diagnostic name to clients' problems can powerfully affect their lives. It can affect many aspects of their functioning—self-esteem, career opportunities, eligibility for many kinds of insurance, vulnerability to rejection and ridicule by others, and educational placement. Some kinds of diagnoses also influence whether the clients' health insurance will reimburse them for counseling expenses, whether licenses to practice an occupation will be granted, and even whether the state will grant a person the right to drive a car. For instance, people who have been diagnosed as chemically dependent are often required by law to reveal that diagnosis when they apply for a driver's license. Similarly, some career options are unavailable to someone with a history of mental or emotional disorders. Of course, such discrimination is unlikely to be legal, but legal prohibitions have not eliminated such practices.

Second, diagnosis has ethical dimensions because it is an inherently imperfect process. Even though behavioral science has advanced substantially over the last 50 years, our knowledge of psychological functioning is still limited and our capacity to gather sufficient information about the functioning of a given individual is also restricted. In the real world, neither clients nor third-party payers usually engage in truly thorough assessment. (The increasing pressure of insurers and managed care companies for "instant" diagnosis is in itself an ethical dilemma—addressed in greater detail in Chapter 14.) As Anastasi (1992) points out, the human tendency to seek quick answers to dilemmas also flaws the process, as does the inclination of diagnosticians to emphasize information received early in the interview over data gathered later (Meehl, 1960).

The diagnostic systems currently used are also far from ideal. The research evidence supporting the categories is uneven, the categories themselves are often overlapping and inconsistent, and they are vulnerable to gender and racial bias (Comer, 1996). There are unresolved philosophical debates about what constitutes a dysfunction (Wakefield, 1992). These imperfections place a heavy burden on the practitioner trying to use the diagnostic system appropriately so that its flaws do not result in harm to clients. Even well-trained counselors do not always arrive at the same diagnosis for identical symptoms using the DSM-IV, partly because of the overlapping categories (for example, see Kirk & Kutchins, 1992).

Third, the mere existence of diagnostic identifiers means that mental health professionals may be biased in favor of using them, even when the diagnosis is unjustified. Two classic studies illustrate this tendency. One was conducted by Langer and Abelson

(1974). In this research, therapists were more likely to diagnose as psychologically disturbed people identified as "patients" than people labeled "job applicants." The other study, even more famous, is that of Rosenhan (1973), in which pseudopatients got themselves admitted to mental hospitals based on their statements that they had been hearing voices. Once admitted, they displayed no other symptoms and denied any recurrence of the voices. In fact, they were instructed to behave as normally as possible from admission forward. No pseudopatient was ever identified as normal by the staff despite some lengthy hospital stays, and all had psychiatric diagnoses on their charts at discharge, although some charts were marked "in remission." (Ironically, the regular patients often questioned the pseudopatients about the legitimacy of their problems, but the staff never voiced such concerns.) Although others have severely critiqued Rosenhan's research (for example, Spitzer, 1975), the point is that whatever its flaws, Rosenhan's study does demonstrate the tendency of mental health professionals to skew the information they receive to fit preexisting categories. The inclination to "pathologize" normal behavior can also be seen in less dramatic ways when counselors mistake normal feelings of bereavement for depression, or label ordinary adolescent rebellion as "conduct disorder." The counselor's first responsibility in assessment is to evaluate available evidence as objectively as possible, without presupposing that if a person is in the client role he or she must have a disorder. Counselors who jump ahead to naming a problem before they have verified that one exists are showing a bias inconsistent with the profession's ethics.

Fourth, in societies where stigma attaches to mental and emotional disorders or any kind of psychological problem, assigning an official diagnostic name to the client's pain can have powerful psychological effects in itself. Clients may feel ashamed or embarrassed, or resist such a designation, and their coping skills may be sorely tested. Clients may become despondent and erroneously conclude that they are hopelessly crazy or flawed. They may even act out in inappropriate or self-destructive ways. However, clients may also have a powerful positive reaction to the designation. Some may be relieved that there is a "name" for the confusing pattern of thoughts, feelings, and behaviors that they have been experiencing. Instead of engendering hopelessness, the name for their previously overwhelming problem encourages them to believe that they can be helped and stirs energy for real change. Thus, identifying what has seemed hopelessly confusing and unspecified can be a turning point in the therapeutic process. Regardless of the specific reaction, though, its strength means that counselors must act responsibly to communicate their assessments and help clients deal productively with them. Moreover, as noted earlier, the stigmatizing of mental health problems also places the client at risk for rejection or mistreatment by others.

Fifth, as Matarazzo (1986) points out, the process of arriving at the diagnosis, of prodding the client for details of his or her experience, is in many ways an invasion of privacy no less severe than a physical examination by a medical doctor or an audit by the Internal Revenue Service. Whenever a professional invades the privacy of another, certain conditions should exist: good reason for the invasion, potential for benefit, competent engagement in the activity itself, and the client's consent. Finally, not keeping information from the assessment confidential is a serious violation of the client's privacy.

Counselors often lose sight of the threat that diagnosis represents to clients. Raimy (1975) suggests that people who voluntarily enter counseling have two underlying worries in addition to their presenting problems. First, they fear that counselors will confirm their worst fear—that they are truly crazy. Second, clients mistakenly believe that the problems they have are so unique and distinctive from those of other people that no one else can possibly understand or help them. The latter belief means that clients expect to be misunderstood and to remain isolated from others. Coming to a clear definition of the problem evokes the first deep-seated fear: Clients think the diagnosis will confirm and make even more real their belief that they are crazy. Clients' second underlying worry sometimes results in a resistance to diagnosis, an incapacity to believe that others have indeed had similar problems. Eventually, a skilled and compassionate counselor can help a client revise such assumptions, but in the meantime the counselor needs to be sensitive to the invasion and threat that diagnosis and testing represent.

Sixth, diagnostic competence can lead to the temptation to misuse it. Specifically, it can lead to casual diagnosis, diagnosis of people with whom one does not have a professional relationship. For example, counselors and therapists may be tempted to use their diagnostic skills to interpret the behaviors of politicians, disfavored colleagues, troublesome students, or others in their personal lives. Those who do so may damage the reputation of the profession and lead people who may be considering professional help to wonder about how counselors will judge them. When mental health professionals succumb to the temptation to use diagnostic terms in casual settings, they encourage the misimpression that diagnosis is simple, magical, or dehumanizing. The APA code is the most explicit on this point: "Psychologists perform evaluations, diagnosis, or interventions only within the context of a defined professional relationship" (Section 2.01).

Still another misuse of diagnosis is to use it as a way to enhance insurance reimbursement for services rather than a way to an accurately state client problems. Pope et al. (1987) found that 35% of their sample admitted to this practice at least sometimes. Of these, 3.5% reported that they did so very often. Such behavior is not only inconsistent with ethical standards, it is also illegal, and would likely be called insurance fraud in most situations. Peterson (1996) notes that inappropriately using a diagnostic category to obtain insurance reimbursement is the most common type of financial misconduct to come before ethics committees, licensing boards, and the courts.

Diagnosis can also be used to harm or discredit people who are already objects of discrimination and disfavor in the society. As Weisskopf-Joelson (1980) noted, diagnosis can serve as a form of social control. She gives the example of labeling slaves who ran away from their masters as mentally disordered. Another problem with social diagnosis is evident in the tendency for members of minorities to receive more severe diagnoses than their majority counterparts for the same symptoms. For example, African-Americans and

Hispanics are more likely to receive diagnoses of schizophrenia than their European-American counterparts (for example, see NIMH, 1980; Manderscheid & Barrett, 1991; Pavkov, Lewis, & Lyons, 1989). In schools, ethical and legal challenges have been raised to many forms of educational and psychological testing, using evidence that such measures tend to discriminate against African-American and Hispanic children (Walsh & Betz, 1995). The now famous research by Broverman and her colleagues (Broverman, Broverman, Clarkson, Rosencrantz, & Vogel, 1970) first highlighted how professionals show gender bias against women. They found that mental health professionals used different adjectives to define a healthy male and a healthy female, but the same professionals used nearly identical adjectives to describe healthy males and healthy adults. In other words, the descriptions for healthy woman and healthy adult differed significantly. Their research pointed out the existence of gender bias in professional judgment about mental health and sparked a number of other studies that found similar conclusions. Gender bias in assessment does not always affect females alone, however. A study by Robertson and Fitzgerald (1990) illustrates this problem. These authors found that counselors diagnosed males in nontraditional roles in the home as more disturbed than males whose behavior aligned more closely with gender expectations. Other scholars suggest that the behaviors that are labeled as *disorders* or *dysfunctions* reflect the prejudices of society. Kaplan (1983) challenges the profession to explain why behaviors commonly found in women in Western society are labeled as pathological when parallel behaviors in men are not. She questions why the official nosology for psychiatric disorders identifies nonassertiveness and loyalty to loved ones even when they are cruel, as dysfunctional, but fails to categorize difficulty expressing feelings, resistance to emotional closeness, and aggressiveness in interpersonal relationship as disorders. The former characteristics are more common among women; the latter, among men. A final example is equally disturbing. Despite the fact that homosexuality has not been identified as a mental disorder since 1973, a national survey of psychologists (Pope et al., 1987) found that 5.3% of the respondents believed that treating homosexuality per se as pathological was *unquestionably ethical*. Several years later when counselors were asked to respond to the same item, 14% of them made the same endorsement (Gibson & Pope, 1993). Taken together, these findings amply demonstrate the vulnerability of misuse of diagnosis for people from minority or oppressed groups.

This research also shows that defining of a behavior as functional or dysfunctional does not take place in a social or cultural vacuum. A particular behavior must be understood in its cultural context. Behaviors that appear bizarre in one society are viewed as normal and desirable in another. The variability in bereavement responses across cultures illustrates this fact. In some cultures, uncensored emotionality is encouraged and seen as completely normal, while regarded in others as extreme and dysfunctional. Similarly, what one culture calls "appropriate assertiveness," another may label "disrespectful arrogance." Thus, counselors who fail to take into account the social and cultural components of current definitions of health and disorder may erroneously designate a normal behavior as symbolic of psychopathology.

Finally, a diagnosis can become a "self-fulfilling prophecy." A person with an erroneous diagnosis of major depression may begin to interpret his or her normal variations in mood accordingly, and may overreact to them. Others may begin to treat that person differently. In time, the focus on low mood can change behavior and thinking, and that person's ordinary bereavement or adjustment problems may grow into the depressive disorder it has been labeled.

In summary, diagnosis is a powerful tool that counselors must learn to use responsibly so that it can help rather than harm the client. Its misuse can stem from a variety of causes, but underlying them all seems to be an insensitivity to the implications of diagnosis, insufficient skill with diagnosis, or an ignorance of the limitations of current diagnostic systems.

Professional Ethical Standards for Diagnosis

The ACA *Code of Ethics* states the following about diagnosing psychological disorders:

Section E.5: Proper Diagnosis of Mental Disorders

a. Proper diagnosis

Counselors take special care to provide proper diagnosis of mental disorders. Assessment techniques (including personal interview) used to determine client care (e.g., locus of treatment, type of treatment, or recommended follow-up) are carefully selected and appropriately used.

b. Cultural sensitivity

Counselors recognize that culture affects the manner in which clients' problems are defined. Clients' socioeconomic and cultural experience is considered when diagnosing mental disorders.

The Ethics of Testing

The central ethical obligations in testing can be divided into (a) responsibilities of those who construct, market, and score psychological or educational tests, and (b) the responsibilities of mental health professionals who use tests with clients. Not only do the ACA and APA codes of ethics include extensive comment on these issues, but other guidelines and statements are also available for counselors and therapists, including the following:

- *Standards for Educational and Psychological Tests* (APA, 1985), the outcome of a joint effort of APA, the American Educational Research Association (AERA), and the National Council on Measurement in Education (NCME). This document is currently under revision, and the next version is scheduled for publication in 1998.
- *Code of Fair Testing Practices in Education,* published by the Joint Committee on Testing Practices (1988), a cooperative effort of the above-named organizations and

ACA, the Association for Measurement and Evaluation in Counseling and Development, and the American Speech-Language-Hearing Association.

■ *Guidelines for Computer-Based Tests and Interpretations,* issued by the American Psychological Association (1986).

■ *Statement on the Disclosure of Test Data,* published by the APA Committee on Psychological Tests and Assessment (1996).

Taken together, these documents give clear direction for responsible test construction and use. Familiarity with the terminology used in these standards facilitates their interpretation. A *test developer* is the person or organization that constructs and publishes a test. A *test user* is the professional who has decided to administer and/or interpret a test to a given population. A *test taker or examinee* is the person who will actually be completing the measure. We will first review the standards for test developers.

Ethics for Test Developers

The fundamental ethical directives for test producers are to use the best possible scientific methods in devising their measures and to keep the welfare of the consumer as their highest priority. Professional standards for those who produce and offer tests for clinical and educational applications demand that test developers prepare instruments with substantial evidence to support their validity and reliability, with appropriate test norms, and with a clear and complete test manual. According to this standard, an acceptable manual elaborates research evidence, describes appropriate applications, and honestly conveys strengths and weaknesses of the test. In addition, test developers are required to furnish evidence of the appropriateness of the test for groups of different racial, ethnic, and linguistic backgrounds. Current standards also encourage developers to provide data that will help users interpret results accurately and avoid common misinterpretations of results. Tests suited only for research should be clearly distinguished from those with clinical and educational applications. Counselors interested in developing a test for counseling or educational application should consult the most recent edition of the *Standards for Educational and Psychological Tests* for a full description of the kinds of data needed before a new test is distributed.

In their marketing activities, producers must truthfully represent the test and make the test available only to professionals who can show they are qualified to use it. In other words, their drive to profit from their creation must be superseded by their commitment to the welfare of the test's intended audience. Most test developers demand that people who buy tests provide evidence of their competence to use the measure responsibly. Users must typically disclose their degrees, licenses, graduate courses, and training in the use of the requested instrument. Graduate students seeking to use tests in completing theses and dissertations must name and provide information about the qualifications of the responsible supervisor. The research by Eyde, Moreland, and Robertson (1988) suggests that publishers' compliance with these standards is far from universal, but the counselors' obligation to limit their use of tests to those in which they have received training stands, regardless.

The ACA and APA codes delineate the following standards for test developers:

APA *Ethical Principles,* **Section 2.03: Test Construction**

Psychologists who develop and conduct research with tests and other assessment techniques use scientific procedures and current professional knowledge for test design, standardization, validation, reduction or elimination of bias, and recommendations for use.

ACA *Code of Ethics,* **Section E.12: Test Construction**

Counselors use established scientific procedures, relevant standards, and current professional knowledge for test design in the development, publication, and utilization of educational and psychological assessment techniques.

Ethics for Test Users

Those who give tests have two sets of people to whom they have ethical obligations: test developers and test takers. Our discussion begins with a description of the former. Because virtually all tests are copyrighted and dependent on the unfamiliarity of test takers with their particular items, test users have a duty to protect the security of a test from unwarranted uses. This obligation means that counselors must keep testing materials in their possession and prevent copying or other forms of dissemination of test items. Test developers have typically made a substantial investment to develop a valid and reliable measure of a construct. Thus they have a right to fair profit from that creation, and a right to control the ways in which that material is disseminated. If counselors learn of others who are violating this obligation, they are mandated to act to prevent such misuse of tests. For example, if a school counselor sees a teacher revealing test items to students in her class, the counselor must intervene to stop the practice. He or she must then determine whether the extent of the breach of test security was sufficient to invalidate the anticipated use of that measure.

This standard means that the practice of sending a standardized test home with clients to complete at their leisure is incompatible with the duty to protect test security and to attempt to obtain valid results from test takers. Surprisingly, many professionals seem unaware of this prohibition. Pope et al. (1987) reported that 24.3% of the psychologists they sampled sent tests such as an MMPI home with clients to be completed. Counselors seem equally ignorant. In a recent study 26% of counselors failed to see the ethical problem in sending a test home with a client (Gibson & Pope, 1993). As soon as clients walk out of the office with the test, counselors have lost control of it and have no guarantee that the measure will be returned to them or properly used. Sending a test home with a client is unsatisfactory for clinical reasons as well. In this circumstance the counselor has no assurance of the conditions under which the client took the test. The client may have failed to follow instructions, violated time constraints, or consulted with others about test items that ought to have been independently completed. In fact, counselors cannot even be certain that the test results they receive were those of the client. Perhaps a roommate or family member answered the questions, or perhaps responding to the items became a group project, with extensive discussion of the appropriate responses. If any of these events occur, the counselor cannot trust the meaningfulness of the results and the entire enterprise has become useless and counterproductive. Consequently, counselors should be resourceful about finding ways to get clients to complete instruments under more controlled conditions. If necessary, they should postpone the testing procedure until such arrangements can be made. The ACA code is quite explicit on this point:

ACA *Code of Ethics,* Section E.7: Conditions of Test Administration

a. Administration conditions

Counselors administer tests under the same conditions that were established in the standardization of the tests. When tests are not administered under standard conditions or when unusual behavior or irregularities occur during the testing session, those conditions are noted in interpretations, and the results may be designated as invalid or of questionable validity.

c. Unsupervised Test Taking

Counselors do not permit unsupervised or inadequately supervised use of tests or assessments unless the tests or assessments are designed, intended, and validated for self-administration and scoring.

Because tests are copyrighted, it is both unethical and illegal for mental health professionals to attempt to use such materials to develop their own tests or otherwise plagiarize existing measures. Counselors who are tempted to extract items from various published tests to create their own measure of a construct should refrain from such behavior. Test publishers may seek legal redress, and the practice violates a counselor's obligation to respect the rights of professional colleagues. The reliability and validity of such a homemade test are also unknown, rendering its scores meaningless as well. Both the ACA and APA standards address this issue, using almost identical wording:

ACA *Code of Ethics,* Section E.10: Test Security

Counselors maintain the integrity and security of tests and other assessment techniques consistent with legal and contractual obligations. Counselors do not appropriate, reproduce, or modify published tests or parts thereof without acknowledgment and permission from the publisher.

APA *Ethical Principles,* Section 2.10: Maintaining Test Security

Psychologists make reasonable efforts to maintain the integrity and security of tests and other assessment techniques consistent with law, contractual obligations, and in a manner that permits compliance with the requirements of this Ethics Code.

Finally, when counselors use tests, they are bound to store the instruments and related materials in a secure place so that people who should not have access to them are prevented from gaining it. A secure place would be a locked cabinet or room to which only the counselor has a key. If other people whom the counselor supervises are to have access to the test or assist in its administration, the counselor is obligated to ensure that they operate by the same standards of test security.

Obligations to Test Users

The ethical responsibilities of counselors to the people to whom they administer tests are extensive and deserve detailed discussion. The first duty is *competence*. Weiner (1989) has remarked, "it is possible in psychodiagnostic work to be competent without being ethical, it is not possible to be ethical without being competent" (p. 829). Testing procedures are deceptively simple to the untrained person. At first glance the interpretation of personality inventories, achievement test scores, or other measures appears straightforward and uncomplicated. That appearance is very misleading. The process of choosing the right test for the intended purpose and audience requires sound professional judgment and competence to understand test manuals and research data. Similarly, proper test administration is crucial to a meaningful outcome to the process. Proper administration requires more than the ability to follow test instructions; it also demands knowledge of how to adapt the testing conditions to unique client circumstances without jeopardizing the validity of the results. For instance, mental health professionals should know how to modify, without invalidating the results, the administration of an individual intelligence test to a person who stutters, and should then know how to account for this modification in a report of results. Finally, interpreting scores and communicating those findings to clients are often the most demanding tasks of all. The ethics codes and scholarly writings (for example, Anastasi, 1992; Pope, 1992) devote extensive attention to this topic.

What are the determinants of competence in these tasks? They are

- Formal study of the particular measures, including careful review of research, test manuals, and other related materials
- A background in statistics and measurement sufficient to understand the reliability, validity, norms, and descriptive data provided by the test publishers
- A knowledge of the strengths and limitations of the test and its proper applications with diverse populations
- A period of supervised experience in its use, including interpretation of the results to clients, after which a competent supervisor judges the counselor to be competent also.

The length of time for developing such competencies will vary depending on the background of the professional and the particular instrument. Instruction in complex personality tests such as the Minnesota Multiphasic Personality Inventory (MMPI) (Hathaway & McKinley, 1943), the MMPI-2 (Butcher, Dahlstrom, Graham, Tellegen, & Kaemmer, 1989), or the Rorschach (Rorschach, 1951) will require a significant investment of time and energy extending over many months. In our training program, for example, mental health counselors must have courses in statistics, educational measurement, psychopathology, and an introductory course on psychological testing before registering for the MMPI course. After successfully completing the MMPI course, they must enroll in an 11-week internship in testing in which they must administer, score, and interpret the instrument to appropriate clients. Their written test reports must be reviewed as well. Only after all these educational challenges are met are students deemed ready to use that test in practice. Even then, they are instructed that they should find additional supervision in testing until they are licensed. Of course, not all tests require this kind of protracted study, but each requires a similarly systematic approach to developing competence. Walsh and Betz (1995) suggest that the greater the likelihood that a test can be misused, the more stringent the criteria for competency should be. Rigorous, comprehensive knowledge is the minimum standard for true competence in using any test responsibly.

Possessing a particular graduate degree is not in itself proof of competence. Nor does competence in the use of one test or one group of tests imply competence in any other test. Competence must always be determined on the basis of the particular training and experience of a given individual with a graduate degree in a mental health field. Historically, psychology programs have tended to have stronger training in testing, but not all psychologists have graduated from programs that fit this definition. Similarly, counseling and social work programs have tended to be less thorough in this area, but particular programs may be exceptionally comprehensive in this domain. The judgment about competence then is always determined on the basis of the individual's experience and background.

Professional standards not only mandate that practitioners act responsibly themselves, but also that they intervene when tests and assessment procedures are used by those who are not qualified to employ them. (See the APA *Ethical Principles,* Section 2.06.) This mandate stems from the risk of misuse and harm to clients (APA, Committee on Psychological Testing and Assessment, 1996). The APA standard also states that psychologists should not take any action that promotes the use of assessment procedures by incompetent individuals.

In some states there have been legal challenges to the use of psychological tests by nonpsychologists, and some of the legal issues are not resolved (Marino, 1995). In Ohio, however, the state attorney general ruled against the position that only psychologists could use procedures labeled as psychological (Montgomery, 1996), thereby supporting the rights of other competent mental health professionals to administer tests. In any case, at this time, the ethical standard is competence, not type of license. Needless to say, counselors should follow legal developments in their states to ascertain the legal standard that affects them.

Anastasi (1988) describes a second important aspect of the ethics of testing. She argues that tests should meet a standard of *relevance* to the needs of a particular client. Tests are justified only when they are demonstrably relevant to the achievement of the client's goals. Testing for its own sake, or because of an institutional mandate, is inappropriate. As long as tests represent a stressor, invade privacy, and are subject to misuse by unskilled persons, the criterion of relevance must be met. Tests used for other reasons, such as research, may be used only with explicit informed consent to that use.

A third important ethical mandate for test users is *multiple criteria for decision making.* This means that tests never serve as the sole criterion on which clinical or educational decisions are based. Anastasi calls this the "hazard of a single score" (1992, p. 611). Tests are limited in their predictive ability and the occasions in which they present invalid or unreliable results are not always apparent to the test user. Thus, all decisions that will affect a client's future must be founded on multiple criteria. For example, depression should never be diagnosed on the basis of an elevated score on a test. Counselors must find independent corroborating evidence to make such a diagnosis. That evidence should come from multiple sources, ideally including personal interview, behavioral manifestations, reports from significant others, and so on. Ibrahim and Arrendondo (1986) cogently state this obligation, arguing that competent assessment should be "multisource, multilevel, and multimethod" (p. 350). In parallel fashion, no academic placement for a child should be completed on the basis of test scores alone. The likelihood of error and harm to the client from reliance on test data alone is simply too great.

Finally, counselors should understand their responsibilities when asked to make inferences on the basis of test results. In other words, they have a duty to acknowledge the limitations of tests in making inferences about behaviors not directly assessed by the test. A counselor may wish to know whether the test results support a diagnosis or whether they can help predict future violence or suicidality. Whenever asked to make such inferences, counselors recognize that they cannot be as sure of their judgments as they may be of their description of current functioning based on test results. Predicting future behavior is especially difficult. For example, a therapist can be more confident that an elevation on a depression scale indicates current dysphoria than that the elevation is an indicator of future mood. Thus, the comments of counselors related to such inferences must not go beyond the available evidence and must include material that acknowledges the limitations of tests whenever attempting to make global statements or predictions (Weiner, 1989).

The American Psychological Association has published a set of case studies of ethical issues in using tests that can help counselors examine the application of these ethical standards for test usage to specific situations (Eyde et al., 1993). Readers who plan to conduct testing as part of their professional practice are urged to consult this and the other resources listed in the recommended readings for further guidance.

Client Rights in Testing

Ethical standards delineate a number of rights for clients and accompanying responsibilities for the professionals, to ensure that client rights are protected. Foremost among these is the right to *informed choice* about tests. Clients should be informed about the purposes, tasks, uses, and implications of the proposed testing, including any risks and benefits that may result. If testing data will be used in any decision making, clients should be told about that potential. For example, if an MMPI will be employed to help determine a client's eligibility for a special treatment program, that should be disclosed. Similarly, if an educational test will have a role in deciding the appropriateness of special services, that information should be communicated to the child and the parents. Clients have a right to have their questions about a test answered, although test items and other data that might compromise test security or the validity of results should be excepted from this general guideline. If copies of test reports are to be kept in a client's file, that should be explained as well. Needless to say, clients should also understand that they have the right to refuse testing or to withdraw their consent at any time. The specific wording of the ACA code is as follows:

> **ACA** *Code of Ethics,* **Section E.3: Informed Consent**
>
> a. Explanation to clients
>
> Prior to assessment, counselors explain the nature and purposes of assessment and the specific use of results in language the client (or other legally authorized person on behalf of the client) can understand, unless an explicit exception to this right has been agreed upon in advance. Regardless of whether scoring and interpretation are completed by counselors, by assistants, or by computer or other outside services, counselors take reasonable steps to ensure that appropriate explanations are given to the client.

The APA code does not deal separately with informed consent to assessment. Section 4.02 identifies therapy and "related procedures" as needing informed consent and thus should be applied to assessment.

The ACA code highlights another aspect for informed consent. Section E.7.d states, "Prior to test administration, conditions that produce most favorable test results are made known to the examinee." In other words, clients should be told the conditions that might produce the most favorable results, if research indicates such a set of circumstances. For example, if research suggests that sufficient rest and a positive test-taking attitude are likely to improve performance on an achievement test, clients should be told about the influence of these factors before the testing.

The second client right is to *feedback* about the results of the testing. For many years, feedback was regarded as optional, left to the discretion of the professional. In some hospitals and outpatient clinics, new clients were routinely given a battery of tests without any provision for feedback. Some counselors even believed it unwise to share such data. As recently as 1983 Berndt found that only a minority of clinicians were enthusiastic about providing feedback. Others in his study favored a limited amount of feedback, with some stating that they shared only positive results. A few of Berndt's respondents indicated that practical considerations prevented feedback, implying that regular feedback was an unrealistic goal in the real world. The consumer rights movement was one important factor in changing that view, but there are still sites where this right is not honored. The current standard is clear, however—unless a person waives his or her right to feedback before testing or if a law prevents it, the professional is bound to provide an interpretation of the results. The codes state the following:

APA *Ethical Principles*, Section 2.09: Explaining Test Results

Unless the nature of the relationship is clearly explained to the person being assessed in advance and precludes provision of an explanation of the results (such as in some organizational consulting, preemployment or security screening, and forensic applications), psychologists ensure that an explanation of the results is provided using language that is reasonably understandable to the person being assessed or to another legally authorized person on behalf of the client. Regardless of whether the scoring and interpretation are done by the psychologist, by assistants, or by automated or other outside services, psychologists take reasonable steps to ensure that appropriate explanations are given.

ACA *Code of Ethics,* Section E.1.b

They respect the client's right to know the results, the interpretations made, and the bases for conclusions and recommendations.

Direct communication with the client about results has been mandated for several reasons. First, tests are fallible and clients ought to have an opportunity to respond to erroneous or misleading conclusions. The opportunity to correct such errors is especially important if test data will influence decisions made about the client's future. Discussion of results also assists the counselor in evaluating the reliability and validity of findings and in accurately interpreting subtle or confusing findings from the test. A moderate elevation on the L (lie) scale of the MMPI may mean that the test taker was attempting to create a good impression in a very unsophisticated way, or it may mean that the person has had an unusually strict religious upbringing. A discussion with a client about historical or current life circumstances can also help the counselor decipher the more accurate interpretation of that scale and state with greater confidence the meaning of test scores.

As Matarazzo (1986) notes, testing is not always easy for a client. The process often raises anxiety about the results, pushes clients to focus on uncomfortable aspects of their experience, and is often tedious and intellectually demanding. Counselors, who have typically thrived in academic settings and testing situations, tend to overlook the onerous connotation of the task for clients whose academic experiences were less rewarding. For some clients, the effort expended just to read the words on the page is substantial. Even for clients who are at home with the intellectual aspects of testing, there are still costs. For example, a person suffering from depression or anxiety must work exceptionally hard sometimes just to focus enough to answer the questions and stay on task. In short, clients are making a considerable investment when they agree to testing, and clear, accurate feedback in language they can understand is a fair return for that investment.

A final reason for conducting a feedback session is that there is some evidence that it has therapeutic value. In one study (Finn & Tonsager, 1992), clients who received feedback on their MMPI results experienced significant reductions in symptoms and distress. They also reported no negative consequences from the feedback; instead, they were overwhelmingly positive about the experience. This finding is consistent with the views of other scholars that feedback benefits client–counselor rapport, client cooperation, and good feelings about tests and about mental health professionals (for example, see Dorr, 1981; Finn & Butcher, 1991; Fischer, 1986).

Pope (1992) identifies three reasons why counselors are sometimes reluctant to give feedback: (1) because they find giving bad news uncomfortable, (2) because they do not want to do the hard work of translating technical jargon into language the client can understand, and (3) because the test results do not contain the kind of clear and unambiguous findings the client has hoped for (p. 268). When experiencing such reactions, counselors should seek out advice and supervision about how to proceed skillfully and responsibly. If such reactions occur frequently, a counselor's competence in using the test is probably less than adequate, because competence in testing necessarily includes the capacity to explain negative findings sensitively, to translate jargon easily, and to discuss the limitations of tests openly.

The professional standards are rather vague in describing precisely what is meant by feedback. Does it mean sharing every descriptor associated with every scale? Does it require both verbal and written feedback? Can it be limited to a few sentences of general comments? How can the obligation to feedback be balanced against the publisher's right to security for the test? The general guideline that seems most prudent is to provide as full a description as time, interest, and test security allow, omitting or postponing review of results that the counselor judges would be harmful to the client's current well-being. It is important to note that the codes do not require feedback under all circumstances. If a counselor chooses to omit discussion of particular aspects of a test, the counselor's decision must be based on an objective consideration of the client's welfare, not on a wish to avoid an uncomfortable undertaking. Such a judgment should stand up to the "clean well-lit room standard" and be periodically reviewed so that if a client's state of mind changed to be receptive to those findings, the counselor would be in a position to disclose them.

When presenting feedback to clients, counselors are obliged to remind clients about the fallibility of tests and to present results in the form of hypotheses rather than conclusions. The test does not contain "absolute truths" about them; rather, it offers hypotheses that may be helpful in understanding their concerns and behavior and in suggesting treatment strategies. Counselors should prepare carefully for feedback sessions and be fully familiar with the findings. They should be alert to the ways people can misunderstand scores and data and take extra care to be precise in their descriptions (Pope, 1992). Each feedback session should include a focus on the client's experience while taking the test and on his or her goals for the session. The importance of plain, clear language understandable to the client is crucial to compliance with both the spirit and the letter of the requirement here. Jargon does not communicate, nor does it advance client trust in the counselor's expertise. Even when counselors meet this criterion, they can err in another way—overwhelming the client with lengthy descriptions that the client cannot absorb in one session. This error occurs when trying to "cover the test" rather than to enlighten the client about its findings. With such a misconception, counselors can end up talking at length, giving the client little opportunity to question or respond, and generally defeating the purpose of feedback, that is, to inform the client and work collaboratively with the client to determine the meaning and impact of the test results for future sessions.

Statutes and case law may affect the provision of feedback in some states and some settings. For example, when courts mandate psychological testing to determine a person's competency to stand trial there may be no legal obligation at all to provide the client with information about test results (APA, Committee on Psychological Testing and Assessment, 1996). The court may even prohibit feedback. In that circumstance, the counselor may follow legal rulings without worry about ethical penalties. If possible and permissible within that setting however, counselors should seek to give some information to test takers, in recognition of their basic human rights.

Sometimes test results provide information that must be acted on (Pope, 1992). For example, a test may suggest a high probability of suicide or a substance abuse problem in a 12-year-old. In such an event, a counselor's duty to protect is evoked, at least insofar as the counselor must explore whether the test finding is accurate. If additional investigation reveals that the test result is supported by other information, the counselor should act to prevent the likely harm.

When mental health professionals are employed as consultants and evaluators for organizations, they often have no direct relationship with the test takers. An organization may use tests to screen inappropriate candidates, or a court may seek to gather data to make a custody determination. In such instances, test takers may be asked to waive their right to receive test results. A mental health professional may honor such a waiver, provided the person agreed to it *prior to the testing*. In other words, the only exception to the client's right to an explanation of test findings is an a priori agreement to that effect.

The time that should be devoted to feedback will vary from client to client and from test to test. Practical concerns about the pressures imposed by managed care and brief therapy have a place in the discussion. However, the central determinants to the decision about how much time should be devoted to this task should be

- The client's satisfaction that he or she understands the meaning and implications of the test results
- The counselor's assessment that the feedback session has been sufficient to clarify any confusions in the test findings or elucidate any subtle results
- Their mutual agreement about the ways in which test results should influence future treatment planning
- The implications of the release of these findings to others if the client agreed to the release prior to the testing

The process of providing clients with feedback about test results should be documented in the case record, along with the client's comments about the feedback and any aspects of the testing that need additional follow-up.

Clients also have the right to protection against another form of misuse of test results, that is, the inappropriate use of outdated or obsolete test findings. This standard stems from the reality that tests sample behavior in a single time period (Anastasi, 1992), which cannot have perpetual validity. Both codes unambiguously refer to this topic:

ACA *Code of Ethics*, Section E.11: Obsolete Tests and Outdated Test Results

Counselors do not use data or test results that are obsolete or outdated for the current purpose. Counselors make every effort to prevent the misuse of obsolete measures and test data by others.

APA *Ethical Principles*, Section 2.07: Obsolete Tests and Outdated Test Results

(a) Psychologists do not base their assessment or intervention decisions or recommendations on data or test results that are outdated for the current purpose.

(b) Similarly, psychologists do not base such decisions or recommendations on tests and measures that are obsolete and not useful for the current purpose.

The point at which tests become outdated or obsolete varies with the individual measure, the construct being assessed, and the person being evaluated. Depressed mood, for example, may be highly changeable and scores of that construct rapidly outdated, but measures of extroversion or spatial relations may be stable for an extended period. Judgments about this issue must be made on an individual basis according to the state of the science of measuring the relevant construct. Any test used to predict a future behavior, such as performance in graduate courses, becomes obsolete as soon as actual performance is known.

Release of Test Data

The appropriate release of test data has gained considerable attention in the professional community in recent years (Shapiro, 1991). Courts, lawyers, and clients themselves have sought access to test results. They have asked for test reports and even for raw data, including test questions, answer sheets, scoring materials, and the like. Deciding about the conditions under which the release of such data is appropriate is a complex endeavor in which the counselor must weigh competing rights and discrepant legal and ethical mandates. On the one hand, professionals are bound to protect the rights of test producers, and on the other, they must honor their clients' rights to results. Similarly, they must protect against misuse of results by unqualified professionals, but they must not ignore legal mandates to produce testing data. Fortunately, both the ethics codes and scholars address this issue at some length. The codes state the following on this topic:

ACA *Code of Ethics,* **Section E.3**

b. Recipients of Results

The examinee's welfare, explicit understanding, and prior agreement determine the recipients of test results. Counselors include accurate and appropriate interpretations with any release of individual or group test results.

ACA *Code of Ethics,* **Section E.4. Release of Information to Competent Professionals**

a. Misuse of Results

Counselors do not misuse assessment results, including test results, and interpretations, and take reasonable steps to prevent the misuse of such by others.

b. Release of Raw Data

Counselors ordinarily release data (e.g. protocols, counseling or interview notes, or questionnaires) in which the client is identified only with the consent of the client or the client's legal representative. Such data are usually released only to persons recognized by counselors as competent to interpret the data.

APA *Ethical Principles,* **Section 2.02**

(b) Psychologists refrain from misuse of assessment techniques, interventions, results, and interpretations and take reasonable steps to prevent others from misusing the information these techniques provide. This includes refraining from releasing raw test results or raw data to persons, other than to patients or clients as appropriate, who are not qualified to use such information.

The wording in each code varies somewhat, leading to different conclusions about what is ethical depending on which code is used, but there is some common ground. Both documents assert that test results should not be released to people who are not qualified to interpret them. These standards impose a responsibility on the counselor whose client is requesting a release of data, to ascertain the qualifications of those who seek such information. Tranel (1994) recommends that professionals uncertain about the competencies of the requesting party should seek from that person a curriculum vitae or similar documentation to verify qualifications. Because one's discipline or license does not guarantee competence in interpreting any particular test, the duty to acquire evidence of qualifications extends very broadly. Sometimes other professionals are offended by such inquiries, and uncomfortable exchanges can ensue. Nevertheless, counselors cannot allow the discomfort of such interactions to interfere with their resolve to follow the ethical standards. Usually, citing these standards when requesting such documentation defuses the conflict, but even if that strategy is unsuccessful, releasing test data to unqualified people presents such a high risk of harm to client welfare that counselors are obliged to stand firm on this point. Note the repeated emphasis in both codes on the importance of avoiding misuse of test results.

When clients are requesting the release of test results to people who the counselor believes are unqualified to handle that information responsibly, the counselor should discuss his or her reservations with the client at length. When clients know that counselors are trying to act in their best interests, they are usually amenable to alternative arrangements. The goal of this conversation should be to identify an alternative person who is qualified that both agree is otherwise suitable to receive the results.

The caution needed in determining whether the data can be released to a particular party does not mean that professionals should aim to keep test data to themselves whenever possible. On the contrary, when clients consent, the sharing of client information among responsible and competent professionals usually results in better service for clients, improving their chances of therapeutic gain. In this situation, a spirit of cooperation and collaboration is to be fostered, and no reluctance about the release is needed.

The codes differ in other respects on release of test information. The APA code suggests that test results and raw data may be released to clients, but the ACA code is silent on this issue, mentioning only release to qualified persons. Not all scholars have interpreted the APA code in that way, though. Tranel (1994) believes it means that psychologists should explain and interpret findings for clients and typically allow for client access to written reports of testing, but he asserts it does not imply that raw data should be released directly to clients. Bersoff (1995) questions his interpretation. Canter et al. (1994) state that the code was worded in that way to acknowledge that in some jurisdictions, clients have a legal right to raw data. They also suggest, though, that under other circumstances, psychologists should release raw data only to qualified people. Until the exact meaning of this standard is clarified, those bound to follow the APA code should act cautiously, looking first for a way to achieve the client's goal without the release of raw data to a client unqualified to interpret them, if state laws allow for such an alternative.

Increasingly, test materials are subject to requests from attorneys and judges for use in court proceedings. Counselors should follow the same guidelines for responding to such requests as they use for any other material that may be privileged. (See Chapter 5 for a fuller discussion of privileged communication.) If a court orders disclosure of raw data and test materials, the counselors are placed in an untenable position. One set of ethics and laws demands that they not violate copyright and proprietary interests of test publishers and that they zealously guard against test misuse, whereas the other requires them to produce all documents included in a court order. When faced with such a dilemma, scholars (for example, Tranel, 1994) advise that mental health professionals explain the conflict to the court, and work to see that the materials are released to another qualified professional and are somehow protected from widespread dissemination. In this situation a judge sometimes agrees to view materials "in camera" or to send them directly to a qualified professional named by the court for the purpose of interpreting them. Tranel (1994) suggests that courts are often amenable to such actions and show some understanding of the dilemma faced by the mental health professional. The document produced by the APA Committee on Legal Issues (1996) is also an important resource in this situation.

Responsible Use of Test Interpretation Services

Counselors and therapists often contract with scoring and interpretation services for the psychological tests they administer to clients. Practitioners view these services positively as timesavers that relieve them of the onerous task of scoring often complex instruments. Along with the scores or personality profile data, these services frequently furnish a typed interpretation of the results. Although the use of such procedures is not inherently unethical, important conditions must be met before their use is ethically justified.

First, the interpretations such services provide must be based on criteria that have been subject to validation, and these results should be made available to subscribers to the service. Matarazzo (1986) has criticized the scoring criteria employed by the services because they have not presented evidence that the criteria are supported by scientific evidence, nor have the criteria been offered for objective review by other scholars. This omission is particularly important because the reports are packaged to appear so professional, complete, and sound that they seem more scientific than they really are. Anastasi terms this "the hazard of illusory precision" (1992, p. 611). Second, according to Matarazzo these interpretive reports do not generate multiple interpretations of results, even though for some combinations of scores multiple interpretations are indeed possible. He argues that he has found the reports less plausible than the interpretations of respected colleagues. Other criticisms have been made about computerized reports. Bersoff and Hofer (1991) contend that such reports fail to be individualized and cannot take into account the unique characteristics of the test taker. In addition, they argue that these reports are "bland, impersonal, and nonspecific" (p. 243).

The most crucial danger of interpretive services is that counselors and therapists not otherwise competent to interpret tests will employ these interpretations in their work and present these results to clients. The *Guidelines for Computer-Based Tests and Interpretations* (APA, 1986) condemns this practice and recommends that computerized test interpretations be used only "in conjunction with professional judgment." *The Standards for Educational and Psychological Tests* (APA, 1985) take the same position. A national survey of psychologists found that practitioners voiced concern about unqualified people using these interpretations as one of the primary ethical issues facing them in assessment (Pope & Vetter, 1992). The responsibility of the test user to ascertain the validity and appropriate interpretation of results does not diminish just because an organization with no firsthand knowledge of the client has written a report. The only responsible way to use such material is as a "second opinion." Counselors who would not be judged competent to interpret an instrument in the absence of such a report must not use these reports. These materials should serve as aids to accurate assessment of test results, not as substitutes for clinician deficiencies. Bersoff and Hofer point out that if there are legal challenges to the use of computer scoring and interpretations, both the test user and the organization that provides that service are likely to be listed as defendants. Test users who are unable to demonstrate their independent competence in that test would be particularly vulnerable to a malpractice claim.

The ACA code speaks primarily to the duties of those who develop scoring and interpretation services. The APA code offers a similar statement but also discusses more fully the obligations of users of these services.

ACA *Code of Ethics,* **Section E.9: Test Scoring and Interpretation**

c. Testing services

Counselors who provide test scoring and test interpretation services to support the assessment process confirm the validity of such interpretations. They accurately describe the purpose, norms, validity, reliability, and applications of the procedures and any special qualifications applicable to their use. The public offering of an automated test interpretation service is considered a professional-to-professional consultation. The formal responsibility of the consultant is to the consultee, but the ultimate and overriding responsibility is to the client.

APA *Ethical Principles,* **Section 2.08: Test Scoring and Interpretation Services**

(a) Psychologists who offer assessment or scoring procedures to other professionals accurately describe the purpose, norms, validity, reliability, and applications of the procedures and any special qualifications applicable to their use.

(b) Psychologists select scoring and interpretation services (including automated services) on the basis of evidence of the validity of the program and procedures as well as other appropriate considerations.

(c) Psychologists retain appropriate responsibility for the appropriate application, interpretation, and use of assessment instruments, whether they score and interpret such test themselves or use automated or other services.

Multicultural Issues in Testing

The codes of ethics exhort mental health professionals to be alert to the ways in which gender, age, race, ethnicity, national origin, religion, sexual orientation, disability, language, or socioeconomic status may affect the appropriate administration or interpretation of assessment tools (APA *Ethical Principles,* Section 2.04). The ACA code attends both to the ethics of selecting tests for culturally diverse populations and to their appropriate administration and interpretation:

ACA *Code of Ethics,* **Section E.6: Test Selection**

Counselors are cautious when selecting tests for culturally diverse populations to avoid inappropriateness of testing that may be outside of socialized behavioral or cognitive patterns.

ACA *Code of Ethics,* **Section E.8: Diversity in Testing**

Counselors are cautious in using assessment techniques, making evaluations, and interpreting the performance of populations not represented in the norm group on which an instrument was standardized. They recognize the effects of age, color, culture, disability, ethnic group, gender, race, religion, sexual orientation, and socioeconomic status on test administration and interpretation and place test results in proper perspective with other relevant factors.

These standards, the *Guidelines for Providers of Psychological Services to Ethnic, Linguistic, and Culturally Diverse Populations* (APA, 1993b) and the scholarship on multiculturalism underscore the importance of three particular issues: First, because there is no such thing as a culture-free test (Anastasi, 1988; Walsh & Betz, 1995), counselors should decide on assessment instruments and interpret them in light of the client's cultural background. This position is echoed by Sue, Arrendondo, and McDavis (1992), who have offered standards for competency to counsel in a multicultural society. These authors contend that counselors need *knowledge* of how potential bias may affect the interpretation of test results and *skill* in using measures for the benefit of diverse clients. (See the next chapter for more discussion of these competencies.)

One important consideration in this area is the availability of normative data for the client's population. When tests do not have norms for particular cultural groups, alternative measures should be sought. If no alternatives exist, those results should be interpreted with great caution. For example, a mental health agency should not use the original MMPI for personality assessment with Latino or Asian-American clients if the MMPI-2 can be substituted because the newer measure has included members of those populations in its norm group. The counselor's responsibility does not end with the use of the newer test. It extends to becoming familiar with subsequent research on scores of those populations on the test, because such research can be crucial to accurate interpretation of a particular score or ambiguous finding.

Second, counselors should also carefully examine tests for content bias (Walsh & Betz, 1995). Content bias occurs when the items in a test are differentially familiar to different cultural groups. Test items that ask respondents about deciduous trees may be impossible for Native Americans from the desert Southwest to respond to because they have no such trees in their environment. Similarly, urban dwellers may be unable to give meaningful responses to items that require knowledge of rural or suburban settings. Sensitivity to the impact of such items on the conclusions drawn from a test is crucial to avoid misinterpretation of the results. A desire to eliminate content bias in items has been a factor in the recent revision of several well-known personality inventories (such as the MMPI-2). Content bias has been the focus of much debate in the literature on tests of cognitive abilities with culturally diverse populations. Scholars have presented cogent arguments that lower scores from diverse groups on such measures are at least partially caused by content bias (Lonner & Ibrahim, 1996).

Third, because of counselors' duty to avoid discrimination and to intervene whenever possible to stop it, counselors should be alert to the ways their test reports are used with culturally diverse clients. The best known legal case involving discrimination on the basis of test results was *Larry P. v. Riles* in California (1979). In that case the court found that school officials had misdiagnosed a student and misused intelligence test results in a way that resulted in significant, perhaps permanent, harm to that child. This case acted as the impetus for reexamination of the testing practices with minority students in California and other states. That case is a blatant example of the problem, but there are many more less dramatic violations of client rights. Too often test reports are superficially understood and then used in a discriminatory fashion. School officials who expect Mexican-American students to have lower scores on achievement tests will be less likely to carefully interpret such test results and to account for the impact of culture and linguistic variables. They may overinterpret slight differences favoring European-American students, when an accurate analysis of the findings would reveal no meaningful difference in performance by ethnic group. In this situation, if many of the Mexican-American students spoke English as a second language, their almost equal scores to the European-American students might realistically be viewed as indicators of higher achievement potential, given their comparative language disadvantage. Counselors must work energetically both to develop the competence to see the influence of such factors and to communicate appropriate ways to interpret tests to other professionals. One especially helpful guide to competent and responsible assessment for diverse populations is *The Handbook of Multicultural Assessment,* written by Suzuki, Meller, and Ponterotto (1996). In essence, the standards and literature on this issue point to the importance of counselors' personal commitment to nondiscrimination and appreciation of cultural differences. The counselor must be alert to both intended and unintended discrimination, as both have negative impact on clients. In this context, the virtue of commitment to social justice and fair treatment for all takes on special importance.

Tests in Employment Settings

Psychological tests have found increasing use in employment settings over the last 20 years (Hogan, Hogan, & Roberts, 1996). They have been used primarily to assist in hiring and promotion. Intelligence tests, measures of verbal and mathematical reasoning, vocational aptitude batteries, and personality inventories are most commonly chosen. The newest trend is the use of "integrity tests" aimed at predicting a job applicant's honesty and attitudes toward theft (Camera & Schneider, 1994). When any tests are used in employment settings, there are several ethical issues to be dealt with:

- Has performance on the instrument under consideration been demonstrated by scientific evidence to be related to the job performance it ought to predict? Legal rulings have also emphasized that the standard for acceptability of such testing is a demonstrated relationship to the variables of interest in the employment setting.
- Has the publisher of the test followed ethical guidelines and avoided sacrificing the welfare of the test taker on the altar of profit?
- Do the people who select, administer, score, and interpret the results have the necessary competencies for those tasks, and do they work to restrain misuse by unqualified individuals?
- Do those who are asked to take such tests understand their rights, and are their dignity and confidentiality appropriately honored?
- Do the tests avoid discrimination against people for reasons unrelated to job performance? Are there no significant differences in rejection rates for different racial and ethnic groups? (Cronbach, 1984)

- Have the limitations and reservations about the test been acknowledged and taken into account in interpreting results?
- Are test results used in conjunction with other information so that they are not the sole criterion on which any decision is based? Does the test provide more accurate information than alternative selection procedures? (Cronbach, 1984)
- Does state law allow the kind of testing under consideration? For example, Massachusetts prohibits integrity testing for job applicants (Camera & Schneider, 1994). Integrity testing involves the use of psychological tests to assess honesty in work behavior.

If all these questions can be answered affirmatively, the use of testing in such environments is more likely to be consistent with current ethical standards.

Laws That Affect Testing

Counselors who employ tests should be aware of several federal laws that affect their work. The implications of such laws are especially widespread in educational and employment settings.

- Family Educational Rights and Privacy Act of 1974, or FERPA (the Buckley Amendment). This law protects the rights of parents and guardians to view their child's academic records and to control who else may have access to them.
- The Education for All Handicapped Children Act (Public Law 94-142). This law was enacted to guarantee the rights of children with disabilities to an equal education and specifies that parents' consent is required prior to testing their child. It also mandates a fully informed parental consent to testing and access of parents to test protocols when testing is completed. The law requires that tests be in the child's language and be appropriate for the intended use.
- Public Law 101-336 (the Americans with Disabilities Act of 1990). This legislation protects the rights of people with disabilities and mandates that testing be appropriate for the individual, that it not be used to discriminate in employment options for people with disabilities, and that reasonable accommodations be made in testing for such people.

CASES FOR DISCUSSION

The Case of Lee

Lee, a 14-year-old eighth-grade student, is being considered for placement in advanced classes in high school. Lee's parents immigrated to the United States from Korea five years ago, and the whole family recently became U.S. citizens. Lee learned English quickly after his arrival in the United States, but he had no exposure to English in Korea. His test scores in mathematics and verbal reasoning place him at the 86th percentile for eighth-graders in his district. The district uses a cutoff score of the 90th percentile to assign students to advanced classes. Lee has earned *A*'s in both math and English classes. His teachers believe Lee is appropriate for advanced placement, but the guidance counselor is concerned about his test score. The counselor suggests a compromise—enroll Lee in the advanced mathematics class only. She cites two reasons for the suggestion: the evidence that Asian-American students tend as a group to excel in math and the fact that Lee learned English only five years ago. Is her suggestion consistent with the ethical guidelines for counselors?

The Case of Miranda

After several counseling sessions that included some psychological testing, Miranda's counselor, Mr. Edwards, believes that this client's problems fit the criteria for two different diagnostic categories. For one of these categories Miranda's insurance company will reimburse services, for the other she is likely to be denied such payment. Because Miranda is motivated for counseling and is experiencing real emotional discomfort from her problems, Mr. Edwards is leaning toward using the diagnosis that is acceptable to the insurance company. He reasons that because he can justify either diagnosis, he is acting in accordance with ethical standards. Do you agree?

Analysis of the Cases

A number of ethical considerations arise in the case of Lee. The central ethical principles involved are justice and beneficence, the obligation to treat this student fairly and to help him progress academically. The provisions in the codes raise a number of questions to be resolved.

1. Are there norms for Asian-American students or for English-as-a-second-language students for the achievement test that was employed? If not, was appropriate caution used in interpreting Lee's results?

2. Is the counselor interpreting the percentile score appropriately, taking into account the psychometric evidence on the test? In particular, does she understand how the standard error of measurement affects the meaning of the 86th percentile in comparison to the 90th percentile?

3. Was the test appropriate in other ways for Lee? What level of content or selection bias was present in the items that might have distorted the young man's true score?

4. Is the counselor using the test score appropriately, as one factor among several criteria for placement? Has the counselor considered that for students whose native tongue is not English, Lee's score may actually show greater potential than an English speaker's score just a few points higher?

5. To what degree does the counselor's compromise represent a stereotype about Asian students and a failure to see Lee as an individual? Is the counselor unintentionally racist in this instance?

6. What evidence is there to support her assumption that five years' experience with English is insufficient for placement in advanced classes or that the test is a better predictor of high school success than middle school grades or teacher recommendation?

7. To what degree have the school personnel involved Lee and his parents in the decision making? Have they honored the family members' rights to autonomy?

8. Will more harm come to Lee if he attempts the advanced classes and does not succeed or if he is denied the opportunity to enroll in them? Conversely, which option has the potential to provide the most benefit to Lee?

Without answers to these questions, it is difficult to come to a definitive judgment on the ethics of the counselor, but the brief evidence presented is enough to instill doubt that the counselor is in compliance with the letter or the spirit of the codes. At the least, she seems unequal to the challenge of properly interpreting test scores and insufficiently in awe of the power she wields to help or harm.

The case of Miranda deals with the counselor's effort to meet a true need for counseling that Mr. Edwards sees in Miranda, without depriving her of insurance reimbursement for those services. He seems motivated by an interest in doing good for this individual. In this case, too, though, more information is needed before his behavior can be deemed ethical. Specifically, one should resolve the following questions:

1. Is his analysis that the two diagnostic categories are equally valid for this client supported by objective evidence? Would competent colleagues be likely to arrive at a similar conclusion?

2. Has he taken into account how cultural variables may influence the appropriate diagnostic category for Miranda?

3. To what degree does Mr. Edwards's interest in insurance reimbursement reflect a true commitment to the welfare of the client rather than an interest in reliable payment for his services?

4. What implications would the use of the reimbursable diagnosis have for the client, other than payment for counseling? Does this diagnosis indicate a more severe mental illness? Would the use of such a category have negative impact on the client's life?

5. To what degree is the client informed and involved in the decision-making process about the appropriate diagnostic category? Does she understand the implications of submitting for reimbursement? Because the effects all fall on Miranda, is she being given the freedom to make the final decision about this issue?

If Mr. Edwards's conclusion is supported by evidence, by competent colleagues, is freely chosen by a fully informed client, and is not motivated by self-interest or a desire to trick the insurer, then he has probably not violated an ethical standard. However, providing adequate answers to all those conditions may be more difficult than it first appears.

SUMMARY

The ethical standards applicable to assessment activities are based on the significant power the counselor wields in this role. The imperfections in diagnostic systems and testing instruments, coupled with their vulnerability to misinterpretation by unqualified persons, also add to their power. Counselors, however, cannot avoid the task of assessing client problems on the grounds that assessment tools can be misused. Without a clear definition of the client's issues, the counselor's ability to provide effective treatment is significantly impaired. Thus, counselors must proceed carefully and diligently in assessment activities, mindful of the rights and responsibilities of all involved.

When engaged in diagnosis, counselors must be careful to act competently, without discrimination or unintentional racism, and give clients clear information about the meaning and implications of the diagnosis. They should fully recognize the strengths and weaknesses of current diagnostic systems and the impact of such identifiers on clients.

Similarly, when using psychological or educational tests, counselors should have extensive skill and training in order to use the findings in suitable ways with a given individual. They must possess the knowledge and skill to discriminate between valid and invalid findings and to take into account the cultural and social background of the test taker. They must not encourage those unqualified for the activity to engage in it, nor should they use outdated test results in their work. In most instances, clients have a right to feedback about the test. The exact nature of that feedback is not prescribed by the code, but it must convey as accurate and full a picture of the results as circumstances allow. The history of the profession is replete with examples of counselors misinterpreting test results with diverse and oppressed populations, so counselors must be especially vigilant not to repeat those violations and to stay current with the literature on multicultural aspects of assessment. When tests are used in employment settings, their scores must be correlated with job characteristics and test takers must understand their rights in such a situation. Counselors would also be well advised to know how the laws in their jurisdictions affect the assessment process, as state laws vary and change rapidly.

Not only are counselors bound to protect the rights of clients, they also have a responsibility to honor the rights of test producers, acting in ways that recognize their legal rights to ownership of and fair profit from test materials. Therefore, counselors must guard against violations of test security, must not plagiarize test materials, and must seek the option to use such materials only when qualified to do so. In turn, test producers are obligated to provide scientific evidence of the reliability and validity of their tests and other related materials in test manuals. They should assist counselors in the responsible use of assessment tools as much as possible.

DISCUSSION QUESTIONS

1. Do you think the flaws in the current diagnostic system used in mental health make it impossible to use responsibly? Why or why not? If not, how would you improve the diagnostic system?

2. Do you believe the benefits of employment testing outweigh its liabilities? Why or why not?

3. Research shows that some professionals do not give clients negative feedback from testing; they report only positive results. What do you think about the ethics of this practice?

4. Currently test producers are asked by professional associations to market their tests only to qualified users. Is that a fair request in a free-enterprise system? What would happen if that restriction did not exist?

5. Some have argued that testing should not be used at all in educational settings with culturally diverse students. They have contended that the risk of test results being misused is so great with this population that they should never be a part of educational decision making. What's your analysis of this argument?

RECOMMENDED READINGS

American Psychological Association. (1985). *Standards for psychological and educational tests.* Washington, DC: Author.

American Psychological Association. (1986). *Guidelines for computer-based tests and interpretations.* Washington, DC: Author.

American Psychological Association, Committee on Psychological Tests and Assessment. (1996). Statement on the disclosure of test data. *American Psychologist, 51,* 644–648.

Anastasi, A. (1992). What counselors should know about the use and interpretation of psychological tests. *Journal of Counseling and Development, 70,* 610–615.

Eyde, L. D., Robertson, G. J., Krug, S. E., Moreland, K. L., Robertson, A. G., Shewan, C. M., Harrison, P. L., Porch, B. E., & Hammer, A. L. (1993). *Responsible test use: Case studies for assessing human behavior.* Washington, DC: American Psychological Association.

Hogan, R., Hogan, J., & Roberts, B. W. (1996). Personality measurement and employment decisions: Questions and answers. *American Psychologist, 51,* 469–477.

Joint Committee on Testing Practices. (1988). *Code of fair testing practices in education.* Washington, DC: American Psychological Association.

Suzuki, L. A., Meller, P. J., & Ponterotto, J. G. (1996). *Handbook of multicultural assessment.* San Francisco: Jossey-Bass.

11

Ethical Counseling in a Multicultural Society
The Promise of Justice

American society has always been culturally diverse, but for many years mental health professions largely ignored the impact of that diversity on their work. Wrenn (1962, 1985) aptly described counseling as "culturally encapsulated." In recent years, however, these professions have moved the topic from the periphery of their consideration toward the center. Attention to multicultural issues has become so intense that some have called this movement psychology's "fourth force" (Pedersen, 1991a). Many scholars contend that the issue has not yet achieved the prominence it deserves (for example, see Pedersen, Draguns, Lonner, & Trimble, 1996; Sue, 1995), but the progress that has been made is undeniable.

Several factors account for this shift. Demographic changes are the most obvious cause. Racial and ethnic groups referred to as "minorities" now comprise a larger percentage of the population and the labor force than ever. Projections are that within the next 50 years, those who have been minorities will become a numerical majority in the United States (Sue, 1995). In many urban communities, that transformation has already occurred (Sue et al., 1992). Population groups of that size garner attention, not only for their magnitude, but for the expanding political and social power their size commands. Second, in the latter half of the twentieth century, the legal system has provided increasing recognition of the rights of minority groups through federal statutes such as the Civil Rights Act of 1964 and the Americans with Disabilities Act of 1990 (Public Law 101-336). Not all efforts to increase minority rights were successful (note the failure of the Equal Rights Amendment), but the momentum was clearly in this direction. Third, as professional education became more available to groups previously denied access, the professions themselves included more members of culturally diverse groups. These professionals, along with other scholars, have actively fostered consideration of multicultural issues. They have also pushed the profession toward a fuller acknowledgment of its own history of failures in treating culturally diverse groups and of the harm that racist and ethnocentric attitudes can cause others (for example, see Ridley, 1995; Sue & Sue, 1990). In addition, scholarship in cross-cultural psychology has blossomed in this period, providing a rich conceptual base for that agenda. Finally, the reemergence of interest in professional ethics over the last two decades has also played a small role, placing the profession's fundamental ethical principles and virtues at the forefront of professional concern. Attention to multicultural issues is a natural outgrowth of discussions of respect for autonomy, fairness, and the obligation to do good for others. At its core, professional ethics is about commitment to reducing the suffering of other people (Fowers & Richardson, 1996). One cannot honor that commitment without working to eliminate racism, oppression, and stereotyping, which cause much suffering in modern society.

In this context, it is not surprising that the ethical implications of the multicultural society have been extensively discussed. The most recent versions of the ethics codes of ACA (1995) and APA (1992) show an unprecedented concern for this topic. Moreover, the associations have published additional guidelines to enhance responsible practice with diverse clients. This chapter reviews those materials, discusses the scholarly literature that critiques the codes, and examines other features of professional ethics in a multicultural society that are not yet addressed by the codes. Its central theme is that ethics requires counselors to break free from cultural encapsulation and develop a set of competencies and commitments for productive work with diverse groups. Achieving this goal for all professionals is crucial if the ethical ideals of the profession are to be met, especially because the history of the profession is marred with incidents of ignorance, insensitivity, and ethnocentric bias.

The Language of Multicultural Counseling

A set of definitions of terms used in this chapter is a necessary preamble to the discussion:

- A *minority* is a group that has suffered discrimination or been oppressed. It is typically smaller in size as well as power than a majority cultural group, but it need not be small to be considered a minority. Minority status is primarily a function of access to power and history of oppression.
- *Culturally diverse clients* are clients from any group that is represented in the preceding definition of minority or is otherwise of a different cultural tradition from the counselor.
- *Multicultural counseling* is any counseling situation in which the cultures of the client and the counselor differ. In some writings the terms *cross-cultural* or *transcultural counseling* are used.
- *Culture* is the "set of shared meanings that make social life possible" (Fowers & Richardson, 1996, p. 610). These meanings form the structure of social interaction and give members of the culture a set of standards and norms for behavior. In this chapter *culture* is used broadly, including not only ethnicity and nationality, but also encompassing demographic variables (such as age, gender, sexual orientation, and physical disability) and affiliations (such as religion).

- *Ethnicity* is a shared identity derived from shared ancestry, nationality, religion and race (Lum, 1992).
- *Multiculturalism* is a "social-intellectual movement that promotes the value of diversity as a core principle and insists that all cultural groups be treated with respect and as equals" (Fowers & Richardson, 1996, p. 609).

The Context of the Current Ethical Standards

To fully appreciate the ethical standards for counselors in a multicultural society, one must acknowledge not only that there are many cultural traditions beyond one's own, but also that not all cultural groups have equal power in our society. Many have been subject to oppression and discrimination, and the prejudicial attitudes and behaviors that allowed such violations of human dignity to occur are far from extinct. Furthermore, counselors need to recognize that they themselves are not immune from the prejudicial attitudes that characterize Western society and that they can inadvertently perpetuate oppression and discrimination even if they abhor prejudice and want to practice sensitively (Sue, Ivey, & Pedersen, 1996). Counselors internalize society's biases just as other citizens do, and these biases frequently play themselves out in unconscious ways. For example, if a counselor locates a practice so as to be inaccessible to public transportation, he or she is probably not deliberately discriminating or choosing to deny access to particular segments of the population. Nevertheless, the effect is still discriminatory insofar as it denies access to people without their own cars—a group likely to contain a greater proportion of minority clients. The implicit message is that counseling is meant to serve people with resources and that those without private transportation do not even figure into the equation when deciding on a suitable location for the practice. A counselor confronted about this problem would be likely to respond, "I just didn't think about that." Or, to cite a different example, a school counselor might accept without challenge a Latina's request to drop out of physics because it's too demanding, when that same counselor might actively encourage a European-American boy to persevere or help him get tutoring to succeed in the course. The counselor need not have a conscious belief that Latinas are less intelligent or less deserving, he or she may just have lower expectations for Latino people (or for girls), without ever being aware that that assumption is operating. That belief has been absorbed from the negative messages and stereotyping in the culture. Recent literature on the differential treatment of boys and girls in American classrooms provides still another vivid example of unconsciously prejudicial behavior (Bailey, 1996). Ridley (1995) refers to such acts as "unintentional" racism or sexism. The harm such acts cause is no less real because they are unintended, however. For that reason, much of the effort in promoting effective and responsible service for diverse populations has focused on helping counselors become aware of such hidden beliefs and attitudes so that fairer judgments can be made.

Of course, unintentional bias is not the only form of bias counselors may exhibit. Sometimes counselors consciously endorse prejudiced beliefs and attitudes. As was mentioned in Chapter 10, as late as 1993 14% of counselors still equated homosexuality with psychopathology, even though the professions had definitively stated more than a decade before that homosexuality was not a psychological disorder (Gibson & Pope, 1993). Endorsing of such beliefs and attitudes directly contradicts the provisions of the ethics codes of every major mental health association.

The Codes of Ethics on Multicultural Counseling

The 1995 ACA code speaks to the topic of multicultural counseling in the first paragraph of its preamble. Sue (1995) notes this placement as an important symbol of the centrality of this issue to ethical practice. The section reads,

> The American Counseling Association is an educational, scientific, and professional organization whose members are dedicated to the enhancement of human development throughout the lifespan. Association members recognize diversity in our society and embrace a cross-cultural approach in support of the worth, dignity, potential, and uniqueness of each individual.

In addition, the ACA code contains another 13 references to diversity issues in its 1995 version, divided among nearly all sections of the code.

The 1992 revision of the APA *Ethical Principles* also includes numerous references to diversity issues, including a statement in its introductory General Principles that reads,

> **Principle D: Respect for People's Rights and Dignity**
> Psychologists accord appropriate respect to the fundamental rights, dignity, and worth of all people. They respect the rights of individuals to privacy, confidentiality, self-determination, and autonomy. . . . Psychologists are aware of cultural, individual, and role differences, including those due to age, gender, race, ethnicity, national origin, religion, sexual orientation, disability, language, and socioeconomic status. Psychologists try to eliminate the effect on their work of biases based on these factors, and they do not knowingly participate in or condone unfair discriminatory practices.

Taken together, the other sections of the codes that refer to multicultural issues deal with the promotion of client welfare, competence to practice with diverse populations, avoidance of discriminatory behavior, and training and research issues.

Promoting Client Welfare

The sections of the ACA code that concern the promotion of client welfare identify prohibited behavior—discrimination (Section A.2.a), call members to respectful appreciation of cultural differences (Section A.2.b), and caution professionals against imposing personal values on clients in a diverse society (Section A.5.b). This material makes the exhortation in the preamble more specific as well as enforceable. These sections highlight the degree to which counseling cannot be separated from personal values and beliefs, and stem from the recognition that the power of the counselor can easily be misused. These sections remind professionals that this occupation is one of service to others, not self-service. When counselors operate in a biased or monocultural way, they are serving their own needs, not those of their clients.

Competence with Multicultural Populations

As discussed in Chapter 6, competence to practice means a professional has the knowledge, skill, and diligence required for the tasks he or she undertakes. There are two references to multicultural competence in the ACA code. The first is in the section explaining the boundaries of one's competence, and states, "Counselors will demonstrate a commitment to gain knowledge, personal awareness, sensitivity, and skills pertinent to working with a diverse population" (ACA, *Code of Ethics,* Section C.2.a). The second reference extends that responsibility to continuing education responsibilities, "and keep current with the diverse and/or special populations with whom they work" (ACA, *Code of Ethics,* Section C.2.f).

The APA code addresses the topic as follows:

Section 1.08: Human Differences

Where differences of age, gender, race, ethnicity, national origin, religion, sexual orientation, disability, language, or socioeconomic status significantly affect psychologists' work concerning particular individuals or groups, psychologists obtain the necessary training, experience, consultation, or supervision necessary to ensure the competence of their services, or they make appropriate referrals.

Unfortunately, these sections do not elaborate on the specific components of multicultural competency. Other scholars have addressed that question. Sue and Sue (1990) laid out three broad dimensions of this competency. These dimensions are (1) self-awareness so that one's values, biases, personal beliefs, and assumptions about human nature are known; (2) understanding without negative judgments of the worldviews and assumptions of culturally diverse clients; and (3) skill in using and developing counseling interventions appropriate with diverse clients. Other authors have organized the necessary multicultural competencies as appropriate beliefs and attitudes, cultural knowledge, and practical skills. Sue et al. (1992) synthesized the literature into a document entitled *Multicultural Counseling Competencies and Standards,* and the Association for Multicultural Counseling and Development, along with the Association for Counselor Education and Supervision, later endorsed these standards. This document was expanded in 1996 (Arrendondo et al.). These guidelines identify the following beliefs and attitudes about oneself, about the client, and about intervention strategies as essential components of competency:

■ Awareness of the influence of one's own cultural heritage on his or her experiences, attitudes, values, and behaviors and the ways in which that culture limits or enhances effectiveness with diverse clients

- Comfort with cultural differences and with clients from diverse cultures, developing an attitude that values and appreciates cultural difference rather than disparages or tolerates it
- Honesty with self about negative emotional reactions and preconceived notions about other cultures, recognition of the harmful effects such reactions can have on clients, and commitment to work on changing such attitudes
- Respect and appreciation for culturally different beliefs and attitudes, by honoring natural community support networks and valuing bilingualism, for example

The document also details a knowledge base for counselors that includes a strong foundation of self-knowledge and a solid background in the particular cultures from which one's clients will be drawn:

- Comprehension of how one's own culture affects one's definition of normality–abnormality and the process of counseling
- Understanding of the implications of racism, oppression, and stereotyping on a personal and a professional level, including acknowledgment of one's own racist attitudes
- Familiarity with the literature on social impact on others, with special attention to the effect of one's communication style on diverse clients
- Appreciation of the cultural heritage of diverse clients with whom one is working and the impact that cultural identity development may have on clients
- Sensitivity to the ways in which culture may affect specific client attributes such as personality development, career choice, help-seeking behavior, manifestation of psychological distress, and so on
- Comprehension of the influence of social and political factors on culturally diverse clients, with appreciation of the harm that racism can inflict on individual functioning
- Knowledge of the aspects of traditional counseling that may clash with a particular client's culture, including assessment tools and intervention strategies
- Appreciation of institutional barriers that impede access to counseling for many culturally diverse clients
- Familiarity with cultural norms and practices regarding family structure
- Understanding of how the cultural group uses family and community resources to help people in distress
- Appreciation of the ongoing problems of discrimination and oppression that may have particular impact on culturally diverse clients in a given community

Finally, the document elaborates on a number of skills or activities that counselors should acquire to be effective multicultural counselors (the theme of this section is active engagement in activities that enhance skills):

- Pursuit of activities that enhance understanding of one's own culture and limit the degree to which the prejudiced attitudes of the culture affect one's behavior

- Active involvement in activities that expand knowledge of cultural groups that is both intellectual and experiential
- Versatility in verbal and nonverbal helping responses and judgment about when to use each appropriately
- Skill in helping clients intervene effectively with institutional barriers to their goals
- Capacity to use community resources, such as traditional healers, when appropriate
- Bilingualism, or at least a willingness to appreciate the client's desire to use a first language in counseling and make an appropriate referral
- Expertise in the responsible use of assessment tools with diverse populations (Lonner & Ibrahim, 1996)
- Active involvement in activities in the community meant to reduce prejudice and enhance cross-cultural knowledge
- Skill in educating diverse clients to the counseling process in ways that make sense to them

APA's *Guidelines for Providers of Psychological Services to Ethnic, Linguistic and Culturally Diverse Populations* (1993b) echoes the same themes, with somewhat greater emphasis on the impact of bias on diagnosis and assessment. This document also provides examples that help flesh out the concepts embedded in both sets of guidelines. For instance, the APA publication uses the "healthy paranoia" of oppressed groups to illustrate the ways diagnosis must take cultural factors into account if it is to be accurate. All too often that suspicion is treated as pathological when it is indeed functional to the environment of that client.

Several objective measures to help counselors assess their level of multicultural competency have recently been developed. The test with the most evidence of reliability and validity is the *Multicultural Counseling Inventory* constructed by Sodowsky, Taffe, Gutlin, and Wise (1994). These instruments examine the skills, knowledge, and attitudes of counselors toward multicultural populations. Counselors who are unsure about their current competency might find one of these measures useful and should consult Pope-Davis and Dings (1995) for a review of the literature on these instruments.

A Critique of the Current Ethics Codes

Critics of the ethics codes note that the ethical principles that underlie its tenets are not universally endorsed by all cultures. The emphasis on respect for the autonomy of the individual that girds the entire social and political structure in Western societies is notably absent in some Eastern cultures. Instead, those cultures give primacy to the health and well-being of the group or the family. In this and other ways, the codes, the critics say, have abrogated their responsibility to acknowledge this diversity in ethical values. Consequently, in this view, the codes fail to help practitioners deal responsibly with such conflicts in fundamental ethical values and are negligent in their responsibility to protect the public from poor service.

This debate highlights some of the thorniest ethical dilemmas that counselors confront in their work. How should one respond when the situation of the client seems to compromise his or her personal freedom and dignity, yet is condoned or encouraged by his or her culture? For example, what is the ethical response when a client's culture refuses to allow girls to attend school, or condones a kind of indentured servitude of some classes that is not far removed from slavery? Is there a point at which respect for the cultural tradition of the client gives way to universal human values? If so, who makes the decision about which values are universal? Does that come from the individual counselor or from somewhere else? LaFromboise, Foster, and James (1996) wrestle with these questions, suggesting that professionals must avoid both ethical absolutism (a rigid, dogmatic adherence to a particular set of ethical values) and ethical relativism (an equal acceptance of all ethical values). Instead, they recommend a middle position that allows for diversity in values, but is not so relativistic as to deny the existence of any universal human principles.

Cautions About a Multicultural Perspective

There are two extremes to be avoided in a multicultural perspective. One extreme is implied in the preceding discussion, that is, the failure to take culture into account in the therapeutic process. The second extreme to be avoided is the failure to acknowledge intracultural variations and individual differences. Within the African-American community, for example, are many subcultures, and it is mistaken to assume a uniformity in culture that simply does not exist. Not all people from the same cultural group are identical, even if they share a subculture. Their individual beliefs, values, practices, and assumptions may vary substantially from those that typify their culture in general. Cultural groups overlap, too. A person may have an Asian mother, an African-American father, a Latina stepmother, and be gay. In this situation, many cultures have contributed to his development and current functioning, and it would be inappropriate to single out any one group as "his culture." Pedersen (1991b) makes the point that each interpersonal encounter is a multicultural encounter. Cultural traditions, then, must be seen as hypothetical influences on individuals until evidence shows that they are operative. In other words, a balance is to be achieved that gives cultural variables their appropriate consideration without either overemphasizing or ignoring their influence on human behavior. Counselors who find themselves thinking thoughts such as "She's Native American, so she must feel . . . " or "He's Latino so he must think . . . " are falling victim to the very racist behavior they may be trying to avoid.

Counselors should also be cautious in interpreting the literature on cultural factors in counseling. That literature is still developing and is in a state of flux. In this context, knowledge is never absolute and quickly becomes outdated. The perspectives currently held on the influence of culture on behavior are not fully formed and ought to be viewed with some caution by practitioners. Thus, counselors have an obligation to stay current with this rapidly changing literature.

Finally, scholars on this topic note that attention to issues of cultural diversity is not limited to white counselors. They are not the only cultural group that has internalized racist messages from the society, and they are not the only professionals who will encounter clients whose cultural background differs from their own. Any cultural group can stereotype or assume that its cultural tradition is the best or the only way to organize social reality. Of course, white counselors, as the majority in the professions, and as the beneficiaries of the current social structure, have an especially strong obligation to develop and maintain multicultural sensitivity. An commitment to multicultural sensitivity and competence is a necessity for all counselors, however.

Cases for Discussion and Analysis

Consider the following questions for each case:

- How important is the client's cultural context in assessing the client's issues and determining treatment options?
- What is your emotional reaction to the problem the client presents?
- How do you think your personal values would affect your capacity to counsel these people?
- What multicultural competencies do you think are necessary to do effective counseling in each of these cases?

The Case of Daniel

Daniel is a 23-year-old Orthodox Jew whose family has arranged a marriage for him, the accepted practice in his community. His reaction to this marriage has caused him so much distress that the rabbi recommended counseling. In session Daniel reveals that he is ambivalent about the marriage. On the one hand, he wants to follow the tenets of his religion, which places such strong emphasis on the importance of marriage for a Jewish man, but on the other, he knows he feels nothing for the woman his family has chosen. Daniel says he wants to marry eventually, but feels completely unready now. He feels trapped. To violate his parents' choice would be inconsistent with the expectations of his religion and would risk his family's goodwill and his community's acceptance, but he feels strongly unsuited to this woman at this time. He asks his counselor to help him find a way to be more accepting of his parents' and community's choice for him.

The Case of Roberta

Roberta has come to counseling with her aunt, Mary Begay. Roberta is a Navajo who lives on the reservation with her father, stepmother, and four stepbrothers. She has been detached from the family and acting in ways very atypical for Roberta. They are all worried about her, especially her aunt. Ms. Begay tells of a recent episode that she calls "moth madness," and Roberta acknowledges that this occurred. The counselor wonders if Roberta has developed an insect phobia, and questions her extensively about her fears. Her responses do not point to a phobia, and the counselor is unsure of how counseling ought to proceed, but the client is willing to return to counseling again to explore the matter further. The counselor tentatively diagnoses an adjustment disorder, but is unsure of the cause of Roberta's distress.

The Case of Mervin

Mervin is an 17-year-old African-American teenager who was found living on the streets and sent to counseling by the courts. He is now in a foster home. His mother and father died recently of AIDS complications. His father was a hemophiliac who infected his mother with the virus before he was diagnosed. Mervin does not establish eye contact easily with his European-American counselor and has trouble sitting still for a whole session. The boy says that he wants to be left alone to finish high school, get a job, and get enough money to live on his own. He resists discussing his feelings about his parents' deaths or his current situation. He seems skeptical about the counselor's intentions and seems to have concluded that counseling is something to be patiently endured until the counselor gets tired of it.

The Case of Calvin

Calvin is a 20-year-old architecture student who comes to counseling because of procrastination. Calvin is of Korean ancestry, and his father is a scientist. As the counseling session progresses, Calvin's problem becomes clearer. He procrastinates because he has little interest in architecture. He loves to sculpt and has taken several electives in art. His behavior and affect reveal that sculpture is his true interest, but Calvin turns away suggestions that he may want to consider another major besides architecture. Instead of talking about his own interests, he discusses the long line of scientists in his family and his need to choose a profession with at least some relation to science. He asks the counselor to focus on the procrastination problem, because he cannot really consider other majors.

Analysis of the Cases

In each of these cases, understanding the client's culture is a crucial component of ethical and effective counseling. Daniel, for example, lives in a religious community whose values, traditions, beliefs, and goals probably define almost every aspect of his life. He is part of a group that has been victimized by discrimination and oppression and that prefers minimal interaction with other cultures. His problem stems from a clash between personal wishes and cultural norms. Similarly, Roberta comes from a community that has suffered discrimination and oppression and has learned to be careful in interactions with non-Indians. The cultural norms of her tribe have probably defined her values and beliefs. She may view counseling as a last resort and be skeptical about its capacity to help. The specific problem she mentions, "moth madness," is specific to her culture and is not part of most formal diagnostic systems used in counseling, so it is not meaningful outside the client's culture unless others have been taught its definition. Next, Mervin may have learned not to trust whites easily and to be uncomfortable with other people involving themselves in his personal affairs. Finally, Calvin has placed his family's expectations for his profession above his personal desires, a typical choice in Asian-American culture (Sue & Sue, 1990), but one that conflicts with the dominant U.S. cultural values of individual freedom of choice and action.

Thus, culture is a major influence on the development and definition of the problems these people are experiencing and has impact on the selection of an appropriate treatment strategy. A counselor who is unfamiliar with the Navajo concept of moth madness will have little sense of what Roberta is experiencing, and without asking questions and consulting with others will likely misdiagnose and mistreat this girl. (Moth madness is a seizurelike experience that typically follows incestuous dreams or thoughts in Navajo culture.) Similarly, a counselor who frames Daniel's or Calvin's problem as depression and anxiety stemming from a lack of assertiveness or a failure to appropriately separate from family may create greater pain and will have little success in selecting an intervention that alleviates their pain. Mervin might be misunderstood as hostile, unfeeling, or unable to form close social bonds if his counselor fails to take the cultural context of his behaviors into account. Under such circumstances, his real difficulties are unlikely to be remedied.

Each of these cases probably stirs an emotional reaction in those who imagine themselves in that counselor's position. The view that one's family has the right to choose one's marriage partner is a perspective that few in Western society hold, that most disagree with strongly, and that seems contradictory to the central concept of individual freedom. It probably evokes confusion, anger, and suspicion in counselors from Western cultures. At an intuitive level, many counselors probably believe that Daniel's lack of choice is morally wrong. Roberta's counselor may react with puzzlement and discomfort, or she may approach her with benevolent condescension for her use of such quaint language. The implication in the case description, that the counselor failed to ask the client the meaning of moth madness, suggests either a discomfort with such a strange wording or a naive assumption that it is equated with an insect phobia. Such behavior epitomizes what Wrenn (1962) termed "cultural encapsulation."

Mervin's counselor may react to his behavior and attitude with frustration and may misinterpret the client's response as showing a personal dislike of the counselor. The counselor might assume that Mervin's parents were infected with the HIV virus through intravenous drug use because of a stereotype about heterosexual African-Americans who are HIV infected. Mervin may have experienced this reaction previously from those who did not know his family.

Finally, in the case of Calvin some of the same emotions may emerge. Some counselors may feel angry with the cultural value that minimizes the importance of individual career choice. They may even disbelieve the family influence as a primary factor and wonder if Calvin has some deeper psychological problem that prevents him from doing what he wants. In this instance too, some counselors may believe that the family is morally wrong to impose a career choice on a young adult. In any of these cases, a counselor can also feel the urge to rescue the client and show him or her a different (better?) way of understanding self and relating to family and others.

Multicultural Counseling Competencies

The competencies essential to avoid the many pitfalls just described include an *attitude of openness* toward other cultural views of the world. Understanding the influence of one's cultural heritage on one's own development, values, beliefs, and social behaviors is a prerequisite for this attitude. If one sees the roots of one's behaviors in culture, one is less likely to assume their universal truth or generalizability. In Daniel's case, a counselor would need a willingness to understand the history and function of the arranged marriage tradition in that culture and to identify its origins in a different philosophy of individual freedom. He or she should also be familiar with the implications of the choices Daniel is considering for his social, occupational, and individual functioning. If the counselor is likely drawn to encouraging the client to refuse the marriage at this point, he or she should understand that such a path may carry with it enormous costs for Daniel and may therefore not be in his best interests. That open mind is a prerequisite for helping a client sort out available alternatives and come to a free, self-made choice. Without it, the counselor has a hidden agenda of pushing the client toward a particular action. In the end, it is the client who must live with the consequences of the decision, not the counselor.

Second, a counselor must have *knowledge of the specific culture*. This is especially obvious in the case of Roberta. Ignorance of common cultural phenomena seem to be causing the counselor to badly misdiagnose the problem. Knowledge of the culture is also crucial when clients are torn between following the path typical of their culture and breaking off in a different direction. Knowledge would prevent Calvin's counselor from minimizing his parents' role in career decision making or underestimating the difficulty of violating that expectation.

Third, a counselor must be *competent in involving other support people* from the culture. Knowing when and how to engage the rabbi in Daniel's decision making (assuming, of course, that Daniel agrees) could be a crucial factor in resolving the dilemma. In Roberta's case, the counselor did not seem to understand the aunt's role or availability as a resource, nor did she seem to know to contact a healer from the tribe who might shed light on the situation. In these scenarios, all clients spoke English, but if they did not, this competency also implies the capacity to use the client's language, select a competent interpreter, or refer appropriately. Counselors should know how to seek out support for themselves, through consultation with peers and supervisors, to become better informed about the client's culture.

Fourth, the counselor needs to *modify interventions* or use interventions designed for cross-cultural counseling. Standard approaches to decision making or problem solving do not sufficiently account for the cultural aspects of situations such as Mervin's or Calvin's. Counselors must be skilled enough to adapt them or to use alternative approaches developed for cross-cultural counseling. For example, if Daniel decides to express his feelings about the marriage to his parents, the counselor must be competent in adapting traditional methods for effective interpersonal communication or assertive self-statements to this cultural context. The work of Pedersen (for example, see 1994) and the book edited by Ponterotto, Casas, Suzuki, and Alexander (1995) are important resources in developing such competencies.

Counselors must also *develop a tolerance for ambiguity and divergent views of right and wrong*. When counseling clients such as Daniel, Calvin, or Mervin, counselors need the ability to accept that others do not have the same philosophy, worldview, or system of morality. They must be able to tolerate the discomfort that watching a young person enter into an arranged marriage is likely to provoke. In parallel fashion, they must learn to accept Mervin's choice not to participate fully in counseling, if that is his decision. In essence, this competency springs from the principle of respect for autonomy. If clients freely elect a path and have considered its alternatives, counselors have a duty to respect that choice—provided, of course, it is not a serious risk to the client or others.

SUMMARY

American society has never been culturally homogeneous, but recent and projected changes in population demographics will render it truly heterogeneous. In fact, by early in the twenty-first century, ethnic groups that have long been labeled *minorities* will collectively outnumber the rest of the population. These changes mean that counselors will need skills, beliefs, and attitudes that equip them for providing effective service to culturally diverse clients. The current versions of the codes of ethics place substantial emphasis on multicultural issues. Commitment to principles of equality and justice has never been more important. Along with the desire to be fair and accessible, one must have specific competencies in multicultural counseling to achieve that goal. These competencies include self-awareness that encompasses understanding of one's own cultural heritage and the impact of racism and discrimination on self and others. They also include knowledge about other cultures and the impact of culture on human behavior, with special emphasis on cultural effects on expressions of distress and dysfunction and on responses to counseling. Finally, competent counselors in a multicultural society will also possess skills in transcultural counseling techniques and in adapting other counseling interventions to meet the needs of a diverse clientele.

In the course of their work with diverse populations, counselors will confront dilemmas that are exceptionally difficult to resolve because some of them involve conflicts about deep personal values and beliefs. When this happens, counselors should act cautiously, seek consultation from those more knowledgeable about the client's culture, and refer to the abundant literature on responsible multicultural counseling and therapy.

DISCUSSION QUESTIONS

1. Do you believe the competencies outlined in this chapter are sufficient to equip counselors to work with clients from different backgrounds? Are there other competencies you think should be added to this list? (Explain.)

2. Racism, sexism, and other forms of stereotyping are certainly not extinguished. Sometimes they even seem to be getting worse. What is the responsibility of a counselor in the face of such eruptions of prejudice?

3. Some scholars suggest that all counseling should be seen as cross-cultural. Does this view make sense to you? Why or why not?

4. Language barriers have been one important reason that diverse populations have had less access to counseling. Should competency in a second language be added as a requirement of professional training to address this problem? Is using an interpreter a good solution to this deficiency?

5. Racist counselors still practice, and otherwise well-intentioned counselors still act in racist ways sometimes. How do you think a counselor should react when he or she encounters racist behaviors in colleagues?

6. Do Asian, African-American, and Latino counselors need to be as vigilant about self-monitoring for unconscious racism as European-American counselors? Why or why not?

RECOMMENDED READINGS

American Psychological Association. (1993). *Guidelines for providers of psychological services to ethnic, linguistic and culturally diverse populations.* Washington, DC: Author.

Arrendondo, P., Toporek, R., Brown, S. P., Jones, J., Locke, D., Sanchez, J., & Stadler, H. (1996). Operationalization of the multicultural counseling competencies. *Journal of Multicultural Counseling and Development, 24,* 42–78.

Pedersen, P. B. (1994). *A handbook for developing multicultural awareness* (2nd ed.). Alexandria, VA: American Counseling Association.

Pedersen, P. B., Draguns, J. G., Lonner, W. J., & Trimble, J. E. (1996). *Counseling across cultures* (4th ed.). Thousand Oaks, CA: Sage.

Ponterotto, J. G., Casas, J. M., Suzuki, L. A., & Alexander, C. M. (Eds.). (1995). *Handbook of multicultural counseling.* Thousand Oaks, CA: Sage.

Pope-Davis, D. B., & Dings, J. G. (1995). The assessment of multicultural counseling competencies. In J. G. Ponterotto, J. M. Casas, L. A. Suzuki, & C. M. Alexander (Eds.), *Handbook of multicultural counseling* (pp. 287–311). Thousand Oaks, CA: Sage.

Ridley, C. R. (1995). *Overcoming unintentional racism in counseling: A practitioner's guide to intentional intervention.* Thousand Oaks, CA: Sage.

PART THREE

Ethical Issues in Special Settings

12

The Ethics of Supervision
Modeling Responsible Behavior

To understand the central concerns in the ethics of supervision, we must begin by clarifying several misperceptions of the nature of supervision in counseling and psychotherapy.

The Ethics of Supervision: Myths and Realities

One myth about supervision is that it is an activity at the periphery of the profession, occupying a small and rather insignificant proportion of a professional's time. Yet competent and ethical supervision is an integral part of effective practice. According to Osipow and Fitzgerald (1986), 64% of counseling psychologists regularly spend time supervising other professionals. Moreover, the scholarly literature abounds with references to the crucial importance of supervision in developing and maintaining professional competence (for example, see Loganbill, Hardy, & Delworth, 1982; Stoltenberg & Delworth, 1987). Ethical and legal guidelines view supervision as a prerequisite for competence and credentialing.

Nevertheless, little objective evidence is available about the quality or effectiveness of most supervision. The meager evidence that has been accumulated is not especially encouraging. It shows that the quality of supervision is not uniform and not always consistent with current professional standards. For example, ethics complaints and malpractice claims relating to supervision are rather common. In 1985, VanHoose and Kottler concluded that negligent supervision was a leading cause in many malpractice suits. In addition, some of the most famous malpractice cases in the history of mental health have stemmed at least partly from inadequacies in supervision (for example, Tarasoff, 1974, 1976). Slovenko (1980) argued that had the supervising mental health professional in the *Tarasoff* case handled his supervisory duties responsibly, the plaintiffs might not have been able to show negligence. Survey research also shows that some supervisors exploit their supervisees and act with disregard for their responsibilities in that role and with disdain for the rights of the supervisee (for example, see Allen, Szollos, &

261

Williams, 1986). My own experience as a counselor educator and supervising psychologist certainly confirms that lapses in competent supervision occur frequently, and episodes of exploitive supervision are all too common.

Three factors may explain the discrepancy between the desired and actual state of supervision. The first factor is the rather common practice of equating competence as a practitioner with competence as a supervisor. Both the ethics codes and the literature on supervision strongly belie this assumption (Bernard & Goodyear, 1992; Vasquez, 1992). They view skill and experience as a practitioner as a necessary but not sufficient condition for competence in supervision. In this chapter I examine the components of supervisor competency presented in the codes and the literature.

Supervision is a process that involves multiple roles (Bernard & Goodyear, 1992; Sherry, 1991). The supervisor is a teacher, mentor, adviser, consultant, and evaluator to the supervisee as well as a counselor (from a distance) to the clients of the supervisee. Successfully managing these multiple roles requires knowledge, self-awareness, and experience. Thus, the second factor that helps explain some lapses in responsible supervision is a professional's inability to handle these varied roles simultaneously. The following pages elaborate on this issue and provide recommendations for success in this task.

The third and final factor that relates to improper supervision is the inability of the supervisor to place the welfare of the supervisee or the supervisee's clients over his or her own interests. When this happens, supervisees get exploited. The form of such misbehavior varies substantially, from the imposition of personal values, to sexual harassment and financial exploitation. Its results regularly depreciate the effectiveness of the supervisory experience, compromise the value of the counseling experience to the clients, and sometimes traumatize the supervisee (Allen et al., 1986; Slimp & Burian, 1994). The following pages examine in more detail the forms such exploitation takes and ways to minimize that risk.

The content of this chapter is drawn not only from scholarly writings and the codes of ethics of the professions, but also from two other important documents. Both have been developed and published under the auspices of the Association for Counselor Education and Supervision (ACES), a division of ACA. Neither has the same power of enforcement as the codes, but both guide professionals seeking to act in accordance with the highest ethical values. The first document, *Standards for Counseling Supervisors,* was published in 1990. ACA formally adopted these standards during 1989. The second document developed by ACES is entitled *Ethical Guidelines for Counseling Supervisors* (1993). It attends to a broader range of issues in supervision and is especially useful in clarifying the ethical dimensions of role conflicts, in elucidating the supervisor's obligations to the client and supervisee, and in administering supervisory placements.

Competence to Supervise

To understand the ethical and legal dimensions of competence in supervision, we must retrace our steps to the components of competent practice. As you recall, competence requires knowledge, skill, and diligence in work with real clients. Novice counselors are deemed competent after they demonstrate to supervisors sufficient levels of these qualities in work with a variety of clients. Supervisors, then, are the final gatekeepers of the profession, who act as the last checkpoint against the admission of unskilled or untherapeutic people into the professional community. The process of determining which novices are competent demands careful and sustained attention to the activities of the supervisee. Untrained supervisors are unlikely to meet those demands. When they fail in this ethical duty, they damage the profession, the public, and probably the person inappropriately admitted to the profession.

The ACES Standards for Counseling Supervisors (1990) elaborate in great detail the characteristics and competencies of effective supervisors. In this way they provide a road map for professionals who want to assess their supervisory competence. The characteristics identified by these standards are summarized as follows:

- Competence as counselors themselves, including skills in assessment and intervention, case conceptualization and case management, recordkeeping, and evaluation of counseling outcomes
- Attitudes and traits consistent with the role, such as sensitivity to individual differences, motivation and commitment to supervision, and comfort with the authority accompanying that role
- Familiarity with the ethical, legal, and regulatory dimensions of supervision
- Knowledge of the professional and personal facets of the supervisory relationship and the impact of supervision on the supervisee
- Understanding of the methods and techniques of supervision
- Appreciation of the process of counselor development and its unfolding in supervision
- Capacity to evaluate a supervisee's counseling performance fairly and accurately and to provide feedback to facilitate growth
- Grasp of the rapidly expanding body of theory and research on counselor supervision

Both the length and complexity of this list demonstrate that competence as a practitioner is but a small part of responsible supervision. In light of these standards, the notion that supervisory skills are acquired through "on-the-job-training" or by osmosis is clearly incorrect. When researchers (Navin, Beamish, & Johanson, 1995) used this document to ascertain the competence of counselors currently in the supervisory role, many fell short, especially of the standard relating to training in supervision. Other research also supports this conclusion (Hess & Hess, 1983). Even supervisees seem unsure of the supervisory training of those who oversee their work. A survey of psychologists by McCarthy, Kulakowski, and Kenfield (1994) found that 72% of the sample were uncertain about whether their supervisors had training in supervision.

Of course, ethical standards deal with more than objective knowledge and observable skill. They also place considerable emphasis on the attitudes and values of the supervisor, requiring the same kind of diligence in supervisory responsibilities that is expected in direct service. Also embedded in the standards and the other literature on supervision (for example, Leong & Wagner, 1994) is a mandate for sensitivity to individual differences and the special concerns of culturally diverse supervisees.

The ACA ethics code addresses the topic, at least in very general terms:

Section F.1.f: Supervision Preparation

Counselors who offer clinical supervision services are adequately prepared in supervision methods and techniques. Counselors who are doctoral students serving as practicum or internship supervisors to master's level students are adequately prepared and supervised by the training program.

The APA code focuses its comments on the need for the professional to assign responsibilities to supervisees in appropriate ways and to provide them with proper oversight:

Section 1.22: Delegation to and Supervision of Subordinates

(a) Psychologists delegate to their employees, supervisees, and research assistants only those responsibilities that such persons can reasonably be expected to perform competently, on the basis of their education, training, or experience, either independently, or with the level of supervision usually provided.

(b) Psychologists provide proper training and supervision to their employees or supervisees and take reasonable steps to see that such persons perform services responsibly, competently, and ethically.

(c) If institutional policies, procedures, or practices prevent fulfillment of this obligation, psychologists attempt to modify their role to correct the situation to the extent feasible.

Responsible Use of Supervisory Power

Supervision is often an emotionally intense experience for supervisees. They are coping with the heavy emotional demands of clinical work and are in the midst of making important decisions about their professional futures (Slimp & Burian, 1994). Moreover, supervisees have limited ability to protect themselves when their supervisors act inappropriately. The supervisory relationship also involves a strong emotional connection between those involved, and parallels therapy in some regards. Reactions similar to transference and countertransference happen frequently, and supervisors often become aware of the ways in which the personal problems of supervisees affect their functioning with clients (Bernard & Goodyear, 1992). Supervisees also look to their supervisors as models of professional behavior (Vasquez, 1992). So supervisors who act unethically may be "teaching" those under their influence to engage in those behaviors. At the very least, though, supervisors who misuse their influence are losing an opportunity to show less experienced colleagues the proper behavior of a professional. For all these reasons, the person in the supervisory role has substantial power and can use it to help or harm supervisees.

The codes of ethics and guidelines address issues of power and exploitation in broad terms, grouping together many classes of people over whom professionals may have authority. The codes' most specific comments deal with sexual exploitation:

ACA *Code of Ethics,* **Section D.1.k**

Counselors do not engage in exploitive relationships with individuals over whom they have supervisory, evaluative, or instructional control or authority.

ACA *Code of Ethics,* **Section E.1.b: Relationship Boundaries**

Counselors clearly define and maintain ethical, professional, and social relationship boundaries with their students and supervisees. They are aware of the differential in power that exists and the student's or supervisees's possible incomprehension of that power differential. Counselors explain to students and supervisees the potential for the relationship to become exploitive.

ACA *Code of Ethics,* **Section E.1.c: Sexual Relationships**

Counselors do not engage in sexual relationships with students or supervisees and do not subject them to sexual harassment.

APA *Ethical Principles,* **Section 1.19: Exploitative Relationships**

(a) Psychologists do not exploit persons over whom they have supervisory, evaluative, or other authority, such as students, supervisees, employees, research participants, and clients or patients.

(b) Psychologists do not engage in sexual relationships with students or supervisees in training over whom the psychologist has evaluative or direct authority, because such relationships are so likely to impair judgment or to be exploitive.

Avoiding Unhealthy Dependency

Kurpius, Gibson, Lewis, and Corbet (1991) assert that supervisors who foster an unhealthy dependency on them are also misusing their power. The goal of supervision is not to have the supervisee deferring all judgment to the supervisor, but rather to help the supervisee develop the skills, judgment, and confidence to accurately discriminate when to work independently and when to seek assistance. At first, of course, novice counselors are rather dependent on their supervisors for guidance, reassurance, and practical strategies. This kind of dependence at this stage of development is not problematic. What is problematic is a supervisory style that fails to encourage independence, or worse, actively encourages dependency. Supervisors who are uncertain whether their behavior meets this standard should evaluate it in light of the "clean, well-lit room standard" (Haas & Malouf, 1995) and seek consultation.

Limiting the Number of Supervisees

Responsible use of power in supervision encompasses more than avoiding exploitive behaviors. Four other dimensions exist. One is the responsibility to limit the number of supervisees to a manageable level so that the needs of supervisees and their clients are met (ACES, 1990). What number of supervisees is manageable? The answer depends on several factors:

- The experience and competence of the supervisor as therapist and as supervisor
- The experience and competence of the supervisee
- The time available for supervision activities
- The nature of the client population served
- The existence of any state laws or regulations that stipulate a maximum number of supervisees

In general, when the demands of the population served and the needs of the supervisee are high, and the competence or time availability of the supervisor is low, fewer people should be supervised. Regulatory bodies often set a maximum of three to five supervisees per licensed professional. The American Association of State Psychology Boards recommends no more than three supervisees per psychologist (AASPB, 1979). These limits are sensible, given the often intense demands of the supervisory process and the legal dimensions of supervision. (The latter will be discussed in subsequent sections of this chapter.) However, that regulation does not imply that it is ethical for all licensed professionals to take on that number of supervisees. Such a judgment should be based on the criteria listed earlier. In some cases, there is no ethical justification for even a single supervisee. Counselors who tend to accept many supervisees need to examine their motivation. If supervision is being used as a method of increasing income or professional reputation, then the practice is misguided. The only supportable justification for multiple supervisees is public need, commitment to training, and interest in the development of the people being supervised.

Three other aspects of supervision are important to address. First, supervision must be a face-to-face activity (ACES, 1993), and the supervisor should have face-to-face interaction with clients if necessary. Supervision by memo or telephone is not a substitute for person-to-person contact, except in rare circumstances. Nor is "review of case notes" a viable alternative, though the research by Navin et al. (1995), shows that such a practice is rather common. The need to arrange in-person meetings puts a practical limit on the number of supervisees. Second, not all states stipulate a maximum number of supervisees for all professions. In Ohio, for example, there is no regulation governing the number of supervisees a psychiatrist can oversee at one time. When such regulatory gaps exist, the determination of a prudent and responsible number of supervisees is left to the individual practitioner. Third, a supervisee cannot shift all the responsibility for decision making about this matter to the supervisor. A supervisee is also responsible for knowing and abiding by the ethical and legal standards governing practice. Thus, any professional is obliged to refuse to accept supervision from someone who has an excessive load of supervisees. In this situation, the counselor needs to make alternative arrangements and, if possible, to tactfully inform the supervisor about the reason for that decision.

Informed Consent to Supervision

The second aspect of responsible use of power to consider is that of respecting the supervisee's autonomy. One important way to honor this autonomy is through developing informed consent to supervision. It is the responsibility of the supervisor to ensure that the supervisee understands and freely consents to the conditions of supervision. McCarthy, Sugden, Koker, Lamendola, Maurer, and Renninger (1995) identify seven specific topics that the supervisor ought to address in the informed consent process. Supervisees should be instructed, first, about the *purposes of supervision,* that is, to foster their development as competent professionals and to protect the welfare of their clients. Second, they also have a right to know the *qualifications, credentials, style, and theoretical orientation of the supervisor* as consumers of a professional service. Third, they should be briefed about the *logistics* of supervision—times, frequency, emergency procedures, paperwork, and other demands imposed by licensing boards or internship requirements. Supervisors should also provide the name of at least one other professional whom the supervisee might contact in the event that the supervisor was unreachable in a crisis. In addition (fourth), supervisees have a right to understand the *process and procedures* for supervision, including the roles, expectations, and responsibilities of each person. For example, if a supervisor expects a supervisee to prepare for their meetings in a particular way, such an expectation should be communicated. Frequently, supervision involves reviewing tape recordings of sessions with clients. In this event, developing informed consent with the client would include explanation of taping procedures and the ways the tapes will be used in supervision.

Fifth, and perhaps the most crucial, of all the guidelines suggested by McCarthy and her colleagues states that supervisees should be instructed about the *procedures for evaluating their performance.* This recommendation is supported by the ethics codes (APA, Section 6.05, and ACA, Section F.2.e). Evaluation procedures must include provisions for frequent, objective feedback sessions about performance and specific recommendations for remedying deficiencies. Supervisors' evaluation procedures should also aim at building the supervisees' skills in accurate self-evaluation (Disney & Stephens, 1994). Supervisees in danger of failing must be informed about this risk immediately. They should also be briefed about the particular areas of deficiency and the level of improvement necessary to remain in good standing (Bernard & Goodyear, 1992). To avoid confusion, written evaluations are essential. Many ethics complaints regarding supervision involve violations of these evaluation guidelines. Too often supervisees misunderstand the role of the supervisor and/or misjudge their progress in supervision. Supervisees have much at stake in the process and have often had little prior experience with individual supervision as a method of evaluation. Consequently, comprehensive attention to this issue is crucial. Allen et al. (1986) found that supervisors judged by psychology interns to be ideal were clear, thorough, and respectful in their evaluation procedures. Robiner, Fuhrman, and Bobbitt (1990) have proposed an instrument called the Minnesota Supervisory Inventory (MSI) that supervisors may use to ensure objective and comprehensive feedback.

The sixth component of informed supervision, according to McCarthy et al., is *instruction in the ethical and legal issues in supervision and practice.* Ethics education in graduate programs tends to focus more on direct service issues than on teaching and supervision concerns (Welfel & Hannigan-Farley, 1996), so that supervisors cannot be confident that their supervisees are educated about these topics. Even if the material was discussed in ethics courses, prudent supervisors remind supervisees about the ethical and legal standards that affect their interactions, providing copies of the codes and guidelines for supervisees to refer to as needed. As mentioned, the ACA code specifically charges supervisors with the duty to instruct supervisees about the boundaries of their relationship.

Finally (seventh), McCarthy et al. recommend that supervisors use a *written informed consent document* that contains information relevant to each of the six areas just described, for each person to sign as a contract for their work together. This practice protects the legal rights of both parties and also symbolizes the dignity and autonomy of each. It formalizes their mutual commitment to the learning process and the welfare of the clients. (McCarthy et al. include a sample contract in the appendix to their article that can serve as a model for others to use.)

Other scholars recommend documenting each supervisory session, both to improve evaluation of supervisees and to monitor the care given to clients (Harrar, VandeCreek, & Knapp, 1990). The content of these documents should include five items:

- Date and time for the meeting
- A listing of cases discussed
- Notes about client progress
- Recommendations to the supervisee
- Issues for follow-up in future meetings

If the supervisee is having significant difficulty in meeting client needs or learning required concepts, documentation of the meeting should also contain a plan for remedying of those deficiencies. These records should be kept in a confidential file, accessible to supervisor and supervisee. Bridge and Bascue (1988) have published a one-page form that efficiently meets these requirements.

Sensitivity to Issues of Diversity

The third aspect of responsible use of power relates to the sensitivity of the supervisor to issues of diversity. In particular, the supervisor is obligated to avoid actions that reflect gender, ethnic, age, religious, or sexual orientation bias. The ACES standards (1990, p. 30) address this topic directly in Section 4.1:

> The counseling supervisor:
> demonstrates knowledge of individual differences with respect to gender, race, ethnicity, culture and age and understands the importance of these characteristics in supervisory relationships.

Unfortunately, research shows that insensitivity about these issues is not unknown. In the Allen et al. (1986) study, such behaviors were a major factor in earning counselors the designation "worst supervisor." Even well-intentioned supervisors can exhibit inappropriate behaviors. Williams and Halgin (1995) point out that in the hope of fostering congenial relationships, European-American supervisors of African-American supervisees often avoid discussing their racial difference. That avoidance is likely to have the opposite impact. Similarly, these scholars suggest that supervisors sometimes show insensitivity to the impact of their power over African-American supervisees. They fail to understand the supervisees' level of discomfort with the one-down position in a society that has so often discriminated against their race. It is interesting to note that in one of the few empirical studies of cross-cultural supervision, Vander Kolk (1974) found that at the start of the supervision experience, African-American students anticipated less acceptance and empathy from their supervisors than did their European-American counterparts.

In parallel fashion, supervisors can hold different objectives or behaviors unfairly based on the age, gender, religion, sexual orientation, or cultural background of supervisees. They may even discriminate on the basis of these factors in accepting students to supervise. Again, Allen et al. (1986) found that students who encountered supervisors who acted in these ways labeled those professionals as bad supervisors.

Bernard and Goodyear (1992) offer some suggestions for minimizing these problems. First, supervisors must reject the "myth of sameness" and acknowledge the reality and contributions of cultural diversity. Second, they must understand that their own views of the world may not be shared by their supervisees and that this difference does not represent a deficiency in anyone. Third, they encourage supervisors to devote the same energy to appreciating cultural diversity in supervision as they may use in understanding how cultural diversity affects therapy relationships. They must also be committed to self-monitoring their own behavior and to developing the knowledge and skills required for effective cross-cultural supervision. Vasquez (1992) offers another valuable recommendation: Supervisors of culturally diverse professionals ought to become familiar with the special challenges inherent in integrating ethnic identity with professional identity.

Other Personal Values and Beliefs

Supervisors also need to be aware of the ways in which other personal beliefs and values may affect the supervisory process. This responsibility closely parallels the counselor's duty with clients; hence, the following sections of the ethics codes are relevant:

> **ACA** *Code of Ethics,* **Sections A.5.a and A.5.b**
>
> a. Personal needs
>
> In the counseling relationships, counselors are aware of the intimacy and responsibility inherent in the counseling relationships, maintain respect for clients, and avoid actions that seek to meet their personal needs at the expense of clients.
>
> b. Personal values
>
> Counselors are aware of their own values, attitudes, beliefs, and behaviors and how these apply in a diverse society, and avoid imposing their values on clients.

> **APA** *Ethical Principles,* **Principle B: Integrity**
>
> Psychologists seek to promote integrity in the science, teaching and practice of psychology. . . . Psychologists strive to be aware of their own belief systems, values, needs and limitations and the effects of these on their work.

By substituting the word *supervisee* for *client* in the preceding sentences, a counselor can obtain a good sense of the goal of this recommendation for supervision. Because of the limited power of the supervisee, the person in authority must be able to separate professional from personal beliefs and values and to use only the former in teaching and evaluating the supervisee. Consider the following situation:

Dr. Ziblinsky supervises two predoctoral interns at a college counseling center. She also serves on the board of directors of the Planned Parenthood agency in her community. One of her interns, Mr. Appleton, is an active participant in the local Right-to-Life group. Dr. Ziblinsky learns of Mr. Appleton's involvement in that organization a few months into the internship. Soon thereafter, she begins assigning female clients to the other intern, in the belief that Mr. Appleton's personal values would prevent him from effectively counseling female students about reproductive issues. Dr. Ziblinsky also finds herself being more businesslike and task oriented with Mr. Appleton than with the other intern. When Mr. Appleton realizes what is happening, he asks for a private meeting with her to discuss the matter. In that meeting, Dr. Ziblinsky defends her decision, arguing that it is in the best interests of the students who seek counseling at the center.

In this scenario, Dr. Ziblinsky has failed to distinguish personal from professional belief. She has allowed her own strong beliefs about reproductive issues to inappropriately influence her professional judgment about a supervisee. She is preventing Mr. Appleton from seeing female clients based on speculation rather than on any evidence that he intends to impose his beliefs on clients. Thus, this supervisor acted unethically. First, the frequency with which female clients seek counseling about an unexpected pregnancy is rather low. It certainly happens, but most female clients have other issues. To eliminate all female clients from his calendar is an overreaction to a relatively low-probability event. Second, even if a client does present with an unexpected pregnancy, Dr. Ziblinsky has no evidence that her intern will attempt to impose his personal beliefs on that client. Mr. Appleton may have already thought through this issue and decided on a strategy to refer the client to another counselor under this circumstance. In addition, Dr. Ziblinsky is violating professional standards insofar as she is allowing her disdain for this intern's personal beliefs to affect her behavior in supervision. She has begun a pattern of treating Mr. Appleton differently from the other intern. This is discrimination based on a characteristic that has not shown any relevance to his competence as a professional. The intern also needs to have broad training. Preventing him from counseling women limits his training and his competence. Such limits should be imposed only when justified by evidence of incompetence or misconduct. Then she further complicates her ethical error by failing to recognize the problem when her intern speaks to her about it. The supervisor has thereby missed an opportunity to change her behavior to comply with her duty to this student. In short, in the name of doing what she believes to be the right thing for women with unexpected pregnancies, she has failed to act responsibly. Her initial motivation was not self-interested, because she did not personally profit in any way from her decision, but it was self-absorbed and inattentive to her duties to the intern. If she continues her current behavior, Dr. Ziblinsky will violate all five ethical principles—beneficence, nonmaleficence, justice, fidelity, and respect for autonomy.

When faced with such issues in supervision, supervisors ought to ask themselves the following questions:

- Is this belief or value truly relevant to professional behavior?
- Am I treating supervisees or their clients unfairly by my actions?
- Am I fostering the growth of the supervisee by this action?
- Would objective colleagues be likely to come to the same conclusion?
- What alternatives to the course of action under consideration may better comply with professional standards?
- Will supervision or therapy assist me in meeting my obligations to the supervisee?
- If I have already acted in inappropriate ways, how can I undo or minimize the harm that has already been done?

Supervisors are also obliged to respect differences in theoretical orientation. Indeed, the ACES guidelines (1990, Section 3.08) mandate that supervisors have an important role in helping those in their charge to develop their own theoretical orientation. Failure to respect theoretical differences implies that one already has "the truth" about effective therapy. Such an attitude is not only disrespectful of the autonomy of others, it is also inconsistent with scientific evidence. No research shows that one theoretical approach to counseling is superior to all the others. Thus supervisors ought not criticize supervisees for using alternative approaches as long as the intern is competent and can show the relevance of the approach to a client's problem. If a supervisor has a strong investment in a particular theory or method, that investment should be made known to the supervisee before the relationship begins, so that he or she can make an informed decision about whether to engage in this supervisory relationship. Of course, if a supervisee is using an approach that one believes will be counterproductive or ineffective, then the supervisor is obligated to suggest alternatives. The encouragement of alternative strategies should be based on objective analysis rather than on personal preferences or overidentification with a theory.

Responsibilities for Client Welfare

Supervisors have ultimate legal and ethical responsibility for the welfare of their supervisees' clients. When counseling supervisors have competent, diligent supervisees who foster the welfare of their clients, there is little conflict between their obligations to both parties. However, when supervisees act in ways that do not positively affect the well-being of clients, supervisors feel conflicting obligations. On the one hand, they must help supervisees overcome problems so that they can continue to develop as professionals. If a supervisor intervened with every mistake, supervisees would not be able to improve their skills, and if high levels of competence were established for novice professionals to work with clients, very few would attain the standard. On the other hand, supervisors must protect the welfare of the client from inept care. How can a supervisor meet both these obligations? The ACES *Guidelines* are helpful in this regard. They establish that both are important duties, but that the supervisor's first responsibility is to the client. The duty to the supervisee's development as a professional is secondary. The ACA code reiterates that message in its opening standard:

ACA *Code of Ethics,* Section A.1: Client Welfare

The primary responsibility of counselors is to respect the dignity and to promote the welfare of clients.

The APA code uses a wider lens in viewing the issue, grouping together the obligations of psychologists to act with concern for the welfare of all parties with whom they interact:

APA *Ethical Principles,* Principle F: Concern for Others' Welfare

Psychologists seek to contribute to the welfare of those with whom they interact professionally. In their professional actions psychologists weigh the welfare and rights of their patients or clients, students, supervisees, human research participants, and other affected persons, and the welfare of animal subjects of research. When conflicts occur among psychologists' obligations or concerns, they attempt to resolve these conflicts and to perform their roles in a responsible fashion that avoids or minimizes harm.

The best remedy for the problem, of course, is prevention. Supervisors must thoroughly assess the skills of the supervisee at the beginning of the experience and must assiduously monitor changes. Novice counselors should be carefully supervised so that errors can be prevented or minimized when they occur. The complexity of cases they are given should match their prior training and experience, and the clients they serve should understand the nature of the counseling they are receiving and the recourse they have if dissatisfied. None of these responsibilities can be met with a laissez-faire style of supervision. Supervisors should be guided by the goal of maximizing student learning without risking client welfare.

Vasquez (1992) notes that interns and others under supervision sometimes suffer distress that impairs their functioning in the professional role. They are not immune from the problems that can afflict other professionals—substance abuse, major mental illness, grief, loneliness, or marital dissatisfaction. Thus she recommends that supervisors be alert for such difficulties and intervene as soon as such problems begin to compromise a supervisee's work. The ACA *Code of Ethics* and the ACES document (1993) support this recommendation (ACA, Section F.3; ACES, Section 2.12). Lamb, Cochran, and

Jackson (1991) have defined impairment more broadly, to encompass two other characteristics. One is an unwillingness to comply with professional ethical standards, and the second is an inability to meet minimum criteria for competence. Regardless of the scope of an individual supervisor's definition of impairment, it is clear that supervisors are obliged to monitor supervisee progress and intervene when meaningful deficits occur to protect client welfare and to facilitate supervisee development. Lamb et al. have offered a comprehensive set of guidelines to aid in identifying and remedying intern impairment. These guidelines emphasize the importance of frequent communication among supervisors, regular feedback meetings with supervisees, and formal procedures for responding to impairment when other efforts are insufficient. When such interventions are unsuccessful, probation or dismissal may become necessary. (See Frame & Stevens-Smith, 1995, for a discussion of legal and ethical issues in dismissing students from academic programs for other than academic reasons.)

The responsibility of the supervisor to the client extends to two other areas. First, the supervisor is bound to oversee the confidentiality of client disclosures and records. This duty behooves supervisors to educate and monitor those they oversee regarding confidentiality standards and procedures. It also means that they make sure clients have been informed about and consented to the supervisee's communications with the supervisor. Second, when sessions are to be recorded or observed, supervisors should ascertain that clients have agreed to the practice and understand how the recordings will be used. They also monitor the care supervisees take over the confidentiality of those tapes. If a client refuses consent for taping, the supervisor must judge whether the supervisee is capable of providing competent service in the absence of such monitoring. If the supervisor concludes that recording is essential for competent service or is a requirement for the supervisee, he or she must help the supervisee communicate that to clients and obtain alternate care for the client that does not involve the use of recording devices. Prudent supervisors guard the client's right to autonomy about recording and recognize the obligation of the institution to provide competent, beneficial service to that client.

Dual-Relationship Issues

Sexual exploitation is not the only form of dual relationship to which supervisors are vulnerable. Because of the close, collegial nature of supervisory relationships, those in authority can lose track of the evaluative aspect of those relationship and begin to see supervisees as friends or fully qualified colleagues. If you recall the case of Yolanda from Chapter 2, she was at risk for entering a dual relationship with her supervisee when she wanted to invite her supervisee to join her in social and community activities. Because the boundaries between supervisee and supervisor can get blurred even more easily than boundaries in other professional relationships, counselors must be vigilant about monitoring their behavior and should set clear limits. The codes do not absolutely forbid social or business relationships with supervisees, but they strongly caution against them. The responsibility to place client welfare ahead of the supervisee's experience means that the supervisor must be able to clearly see what is happening with the client and have the energy to intervene when needed. Social or business relationships compromise that capacity. In a dual relationship, counselors can come to prize their friendship or financial connection to the supervisee more than they value a client's welfare. When a counselor is in doubt about the ethics of a particular relationship, he or she should consult with colleagues for guidance. Research suggests that boundary violations occur rather frequently. For instance, Navin et al. (1995) reported that 25% of their sample of field supervisors were aware of social interactions between supervisors and trainees that they viewed as incompatible with the supervisors' duties.

Supervisors are sometimes tempted to serve as counselors for those they supervise. In a survey of counselors at college counseling centers, Sherry et al. (1991) found that 48% of respondents admitted such behavior at least on rare occasions. Of these, 3% acknowledged treating supervisees at least fairly often. The therapylike nature of supervision makes this role slippage understandable, but not ethical. Whiston and Emerson (1989) identify several specific problems with this practice. First, it can compromise a supervisor's objectivity about both the supervisee and the client and thereby interfere with one's duty to both. In addition, it diminishes the capacity of supervisors to carry out their responsibility to the profession and the public to act as gatekeeper against admitting ineffective individuals into the profession. Second, the client/supervisee is not only even more vulnerable to a supervisor's misuse of power, but he or she is also likely to be confused about which rules apply when. A supervisee might be reluctant to reveal personal information in counseling, fearing its impact on supervision. Moreover, they point out that when such a dual relationship is occurring, another violation must have preceded it—a failure of informed consent. Consent probably has not been properly obtained. Its voluntariness is certainly in doubt if the supervisor proposed the counseling sessions. Finally, if there are any group supervision activities occurring, a dual relationship with one supervisee complicates the process of group supervision. If other group members know of the counseling activity, they may be uncomfortable and fail to take full advantage of the experience. Similarly, the supervisee in the dual relationship may have worries about the confidentiality of counseling information and about the way he or she will be evaluated in the supervision.

The wording of the ACA code on this issue suggests that the profession finds that reasoning cogent:

ACA *Code of Ethics,* Section F.3.c

If students or supervisees request counseling, supervisors or counselor educators provide them with acceptable referrals. Supervisors or counselor educators do not serve as counselor to students or supervisees over whom they hold administrative, teaching or evaluative roles unless this is a brief role associated with a training experience.

Unfortunately, many practitioners seem oblivious to the ethical implications of counseling supervisees. In 1987, 13% of psychologists labeled this practice as ethical (Pope et al., 1987). Four years later, Gibson and Pope (1993) found that 44% of the counselors participating in their survey endorsed this view.

At first glance, avoiding an intense counseling component of supervision seems inconsistent with the recommendation to monitor the effect of supervisees' personal problems on their work. However, ethics scholars provide a reasonable resolution of the dilemma. The bedrock of their scholarship is a recognition of the limits on the depth and breadth of exploration of personal issues in supervision. Whiston and Emerson (1989) offer guidelines for distinguishing supervision from counseling. First, as the ACES *Guidelines* also advise (Section 2.11), any discussion of personal issues should focus on their relationship to professional development. Personal issues that appear irrelevant to professional functioning have no place in a supervisory discussion. Second, the function of the supervisor is to *identify* personal problems that may be inhibiting the supervisee's performance, not to *resolve* those issues. The latter is the task of a counselor with no conflicting role obligations, to whom the supervisor may refer the supervisee. Third, when supervisees reveal personal matters in connection with a case discussion, supervisors should limit their responses to basic empathy and understanding of the issue and should refrain from interpretations or comments that would make deep exploration of personal matters more likely. Supervisors ought not to act in a cold and unfeeling way in response to such supervisee disclosures, however. Supervisor warmth is a highly valued quality among interns and facilitates their development (Allen et al., 1986). Thus, supervisors should show compassion and concern but refrain from moving into deeper therapeutic territory. Moreover, supervisees who are informed about the distinction between therapy and supervision are better able to respect the boundaries between those two activities and to understand the meaning of supervisors' responses to personal issues. For example, if a supervisee reveals that he is distracted by news that his parent has been diagnosed with advanced cancer, a supervisor may discuss the matter with him, show sympathy, and ask whether there is any way in which she can be of assistance. None of those actions involves deep probing into personal issues.

What if students do not request counseling or seem unaware of the need for it? Wise, Lowery, and Silverglade (1989) suggest that students' capacity to respond to a supervisor's recommendation to seek counseling may be related to their stage of professional development and trust of the supervisor. They suggest that students who have moved beyond their initial fears of incompetence and focus on specific counseling techniques are more likely to be receptive to such advice.

Layered Supervision

To become a competent supervisor, one must have supervised experience in supervision (along with knowledge and diligence, of course). Graduate programs often provide internships in supervision to advanced students by having them oversee the work of beginning students. Doctoral students commonly supervise master's-level students, for example. In the long run, this practice benefits the profession, the public, and the supervisees. However, it also raises difficulties. For example, when there are several layers of supervision the professionals who have the ultimate responsibility for the client find more distance between them and the client. Their sense of the client's progress is obscured. They must develop careful and consistent data-gathering methods to overcome this weakness. Second, they have responsibilities for the learning of not one, but two supervisees, whose needs, skills, and attitudes may vary significantly. They must work energetically to monitor the students' progress and to facilitate their learning. Third, supervisors must be especially alert for compromised confidentiality of client disclosures and violations of client autonomy rights. The more people who hold confidential information, the more likely that inadvertent breaches will occur. Fourth, when supervision is layered, the responsibility for client welfare may be diffused and problems may be missed, because each professional assumes another was responsible. The supervisor at the top layer must guard against such a diffusion of responsibility. Finally, as Herlihy and Corey (1996) note, even when layered supervision is carried out within the boundaries of the ethical standards, the experience of being supervised by other students can be uncomfortable. Thus supervisors need to appreciate this discomfort and keep discussion lines open so that those who are ill at ease with the arrangement feel they may voice their concerns and get them resolved.

Legal Aspects of Supervision

Two kinds of legal issues are of special concern to mental health professionals involved in supervision: (1) the liability of supervisors for both their own actions and the actions of supervisees and (2) the legal rights of professionals under supervision.

Liability Issues

The most important legal issue in supervision relates to the degree of liability a supervisor bears for the actions of supervisees. To understand the liability issues, one must begin with the nature of the service a client has a right to expect when working with a supervisee. As Harrar et al. (1990) point out so perceptively, when a client agrees to such counseling, he or she is *not* consenting to substandard or harmful care. The contract implicit in that consent is for the service providers to give competent, helpful service. When that does not occur, clients have been wronged and it is their right to seek redress. If incompetent care is given, the client may point to all parties in the relationship as responsible for the harm that has happened. Thus, supervisors are liable for their own actions *and* for the negligent acts of those they supervise. Harrar et al. define the first kind of liability as *direct liability*. It parallels the liability any practicing mental health professional would have in relation to negligence in his or her work. In other words, this form of liability holds when the harm to the client occurred at least partly because the supervisor failed to conduct supervision in accordance with ethical and legal standards. Supervisors may be directly liable under a variety of circumstances, including, but not limited to the following: failing to meet with supervisees, neglecting important client information that supervisees share with them, or assigning clients to supervisees who are inadequately trained to deal with the clients' concerns.

Vicarious liability also exists for supervisors. The Latin term associated with this concept is *respondeat superior*, and it means "Let the master respond." It means that supervisors may be held liable for the actions of their supervisees even when the supervisors have not been negligent in carrying out their supervisory duties. The rationale behind this principle is based on the profit supervisors gain from their supervisees and on their power over them. (The term *profit* is defined broadly and need not be monetary.) Because supervisors choose whom they will accept as supervisees, regularly decide whether supervisees will be allowed to continue in the professional capacity, and benefit when supervisees perform admirably, the law has reasoned that supervisors ought to share the financial burdens for the misconduct of subordinates (Disney & Stephens, 1994; Harrar et al., 1990). Vicarious liability applies only to actions "within the course and scope of the supervisory relationship" (Disney & Stephens, 1994, p. 15) and is tempered by other factors such as the extent of the supervisor's power over the subordinate, the aspect of the counseling in which the negligence occurred, the particular circumstances of the actions, the motivation of the supervisee, and the likelihood that the supervisor could have reasonably predicted the supervisee's action. Vicarious liability also assumes that the subordinate has voluntarily chosen to be under the supervisor's guidance and direction (Harrar et al., 1990). In short, even exemplary supervisory behavior does not greatly reduce the risk of vicarious liability. Vicarious liability might occur if a supervisee provides incompetent service to a client but has withheld relevant information about the course of treatment from the supervisor. A supervisor might also be held liable, for example, if a supervisee disclosed confidential information to someone outside the workplace.

Given these facts, one may wonder why mental health professionals agree to take on the responsibilities of supervision in the first place. Are they ignorant of the liability issues? Do they value supervision so much that they willingly accept the risk? Do they act grudgingly, feeling there is little alternative? Based on the available evidence, ignorance of this legal standard probably is the most significant factor, but no definitive research exists on that issue. Regardless, supervision is vital to the future of the profession and the provision of quality services to the public. Competent professionals, then, must find ways to minimize their risk. Bernard and Goodyear (1992) recommend that supervisors establish an open, trusting relationship with supervisees so that supervisees are willing to discuss all aspects of their work with clients in supervisory sessions. I would add to that a requirement that supervisees record counseling sessions so that supervisors can hear or see exactly what has transpired in session. Even though supervisors may not have the time to review a complete recording of every supervisee session, as long as a tape exists the option is available if needed. Moreover, tapes encourage supervisees to share more fully with supervisors in their discussions, as they recognize that supervisors may well learn about the events in counseling through the tape, anyway. A comprehensive orientation to the supervision experience that focuses on ethical and legal issues and allows the supervisor to carefully assess supervisee strengths and weaknesses may also reduce the likelihood of subordinate misconduct or client disservice. Finally, Bernard and Goodyear encourage professionals to stay current with legal developments that may affect them and to take special care in documenting supervision when supervisees are acting incompetently. A good record of supervision will at least minimize direct liability. Liability insurance for supervisors is also in order. It does not prevent problems, but it may reassure professionals that their financial resources are not vulnerable to a lawsuit.

Due Process Rights

When working in public institutions, supervisees have the same due process rights against unfair government action as do other citizens. These rights derive from the Fourteenth Amendment to the U.S. Constitution and prevent states from taking actions against individuals without giving them notice and opportunity to oppose such action. Those who work for private organizations have due process rights if the policies and procedures of the organization stipulate them. Many private universities, hospitals, and community agencies recognize this right. Applied to supervision, this means that the supervisee has a legal right to supervisory feedback, periodic evaluations, and opportunities to file grievances about actions they think have been unfair. Bernard and Goodyear (1992) argue that some of the most egregious violations of trainees' due process rights occur when they receive negative final evaluations without any prior warning that their performance is significantly substandard. To avoid such violations, they advise professionals to periodically communicate negative performance evaluations in specific terms that include the changes that would be deemed adequate performance. Such an action prevents misunderstanding about how much improvement is sufficient for success. Due process rights are meant to protect supervisees from arbitrary action based on incomplete, irrelevant, or untrue evidence. Such rights do not mean that all supervisees have the right to a passing grade or a positive evaluation; the duty of the supervisor is also to protect the public from incompetent professionals. Instead, due process suggests that supervisors must be sensitive to the implications of negative findings on those they oversee and must ensure that negative judgments are fair and appropriate.

Relations with Third-Party Payors

Frequently, clients of unlicensed supervisees are submitting the costs of their care for reimbursement by insurers, who before providing payment, typically require evidence that the supervisee is supervised by a licensed mental health professional. Some unscrupulous but energetic supervisors have used this mechanism to increase their incomes. The most egregious cases have involved supervisors overseeing the work of dozens of supervisees and submitting the claims as though they themselves had provided the service (Harrar et al., 1990). As already mentioned, supervision under these conditions fails to meet the standard for competent oversight and thereby violates ethical rules. If it also deceives the third-party payor about the nature of the service provided, the practice is likely to be illegal, too, as a form of insurance fraud. Neither private insurers nor government agencies allow this behavior. In fact, they have aggressively pursued legal action against serious violators. For all these reasons, supervisors are cautioned to be exceedingly cautious about practices that may be inconsistent with guidelines and contracts, and to educate those they oversee about the proper methods for submitting claims.

SUMMARY

When people take on supervisory responsibilities, they must keep in mind a number of ethical obligations and legal duties. Not only must they demonstrate competence to supervise as well as competence to practice, they must also guard the rights of the supervisee to a beneficial learning experience with fair and appropriate feedback about performance. Even more important than the progress of the trainee, though, is the welfare of the clients served by the trainee. A supervisor holds both ethical and legal responsibility for clients' welfare, and when the needs of the supervisee conflict with those of the clients, the codes mandate that clients' concerns take precedence. The legal requirement to care for the client stems from the client's right to competent service regardless of the counselor's level of training.

Supervisors are also ethically bound not to engage in activities that exploit their supervisees. They are especially cautioned to avoid sexual contact, insensitivity to issues of diversity, and introjection of personal values into the professional relationship. Supervisors who fail to act responsibly themselves, or who have supervisees who act unethically, are held liable for the consequences. The latter principle is called *vicarious liability*. Similarly, those who violate the due process rights of trainees or clients' rights to confidentiality can be held legally responsible for those failures. Finally, supervisors need to be attuned to their legal and ethical obligations when working with third-party payors, and to be scrupulously accurate about reporting services rendered by supervisees.

DISCUSSION QUESTIONS

1. Many current supervisors indicate that they have had little formal training in supervision. Given the standards you have read, how would you address this problem? Should such training be mandated? Should there be a test for supervision? What other ideas do you have?

2. A substantial minority of supervisors in one study referred to supervisees as "friends." Some strongly believed that their personal connection to the trainee enhanced rather than compromised their supervision. Is there any merit to that view? If you were consulting with them about this issue, how would you respond?

3. What do you believe is the ethically ideal way for a supervisor to respond to a sincere, well-motivated, but incompetent performance by an intern? How long should a supervisor allow an intern whose interactions with clients are unsatisfactory to continue to try to improve?

RECOMMENDED READINGS

Association for Counselor Education and Supervision. (1990). Standards for counseling supervisors. *Journal of Counseling and Development, 69,* 30–32.

Association for Counselor Education and Supervision. (1993). Ethical guidelines for counseling supervisors. *Counselor Education and Supervision, 34,* 270–276.

Disney, M. J., & Stephens, A. M. (1994). Legal issues in clinical supervision. In T. P. Remley (Ed.)., *ACA Legal Series* (Vol. 8). Alexandria, VA: American Counseling Association.

13

Counselors as Teachers and Researchers
Integrity, Science, and Care

Many counselors are involved in training the next generation of professionals and in research to advance the science of the profession. Some professionals devote their entire careers to these endeavors. The central ethical issues embedded in these activities mirror those of direct service activities: competence, responsible use of power, and promotion of the welfare of those under their care. This chapter discusses how each obligation is met when teaching and conducting research.

The Ethics of Teaching

Our society views teachers ambivalently. On the one hand, they are held in high regard: "What office is there which involves more responsibility, which requires more qualifications, and which ought, therefore, to be more honourable, than that of teaching?" (Martineau, 1837). On the other hand, they are viewed with disdain and distrust: "He who can, does. He who cannot, teaches" (Shaw, 1903). Even those who see some value in teaching are concerned about its potential for abuse: "A teacher should have maximal authority, and minimal power" (Szasz, 1973). This ambivalence stems partly from the high hopes that citizens have for education and partly from their frequent disappointments over unrealized hopes. The enterprise of teaching others to be effective counselors and therapists is also fraught with potential for good or ill. When good occurs, the next generation is entrusted with the wisdom of the past and encouraged to extend it, and when bad happens, either incompetent people are admitted to the profession, or qualified people are discouraged from it. Szasz's wish to contain the power of the teacher cannot be realized, though. Instead, the task of the profession is to ensure that its teachers use their power responsibly.

Unfortunately, the literature on the ethics of training mental health professionals is not as abundant as the publications on ethics in counseling, but there are still valuable resources available. Several experts have addressed the issue, the recent versions of the ethics codes speak to this activity, and some empirical studies have been conducted. The central ethical issues in this body of literature deal with competence to teach, the responsible use of power, the management of multiple and sometimes conflicting role obligations, and the duties to the profession, the students, and the public.

Competence to Teach

Faculty who teach counselors ought first to be competent practitioners. In addition, they must be knowledgeable about their subject matter, prepared for their work, and put fair effort into facilitating student learning. Nearly all psychology faculty acknowledge occasional incidences of inadequate preparation for classes, but the number who admit teaching material they have not mastered is also surprisingly high—38% (Tabachnick et al., 1991). Moreover, they revealed that they engaged in this practice more than rarely. The percentage of counselor educators who report teaching material for which they are not competent is almost identical—36%, according to Schwab and Neukrug (1994). Faculty also have a responsibility to present information fairly, and to distinguish between personal opinions and established theory and research. The 1990 APA code (no longer in effect) succinctly stated this duty: "[A]s teachers psychologists perform their duties on the basis of careful preparation so that their instruction is accurate, current, and scholarly" (Principle 2b). In the same survey, nearly 4% admitted bias in teaching is a frequent practice. The obligation to stay current in a rapidly changing discipline is especially important. Tabachnick et al. (1991) found uneven compliance with this standard. In that study, 36% of teaching psychologists admitted teaching a course without updating lecture notes.

When presenting material for which scientific support is scarce, that limitation needs to be clearly stated. In other words, cutting-edge, speculative, or experimental material should be labeled as such. This recommendation does not mean that faculty must curtail their presentations to long-established constructs, but it does suggest that students should be informed about the distinction between concepts in the mainstream of professional thinking and those too new or speculative to be widely accepted. For example, in teaching innovative therapeutic techniques such as eye movement desensitization (Herbert & Mueser, 1992; Shapiro, 1995), faculty should give students a sense of both the promise and the limitations of the technique, including discussion of the research evidence. Professors who keep in mind the ultimate goal of teaching—to educate practitioners who will be capable of making objective, informed, independent judgments about the merits of innovations—will be better equipped to make wise decisions about such matters. If there is substantial debate about the merits of a particular theory or method, both sides of the argument should be presented. Of course, faculty need not hide their own perspectives from students. Showing students the rationale for one's personal assessments about unsettled issues in the field can help students develop appropriate criteria for making similar judgments themselves. However, neither demeaning others who hold different views nor dismissing the valid positions of others is consistent with ethical standards. Here is ACA's statement on this subject:

ACA *Code of Ethics,* **Section F.2.f: Varied Theoretical Positions**
Counselors present varied theoretical positions so that students and supervisees may make comparison and have opportunities to develop their own positions. Counselors provide information concerning the scientific basis of professional practice.

APA's guideline is written in more general terms, but conveys a similar message:

APA *Ethical Principles,* **Section 6.03: Accuracy and Objectivity in Teaching**
(a) When engaged in teaching or training, psychologists present psychological information accurately and with a reasonable degree of objectivity.

Canter et al. (1994) interpret this standard to apply when faculty "abandon normally recognized standards of professionalism" and caution that it cannot be used to accuse those with divergent theoretical orientations of unethical practice (p. 117).

In many universities faculty are asked to teach courses not directly related to their research and teaching expertise. When such requests are made, faculty must evaluate whether their training and experience are sufficient to perform competently, just as practitioners need to judge whether a particular activity falls within their boundaries of competence. When professors determine that a subject falls outside their areas of competence, they must decline to teach it unless they can obtain continuing education beforehand. The statement from the ethics codes on working within the boundaries of one's competence apply equally to teaching as to therapy. (See Section C.2.a of the ACA code and Section 1.04 of the APA code.) Such determinations ought to be objectively made, with consideration of the legitimate needs of the curriculum and the students. Faculty who are tempted to use a competency argument to justify refusing a course that is unappealing for other reasons are not acting with fairness or beneficence.

Responsible Use of Power

As discussed in relation to supervision and in Chapter 7, sexual harassment, sexual exploitation, and related abuse of the less powerful position of students happen rather frequently in graduate programs in counseling and psychology. In published research, the mean percentage of faculty who admit sexual contact with students is 8.8%. In one study, almost one-third of female psychology graduate students reported incidents of sexual harassment (Glaser & Thorpe, 1986). In another study, psychology internship directors singled out faculty–student sexual contact as a continuing blind spot for those who teach (Welfel, 1992). The attention sexual harassment has received in the media in the last decade does not seem to have eliminated the problem, because even recent researchers found 11.7% of students experiencing harassment (Mintz et al., 1994).

Blevins-Knabe (1992) offers some insights into the reasons sexual harassment occurs in higher education. She suggests that faculty are blind to the implications of their actions. They tend to perceive their behavior as friendly and supportive, but students find it harassing. She also hypothesizes that labeling such actions with such benign words stems from their reluctance to admit their sexual motivation. Sometimes both faculty and students are willing participants in sexual relationships. When sexual relationships are consensual, Blevins-Knabe believes that shared professional interests, personal insecurities in the students, unresolved personal issues in faculty, and sex role socialization factors all are influential. Interestingly, though, when viewed in retrospect, neither faculty nor students perceive "consensual" relationships as freely chosen or beneficial to the personal or professional development of either party (Glaser & Thorpe, 1986; Miller & Larrabee, 1995; Pope et al., 1979; Robinson & Reid, 1985). There are also effects on other students who hear discussion of sexual advances by faculty to their peers. Adams, Kottke, and Padgit (1983) reported that 13% of female students and 3% of male students tried to avoid working with faculty known or rumored to have made sexual advances to other students. Of course, some faculty prey on vulnerable students and are exclusively motivated by self-interest, but others initiate sexual contact because of personal dissatisfactions, life crises, or neurotic tendencies. None of these reasons justifies such involvement. The current ethics codes are the first to explicitly forbid sexual contact with current students (ACA, Section F.1.c; APA, Section 1.19b). Thus, faculty need to set clear boundaries in their relationships with students and seek out professional assistance when tempted to initiate sexual relationships.

Sexual contact is not the only abuse of faculty power, nor is it likely to be the most common in practice. Faculty exploit students' needs for professional success and clinical or research experience as well. They also abuse their power when they discriminate on the basis of characteristics unrelated to academic performance and when they fail to be sensitive to the implications of their decisions on students' or colleagues' futures. Here are some examples of such abuses:

Professor Yelter assigns research topics to students in her course according to the content areas she needs to include in her book in progress. The topics for some of these papers are only peripherally related to course content, and students have no option to change topics. When the papers are submitted, she attends only to the quality of the reference list, rather than the analysis of the topic. She grades according to the potential usefulness of the students' work to her book.

Dr. Marsher encourages discussion in his classes. When many students have raised their hands to respond to an issue he has raised, he almost always acknowledges male students first. In addition, he is more likely to give male students time to develop their thoughts and respond to differing perspectives. His typical interaction with female students is briefer and less patient.

Doctoral students assigned to Professor Pastione soon learn that if they wish to receive a positive letter of reference from her for positions after they graduate, they should volunteer to help her with her research projects. If they are involved in other faculty research or do not have the time to volunteer for Professor Pastione, they ought to find another adviser because she will not support them, no matter what their other competencies or experiences.

In the first case, Professor Yelter is using students in the class as unpaid, unacknowledged research assistants. Moreover, she is placing her own interests ahead of their learning and providing them with no viable alternative to the plan she has established. Such an action is contrary to the ethical principles of beneficence and respect for autonomy. It is also inconsistent with the sections of the codes that require faculty to "conduct training programs in an ethical manner and serve as role models for professional behavior" (ACA, *Code of Ethics,* Section F.1.a), to give students credit for research contributions (ACA, *Code of Ethics,* Section F.1.d), and to avoid exploitive relationships (APA, *Ethical Principles,* Section 1.19). Dr. Yelter's ethical problems do not end there. Her behavior also violates the stipulations in the codes dealing with objectivity in assessment:

> **APA *Ethical Principles,* Section 6.05**
> (b) Psychologists evaluate students and supervisees on the basis of their actual performance on relevant and established program requirements.

Needless to say, Professor Yelter ought to stop this practice, assign topics directly related to course content, and use fair and objective grading criteria. If she needs research assistance with her project, she can hire someone. If a student elects to volunteer for that job in order to gain experience, that arrangement would also be ethical provided the student's efforts were acknowledged and other forms of exploitation were avoided. She also could benefit from remedial education about the power she holds over students who may not feel free to challenge her requirements or question their grades. Her current actions stand in direct opposition to acting as an appropriate professional role model.

Dr. Marsher is engaging in gender bias. This behavior is inappropriate because it gives unfair advantage to some students on the basis of a characteristic irrelevant to professional competence or performance. It violates sections of the code that proscribe discrimination (ACA *Code of Ethics,* Sections C.5.a , D.1.i; APA, *Ethical Principles,* Sections 1.10, 1.12). Probably Dr. Marsher is unaware of this aspect of his behavior. His ignorance of its existence does not excuse it, however. Students currently enrolled in his courses may feel unable to communicate their experience to him for fear of retribution. Once grades are submitted, though, those who will not be participating in additional courses with Dr. Marsher are ideal candidates to address the matter, through course evaluations, conversations with the professor, or discussions with other faculty in the program. Needless to say, if other faculty learn of this behavior, they too have an obligation to address it with Dr. Marsher, assuming that the student involved does not object to such an approach.

The essence of Professor Pastione's ethical problem is the way in which she has transformed a basic obligation of her position, the writing of letters of recommendation, into a "service for sale" in exchange for labor on her projects. Students willing to work "earn" a positive evaluation, apparently without regard for their actual capacities as counselors. This practice not only exploits the students' vulnerabilities, it also violates the professor's obligation to gatekeep, to act to ensure that only competent students are admitted into the profession. The ACA code is quite explicit on this issue, although it substitutes the term *endorsement* for *recommendation:*

ACA *Code of Ethics,* **Section F.1.h: Endorsement**

Counselors do not endorse students or supervisees for certification, licensure, employment, or completion of an academic or training program if they believe students or supervisees are not qualified for the endorsement. Counselors take reasonable steps to assist students or supervisees who are not qualified for endorsement to become qualified.

Professor Pastione has also violated her duty to respect autonomy and avoid harm to those she oversees. Unless assisting this faculty member with her research is an explicit condition of admission or progress in the doctoral program fully disclosed in writing at the time of application, her demand violates students' rights to informed consent to educational procedures. However, as long as Professor Pastione uses research assistance as the "quid pro quo" of evaluation, no degree of informed consent could transform her behavior into an ethically acceptable practice.

ACA *Code of Ethics,* **Section F.2.a: Orientation**

Prior to admission, counselors must orient prospective students to the counselor education or training program's expectations, including, but not limited to the following: (1) the type and level of skill acquisition required for successful completion of the training; (2) subject matter to be covered; (3) the basis for evaluation; (4) training components that encourage self-growth or self-disclosure as part of the training process; (5) the type of supervision settings and requirements of the sites for required clinical field experiences; (6) student and supervisee evaluation and dismissal policies and procedures; and (7) up-to-date employment prospects for graduates.

APA's *Ethical Principles* communicate the same position in Section 6.02. In addition, Professor Pastione harms students in several ways. Those who reject participation in her project, unaware of the consequences, are injured by the unexpected and unfair endorsement they receive. Other students may not have the luxury of working for free, needing to support themselves through graduate school. These people are also harmed. The professor's practice may even cause harm to those who get an undeserved positive reference. Students whose talents lie in another field are not necessarily better off for earning a credential they do not deserve. In the long run, these students may be better helped by learning at this stage that they are not competent enough for a counseling career. The pain in that event may be significantly less than the pain of a malpractice suit, lost positions, or other problems that stem from incompetence in the field. Even more important, Professor Pastione may be harming the public served by these ineffective students. The solution? Obviously, Professor Pastione must stop this practice, recruit research assistants in a more appropriate fashion, and base comments in letters of evaluation on actual performance. She should also seek to redress the wrongs she has done in past letters of reference, sending revised copies to students for future use.

None of these faculty is adhering to the opening section of ACA's standards for counselor educators, for none is acting as positive role models for students:

ACA *Code of Ethics*, Section F.1.a: Educators as Teachers and Practitioners
Counselors who are responsible for developing, implementing, and supervising educational programs are skilled as teachers and practitioners. They are knowledgeable regarding the legal, ethical, and regulatory aspects of the profession, are skilled in applying knowledge, and make students and supervisees aware of their responsibilities. Counselors conduct counselor education and training programs in an ethical manner and serve as role models for professional behavior. Counselor educators should make an effort to infuse material related to human diversity into all courses and/or workshops that are designed to promote the development of professional counselors.

Neglect of Responsibilities: Another Form of Misuse of Power

Keith-Spiegel (1994) makes a point about psychology educators that applies to faculty in related professions. The mandate to avoid harm is more complex to interpret in the teacher role than in the role of counselor or therapist. Clearly, a teacher wishes not to cause harm to students, but when students' work is substandard or their attitude irresponsible, a teacher's concern about harm to students must be balanced against his or her duty to the clients whom the student may serve and the reputation of the profession. As discussed in Chapter 3, admitting people who are unable or unwilling to abide by professional standards does not inspire public trust. Thus, faculty who fail to prevent unqualified people from practicing are overlooking one of their major responsibilities. The goal of faculty is, of course, to help all students meet the standards set for competence, but when that fails, they must not accept unqualified people. Again, the ACA code speaks to this issue most directly, specifying procedures for dealing with student deficiencies:

ACA *Code of Ethics*, Section F.3.a: Limitations
Counselors, through ongoing evaluation and appraisal, are aware of the academic and personal limitations of students and supervisees that might impede performance. Counselors assist students and supervisees in securing remedial assistance when needed, and dismiss from the training program supervisees who are unable to provide competent service due to academic or personal limitations. Counselors seek professional consultation and document their decision to dismiss or refer students or supervisees for assistance. Counselors assure that students and supervisees have recourse to address decisions made to require them to seek assistance, or dismiss them.

The following case exemplifies a common ethical failure to meet this standard:

Dr. Dorian is an untenured faculty member who hopes to achieve tenure in a few years. In his university, competent teaching and good relationships with students figure prominently in tenure review. Dr. Dorian has a student in counseling practicum whose performance is unsatisfactory. His substantial efforts to help this student to improve his performance have been fruitless. Moreover, the student does not seem to understand the limits of his competency and tends to take on cases for which he is unqualified. Dr. Dorian believes this student ought not to pass practicum, but he also fears that this vocal and well-connected student will file a grievance over a failing grade and attempt to focus the attention of university administrators on his situation. In light of the complications a failing grade will cause for him, Dr. Dorian decides to pass this student.

To comply with the ethical standards, Dr. Dorian should record the grade he believes the student earned, in spite of the discomfort that may ensue. If Dr. Dorian has documented his repeated interventions to help the student remediate his problems, responding to a grievance or other inquiry is not difficult. In most universities students must demonstrate that grading procedures were arbitrary or discriminatory—a rather difficult standard to meet. It seems that Dr. Dorian's anxiety about tenure is overriding his judgment. At a deeper level, Dr. Dorian may think ethical behavior is a matter of convenience. When standards are easy to follow, he may willingly comply, but when compliance causes him personal discomfort, he breaks the rules. Such behavior is unprofessional.

Other violations of this standard are not so blatant. Some derive from a good-hearted desire on the part of faculty to help all students reach their full potential. This aim is admirable and ought to be a guidepost for faculty behavior. It becomes problematic, however, when students who do not perform competently are allowed to progress. Faculty cannot lose sight of their obligations to such students' potential clients. In this situation, faculty ought to focus on helping students redirect their career goals if remediation efforts fail. At other times, overcrowded classes make careful assessment of each student's competencies difficult. Faculty overwhelmed by their teaching load, research responsibilities, and administrative demands may succumb to giving all students "the benefit of the doubt" rather than engage in the difficult task before them. Neither overwork nor compassion for an individual student are sufficient justifications for actions that defy a professional standard, although 10% of psychology faculty admitted that the likeability of a student had influenced their grading (Tabachnick et al., 1991).

Obligations to Colleagues

Of course, faculty have obligations to colleagues as well as to students. The Preamble to the APA *Ethical Principles* captures these responsibilities well:

> **APA *Ethical Principles*, Principle B: Integrity**
> Psychologists seek to promote integrity in the science, teaching and practice of psychology. In these actions, psychologists are honest, fair and respectful of others. . . .

The next case illustrates misconduct toward colleagues:

Professor Caste is asked by faculty at another university to review the promotion file of a colleague, because he is an expert in the same field as the candidate. Professor Caste agrees. His two-paragraph letter arrives several weeks later. It shows very little attention to the file of materials submitted to him. Not only does Professor Caste's letter show no evidence of having read the most important materials submitted for review, but it miscounts the total number of publications, misinterprets others, and makes inferences not supported by the evidence. Professor Caste ends his letter with a negative recommendation for promotion.

This behavior is inconsistent with the provisions of the codes that deal with avoiding harm and acting competently. Universities regularly rely on external evaluations of scholarship, and professionals asked to undertake this duty must carry it out diligently. Professor Caste's negligence may have cost a worthy teacher a promotion, or even a job, if a tenure decision was involved. The best way for Professor Caste to remedy his mistake (in the unlikely event that he recognizes the error of his ways) is to send a retraction of his initial letter admitting the inadequacies in his first review, along with a replacement letter that fairly evaluates the candidate's work. If the promotion has been denied, he ought to encourage the university to reconsider its decision and share his communications with the candidate. He also owes an apology to the candidate. In the absence of such action or other attempt to undo the harm caused, the candidate for promotion would certainly be justified in filing an ethics complaint against him.

Nonsexual Dual Relationships

Faculty and students often have several different kinds of professional contacts. A student may serve as research assistant, pupil in a class, collaborator on a manuscript, and supervisee in practicum seminar to the same faculty member simultaneously. Consecutive involvement in multiple roles is even more common with students and faculty. For example, my current research assistant is simultaneously a teaching intern under my supervision, and a collaborator on a manuscript in preparation. In prior terms she has been enrolled in clinical practicum, academic courses, and independent studies with me. Are either of us acting unethically? Many would see no ethical dimension to our multiple types of interaction. In fact, multifaceted and prolonged connections between faculty and students, usually termed *mentoring relationships,* are often viewed as desirable, both by scholars and by the parties involved (Bogat & Redner, 1985; Bowman, Bowman, & DeLucia, 1990; Bowman, Hatley, & Bowman, 1995). Some scholars associate mentoring with higher student achievement, satisfaction, and persistence in academic programs (for example, see Bean & Kuh, 1984).

Still, some ethics scholars have expressed caution about multiple connections with students (for example, see Kitchener, 1992). They can blur the objectivity of the professional, incur jealousy or misunderstanding in other students (Bowman et al., 1995), and make other boundaries that ought to be observed harder to maintain. For instance, faculty working closely with students may begin to use students as confidants about personal matters, socialize extensively with those students, or otherwise forget the distinction between professional and personal relationships. When students become more like friends than students, faculty may have difficulty honoring their responsibilities as gatekeepers in the profession. The power imbalance in the relationship cannot be ignored either, because it diminishes the reciprocity that characterizes ordinary friendships. In most cases, the faculty member probably feels freer than the student to express feelings, ask favors, or seek emotional support. At some level, the student is aware that the faculty member has tremendous influence over his or her future. For these reasons the codes caution professionals to honor boundaries (ACA, *Code of Ethics,* Section F.1.b.; APA, *Ethical Principles,* Section 1.17). The three criteria used in the APA code to evaluate the advisability of a particular dual relationship are worth reviewing here. A dual (or multiple) relationship is inappropriate when (1) it would impair the professional's objectivity, (2) interfere with carrying out one's professional duties, or (3) might harm or exploit the other person.

Honoring boundaries is a rather abstract term. In relation to faculty–student relationships, I believe it means:

- Refraining from using the student as a confidant about personal matters or about matters of frustration with colleagues
- Ensuring that the bulk of the time spent together focuses on professional rather than personal issues. Friendly interactions are certainly not to be avoided, but a preponderance of talk about social events is inadvisable. (One should keep in mind that in virtually all interactions, the goal of the student is to learn from the faculty member.)
- Declining repeated one-on-one social engagements in favor of group events.
- Setting limits to exploration of personal stresses or dilemmas that the student is experiencing, or referring the student to another counselor, just as one ought to do as a clinical supervisor.
- Refusing a mentoring relationship with relatives or with students with whom one has had a prior or ongoing personal relationship.
- Clarifying the parameters of the relationship and the roles at the onset so that both student and faculty member understand the nature of the interaction and the relevant contents of the ethics codes.
- Making mentoring activities available to a variety of students.
- Consulting with colleagues periodically about mentoring issues so that one can deal with minor problems and receive external feedback about the relationship.
- Allowing students who wish to withdraw from a mentoring relationship to do so with dignity and without retribution.

Using these criteria and the decision-making model from Chapter 2, consider the ethics of the following situations:

A graduate student runs a house-painting service in the summer. She uses the earnings from this business to fund her education for a doctoral degree. A faculty member who notices a flyer advertising her business on a bulletin board contracts with the student to have his house painted next summer. The student will be enrolling in his group therapy course the following fall.

A faculty member has a part-time psychotherapy practice. She asks an especially talented student, who has recently graduated, to join the practice.

A student's family has suffered a devastating house fire that has disabled her parents. Because her parents had been funding her education and are no longer in a position to do so, she fears she will not be able to continue enrollment next quarter. She has applied for financial aid but is unlikely to receive the aid in time for registration. Her advisor, on hearing of her situation, writes her a check for next quarter's tuition, telling her she can repay the loan when her financial aid gets straightened out.

A professor's car is out of service. One of the students in his class lives nearby. The professor asks that student for a ride to campus the next day.

In recent research Bowman et al. (1995) surveyed students and faculty to ascertain their views on the ethics of several kinds of dual relationships. They included vignettes dealing with social, monetary, mentoring, and sexual contacts. As expected, virtually all respondents found sexual contacts inappropriate, but there was little unanimity in other responses. No more than three-quarters of the sample came to agreement on the ethics of faculty who hire students to baby-sit, maintain a concurrent friendship with a student or have students as primary social contacts, or keep silent from other faculty a student's slur against homosexuals, made in a social setting. This disparity in response speaks to several issues, including the general lack of attention this topic has received in the professional literature, the abstractness of the codes on this matter, and the conflict in professional and personal obligations. In other words, both faculty and students seem to recognize the complexity of ethical decision making in this area and the degree to which a particular activity must be evaluated in its context. The survey by Tabachnick and her associates (1991) suggests similar uncertainty about the ethics of nonsexual faculty–student contacts. Nearly 49% labeled asking a student for a small favor (such as a ride home) as ethical under many or all circumstances, and 37% saw it as rarely or never ethical. Similarly, 29% of faculty viewed lending students money as ethical in most or all situations, but 50% held a contrary view.

Faculty who are tempted to take rigid stances in opposition to all forms of dual connections with students are probably overreacting to the risks, and sidestepping their ethical obligation to foster the development of their students. Lloyd (1992) has remarked that some faculty seem to have a "mentoring phobia." Although that characterization seems strongly worded (and inconsistent with research evidence), it does put a name to the discomfort and worry some faculty feel about their relationships with graduate students. Careful consideration of ethical guidelines, and the preceding criteria for managing multiple professional contacts, should reduce the risks of such relationships without compromising their potential benefits. (Those who seek examples of other hypothetical cases that have ethical dimensions, can see Keith-Spiegel, Wittig, Perkins, Balogh, and Whitley, 1993.)

Personal Growth Experiences

The emotional stability of the mental health professional is crucial to the success of counseling. Many ethics complaints result from character flaws, neurotic tendencies, or other deficiencies in coping with personal stresses. For these reasons counselor educators have a duty to ensure that students have the emotional stability and temperament for the profession and that the personal issues that may be impeding their effectiveness are identified and resolved.

Experiences that increase empathy with clients, give students opportunities to "walk in clients' shoes," and involve students in experimental learning are all valued by mental health professions as crucial teaching tools in the training process. These same experiences also help students become aware of the ways in which their own emotions, defenses, and coping strategies affect their capacity to work effectively with clients. Thus many programs interweave personal growth experiences in the curriculum. In counseling labs, students frequently practice counseling skills on each other, in group classes they engage in group experiences, and in testing courses they often take the psychological tests they are studying. The inclusion of such personal growth experiences has been controversial, partly because it pits a student's right to privacy against the profession's responsibility to admit only competent professionals to the field (Corey et al., 1993). Counselor educators have divided views of the ethics of such experiences (Schwab & Neukrug, 1994). The ACA code has provided standards for such experiences so that professionals can adequately balance competing ethical values:

> **ACA** *Code of Ethics,* **Section F. 3.b: Self-Growth Experiences**
> Counselors use professional judgment when designing training experiences conducted by the counselors themselves that require student or supervisee self-growth or self-disclosure. Safeguards are provided so that supervisees and students are aware of the ramifications their self-disclosures may have on counselors whose primary role as teacher, trainer, or supervisor requires acting on ethical obligations to the profession. Evaluative components of experiential training experiences explicitly delineate predetermined academic standards that are separate and not dependent on the student's level of self-disclosure.

The appropriate use of such experiences depends on adequate informed consent, on a boundary between materials subject to grading and the type or quality of self-disclosure in the experience, and on an agreement that the faculty member acts in all possible ways to respect the dignity of the student. Because at times faculty are obligated to re-

veal or follow up on disclosures in growth experiences, students should clearly understand, prior to the experience, the circumstances that would require such action. For
example, a student should be informed that comments about child abuse or neglect
made in the presence of a mental health professional cannot be held in complete confidence. The counselor educator must take appropriate action to report that abuse. Similarly, if a student reveals a strong dislike for another racial group with whom she is likely
to work, a faculty member must pursue that matter with the student. Because so much
may be at stake for them, students ought to understand in advance the implications of
disclosures. Faculty involved in growth experiences may find that written documents
are helpful accompaniments to oral review of these issues with students.

When a course involves a significant amount of self-disclosure or involvement in
personal growth activities, programs sometimes use part-time faculty. These faculty are
less involved in other dimensions of the program, and are less likely to have continuing
contact with students, so both students and faculty may approach the experience more
comfortably and confidently. If the part-time faculty member is competent in the task
and if the student is more open to disclose and participate, student growth may occur at
a faster rate than with a regular faculty member. This option is not essential or always
feasible, but it eases the ethical complications for all involved. Patrick (1989) also recommends avoiding placing the student in the client role in peer counseling whenever
possible, suggesting instead that students from other programs in the university would
be more appropriate.

Faculty overseeing such experiences have a demanding task. The codes provide
guidance, but ultimately, they must make difficult judgments. Student deficiencies are
often on the border between competence and incompetence, and between outrageous
and simply undesirable. Following a systematic strategy for ethical decision making is
crucial in such ambiguous situations, as is consultation with colleagues. Rigorous admissions standards help reduce the problem, but do not eliminate it.

An Ethics of Care

Kitchener (1992) highlights a fundamental ethical issue for faculty in mental health.
Commitment to teaching is not the only reason mental health professionals become
educators. Many find research, consultation, and community involvement at least as important. Indeed, universities often make rewards for faculty contingent on activities outside the classroom. Inadequacies with students or in instructional approach are regularly
overlooked by institutions when faculty bring in research grants or consulting contracts
to the university. One can invest in other activities, of course, not only because they can
reflect positively on the training program and advance knowledge, but also because of
personal enjoyment. However, counselors ought not sacrifice competent and caring
teaching to attend to other responsibilities. Applying Nodding's concept of an ethics of
care (1984), Kitchener points out that faculty who fail to care about the program, the

courses, and the students are inadequate role models who are failing to promote the welfare of those they serve. Such an uncaring attitude is not a minor ethical deviation; it runs contrary to the profession's deepest ethical values.

The Ethics of Research

Most counselors, psychologists, and social workers do not identify themselves as researchers. Instead, they perceive research as an activity for those in academia or in specialized research settings. Although much attention has been given to developing graduate curricula to train competent scientist-practitioners, in reality most graduates fit that definition only insofar as they are consumers of research. Economic and societal changes seem to be fueling a challenge to this distinction for mental health practitioners. The demand for accountability and outcome data in both mental health and educational settings suggest that over the next decade a much wider sampling of professionals will be involved in designing and implementing research and evaluation activities (Eisen & Dickey, 1996; Sexton et al., 1997). For example, managed health care systems are seeking data not only on the effectiveness of given treatments with particular clients, but also information about the outcomes of a specific form of treatment or setting (Wedding, Topolski, & McGaha, 1995). Schools and community agencies are experiencing increased pressures for accountability. Consequently, the days may be passing when practicing professionals could relinquish involvement in research and evaluation. Third-party payors, especially, are seeking more evidence that treatments are effective and produce the outcomes that practitioners expect. Not only must practitioners refurbish clinical research skills, but they must also reacquaint themselves with ethical issues in research in clinical and educational settings. This section highlights the major ethical issues practitioners will confront and directs them to appropriate resources for future study. The essential ethical responsibilities of the researcher are (1) to develop scientifically acceptable research protocols that are worth participants' time and have a reasonable chance of yielding meaningful findings, (2) to protect the rights of participants (both human and animal) in the research process, (3) to report results fairly and accurately, and (4) to cooperate with colleagues and share research data. Students who seek more detailed information about planning research to conform to ethical standards may find Sieber (1992) a useful resource.

Good Science and Good Ethics

Most research in our field requires the participation of human beings. Some forms of research carry risks to participants. A researcher who wants to examine the social and emotional effects on children whose parents have HIV disorders is exposing those children and their parents to a psychological risk. In revealing information that the researcher requests, participants may feel painful emotions or become aware of problems they had not yet recognized. The parents and children may encounter some difficulties in their interactions subsequent to the research interview. These risks are not insurmountable, and may be worth enduring for the information gained. However, if the research design is not scientifically rigorous, the chance of making valid and meaningful conclusions is almost nonexistent. Substantial flaws in the design might even lead to results that contradict the actual state of affairs. In either event, it is unfair to subject people to the psychological risks of such research without the potential for scientific gain.

Rosenthal (1994) takes this analysis one step further. He contends that poorly designed and executed research is unethical even if the participants are not at risk for harm or discomfort. He argues that participants are donating valuable commodities, such as their time, attention, and cooperation. These commodities are no less valuable in low-risk research than in higher-risk research. In an interesting analogy, he encourages researchers to view participants as kind of "granting source," to whom investigators have obligations. Poorly designed research not only wastes people's time and prevents them from engaging in other activities for that interval, but also makes people more skeptical about the value of research participation and makes it more difficult for other researchers with more meritorious projects to recruit participants. In terms of the ethical principles, inadequate research designs violate the duty to beneficence and to fidelity even if they avoid risk of harm. Gelso (1985) frames this question as one of rigor and relevance. Meritorious research attends to both the rigor of the research design and the potential of the research to be relevant to practice.

Good science also assumes sensitivity to issues of diversity. Researchers, for example, who make generalizations to both genders on the basis of research with only one gender are acting inappropriately. Similarly, researchers who fail to acknowledge the limitations of their samples in cultural or ethnic diversity are ignoring an important aspect of scientific rigor and making their findings vulnerable to misuse, particularly with populations not represented in their samples. The ACA code comments, "Counselors are sensitive to diversity and research issues with special populations. They seek consultation when appropriate" (Section G.1.f).

The codes of ethics attend only indirectly to this issue, and unfortunately, are rather general and uninformative about the importance of good science to good ethics. For example, the APA *Ethical Principles* state, "Psychologists design, conduct, and report research in accordance with recognized standards of scientific competence" (Section 6.06).

How can a practitioner ensure that a study is of sufficiently high quality to justify the risks? Obviously, good science requires researchers who are competent to conceptualize, design, and analyze data in their projects and are knowledgeable about recent research on the same topic. Practitioners with weaknesses in any of these domains should seek training and consultation before embarking on research that involves human or animal subjects.

Protecting the Rights of Research Participants

Ensuring that a project has scientific merit is only one component of ethical research. Scientific gains cannot be made at the cost of the health or well-being of participants. History has taught many lessons about the devastation such blind devotion to science can inflict when the rights of participants are ignored. The Tuskegee experiments, the injection of live cancer cells into chronically ill patients in the 1960s, and the electronic surveillance of jury rooms without jurors' knowledge are just three of the most notorious of such examples of research harmful to people (Katz, 1972). The mental health professions have attempted to prevent the recurrence of such misconduct by giving this topic extensive coverage in the ethics codes. In fact, protecting the rights of participants receives more attention in the codes than any other issue in research ethics. In essence, these documents require

- Fair and noncoercive recruiting of participants that honors their dignity.
- Responsibly and appropriately using incentives to participate, avoiding the use of incentives so enticing that they are practically impossible to refuse.
- Communicating informed consent procedures in ways participants can comprehend.
- Vigorously protecting the rights of those vulnerable to abuse (such as prisoners or institutionalized patients) or those incompetent to give consent.
- Providing for children to "assent" to research, even though the formal consent for such participation must come from parents and guardians (Powell & Vacha-Haase, 1994).
- Avoiding deception about particulars of the research unless deception is justified by the scientific merit of the study and no good alternatives exist (Lindsey, 1984).
- Describing of the results of research to participants if they wish, as soon as the data are ready for dissemination. (This process is also referred to as *debriefing.*)
- Protecting the anonymity of research participants and the confidentiality of their disclosures unless they explicitly consent to release of personal information.
- Overseeing others involved in the research, such as graduate students and technical staff, so that they do not violate participants' rights.

Many of the ethical mandates just listed have also been codified into laws or regulations. Thus penalties for their violation can extend beyond the discipline of a professional association. As part of regulations governing human research subjects, the federal government has mandated the creation of institutional review boards (IRBs) at research institutions to approve and oversee the conduct of any research that involves risk of harming human subjects (U.S. Department of Health and Human Services, 1995). Much of the responsibility of institutional review boards is directed toward ensuring that researchers respect participants' rights and minimize risks. These committees have the power to approve, reject, or mandate changes in research proposals that come before them and to monitor ongoing research for compliance with legal mandates. A negative vote by an IRB prevents research from going forward, and an unfavorable review of research in progress can stop its continuance. In psychological or clinical research, IRB review panels are especially attentive to the completeness and comprehensibility of informed consent procedures, the voluntariness of participation, and the protection of the confidentiality of information received. They also examine research proposals to ensure that participants understand that they can withdraw from research at any point without penalty and that they can contact researchers with questions at any point in the process. All investigators connected with an institution must have their research approved by an IRB. This duty applies to students, faculty, volunteers, and to other paid employees.

Mental health researchers rely on animal research less commonly than their counterparts in basic social science, but there have been important studies, particularly using primates, in which mental health researchers have been involved. In the last two decades, the animal rights movement has severely criticized the use of animals in psychological and medical research as inherently cruel (Galvin & Herzog, 1992; Keith-Spiegel & Koocher, 1985). The philosophical debate about the morality of animal research is not resolved, but this movement has caused several changes, including more federal regulation, clearer ethical standards, and the emergence of institutional review boards at organizations that conduct animal research (Bersoff, 1995). Therefore, it behooves mental health professionals to be aware of the ethical guidelines for research with animals. In 1993 the APA published the *Guidelines for Ethical Conduct in the Care and Use of Animals* (1993a) which explain the circumstances under which animal research is justified, the responsibilities of those who care for the animals, the conditions for humanely housing animals, the appropriate experimental and field research procedures, and the responsible use of animals for educational purposes. These standards were designed to help prevent the abuses of animal welfare that helped fuel the protests by animal rights activists, and to ensure that meritorious research can continue.

Fair and Objective Reporting of Results

Once data are collected and analyzed, researchers have several more ethical obligations. The most basic of these obligations is not to misrepresent the results in any publication or communication of them to participants or colleagues. Unfortunately, this form of research misconduct has occurred on more than one occasion. Miller and Hersen (1992) cite several notorious examples of such misconduct. Investigators have fabricated data, changed findings, selectively reported only supportive results, and engaged in a variety of efforts to mislead the public about the nature of their findings. Needless to say, all such actions constitute research fraud and are highly unethical. The codes are quite explicit on this point:

> **APA** *Ethical Principles,* **Section 6.21: Reporting of Results**
>
> (a) Psychologists do not fabricate data or falsify results in their publications.
>
> (b) If psychologists discover significant errors in their published data, they take reasonable

steps to correct such errors in a correction, retraction, erratum, or other appropriate publication means.

ACA *Code of Ethics,* Section G.3: Reporting Results

a. Information affecting outcome

When reporting research results, counselors explicitly mention all variables and conditions known to the investigator that may have affected the outcome of a study or the interpretation of data.

b. Accurate results

Counselors plan, conduct, and report research accurately and in a manner that minimizes the possibility that results will be misleading. They provide thorough discussions of the limitations of their data and alternative hypotheses. Counselors do not engage in fraudulent research, distort data, misrepresent data, or deliberately bias their results.

Violations of this kind seem to happen when researchers' self-interest overtakes their judgment and when research environments push hard for productivity without regard for professional standards of conduct.

One other cause of trimming or altering research data must be acknowledged. In small, single-authored studies, the principal investigator is often the only person who has access to the raw data. Investigators conducting this kind of research tend to have little supervision and relatively small chance of being caught if they alter the data. When researchers have much riding on the outcome of a study, they can be vulnerable to altering data to fit their expectations. Consequently, the ethics of research depend on the integrity of the individual researcher and the commitment of research centers to properly oversee all projects underway at their institutions. Researchers who are tempted to turn a blind eye to the ethical standards in this matter and who cannot be swayed by an appeal to the ethical values of the profession, are well advised to remember two things: Even a small misrepresentation of the data can ruin a career and a reputation, and enforcement of standards in this arena is improving.

Sometimes researchers obtain findings that are contrary to their expectations or to their current theory. In this situation, an investigator may be tempted not to publish these results. However, not publishing such findings also runs counter to the duty to accurately communicate results, and is inappropriate. Hiding such results may mean that other researchers pursue unproductive paths and that a more complete explanation of the phenomenon of interest is delayed. Once again, the professional's responsibility is to serve the greater good rather than his or her own personal preferences.

Cooperation with Research Colleagues

The ultimate goal of clinical research is to add to the profession's understanding of human behavior. Research serves a social good insofar as it informs professionals about matters that affect the efficacy of their work with clients. The aim of research is not to build the reputation of an investigator or to gain anyone job security or financial reward, although these outcomes may be secondary benefits of good research. Thus, research is by definition a cooperative endeavor in which research findings are shared with colleagues and peer criticism is conducted in an educative rather than punitive fashion. Withholding information or data from colleagues who are making good-faith requests for data is unethical precisely because it contradicts the fundamental purpose of research. Of course, it is important to acknowledge that researchers are often in competition with each other for funding, promotions, or public acclaim. To some degree this competition can motivate researchers to conduct more rigorous research, but it can also spark hostile and uncooperative attitudes among those working in the same field. ACA's wording on the subject is as follows:

> **ACA** *Code of Ethics,* **Section G.3.c**
> Counselors communicate to other counselors the results of any research judged to be of professional value. Results that reflect unfavorably on institutions, programs, services, prevailing opinions, or vested interests are not withheld.

Researchers are also advised to retain raw data for a number of years so that other qualified researchers may have access to it if they wish to reanalyze the data. The code does not specify an exact interval for retaining such data, but it is prudent to keep data for at least 10 years. Now that a great deal of data can be stored on a small computer disk, it may be feasible to keep raw data indefinitely. The only caution about such sharing of data relates to the rights of research participants. The APA code deals with this issue succinctly:

> **APA** *Ethical Principles,* **Section 6.25: Sharing Data**
> After research studies are published, psychologists do not withhold the data on which their conclusions are based from other competent professionals who seek to verify the substantive claims through re-analysis and who intend to use such data only for that purpose, provided the confidentiality of the participants can be protected and unless legal rights concerning proprietary data preclude their release.

Credit for Publication of Research Findings

The same pressures that sometimes influence the willingness of professionals to share data also affect their attitudes toward research publications. In a "publish or perish" environment, researchers may become overconcerned about the number of their publications and less attentive about their quality or their actual contribution to the study. Some have been known to "trade authorships" in exchange for favors. Both codes speak directly to this issue, and their messages are clear. They dictate that professionals accept authorship on work in which they have made a significant contribution. The order of authorship ought to reflect the level of contribution to the research and writing. Second, no counselors or psychologists may take credit for publications with which they were uninvolved. A role as director or department chair at the time a project was conducted, for example, does not constitute involvement. Third, when student theses or dissertations are published, students have first authorship if the adviser's name also appears on the publication. Generally, advisers should consider a second authorship only if they were substantially involved in the research (APA Ethics Committee, 1983). In other faculty–student research collaborations, faculty are obliged to respect the contributions of students and give them appropriate credit for their work (Fine & Kurdek, 1993; Goodyear, Crego, & Johnston, 1992). Finally, when submitting a manuscript for publication, it should be sent only to one journal at a time. Duplicate submissions are expressly prohibited. However, if one journal chooses not to publish the manuscript, of course the author may send the manuscript to another journal.

Special Ethical Concerns for Counseling and Therapy Researchers

There are four special concerns of researchers in counseling and psychotherapy process and outcome. The first relates to experimental design. Research that explores the usefulness of counseling interventions usually employs comparison groups. One or more groups receive the experimental treatment, and another receives either a standard treatment or a placebo. Because all participants might benefit from the new treatment for their problems, one must question whether it is ethical to withhold the experimental treatment. Several factors should be considered when designing such research. First, there is no assurance that the experimental treatment will be helpful; it may have no effect or may even be counterproductive. Second, without comparison groups, no one can be sure of the effects of the new treatment in comparison to other approaches, and its real usefulness to practitioners cannot be determined with confidence. Third, usually experimental treatments are not truly withheld, but rather delayed. When comparison groups are used, the standard of practice is to offer the new treatment to those groups once the initial round is complete. Researchers who are considering a research design that does not at least offer a delayed exposure to an experimental treatment found useful after a first round of experimentation are not acting consistently with current guidelines.

The second special concern deals with the impact of treatments on participants. Whenever research is being conducted on clinical populations, researchers have an obligation to be alert for deterioration effects on any participants and to intervene if the deterioration puts a participant at risk. In this situation, the scientific profit must be sacrificed to the well-being of the individual. An appropriate referral must be made. Those who volunteer for such research should also clearly understand this option at the time they give consent for participation.

The third special issue concerns the accessibility of written information about clients and the need for client consent to such activities. Research that reviews client records without the actual participation of the client is controversial. Since no one is put at risk or inconvenienced, in one sense no consent for this research seems necessary; however, a review of client records is probably not within the expectations clients had when they consented to counseling. A commitment by the researcher to honor the confidentiality of the documents lessens the ethical concerns somewhat, but the practice is still not fully consistent with respect for the client's dignity and privacy. Thus, when possible, it seems best to obtain client consent before review of any records or to include a provision for that consent in the general consent obtained at the onset of counseling or therapy. If neither of these options is feasible, perhaps the clinicians involved with the clients can remove all identifying data from the records before researchers use them.

The fourth special concern is the provision of feedback. The ethics codes mandate that participants be given feedback about the outcomes of research if they are interested in that information (ACA, Section G.2.g; APA, Section 6.18). Some research suggests that feedback to participants about the results of a study is frequently neglected, however. McConnell and Kerbs (1993) found that more than 30% of the researchers in their study failed to provide the feedback they had agreed to provide when people were asked to participate in their studies. According to the authors, this happened largely because researchers gave feedback a low priority. They seemed to know what they ought to do, but could not put together the energy to accomplish it. To avoid this problem, researchers ought to realign their priorities and structure their time better to honor their duty to feedback. The failure to follow up may diminish participants' willingness to volunteer for future studies.

SUMMARY

The ethical issues of teaching closely parallel supervision. The faculty member has obligations not only to students, but also to the public whom those students will serve, and to the profession. Faculty members violate ethical standards when they teach without proper knowledge, without proper sensitivity to individual differences, or with nonobjective techniques. They are also guilty of misconduct when they exploit their students' needs for positive evaluations, research experience, or clinical involvement. Faculty who act irresponsibly with colleagues are no less guilty of misconduct.

Because faculty are encouraged to act as mentors to students, they must be careful not to take mentoring past the boundary of an appropriate professional contact. Boundaries of faculty–student relationships need not be drawn as rigidly or as small as boundaries between clients and therapists, but they still exist. An ethics of care and respect for student autonomy is one useful guide to effective, responsible teaching and advising.

Researchers have several important ethical obligations, including conducting research studies that are of sufficient quality to contribute to knowledge, protecting the rights of human and animal participants, communicating and sharing research results with the professional community, avoiding fraudulent or misleading publication of results, and claiming authorship only when justified. Researchers must give priority to their responsibilities to honor the dignity of participants and help advance science over their personal interests.

DISCUSSION QUESTIONS

1. Some counseling and psychotherapy training programs require students to obtain individual counseling during graduate school. Assuming counseling is not provided by the teaching faculty, what do you see as the ethical dimensions of this practice?

2. How should faculty members deal with insensitive and prejudiced comments they overhear students making outside the classroom?

3. Some doctoral programs strongly encourage doctoral students to do their dissertations in the same areas as faculty research. They are not prohibited from choosing other options, but they get little support for such choices. Is this an ethical violation? Why or why not?

4. Much research in our field involves "convenient samples," such as college or graduate students, rather than other, less accessible groups in society. What ethical issues does such a practice engender?

5. Complete objectivity in research is impossible. Researchers naturally "hope" for particular outcomes for their studies. How can those involved in research deal effectively with the ethical implications of their disappointment when research findings contradict their expectations?

RECOMMENDED READINGS

American Psychological Association. (1982). *Ethical principles in the conduct of research with human participants.* Washington, DC: Author.

Fine, M. A., & Kurdek, L. A. (1993). Reflections on determining authorship credit and authorship order on faculty–student collaborations. *American Psychologist, 48,* 1141–1147.

Keith-Spiegel, P., Wittig, A. F., Perkins, D. V., Balogh, D. W., & Whitley, B. E., Jr. (1993). *The ethics of teaching: A casebook.* Muncie, IN: Ball State University.

Rosenthal, R. (1994). Science and ethics in conducting, analyzing, and reporting psychological research. *Psychological Science, 5,* 127–134.

Sieber, J. E. (1992). *Planning ethically responsible research: A guide for students and internal review boards.* Newbury Park, CA: Sage.

Tabachnick, B. G., Keith-Spiegel, P. S., & Pope, K. S. (1991). Ethics of teaching: Beliefs and behaviors of psychologists as educators. *American Psychologist, 46,* 506–515.

14

Ethics in Community and Consulting Settings

Avoiding Conflicts of Interest

In the early history of mental health work, most practitioners were employed by large institutions—schools, hospitals, colleges, or government agencies. The advent of licensing for mental health professionals several decades ago resulted in a whole host of new employment opportunities, including the option to "hang out a shingle" and practice independently. Even more options came with the enactment of federal and state community mental health legislation in the 1960s. Thirty years after these changes, a minority of counselors, psychologists, and social workers work for large institutions. Many are employed by local mental health agencies, group practices, or function in solo practices. Professionals who are employed by large institutions such as schools or hospitals now often operate part-time private practices. In addition to the ethical issues already enumerated in the previous chapters, there are also special ethical concerns for those who work in these settings. This chapter addresses those special issues, focusing on ethical standards for client contacts, relationships with other professionals, obligations to third parties (such as insurers), and ethical considerations in consultation and forensic activities.

Responsibilities to Clients

Counselors have six major types of responsibilities to clients discussed in this section. These responsibilities are not necessarily unique to community and private practice, but probably are more salient for practitioners in these settings.

Advertising Services and Soliciting Clients

Both independent practitioners and community agencies funded by outside sources depend on a steady flow of clients and "billable hours" to survive. Thus, mental health professionals in the community are motivated to inform people about their services and encourage those who may benefit to use them. For many years, advertising of mental health services was severely curtailed by ethical standards. In that era, advertising was limited to brief, descriptive entries in telephone and service directories. To market counseling services in a manner similar to the marketing of other consumer products was judged unseemly and risky to the consumer. In the late 1980s the Federal Trade Commission challenged the legality of such restrictions and caused a dramatic change in the professions' standards for advertising. (For a fascinating account of the confrontation between the FTC, with its emphasis on free speech and free trade, and the APA, with its emphasis on protection of the public and the reputation of the profession, see Koocher, 1994a). Currently the guidelines for advertising deal primarily with prohibitions of deceptive practices and direct, in-person solicitation. They also restrict the use of testimonials. The wording in the APA document is illustrative:

APA *Ethical Principles,* Section 3.01: Definition of Public Statements

Psychologists comply with the Ethics Code in public statements relating to their professional services, products, or publications or to the field of psychology. Public statements include but are not limited to paid or unpaid advertising, brochures, printed matter, directory listings, personal résumés or curriculum vitae, interviews or comments for use in media, statements in legal proceedings, lectures and public oral presentations, and published materials.

Section 3.02: Statements by Others

(a) Psychologists who engage others to create or place public statements that promote their professional practice, products, or activities retain professional responsibility for such statements.

(b) In addition, psychologists make reasonable efforts to prevent others whom they do not control (such as employers, publishers, sponsors, organizational clients, and representatives of the print or broadcast media) from making deceptive statements concerning psychologists' practice or professional or scientific activities.

(c) If psychologists learn of deceptive statements about their work made by others, psychologists make reasonable efforts to correct such statements.

(d) Psychologists do not compensate employees of press, radio, television, or other commercial media in return for publicity in a news item.

(e) A paid advertisement relating to a psychologist's activities must be identified as such, unless it is already apparent from the context.

Section 3.03: Avoidance of False or Deceptive Statements

(a) Psychologists do not make public statements that are false, deceptive, misleading, or fraudulent, either because of what they state, convey, suggest, or because of what they omit, concerning their research, practice, or other work activities or those of persons or organizations with which they are affiliated. As examples (and not in limitation) of this standard, psychologists do not make false or deceptive statements concerning (1) their training, experience, or competence; (2) their academic degrees; (3) their credentials; (4) their institutional or association affiliations; (5) their services; (6) the scientific or clinical basis for, or results or degrees of success of, their services; (7) their fees; or (8) their publications or research findings.

(b) Psychologists claim as credentials for their psychological work, only degrees that (1) were earned from a regionally accredited educational institution or (2) were the basis for psychology licensure by the state in which they practice.

Section 3.05: Testimonials

Psychologists do not solicit testimonials from current psychotherapy clients or patients or other people who because of their particular circumstance are vulnerable to undue influence.

Section 3.06: In-person Solicitation

Psychologists do not engage, directly or through agents, in uninvited in-person solicitation of business from actual or potential psychotherapy clients or other persons who because of their particular circumstance are vulnerable to undue influence.

From these statements, it is clear that professionals are free to market their services in any way that avoids exploiting current or former clients or deceiving potential clients. Counselors may even solicit testimonials from satisfied former clients, as long as those clients are not vulnerable to undue influence, although this is a practice fraught with problems and not recommended by most ethics scholars (for example, see Koocher, 1994b). The dangers inherent in such freedoms are clear, and the duty to maintain the boundaries between legitimate marketing and misleading advertising falls squarely on the shoulders of the individual professional. Counselors considering advertising should ask themselves the following questions:

- Is the description of the service fair, honest, and as comprehensive as possible given the format?
- Are my credentials and training presented accurately?
- Does the advertisement help members of the public obtain services they want?
- If a testimonial is included, was it received from someone not under undue influence from me, and have I developed a plan for helping the person involved deal with any unintended consequences from his or her involvement in the testimonial?
- Would my peers agree that the advertisement complies with professional standards?
- Have I done all I can to guarantee that others involved in the advertising will abide by the ethical standards for advertising?
- Does the way I am advertising bring credit to the profession and promote public confidence in it?

Sturdivant (1993) points out that advertising professional services can serve the public as well as benefit the mental health provider. She argues that people cannot access services they do not know about or understand. Marketing can act as an educational tool that acquaints the public with resources they would not otherwise learn about. Her argument presumes that when a professional markets mental health or counseling services, that professional has already assessed the needs of the community and designed services to address those needs. She refers to research by the Ohio Psychological Association showing that consumers respond positively to marketing information about counseling and psychotherapy and that marketing results in increased respect for the profession. Nevertheless, counselors must carefully evaluate whether advertisements and other marketing efforts meet applicable standards.

Public Statements and Other Interactions with the Media

As is evident from the sections of the APA code cited earlier, counselors and therapists also come into the public eye by making statements about news events, discussing their research and writings, and giving interviews over print and broadcast media. For example, when a national news organization wishes to do a story on a psychological disorder (such as agoraphobia or attention deficit disorder), reporters often seek out experts in the field. Similarly, when analyzing the aftermath of a disaster, reporters often ask mental health professionals to comment on the psychological and social implications of the disaster. Conducted ethically, such interactions inform and educate the public and bring credit to the profession. However, professional standards are sometimes violated. The most common violations are failing to present one's credentials accurately, making claims not supported by evidence, drawing conclusions based on intuition or a cursory review of the situation, and attempting to do therapy rather than education. The following are case examples of some of these violations:

Dr. Doppert and the Television Talk Show

Dr. Doppert, a well-known marriage and family counselor in a major city, has agreed to participate in a television talk show on the subject of how couples recover from an episode of infidelity. The format is for two such couples to appear before a live audience to describe their experiences. At the end of the show, Dr. Doppert is to come on stage and spend five minutes with each couple to "help them heal" from the wounds of infidelity. When the show is taped, the therapist takes the assigned part and works with each couple before a live audience with the cameras running. Aside from introductions and watching the earlier portion of the show, she has had no contact with the couples. Because the segment ran behind schedule, the counselor had three minutes on the air to help each couple express their feelings about infidelity. At the end of taping she said good-bye to each couple and gave them her business card. Dr. Doppert was not paid for the time, but her book and practice were both mentioned when she was introduced to the audience.

Dr. Bewinger and the Book Tour

Dr. Bewinger has written a book challenging conventional understanding of obsessive-compulsive disorder, suggesting that it is largely caused by improper diet. His conclusions are based on his therapeutic practice treating clients with this disorder. He has conducted no formal research studies and provides only anecdotal evidence for his claims. When asked for specifics, Dr. Bewinger reluctantly reveals that he has treated 12 clients successfully with this method. In the introduction to the book, four of those clients offer testimonials to the value of the approach, and one tours with him to promote the book. Moreover, Dr. Bewinger does not dispute the public announcements that refer to him as a psychologist, although he is actually a licensed mental health counselor. (Please note that the hypothesis about the etiology of obsessive-compulsive disorder presented in this scenario has *no basis in fact* and was created solely for this case.)

Mertice Mentrison

Mertice has a Ph.D. in American history and an M.Ed. in counseling. Nevertheless, all the public announcements about her work as a substance abuse counselor use the title "Doctor."

All of these mental health professionals are violating the ethical standards listed earlier. Dr. Doppert's practice of intervening therapeutically with talk show guests violates the standard of providing care only within a professional relationship (APA, Section 1.03). It also violates stipulations about informed consent, confidentiality, and not risking harm to clients. Through her participation, she is also giving all who see the show a false impression of the therapy process and of acceptable practices for marriage and family therapists. In addition, she is placing the chance to promote her book and practice ahead of the rights or needs of the couples on the show. Given the standards for public announcements, Dr. Doppert's only ethical role in the show would be to provide information to the audience about the kinds of psychological and relationship difficulties that research shows commonly occur after infidelity. She should not in any way give the impression that she is providing a therapeutic service to the couples in a few minutes on television. She also should make efforts to ensure that the host or others do not communicate that she is appearing for the purpose of providing counseling in any form to the individual couples. DeTrude (1996) cautions professionals against thinking they can exert this level of control in a live talk show. The pressure of the host and audience to break down boundaries may be overwhelming, compromising both the dignity of the client and the professionalism of the counselor.

Dr. Bewinger's claims about his new treatment for obsessive-compulsive disorder violate Section 3.03 of the APA's code because they are misleading and do not give any scientific basis for his conclusions. They also seem to be motivated more by his desire to sell books than by any commitment to science or good treatment for this disorder. From the information provided, it is difficult to determine whether the testimonials he includes violate the standard of "undue influence." His conduct also contradicts the standard about misrepresenting his credentials, because he is not actively trying to keep others from characterizing him as a psychologist. His misconduct represents a flagrant disregard for client welfare, scientific truths, and impact on former clients. This counselor is discrediting the profession and encouraging people who may have a serious emotional disorder to seek an unproved treatment, thus delaying their access to treatments that may truly help them.

Ms. Mentrison is clearly disregarding both APA's code cited and ACA's code (Section C.4.e), which proscribe use of the title "Doctor" unless a person's degree is in counseling or a closely related field. Since historians have no training in counseling, psychology, or human development as part of their doctoral programs, there is no justification for using that title. Ms. Mentrison is attempting to deceive the public into believing she has a credential she does not possess.

Payment Issues

The amount of money a counselor or therapist in private practice earns depends on the number of sessions conducted for payment. Even Freud himself was well aware of this issue, complaining frequently about his money problems (Freud, 1954). The more sessions for which the practitioner is paid, the larger his or her paycheck. Thus, the primary ethical issue for those in private practice is coping with the conflict of interest inherent in this arrangement. Consider the following situations:

Ms. Amberside, a mental health counselor in private practice, is planning a expensive wedding trip to the Caribbean, for which she is saving money. Mr. Klepper has been in her care for some time for treatment of panic disorder. He met his treatment goals two months ago but remains in therapy because he is reluctant to terminate. He says he enjoys his weekly session and worries that the panic attacks will recur if he ends therapy. Mr. Klepper writes a check for therapy each week and never misses a payment. Ms. Amberside decides that her client should be able to terminate when he is ready, and that he is doing no one harm by extending his time in therapy beyond necessity.

Dr. Wrankley is seeing a client who has been mandated for counseling by the court. The court reimburses the therapist for these sessions at his full rate. This woman agrees to the arrangement because she sees it as her "least worst option," but she reluctantly attends counseling and spends most of her sessions in rather superficial discussion of her problems. She resists Dr. Wrankley's efforts to focus on deeper therapeutic issues and is making minimal progress. Dr. Wrankley recently established his practice and is struggling to meet expenses. Because he needs the income from the court, he allows the client to continue her current pattern in sessions. His reports to the court focus on her dependable attendance and describe the small changes she has made thus far and deemphasize her resistance to therapy. He does not lie to the court, but his correspondence less than completely reveals his true professional judgment about the client's therapeutic progress to date.

Both Dr. Wrankley and Ms. Amberside are engaging in what Cummings (1995) has called *unconscious fiscal convenience*, overlooking important therapeutic dimensions of counseling because attending them would conflict with the practitioner's financial self-interest. Such professionals are not maliciously exploiting their clients, but they do fail to see that the underlying motivation for their therapeutic decisions stems from their need for the money these clients provide. Thus both are acting unethically. Ms. Amberside should instead be helping Mr. Klepper cope with the stress of termination and develop alternative environmental supports. Similarly, Dr. Wrankley ought to stop colluding with his client to deceive the court and should begin to encourage his client's more active involvement in therapy. Moreover, he should immediately provide more complete reports of her therapeutic progress to the court, informing his client of this action before he does so.

To avoid such ethical lapses, counselors in private practice ought to engage in regular peer consultation and supervision about the financial management of their cases. Making the criteria for therapeutic decision making known to trusted colleagues is, in effect, using the "clean, well-lit room standard" (Haas & Malouf, 1995). This procedure acknowledges the difficulty in viewing clients objectively when one's financial well-being is at stake and provides an potentially effective method to prevent significant abuses.

Even counselors who are motivated by altruism and are insightful about the conflict-of-interest potential in private practice are often uncomfortable discussing money matters with their clients. They want to hurry past the financial details and focus on therapeutic issues. Although such an attitude is understandable, it is also fraught with risks. Clients who are unclear about the costs of counseling are not giving truly informed consent. Under these circumstances, clients may be more likely not to comply with payment conditions or may feel anger or resentment toward the counselor. According to the ACA code, clients must understand the financial aspects of therapy as well as other aspects:

> ### ACA *Code of Ethics,* Sections A.10.a: Advance Understanding
> Counselors clearly explain to clients, prior to entering the counseling relationship, all financial arrangements related to professional services including the use of collection agencies or legal measures for nonpayment.

As the last sentence of this section suggests, informed consent about payment issues is especially important if clients fail to honor their financial obligations. In that situation, sometimes counselors must decide whether to contract with collection agencies or pursue legal action to get paid. Because such methods compromise confidentiality, clients must fully understand the implications of nonpayment. Interestingly, almost 4% of the legal claims filed against psychologists involved counter suits over collection of fees (Peterson, 1996). Of course, counselors are not obligated to employ collection agencies to obtain delinquent payments, but they are not prevented from doing so, provided the client had prior warning that such methods might result from nonpayment. Even if a client has consented to collection or other legal means to recover payment, a prudent professional is well advised to remind the client of that agreement before taking that step, so the client has the option to provide payment and avoid such actions. As a matter of fact, the APA code includes that stipulation. Knapp and VandeCreek (1993) provide other recommendations for responsible use of collection services, including oversight of the means by which these services attempt to collect payment.

When clients are delinquent in paying, professionals are sometimes tempted to withhold copies of their records from subsequent therapists until payment is rendered.

This practice is a form of "holding the records hostage" and is unethical. In fact, it is explicitly prohibited by the APA code (Section 5.11). The ACA code implies that such a practice is inconsistent with current standards, but is not as explicit on the subject (Section B.4).

The ACA code of ethics also mandates that counselors provide some services on a *pro bono* basis,—that is, without fee—as a way of keeping in focus one's commitment to public welfare (see Section A.10.d). The APA, NASW, and AAMFT codes likewise encourage pro bono work. Recent research suggests that many psychologists follow this guideline (Knapp, Bowers, & Metzler, 1992). All codes also note that in establishing fees, professionals ought to consider client's financial circumstances. Many professionals use a sliding scale, adjusting the fee to a clients' level of income. Lien (1993) has questioned the ethical value of the sliding scale, but this practice is generally viewed as a responsible way to make services available to people with low incomes. Of course, counselors have a right to a reasonable income and have no ethical obligation to suffer significant financial hardship to comply with this mandate. The goal is to be as sensitive and accommodating to the financial situations of clients as is reasonable.

Interruption or Termination of Services

In personal relationships, adults can discontinue a personal relationship whenever they wish. They risk hurting a friend's feelings or receiving angry feedback, but there are no other significant consequences for them. Counselors, however, have no such freedom once they have embarked on a professional relationship with a client. A failure to provide needed services is usually termed *abandonment*. Counselors who abandon clients are violating explicit provisions of the codes (ACA, Section A.11.a; APA, Section 4.09). This standard is rooted in the profession's devotion to client welfare and to the protection of its reputation. Counselors who stopped counseling on a whim or out of dislike for clients diminish public confidence in the profession and damage the clients involved. Of course, sometimes counselors must terminate service in the middle of counseling. They may obtain new employment, retire, or get sick. In such circumstances, the codes specify that counselors must help clients find appropriate referrals and must do all they can to smooth the transition to the new counselor. A similar approach is advised if a client fails to pay for counseling as agreed. The counselor may refer the client to free services, but must do all that is required to facilitate the transition. If other services are not immediately available, counselors may not abandon clients in need because of nonpayment of fees. When interruptions in service are foreseeable (such as an elective surgery scheduled weeks in advance), counselors ought to plan for them. They should refrain from accepting new clients and should refer current clients to other mental health professionals.

Counselors in a sole private practice must also make provisions for another professional to handle their caseloads in the event of their sudden death or disability. Those in larger agencies should see that policies and procedures for referral in this circumstance are in place at their agency. Because clients become attached to specific counselors and are often in the midst of emotional stress and disruption, counselors have a special duty to take all reasonable steps to ensure that clients will be well served in their absence. Bram's (1995) review of the literature in psychology suggests that this standard is frequently violated when therapists underestimate their clients' needs for interim service in their absence. Counselors who had been disabled for several months tended to minimize the impact of their disability on clients and to make only haphazard arrangements for referral in the interval. Pope and Vasquez (1991) have identified several issues to be addressed if a counselor is incapacitated for a lengthy period:

- Who will provide both ongoing treatment and crisis intervention for clients?
- Who will notify clients about the therapist's absence?
- How can clients and others obtain information about the therapist's course of recovery?
- How will the therapist's records be handled, and who will have access to them?

These authors also caution practitioners in private practice to carefully think through a "worst-case scenario," to help protect the welfare of clients from negative effects of an interruption of service. A planful, proactive approach to such eventualities is an ideal strategy.

Records

Counselors are obliged to keep records of counseling and psychotherapy, both to benefit clients and to help other professionals provide effective service. Records can also help researchers study therapeutic processes and outcomes. This obligation is codified in the ethical standards and further supported by statute and case law. The ACA code contains the following statement on the subject:

> **ACA** *Code of Ethics,* **Section B.4.a: Requirement of Records**
> Counselors maintain records necessary for rendering professional services to their clients and as required by laws, regulations, or agency or institutional procedures.

The APA code uses similar wording in Section 1.24. Moreover, APA has issued *Record Keeping Guidelines* (1993c), providing detailed information about the content, construction, and retention of mental health records. Although some professionals decry such guidelines as an intrusion of bureaucracy and paper trails into therapeutic work, most scholars find the current standards valuable for maintaining quality care to clients and for protecting professionals whose work is challenged by disciplinary boards, lawsuits, or third-party payors (Barnett, 1994; Soisson, VandeCreek, & Knapp, 1987). These APA guidelines specify the content that ought to be included in professional records:

- Information relevant to the nature, delivery, progress, or results of services
- Identifying data, dates and types of services, fees, assessment and testing data, plans for intervention, consultations, summaries, and any release of information obtained

■ Data in sufficient detail for subsequent mental health professionals to plan adequately for future care

Piazza and Baruth (1990) recommend that six categories of information be included in counseling records: identifying information, assessment information, treatment plans, case notes, termination summary, and other data such as consent forms, copies of correspondence, and releases.

Oversight of Other Staff. The APA *Record Keeping Guidelines* (1993c) also indicate that psychologists are responsible both for maintaining the confidentiality of the records and for overseeing of any other staff who may have contact with the records. Licensed practitioners from other professions would also be wise to honor this guideline. Professionals who work in large agencies or practices must educate support personnel about confidentiality issues and guard against careless or thoughtless procedures for handling client records. Nonclinical personnel should read only those data from client files needed for billing and related purposes. It is important to note that this guideline applies to all workers at agencies and practices without clinical licenses. Administrative directors with business degrees have no more right to access therapy notes than do typists or receptionists. Moreover, clinicians have no right to read the records of other practitioners without a legitimate professional reason.

Forms of Records. Records may be maintained in more than one medium (written document, computer data, taped material), but the professional is responsible for the confidentiality of records regardless of the medium. Professionals who store client data on computers must be especially attuned to the security of those files and must prevent others from accessing confidential material. Sampson et al. (1997) point out that confidentiality of records may be compromised when client information is transmitted over computer networks. Computer experts note that files "deleted" from hard drives and disks are not truly deleted and can regularly be recovered by competent computer technicians. (That circumstance may comfort those who inadvertently delete important records, but it is unsettling for the confidentiality and privacy of most people.) Counselors who use laptop computers for storage of client records because of their portability and convenience need to take extra care to minimize the risk of theft of those computers or the risk of damage to client records if the equipment is damaged. Similarly, the increasingly common use of fax (facsimile) machines to send records should be done with care. As soon as a record is faxed to another telephone number, the professional loses control over the record. One should ensure that the receiving professional (or a designated staff person) is available to take control of the facsimile as soon as it is sent.

Many agencies stipulate that written client records may never leave the building without a signed release from the client. Such a policy helps prevent inadvertently compromising confidentiality.

Retention of Records. Some states and provinces have laws that mandate that therapeutic records be retained for a certain length of time. In the absence of any state laws governing this issue, APA recommends that complete records for adult clients be maintained for at least 3 years after service has ended, and that a summary of records be kept for another 12 years. For minors, records ought to be kept until 3 years after the age of majority (age 18). Thus, if a client saw a therapist even once 3 years after their initial appointment, complete records of the treatment must be kept for 6 years from the first appointment. For this person, a professional would be required to retain at least a summary of records for another 12 years, for a grand total of 18 years of records for this client's visits.

Disposal of Records. Because some information stored in client records can become outdated and invalid, the ethics codes stipulate that professionals attend to the time-limited validity of some information in client records and that they alert others who may seek such records to the existence of outdated data. (The results from standardized tests are one example of material in a client's record that may become outdated.) When any portion of a record is disposed of, professionals must maintain the client's confidentiality. Practically, this may mean shredding all documents before placing them in trash containers or recycling bins. Shredding prevents people who collect the trash from accessing confidential information.

Value of Records for the Professional. Obviously, the primary goals in keeping records of therapeutic contacts are to provide high-quality service for clients and to maintain continuity of service if different caregivers are involved. A secondary purpose is to document that good care was provided, if questions about that care are raised in court or in disciplinary hearings. Appelbaum and Gutheil (1991) have referred to documentation and consultation as the "twin pillars of liability protection" (p. 201). Regardless of one's personal feelings about the merits of keeping the kind of records described in the APA guidelines recordkeeping is rapidly becoming a "legal standard of care" for counseling and psychotherapy. In fact, the failure to keep adequate records has been used as evidence of poor care in court proceedings (Soisson et al., 1987). Some therapists have lost their licenses because they failed to keep appropriate records (Anderson, 1996). The courts, too, tend to conclude that if there is no record of good care, there is no good care (Soisson et al., 1987).

A good record also protects a therapist in high-risk situations, such as a threat of suicide or injury to others. In that circumstance, scholars recommend special care for documentation, including not only the ultimate judgment reached, but also a review of the factors evaluated to reach that judgment and of sources consulted in the process. Professionals who detail such information in the record are less likely to be judged negligent in court, even if their decision turned out to be wrong (Peterson, 1996; Soisson et al., 1987).

Ownership of Records. Records of mental health care are considered in most jurisdictions to be the property of the professional, but clients typically have access to copies of those records and control their dissemination (Soisson et al., 1987). Anderson (1996) explains this concept quite succinctly: "You own the records, but your clients own the information contained in them" (p. 94). Consequently, mental health professionals ought to enter record notes that they would be willing to have the client read. Emotional statements, summary judgments, and personal opinions have no place in the record. Any information that might embarrass or harm the client or others should be omitted. Some scholars suggest that counselors write records collaboratively with clients, to increase their involvement in the process, reduce their worry about what the records may contain, and lessen the risk of a malpractice claim (Anderson, 1996; Mitchell, 1991). Once again, though, because the legal requirements for recordkeeping vary from state to state, all mental health professionals should stay abreast of laws in their states related to this issue.

Ethics of Dual Records. Some counselors and therapists keep dual records. One set is the official record of services, and the other is their personal notes on the case. The latter allows the counselor to sort through feelings and reactions to the counseling process. Thus far, only official notes have been successfully obtained for court proceedings and disciplinary hearings (Anderson, 1996). Although one cannot predict whether this legal precedent will be maintained in the future, there does not seem to be justification to advise professionals who engage in this practice to change it. However, personal notes ought to always be anonymous, secure, and devoted primarily to the counselor's issues with the case, rather than the client's. Personal notes should always be a supplement to the record, not a substitute for it.

Involuntary Commitment

Counselors in community agencies or private practice sometimes see clients who cannot meet their own basic needs and/or who represent a threat to themselves or others. For instance, a person may be experiencing hallucinations and delusions that include beliefs that any food given to her is poisoned and that if she falls asleep someone will stab her. In this mental state the person cannot eat or sleep or otherwise meet basic needs. She may also refuse to accept hospitalization because of these delusions and hallucinations. In such situations a person probably cannot safely be free, and thus, counselors and therapists sometimes ask the courts to place that person in a protected environment until the person has stabilized. If such placement happens without the person's consent , it is called "involuntary commitment" to a psychiatric unit or hospital (Swenson, 1997). Needless to say, deciding to take away someone's freedom, even temporarily, is a serious matter that has both legal and ethical dimensions. There are many examples of people who were sent to mental institutions because they held deviant or unconventional beliefs and behaviors, but who were not truly mentally ill.

Currently, all states have elaborate procedures to be undertaken to ensure that the rights of the person are not violated any more than necessary and that the hospitalization is truly unavoidable. The specific criteria vary from state to state, but the general standard for such placement is to find "the least restrictive environment possible" while still protecting the safety of the individual (Swenson, 1997). Usually a preliminary hearing must be conducted so that a judge can determine whether the action is legally warranted. Counselors involved in decision making about involuntary commitment must be trained to assess mental and emotional disorders, be familiar with the laws and regulations applicable in their jurisdiction, and be respectful of the dignity of the person involved. Counselors may breach confidentiality and ignore informed consent provisions only as necessary to transfer the person to a safe environment. An involuntary commitment procedure is not a license to throw aside all usual protections of client rights and privacy. For example, if police are called to transport a client to a hospital, the officers should be given only that information they need to safely complete the transportation. They do not need detailed personal information irrelevant to their assignment. The fundamental criteria to guide counselors' decision making are respect for their clients' inherent worth and dignity, and promotion of their welfare.

Counselors deciding whether a given individual requires commitment are often facing complex and contradictory situations. As mentioned in Chapter 5, determining dangerousness is difficult. Sometimes even the best efforts of mental health professionals cannot guarantee the safety of clients and their families, but practitioners owe competent and diligent care to all involved. Counselors dealing with such complex situations can gather enough relevant information, carefully assess dangerousness according to accepted criteria, and work to identify the least restrictive environment possible that will protect both the client and others at risk (Bednar et al., 1991). In the current funding environment, substantial obstacles often hinder committing even those who meet every professional criterion for hospitalization. The problems of hospitalizing a person without insurance can be daunting. If the person to be involuntarily hospitalized is a minor, parental consent may be all that is required, although in some states a court hearing is also mandated (Ellis, 1996). Throughout this frustrating and confusing process, counselors should maintain a steadfast commitment to the client's welfare and to an outcome that benefits the client, compromises his or her rights as little as possible, and also helps protect others at risk.

Responsibilities to Colleagues

Counselors and therapists have obligations to conduct their interactions with other professionals in a way that honors their dignity, brings credit to their own profession, and avoids exploiting clients.

Cooperation and Respect

The generous federal funding that sparked the community mental health movement in the 1960s has long since disappeared, and now agencies are rivals in the battle for limited government and foundation resources. Private practitioners compete with agencies and with each other for the limited numbers of voluntary clients. Most seek to become "preferred providers" for managed care networks, to gain access to insured clients. In such an environment, professionals may feel tempted to forget their shared purpose of public service and to attend instead to the race for funds and clients. The directives in the codes caution professionals against such oppositional attitudes toward peers and encourage them instead to actively collaborate with other mental health professionals. Such a perspective not only benefits the public, but also serves the long-term interest of the professions, enhancing both access and quality of services. Counselors who take a short-term perspective or who center their energies on this month's billable hours may feel tempted to accept without question clients already receiving service elsewhere, or even try to lure clients away from other practitioners. Keith-Spiegel and Koocher (1985) label the latter practice "pirating." The codes strongly recommend against such practices:

> **ACA** *Code of Ethics,* **Section C.6.e: Clients Served by Others**
> When counselors learn that their clients are in a professional relationship with another mental health professional, they request releases from clients to inform the other professionals and strive to establish positive and collaborative professional relationships.

> **APA** *Ethical Principles,* **Section 4.04: Providing Mental Health Services to Those Served by Others**
> In deciding whether to offer or provide services to those already receiving mental health services elsewhere, psychologists carefully consider the treatment issues and the potential patient's or client's welfare. The psychologist discusses these issues with the patient or client, or another legally authorized person on behalf of the client, in order to minimize the risk of confusion and conflict, consults with the other service providers when appropriate, and proceeds with caution and sensitivity to the therapeutic issues.

Of course, if clients are dissatisfied with their therapists or strongly believe that supplemental care is needed, counselors must respect their rights to seek other care. As consumers, clients are free to choose as long as the professional does not judge the change in caregivers to be harmful to the welfare of the client. When two or more mental health caregivers are involved simultaneously in the care of a client, frequent communication among them is desirable, provided the client agrees to such contacts. If a client is not willing to allow such communications, then the professional must make an independent judgment about whether good care can be provided within that restriction. If a professional concludes that such a restriction represents a potentially harmful situation for the client, he or she should disclose that conclusion to the client, attempt to renegotiate the arrangement or, if the renegotiation is not successful, should ask the client to see the other professional exclusively. Of course, termination and referral should not be done abruptly and ought not to be conducted in a way that causes the client additional distress. In essence, where supplemental or alternative counseling appears contrary to clients' therapeutic needs, counselors must balance their obligations not to abandon clients against their duty to avoid harm to those clients. Supervision and consultation are important resources to help counselors sort through such issues.

A second important aspect of cooperation and respect among colleagues relates to the interactions among the different mental health professions. Disagreements about what services individual professions are competent to provide have erupted during the recent history of psychiatry, psychology, counseling, and social work. Professionals schooled in one discipline may view differing training models with suspicion and tend to limit referrals and professional contacts to those with the same degree. Depending on one's perspective, this tendency to disdain related professions may be rooted in financial self-interest or in legitimate concern about the quality of services available to the public. The codes address this issue as follows:

> **APA** *Ethical Principles,* **Principle B: Integrity**
> Psychologists seek to promote integrity in the science, teaching, and practice of psychology. In these activities psychologists are honest, fair, and respectful of others.

> **APA** *Ethical Principles,* **Principle C: Professional and Scientific Responsibility**
> Psychologists consult with, refer to, or cooperate with other professionals and institutions to the extent needed to serve the best interests of their patients, clients, or recipients of their services.

> **APA** *Ethical Principles,* **Section 1.09**
> In their work-related activities, psychologists respect the rights of others to hold values, attitudes, and opinions that differ from their own.

The ACA code is even more specific on this issue:

> **ACA** *Code of Ethics,* **Section C.6.a: Different Approaches**
> Counselors are respectful of approaches to professional counseling that differ from their own. Counselors know and take into account the traditions and practices of other professional groups with which they work.

Thus, behaviors that disparage the competence or value of other professions, that suggest to clients that other professions are inherently less worthy than one's own, and that are based more on self-interest than on public need are not only unseemly, but also contradict the values and standards expressed in professional codes. In the current competitive climate, practitioners will probably experience frustrations that lead to less than charitable thoughts about their fellow professionals. However, they must guard against expressing those feelings to clients or colleagues whom they may influence. Counselors and therapists should aim at finding ways to work together to counteract some of the social and political realities that limit or deny citizens access to quality mental health care.

Fee Splitting

The term *fee splitting* refers to the practice of paying a fee to someone who provides referrals or receiving a fee from a professional to whom one sends referrals. In colloquial terms, fee splitting is a kind of "kickback." The codes of ethics of all mental health professions prohibit such arrangements unless the fee can be traced to a specific service provided. A fee for a referral in the absence of a service is unethical. (See, for example, Section 1.27 of the APA code and Section D.3.b of the ACA code.) The rationale for this prohibition is the risk to client welfare inherent in fee splitting. If counselors personally gain from a referral, they are vulnerable to making referral decisions based on their own gain rather than on the best interest of clients. Many other professions, such as law and medicine, carry similar wording in their codes of ethics. Unfortunately, some counselors seem unaware of this prohibition. Gibson and Pope (1993) found that 8% of their sample endorsed this activity as ethical.

The prohibition of fee splitting raises questions about several rather common practices in private practice. Sometimes one professional whose name is on a practice (for example, Dr. Enterprising and Associates) receives a percentage of the income of the other professionals in the practice for each client they see. The associates are not employees of Dr. Enterprising, but they subcontract with him or her for space, support services, and the like. In light of the code, ethics scholars have expressed concern about this practice (Haas & Malouf, 1995; Koocher, 1994b; Peterson, 1996). In their analysis of the APA code, Canter et al. (1994) suggest that such fees are acceptable if the professional to whom the fee is paid offers some services to the referring professional. For example, if Dr. Stern uses office space, secretarial services, and utilities in Dr. Mahmoud's practice, Dr. Stern may pay a fee to Dr. Mahmoud for referrals she receives from him. The fee should be reasonable, in light of the expenses Dr. Mahmoud undertakes for the work of Dr. Stern. Moreover, the nature of the financial arrangement between Dr. Mahmoud and Dr. Stern should be disclosed to the clients involved. Keeping such arrangements hidden from clients or those who pay for services is inappropriate. However, if Dr. Mahmoud and Dr. Stern had completely separate practices and Stern paid her counterpart for referrals, that arrangement would violate the code, because Dr. Mahmoud would be providing no service to the client directly or indirectly.

Questions have also been raised about the ethics of participating in provider networks or referral services. The consensus of current opinion is that professionals may ethically participate in health maintenance organizations, preferred provider organizations, or referral services, such as those often operated by state or local psychological associations, as long as that relationship is disclosed to clients, does not violate the client's best interests, and the fee paid is justified based on services or expenses involved (Canter et al., 1994; Koocher, 1994b). Peterson (1996) suggests that open communication with clients about these issues also helps reduce the risk of the appearance of a conflict of interest.

As competition to provide services increases in the decades ahead, and third-party payors figure ever more prominently in access to care, counselors need to be sensitive to the ethical dimensions of the financial agreements they reach with insurers and other providers, and to ensure that all decisions about client care are based on the needs of clients irrespective of the financial implications for themselves. Counselors should also guide such decisions by current state laws on fee splitting, as these often vary substantially from one jurisdiction to the next (Peterson, 1996).

Responsibilities to Third Parties

The era is rapidly ending in which the interactions between a counselor and a client concerned no one other than the parties involved. Others are becoming involved in the counseling process, either because the client has been ordered into counseling as a result of a legal proceeding or because an insurer is paying for services. This section discusses the counselor's ethical responsibilities to these third parties.

Mandated Therapy

American courts are increasingly mandating that people enter counseling and therapy as a condition of their sentence. Teens who shoplift, belong to gangs, run away, or engage in drug violations are sometimes mandated to get counseling. College students who act disruptively may be pushed into counseling (Amada, 1993). Adults who drive drunk, have neglected or abused their children, or been found guilty of stalking often "choose" counseling over jail or loss of rights. Similarly, children with learning disabilities or with aggressive behavior patterns may be sent to counseling by the courts or parents. Licensing boards often add counseling to their rehabilitation procedures for professionals found guilty of misconduct. As mentioned in Chapter 6, there are important concerns about informed consent to counseling under such circumstances. First, the counselor and mandated person must be clear about who the client is and to whom the counselor owes allegiance. If an outside body has dictated the goals of counseling, then the counselor must make an independent judgment about the appropriateness of those goals for this individual. The involvement of a third party in the decision to enter counseling does not diminish one's responsibility to do good and avoid harm. Nor is one's duty to promote the well-being of the individual client reduced if a court is involved. If counselors believe that clients will be unable to profit from the type of counseling recommended by the courts, they must communicate their concerns to the mandating party. Counselors should also present alternatives to the mandated treatment, if any are available.

Clients need to understand that they have some choice about participating, even though the alternative to counseling is not especially appealing. In addition, clients need to understand the limits of confidentiality. If counselors are to submit regular reports to a board or court, clients must comprehend the nature of the reports and the possible consequences of such reports. Further, reporting to a third party sometimes becomes a "slippery slope" for breaches of confidentiality. Any disclosures to other parties ought to be limited to information relevant to the court's concerns. Next, not all counselors are competent to work with mandated clients. Competency in this realm requires knowledge, experience, and skill (Patterson & Welfel, 1994). Finally, counselors must avoid the temptation of viewing mandated clients as "second-class" clients because they are involuntary. They ought to be accorded the same level of respect as any person who engages voluntarily in the process. Here is the wording from the codes on this issue:

ACA *Code of Ethics,* **Section C.5.c: Reports to Third Parties**
Counselors are accurate, honest and unbiased in reporting their professional activities and judgments to appropriate third parties including courts, health insurance companies, those who are recipients of evaluation reports and others.

APA *Ethical Principles,* **Section 1.21: Third-Party Requests for Services**
(a) When a psychologist agrees to provide services to a person or entity at the request of a third party, the psychologist clarifies to the extent feasible at the outset of the service, the nature of the relationship with each party. This clarification includes the role of the psychologist (such as therapist, organizational consultant, diagnostician, or expert witness), the probable uses of the services provided or the information obtained, and the fact that there may be limits to confidentiality.

(b) If there is a foreseeable risk of the psychologist's being called upon to perform conflicting roles because of the involvement of a third party, the psychologist clarifies the nature and direction of his or her responsibilities, keeps all parties appropriately informed as matters develop, and resolves the situation in accordance with this Ethics Code.

Interactions with Insurers, Managed Care Providers, and Other Payors

Some of the most agonizing ethical dilemmas for those practicing in community settings have arisen because of interactions with outside payors. On the one hand, the availability of reimbursement for mental health care has dramatically increased access to care. On the other hand, it has diminished both the freedom of providers to treat clients independent of outside concerns, and the privacy of clients. Moreover, the limits set on the kinds or duration of care that can be reimbursed have prompted many mental health professionals to view access to quality care, particularly under managed care, as a sham. Its severest critics refer to managed care as the rape of psychotherapy (Fox, 1995) or as invisible rationing (Miller, 1996). Decision making about reimbursement for care may be made by people who have no contact with the client and who use criteria that oversimplify research findings or have no known scientific validity. Counselors whose clients are denied reimbursement for care that the counselors believe is essential are placed in a difficult position. They then must provide care at lower cost, without reimbursement, or ask clients to pay out-of-pocket. Moreover, insurers allow people to be reimbursed for services only when the professionals involved in the case meet their standards. Often, that means being listed on a network of preferred providers. Professionals who do not wish to contract with the insurer in that way are effectively prevented from working with clients insured by that company. The criteria for getting listed are highly variable. Some counselors with sterling credentials and proven records are denied, while others whose skills are unproved are accepted. Counselors can be removed from such lists whenever the insurers wish, and usually have little recourse. Fear of being removed from lists of approved providers places decision making about clients' needs under a shadow of worry about reprisals for recommending expensive or prolonged care.

Clients, too, face tough decisions—to see an insurer-approved professional and get help in paying for therapy, or to strike out on their own and fund counseling themselves. To challenge the limits reimbursers place on the length or type of therapy, they must often be willing to surrender some privacy, because the typical channels of complaint are through their employers. If they want their employers to lobby on their behalf, they must give them information about problems and treatment. To help consumers and professionals deal with these problems, the professional associations of 17 mental health disciplines, including counseling, psychology, social work, and family therapy, have produced a document that outlines the rights of clients in managed mental health plans (Sleek, 1997). Its ultimate goal is to protect clients from substandard care.

Most practitioners rue the day that managed care entered the arena. An APA survey found that 80% of psychologists viewed the impact of managed care on mental health negatively (Committee for the Advancement of Professional Practice, 1995). However, there are no signs that this model of payment for mental health care will disappear in the near future. How can counselors and therapists cope with this form of reimbursement and still abide by standards for care set by their professions, licensing boards, and often by law? The following is a primer for ethical survival in this context. Readers are urged to consult the sources listed in the recommended readings for a fuller discussion of these issues. I begin with a clearer definition and brief history of managed care.

Definition, History, and Data on Managed Care. Managed mental health care involves efforts by companies to control the costs of services and prevent payment for services that are ineffective, unnecessary, or counterproductive. It seeks to achieve this goal by regularly reviewing use of services, contracting with limited numbers of practitioners who agree to set fees for service, and preauthorizing care (Corcoran & Winslade, 1994). It originated as a response to the escalating costs of health care and was superimposed on outpatient mental health, even though costs for outpatient mental health care were not increasing at the same high rate as other forms of health care, and despite the fact that outpatient mental health care is only a small piece of the overall cost of health care in the United States (Iglehart, 1996). Critics charge that the current mode of operation of most managed care companies stems primarily from profit motives and not from any overriding commitment to efficient, quality care (for example, see Miller, 1995, 1996; Wrich, 1995). There are several variants of managed health care companies—health maintenance organizations, preferred provider organizations, and point-of-service plans. Almost all forms limit the numbers of outpatient sessions allowed annually, and significantly restrict access to inpatient care. A review of research on psychologists' experiences with managed care indicates, as noted, that they view the impact of managed care negatively, and have experienced many episodes when necessary care was denied or delayed (Miller, 1996). A few studies that have compared the outcomes of depressed clients in traditional fee-for-service arrangements with client outcomes in managed care found that managed care clients were more frequently underdiagnosed and had significantly worse outcomes (Rogers et al., 1993; Wells et al., 1989). However, empirical research on the impact of managed care on diagnosis and treatment is still too limited to draw meaningful conclusions.

Special Ethical Concerns in Managed Care.   When professionals are considering signing a contract with a managed care company, they need answers to each of the following questions before they agree to participate:

1. Does the financial arrangement with the company let the practitioner make independent professional judgments based on the client's needs and goals (Haas & Cummings, 1991)? Does it minimize conflict-of-interest issues?

2. Are the people who are conducting the preauthorization of care and the periodic review of services trained professionals capable of understanding diagnostic and treatment issues and able to use protocols for care responsibly? Are those protocols derived from scientific evidence? If so, what is that evidence?

3. Are resources available to meet special client needs and take into consideration unique variables that may affect an individual client's need for services? What resources are available? How well does the organization avoid a "one size (brief) fits all" approach to therapy?

4. How well does the system respond to the particular needs of culturally diverse populations (Newman & Bricklin, 1991)?

5. To what degree does the process of preauthorization of care and utilization review intrude into client privacy (Haas & Cummings, 1991)? Is this intrusion excessive?

6. Are there reasonable protections of confidential therapeutic information in place within the managed care company? Is access limited to those who have a professional role to play, and do those professionals comprehend their obligations to protect the privacy of clients (Scarf, 1996)?

7. How accurate is advertising for enrollment in the plan? Are enrollees clearly informed about the limits of mental health benefits ?

8. Does the managed care plan respond positively, or at least neutrally, to the actions of professionals who take a comprehensive approach to informed consent, including explaining the limits of confidentiality, payment issues, and the like related to their use of the managed care plan for reimbursement of services? To what degree does the plan it recognize that professionals have a duty to disclose the potential impact of managed care on treatment as well as the possibility that reimbursement for care may be terminated before treatment goals are reached (APA *Ethical Principles,* Sec-

tion 1.25e; Appelbaum, 1993)? Does it allow professionals to disclose the nature of their contractual obligations to the company?

9. Does the managed care provider give a fair and reasonable hearing to requests for exceptions to standard care based on individual client needs, and does it refrain from punishing professionals who make such requests?

Professionals must still be vigilant for ways in which their duty to promote client welfare may conflict with their obligations to the managed care organization. The experience of mental health professionals in interacting with managed care providers shows that ethical issues are likely to occur on a regular basis. (Of course, ethical issues also occur regularly in fee-for-service settings.)

Mental health professionals should also be advised that the standards of care used to make judgments about malpractice claims do not vary because of the limits of insurance or managed care policies (Appelbaum, 1993). Counselors cannot base decisions about mental health care on insurance or other financial considerations but should focus decisions more narrowly on the welfare of the clients. Similarly, there is some suggestion in the law that mental health professionals need to act assertively when insurers deny coverage for treatment that they believe is necessary. Appelbaum (1993) refers to this standard as "the duty to appeal adverse decisions" and recommends that counselors and therapists act as advocates on their clients' behalf when care has been refused. Appelbaum also points out that the ethical and legal standards about abandonment and interruption of services are not suspended in managed care settings. Clients, of course, may elect not to continue treatment after reimbursement ends, but the choice should be in their hands and they should understand the implications of ending treatment prematurely.

In sum, practitioners must guard against shifting the responsibility for adequate client care to the managed care company. They must guide decisions by the principle of competent diagnosis and treatment and must energetically work toward that goal regardless of the funding source for services provided. Counselors and therapists should not relinquish all their power to insurers.

Evidence of Ethics Violations in Dealing with Third-Party Payors. Counselors who feel frustrated by the power third-party payors exert over their clients' access to mental health care and their own access to income, may be tempted to use more severe diagnoses than warranted, in order to receive additional time in therapy, or to otherwise change diagnoses to meet reimbursement criteria. In fact, between 1990 and 1993, 15% of the ethics claims filed with the APA Ethics Committee dealt with this form of misrepresentation (Peterson, 1996). Similarly, most of those responding to Pope et al. (1987) reported that they had altered an insurance diagnosis to meet reimbursement criteria. As mentioned already, if there is no objective, clinically justifiable reason for a change in diagnosis, this practice violates ethical standards (ACA, *Ethics Code,* Section C.5.c; APA, *Ethical Principles,* Section 1.26). It is also fraudulent and subject to legal penalties.

The Ethics of Consultation

Counselors in community agencies often act as consultants, either to other individual professionals or to organizations and groups. School counselors frequently function in this role as well (Dinkmeyer, Carlson, & Dinkmeyer, 1994). When consulting, they apply their professional expertise to the questions, problems, or needs of those who seek their services. Often consultants must first help identify the needs to address and/or goals to achieve, as consultees may have only vague ideas about such matters. Consultation is increasingly common among mental health professionals (Dougherty, 1990), largely sparked by the Community Mental Health Act of 1963 (Brown, Pryzwansky, & Schulte, 1991). Graduate training in consultation is uneven (Newman, 1993), and the ethics codes have been criticized for giving this activity insufficient attention (Robinson & Gross, 1985). The APA code limits its specific comments to issues relating to individual therapy (Sections 1.20 and 5.06). The 1995 ACA code devotes one full section (D.2a–d) and two subsections (B.6.a and B.6.b), to the topic, but neither code provides comprehensive ethical guidelines for consultants or directly addresses organizational consulting. Fortunately, scholars have written extensively on the ethics of consultation, and are a valuable resource. Newman (1993), for example, identifies four crucial ethical issues in consultation: (1) the relationships between the people involved, including the confidentiality of information disclosed; (2) the influence of the consultant's values on the process; (3) the competence of professionals who consult; and (4) the selection and implementation of interventions. What follows is a brief review of each ethical dimension. To this list, I add consideration of the ethics of financial matters. Those interested in an in-depth analysis of this topic should refer to Newman (1993), Dougherty (1990), or Robinson and Gross (1985).

Consultation Relationships

Consultation relationships are triadic rather than dyadic (Brown et al., 1991). In every such relationship, there is the consultant, the consultee, and the consultee's client system. However, the client system does not hire the consultant, shape the consultant's responsibilities, or sometimes even know a consultation is underway. Yet, ultimately, consultants influence the client system and are responsible for the ways their actions affect that system. Mental health professionals who are not attuned to the implications of their work on these rather invisible participants can violate their rights and impair the ways the system impacts them. For example, the director of a large mental health agency may contract with a consultant to help increase the staff's productivity and generate more revenue for the agency. The impact of the consultant's work will be felt not only by the staff but also by the clients whom the agency serves. In some ways, both staff and consumers are part of the client system, although they had no voice in deciding whether to hire a consultant or in setting the initial goals for the arrangement. Yet both groups may experience the greatest impact of any recommendations implemented after the consultation. Newman (1993) cautions consultants to stay aware of all three participant groups in consultation, to be sensitive to the effects of their work on all parties, and to avoid situations in which their work may be used to the detriment of the client system. A wise consultant seeks to involve all parties in designing a consultation agreement at the earliest possible stage. Such involvement not only demonstrates greater respect for client rights and autonomy, but it also improves the chances of the project's success, and helps identify related goals or problems. By including all parties, the consultant may learn, for example, that a given problem is a bookkeeping or reimbursement matter rather than a lack of client contact.

Newman (1993) also points out that managing confidentiality and informed consent is more complicated in consultation situations, especially when the consultation is aimed at organizational change. How should a consultant handle one-on-one disclosures from employees? Are they confidential? Consultants need to be clear about their purpose and relationship with each employee with whom they interact and to forewarn any person when material cannot be kept confidential. A consultant hired to help smooth the merger of two mental health agencies should very directly tell the clients if he or she believes that keeping individual confidences may conflict with achieving the broader institutional goals. In other words, the limits of confidentiality should be clearly spelled out to all involved. What is less complicated, of course, is the consultant's obligations to keep information related to the organization or people involved confidential from those who have no right to that information. Such disclosures are simply wrong.

As discussed in Chapter 6, informed consent refers to the free and educated choices of people about matters that affect them. In organizations, senior executives often make decisions about hiring consultants and about the work those consultants will be doing. Employees and clients have less involvement and less power than the executives. Employees who disagree with the process or goals or consultation may be reluctant to voice those concerns, for fear of losing status or other repercussions. Consultants need to be sensitive to the hierarchical nature of organizations and work skillfully with all parties to approach ideal voluntary consent as closely as possible. Counselors can educate executives, for example, about the value of not coercing employees, and they can respect employees and encourage them to relinquish unwarranted caution.

Finally, consultants must also be alert to dual-relationship issues. Not only must they avoid sexually exploiting people they serve, but they must also be sensitive to nonsexual dual relationships that may compromise their objectivity. Consultants often work intensively with a few individuals in an organization. Such intensive contact can lead to inappropriate blending of roles. Consultant and friend, or consultant and business partner, are two such contacts that probably present ethical problems. When a consultant develops a personal relationship with one partner in consultation, he or she is vulnerable to ignoring the interests of the other partner. Moreover, when one is a business partner of a psychologist in a group practice and simultaneously a consultant on productivity, it is easy to lose track of the needs and rights of the clients and the other employees.

Values

The values of the consultant are important in two respects (Newman, 1993). First, because consultants cannot be value free, they must become aware of the ways in which their values influence consultation process and outcome. Such awareness will help the professional avoid unconsciously imposing personal values in ways that are unproductive for the client. Second, consultants should be prepared to respond to conflicting values in their projects. Conflicts are not inherently destructive, but they can be harmful if ignored or improperly handled. The consultant who is committed to collaboration to address problems may have significant conflict with directors who believe in a more authoritative and centralized approach to management, unless both parties can openly discuss and resolve the issue.

Competence

Many mental health professionals provide consultation in the middle and late stages of their careers, but relatively few have formal academic training in consultation. Scholars decry this situation, both because of the risk to clients and because of lost opportunities to have beneficial impact on consultees and client systems (for example, see Crego, 1985, Lowman, 1985). Practitioners seem to make the same mistake in thinking about competence to do consultation that they make in thinking about competence to supervise—they embrace the myth that clinical skills are sufficient. However, scholars agree that there is a body of knowledge to be learned in formal training, a set of skills that need to be practiced under supervision, and a capacity for judgment that is acquired with experience (for example, see Dougherty, 1990). Lowman (1985) notes that most counselors and therapists would be appalled if people without any counseling training presented themselves as counselors, yet counselors sometimes offer themselves as consultants without having been trained to consult. The tendency to misjudge the knowledge required for consulting does not release any professional from the obligation to work within the boundaries of competence. Practitioners without formal training and a history of supervised experience in consultation must refrain from presenting themselves as having such a background.

Finally, competence to consult in one setting does not imply competence in all consultation settings or activities. A professional competent to provide case consultations may not be the best resource for organization issues. Similarly, personal problems or preexisting relationships may compromise competence to be effective with a given client. The obligation to evaluate competence and to ensure that it is maintained always lies with the individual professional. Those who represent themselves as skilled consultants must be prepared to demonstrate the sources of their knowledge and be ready to take responsibility for harm their interventions cause.

Ethical Issues in Intervention

Because of the triadic relationships among consultant, consultee, and client system in mental health, consultants should keep the effects of their interventions on clients in the forefront of their thinking. Moreover, they need to be alert for ways in which others might misuse their findings, and work to prevent such misuse. Executives who seem to want to use a consultant report to dismiss older employees, for example, must be energetically dissuaded from such action. If persuasion fails, consultants should withdraw from the project. In other words, consultants cannot shift to others the responsibility for the ways those others use their recommendations.

Consultants sometimes advocate interventions without sufficient forethought. Even well-designed interventions that are likely to do much good may also carry some negative consequences. Counselors cannot ignore negative impacts because the cost–benefit ratio is positive. Instead, they must seek to prevent or minimize those side effects as much as possible. Consultants must be sensitive to the power they exert and use it responsibly.

Finally, consultants should base interventions and recommendations on empirical findings to the highest degree possible (Newman, 1993). They should distinguish experimental or untested recommendations from those well supported by prior research. Empirical data cannot always provide direct guidance for every consulting situation, and a consultant who expects to export findings from other settings wholesale into the current situation is likely to be disappointed. Research is not a cookbook for consultation (Newman, 1993), but rather a foundation for effective interventions.

Fees for Consulting

Why do many professionals become involved in consultation at some point during their careers? This involvement stems partly from the challenge and variety of the activity, partly from the status inherent in it, and partly from the financial gain to be had, especially in organizational consulting. A well-reputed consultant can earn a handsome living. If one is competent, conscientious, and committed to the public good, that reimbursement is well deserved and not an ethical issue. However, at times the opportunity for significant income clouds a professional's judgment. Such a person may accept consulting contracts without true competence, for the financial gain, or may ignore findings and interventions inconsistent with the hopes and expectations of whoever is writing the checks. In the latter situation, consultation becomes telling the executives what they want to hear and is a sham from which no one is likely to benefit, even the executives. This is a true conflict of interest. Consultants should ensure that their methods, findings, and suggested interventions serve the best interests of consultees and client systems.

Needless to say, consultants who prolong or extend consulting contracts to enhance their incomes are acting unethically, as are consultants who simultaneously encourage the consultee to become dependent in order to serve the consultant's own needs. For example, a consultant who encourages a board of directors to replace its director and then maneuvers herself into the director's position is flagrantly violating ethical principles.

Records of Consultation

Just as records of counseling and psychotherapy improve service to clients and help protect professionals against claims of negligence or misconduct, so too, records of consulting increase the likelihood of effective service. Consultants should have written contracts setting out the relationship, fees, goals, and practical aspects of the consultation. Issues of confidentiality and informed consent should be addressed in such contracts, along with any unique elements of the consultation. Similarly, consultants should keep progress notes and document any areas of concern or disagreement with special care. A copy of all reports to the consultee should be retained, along with copies of correspondence and telephone contacts. Consultants should protect the confidentiality of these records in the same way counseling records are protected.

The Ethics of Forensic Activities

The term "forensic mental health work" refers to those professional activities of a psychologist, counselor, or social worker that involve, primarily, courts of law. These include, but are not limited to the following:

- Conducting child custody evaluations for a divorce court
- Acting as an expert witness in a legal case
- Serving as consultant to attorneys on jury selection or other aspects of trials
- Assessing a defendant's competence to stand trial;
- Providing psychological information about a convicted person to the court prior to the penalty phase of a trial

In each situation the court or an agent of the court employs or mandates the mental health professional to provide professional advice relevant to court business in civil or criminal cases. The ethics of forensic activities have received increasing attention in the literature over the last decade for several reasons. First, the courts are seeking out such advice more often (Haas, 1993). Second, the roles and loyalties of professionals who participate in forensic work are often confusing and conflicting (Bersoff & Koeppl, 1993). The demands, cultures, and norms of the courtroom and the community counseling center are very different (Melton, 1994), and to act ethically counselors need knowledge of these differences (Anderton, Staulcup, & Grisso, 1980; Weikel & Hughes, 1993). Third, the professional sometimes has significant power in this role. A judge, for example, may rely heavily on a psychological evaluation of parents in making child custody decisions or in competency hearings for elderly people. Finally, the ethics of forensics have earned their prominent place partly through dishonor. The existence, even in small numbers, of "hired guns" and experts who will argue for any side that pays them for testimony has placed a cloud of suspicion over the matter (Huber, 1991; Pope & Vetter, 1992). Some critics have nothing but disdain for expert testimony. Szasz (1973) referred to testimony by psychiatrists as "Mendacity masquerading as medicine." However, there is nothing inherently unethical in providing professional services to a court. In fact, when conducted with allegiance to high ethical standards, such activities can bring credit to the profession. In the situations just mentioned, a competent mental health professional committed to using his or her skill responsibly can improve the likelihood that the court will make a fair and reasoned evaluation of the questions before it.

Psychologists and psychiatrists have had more intensive involvement in these roles than other professionals, but counselors and social workers are increasingly present in the courtroom (Bersoff, 1995; Foster, 1996). Child welfare cases may even include a larger proportion of counselors and social workers than psychologists. As more states license counselors and social workers as independent practitioners, their visibility in forensic activities will expand further. Thus, questions about the ethics of forensics are the proper domain of all mental health professionals.

The central ethical questions to consider when engaging in such activities are listed as follows. These derive from the writing of ethics scholars, published specialty guidelines (APA, 1994; Committee on Ethical Guidelines for Forensic Psychologists, 1991), and the ethics codes. The 1992 version of the APA *Ethical Principles,* for example, devotes an entire section to forensic activities (APA, Sections 7.01–7.06), extending its coverage of this issue significantly (Perrin & Sales, 1994). Those who seek a complete discussion on this topic may see the recommended readings at the end of this chapter. Here are the central questions:

Competence
1. Do I have the requisite knowledge about the issue before the court and about the law as it applies to my involvement? Is that knowledge current? Do I have enough time for the task to perform it competently?
2. Do I have a clear picture of the boundaries of my competence in this situation, and can I ensure that I will not be pressured to violate those boundaries?
3. Can I operate so that my personal values and beliefs do not compromise my capacity to provide good service?
4. Can I competently supervise my staff so that they too act within the boundaries of their competence?
5. Do I know and have access to all relevant codes and professional guidelines relevant to forensic work?
6. Do I have knowledgeable colleagues with whom I may consult if that becomes advisable?

7. Am I prepared to make available to the court the scientific data that support my conclusions or recommendations?

8. If an emergency arises, do I provide necessary care, assuming I am competent to provide it?

Informed Consent

1. Do all parties involved understand my role, my competence and its limits, the fees, duration, and other practical matters related to the activity?

2. Is there a written informed consent form for clients to sign and a written contract with court personnel?

3. Have I reviewed informed consent issues with clients myself and not relegated that duty to others? Do clients understand how evaluative data will be used and how my role differs from the role of a therapist?

4. Have I respected the civil rights of all involved?

Dual Relationships

1. Have I avoided or minimized potential conflicts of interest in the situations, or declined to participate if the conflict cannot be resolved?

2. Have I avoided dual relationships and exploitation of clients?

3. Have I made court personnel aware of any potential conflicts?

4. Have I declined to act as an evaluator, or expert witness for people who have been my clients, because of the potential conflict (Greenberg & Shuman, 1997)?

5. Have I avoided using undue influence in the process?

6. Have I declined to accept as clients individuals for whom I served as court evaluator?

Confidentiality

1. Do the parties involved understand confidentiality and its limits in this situation? Do clients know that court-mandated evaluations will be shared with the court, for example?

2. Are the records I keep secure?

3. Do I maintain confidentiality of any disclosures not relevant to the business of the court, unless otherwise released?

4. Do I honor my obligation not to breach confidentiality with any people outside of the situation unless I have appropriate releases?

Fees

1. Are my fees fair?

2. Have I refused any contingency-based form of payment, that is, any payment based on the outcome of a case?

Communications

1. Have I ensured (as much as possible) that reports, testimony, and the like generated from my services are communicated honestly and without deception?

2. Have I acted to correct any misrepresentations of my work?

3. Do I advertise my services in a way that honestly and fairly represents my competencies?
4. Do I understand the implications of my role, especially as expert witness, for the reputation of the profession, and am I committed to acting in ways that bring credit to the profession?

Child Custody Evaluations
1. Do I have the specialized competence required to conduct such evaluations (APA, 1994; Stahl, 1994)?
2. Do I keep the best interests of the child in the forefront of my considerations and know how to deal with the ambiguity inherent in that criterion (Oberlander, 1995)?
3. Do I interview all involved and use multiple sources of data in making my evaluation?
4. Do I fairly assess all data sources?
5. Do I know how to deal responsibly with children's preferences for one parent (Oberlander, 1995)?
6. Do I refrain from agreeing to conduct such an evaluation if I have a preexisting relationship with any party or any connection that may compromise my objectivity and effectiveness?

In light of these questions, consider the following cases:

A clinical social worker is asked to make a child custody assessment in a divorce action. He interviews both children and the father in person. The mother needed emergency surgery and could not keep her scheduled interview. The interview was postponed one day, and the social worker went to the mother's hospital room for the interview. The mother was in pain and still somewhat groggy from the medication and anesthesia. The social worker submitted her report and recommendations based on these interviews and other available data.

A psychologist is asked to evaluate the competence to stand trial of a woman who is charged with killing her twin infant sons they slept in their cribs. The woman's mental health records show a history of paranoid schizophrenia, and she was noncompliant with medications for several weeks prior to the violence. The psychologist is in her third month of pregnancy with twins herself, and she finds herself repulsed and frightened by this woman's actions. She believes she cannot deal with this case at this time and declines to participate, referring the case to a colleague.

A social psychologist has become a sought-after consultant to defense lawyers regarding jury selection. He uses his considerable expertise in human social behavior to help defense lawyers obtain sympathetic jurors. He keeps records of his effectiveness, and those records show that his advice generally results in impaneling juries more sympathetic to the defendant.

The psychologist who recognizes the impact of her personal situation on her capacity to provide objective, professional service is acting in compliance with the professional standards, and is making a judgment consistent with the best interests of the client. The social worker who uses unreliable information on which to base a custody evaluation is violating guidelines, however. A bedside interview while a person is still under the influence of anesthesia and pain medication is an insufficient basis for making generalizations about that person's fitness as a parent. In this situation, other pressures seem to have overtaken responsible judgment and promotion of the client's welfare. Moreover, the error is serious because the stakes are so high in this case.

A judgment about the ethics of the social psychologist's behavior needs more careful consideration. The U.S. system of jurisprudence is built on the right of a person to a zealous defense against any charges against him or her. The expertise of the social psychologist can be appropriately used to help defendants obtain jurors who are not likely to be biased against the person on trial and who will otherwise attempt to keep an open mind about the legal proceedings. His work is more likely to be within the ethical boundaries of the profession if his judgment about what constitutes a "sympathetic jury" is based on scientific evidence, not on personal whim or other idiosyncratic criteria. Similarly, if his judgments rely on stereotypes alone—for example, a European-American defendant should have a European-American jury—they deviate from the ethical standards of the profession and fail to bring credit to it.

SUMMARY

Counselors in community and private practice settings must wrestle with conflict-of-interest dilemmas. They must balance their own need for and right to a fair profit from their work against clients' rights to services and their roles as professional helpers. In addition, outside parties, especially those who provide payment for professional services, often affect the relationship between counselor and client. There are six central ethical mandates for community counselors. The first is to recruit clients with fair, complete, and honest descriptions of their capabilities and credentials and to avoid direct solicitation of potential clients. Second, the fees charged for services ought to be fair, clearly communicated, and sensitive to the financial status of the client. Professionals have a right to a fair income, but they are not allowed to place their own financial gain ahead of the welfare of clients. Third, if service must be interrupted, mental health professionals ought to have in place mechanisms for alternate care so that clients' therapeutic progress will be minimally disrupted by the interruption. Fourth, records of services ought to be up-to-date, accurate, and confidential so that competent service can be provided and privacy can be protected. Those records should be maintained for sufficient time for follow-up care to be provided, and disposed of in ways that guarantee client privacy. Fifth, if outside sources mandate therapy, the professional gives primary allegiance to the client, with due respect for the rights of the third parties and informed consent for all involved. Sixth, if clients need to be hospitalized against their wishes, the procedures used should be respectful to clients and minimally restrict their freedom.

Relationships with colleagues in the community are built on respect, honesty, and fairness. Turf wars, private judgments about competencies, and disagreements among professional disciplines ought not to be carried into the consulting room. Financial arrangements between colleagues should be open to client inspection and free from any hint of fee splitting or other forms of kickbacks.

When dealing with outside payors for counseling and psychotherapy, counselors must advocate for their clients for needed services and for limited intrusion into their clients' rights to privacy. Moreover, they must assess appropriate diagnosis and treatment separately from insurance and financial considerations. The frustrations with insurers that mental health professionals commonly experience do not excuse any misrepresentations in diagnosis and treatment to those payors.

Finally, when consulting or engaging in forensic activities, mental health professionals need to recognize that those specialties require professionals to have focused training and experience before they can assert competency. The tenets of good science, informed consent, confidentiality of records and disclosures, avoidance of dual relationships and exploitation, and sensitivity to individual differences and cultural background apply as strongly to these undertakings as they do to therapy relationships.

DISCUSSION QUESTIONS

1. As mental health professionals feel increasing competitive pressures for limited financial resources, how can they better manage the competition between disciplines and avoid some of the disagreements that have plagued mental health professions in recent decades?

2. Do you agree that fee splitting is wrong? Does the distinction between fee splitting between individual professionals and participation in "provider networks" or referral services seem meaningful to you? Why or why not?

3. Some mental health professionals have welcomed the changes in advertising ethics spurred by the Federal Trade Commission, but others have decried those changes. How do you view the current standards for advertising and soliciting clients, especially the freedom to use testimonials?

4. Many have challenged the current standards for recordkeeping as bureaucratic and designed primarily to protect the mental health professional. Do you agree with this view?

5. Some mental health professionals have refused to deal with insurers and managed care companies, asking their clients to handle that paperwork. They argue that their role is to provide clients with information relevant to their treatment and diagnosis and then to empower clients to deal with their insurers. Discuss the merits and deficiencies in this approach to managed care.

6. In an era in which funding for counseling and therapy services is limited, activities such as consulting and forensic work seem especially enticing to underpaid mental health professionals. Should there be a special credentialing process or other gate-keeping mechanism to ensure that only competent professionals offer their services in these arenas? If so, what would you recommend?

RECOMMENDED READINGS

Amada, G. (1993). Some ethical considerations: A commentary on "Between Cordelia and Guido: The consultant's role in urgent situations." *Journal of College Student Psychotherapy, 7,* 23–34.

American Psychological Association. (1993). *Record keeping guidelines.* Washington, DC: Author.

American Psychological Association. (1994). Guidelines for child custody evaluations in divorce proceedings. *American Psychologist, 49,* 677–680.

Appelbaum, P. S. (1993). Legal liability in managed care. *American Psychologist, 48,* 251–257.

Committee on Ethical Guidelines for Forensic Psychologists. (1991). Specialty guidelines for forensic psychologists. *Law and Human Behavior, 15,* 655–665.

Haas, L. J., & Cummings, N. A. (1991). Managed outpatient mental health plans: Clinical, ethical and practical guidelines for participation. *Professional Psychology: Research and Practice, 22,* 45–51.

Knapp, S., & VandeCreek, L. (1993). Legal and ethical issues in billing patients and collecting fees. *Psychotherapy, 30,* 25–31.

Newman, J. L. (1993). Ethical issues in consultation. *Journal of Counseling and Development, 72,* 148–156.

Oberlander, L. B. (1995). Ethical responsibilities in child custody evaluations: Implications for evaluation methodology. *Ethics and Behavior, 5,* 311–332.

Piazza, N. J., & Baruth, N. E. (1990). Client record guidelines. *Journal of Counseling and Development, 68,* 313–316.

Sampson, J. P., Kolodinsky, R. W., & Greeno, B. P. (1997). Counseling on the information highway: Future possibilities and potential problems. *Journal of Counseling and Development, 75,* 203–212.

Soisson, E. L., VandeCreek, L., & Knapp, S. (1987). Thorough record keeping: A good defense in a litigious era. *Professional Psychology: Research and Practice, 18,* 498–502.

Stahl, P. M. (1994). *Conducting child custody evaluations: A comprehensive guide.* Thousand Oaks, CA: Sage.

15

The Counselor in the Schools
Applying Professional Standards
to the Educational Culture

Many of the ethical issues school counselors face are not unique to their setting. Anyone working with minors must grapple with the complications that the age of their clients bring both to informed consent and confidentiality. All professionals who are part of large, public organizations must deal with accountability issues and delicate relationships with administrators. Both community and school counselors must respond sensitively and competently with culturally diverse clients (Hobson & Kanitz, 1996). However, several ethical challenges specific to school counseling deserve attention. These issues are (1) the conflict between the open communication norms among educators and the confidentiality norm of the counseling profession, (2) the obligation to assist students experiencing personal and social difficulties and the frequent resistance of parents and communities to counseling for those problems, (3) the ethics of peer counseling and peer mediation; (4) the need to follow sometimes conflicting state and federal laws about parental rights to educational information about their children, and (5) the obligations of school counselors with suicidal students. The ethical standards that guide this discussion are the ACA *Code of Ethics* and the *Ethical Standards* of the American School Counselor Association, or ASCA (1992). The former document is enforceable for all members of ACA, and the latter is meant to be used as a guideline to supplement the code, focusing attention on the ethics of school counseling. (A copy of the ASCA standards is included in Appendix G.)

Clash of Cultures: Open Versus Closed Communication Systems

Many school counselors begin their careers as teachers. In a teaching role, they learn the value of open communication with other school personnel. Educators tend to believe that effective teaching depends on adequate knowledge about all factors that affect student learning. The norm for teachers is to share information with others in the school who interact with their pupils. A teacher who is concerned about his student's health or cleanliness, for example, would not hesitate to discuss those concerns with the school nurse. In fact, a failure to consult with other educators about one's concerns would be seen as shirking a responsibility of good teaching. Such consultation serves a social purpose as well—it becomes an outlet for adult-to-adult conversation in a workday that is dominated by adult-to-child communications. It helps maintain the web of social connections between the adults in a building (Ferris & Linville, 1985). The counseling "culture" is significantly different. Counselors are taught that the information clients share is confidential and that communication of that information is allowed only with client knowledge and permission or with the best interests of the child in mind. Counselors are not allowed to use specific client matters as a means of fostering adult-to-adult conversation. This clash of cultures not only makes the transition from the role of teacher to counselor more difficult for novices, but also complicates the work of the experienced school counselor. Teachers and administrators expect them to communicate openly about students and see themselves as equals, with just as much concern for the best interests of students as counselors have. When counselors are not forthcoming about matters disclosed by students, other educators can be confused and even offended. In time, teachers who misunderstand counselors' reticence may come to view the counselors as less than "team players" and may feel more reluctance to refer students for counseling. The institutional pressures on counselors to conform to school norms can be substantial (Schulte & Cochrane, 1995).

School counselors often feel caught between these two cultures. On the one hand, they want acceptance, respect, cooperation, and referrals from other school personnel, all of which seem to require open communication to obtain, and on the other, they want to honor the confidentiality of student disclosures to maintain trust. At first glance, the two desires seem mutually exclusive, but there are responsible ways to resolve the conflict. Consider the following situations:

The Case of Reggie

Reggie is a fifth-grade student whose behavior has deteriorated over the last two months. He used to be an involved, conscientious student who wanted to learn. Now he seems to spend most of his time in class with his head on his desk or his gaze out the window. He is not submitting homework and is failing. After consulting with other teachers, the math teacher, Mr. Kearns, learns that Reggie behaves this way in all classes, and he refers the student to the school counselor, Dr. Jeffers. After a few counseling sessions and an explanation of confidentiality to Reggie and his mother, the child begins to reveal information about his personal life. His mother was recently diagnosed as HIV positive. Simultaneously, he learned that his mother had abused intravenous drugs until she became pregnant with him. Reggie feels sad, angry, and betrayed. Both Reggie and his mother do not want her illness or other matters about their personal lives disclosed to anyone else at school. Mr. Kearns has felt frustrated by the counselor's lack of response to his questions about Reggie, and has asked the principal for a meeting among all educational personnel involved with Reggie to discuss the child's deteriorating behavior. Dr. Jeffers is asked to attend. The teacher and principal are truly concerned for Reggie's well-being and want the counselor to help them help this student.

The Case of Gloria

The lunchtime conversation in the teacher's room focuses on a sophomore named Gloria, whose mother was shot while robbing a bank several years ago. The mother is incarcerated, and the father has been emotionally unstable since the robbery. The father frequently comes to school dressed in his pajamas and accuses staff of trying to poison his daughter. The father has refused psychological treatment. Gloria has become painfully shy and often skips school for days after her father's visits there. Today's lunchroom conversation is recounting the father's most recent visit, and the emotions expressed around the table are a mixture of sympathy for the girl and laughter at the wild accusations and outrageous behavior of her father. The counselor takes a seat at the table and is asked what she thinks about all this.

Case Analysis

In Reggie's case, the ethical standards are clear. If both Reggie and his mother are adamant about keeping counseling disclosures confidential, the counselor must abide by their wishes. None of the exceptions to confidentiality apply here; there is no child abuse, no imminent danger to Reggie or threat to another, no court order, and no parental permission or request to disclose. The ASCA *Ethical Standards* use these words about confidentiality:

> **Section A.9: Responsibilities to Students**
>
> The school counselor protects the confidentiality of information received in the counseling relationship as specified by law and ethical standards. Such information is only to be revealed to others with informed consent of the counselee and consistent with the obligation of the counselor as a professional person.

> **Section B.2: Responsibilities to Parents**
>
> Informs parents of the counselor's role with emphasis on the confidential nature of the counseling relationship between the counselor and counselee.
>
> Treats information received from parents in a confidential and appropriate manner.

> **Section C.2: Responsibilities to Colleagues**
>
> Promotes awareness and adherence to appropriate guidelines regarding confidentiality, the distinction between public and private information, and staff consultation.

Is the counselor's only choice to alienate colleagues and remain silent in the meeting? Fortunately, there are other options at this point. The counselor would be well advised to discuss with Reggie and his mother the teacher's concern about the child's academic performance, give his mother information about the meeting, seek guidance about exactly what information, if any, the counselor may reveal in that meeting, and ask permission from the principal to invite Reggie's mother and/or Reggie to the meeting. (The counselor may also wish to refer the family for family counseling and support in dealing with the difficult problem facing them. Such support may further assist Reggie to cope better with his mother's illness and history.) Before any conference about the student, the counselor ought to meet privately with the teacher and the principal to explain the confidentiality requirements and the limits they place on free and full discussion of counseling sessions. Description of any state and federal laws that seem relevant would also help other educators understand the dilemma posed by their request for counseling information.

The counselor can avoid a great deal of the aggravation in such situations by educating faculty and administrators about the roles and responsibilities of school counselors before a problem erupts (Tompkins & Mehring, 1993; Watson, 1990). A straightforward inservice education program would reassure colleagues that the goal of the counselor is to help teachers help students, but that the legal and ethical parameters under which counselors work means that they must disclose student revelations carefully, if at all. Ferris and Linville (1985) and Cooney (1985) advise written policies on confidentiality and written referral procedures. In addition, Tompkins and Mehring (1993) recommend that communication about confidentiality obligations begin at the time a professional is interviewing for a position. By initiating such a discussion, a counselor can get a clearer sense of the knowledge and receptivity of other educational personnel to confidentiality of counseling disclosures.

In the second case, the lunchroom discussion about the sophomore's troubles and her father's unusual behavior seems geared more to entertain the teachers than to promote the best interests of the student or her parent. Lunchroom discussions are not structured professional interactions clearly planned to benefit students. They can often deteriorate into gossip (Watson, 1990). Moreover, teachers in the room may have no interaction with Gloria, and therefore, have no need or right to know anything about her. For the counselor to participate in any discussion of the people involved would demean those individuals and would not bring credit to the counselor or to the profession. Therefore, the counselor should find a way to divert the group's attention to another issue and avoid comment on this topic. The manner of the diversion and the refusal to discuss this issue need not be made in a morally superior or self-righteous way. When such dramatic events occur, it is natural for people to wish to talk about them later. For counselors, especially, that natural human desire must be superseded by their professional obligations. As with the last scenario, educating teachers to the unique responsibilities of counselors might have alleviated the pressure the counselor felt to participate. Perhaps, though, the only truly safe way to avoid such discussions is to refrain from sitting in the lunchroom or teacher's lounge when such events are likely to become the focus of conversation. Participation in such gossip can have legal as well as ethical consequences. Under such circumstances, all school personnel are vulnerable to claims of defamation of character (Fischer & Sorenson, 1996). Moreover, counselors would be well advised to assist colleagues who participate in such lunchroom gossip to understand the legal and ethical implications of their behaviors.

School counselors need not think of other educators in an adversarial way, however. When students and parents are informed about the potential value of sharing information with relevant teachers and administrators and when they have control over the material that is revealed, they often agree to such releases. In the first case, Reggie and his mother may want to tell school officials something, and the counselor can help them articulate the kind of communication that would feel comfortable for them. For example, they may want to tell teachers that a member of Reggie's family is ill with a chronic disease and Reggie is quite distracted and worried about that. Counselors must balance the value such disclosures would have for the child's education against the risk of other people incidentally or intentionally violating guidelines for the proper use of that information. The counselor can help all parties define the clients' views of appropriate and inappropriate uses of the disclosures, and thus help reduce the risk of violating the clients' wishes. The ASCA standards speak to this point:

Responsibilities to Colleagues and Professional Associates
The school counselor

(1) establishes and maintains a cooperative relationship with faculty, staff, and administration to facilitate the provision of optimum guidance and counseling services.

(2) promotes awareness and adherence to appropriate guidelines regarding confidentiality, the distinction between public and private information and staff consultation.

Research on the compliance of school counselors with these directives is limited. Two studies by Wagner (1978, 1981) suggested that approximately one-quarter of the counselors sampled admitted engaging in informal communications with others about clients. Most who engaged in this practice did not view it as ethical though. Such frequent participation in a practice they acknowledged as unethical suggests that the open communication culture of the school powerfully influences counselor behavior.

Davis and Ritchie (1993) advise school counselors to inform administrators about any counselor activity that is likely to have legal repercussions for the school. If, for instance, a counselor decides to hospitalize a student in the midst of a psychotic episode without parental consent (because the parents could not be reached), he or she should tell the principal about the action and its rationale, that is, the parents' unavailability and the safety risk to the student. This situation has potential legal ramifications, because the parents may claim that the action violated their right to consent and damaged the reputation of the family. At the same time, Davis and Ritchie caution counselors to use prudent judgment about such consultations, resisting the temptation to break confidentiality for any activity that has any potential for legal complications. However, in situations in which legal action is a significant possibility, administrators should be informed. After all, administrators will be in a better position to help and defend the school counseling program if they are aware of the situation.

Privilege for School Counselors

In this litigious era courts are increasingly likely to call school counselors in to testify about their work with parents or students (James & DeVaney, 1995). They may sub-poena a counselor to testify in a custody hearing for a child with whom the counselor has had extensive contact, or ask a counselor to produce a client's counseling records. If counselors violate confidentiality and reveal information that ought to have been kept private, they themselves can be brought to court to defend against charges of malprac-tice or defamation of character (Fischer & Sorenson, 1996). For these reasons school counselors need to become aware of the laws about privileged communication in their states. Fischer and Sorenson (1996) identify 18 states where the clients of school coun-selors can assert at least limited privilege in state courts. These states include Alabama, Arkansas, Idaho, Indiana, Iowa, Kansas, Maine, Michigan, Missouri, Montana, Nevada, North Carolina, North Dakota, Ohio, Oregon, Pennsylvania, South Dakota, and Vir-ginia. In other states, no statutory privileges are established for school counselors. The 1996 U.S. Supreme Court decision in *Jaffee v. Redmond* may spur further extensions of privilege (Remley, Herlihy, & Herlihy, 1997), so school counselors should stay alert for legal changes that affect confidentiality. Counselors who practice in states with some level of privilege for clients of school counselors have a responsibility to educate other school personnel about the meaning and implications of that privilege for their work.

Parental and Community Values That Diverge from Professional Values

Kaplan (1996) describes the challenges that some parent groups and political organiza-tions are bringing to school counseling. Their aim is to give parents increased control over the schooltime activities of their children. Some groups oppose the involvement of school counselors with children in any personal, social, or career development activity unless parents give their express consent. In this view, counselors ought to restrict their work with children to activities such as schedule planning, educational testing, and edu-cational problem solving. According to Kaplan (1996), some of these groups want counselors and other educators to refrain from teaching decision-making skills or using programs designed to foster self-esteem and self-confidence in children. Some groups believe that by teaching decision-making skills, counselors are undermining parental authority and religious teachings. Similarly, they challenge the appropriateness of inter-ventions designed to increase self-esteem because they believe they lessen the level of obedience children show to those in authority. In such cases, the values of parents seem contradictory to central educational values in the mainstream of democratic societies (Kaplan, 1996).

Kaplan (1996) also contends, though, that this movement raises some important questions for counselors to consider. Parents who want to make informed decisions about the counseling activities in which their children participate deserve that right. Similarly, because parents bear the primary responsibility for their children, they deserve to know a great deal about the disclosures those young people make to other adults. Kaplan suggests that school counselors have some accountability for this growing opposition to their profession. In her view some counselors have failed to acknowledge legitimate parental rights or have delved into personal and social problems of students that are beyond the limits of their competence to treat. They have tended to view parents as adversaries rather than allies in helping children. In these ways counselors have risked harm to clients and created resentment among family members. These problems have occurred even with well-intentioned counselors motivated solely by a desire to promote their students' development. Research by Ritchie and Partin (1994) suggests that less than 10% of school counselors in Ohio seek the consent of parents even when they are counseling students on a regular basis.

Kaplan (1996) recommends parental and community education about counseling programs as a partial remedy to such misunderstandings. Parents are often reassured to learn that counselors do not intend to work outside the boundaries of their competence, that they will honor the rights of parents to information about students, and that they will be respectful of family values that run contradictory to some counseling programs. A practical way to educate families about school counseling programs is to develop and distribute a handbook including the credentials of school counselors, the mission of the program, and its policies and procedures about interaction with parents.

Of course, none of these remedies is a panacea for opposition by political and parent groups who strongly oppose counseling in the schools. Counselors whose very jobs may be at stake in some communities need to demonstrate the value of their programs to the community, to collaborate with other professionals and professional associations to preserve such services for students, and to keep as their guiding principle the best interests of the students they serve. Counselors can avoid some of these problems by taking into account community values as they carry out their duties. This does not mean counselors ought to be slaves to community preferences. Rather, it means that with sensitivity to the prevailing community norms, counselors are better equipped to anticipate resistance to interventions and act to prevent its occurrence in the first place.

Sometimes communities hold values that are inherently contradictory to the values of the counseling profession (Davis & Ritchie, 1993). Communities in which there is strong opposition to discussing sexuality or drug abuse in the schools can pose a problem for counselors whose students raise these issues. If the community frowns on providing contraceptive information, should a counselor refuse to provide a referral for contraceptive information to a student who seeks it? Should a counselor disclose to parents all student comments about drug experimentation in a community that expects such disclosures? In a community that has little tolerance or understanding of gay, lesbian, or bisexual orientations, should counselors help students who have questions about sexual identity? These are complicated questions, and the answers depend on a number of factors: the age and maturity of the student, the student's willingness to involve parents, the likelihood that the parents' response will not harm the child, the school policy on such matters, and the applicable laws and professional standards. No one benefits if counselors enrage a community and arouse its opposition to the whole counseling program. However, counselors cannot ignore the needs of adolescents who seek information and service about sensitive issues. Indeed, gay, lesbian, and bisexual students are at substantial risk for suicide, conflicts with family, and violence from others (Besner & Spungin, 1995). Strong parental and community values against sexual intimacy before marriage or drug experimentation will not guarantee that every student will act in accordance with those values. Ultimately, school counselors must make such decisions with the best interests of their students as the main priority.

In some situations, state and federal laws protect the rights of counselors to advise adolescents about sensitive issues. Anderson (1996) and Fischer and Sorenson (1996) suggest that counselors who give adolescents competent advice and referrals to appropriate resources for birth control information are not likely to be successfully sued for malpractice. State laws often do not give counselors the same freedom about discussions of abortion, although there is great variability in state statutes on this matter. Counselors need to be cautious and alert to legal limitations on their comments when a pregnant student wants to discuss abortion. Anderson (1996) advises counselors to be especially circumspect about sharing their personal views on this highly controversial matter. Once again, the ideal resolution is to help the teenager involve her parents in the decision making. The law is silent or unclear on other sensitive matters that do not involve abuse, neglect, or clear and imminent danger. The ASCA code recognizes the rights of both students and parents, but it also affirms the appropriateness of a wide focus for school counseling on educational, personal, and social dimensions of development:

Responsibilities to Pupils
The school counselor

(1) has a primary obligation and loyalty to the pupil who is to be treated with respect as a unique individual, whether assisted individually or in a group setting.

(2) is concerned with the total needs of the student (educational, vocational, personal, and social) and encourages maximal growth of each counselee.

Responsibilities to Parents
The school counselor

(1) respects the inherent rights and responsibilities of parents for their children and endeavors to establish a cooperative relationship with parents to facilitate the maximal development of the counselee.

(2) is sensitive to changes in the family and recognizes that all parents, custodial and noncustodial, are vested with certain rights and responsibilities for the welfare of their children by virtue of their position and according to law.

The Ethics of Peer Helping Programs

Peer support programs exist under many names—peer counseling, peer support, peer intervention, peer facilitation, peer mediation, and peer conflict resolution. Their central feature involves training students to act as support people for other students who have problems or are at risk for developing problems. Peer helper programs have become more common over the last two decades, as schools try to increase student access to support services without increasing costs (Morey, Millton, Fulton, Rosen, & Daly, 1989). Low cost has not been the only factor in their expansion, however. They have been viewed as valuable gateways to attract reluctant students to counseling services they need. Adolescents in particular are often hesitant to reveal their problems to adults. The original peer helping concept was construed as limited to developmental concerns and peer tutoring (Anderson, 1976). According to Lewis and Lewis (1996), many peer helping programs have been initiated as a response to serious mental health issues—suicide, drug and alcohol abuse, eating disorders, and depression. Peer intervention programs for such problems have expanded beyond the high school level. Herring (1990) advocates peer helping programs for suicide prevention at the middle school as well, and many peer helping programs have been developed in elementary schools (Myrick, Highland, & Sabella, 1995).

How effective are these programs in meeting their goals, and what ethical problems arise from their use? According to Lewis and Lewis (1996), much of the evidence about the effectiveness and outcomes of peer helping programs is anecdotal rather than empirical. Program effectiveness is not always measured by meaningful, objective criteria, so that the true impact of these interventions is still not determined. Lewis and Lewis urge more research and evaluation in order to better assess the power of such programs. They go on to question the merit of using peer helping models for serious mental health problems in the absence of such outcome data. They state, "there is not yet a body of evidence documenting the effectiveness, or the safety, of using peer helping programs to address problems beyond the basic academic and developmental issues they were initially intended to address" (p. 312). To the degree, then, that counselors cannot demonstrate either the merit or the safety of such programs, there is serious question about the ethics of their use.

In addition, peer helping programs require high levels of supervision, both at initiation and throughout the program. Helpers must be carefully chosen, well trained, and continuously monitored to ensure that they are skilled enough to provide support services and that they do not exceed the limits of their competence. In their research Lewis and Lewis (1996) found a disturbing pattern. Many of the educators responsible for peer helping programs were not trained counselors. Thus, in those cases, there were no professionals with the requisite training and experience to accomplish important supervisory tasks. In those circumstances, neither the helpers nor the supervisors have the competence to assess the seriousness of a student's emotional problem or to decide on appropriate treatment. Needless to say, given the risks of peer counseling, supervision by trained counselors knowledgeable in supervision of volunteers appears to be a minimal requirement for an ethical program. The ASCA *Ethical Standards* (1992) speak directly to this issue:

Responsibilities to Students

The school counselor:

(15) has unique responsibilities in working with peer programs. In general, the school counselor is responsible for the welfare of students participating in peer programs under his/her direction. School counselors who function in training and supervisory capacities are referred to the preparation and supervision standards of professional counselor associations.

Noncounselor supervisors are unlikely to understand guidelines for confidentiality, dual relationships, informed consent, and the myriad other professional guidelines for responsible helping services. School counselors therefore ought not to support the use of noncounselors in overseeing peer helping programs.

The role demands on students who volunteer to be peer helpers are substantial. Professionals responsible for such programs see benefits to those volunteers, but some wonder whether they are overburdened for their developmental level when they are asked to cope with serious mental health issues (Lewis & Lewis, 1996; Morey et al., 1989). In Lewis and Lewis's study of 263 peer programs in Washington State, they found two completed suicides by peer helpers. Two incidents is not a sufficient basis for a sweeping conclusion about the risks of the helper role, but these events illustrate the need to screen candidates carefully, monitor stress, and supervise closely. Regardless of the precautions, there is still reason to question whether adolescents or preadolescents ought to be put at risk for such stress under any circumstances. Burnout and secondary posttraumatic stress are real dangers even for trained professionals (Ackerly et al., 1988; Figley, 1995; Raquepaw & Miller, 1989). There is no evidence that young people are any less vulnerable to these problems.

Even peer counseling programs that limit their focus to conflict resolution or developmental and educational issues must cope with potential ethical issues regarding confidentiality of student disclosures. Adolescent volunteers must, of course, be oriented to the importance of confidentiality, and reminded periodically about it, but their immaturity suggests that those precautions may still not prevent violations of confidentiality. Students using peer counseling services ought to understand the limits of confidentiality when they use such services, and supervisors should be prepared to respond when trust is broken. Volunteers should be ready to share all student disclosures with supervisors, and users should be informed about such consultation. In addition, guidelines ought to be established to avoid dual-relationship problems and so that volunteers know the rules for assisting friends.

In short, when school counselors initiate or take responsibility for existing peer counseling programs they must be prepared to devote extensive time and energy to the task of administering and supervising these programs. Moreover, they ought to systematically evaluate the outcomes of such programs on both the helpees and the volunteers and revise or eliminate ineffective or harmful aspects of the program accordingly.

Legal Issues for School Counselors: State and Federal Statutes

The legal issues that concern school counselors derive from the laws passed by Congress and state legislatures and from case law, especially in the area of negligence and malpractice.

There are state and federal statutes that directly affect the work of the school counselor. (A complete discussion of these laws is beyond the scope of this chapter. Readers should refer to Fischer and Sorenson, 1996, for a thorough review of legal rulings in this area.) One of the most important of these laws is the Family Educational Rights and Privacy Act (FERPA) enacted in 1974 (commonly referred to as the Buckley Amendment). This act contains four major sections, all of which are designed to ensure that parent's rights to information about their children's education are honored. Part 1 ties the availability of federal funding to parental access to school records. If schools fail to provide parents such access, they are not eligible for federal funding. Because federal money is crucial to the operation of most school districts, virtually all allow parents to inspect school records. Students who are 18 or older also have the same rights as parents of younger children. Part 2 requires parental consent for medical, psychiatric, or psychological evaluations of a child under 18 or for participation in "any school program designed to affect or change the personal behavior or values of a student" (Baker, 1996, p. 282). Part 3 prevents unauthorized people from viewing the educational records of children. Only school officials directly involved in the education of a student may have access to his or her records. Directory information is excepted from this policy, however, and schools can release it without parental consent under certain conditions (McCarthy & Sorenson, 1993). Moreover, if a child is transferring from one school to another, schools can also transfer records without express parental consent, as long as they notify parents about the transfer. Finally, if subpoenaed by a court, schools may produce educational records if they are germane to the issue before the court. The final section empowers the U.S. secretary of education to develop regulations relevant to student privacy.

FERPA implies that students and/or their parents own the information in official school records, ought to have free access to that information, and have the right to control who else gains access to educational records aside from school officials. This law does not alter the confidentiality of communications otherwise protected by law and does not cover private records of school counselors or teachers, provided those private records are not shared with others. The latter stipulations provide some leeway for school counselors to have confidential communications with students and to keep separate records of such communications. In fact, given the stipulations of FERPA and related laws, school counselors would be well advised to keep all records of counseling completely separate from the official educational record of the student (Anderson, 1996). However, they should note that if records of counseling are not truly private and are shared with other counselors or teachers, then those documents are considered educational records and should be available to parents (Fischer & Sorenson, 1996). According to Sorenson and Chapman (1985), noncompliance with this provision is high, as 66% of school counselors did not grant parents access to files that were shared with other school personnel. In a more recent study, Davis and Mickelson (1994) also found that most school counselors did not understand parental rights to records.

In this age of blended families and noncustodial parents, it is important to note that FERPA gives the same rights to noncustodial parents that it extends to custodial parents (Anderson, 1996). Surprisingly, Sorenson and Chapman (1985) found that this aspect of FERPA was also frequently violated. Seventy-seven percent of school counselors they surveyed reported school policies that denied noncustodial parents equal access to school records. If a counselor is dealing with sensitive information that may negatively affect a child if disclosed to either parent, the counselor needs to make a judgment about disclosure based on the best interests of the child. Careful consultation and supervision are in order under such circumstances. FERPA and other laws should not be interpreted to supersede the health and welfare of any child.

Other federal and state laws also provide for parental access to student files. The Americans with Disabilities Act of 1990 is one such example. That law stipulates, for example, that if parents are disabled, the school is responsible to provide information in the records in a form they can understand (McCarthy & Sorenson, 1993). If parents do not speak or read English, the school must provide information in a language they can understand.

Liability for School Counselors: An Emerging Reality

Not long ago, the folklore of the profession suggested that school counselors were insulated from most kinds of malpractice liability. The myth was that their peers in community agencies, hospitals, and private practice were targets for such actions, but that they were immune, either because of legal protections for educators or because of the relative invisibility of their counseling activities. Such beliefs are, unfortunately, inconsistent with current realities. School counselors can and do get sued (Fischer & Sorenson, 1996). Claims of malpractice are still less common for school counselors than for mental health counselors, but they are increasing. Fischer and Sorenson (1996) identify six activities that make school personnel vulnerable to malpractice claims. These include (1) administering drugs, (2) giving birth control advice, (3) giving abortion-related advice, (4) making statements that might be defamatory, (5) assisting in searches of student lockers, and (6) violating confidentiality and privacy of records. As already mentioned, counselors who stay informed about federal and state laws regarding contraceptive and abortion discussions with minors and who act competently are not likely to be successfully sued for their activities in this domain. Similarly, close allegiance to confidentiality and privilege obligations dramatically reduces potential liability for defamation or other violations of privacy. When school counselors are involved in searches of student lockers, cars, or other possessions, they must take care that they abide by current policies and laws affecting such searches and that the privacy of the student is limited only to the degree necessary.

Liability for Student Suicides

One of the emerging sources of malpractice claims stems from student suicides. Until 1991, claims against school counselors related to student suicides resulted in little liability for counselors (Fischer & Sorenson, 1996). In that era, the courts generally ruled that a duty of care could not be imposed on school personnel who did not have sufficient training in diagnosing mental disorders. A Maryland court reversed that trend, finding that a school counselor could be held liable for a student suicide (*Eisel v. Board of Educ.,* 1991). In that case, a 13-year-old girl's suicidal comments to her friends were reported by those friends to a school counselor. That counselor, in turn, informed the counselor assigned to the girl to whom the statements had been attributed. The two counselors called the girl into their office and asked her about the matter. The girl denied making those statements. The counselors did nothing further, and later that day the girl was shot in a suicide pact with another student. The court ruled that the school counselor did indeed have a special relationship with the student and a duty of care to act to prevent this suicide. Specifically, they faulted the counselor for not notifying the parents of the information the counselor had received about their daughter's suicidal comments. The court recognized that school counselors may not be able to control students to the same degree as professionals in hospitals and other restricted settings, but they asserted that counselors still have a duty to intervene to lessen foreseeable risks by informing the parents (Pate, 1992). Had the counselor in this case told the parents about the suicide threat, her liability probably would have ended at that point (Remley & Sparkman, 1993), unless the counselor had reason to expect that the parents would not respond appropriately. Sometimes adults deny the risk of suicide among young people (Wellman, 1984). In such circumstances, the counselor may need to act more energetically to ensure that the parents act to protect the child.

In the Eisel case, the central issue was the foreseeability of the risk to the student and the counselors' very limited response to a life-threatening problem. It is important to note that in this case Ms. Eisel was not an ongoing client of the school counselor, but rather a member of the student body assigned to that counselor. Once the counselor sought out Ms. Eisel to question her about her suicidal intentions, a special relationship was created. If future courts rule in similar ways, this suggests that school counselors cannot ignore risks to those with whom they have little ongoing contact. The obligation of the counselor is to take reasonable steps to prevent suicide among all students for whom they have responsibility. This case also underscores the value of attending to comments of other students. Counselors need to evaluate the veracity of remarks of other youngsters, and to follow up when they believe the information conveyed may be true.

These events should not cause school counselors to overreact to potentially suicidal situations, however. Remley and Sparkman (1993), for example, caution counselors not to make hasty, emotional judgments about suicidal risk. Physical restraint of students or calls to emergency personnel are rarely called for. Instead, school counselors ought to make careful, reasoned assessments of risk, and act in an expeditious but not rash way when they judge risk to be high.

Because suicide mortality increases significantly over the adolescent years (Diekstra, 1995), Sheeley and Herlihy (1989) suggest that school counselors consider implementing suicide prevention programs at their schools. Such programs alert adults and youngsters in the school to the warning signs for suicide and give them guidelines for responding. Prevention activities are helpful in reducing risk and in responding to serious mental health problems among adolescents. There is no legal obligation to have such a program, however. Remley and Sparkman (1993) argue that liability fears form an unsound basis for their creation. The principle of beneficence, not self-protective impulses, should drive all such programs.

When suicide does occur, counselors should provide support services for the student body to help them grieve and come to grips with the loss. The suggestion that adolescents are sometimes at risk for "copycat" suicides also adds merit to this recommendation (Sheeley & Herlihy, 1989). Many schools have relationships with community mental health centers, and professionals from both settings work together to provide crisis intervention. Such interventions are consistent with the ethical and legal obligations of the profession.

D. H. Henderson (1987) reminds school counselors that the duty of care is not limited to issues of suicide or injury to others. School counselors bear a legal and ethical obligation to act in other types of foreseeable risks. For example, he suggests that counselors ought to refer students to appropriate care when they display evidence of severe mental and emotional dysfunction. Usually the best way to implement this duty is to get the youngster to agree to the parents' involvement. In the absence of that agreement, counselors must make their judgment on the basis of the child's best interests.

SUMMARY

The ethical and legal issues confronting school counselors overlap significantly with those facing community counselors. Standards for competence to practice, informed consent, confidentiality, dual relationships, and fair assessment practices are applicable across all settings. However, five rather unique ethical challenges face school counselors. The first is the clash between the open communication patterns among educators and the limits of communication among professionals imposed by confidentiality standards and privilege laws. Counselors who understand such limits themselves and work to educate other school personnel about the impact of confidentiality on peer relationships are more likely to serve students, the school, and the profession effectively. On occasion, the open pattern of communication in school includes gossip and informal communications among educators. The ethics of school counseling clearly prohibit participation in such conversation. In fact, gossiping about students may leave counselors vulnerable to legal charges of defamation of character. Second, counselors must be prepared to work with parents and communities whose values differ from the fundamental values of the counseling profession. They must be respectful of parental rights, but also sensitive to the needs of the child. In many states, the right of school counselors to help children with matters relating to contraception, abortion, and other sensitive issues is legally protected, provided counselors work within the boundaries of their competence and do not insert their personal views into the counseling interaction. An active program of community education about counseling programs, coupled with evidence of program effectiveness, can reduce resistance and suspicion of counselors. Third, counselors who develop and oversee peer counseling programs must ensure that the programs are helpful to student volunteers and to those they serve. Peer helping programs should be supervised by counselors and should be limited to developmental and educational concerns because there is no clear evidence that such programs can responsibly assist young people with more serious mental health concerns.

Ethical school counselors should be familiar with the provisions of the Family Educational Rights and Privacy Act of 1974 and related laws dealing with special education and the rights of those with disabilities. Because state and federal laws affecting education change so rapidly, school counselors bear a responsibility to keep current with those changes and to ensure that school policies are consistent with statutes. Finally, school counselors are not immune to malpractice claims, although such claims occur somewhat less frequently for them than for other mental health professionals. Courts in recent years have tended to view school counselors as having a duty of care to prevent foreseeable danger to students by involving parents or other adults to help keep the student safe and secure the needed care.

DISCUSSION QUESTIONS

1. Schools often have policies that all drug use information that comes to the attention of staff must be reported to administrators. Thinking of potential scenarios with students, at what point do you think it advisable for counselors to report drug use and at what point should they honor confidentiality?
2. School counseling has endured substantial criticism in recent years for many of its activities. For example, self-esteem programs have been labeled as too humanistic, and drug and alcohol support groups have been called too intrusive into family matters. When such criticisms are made about school counseling, what do you see as the ethical obligations of the school counselor?

3. Do the confidentiality requirements for school counselors make it difficult for them to establish strong professional ties with other school personnel? Do those requirements make personal friendships with other staff more difficult?

4. How would you respond to the criticism that peer helping programs place helpers and helpees at risk when they attempt to deal with issues such as depression, suicide, drug use, and related problems? How would you balance the risks of such programs against their potential value to students?

5. What do you see as the ethical issues involved in suicide prevention and crisis intervention programs?

6. Should school counselors be immune from liability claims?

RECOMMENDED READINGS

American School Counselor Association. (1992). *Ethical standards for school counselors.* Alexandria, VA: Author.

Fischer, L., & Sorenson, G. P. (1996). *School law for counselors, psychologists, and social workers* (3rd ed.). White Plains, NY: Longman.

Kaplan, L. S. (1996). Outrageous or legitimate concerns: What some parents are saying about school counseling. *The School Counselor, 43,* 165–170.

Lewis, M. W., & Lewis, A. C. (1996). Peer helping programs: Helper role, supervisor training and suicidal behavior. *Journal of Counseling and Development, 74,* 307–313.

Remley, T. P., Jr., & Sparkman, L. B. (1993). Student suicides: The counselor's limited legal liability. *The School Counselor, 40,* 164–169.

PART FOUR

When Prevention Fails: Ethical Responses to Unethical Behavior

16

Recovering from Ethical Missteps
Responsibility and Rehabilitation

The typical mental health professional probably spends 30 to 40 years practicing the craft. Even those who undertake this profession as a second career are likely to work for 20 years or more. In that span of time ethical mistakes of varying seriousness will almost certainly occur. As discussed in Chapter 1, many mental health practitioners admit both intentional and unintentional violations of ethical standards (Pope et al., 1987; Sherry et al., 1991), but very few of those violations are reported to any disciplinary body (Pope & Vasquez, 1991). Inadvertent disclosures of confidential information are especially common examples of these missteps (Pope et al., 1987). Counselors who fail to acknowledge their vulnerability to misconduct are naive at best, and frightening at worst. The novelist D. H. Lawrence speaks with conviction on the subject: "This is the very worst wickedness, that we refuse to acknowledge the passionate evil that is in all of us. That makes us secret and rotten" (1915, reprinted in Zytaruk & Boulton, 1981). In its essence, ethical practice is not about expecting perfection; rather, it is about taking responsibility for one's actions (whether ethical or unethical) and keeping the improvement of one's clients as the central aim. In some ways, one of the truest tests of a professional's commitment to ethical practice is the way that person reacts when he or she deviates from that path, especially when disciplinary bodies are not likely to discover that deviation. This capacity to acknowledge one's failings and act to ameliorate their negative effects in the absence of external reprimands is closely related to the virtue ethics about which Meara, Schmidt, and Day (1996) write so eloquently. Virtuous professionals believe so strongly in the ethical values of the profession that they hold themselves accountable even when others do not. The ethical principles underlying this personal accountability are beneficence and fidelity.

Unfortunately, the ethics codes do not address this issue directly. Instead, they deal with the professional's responsibility to know the codes, act in accordance with them, and consult with others when in doubt (ACA, Section H; APA, Sections 8.01–8.07). In the same sections, the codes also describe strategies for handling the questionable behaviors of colleagues, but are largely silent on one's duty after recognizing one's own ethical misconduct as a professional. The ethics literature also addresses the issue of colleague misconduct (for example, Levenson, 1986) and response to others' accusations (Chauvin & Remley, 1996), but contains little reference to recovery from one's own misconduct. Principle C of the APA *Ethical Principles* (1992) touches on the matter in its statement "Psychologists . . . accept appropriate responsibility for their behavior." Similarly, the following section of the ACA *Code of Ethics* seems relevant:

ACA *Code of Ethics,* Section C.2.d: Monitor Effectiveness

Counselors continually monitor their effectiveness as professionals and take steps to improve when necessary.

The ethics codes emphasize prevention of misconduct, and this emphasis is both understandable and noble, but any discussion of professional ethics that attends only to prevention is ultimately insufficient, in the light of human nature, research evidence about misconduct, and the limitations of current reporting mechanisms. Not discussing remediation leads to the mistaken impression that mistakes are rare or avoidable. In this context, practitioners are more likely to view their ethical violations as problems that ought to be kept secret and hidden away. The focus of this chapter, then, is on frank and open attention to ethical violations and on recommendations for coping responsibly with one's own mistakes. Because these recommendations are not codified in any official document, they are advisory, not enforceable. Their aim is to encourage mental health professionals to understand accountability at its most fundamental level. The foundation for these recommendations derives partly from the literature on the rehabilitation of offending counselors and psychotherapists (for example, see Schoener & Gonsiorek, 1988). The two essential questions that professionals need to answer when confronting their own mistakes are

- What damage have I done, and how can I undo or ameliorate that damage?
- What steps should I take to ensure that I do not repeat this mistake?

Assessing and Responding to the Damage

Once a professional has become aware of a problematic behavior, the first step is to determine how much harm has been caused. Assessing harm to the client is the top priority, followed by damage to colleagues, others in the community, and to the reputation of the profession. Consulting with a trusted colleague can be very helpful. Colleagues are usually objective, knowledgeable, and often able to identify biases of which the individual is unaware. Colleagues can sometimes act as intermediaries with disaffected clients or colleagues who resist additional contacts with the offending counselor because of their negative experience. For example, a colleague might telephone a client to explore ways in which the client's needs can be met. Perhaps a client would be willing to make an appointment with a different counselor or participate in a meeting with the counselor with other professionals present to find an acceptable solution to the difficulty.

Once the level of damage is determined, the next step is to develop a strategy that will ameliorate that harm. The more serious the infraction, the more complicated the remediation is likely to be. A counselor who has for weeks provided incompetent service because of alcohol abuse has a much greater task in this regard than a therapist who acted incompetently on a single day because of illness or personal crisis. In the latter case, providing a day's worth of sessions without cost to compensate for the day of poor service may be all that is required as long as the incompetent sessions did not inflict significant damage on clients.

The therapist seeking to compensate for weeks of incompetent service faces a more difficult task. The length of the incompetent service also increases the likelihood of meaningful negative effects for clients. A depressed client who receives inadequate therapy for six weeks will probably suffer more than one who gets a single bungled session. Clients may have terminated counseling prematurely and may be unwilling to engage in counseling again because of their bad experience. In those cases, the counselor can do little to ameliorate the damage done. The ill effects may extend not only to clients, but also to the client's family members and friends, to whom the counselor has little or no access. Colleagues may have suffered emotional stress or financial loss during the period of impairment. Some attention to remedying negative impact on them is also in order. Obviously, in this kind of situation, the counselor's capacity to remedy the harm is limited. If the original victims of the misconduct are inaccessible, then professionals may perform the equivalent of the "community service" penalty that criminal courts often impose for minor offenses. The point of such actions is to act to compensate the community for misbehaviors. Community service activities serve two purposes. They balance the scales in a small way, and they remind those involved of their responsibilities to the broader community.

One cautionary note is in order here. Ethical ideals do not require a herculean effort to ameliorate all ill effects. The crucial feature of all such efforts is one's good-faith commitment to help those he or she has harmed and to address the damage to the profession's reputation in the community. Consultation can assist here too, in sorting out reasonable from unreasonable efforts and in devising a workable plan to remedy damage.

The impact of remedies on those who suffered the original ill effects must also be assessed. Put plainly, if the cure is worse than the disease, it's no cure at all. Because the most important ethical standard is the welfare of the client, remediation efforts that jeopardize that welfare have no place in recovery from an ethical misstep. For example, if a counselor reveals a client name to a colleague in a lunchtime chat, that counselor probably has violated the ethics code. The purpose of the discussion with the colleague was not professional, not in the client's best interest, and there was no client release for the disclosure. When the counselor recognizes the blunder, he or she needs to carefully examine the best way to remedy that mistake. Speaking with the colleague again to acknowledge the error and asking the colleague to honor confidentiality is one remedy that injures no one. Whether the violation is best disclosed to the client depends on its effects on the client, especially because it is a minor infraction with little likelihood of negative consequences for that client. If an objective assessment of a remedy reveals that it risks additional harm to a client, the counselor should seek alternative remedies. Because the task of implementing a remedy is emotionally stressful, however, particularly when it involves disclosure to a client, counselors may be tempted to rationalize that all such disclosures will be harmful and should not be done. The criterion for judging the appropriateness of a remedy is the long-term welfare of the client rather than the immediate self-interest of the counselor. Consultation is essential here, too, in sorting out reasonable and helpful interventions from unreasonable or self-serving ones.

Rehabilitating the Counselor

A counselor who has erred begins the process of recovery with an honest self-evaluation that unflinchingly recognizes the mistakes made and seeks out the causes so that they will be less likely to recur. The goal here is not to engender guilt or shame, but rather to gather energy for the process of change. The nature of the rehabilitative activities will vary significantly with the violation. For minor infractions, one may need simply to reread the ethics code and consult with colleagues for a period to verify that one is interpreting the code in an acceptable way. For more serious matters, a formal plan for rehabilitation is in order. That plan may include

- Therapy for the counselor if personal problems or character flaws are at the root of the misconduct.
- Reduction in the scope of one's practice to reduce risk. (A person who has violated sexual contact prohibitions, for instance, is well advised to refrain from accepting clients who are likely to spark that person's sexual desires.)
- A temporary moratorium on therapeutic work until stability is regained.
- An arrangement with another counselor to closely supervise one's practice so that any problematic behaviors can be quickly identified and stopped.
- A program of self-education or formal ethics education to gain a better understanding of the codes and the ethical values of the profession.
- Enrollment in training experiences that improve clinical competency.

This list is not comprehensive. Rehabilitation activities should be tailored to the individual violation and to the violator's characteristics. Similarly, the period of time devoted to rehabilitation will vary widely. Approaches to subsequent offenses in the same domain ought to be treated more aggressively than first offenses, but even first offenses ought not to be ignored. Finally, even when the rehabilitation period seems complete, because of human frailty the professional ought to periodically engage in supervision activities that ensure that no slippage has occurred.

Compassion and Empathy

There is one additional value in personal accountability: compassion. It reminds professionals that we are all vulnerable to ethical missteps and deters us from adopting an attitude of moral superiority toward counselors who have been accused of misconduct. By recognizing our own mistakes, we gain compassion and empathy for others. As Jerome (1889) wrote more than a hundred years ago, "It is in our faults and failings, not in our virtues, that we touch each other and find sympathy. . . . It is in our follies that we are one." Thus, when others seek us out for consultation after an infraction, we are more likely to take an approach of seeking rehabilitation rather than punishment, of giving sympathy rather than harsh personal judgment. This compassion is not incompatible with full accountability for behavior; it is the fullest application of ethical ideals.

CASES FOR DISCUSSION

The following cases are representative examples of ethical missteps that others are unlikely to file complaints about (or even know about). They highlight both the need for remedies for misconduct, and the difficulty in implementing it on occasion. They also raise interesting questions about rehabilitation. Reflect on each case, come to a conclusion about the ideal ethical remedy, and plan for rehabilitation.

The Case of Dr. Portrain

Dr. Portrain, a psychologist, attended a one-day seminar on the use of clinical hypnosis for posttraumatic stress. This seminar was his first exposure to hypnosis and was taught by an expert in hypnosis who has received high ratings for the quality of her presentation. Since that seminar, Dr. Portrain has spent several hours reading about hypnosis and has discussed that material with his colleagues. A few days later a man who had barely escaped a serious fire in his apartment building came for counseling. An assessment indicated a moderate level of posttraumatic stress. Dr. Portrain recommended hypnosis as the treatment of choice, omitting any mention of other approaches that might help this client. The psychologist was eager and excited about the ability to employ this new treatment tool so soon after the workshop. The man agreed to hypnosis, and Dr. Portrain conducted three sessions using hypnosis. At the end of those sessions, the man showed no improvement in his symptoms. While watching the man weep over his disappointment about not improving, Dr. Portrain then realized that he had been practicing beyond the boundaries of his competence and had unfairly pushed his client into an experimental treatment without explaining other options.

The Case of Dr. MacDuff

Dr. MacDuff's client, Mr. Betts, reveals to him a very embarrassing event that occurred on his recent honeymoon. The client was relieved to be able to discuss the issue with his therapist and by the end of the session, the client began to appreciate the humor as well as the pain in the situation. The next weekend, Dr. MacDuff was at a party at a neighbor's home. During that party, the host initiated a "Tell us your most embarrassing moment" game and the partygoers agreed to participate. When Dr. MacDuff's turn came, he had difficulty thinking of anything that would spark real laughter in the group. So, he told of Mr. Bett's incident without identifying his client. In fact, he simply referred to the person as an acquaintance. The group enjoyed the anecdote immensely; it was the highlight of the party. The next day he encountered a partygoer in the supermarket who again expressed his enjoyment of Dr. MacDuff's anecdote. At this point, the doctor began to feel uneasy about his behavior and to regret it.

The Case of Ms. Spend

Ms. Spend, a licensed clinical counselor in private practice, has become increasingly frustrated with the demands of third-party payors. Recently, when treating a woman with major depression, the insurance company authorized only five sessions and would not raise that limit. The client decided to pay out-of-pocket for the rest of her sessions, but this represented a hardship to the client, even at reduced fees. The next time Ms. Spend encountered a client insured by the same company, she entered a diagnosis more severe than the client's true symptoms in order to obtain more reimbursement. In this case, the insurer agreed to 10 sessions, a number both the counselor and the client judged adequate for the problem. Two weeks after that client terminated, Ms. Spend attended a seminar on ethical and legal issues in counseling and realized that her behavior with this client was not only unethical, but also probably illegal.

The Case of Ms. Monderly

Ms. Monderly is a licensed clinical social worker who has been in practice for 10 years. She has recently moved to a new community and feels lonely. One day she encountered a client who seemed to have all the characteristics she values in a friend. The client seemed to be experiencing the same feelings about Ms. Monderly. Ms. Monderly decided to refer this client to another therapist after three sessions. The other therapist is an expert in the problem the client was experiencing, but Ms. Monderly's motivation was based primarily on her desire to begin a friendship with this client. Two months after the termination, Ms. Monderly telephoned the client to invite her to a museum opening. They began to attend cultural activities regularly. At one activity a few months later, Ms. Monderly saw a colleague from the practice. The colleague seemed surprised when he recognized the client. His expression of surprise changed to disapproval when the client revealed in their brief conversation that she and Ms. Monderly had become very close friends. Ms. Monderly wondered whether she should have resisted her personal interest in this client and made other efforts to find friends in her new community.

SUMMARY

No mental health professional is immune to unethical practice. Survey data suggest that violations of confidentiality, informed consent, and dual relationships are rather common. Those studies also show that professionals express concern about their past misbehaviors and worry about future missteps. In this context, counselors and therapists ought to recognize their own vulnerability to ethical violations and take personal responsibility for acting to remedy them even if outside disciplinary bodies fail to catch their misconduct. This obligation is not codified in any professional ethical standards and thus, is not enforceable, but is consistent with the ethical ideals of mental health professions to promote the welfare of others and place clients' needs ahead of one's own. Specifically, professionals ought to assess the damage their misconduct has caused, develop a plan for intervening to reduce or compensate for that damage, and then turn their attention to rehabilitation so that they are less vulnerable to that violation in the future.

DISCUSSION QUESTIONS

1. Should the ethics codes contain more explicit references to remedies and rehabilitation? If so, what wording would you find acceptable? If not, why not?
2. Is commitment to the ethical ideal of minimizing damage to clients and others naive and unrealistic in a world of malpractice litigation and disciplinary action by licensing boards?
3. Under what circumstances do you think implementing a remedy for a misstep might be as harmful as the misstep itself? If clients are ignorant of ethical violations, should they be informed?
4. What are the ethical dilemmas for the colleague who acts as a consultant to a professional who discloses a serious ethical violation?

RECOMMENDED READINGS

Jordan, A. E., & Meara, N. M. (1990). Ethics and the professional practice of psychologists: The role of virtues and principles. *Professional Psychology: Research and Practice, 21,* 107–114.

Meara, N. M., Schmidt, L. D., & Day, J. D. (1996). Principles and virtues: A foundation for ethical decisions, policies and character. *The Counseling Psychologist, 24,* 4–77.

References

Ackerley, G. D., Burnell, J., Holder, D. C., & Kurdek, L. A. (1988). Burnout among licensed psychologists. *Professional Psychology: Research and Practice, 19,* 424–431.

Adams, J., Kottke, J. L., & Padgit, J. S. (1983). Sexual harassment of university students. *Journal of College Student Personnel, 24,* 484–490.

Adelman, J., & Barrett, S. E. (1990). Overlapping relationships: Importance of a feminist ethical perspective. In H. Lerman & N. Porter (Eds.), *Feminist ethics in psychotherapy* (pp. 87–91). New York: Springer

Ahia, C. E., & Martin, D. (1993). The danger-to-self-or-others exception to confidentiality. In T. P. Remley (Ed.), *ACA Legal Series* (Vol. 9). Alexandria, VA: American Counseling Association.

Akamatsu, T. J. (1988). Intimate relationships with former clients: National survery of attitudes and behavior among practitioners. *Professional Psychology: Research and Practice, 19,* 454–458.

Allen, G. J., Szollos, S. J., & Williams, B. E. (1986). Doctoral students' comparative evaluations of best and worst psychotherapy supervision. *Professional Psychology: Research and Practice, 17,* 91–99.

Alyn, J. H. (1988). The politics of touch in therapy: A response to Willison and Masson. *Journal of Counseling and Development, 66,* 432–433.

Amada, G. (1993). Some ethical considerations: A commentary on "Between Cordelia and Guido: The consultant's role in urgent situations." *Journal of College Student Psychotherapy, 7,* 23–34.

American Association for Counseling and Development (AACD). (1988). *Ethical standards.* Alexandria, VA: Author.

American Association for Marriage and Family Therapy (AAMFT). (1991). *Code of ethics.* Washington, DC: Author.

American Association of State Psychology Boards (AASPB). (1979). *Guidelines for the employment and supervision of uncredentialed persons providing psychological services.* Montgomery, AL: Author.

American Counseling Association (ACA). (1994). *Policies and procedures for processing complaints of ethical violations.* Alexandria, VA: Author.

American Counseling Association (ACA). (1995). *Code of ethics and standards of practice.* Alexandria, VA: Author.

American Psychiatric Association. (1993). *Principles of medical ethics with annotations especially applicable to psychiatry.* Washington, DC: Author.

American Psychiatric Association. (1994). *Diagnostic and statistical manual of mental disorders* (4th ed.) [DSM-IV]. Washington, DC: Author.

American Psychiatric Association, Ad Hoc Committee on AIDS Policy. (1988). AIDS Policy: Confidentiality and disclosure. *American Journal of Psychiatry, 145,* 541–542.

American Psychological Association (APA). (1973). *Guidelines for psychologists conducting growth groups.* Washington, DC: Author.

American Psychological Association (APA). (1981a). *Ethical principles.* Washington, DC: Author.

American Psychological Association (APA). (1981b). *Specialty guidelines for the delivery of services: Clinical psychologists, counseling psychologists, organizational/industrial psychologists, school psychologists.* Washington, DC: Author.

American Psychological Association (APA). (1982). *Ethical principles in the conduct of research with human participants.* Washington, D. C: Author.

American Psychological Association (APA). (1985). *Standards for psychological and educational tests.* Washington, DC: Author.

American Psychological Association (APA). (1986). *Guidelines for computer-based tests and interpretations.* Washington, DC: Author.

American Psychological Association (APA). (1990). *Ethical principles of psychologists* (amended June 2, 1989). Washington, DC: Author.

American Psychological Association (APA). (1991). *Legal liability related to confidentiality and the prevention of HIV transmission.* Washington, DC: Author.

American Psychological Association (APA). (1992). *Ethical principles of psychologists and code of conduct.* Washington, DC: Author.

American Psychological Association (APA). (1993a). *Guidelines for ethical conduct in the care and use of animals.* Washington, DC: Author.

American Psychological Association (APA). (1993b). *Guidelines for providers of psychological services to ethnic, linguistic and culturally diverse populations.* Washington, D. C: Author.

American Psychological Association (APA). (1993c). *Record keeping guidelines.* Washington, DC: Author.

American Psychological Association (APA). (1994). Guidelines for child custody evaluations in divorce proceedings. *American Psychologist, 49,* 677–680.

American Psychological Association (APA). (1996). *Rules and Procedures.* Washington, DC: Author.

American Psychological Association (APA), Committee on Legal Issues. (1996). Strategies for private practitioners coping with subpoenas or compelled testimony for client records or test data. *Professional Psychology: Research and Practice, 27,* 245–251.

American Psychological Association (APA), Committee on Professional Practice and Standards. (1995). Twenty-four questions (and answers) about professional practice in the area of child abuse. *Professional Psychology: Research and Practice, 26,* 377–383.

American Psychological Association (APA), Committee on Psychological Testing and Assessment. (1996). Statement on the disclosure of test data. *American Psychologist, 51,* 644–648.

American Psychological Association (APA), Committee on Women in Psychology. (1989). If sex enters into the psychotherapy relationship. *Professional Psychology: Research and Practice, 20,* 112–115.

American Psychological Association (APA), Ethics Committee. (1983). *Authorship guidelines for dissertation supervision.* Washington, DC: Author.

American Psychological Association (APA), Ethics Committee. (1994). Report of the Ethics Committee, 1993. *American Psychologist, 49,* 659–666.

American Psychological Association (APA), Ethics Committee. (1995a, October). APA Ethics Committee adopts statement on telephone therapy. *APA Monitor,* p. 15.

American Psychological Association (APA), Ethics Committee (1995b). Report of the Ethics Committee, 1994. *American Psychologist, 50,* 706–713.

American Psychological Association (APA), Ethics Committee. (1996a). Report of the Ethics Committee, 1995. *American Psychologist, 51,* 1279–1286.

American Psychological Association (APA), Ethics Committee. (1996b). Rules and procedures. *American Psychologist, 51,* 529–548.

American Psychological Association (APA), Insurance Trust. (1990). *Bulletin: Sexual misconduct and professional liability claims.* Washington, DC: Author.

American Psychological Association (APA), Task Force. (1975). Report of the task force on sex bias and sex role stereotyping in psychotherapeutic practice. *American Psychologist, 30,* 1169–1175.

American Psychological Association (APA), Task Force. (1978). Guidelines for therapy with women. *American Psychologist, 33,* 1122–1123.

American School Counselors Association (ASCA). (1992). *Ethical standards for school counselors.* Alexandria, VA: American Counseling Association.

Anastasi, A. (1988). *Psychological testing* (6th ed). New York: Macmillan.

Anastasi, A. (1992). What counselors should know about the use and interpretation of psychological tests. *Journal of Counseling and Development, 70,* 610–615.

Anderson, B. S. (1996). *The counselor and the law* (4th ed.). Alexandria, VA: American Counseling Association.

Anderson, D., & Swanson, C. D. (1994). *Legal issues in licensure.* Alexandria, VA: American Counseling Association.

Anderson, R. (1976). Peer facilitation: History and issues. *Elementary School Guidance and Counseling, 11,* 16–25.

Anderson, S. K., & Kitchener, K. S. (1996). Nonromantic, nonsexual posttherapy relationships between psychologists and former clients: An exploratory study of critical incidents. *Professional Psychology: Research and Practice, 27,* 59–66.

Anderton, P., Staulcup, V., & Grisso, T. (1980). On being ethical in legal places. *Professional Psychology: Research and Practice, 11,* 764–773.

Anonymous. (1991). Sexual harassment: A female counseling student's experience. *Journal of Counseling and Development, 69,* 502–506.

Appelbaum, P. S. (1993). Legal liability in managed care. *American Psychologist, 48,* 251–257.

Appelbaum, P. S., & Gutheil, T. G. (1991). *Clinical handbook of psychiatry and the law* (2nd ed.). Baltimore: Williams & Wilkins.

Arrendondo, P., Toporek, R., Brown, S. P., Jones, J., Locke, D., Sanchez, J., & Stadler, H. (1996). Operationalization of the multicultural counseling competencies. *Journal of Multicultural Counseling and Development, 24,* 42–78.

Arthur, G. L., Jr., & Swanson, C. D. (1993). Confidentiality and privileged communication. In T. P. Remley (Ed.), *ACA Legal Series* (Vol. 6). Alexandria, VA: American Counseling Association.

Association for Counselor Education and Supervision (ACES). (1990). Standards for counseling supervisors. *Journal of Counseling and Development, 69,* 30–32.

Association for Counselor Education and Supervision (ACES). (1993). Ethical guidelines for counseling supervisors. *Counselor Education and Supervision, 34,* 270–276.

Association for Specialists in Group Work (ASGW). (1990). *Professional standards for the training of group workers.* Alexandria, VA: American Counseling Association.

Association for Specialists in Group Work (ASGW), Executive Board. (1989). *Ethical guidelines for group counselors.* Alexandria, VA: American Counseling Association.

Aubrey, M., & Dougher, M. J. (1990). Ethical issues in outpatient group therapy with sex offenders. *Journal for Specialists in Group Work, 15,* 75–82.

Bacorn, D., & Dixon, D. (1984). The effects of touch on depressed and vocationally undecided clients. *Journal of Counseling Psychology, 31,* 488–496.

Baer, B. E., & Murdock, N. L. (1995). Nonerotic dual relationships between therapists and clients: The effects of sex, theoretical orientation and interpersonal boundaries. *Ethics and Behavior, 5,* 131–145.

Bailey, S. M. (1996). Shortchanging girls and boys. *Educational Leadership, 53,* 75–79.

Bajt, T. R., & Pope, K. S. (1989). Therapist–patient sexual intimacy involving children and adolescents. *American Psychologist, 44,* 455.

Baker, L. C., & Patterson, J. E. (1990). The first to know: A systematic analysis of confidentiality and the therapist's family. *American Journal of Family Therapy, 18,* 295–300.

Baker, S. B. (1996). *School counseling for the twenty-first century* (2nd ed.). Englewood Cliffs, NJ: Prentice Hall.

Barnett, J. E. (1994). Documentation guidelines and ethical practice in psychotherapy. *Psychotherapy, 31,* 35–39.

Barret, B. (In press). A decision making model for ethical dilemmas in HIV-related psychotherapy. In J. R. Anderson (Ed.), *Ethical issues in HIV-related mental health practice: A casebook and resource manual.* Washington, DC: American Psychological Association.

Bartell, P. A., & Rubin, L. J. (1990). Dangerous liaisons: Sexual intimacies in supervision. *Professional Psychology: Research and Practice, 21,* 442–450.

Bates, C. M., & Brodsky, A. M. (1989). *Sex in the therapy hour: A case of professional incest.* New York: Guilford.

Baumoel, J. (1992). The beginning of the end for the psychotherapist–patient privilege. *Cincinnati Law Review, 60,* 797–826.

Bean, J. P., & Kuh, G. (1984). The reciprocity between student–faculty informal contact and academic performance. *Research in Higher Education, 21,* 461–477.

Beauchamp, T. L., & Childress, J. F. (1983). *Principles of biomedical ethics* (2nd ed.). Oxford, England: Oxford University Press.

Beauchamp, T. L., & Childress, J. F. (1989). *Principles of biomedical ethics* (3rd. ed.). Oxford, England: Oxford University Press.

Becvar, D. S., & Becvar, R. J. (1996). *Family therapy: A systemic integration.* Boston: Allyn & Bacon.

Bednar, R. L., Bednar, S. C., Lambert, M. J., & Waite, D. R. (1991). *Psychotherapy with high-risk clients: Legal and professional standards.* Pacific Grove, CA: Brooks/Cole.

Beeman, D. G., & Scott, N. A. (1991). Therapists' attitudes toward psychotherapy informed consent with adolescents. *Professional Psychology: Research and Practice, 22,* 230–234.

Bennett, B., Bryant, B., VanderBos, G., & Greenwood, A. (1990). *Professional liability and risk management.* Washington, DC: American Psychological Association.

Bergin, A. E., & Garfield, S. L. (1994). Introduction and historical overview. In A. E. Bergin & S. L. Garfield (Eds.), *Handbook of psychotherapy and behavior change* (4th ed.) (pp. 3–18). New York: Wiley.

Bernard, J. L., & Jara, C. S. (1986). The failure of clinical psychology graduate students to apply understood ethical principles. *Professional Psychology: Research and Practice, 17,* 313–315.

Bernard, J. L., Murphy, M., & Little, M. (1987). The failure of clinical psychologists to apply understood ethical principles. *Professional Psychology: Research and Practice, 18,* 489–491.

Bernard, J. M., & Goodyear, R. K. (1992). *Fundamentals of clinical supervision.* Boston: Allyn & Bacon.

Berndt, D. J. (1983). Ethical and professional considerations in psychological assessment. *Professional Psychology: Research and Practice, 14,* 580–587.

Bernsen, A., Tabachnick, B. G., & Pope, K. S. (1994). National survey of social workers' sexual attraction to their clients: Results, implications and comparison to psychologists. *Ethics and Behavior, 4,* 369–388.

Bersoff, D. N. (1994). Explicit ambiguity: The 1992 ethics code as an oxymoron. *Professional Psychology: Research and Practice, 25*, 382–386.

Bersoff, D. N. (Ed.). (1995). *Ethical conflicts in psychology.* Washington, DC: American Psychological Association.

Bersoff, D. N., & Hofer, P. J. (1991). *Legal issues in computerized psychological testing.* Hillsdale, NJ: Erlbaum.

Bersoff, D. N., & Koeppl, P. M. (1993). The relationship between ethics codes and moral principles. *Ethics and Behavior, 3*, 345–357.

Besner, A. F., Spungin, C. I. (1995). *Gay and lesbian students: Understanding their needs.* Washington, DC: Taylor & Francis.

Bisbing, S. B., Jorgenson, L. B., & Sutherland, P. K. (1995). *Sexual abuse by professionals: A legal guide.* Charlottesville, VA: Mitchie.

Bissell, L., & Haberman, P. (1984). *Alcoholism in the professions.* New York: Oxford University Press.

Blevins-Knabe, B. (1992). The ethics of dual relationships in higher education. *Ethics and Behavior, 2*, 151–163.

Bogat, G. A., & Redner, R. L. (1985). How mentoring affects the professional development of women in psychology. *Professional Psychology: Research and Practice, 16*, 851–859.

Bollas, C., & Sundelson, D. (1995). *The new informants: The betrayal of confidentiality in psychoanalysis and psychotherapy.* Northvale, NJ: Aronson.

Bongar, B. (1988). Clinicians, microcomputers and confidentiality. *Professional Psychology: Research and Practice, 19*, 286–289.

Bongar, B. (1991). *The suicidal patient: Clinical and legal standards of care.* Washington, DC: American Psychological Association.

Borum, R. (1996). Improving the clinical practice of violence risk assessment: Technology, guidelines and training. *American Psychologist, 51*, 945–956.

Borys, D. S., & Pope, K. S. (1989). Dual relationships between therapist and client: A national study of psychologists, psychiatrists and social workers. *Professional Psychology: Research and Practice, 20*, 283–293.

Bouhoutsos, J. C. (1984). Sexual intimacy between psychotherapists and clients. In L. Walker (Ed.), *Women and mental health policy* (pp. 207–227). Beverly Hills, CA: Sage.

Bouhoutsos, J. C., & Brodsky, A. M. (1985). Mediation in therapist–client sex: A model. *Psychotherapy: Research and Practice, 22*, 189–193.

Bouhoutsos, J. C., Holroyd, J., Lerman, J., Forer, B., & Greenberg, M. (1983). Sexual intimacy between psychotherapists and patients. *Professional Psychology: Research and Practice, 14*, 185–196.

Bowlby, J. (1951). *Maternal care and mental health.* Geneva: World Health Organization.

Bowman, R. L., Bowman, V. E., & DeLucia, J. L. (1990). Mentoring in a graduate counseling program: Students helping students. *Counselor Education and Supervision, 30*, 58–65.

Bowman, V. E., Hatley, L. D., & Bowman, R. L. (1995). Faculty–student relationships: The dual role controversy. *Counselor Education and Supervision, 34*, 232–242.

Braaten, E. B., Otto, S., & Handelsman, M. M. (1993). What do people want to know about psychotherapy? *Psychotherapy, 30*, 565–570.

Bram, A. D. (1995). The physically ill or dying psychotherapist: A review of ethical and clinical considerations. *Psychotherapy, 32*, 568–580.

Bray, J. H., Shepherd, J. N., & Hays, J. R. (1985). Legal and ethical issues in informed consent to psychotherapy. *American Journal of Family Therapy, 13*, 50–60.

Bridge, P., & Bascue, L. (1988). A record form for psychotherapy supervision. In P. Keller & S. Heyman (Eds.), *Innovations in clinical practice* (Vol. 7) (pp. 331–336). Sarasota, FL: Professional Resource Exchange.

Brosig, C. L., & Kalichman, S. C. (1992). Clinicians' reporting of suspected child abuse: A review of the empirical literature. *Clinical Psychology Review, 12*, 155–168.

Broverman, I. K., Broverman, D., Clarkson, F. E., Rosencrantz, P., & Vogel, S. (1970). Sex role sterotypes and clinical judgments of mental health. *Journal of Consulting and Clinical Psychology, 34*, 1-7.

Brown, D., Pryzwansky, W. B., & Schulte, A. C. (1991). *Psychological consultations: Introduction to theory and practice.* Boston: Allyn & Bacon.

Brown, L. (1988). Harmful effects of posttermination sexual and romantic relationships between therapists and their former clients. *Psychotherapy, 25*, 249–255.

Burke, C. A. (1995). Until death do us part: An exploration into confidentiality following the death of a client. *Professional Psychology: Research and Practice, 26*, 278–280.

Butcher, J. N., Dahlstrom, W. G., Graham, J. R., Tellegen, A., & Kaemmer, B. (1989). *Minnesota Multiphasic Personality Inventory-2 (MMPI-2): Manual for administration and scoring.* Minneapolis: University of Minnesota Press.

California Department of Consumer Affairs. (1990). *Professional therapy never includes sex.* (Available from the Board of Psychology, 1426 Howe Avenue, Sacramento, CA 95825).

Callanan, K., & O'Connor, T. (1988). *Staff comments and recommendations regarding the Senate Task Force on Psy-*

chotherapist and Patient Sexual Relations. Sacramento, CA: Board of Behavioral Science Examiners and Psychology Licensing Committee.

Camera, W. J., & Schneider, D. L. (1994). Integrity tests: Facts and unresolved issues. *American Psychologist, 49,* 112–119.

Canter, M. B., Bennett, B. E., Jones, S. E., & Nagy, T. F. (1994). *Ethics for psychologists: A commentary on the APA ethics code.* Washington, DC: American Psychological Association.

Canterbury v. Spence, 464 F. 2d 772 (D.C. Cir. 1972).

Cassileth, B. R., Zupkis, R. V., Sutton-Smith, K., & March, V. (1980). Informed consent? Why are its goals imperfectly realized? *New England Journal of Medicine, 323,* 896–900.

Chauvin, J. C., & Remley, T. P., Jr. (1996). Responding to allegations of unethical conduct. *Journal of Counseling and Development, 74,* 563–568.

Claiborn, C. D., Berberoglu, L. S., Nerison, R. M., & Somberg, D. R. (1994). The client's perspective: Ethical judgments and perceptions of therapist's practices. *Professional Psychology: Research and Practice, 25,* 268–274.

Clay, R. A. (1997, April). New drugs prolong life for longer than some patients are prepared for. *APA Monitor,* p. 43.

Clayton, S., & Bongar, B. (1994). The use of consultation in psychological practice: Ethical, legal and clinical considerations. *Ethics and Behavior, 4,* 43–57.

Comer, R. J. (1996). *Fundamentals of abnormal psychology.* New York: W. H. Freeman.

Committee for the Advancement of Professional Practice. (1995). *CAPP practitioner survey results.* Washington, DC: American Psychological Association.

Committee on Ethical Guidelines for Forensic Psychologists. (1991). Specialty guidelines for forensic psychologists. *Law and Human Behavior, 15,* 655–665.

Cooney, J. (1985). An ethical approach to teacher referral of children for individual counseling. *Elementary School Guidance and Counseling, 19,* 198–201.

Corcoran, K., & Winslade, W. J. (1994). Eavesdropping on the 50-minute hour: Managed mental health care and confidentiality. *Behavioral Sciences and the Law, 12,* 351–365.

Corey, G. (1995). *Theory and practice of group counseling* (4th ed.). Pacific Grove, CA: Brooks/Cole.

Corey, G., Corey, M., & Callanan, P. (1993). *Issues and ethics in the helping professions* (4th ed.). Pacific Grove, CA: Brooks/Cole.

Corey, G., Williams, G. T., & Moline, M. E. (1995). Ethical and legal issues in group counseling. *Ethics and Behavior, 5,* 161–183.

Corey, M. S., & Corey, G. (1997). *Groups: Process and practice* (5th ed.). Pacific Grove, CA: Brooks/Cole.

Costa, L., & Altekruse, M. (1994). Duty-to-warn guidelines for mental health counselors. *Journal of Counseling and Development, 72,* 346–350.

Coster, J. S., & Schwebel, M. (1997). Well-functioning in professional psychologists. *Professional Psychology: Research and Practice, 28,* 5–13.

Crawford, I., Humfleet, G., Ribordy, S., Ho, F., & Vickers, V. (1991). Stigmatization of AIDS patients by mental health professionals. *Professional Psychology: Research and Practice: 22,* 357–361.

Crawford, R. L. (1994). Avoiding counselor malpractice. In T. P. Remley (Ed.), *ACA Legal Series* (Vol. 10). Alexandria, VA: American Counseling Association.

Crego, C. A. (1985). Ethics: The need for improved consultation training. *The Counseling Psychologist, 13,* 473–476.

Cronbach, L. (1984) *Essentials of psychological testing* (4th ed.). New York: Harper & Row.

Cummings, N. A. (1995). Unconscious fiscal convenience. *Psychotherapy in Private Practice, 14,* 23–28.

Cunningham, S. (1984). Genovese: 20 years later, few heed a stranger's cries. *Social Action and the Law, 10,* 24–25.

Dahlberg, C. C. (1970). Sexual contact between patient and therapist. *Contemporary Psychoanalysis, 5,* 107–124.

Davis, J. L., & Mickelson, D. J. (1994). School counselors: Are you aware of ethical and legal aspects of counseling? *The School Counselor, 42,* 5–13.

Davis, K. L. (1980). Is confidentiality in group counseling realistic? *Personnel and Guidance Journal, 58,* 197–201.

Davis, T., & Ritchie, M. (1993). Confidentiality and the school counselor: A challenge for the 1990s. *The School Counselor, 41,* 23–29.

DeLucia, J. L., Coleman, V. D., & Jenson-Scott, R. L. (1992). Cultural diversity in group counseling. *Journal for Specialists in Group Work, 17,* 194–195.

DeTrude, J. (1996, April). *Therapy and the media: What would the ACA Code of Ethics say?* Paper presented at the annual meeting of the American Counseling Association, Pittsburgh.

Deutsch, C. J. (1984). Self-reported sources of stress among psychotherapists. *Professional Psychology: Research and Practice, 15,* 833–845.

Deutsch, C. J. (1985). A survey of therapists' personal problems and treatment. *Professional Psychology: Research and Practice, 16,* 305–315.

Diekstra, R. F. W. (1995). Depression and suicidal behavior in adolescence: Sociocultural time trends. In M. Rutter (Ed.), *Psychosocial disturbances in young people:*

Challenges for prevention (pp. 212–243). New York: Cambridge University Press.

Dinkmeyer, D., Jr., Carlson, J., & Dinkmeyer, D. (1994). *Consultation: School mental health professionals as consultants.* Muncie, IN: Accelerated Development.

Disney, M. J., & Stephens, A. M. (1994). *Legal issues in clinical supervision.* In T. P. Remley (Ed.), *ACA Legal Series* (Vol. 9). Alexandria, VA: American Counseling Association.

Doromal, Q. S., & Creamer, D. G. (1988). An evaluation of the Ethical Judgement Scale. *Journal of College Student Development, 29,* 151–158.

Dorr, D. (1981). Conjoint psychological testing in marriage therapy: New wine in old skins. *Professional Psychology: Research and Practice, 12,* 549–555.

Dougherty, A. M. (1990). *Consultation: Practice and perspectives.* Pacific Grove, CA: Brooks/Cole.

Drane, J. F. (1982). Ethics and psychotherapy: A philosophical perspective. In M. Rosenbaum (Ed.), *Ethics and values in psychotherapy.* New York: Free Press.

Driscoll, J. M. (1992). Keeping covenants and confidences sacred: One point of view. *Journal of Counseling and Development, 70,* 704-708.

Dubin, S. S. (1972). Obsolescence or lifelong education: A choice for the professional. *American Psychologist, 27,* 486–496.

Dudley, E. (1988, October). *Ethical complaints against family therapists submitted to the AAMFT ethics committee.* Paper presented at the National Meeting of the Association of Marriage and Family Therapists, New Orleans.

Eberlein, L. (1987). Introducing ethics to beginning psychologists: A problem-solving approach. *Professional Psychology: Research and Practice, 18,* 353–359.

Eisel v. Board of Educ., 597 A. 2d 447 (Md. Ct. App. 1991).

Eisen, S. V., & Dickey, B. (1996). Mental health outcome assessment: The new agenda. *Psychotherapy, 33,* 181–189.

Ellis, J. W. (1996). Voluntary admission and involuntary hospitalization of minors. In B. D. Sales & D. W. Shuman (Eds.), *Law, mental health, and mental disorder* (pp. 487–502). Pacific Grove, CA: Brooks/Cole.

Epstein, R. S., & Simon, R. I. (1990). The Exploitation Index: An early warning indicator of boundary violations in psychotherapy. *Bulletin of the Menninger Clinic, 54,* 450–465.

Everett, C. A. (1990). The field of marriage and family therapy. *Journal of Counseling and Development, 68,* 498–502.

Eyde, L. D., Moreland, K. I., & Robertson, G. J. (1988). *Test-user qualifications: A data-based approach to promoting good test use.* Washington, DC: American Psychological Association.

Eyde, L. D., Robertson, G. J., Krug, S. E., Moreland, K. L., Robertson, A. G., Shewan, C. M., Harrison, P. L., Porch, B. E., & Hammer, A. L. (1993). *Responsible test use: Case studies for assessing human behavior.* Washington, DC: American Psychological Association.

Federal Child Abuse Prevention and Treatment Act, 42 U. S. C. 1510 (Supp. 1987).

Federal Education Rights and Privacy Act (FERPA), 20 U. S. C. 1232g. (1982).

Feldman, S. R., Vanarthos, J., & Fleisher, A. B., Jr. (1994). The readability of patient education materials designed for patients with psoriasis. *Journal of the American Academy of Dermatology, 30,* 284–286.

Feldman-Summers, S., & Jones, G. (1984). Psychological impacts of sexual contacts between therapists or other health care professionals and their clients. *Journal of Consulting and Clinical Psychology, 52,* 1054-1061.

Ferris, P. A., & Linville, M. E. (1985). The child's rights: Whose responsibility? *Elementary School Guidance and Counseling, 19,* 172–180

Figley, C. R. (1995). *Compassion fatigue: Coping with secondary traumatic stress disorder in those who treat the traumatized.* New York: Bruner/Mazel.

Fine, M. A., & Kurdek, L. A. (1993). Reflections on determining authorship credit and authorship order on faculty–student collaborations. *American Psychologist, 48,* 1141–1147.

Finn, S. E., & Butcher, J. N. (1991). Clinical objective personality assessment. In M. Hersen, A. E. Kazdin, & A. S. Bellack (Eds.), *The clinical psychology handbook* (2nd ed., pp. 362–373). New York: Pergamon.

Finn, S. E., & Tonsager, M. E. (1992). Therapeutic effects of providing MMPI-2 test feedback to college students awaiting therapy. *Psychological Assessment, 4,* 278–287.

Fischer, C. T. (1986). *Individualizing psychological assessment.* Pacific Grove, CA: Brooks/Cole.

Fischer, L., & Sorenson, G. P. (1996). *School law for counselors, psychologists, and social workers* (3rd ed.). White Plains, NY: Longman.

Fitzgerald, L. F., & Nutt, R. (1986). Division 17 principles concerning the counseling/psychotherapy of women: Rationale and implementation. *The Counseling Psychologist, 14,* 180–216.

Forrester-Miller, H., & Rubenstein, R. L. (1992). Group counseling: Ethics and professional issues. In D. Capuzzi & D. Gross (Eds.), *Introduction to group counseling* (pp. 307–322). Denver: Love Publishing.

Foster, S. (1996, April). Taking the stand as an expert witness. *Counseling Today,* pp. 2, 26.

Fowers, B. J., & Richardson, F. C. (1996). Why is multiculturalism good? *American Psychologist, 51,* 609–621.

Fox, R. E. (1995). The rape of psychotherapy. *Professional Psychology: Research and Practice, 26,* 147–155.

Frame, M. W., & Stevens-Smith, P. (1995). Out of harm's way: Enhancing monitoring and dismissal processes in counselor education programs. *Counselor Education and Supervision, 35,* 118–129.

Freed, D. J., & Walker, T. B. (1988). Family law in the fifty states. *Family Law Quarterly, 21,* 417–572.

Freud, S. (1954). *The origins of psychoanalysis: Letters to Wilhelm Fleiss, drafts and notes (1887–1902).* New York: Basic Books.

Gabbard, G. O. (Ed.). (1989). *Sexual exploitation in professional relationships.* Washington, DC: American Psychiatric Press.

Gabbard, G. O. (1994). Reconsidering the American Psychological Association's policy on sex with former patients: Is it justifiable? *Professional Psychology: Research and Practice, 25,* 329–335.

Galvin, S. L., & Herzog, H. A. (1992). The ethical judgment of animal research. *Ethics and Behavior, 2,* 263–286.

Gantrell, N., Herman, J., Olarte, S., Feldstein, M., & Localio, R. (1989). Prevalence of psychiatrist–patient sexual contact. In G. O. Gabbard (Ed.), *Sexual exploitation in professional relationships* (pp. 27–38). Washington, DC: American Psychiatric Press.

Garcia, J., Glosoff, H. L., & Smith, J. L. (1994). Report of the ethics committee, 1993–1994. *Journal of Counseling and Development, 73,* 253–256.

Garcia, J., Salo, M., & Hamilton, W. M. (1995). Report of the ACA Ethics Committee: 1994–1995. *Journal of Counseling and Development, 74,* 221–224.

Gates, K. P., & Speare, K. H. (1990). Overlapping relationships in rural communities. In H. Lerman & N. Porter (Eds.), *Feminist ethics in psychotherapy* (pp. 97–101). New York, NY: Springer.

Gechtman, L. (1989). Sexual contact between social workers and their clients. In G. O. Gabbard (Ed.), *Sexual exploitation in professional relationships* (pp. 27–38). Washington, DC: American Psychiatric Press.

Geib, P. G. (1982). The experience of nonerotic physical contacts in traditional psychotherapy: A critical investigation of the taboo against touch. *Dissertation Abstracts International, 43,* 0248A. (University Microfilms No. 82-13, 453)

Gelso, C. J. (1985). Rigor, relevance, and counseling research: On the need to maintain our course between Scylla and Charybdis. *Journal of Counseling and Development, 63,* 551–553.

Gibson, W. T., & Pope, K. S. (1993). The ethics of counseling: A national survey of certified counselors. *Journal of Counseling and Development, 71,* 330–336.

Gilligan, C. (1982). *In a different voice: Psychological theory and women's development.* Cambridge, MA: Harvard University Press.

Givelber, D. J., Bowers, W. J., & Blitch, C. L. (1984). *Tarasoff,* myth and reality: An empirical study of private law in action. *Wisconsin Law Review, 1984,* 443–497.

Gladding, S. T. (1992). *Counseling: A comprehensive profession.* New York: Macmillan.

Glaser, R., & Thorpe, J. (1986). Unethical intimacy. A survey of sexual contact and advances between psychology educators and female graduate students. *American Psychologist, 41,* 43–51.

Gonsiorek, J. C., & Brown, L. S. (1989). Post-therapy sexual relationships with clients. In G. R. Schoener, J. H. Milgron, J. C. Gonsiorek, E. T. Luepker, & R. M. Conroe (Eds.), *Psychotherapists' sexual involvement with clients* (pp. 289–301). Minneapolis: Walk-in Counseling Center.

Goodyear, R. K., Coleman, T., & Brunson, B. I. (1986, August). *Informed consent for clients: Effects in two counseling settings.* Paper presented at the annual meeting of the American Psychological Association, Washington, DC.

Goodyear, R. K., Crego, C. A., & Johnston, M. W. (1992). Ethical issues in the supervision of student research: A study of critical incidents. *Professional Psychology: Research and Practice, 23,* 203–210.

Goodyear, R. K., & Shumate, J. L. (1996). Perceived effects of therapist self-disclosure of attraction to clients. *Professional Psychology: Research and Practice, 27,* 613–616.

Gorkin, M. (1987). *The uses of countertransference.* London: Aronson.

Gottlieb, M. C. (1993). Avoiding exploitive dual relationships: A decision-making model. *Psychotherapy, 30,* 41–48.

Gottlieb, M. C., Sell, J. M., & Schoenfeld, L. S. (1988). Social/romantic relationships with present and former clients: State licensing board actions. *Professional psychology: Research and Practice, 19,* 459–462.

Greenberg, S. A., & Shuman, D. W. (1997). Irreconcilable conflict between therapeutic and forensic roles. *Professional Psychology: Research and Practice, 28,* 50–57.

Gregory, J. C., & McConnell, S. C. (1986). Ethical issues with psychotherapy in group contexts. *Psychotherapy in Private Practice, 4,* 51–62.

Guntheil, T., & Gabbard, G. (1993). The concept of boundaries in a clinical practice: Theoretical and risk management dimensions. *American Journal of Psychiatry, 150,* 188–196.

Gurman, A. (1985). On saving marriages. *Family Therapy Networker, 9,* 17–18.

Gustafson, K. E., & McNamara, J. R. (1987). Confidentiality with minor clients: Issues and guidelines for therapists. *Professional Psychology: Research and Practice, 18,* 503–508.

Guterman, M. (1991). Working couples: Finding a balance between family and career. In J. M. Kummerow (Ed.), *New directions in career planning and the workplace* (pp. 167–193). Palo Alto, CA: Consulting Psychologists Press.

Guy, J. D., Poelstra, P. L., & Stark, M. J. (1989). Personal distress and therapeutic effectiveness: National survey of psychologists practicing psychotherapy. *Professional Psychology: Research and Practice, 20,* 48–50.

Haas, L. J. (1993). Competence and quality in the performance of forensic psychologists. *Ethics and Behavior, 3,* 251–266.

Haas, L. J., & Cummings, N. A. (1991). Managed outpatient mental health plans: Clinical, ethical and practical guidelines for participation. *Professional Psychology: Research and Practice, 22,* 45–51.

Haas, L. J., & Malouf, J. L. (1995). *Keeping up the good work: A practitioner's guide to mental health ethics* (2nd ed.). Sarasota, FL: Professional Resource Exchange.

Haas, L. J., Malouf, J. L., & Mayerson, N. H. (1988). Personal and professional characteristics as factors in psychologists' ethical decision making. *Professional Psychology: Research and Practice, 19,* 35–42.

Haley, J. (1976). *Problem solving therapy.* San Francisco: Jossey-Bass.

Hammel, G. A., Olkin, R., & Taube, D. O. (1996). Student–educator sex in clinical and counseling psychology doctoral training. *Professional Psychology: Research and Practice, 27,* 93–97.

Handelsman, M. M., & Galvin, M. D. (1988). Facilitating informed consent for outpatient psychotherapy: A suggested written format. *Professional Psychology: Research and Practice, 19,* 223–225.

Handelsman, M. M., Kemper, M. B., Kesson-Craig, P., McLain, J., & Johnsrud, C. (1986). Use, content and readability of written informed consent forms for treatment. *Professional Psychology: Research and Practice, 17,* 514–518.

Handelsman, M. M., & Martin, W. L., Jr. (1992). The effects of readability on the impact and recall of written consent material. *Professional Psychology: Research and Practice, 23,* 500–503.

Handelsman, M. M., Martinez, A., Geisendorfer, S., Jordan, L., Wagner, L., Daniel, P., & Davis, S. (1995). Does legally mandated consent to psychotherapy en-

sure ethical appropriateness? The Colorado experience. *Ethics and Behavior, 5,* 119–129.

Harding, A., Gray, L., & Neal, M. (1993). Confidentiality limits with clients who have HIV: A review of ethical and legal guidelines and professional policies. *Journal of Counseling and Development, 71,* 297–305.

Hare-Mustin, R. T. (1980). Family therapy may be dangerous to your health. *Professional Psychology: Research and Practice, 11,* 935–938.

Hare-Mustin, R. T., Marecek, J., Kaplan, A. G., & Liss-Levinson, N. (1979). Rights of clients, responsibilities of therapists. *American Psychologist, 34,* 3–16.

Hargrove, D. S. (1982). An overview of professional considerations in the rural community. In P. A. Kelly & J. D. Murray (Eds.), *Handbook of rural community mental health* (pp. 169–182). New York: Human Sciences Press.

Hargrove, D. S. (1986). Ethical issues in rural mental health practice. *Professional Psychology: Research and Practice, 17,* 20–23.

Harlow, H. F. (1971). *Learning to love.* New York: Albion.

Harrar, W. R., VandeCreek, L., & Knapp, S. (1990). Ethical and legal aspects of clinical supervision. *Professional Psychology: Research and Practice, 21,* 37–41.

Hartlaub, G. H., Martin, G. C., & Rhine, M. W. (1986). Recontact with the analyst following termination: A survey of 71 cases. *Journal of the American Psychoanalytic Association, 34,* 895–910.

Haspel, K. C., Jorgenson, L. M., Wincze, J. P., & Parsons, J. P. (1997). Legislative intervention regarding therapist sexual misconduct: An overview. *Professional Psychology: Research and Practice, 28,* 63–72.

Hathaway, S. R., & McKinley, J. C. (1943). *The Minnesota Multiphasic Personality Schedule.* Minneapolis: University of Minnesota Press.

Hayman, P. M., & Covert, J. A. (1986). Ethical dilemmas in college counseling centers. *Journal of Counseling and Development, 64,* 318–319.

Henderson, D. H. (1987). Negligent liability and the foreseeability factor: A critical issue for school counselors. *Journal of Counseling and Development, 66,* 86–89.

Henderson, M. C. (1987). Paradoxical processes and ethical considerations. *Family Therapy, 14,* 187–193.

Hendrick, S. S. (1988). Counselor self-disclosure. *Journal of Counseling and Development, 66,* 419–424.

Heppner, P. P. (Ed.). (1990). *Pioneers in counseling and development: Personal and professional perspectives.* Alexandria, VA: American Counseling Association.

Herbert, J. D., & Mueser, K. T. (1992). Eye movement desensitization: A critique of the evidence. *Journal of Behavior Therapy and Experimental Psychiatry, 23,* 169–174.

Herlihy, B., & Corey, G. (1992). *Dual relationships in counseling*. Alexandria, VA: American Association for Counseling and Development.

Herlihy, B., & Corey, G. (1996). *ACA Ethical Standards Casebook* (5th ed.). Alexandria, VA: American Counseling Association.

Herlihy, B., & Corey, G. (1997). *Boundary issues in counseling*. Alexandria, VA: American Counseling Association.

Herring, R. (1990). Suicide in the middle school: Who said kids will not? *Elementary School Guidance and Counseling, 25,* 129–137.

Herrington, R. (1979). The impaired physician—Recognition, diagnosis and treatment. *Wisconsin Medical Journal, 78,* 21–23.

Hess, A. K., & Hess, K. A. (1983). Psychotherapy supervision: A survey of internship training practices. *Professional Psychology: Research and Practice, 14,* 504–513.

Hetrick, E. S., & Martin, A. D. (1987). Developmental issues and their resolutions for gay and lesbian adolescents. *Journal of Homosexuality, 14,* 25–43.

Hobson, S. M., & Kanitz, H. M. (1996). Multicultural counseling: An ethical issue for school counselors. *The School Counselor, 43,* 245–255.

Hogan, R., Hogan, J., & Roberts, B. W. (1996). Personality measurement and employment decisions: Questions and answers. *American Psychologist, 51,* 469–477.

Hohenshil, T. H. (1996). Editorial: The role of assessment and diagnosis in counseling. *Journal of Counseling and Development, 75,* 64–67.

Holland, T. P., & Kilpatrick, A. C. (1991). Ethical issues in social work: Toward a grounded theory of professional ethics. *Social Work, 36,* 138–144.

Holroyd, J., & Brodsky, A. (1977). Psychologists' attitudes and practices regarding erotic and nonerotic physical contact with clients. *American Psychologist, 32,* 843–849.

Holroyd, J., & Brodsky, A. (1980). Does touching patients lead to sexual intercourse? *Professional Psychology, 11,* 807–811.

Holub, E. A., & Lee, S. S. (1990). Therapists' use of nonerotic physical contact: Ethical concerns. *Professional Psychology: Research and Practice, 21,* 115–117.

Horst, E. A. (1989). Dual relationships between psychologists and clients in rural and urban areas. *Journal of Rural Community Psychology, 10,* 15–24.

Horton, J. A., Clance, P. R., Sterk-Elifson, C., Emshoff, J. (1995). Touch in psychotherapy: A survey of patients' experiences. *Psychotherapy, 32,* 443–457.

Houskamp, B. (1994). Assessing and treating battered women: A clinical review of issues and approaches. *New Directions for Mental Health Services, 64,* 79–89.

Huber, C. H., & Baruth, L. G. (1987). *Ethical, legal and professional issues in the practice of marriage and family therapy*. Columbus, OH: Merrill.

Huber, P. W. (1991). *Galileo's revenge: Junk science in the courtroom*. New York: Basic Books.

Hughes, R. B., & Friedman, A. L. (1995). AIDS-related ethical and legal issues of mental health professionals. *Journal of Mental Health Counseling, 17,* 445–458.

Ibrahim, F. A., & Arrendondo, P. M. (1986). Ethical standards for cross-cultural counseling. *Journal of Counseling and Development, 64,* 349–352.

Iglehart, J. K. (1996). Managed care and mental health. *Health Policy Report, 334,* 131–135.

In re Gault, 387 U. S. I (1967).

Jacob, S., & Hartshorne, T. S. (1991). *Ethics and law for school psychologists*. Brandon, VT: Clinical Psychology Publishing.

Jaffee v. Redmond. 1996 WL 315841 (U. S. June 13, 1996).

James, S. H., & DeVaney, S. B. (1995). Preparing to testify: The school counselor as court witness. *The School Counselor, 43,* 97–102.

Jennings, F. L. (1992). Ethics of rural practice. *Psychotherapy in Private Practice, 10,* 85–104.

Jensen, J. A., McNamara, J. R., & Gustafson, K. E. (1991). Parents' and clinicians' attitudes toward the risks and benefits of child psychotherapy: A study of informed consent content. *Professional Psychology: Research and Practice, 22,* 161–170.

Jensen, R. E. (1979). Competent professional service in psychology: The real issue behind continuing education. *Professional Psychology: Research and Practice, 10,* 381–389.

Jerome, J. K. (1889). *Idle thoughts of an idle fellow*. New York: Dutton.

Johnson, I. H., Santos-Torres, J., Coleman, V. D., & Smith, M. C. (1995). Issues and strategies in leading culturally diverse counseing groups. *Journal for Specialists in Group Work, 20,* 143–150.

Joint Committee on Testing Practices. (1988). *Code of fair testing practices in education*. Washington, DC: American Psychological Association.

Jones, J. H. (1981). *Bad blood: The Tuskegee syphilis experiment—A tragedy of race and medicine*. New York: Free Press.

Jordan, A. E., & Meara, N. M. (1990). Ethics and the professional practice of psychologists: The role of virtues and principles. *Professional Psychology: Research and Practice, 21,* 107–114.

Kalichman, S. C. (1993). *Mandated reporting of suspected child abuse: Ethics, law and policy*. Washington, DC: American Psychological Association.

Kant, I. (1964). *Groundwork of the metaphysics of morals* (H. J. Paton, Trans.). New York: Harper & Row. (Original work published 1785)

Kaplan, L. S. (1996). Outrageous or legitimate concerns: What some parents are saying about school counseling. *The School Counselor, 43,* 165–170.

Kaplan, M. (1983). A woman's view of the DSM-III. *American Psychologist, 38,* 786–792.

Katz, J. (1972). *Experimentation with human beings.* New York: Russell Sage Foundation.

Keeling, R. P. (1993). HIV disease: Current concepts. *Journal of Counseling and Development, 71,* 261–274.

Keith-Spiegel, P. (1994). Teaching psychologists and the new APA ethics code: Do we fit in? *Professional Psychology: Research and Practice, 25,* 362–368.

Keith-Spiegel, P., & Koocher, G. P. (1985). *Ethics in psychology: Professional standards and cases.* Hillsdale, NJ: Erlbaum.

Keith-Spiegel, P., Wittig, A. F., Perkins, D. V., Balogh, D. W., & Whitley, B. E., Jr. (1993). *The ethics of teaching: A casebook.* Muncie, IN: Ball State University.

Kennel, R. G., & Agresti, A. A. (1995). Effects of gender and age on psychologists' reporting of child sexual abuse. *Professional Psychology: Research and Practice, 26,* 612–615.

Kertay, L., & Reviere, S. L. (1993). The use of touch in psychotherapy: Theoretical and ethical considerations. *Psychotherapy, 30,* 32–40.

Kilburg, R. R., Nathan, P. E., & Thoreson, R. W. (Eds.). (1986). *Professionals in distress: Issues, syndromes and solutions in psychology.* Washington, DC: American Psychological Association.

Kirk, S. A., & Kutchins, H. (1992). *The selling of DSM: The rhetoric of science in psychiatry.* New York: Aldine DeGruyter.

Kitchener, K. S. (1984). Intuition, critical evaluation and ethical principles: The foundation for ethical decisions in counseling psychology. *The Counseling Psychologist, 12,* 43–55.

Kitchener, K. S. (1988). Dual role relationships? What makes them so problematic? *Journal of Counseling and Development, 67,* 217–221.

Kitchener, K. S. (1992). Psychologist as teacher and mentor: Affirming ethical values throughout the curriculum. *Professional Psychology: Research and Practice, 23,* 190–195.

Kitchener, K. S., & Harding, S. S. (1990). Dual role relationships. In B. Herlihy & L. B. Golden (Eds.), *Ethical Standards Casebook.* Alexandria, VA: American Counseling Association.

Knapp, S., Bowers, T. G., & Metzler, B. (1992). A survey of Pennsylvania psychologists. *Psychotherapy in Private Practice, 11,* 83–99.

Knapp, S., & VandeCreek, L. (1986). Privileged communication for psychotherapists: An overview. *Psychotherapy in Private Practice, 4,* 13–22.

Knapp, S., & VandeCreek, L. (1993). Legal and ethical issues in billing patients and collecting fees. *Psychotherapy, 30,* 25–31.

Knutsen, E. (1977). On the emotional well-being of psychiatrists: Overview and rationale. *American Journal of Psychoanalysis, 40,* 84–96.

Kohlberg, L. (1984). *The psychology of moral development: The nature and validation of moral stages.* San Francisco: Harper & Row.

Koocher, G. P. (1979). Credentialing in psychology: Close encounters with competence? *American Psychologist, 34,* 696–702.

Koocher, G. P. (1994a). APA and the FTC: New adventures in consumer protection. *American Psychologist, 49,* 322–328.

Koocher, G. P. (1994b). The commerce of professional psychology and the new ethics code. *Professional Psychology: Research and Practice, 25,* 355–361.

Koocher, G., & Keith-Spiegel, P. S. (1990). *Children, ethics and the law.* Lincoln: University of Nebraska Press.

Kottler, J. A. (1982). Unethical behaviors we all do and pretend we do not. *Journal for Specialists in Group Work, 7,* 182–186.

Kottler, J. A. (1994). *Advanced group leadership.* Pacific Grove, CA: Brooks/Cole.

Kurpius, D., Gibson, G., Lewis, J., & Corbet, M. (1991). Ethical issues in supervising counseling practitioners. *Counselor Education and Supervision, 31,* 48–57.

LaFromboise, T. D., Foster, S., & James, A. (1996). Ethics in multicultural counseling. In P. B. Pedersen, J. G. Draguns, W. J. Lonner, & J. E. Trimble (Eds.), *Counseling across cultures* (4th ed., pp 47–72). Thousand Oaks, CA: Sage.

Lakin, M. (1994). Morality in group and family therapies: Multiperson therapies and the 1992 ethics code. *Professional Psychology: Research and Practice, 25,* 344–348.

Laliotis, D. A., & Grayson, J. H. (1985). Psychologist heal thyself. *American Psychologist, 40,* 84–96.

Lamb, D. H., Cochran, D. J., & Jackson, V. R. (1991). Training and organizational issues associated with identifying and responding to intern impairment. *Professional Psychology: Research and Practice, 22,* 291–296.

Lamb, D. H., Strand, K. K., Woodburn, J. R., Buchko, K. J., Lewis, J. T., & Kang, J. B. (1994). Sexual and business relationships between therapists and former clients. *Psychotherapy, 31,* 270–278.

Lambert, M. J., & Bergin, A. E. (1994). The effectiveness of psychotherapy. In A. E. Bergin & S. L. Garfield (Eds.), *Handbook of psychotherapy and behavior change* (4th ed.) (pp. 143–189) New York: Wiley.

Langer, E. J., & Abelson, R. P. (1974). A patient by any other name . . . : Clinician group differences and labeling bias. *Journal of Consulting and Clinical Psychology, 42,* 4–9.

Larry P. v. Riles, 495 F. Supp. at 971 (1979).

Leong, F. T. L., & Wagner, N. S. (1994). Cross-cultural counseling supervision: What do we know? What do we want to know? *Counselor Education and Supervision, 34,* 117–131.

Leong, G. B., Eth, S., & Silva, J. A. (1992). The psychotherapist as witness for the prosecution: The criminalization of Tarasoff. *American Journal of Psychiatry, 149,* 1011–1015.

Levenson, J. L. (1986). When a colleague behaves unethically: Guidelines for intervention. *Journal of Counseling and Development, 64,* 315–317.

Levine, M., Anderson, E., Terreti, L., Sharma, A., Steinberg, K. L., & Wallach, L. (1991, August). *Mandated reports and therapy in the context of the child protection system.* Paper presented at the annual meeting of the American Psychological Association, San Francisco.

Levine, M., & Doueck, H. J. (1995). *The impact of mandated reporting on the therapeutic process: Picking up the pieces.* Thousand Oaks, CA: Sage.

Levy, R. B. (1973). *I can only touch you now.* Englewood Cliffs, NJ: Prentice Hall.

Lewis, M. W., & Lewis, A. C. (1996). Peer helping programs: Helper role, supervisor training, and suicidal behavior. *Journal of Counseling and Development, 74,* 307–313.

Lien, C. (1993). The ethics of the sliding fee scale. *Journal of Mental Health Counseling, 15,* 334–341.

Lindsey, R. T. (1984). Informed consent and deception in psychotherapy research: An ethical analysis. *The Counseling Psychologist, 12,* 79–86.

Lindsey, R. T. (1985, August). *Moral sensitivity: The relationship between training and experience.* Paper presented at the annual meeting of the American Psychological Association, Los Angeles.

Lloyd, A. (1992). Dual relationship problems in counselor education. In B. Herlihy & G. Corey (Eds.), *Dual relationships in counseling* (pp. 59–64). Alexandria, VA: American Counseling Association.

Loganbill, C., Hardy, E., & Delworth, U. (1982). Supervision: A conceptual model. *The Counseling Psychologist, 10,* 3–42.

Lonner, W. J., & Ibrahim, F. A. (1996). Appraisal and assessment in cross-cultural counseling. In P. B. Pedersen, J. G. Draguns, W. J. Lonner, & J. E. Trimble (Eds.), *Counseling Across Cultures* (4th ed.) (pp. 293–322). Thousand Oaks, CA: Sage.

Lowman, R. L. (1985). Ethical practice of psychological consultation: Not an impossible dream. *The Counseling Psychologist, 13,* 466–472.

Luborsky, L., Crits-Christoph, P., Mintz, J., & Auerbach, A. (1988). *Who will benefit from psychotherapy? Predicting therapeutic outcomes.* New York: Basic Books.

Lum, D. (1992). *Social work practice with people of color: A process-stage approach* (2nd ed.). Pacific Grove, CA: Brooks/Cole.

Mabe, A. R. & Rollin, S. A. (1986). The role of a code of ethical standards in counseling. *Journal of Counseling and Development, 64,* 294–297.

Mahoney, M. (1997). Psychotherapists' personal problems and self-care patterns. *Professional Psychology: Research and Practice, 28,* 14–16.

Manderscheid, R., & Barrett, S. (Eds.). (1991). *Mental health in the United States, 1987* (National Institute of Mental Health, DHHS Publication No. ADM-87-1518). Washington, DC: U.S. Government Printing Office.

Manuel, C., Enel, P., Charrel, J., Reviron, D., Larher, M. P., Thorion, J., & Sanmarco, J. L. (1990). The ethical approach to AIDS: A bibliographic review. *Journal of Medical Ethics, 16,* 14–27.

Margolin, G. (1982). Ethical and legal considerations in marital and family therapy. *American Psychologist, 37,* 788–801.

Marino, T. W. (1995, December). Battle for testing rights continues. *Counseling Today,* p. 6.

Maris, R., Berman, A. L., Maltsberger, J. T., & Yufit, R. I. (Eds.). (1992). *Assessment and prediction of suicide.* New York: Guilford Press.

Martineau, H. (1837). *Society in America* (Vol. 3). New York: Saunders & Otley.

Maslach, C., & Jackson, S. E. (1986). *Maslach Burnout Inventory: Manual* (2nd ed.). Palo Alto, CA: Consulting Psychologists Press.

Matarazzo, J. D. (1986). Computerized clinical psychological test interpretations: Unvalidated plus all mean and no sigma. *American Psychologist, 41,* 14–24.

May, W. F. (1984). The virtues in a professional setting. *Soundings, 67,* 245–266.

McCarthy, M. M., & Sorenson, G. P. (1993). School counselors and consultants: Legal duties and liabilities. *Journal of Counseling and Development, 72,* 159–167.

McCarthy, P., Kulakowski, D., & Kenfield, J. (1994). Clinical supervision practices of licensed psychologists. *Professional Psychology: Research and Practice, 25,* 177–181.

McCarthy, P., Sugden, S., Koker, M., Lamendola, F., Maurer, S., & Renninger, S. (1995). A practical guide to informed consent in clinical supervision. *Counselor Education and Supervision, 35,* 130–138.

McCartney, J. (1966). Overt transference. *Journal of Sex Research, 2,* 227–237.

McConnell, W. A., & Kerbs, J. J. (1993). Providing feedback in research with human subjects. *Professional Psychology: Research and Practice, 24,* 266–270.

McGuire, J., Nieri, D., Abbott, D., Sheridan, K., & Fisher, R. (1995). Do *Tarasoff* principles apply in AIDS-related psychotherapy? Ethical decision making and the role of therapist homophobia and perceived client dangerousness. *Professional Psychology: Research and Practice, 26,* 608–611

Meara, N. M., Schmidt, L. D., & Day, J. D. (1996). Principles and virtues: A foundation for ethical decisions, policies and character. *The Counseling Psychologist, 24,* 4–77.

Meehl, P. E. (1960). The cognitve activity of the clinician. *American Psychologist, 15,* 19–27.

Melton, G. B. (1981). Children's participation in treatment planning: Psychological and legal issues. *Professional Psychology: Research and Practice, 12,* 246–252.

Melton, G. B. (1983). Towards "personhood" for adolescents: Autonomy and privacy as values in public policy. *American Psychologist, 38,* 99–103.

Melton, G. B. (1994). Expert opinions: Not for cosmic understanding. In B. D. Sales & G. B. Vandenbos (Eds.), *Psychology in litigation and legislation* (pp. 55–100). Washington, DC: American Psychological Association.

Melton, G. B., Goodman, G. S., Kalichman, S. C., Levine, M., Saywitz, K. J., & Koocher, G. P. (1995). Empirical research on child maltreatment and the law. *Journal of Clinical Child Psychology, 24* (Supp.), 47–77.

Menninger, K. (1958). *Theory of psychoanalytic technique.* New York: Basic Books.

Merta, R. J. (1995). Group work: Multicultural perspectives. In J. G. Ponterotto, J. M. Casas, L. A. Suzuki, & C. M. Alexander (Eds.), *Handbook of multicultural counseling* (pp. 567–585). Newbury Park, CA: Sage.

Merta, R. J., & Sisson, J. A. (1991). The experiential group: An ethical and professional dilemma. *The Journal for Specialists in Group Work, 16,* 236–245.

Meyers, C. J. (1991). Where the protective privilege ends: California changes the rules for dangerous psychotherapy patients. *Journal of Psychiatry and the Law, 19,* 5–31.

Miller, D. J., & Hersen, M. (1992). *Research fraud in the behavioral and biomedical sciences.* New York: Wiley.

Miller, D. J., & Thelen, M. H. (1986). Knowledge and beliefs about confidentiality in psychotherapy. *Professional Psychology: Research and Practice, 17,* 15–19.

Miller, G. M., & Larrabee, M. J. (1995). Sexual intimacy in counselor education and supervision: A national survey. *Counselor Education and Supervision, 34,* 332–343.

Miller, I. J. (1995). Managed care is harmful to outpatient mental health services: A call for accountability. *Professional Psychology: Research and Practice, 27,* 349–363.

Miller, I. J. (1996). Ethical and liability issues concerning invisible rationing. *Professional Psychology: Research and Practice, 27,* 583–587.

Miller, T. R., Scott, R., & Searight, H. R. (1990). Ethics for marital and family therapy and subsequent training issues. *Family Therapy, 17,* 163–171.

Mintz, L. B., Rideout, C. A., & Bartells, K. M. (1994). An national survey of interns' perceptions of their preparation for counseling women and of the atmosphere of their graduate education. *Professional Psychology: Research and Practice, 25,* 221–227.

Minuchin, S. (1974). *Families and family therapy.* Cambridge, MA: Harvard University Press.

Mitchell, R. W. (1991). *Documentation in counseling records.* In T. P. Remley (Ed.), *ACA Legal Series* (Vol. 2). Alexandria, VA: American Counseling Association.

Monahan, J. (1981). *Preventing violent behavior: An assessment of clinical techniques.* Beverly Hills, CA: Sage.

Monahan, J. (1993). Limiting therapist exposure to *Tarasoff* liability: Guidelines for risk management. *American Psychologist, 48,* 242–250.

Montgomery, B. (1996). Ohio Attorney General's Opinion # 96-029.

Morey, R., Millton, C., Fulton, R., Rosen, L., & Daly, J. (1989). Peer counseling: Students served, problems discussed, overall satisfaction, and perceived helpfulness. *The School Counselor, 37,* 137–143.

Morran, D., Stockton, R., & Bond, L. (1991). Delivery of positive and corrective feedback in counseling groups. *Journal of Counseling Psychology, 38,* 410–414.

Morrow-Bradley, C., & Elliott, R. (1986). Utilization of psychotherapy research by practicing psychotherapists. *American Psychologist, 41,* 188–197.

Myers, J. E. B. (1991). When the parents are at war: How to get the child's side of the story. *Family Advocate, 14,* 36–48.

Myrick, R. D., Highland, W. H., & Sabella, R. A. (1995). Peer helpers and perceived effectiveness. *Elementary School Guidance and Counseling, 29,* 278–288.

Napier, A., & Whitaker, C. (1978). *The family crucible.* New York: Harper & Row.

Natanson v. Kline, 186 Kans. 393, 406, 350P. 2d 1093 (1960).

National Association of Social Workers (NASW). (1993). *Code of ethics.* Silver Spring, MD: Author.

National Association of Social Workers (NASW). (1997). *Social work speaks: NASW Policy Statements* (4th ed.) (pp. 156–163). Washington, DC: Author.

National Institute of Mental Health (NIMH). (1980). *Hispanic Americans and mental health services: A compari-*

son of Hispanic, Black and White admissions to selected mental health facilities, 1975. (DHHS Publication No. ADM 80-1006). Washington, DC: U.S. Government Printing Office.

Navin, S., Beamish, P., & Johanson, G. (1995). Ethical practices of field-based mental health counselor supervisors. *Journal of Mental Health Counseling, 17,* 243–253.

Nerison, R. M. (1992). Dual client-therapist relationships: Incidence and consequences to clients. *Dissertation Abstracts International, 54,* 1107B. (University Microfilms No. 93-18, 479).

Neukrug, E. S., Healy, M., & Herlihy, B. (1992). Ethical practices of licensed professional counselors: An updated survey of state licensing boards. *Counselor Education and Supervision, 32,* 130–141.

Newman, J. L. (1993). Ethical issues in consultation. *Journal of Counseling and Development, 72,* 148–156.

Newman, R., & Bricklin, P. M. (1991). Parameters of managed mental health care: Legal, ethical and professional guidelines. *Professional Psychology: Research and Practice, 22,* 26–35.

Newton, L. (1989). *Ethics in America study guide.* Englewood Cliffs, NJ: Prentice Hall.

Nickell, N. J., Hecker, L. L., Ray, R. E., & Bercik, J. (1995). Marriage and family therapists' sexual attraction to clients: An exploratory study. *American Journal of Family Therapy, 23,* 315–327.

Nodding, N. (1984). *Caring.* Berkeley: University of California.

Noel, B., & Watterson, K. (1992). *You must be dreaming.* New York: Poseidon.

Norman, G. (1985). Defining competence: A methodological review. In V. Neufeld & G. Norman (Eds.), *Assessing clinical competence.* New York: Springer.

Nowell, D., & Spruill, J. (1993). If it's not absolutely confidential, will information be disclosed? *Professional Psychology: Research and Practice, 24,* 367–369.

Oberlander, L. B. (1995). Ethical responsibilities in child custody evaluations: Implications for evaluation methodology. *Ethics and Behavior, 5,* 311–332.

Osipow, S., & Fitzgerald, L. F. (1986). An occupational analysis of counseling psychology: How special is the specialty? *American Psychologist, 41,* 535–545.

Otto, R. (1992). The prediction of dangerous behavior: A review and analysis of "second generation" research. *Forensic Reports, 5,* 103–133.

Overholser, J. C., & Fine, M. A. (1990). Defining the boundaries of professional competence: Managing subtle cases of clinical incompetence. *Professional Psychology: Research and Practice, 21,* 462–469.

Paradise, L. V., & Kirby, P. C. (1990). Some perspectives on the legal liability of group counseling in private practice. *Journal for Specialists in Group Work, 15,* 114–118.

Pate, R. H., Jr. (1992). Are you liable? *The American Counselor, 1,* 14–19.

Patrick, K. D. (1989). Unique ethical dilemmas in counselor training. *Counselor Education and Supervision, 28,* 337–341.

Patten, C., Barnett, T., & Houlihan, D. (1991). Ethics in marital and family therapy: A review of the literature. *Professional Psychology: Research and Practice, 22,* 171–175.

Patterson, L. E., & Welfel, E. R. (1994). *The counseling process* (4th ed.). Pacific Grove, CA: Brooks/Cole.

Pavkov, T. W., Lewis, D. A., & Lyons, J. S. (1989). Psychiatric diagnosis and racial bias: An empirical investigation. *Professional Psychology: Research and Practice, 20,* 364–368.

Payton, C. R. (1994). Implications of the 1992 ethics code for diverse groups. *Professional Psychology: Research and Practice, 25,* 317–320.

Pedersen, P. B. (1991a). The multicultural perspective as a fourth force in counseling. *Journal of Mental Health Counseling, 12,* 93–95.

Pedersen, P. B. (1991b). Multiculturalism as a generic approach to counseling. *Journal of Counseling and Development, 70,* 3–14.

Pedersen, P. B. (1994). *A handbook for developing multicultural awareness* (2nd ed.). Alexandria, VA: American Counseling Association.

Pedersen, P. B. (1995). Cross cultural ethical guidelines. In J. B. Ponterotto, J. M. Casas, L. A. Suzuki, & C. M. Alexander (Eds.), *Handbook of multicultural counseling.* (pp. 34–50). Thousand Oaks, CA: Sage.

Pedersen, P. B., Draguns, J. G., Lonner, W. J., & Trimble, J. E. (1996). *Counseling across cultures* (4th ed.). Thousand Oaks, CA: Sage.

Perrin, G. I., & Sales, B. D. (1994). Forensic standards in the American Psychological Association's new Ethics Code. *Professional Psychology: Research and Practice, 25,* 376–381.

Peterson, C. (1996). Common problem areas and their causes resulting in disciplinary action. In L. J. Bass, S. T. DeMers, J. R. P. Ogloff, C. Peterson, J. L. Pettifor, R. P. Reaves, T. Retfalvi, N. P. Simon, C. Sinclair, & R. M. Tipton. *Professional conduct and discipline in psychology* (pp. 71–89). Washington, DC: American Psychological Associaion.

Piazza, N. J., & Baruth, N. E. (1990). Client record guidelines. *Journal of Counseling and Development, 68,* 313–316.

Podbelski, J., & Weisgerber, K. (1988, August). *Differences in moral sensitivity of master's level counselors.* Paper presented at the annual meeting of the American Psychological Association, Atlanta.

Ponterotto, J. G., Casas, J. M., Suzuki, L. A., & Alexander, C. M. (Eds.). (1995). *Handbook of multicultural counseling.* Thousand Oaks, CA: Sage.

Pope, K. S. (1988). How clients are harmed by sexual contact with mental health professionals. *Journal of Counseling and Development, 67,* 222–226.

Pope, K. S. (1989). Therapists who become sexually intimate with a patient: Classifications, dynamics, recidivism, and rehabilitation. *Independent Practitioner, 9,* 28–34.

Pope, K. S. (1990a). Therapist–patient sex as sex abuse: Six scientific, professional and practical dilemmas in addressing victimization and rehabilitation. *Professional Psychology: Research and Practice, 21,* 227–239.

Pope, K. S. (1990b). Therapist–patient sexual involvement: A review of the research. *Clinical Psychology Review, 10,* 477–490.

Pope, K. S. (1992). Responsibilities in providing psychological test feedback to clients. *Psychological Assessment, 4,* 268–271.

Pope, K. S. (1994). *Sexual involvement with therapists: Patient assessment, subsequent therapy, forensics.* Washington, DC: American Psychological Association.

Pope, K. S., & Bajt, T. R. (1988). When laws and values conflict: A dilemma for psychologists. *American Psychologist, 43,* 828.

Pope, K. S., & Bouhoutsos, J. C. (1986). *Sexual intimacies between therapists and patients.* New York: Praeger.

Pope, K. S., Keith-Spiegel, P. S., & Tabachnick, B. G. (1986). Sexual attraction to clients: The human therapist and the (sometimes) inhuman training system. *American Psychologist, 41,* 147–158.

Pope, K. S., Levenson, H., & Schover, L. R. (1979). Sexual intimacy in psychology training. Results and implications of a national survey. *American Psychologist, 34,* 682–689.

Pope, K. S., Sonne, J. L., & Holroyd, J. (1993). *Sexual feelings in psychotherapy: Explorations for therapists and therapists-in-training.* Washington, DC: American Psychological Association.

Pope, K. S., & Tabachnick, B. G. (1993). Therapists' anger, hate, fear, and sexual feelings. National survey of therapist responses, client characteristics, critical events, formal complaints, and training. *Professional Psychology: Research and Practice, 24,* 142–152.

Pope, K. S., Tabachnick, B. G., & Keith-Spiegel, P. S. (1987). Ethics of practice: The beliefs and behaviors of psychologists as therapists. *American Psychologist, 42,* 993–1006.

Pope, K. S., & Vasquez, M. J. T. (1991). *Ethics in psychotherapy and counseling.* San Francisco: Jossey Bass.

Pope, K. S., & Vetter, V. A. (1991). Prior therapist–patient sexual involvement among patients seen by psychologists. *Psychotherapy, 28,* 429–438.

Pope, K. S., & Vetter, V. A. (1992). Ethical dilemmas encountered by members of the American Psychological Association. *American Psychologist, 47,* 397–411.

Pope-Davis, D. B., & Dings, J. G. (1995). The assessment of multicultural counseling competencies. In J. G. Ponterotto, J. M. Casas, L. A. Suzuki, & C. M. Alexander (Eds.). (1995). *Handbook of multicultural counseling* (pp. 287–311). Thousand Oaks, CA: Sage.

Powell, M. P., & Vacha-Haase, T. (1994). Issues related to research with children: What counseling psychologists need to know. *The Counseling Psychologist, 22,* 444–453.

Procidano, M. E., Busch-Rossnagel, N. A., Reznikoff, M., & Geisinger, K. F. (1995). Responding to graduate students' professional deficiencies: A national survey. *Journal of Clinical Psychology, 51,* 426–233.

Raimy, V. (1975). *Misunderstandings of the self.* San Francisco: Jossey-Bass.

Raquepaw, J., & Miller, R. S. (1989). Psychotherapist burnout: A componential analysis. *Professional Psychology: Research and Practice, 20,* 32–36.

Reamer, F. G. (1995). Malpractice claims against social workers: First facts. *Social Work, 40,* 595–601.

Reaves, R. P., & Ogloff, J. R. P. (1996). Liability for professional misconduct. In L. J. Bass, S. T. DeMers, J. R. P. Ogloff, C. Peterson, J. L. Pettifor, R. P. Reaves, T. Retfalvi, N. P. Simon, C. Sinclair, & R. M. Tipton. *Professional conduct and discipline in psychology* (pp. 117–142). Washington, DC: American Psychological Association.

Regehr, C., & Glancy, G. (1995). Sexual exploitation of patients: Issues for colleagues. *American Journal of Orthopsychiatry, 65,* 194–202.

Remley, T. P., Jr. (Ed.). (1991). *Preparing for court appearances. ACA Legal Series* (Vol. 1). Alexandria, VA: American Counseling Association.

Remley, T. P., Jr., Herlihy, B., & Herlihy, S. B. (1997). The U.S. Supreme Court decision in *Jaffee v. Redmond*: Implications for counselors. *Journal of Counseling and Development, 75,* 213–218.

Remley, T. P., Jr., & Sparkman, L. B. (1993). Student suicides: The counselor's limited legal liability. *The School Counselor, 40,* 164–169.

Rest, J. R. (1983). Morality. In J. Flavell & E. Markman (Eds.), *Cognitive development.* In P. Mussen (General Ed.), *Manual of child psychology* (Vol 4, pp. 550–629). New York: Wiley.

Rest, J. R. (1984). Research on moral development: Implications for training counseling psychologists. *The Counseling Psychologist, 12,* 19–29.

Ridley, C. R. (1995). *Overcoming unintentional racism in counseling: A practitioner's guide to intentional intervention.* Thousand Oaks, CA: Sage.

Ridley, C. R., & Tan, S. Y. (1986). Unintentional paradoxes and potential pitfalls in paradoxical psychotherapy. *The Counseling Psychologist, 14,* 303–308.

Ritchie, M. H. & Partin, R. L. (1994). Parent education and consultation about activities of school counselors. *The School Counselor, 41,* 165–170.

Roback, H. B., Ochoa, E., Bloch, F., & Purdon, S. (1992). Guarding confidentiality in clinical groups: The therapist's dilemma. *International Journal of Group Psychotherapy, 42,* 81–103.

Robertson, J., & Fitzgerald, L. F. (1990). The (mis)treatment of men: Effects of client gender role and life style on diagnosis and attribution of pathology. *Journal of Counseling Psychology, 37,* 3–9.

Robiner, W. N., Fuhrman, M. J., & Bobbitt, B. J. L. (1990). Supervision in the practice of psychology: Toward the development of a supervisory instrument. *Psychotherapy in Private Practice, 8,* 87–98.

Robinson, S. E., & Gross, D. R. (1985). Ethics of consultation: The Canterville ghost. *The Counseling Psychologist, 13,* 444–465.

Robinson, W. L., & Reid, P. T. (1985). Sexual intimacies in psychology revisited. *Professional Psychology: Research and Practice, 16,* 512–520.

Rodolfa, E., Hall, T., Holms, V., Davena, A., Komatz, D., Antunez, M., & Hall, A. (1994). The management of sexual feelings in therapy. *Professional Psychology: Research and Practice, 25,* 168–172.

Roeske, N. (1986). Risk factors: Predictable hazards of a health care career. In C. Scott & J. Hawk (Eds.), *Heal thyself: The health of health care professionals.* New York: Brunner/Mazel.

Rogers, W. H., Wells, K. B., Meredith, L. S., Sturm, R., & Burman, A. (1993). Outcomes for adult outpatients with depression under pre-paid or fee-for-service financing. *Archives for General Psychiatry, 50,* 517–525.

Rohrbaugh, J. B. (1992). Lesbian families: Clinical issues and theoretical implications. *Professional Psychology: Research and Practice, 23,* 467–473.

Rorschach, H. (1951). *Psychodiagnostics.* New York: Grune & Stratton.

Rosen, L. D., & Weil, M. M. (1996). Psychologists and technology: A look at the future. *Professional Psychology: Research and Practice, 27,* 635–637.

Rosenhan, D. L. (1973). On being sane in insane places. *Science, 179,* 250–258.

Rosenthal, R. (1994). Science and ethics in conducting, analyzing, and reporting psychological research. *Psychological Science, 5,* 127 -133.

Roy v. Hartogs, 366 NY, S2d 297 (1975).

Royer, R. I. (1985). *Ethical orientation of mental health practitioners: A comparative study.* Paper presented at the annual meeting of the American Psychological Association, Los Angeles.

Rutter, P. (1989). *Sex in the forbidden zone: When men in power—therapists, doctors, clergy, teachers and others—betray women's trust.* Los Angeles: Tarcher.

Salisbury, W. A., & Kinnier, R. T. (1996). Posttermination friendship between counselors and clients. *Journal of Counseling and Development, 74,* 495–500.

Sampson, J. P., Kolodinsky, R. W., & Greeno, B. P. (1997). Counseling on the information highway: Future possibilities and potential problems. *Journal of Counseling and Development, 75,* 203–212.

Satir, V. (1972). *Peoplemaking.* Palo Alto, CA: Science and Behavior Books.

Scarf, M. (1996, June 16). Keeping secrets. *New York Times,* pp. 38–42, 50, 54.

Schank, J. A., & Skovholt, T. M. (1997). Dual-relationship dilemmas of rural and small community psychologists. *Professional Psychology: Research and Practice, 28,* 44–49.

Schoener, G. R., & Gonsiorek, J. (1988). Assessment and development of rehabilitation plans for counselors who have sexually exploited their clients. *Journal of Counseling and Development, 67,* 227–232.

Schoener, G. R., Milgrom, J., & Gonsiorek, J. (1989). Therapeutic responses to clients who have been sexually abused by psychotherapists. In G. Schoener & J. Milgrom (Eds.), *Psychotherapists' sexual involvement with clients: Intervention and prevention* (pp. 95–112). Minneapolis: Walk-In Counseling Center.

Schulte, J. M., & Cochrane, D. B. (1995). *Ethics of school counseling.* New York: Teachers College Press.

Schultz, B. M. (1982). *Legal liability in psychotherapy.* San Francisco: Jossey-Bass.

Schwab, R., & Neukrug, E. (1994). A survey of counselor educators' ethical concerns. *Counseling and Values, 39,* 42–55.

Schwebel, M., Schoener, G., & Skorina, J. K. (1994). *Assisting impaired psychologists* (rev. ed.). Washington, DC: American Psychological Association.

Sekaran, U. (1986). *Dual career families.* San Francisco: Jossey-Bass.

Seligman, M. E. P. (1995). The effectiveness of psychotherapy: The *Consumer Reports* study. *The American Psychologist, 50,* 965–974.

Sell, J. M., Gottlieb, M. C., & Schoenfeld, L. S. (1986). Ethical considerations of social/romantic relationships with present and former clients. *Professional Psychology: Research and Practice, 17,* 504–508.

Sexton, T. L., Montgomery, D., Goff, K., & Nugent, W. (1993). Ethical, therapeutic, and legal considerations in the use of paradoxical techniques: The emerging debate. *Journal of Mental Health Counseling, 15,* 260–277.

Sexton, T. L., & Whiston, S. C. (1994). The status of the counseling relationship: An empirical review, theoretical implications, and research directions. *The Counseling Psychologist, 22,* 6–78.

Sexton, T. L., Whiston, S. C., Bleuer, J. C., & Walz, G. R. (1997). *Integrating outcome research into counseling practice and training.* Alexandria, VA: American Counseling Association.

Shapiro, D. L. (1991). *Forensic psychological assessment.* Boston: Allyn & Bacon.

Shapiro, F. (1995). *Eye movement desensitization and reprocessing: Basic principles, protocols, and procedures.* New York: Guilford Press.

Shaw, G. B. (1903). *Man and Superman.* London: Constable.

Sheeley, V. L., & Herlihy, B. (1989). Counseling suicidal teens: A duty to warn and protect. *The School Counselor, 37,* 89–97.

Shepard, M. (1972). *The love treatment.* New York: Paperback Library.

Sherry, P. (1991). Ethical issues in the conduct of supervision. *The Counseling Psychologist, 19,* 566–584.

Sherry, P., Teschendorf, R., Anderson, S., & Guzman, F. (1991). Ethical beliefs and behaviors of counseling center professionals. *Journal of College Student Development, 32,* 350–358.

Sieber, J. E. (1992). *Planning ethically responsible research: A guide for students and internal review boards.* Newbury Park, CA: Sage.

Siegel, S. J. (1991). *What to do when psychotherapy goes wrong.* Las Vegas, NV: Priority One Consultants.

Simon, R. I. (1991). Psychological injury caused by boundary violation precursors to therapist–patient sex. *Psychiatric Annals, 21,* 614–619.

Simon, R. I. (1992). Treatment of boundary violations: Clinical, ethical and legal considerations. *Bulletin of the American Academy of Psychiatry and the Law, 20,* 269–288.

Simpson case: Confidences survive clients. (1994, September). *National Association of Social Workers Newsletter,* p. 8.

Sleek, S. (1994, December). Ethical dilemmas plague rural practice. *APA Monitor,* 26–27.

Sleek, S. (1997, April). APA backs "bill of rights" for consumers. *APA Monitor,* pp. 1, 17.

Slimp, P. A. O., & Burian, B. K. (1994). Multiple role relationships during internship: Consequences and recommendations. *Professional Psychology: Research and Practice, 25,* 39–45.

Slovenko, R. (1980). Legal issues in psychotherapy supervision. In A. K. Hess (Ed.), *Psychotherapy supervision: Theory, research and practice* (pp. 453–473). New York: Wiley.

Smith, D., & Fitzpatrick, M. (1995). Patient–therapist boundary issues: An integrative review of theory and research. *Professional Psychology: Research and Practice, 26,* 499–506.

Smith, J. L. (1993). Report of the ACA ethics committee: 1992–1993. *Journal of Counseling and Development, 72,* 220–222.

Smith, S. R. (1996). Malpractice liability of mental health professionals and institutions. In B. D. Sales & D. W. Shuman (Eds.), *Law, mental health, and mental disorder* (pp. 76–98). Pacific Grove, CA: Brooks/Cole.

Smith, S. R., & Meyer, R. G. (1987). *Law, behavior and mental health policy and practice.* New York: New York University Press.

Smith, T. S., McGuire, J. M., Abbott, D. W., & Blau, B. I. (1991). Clinical ethical decision making: An investigation of the rationales used to justify doing less than one believes one should. *Professional Psychology: Research and Practice, 22,* 235–239.

Sobel, S. B. (1992). Small town practice of psychotherapy: Ethical and personal dilemmas. *Psychotherapy in Private Practice, 10,* 61–69.

Sodowsky, G. R., Taffe, R. C., Gutlin, T. B., & Wise, S. L. (1994). Development of the Multicultural Counseling Inventory: A self-report measure of multicultural competencies. *Journal of Counseling Psychology, 41,* 137–148.

Soisson, E. L., VandeCreek, L., & Knapp, S. (1987). Thorough record keeping: A good defense in a litigious era. *Professional Psychology: Research and Practice, 18,* 498–502.

Solovey, A. D., & Duncan, B. L. (1992). Ethics and strategic therapy: A proposed ethical direction. *Journal of Marital and Family Therapy, 18,* 53–61.

Somberg, D. R., Stone, G. L., & Claiborn, C. D. (1993). Informed consent: Therapists' beliefs and practices. *Professional Psychology: Research and Practice, 24,* 153–159.

Sonne, J. L. (1987). Proscribed sex: Counseling the patient subjected to sexual intimacy by a therapist. *Medical Aspects of Human Sexuality, 16,* 18–23.

Sonne, J. L. (1994). Multiple relationships: Does the new ethics code answer the right questions? *Professional Psychology: Research and Practice, 25,* 336–343.

Sonne, J. L., Meyer, C., Borys, D., & Marshall, V. (1985). Clients' reactions to sexual intimacy in therapy. *American Journal of Orthopsychiatry, 55,* 183–189.

Sonne, J. L., & Pope, K. S. (1991). Treating victims of

therapist–patient sexual involvement. *Psychotherapy, 28,* 174–187.

Sorenson, G., & Chapman, D. W. (1985). School compliance with federal law concerning the release of student records. *Educational Evaluation & Policy Analysis, 7,* 9–18.

Spitzer, R. L. (1975). On pseudoscience in science, logic in remission and psychiatric diagnosis: A critique of Rosenhan's "On being sane in insane places." *Journal of Abnormal Psychology, 84,* 442–452.

Sporakowski, M. J. (1995). Assessment and diagnosis in marriage and family counseling. *Journal of Counseling and Development, 74,* 60–64.

Stadler, H. A. (1990). Counselor impairment. In B. Herlihy & L. Golden (Eds.), *Ethical standards casebook.* Alexandria, VA: American Association for Counseling and Development.

Stadler, H. A., Willing, K. L., Eberhage, M. G., & Ward, W. H. (1988). Impairment: Implications for the counseling profession. *Journal of Counseling and Development, 66,* 258–260.

Stahl, P. M. (1994). *Conducting child custody evaluations: A comprehensive guide.* Thousand Oaks, CA: Sage.

Stake, J. E., & Oliver, J. (1991). Sexual contact and touching between therapist and client: A survey of psychologists' attitudes and behavior. *Professional Psychology: Research and Practice, 22,* 297–307.

Stanard, R., & Hazler, R. (1995). Legal and ethical implications of HIV and duty to warn for counselors: Does *Tarasoff* apply? *Journal of Counseling and Development, 73,* 397–400.

Steinberg, K. L. (1994). In the service of two masters: Psychotherapists struggle with child maltreatment reporting laws. *Dissertation Abstracts International, 55,* 2412B. (University Microfilms No. AAI8213453.)

Stevens-Smith, P., & Hughes, M. M. (1993). Legal issues in marriage and family counseling. In T. P. Remley (Ed.), *ACA Legal Series* (Vol. 7). Alexandria, VA: American Counseling Association.

Stoltenberg, C. D., & Delworth, U. (1987). *Supervising counselors and therapists: A developmental approach.* San Francisco: Jossey-Bass.

Strasburger, L. H., Jorgenson, L., & Randles, R. (1990). Mandatory reporting of sexually exploitive psychotherapists. *Bulletin of the American Academy of Psychiatry Law, 18,* 379–384.

Strasburger, L. H., Jorgenson, L., & Randles, R. (1991). Criminalization of psychotherapist–patient sex. *American Journal of Psychiatry, 148,* 859–863.

Sturdivant, S. (1993). The ethics of marketing a private practice. *Psychotherapy in Private Practice, 12,* 23–28.

Sue, D. W. (1995). Ethical issues in multicultural counseling. In B. Herlihy & G. Corey (Eds.), *ACA Ethical Standards casebook* (5th ed.). Alexandria, VA: American Counseling Association (pp. 193–204).

Sue, D. W., Arrendondo, P., & McDavis, R. J. (1992). Multicultural competencies and standards: A call to the profession. *Journal of Counseling and Development, 70,* 477–486.

Sue, D. W., Ivey, A. E., & Pedersen, P. B. (1996). *A theory of multicultural counseling and therapy.* Pacific Grove, CA: Brooks/Cole.

Sue, D. W., & Sue, D. (1990). *Counseling the culturally different: Theory and practice* (2nd ed.). New York: Wiley.

Sullivan, T., Martin, W. L., & Handelsman, M. M. (1993). Practical benefits of an informed-consent procedure: An empirical investigation. *Professional Psychology: Research and Practice, 24,* 160–163.

Suzuki, L. A., Meller, P. J., & Ponterotto, J. G. (1996). *Handbook of multicultural assessment.* San Francisco: Jossey-Bass.

Swenson, L. C. (1997). *Psychology and law for the helping professions* (2nd ed.). Pacific Grove, CA: Brooks/Cole.

Szasz, T. (1973). *The second sin.* Garden City, NJ: Anchor.

Tabachnick, B. G., Keith-Spiegel, P. S., & Pope, K. S. (1991). Ethics of teaching: Beliefs and behaviors of psychologists as educators. *American Psychologist, 46,* 506–515.

Talbert, F. S., & Pipes, R. B. (1988). Informed consent for psychotherapy: Content analysis of selected forms. *Professional Psychology: Research and Practice, 19,* 131–132.

Tarasoff v. Regents of the University of California, 118 Cal. Rptr. 129, 529 P. 2d 533 (1974).

Tarasoff v. Regents of the University of California, 131 Cal. Rptr. 14, 551 P. 2d 334 (1976).

Taylor, L., & Adelman, H. S. (1989). Reframing the confidentiality dilemma to work in children's best interests. *Professional Psychology: Research and Practice, 20,* 79–83.

Taylor, L., Adelman, H. S., & Kaser-Boyd, N. (1984). Attitudes towards involving minors in decisions. *Professional Psychology: Research and Practice, 15,* 436–449.

Taylor, R. E., & Gazda, G. M. (1991). Concurrent individual and group therapy: The ethical issues. *Journal of Group Psychotherapy, Psychodrama, & Sociometry, 44,* 51–59.

Teisman, M. (1980). Convening strategies in family therapy. *Family Process, 19,* 393–400.

Thoreson, R. W., Miller, M., & Krauskopf, C. J. (1989). The distressed psychologist: Prevalence and treatment considerations. *Professional Psychology: Research and Practice, 20,* 153–158.

Thoreson, R., Nathan, P., Skorina, J., & Kilburg, R. (1983). The alcoholic psychologist: Issues, problems, implications for the profession. *Professional Psychology: Research and Practice, 14,* 670–684.

Thoreson, R. W., Shaughnessy, P., & Frazier, P. A. (1995). Sexual contact during and after professional relationships: Practices and attitudes of female counselors. *Journal of Counseling and Development, 74,* 84–89.

Thoreson, R. W., Shaughnessy, P., Heppner, P. P., & Cook, S. W. (1993). Sexual contact during and after the professional relationships: Attitudes and practices of male counselors. *Journal of Counseling and Development, 71,* 429–434.

Thorn, B. E., Shealy, R. C., & Briggs, S. D. (1993). Sexual misconduct in psychotherapy: Reactions to a consumer-oriented brochure. *Professional Psychology: Research and Practice, 24,* 75–82.

Tompkins, L., & Mehring, T. (1993). Client privacy and the school counselor: Privilege, ethics and employer policies. *The School Counselor, 40,* 335–342.

Tranel, D. (1994). The release of psychological data to nonexperts: Ethical and legal considerations. *Professional Psychology: Research and Practice, 25,* 33–38.

Truman v. Thomas, California, 611 P. 2d 902, 27 Cal. 3d 285. (1980).

Truscott, D., Evans, J., & Mansell, S. (1995). Outpatient psychotherapy with dangerous clients: A model for clinical decision making. *Professional Psychology: Research and Practice, 26,* 484–490.

U. S. Department of Health and Human Services. (1995). Policy for protection of human research subjects. In D. N. Bersoff (Ed.). *Ethical conflicts in psychology* (pp. 369–377). Washington, DC: American Psychological Association.

Valliant, G. E. (1984). The disadvantages of DSM-III outweigh its advantages. *American Journal of Psychiatry, 141,* 542–545.

Vander Kolk, C. J. (1974). The relationship of personality, values and race to anticipation of the supervisory relationship. *Rehabilitation Counseling Bulletin, 18,* 41–46.

Vanek, C. A. (1990). Survey of ethics education in clinical and counseling psychology. *Dissertation Abstracts International, 52,* 5797B (University Microfilms No. 91–14, 449.)

VanHoose, W. H., & Kottler, J. A. (1985). *Ethical and legal issues in counseling and psychotherapy* (2nd ed.). San Francisco: Jossey-Bass.

Vasquez, M. J. T. (1988). Counselor client sexual contact: Implications for ethics training. *Journal of Counseling and Development, 67,* 238–241.

Vasquez, M. J. T. (1991). Sexual intimacies with clients after termination: Should a prohibition be explicit? *Ethics and Behavior, 1,* 45–61.

Vasquez, M. J. T. (1992). Psychologist as clinical supervisor: Promoting ethical practice. *Professional Psychology: Research and Practice, 23,* 196–202.

Veldick, M. D. (1995). Mandatory report statutes: A necessary but underutilized response to elder abuse. *Elder Law Journal, 3,* 169–190.

Vinson, J. S. (1987). Use of complaint procedures in cases of therapist–patient sexual contact. *Professional Psychology: Research and Practice, 18,* 159–164.

Volker, J. M. (1983, August). *Counseling experience, moral judgment, awareness of consequences and moral sensitivity in counseling practice.* Paper presented at the annual meeting of the American Psychological Association, Toronto.

Wagner, C. (1978). Elementary school counselors' perceptions of confidentiality with children. *The School Counselor, 25,* 240–248.

Wagner, C. (1981). Confidentiality and the school counselor. *The Personnel and Guidance Journal, 59,* 305–310.

Wakefield, J. C. (1992). The concept of mental disorder: On the boundary between biological facts and social values. *American Psychologist, 47,* 373–388.

Walsh, W. B., & Betz, N. E. (1995). *Tests and assessment* (3rd ed.). Englewood Cliffs, NJ: Prentice Hall.

Walter, M. I., & Handelsman, M. M. (1996). Informed consent for mental health counseling: Effects of information specificity on clients' ratings of counselors. *Journal of Mental Health Counseling, 18,* 253–262.

Warwick, D., & Kelman, H. (1973). Ethical issues in social intervention. In G. Zaltman (Ed.), *Processes and phenomena of social change* (pp. 377–417). New York: Wiley Interscience.

Watson, C. H. (1990). Gossip and the guidance counselor: An ethical dilemma. *The School Counselor, 38,* 34–39.

Watson, H., & Levine, M. (1989). Psychotherapy and mandated reporting of child abuse. *American Journal of Psychiatry, 59,* 246–256.

Wedding, D., Topolski, J., & McGaha, A. (1995). Maintaining the confidentiality of computerized mental health outcome data. *Journal of Mental Health Administration, 22,* 237–244.

Weikel, W. J., & Hughes, P. R. (1993). *The counselor as expert witness.* In T. P. Remley (Ed.), *ACA Legal Series* (Vol. 5). Alexandria, VA: American Counseling Association.

Weiner, I. B. (1989). On competence and ethicality in psychodiagnostic assessment. *Journal of Personality Assessment, 53,* 827–831.

Weiner, M. F. (1983). *Therapist disclosure: The use of self in psychotherapy* (2nd ed.). Baltimore: University Park Press.

Weisskopf-Joelson, E. (1980). Value: The enfant terrible of

psychotherapy. *Psychotherapy: Theory, Research and Practice, 17,* 459–466.

Weithorn, L. A. (1983). Involving children in decisions affecting their own welfare: Guidelines for professionals. In G. B. Melton, G. P. Koocher, & M. J. Saks (Eds.), *Children's competence to consent* (pp. 235–260). New York: Plenum.

Welfel, E. R. (1992). Psychologists as ethics educators: Successes, failures, and unanswered questions. *Professional Psychology: Research and Practice, 23,* 182–189.

Welfel, E. R., & Hannigan-Farley, P. (1996). Ethics education in counseling: A survey of faculty and student views. *ICA Quarterly,* 140, 24–33.

Welfel, E. R., & Lipsitz, N. E. (1983). Ethical orientation of counselors: Its relationship to moral reasoning and level of training. *Counselor Education and Supervision, 22,* 35–45.

Welfel, E. R., & Lipsitz, N. E. (1984). The ethical behavior of professional psychologists: A critical analysis of the research. *The Counseling Psychologist, 12,* 31–42.

Welfel, E. R., O'Dell, F. L., & Schuttenberg, E. M. (1991, November). *Burnout in school counselors: An empirical analysis.* Paper presented at the annual meeting of the Ohio Counseling Association, Columbus, OH.

Wellman, M. M. (1984). The school counselor's role in the communication of suicidal ideation by adolescents. *The School Counselor, 32,* 104–109.

Wells, K. B., Hays, R. D., Burman, A., Rogers, W., Greenfield, S., & Ware, J. E., Jr. (1989). Detection of depressive disorder for patients receiving prepaid or fee-for-service care. Results for the medical outcomes study. *Journal of the American Medical Association, 262,* 3298-3302.

Wendorf, D. J., & Wendorf, R. J. (1985). A systemic view of family therapy ethics. *Family Process, 24,* 443–453.

Whiston, S. C., & Emerson, S. (1989). Ethical implications for supervisors in counseling of trainees. *Counselor Education and Supervision, 28,* 318–325

Whiteley, J. M. (1984). A historical perspective on the development of counseling psychology as a profession. In S. D. Brown & R. W. Lent (Eds.), *Handbook of counseling psychology* (pp. 3–55). New York: Wiley.

Wilbert, J. R., & Fulero, S. M. (1988). Impact of malpractice litigation on professional psychology: Survey of practitioners. *Professional Psychology: Research and Practice, 19,* 379–382.

Wilcoxin, A., & Fennel, D. (1983). Engaging non-attending spouse in marital therapy through the use of therapist-initiated written communication. *Journal of Marital and Family Therapy, 9,* 199–203.

Wilkins, M., McGuire, J. M., Abbott, D. W., & Blau, B. I. (1990). Willingness to apply understood ethical principles. *Journal of Clinical Psychology, 46,* 539–547.

Williams, M. H. (1992). Exploitation and interference: Mapping the damage from patient–therapist sexual involvement. *American Psychologist, 47,* 412–421.

Williams, S., & Halgin, R. P. (1995). Issues in psychotherapy supervision between the white supervisor and the black supervisee. *The Clinical Supervisor, 13,* 39–61.

Willison, B. G., & Masson, R. L. (1986). The role of touch in therapy: An adjunct to communication. *Journal of Counseling and Development, 64,* 497–500.

Wilson, L. S., & Ranft, V. A. (1993). The state of ethical training for counseling psychology doctoral students. *The Counseling Psychologist, 21,* 445–456.

Wincze, J. P., Richards, J., Parsons, J., & Bailey, S. (1996). A comparative survey of therapist sexual misconduct between an American state and an Australian state. *Professional Psychology: Research and Practice, 27,* 289–294.

Wise, P. S., Lowery, S., & Silverglade, L. (1989). Personal counseling or counselors in training: Guidelines for supervisors. *Counselor Education and Supervision, 28,* 326–336.

Witmer, J. M., & Davis, T. E. (1996). A question of informed consent. In B. Herlihy & G. Corey (Eds.), *ACA Ethical Standards casebook* (5th ed.) (pp. 187–191). Alexandria, VA: American Counseling Association.

Wolberg, L. R. (1967). *The technique of psychotherapy* (2nd ed.). New York: Grune & Stratton.

Wood, B., Klein, S., Cross, H., Lammers, C., & Elliott, J. (1985). Impaired practitioners: Psychologists' opinions about prevalence and prognosis for intervention. *Professional Psychology: Research and Practice, 16,* 843–850.

Wrenn, C. G. (1962). The culturally encapsulated counselor. *Harvard Educational Review, 32,* 444–449.

Wrenn, C. G. (1985). Afterword: The culturally encapsulated counselor revisited. In P. Pedersen (Ed.), *Handbook of cross-cultural counseling and therapy* (pp. 323–329). Westport, CT: Greenwood.

Wrich, J. T. (1995, March–April). Who's at risk? *EAP Digest,* pp. 19–25.

Yalom, I. (1995). *Theory and practice of group psychotherapy* (4th ed.). New York: Basic Books.

Zane, M. (1990, January 27). $1.5 million verdict against doctor who seduced patient. *San Francisco Chronicle,* p. 4.

Zytaruk, G. J., & Boulton, J. T. (Eds.). (1981). *The letters of D. H. Lawrence* (Vol. 2). New York: Cambridge University Press.

Appendix A

American Counseling Association, Code of Ethics and Standards of Practice

Preamble

The American Counseling Association is an educational, scientific and professional organization whose members are dedicated to the enhancement of human development throughout the life span. Association members recognize diversity in our society and embrace a cross-cultural approach in support of the worth, dignity, potential, and uniqueness of each individual.

The specification of a code of ethics enables the association to clarify to current and future members, and to those served by members, the nature of the ethical responsibilities held in common by its members. As the code of ethics of the association, this document establishes principles that define the ethical behavior of association members. All members of the American Counseling Association are required to adhere to the Code of Ethics and the Standards of Practice. The Code of Ethics will serve as the basis for processing ethical complaints initiated against members of the association.

Section A: The Counseling Relationship

A.1. Client Welfare

a. Primary Responsibility.
The primary responsibility of counselors is to respect the dignity and to promote the welfare of clients.

b. Positive Growth and Development.
Counselors encourage client growth and development in ways that foster the clients' interest and welfare; counselors avoid fostering dependent counseling relationships.

c. Counseling Plans.

Counselors and their clients work jointly in devising integrated, individual counseling plans that offer reasonable promise of success and are consistent with abilities and circumstances of clients. Counselors and clients regularly review counseling plans to ensure their continued viability and effectiveness, respecting clients' freedom of choice. (See A.3.b.)

d. Family Involvement.

Counselors recognize that families are usually important in clients' lives and strive to enlist family understanding and involvement as a positive resource, when appropriate.

e. Career and Employment Needs.

Counselors work with their clients in considering employment in jobs and circumstances that are consistent with the clients' overall abilities, vocational limitations, physical restrictions, general temperament, interest and aptitude patterns, social skills, education, general qualifications, and other relevant characteristics and needs. Counselors neither place nor participate in placing clients in positions that will result in damaging the interest and the welfare of clients, employers, or the public.

A.2. Respecting Diversity

a. Nondiscrimination.

Counselors do not condone or engage in discrimination based on age, color, culture, disability, ethnic group, gender, race, religion, sexual orientation, marital status, or socioeconomic status. (See C.5.a., C.5.b., and D.1.i.)

b. Respecting Differences.

Counselors will actively attempt to understand the diverse cultural backgrounds of the clients with whom they work. This includes, but is not limited to, learning how the counselor's own cultural/ethnic/racial identity impacts her/his values and beliefs about the counseling process. (See E.8. and F.2.i.)

A.3. Client Rights

a. Disclosure to Clients.

When counseling is initiated, and throughout the counseling process as necessary, counselors inform clients of the purposes, goals, techniques, procedures, limitations, potential risks and benefits of services to be performed, and other pertinent information. Counselors take steps to ensure that clients understand the implications of diagnosis, the intended use of tests and reports, fees, and billing arrangements. Clients have the right to expect confidentiality and to be provided with an explanation of its limitations, including supervision and/or treatment team professionals; to obtain clear information about their case records; to participate in the ongoing counseling plans; and to refuse any recommended services and be advised of the consequences of such refusal. (See E.5.a. and G.2.)

b. Freedom of Choice.

Counselors offer clients the freedom to choose whether to enter into a counseling relationship and to determine which professional(s) will provide counseling. Restrictions that limit choices of clients are fully explained. (See A.1.c.)

c. Inability to Give Consent.
When counseling minors or persons unable to give voluntary informed consent, counselors act in these clients' best interests. (See B.3.)

A.4. Clients Served by Others

If a client is receiving services from another mental health professional, counselors, with client consent, inform the professional persons already involved and develop clear agreements to avoid confusion and conflict for the client. (See C.6.c.)

A.5. Personal Needs and Values

a. Personal Needs.
In the counseling relationship, counselors are aware of the intimacy and responsibilities inherent in the counseling relationship, maintain respect for clients, and avoid actions that seek to meet their personal needs at the expense of clients.

b. Personal Values.
Counselors are aware of their own values, attitudes, beliefs, and behaviors and how these apply in a diverse society, and avoid imposing their values on clients. (See C.5.a.)

A.6. Dual Relationships

a. Avoid When Possible.
Counselors are aware of their influential positions with respect to clients, and they avoid exploiting the trust and dependency of clients. Counselors make every effort to avoid dual relationships with clients that could impair professional judgment or increase the risk of harm to clients. (Examples of such relationships include, but are not limited to, familial, social, financial, business, or close personal relationships with clients.) When a dual relationship cannot be avoided, counselors take appropriate professional precautions such as informed consent, consultation, supervision, and documentation to ensure that judgment is not impaired and no exploitation occurs. (See F.1.b.)

b. Superior/Subordinate Relationships.
Counselors do not accept as clients superiors or subordinates with whom they have administrative, supervisory, or evaluative relationships.

A.7. Sexual Intimacies with Clients

a. Current Clients.
Counselors do not have any type of sexual intimacies with clients and do not counsel persons with whom they have had a sexual relationship.

b. Former Clients.
Counselors do not engage in sexual intimacies with former clients within a minimum of two years after terminating the counseling relationship. Counselors who engage in such

relationships after two years following termination have the responsibility to thoroughly examine and document that such relations did not have an exploitative nature, based on factors such as duration of counseling, amount of time since counseling, termination circumstances, client's personal history and mental status, adverse impact on the client, and actions by the counselor suggesting a plan to initiate a sexual relationship with the client after termination.

A.8. Multiple Clients

When counselors agree to provide counseling services to two or more persons who have a relationship (such as husband and wife, or parents and children), counselors clarify at the outset which person or persons are clients and the nature of the relationships they will have with each involved person. If it becomes apparent that counselors may be called upon to perform potentially conflicting roles, they clarify, adjust, or withdraw from roles appropriately. (See B.2. and B.4.d.)

A.9. Group Work

a. Screening.
Counselors screen prospective group counseling/therapy participants. To the extent possible, counselors select members whose needs and goals are compatible with goals of the group, who will not impede the group process, and whose well-being will not be jeopardized by the group experience.

b. Protecting Clients.
In a group setting, counselors take reasonable precautions to protect clients from physical or psychological trauma.

A.10. Fees and Bartering

(See D.3.a. and D.3.b.)

a. Advance Understanding.
Counselors clearly explain to clients, prior to entering the counseling relationship, all financial arrangements related to professional services including the use of collection agencies or legal measures for nonpayment. (A.11.c.)

b. Establishing Fees.
In establishing fees for professional counseling services, counselors consider the financial status of clients and locality. In the event that the established fee structure is inappropriate for a client, assistance is provided in attempting to find comparable services of acceptable cost. (See A.10.d., D.3.a., and D.3.b.)

c. Bartering Discouraged.
Counselors ordinarily refrain from accepting goods or services from clients in return for counseling services because such arrangements create inherent potential for conflicts, exploitation, and distortion of the professional relationship. Counselors may participate in

bartering only if the relationship is not exploitive, if the client requests it, if a clear written contract is established, and if such arrangements are an accepted practice among professionals in the community. (See A.6.a.)

d. Pro Bono Service.
Counselors contribute to society by devoting a portion of their professional activity to services for which there is little or no financial return (pro bono).

A.11. Termination and Referral

a. Abandonment Prohibited.
Counselors do not abandon or neglect clients in counseling. Counselors assist in making appropriate arrangements for the continuation of treatment, when necessary, during interruptions such as vacations, and following termination.

b. Inability to Assist Clients.
If counselors determine an inability to be of professional assistance to clients, they avoid entering or immediately terminate a counseling relationship. Counselors are knowledgeable about referral resources and suggest appropriate alternatives. If clients decline the suggested referral, counselors should discontinue the relationship.

c. Appropriate Termination.
Counselors terminate a counseling relationship, securing client agreement when possible, when it is reasonably clear that the client is no longer benefiting, when services are no longer required, when counseling no longer serves the client's needs or interests, when clients do not pay fees charged, or when agency or institution limits do not allow provision of further counseling services. (See A.10.b. and C.2.g.)

A.12. Computer Technology

a. Use of Computers.
When computer applications are used in counseling services, counselors ensure that: (1) the client is intellectually, emotionally, and physically capable of using the computer application; (2) the computer application is appropriate for the needs of the client; (3) the client understands the purpose and operation of the computer applications; and (4) a follow-up of client use of a computer application is provided to correct possible misconceptions, discover inappropriate use, and assess subsequent needs.

b. Explanation of Limitations.
Counselors ensure that clients are provided information as a part of the counseling relationship that adequately explains the limitations of computer technology.

c. Access to Computer Applications.
Counselors provide for equal access to computer applications in counseling services. (See A.2.a.)

Section B: Confidentiality

B.1. Right to Privacy

a. Respect for Privacy.
Counselors respect their clients' right to privacy and avoid illegal and unwarranted disclosures of confidential information. (See A.3.a. and B.6.a.)

b. Client Waiver.
The right to privacy may be waived by the client or their legally recognized representative.

c. Exceptions.
The general requirement that counselors keep information confidential does not apply when disclosure is required to prevent clear and imminent danger to the client or others or when legal requirements demand that confidential information be revealed. Counselors consult with other professionals when in doubt as to the validity of an exception.

d. Contagious, Fatal Diseases.
A counselor who receives information confirming that a client has a disease commonly known to be both communicable and fatal is justified in disclosing information to an identifiable third party, who by his or her relationship with the client is at a high risk of contracting the disease. Prior to making a disclosure the counselor should ascertain that the client has not already informed the third party about his or her disease and that the client is not intending to inform the third party in the immediate future. (See B.1.c and B.1.f.)

e. Court Ordered Disclosure.
When court ordered to release confidential information without a client's permission, counselors request to the court that the disclosure not be required due to potential harm to the client or counseling relationship. (See B.1.c.)

f. Minimal Disclosure.
When circumstances require the disclosure of confidential information, only essential information is revealed. To the extent possible, clients are informed before confidential information is disclosed.

g. Explanation of Limitations.
When counseling is initiated and throughout the counseling process as necessary, counselors inform clients of the limitations of confidentiality and identify foreseeable situations in which confidentiality must be breached. (See G.2.a.)

h. Subordinates.
Counselors make every effort to ensure that privacy and confidentiality of clients are maintained by subordinates including employees, supervisees, clerical assistants, and volunteers. (See B.1.a.)

i. Treatment Teams.
If client treatment will involve a continued review by a treatment team, the client will be informed of the team's existence and composition.

B.2. Groups and Families

a. Group Work.
In group work, counselors clearly define confidentiality and the parameters for the specific group being entered, explain its importance, and discuss the difficulties related to confidentiality involved in group work. The fact that confidentiality cannot be guaranteed is clearly communicated to group members.

b. Family Counseling.
In family counseling, information about one family member cannot be disclosed to another member without permission. Counselors protect the privacy rights of each family member. (See A.8., B.3., and B.4.d.)

B.3. Minor or Incompetent Clients

When counseling clients who are minors or individuals who are unable to give voluntary, informed consent, parents or guardians may be included in the counseling process as appropriate. Counselors act in the best interests of clients and take measures to safeguard confidentiality. (See A.3.c.)

B.4. Records

a. Requirement of Records.
Counselors maintain records necessary for rendering professional services to their clients and as required by laws, regulations, or agency or institution procedures.

b. Confidentiality of Records.
Counselors are responsible for securing the safety and confidentiality of any counseling records they create, maintain, transfer, or destroy whether the records are written, taped, computerized, or stored in any other medium. (See B.1.a.)

c. Permission to Record or Observe.
Counselors obtain permission from clients prior to electronically recording or observing sessions. (See A.3.a.)

d. Client Access.
Counselors recognize that counseling records are kept for the benefit of clients, and therefore provide access to records and copies of records when requested by competent clients, unless the records contain information that may be misleading and detrimental to the client. In situations involving multiple clients, access to records is limited to those parts of records that do not include confidential information related to another client. (See A.8., B.1.a., and B.2.b.)

e. Disclosure or Transfer.
Counselors obtain written permission from clients to disclose or transfer records to legitimate third parties unless exceptions to confidentiality exist as listed in Section B. 1. Steps are taken to ensure that receivers of counseling records are sensitive to their confidential nature.

B.5. Research and Training

a. Data Disguise Required.
Use of data derived from counseling relationships for purposes of training, research, or publication is confined to content that is disguised to ensure the anonymity of the individuals involved. (See B.1.g. and G.3.d.)

b. Agreement for Identification.
Identification of a client in a presentation or publication is permissible only when the client has reviewed the material and has agreed to its presentation or publication. (See G.3.d.)

B.6. Consultation

a. Respect for Privacy.
Information obtained in a consulting relationship is discussed for professional purposes only with persons clearly concerned with the case. Written and oral reports present data germane to the purposes of the consultation, and every effort is made to protect client identity and avoid undue invasion of privacy.

b. Cooperating Agencies.
Before sharing information, counselors make efforts to ensure that there are defined policies in other agencies serving the counselor's clients that effectively protect the confidentiality of information.

Section C: Professional Responsibility

C.1. Standards Knowledge

Counselors have a responsibility to read, understand, and follow the Code of Ethics and the Standards of Practice.

C.2. Professional Competence

a. Boundaries of Competence.
Counselors practice only within the boundaries of their competence, based on their education, training, supervised experience, state and national professional credentials, and appropriate professional experience. Counselors will demonstrate a commitment to gain knowledge, personal awareness, sensitivity, and skills pertinent to working with a diverse client population.

b. New Specialty Areas of Practice.
Counselors practice in specialty areas new to them only after appropriate education, training, and supervised experience. While developing skills in new specialty areas, counselors take steps to ensure the competence of their work and to protect others from possible harm.

c. Qualified for Employment.
Counselors accept employment only for positions for which they are qualified by education, training, supervised experience, state and national professional credentials, and appropriate

professional experience. Counselors hire for professional counseling positions only individuals who are qualified and competent.

d. Monitor Effectiveness.
Counselors continually monitor their effectiveness as professionals and take steps to improve when necessary. Counselors in private practice take reasonable steps to seek out peer supervision to evaluate their efficacy as counselors.

e. Ethical Issues Consultation.
Counselors take reasonable steps to consult with other counselors or related professionals when they have questions regarding their ethical obligations or professional practice. (See H.1.)

f. Continuing Education.
Counselors recognize the need for continuing education to maintain a reasonable level of awareness of current scientific and professional information in their fields of activity. They take steps to maintain competence in the skills they use, are open to new procedures, and keep current with the diverse and/or special populations with whom they work.

g. Impairment.
Counselors refrain from offering or accepting professional services when their physical, mental, or emotional problems are likely to harm a client or others. They are alert to the signs of impairment, seek assistance for problems, and, if necessary, limit, suspend, or terminate their professional responsibilities. (See A.11.c.)

C.3. Advertising and Soliciting Clients

a. Accurate Advertising.
There are no restrictions on advertising by counselors except those that can be specifically justified to protect the public from deceptive practices. Counselors advertise or represent their services to the public by identifying their credentials in an accurate manner that is not false, misleading, deceptive, or fraudulent. Counselors may only advertise the highest degree earned which is in counseling or a closely related field from a college or university that was accredited when the degree was awarded by one of the regional accrediting bodies recognized by the Council on Postsecondary Accreditation.

b. Testimonials.
Counselors who use testimonials do not solicit them from clients or other persons who, because of their particular circumstances, may be vulnerable to undue influence.

c. Statements by Others.
Counselors make reasonable efforts to ensure that statements made by others about them or the profession of counseling are accurate.

d. Recruiting through Employment.
Counselors do not use their places of employment or institutional affiliation to recruit or gain clients, supervisees, or consultees for their private practices. (See C.5.e.)

e. Products and Training Advertisements.
Counselors who develop products related to their profession or conduct workshops or

training events ensure that the advertisements concerning these products or events are accurate and disclose adequate information for consumers to make informed choices.

f. Promoting to Those Served.
Counselors do not use counseling, teaching, training, or supervisory relationships to promote their products or training events in a manner that is deceptive or would exert undue influence on individuals who may be vulnerable. Counselors may adopt textbooks they have authored for instruction purposes.

g. Professional Association Involvement.
Counselors actively participate in local, state, and national associations that foster the development and improvement of counseling.

C.4. Credentials

a. Credentials Claimed.
Counselors claim or imply only professional credentials possessed and are responsible for correcting any known misrepresentations of their credentials by others. Professional credentials include graduate degrees in counseling or closely related mental health fields, accreditation of graduate programs, national voluntary certifications, government issued certifications or licenses, ACA professional membership, or any other credential that might indicate to the public specialized knowledge or expertise in counseling.

b. ACA Professional Membership.
ACA professional members may announce to the public their membership status. Regular members may not announce their ACA membership in a manner that might imply they are credentialed counselors.

c. Credential Guidelines.
Counselors follow the guidelines for use of credentials that have been established by the entities that issue the credentials.

d. Misrepresentation of Credentials.
Counselors do not attribute more to their credentials than the credentials represent, and do not imply that other counselors are not qualified because they do not possess certain credentials.

e. Doctoral Degrees from Other Fields.
Counselors who hold a master's degree in counseling or a closely related mental health field, but hold a doctoral degree from other than counseling or a closely related field do not use the title "Dr." in their practices and do not announce to the public in relation to their practice or status as a counselor that they hold a doctorate.

C.5. Public Responsibility

a. Nondiscrimination.
Counselors do not discriminate against clients, students, or supervisees in a manner that has a negative impact based on their age, color, culture, disability, ethnic group, gender, race, religion, sexual orientation, or socioeconomic status, or for any other reason. (See A.2.a.)

b. Sexual Harassment.

Counselors do not engage in sexual harassment. Sexual harassment is defined as sexual solicitation, physical advances, or verbal or nonverbal conduct that is sexual in nature, that occurs in connection with professional activities or roles, and that either: (1) is unwelcome, is
offensive, or creates a hostile workplace environment, and counselors know or are told this;
or (2) is sufficiently severe or intense to be perceived as harassment to a reasonable person in
the context. Sexual harassment can consist of a single intense or severe act or multiple persistent or pervasive acts.

c. Reports to Third Parties.

Counselors are accurate, honest, and unbiased in reporting their professional activities and
judgments to appropriate third parties including courts, health insurance companies, those
who are the recipients of evaluation reports, and others. (See B.1.g.)

d. Media Presentations.

When counselors provide advice or comment by means of public lectures, demonstrations,
radio or television programs, prerecorded tapes, printed articles, mailed material, or other
media, they take reasonable precautions to ensure that (1) the statements are based on appropriate professional counseling literature and practice; (2) the statements are otherwise
consistent with the Code of Ethics and the Standards of Practice; and (3) the recipients of
the information are not encouraged to infer that a professional counseling relationship has
been established. (See C.6.b.)

e. Unjustified Gains.

Counselors do not use their professional positions to seek or receive unjustified personal
gains, sexual favors, unfair advantage, or unearned goods or services. (See C.3.d.)

C.6. Responsibility to Other Professionals

a. Different Approaches.

Counselors are respectful of approaches to professional counseling that differ from their
own. Counselors know and take into account the traditions and practices of other professional groups with which they work.

b. Personal Public Statements.

When making personal statements in a public context, counselors clarify that they are
speaking from their personal perspectives and that they are not speaking on behalf of all
counselors or the profession. (See C.5.d.)

c. Clients Served by Others.

When counselors learn that their clients are in a professional relationship with another
mental health professional, they request release from clients to inform the other professionals and strive to establish positive and collaborative professional relationships. (See A.4.)

Section D: Relationships with Other Professionals

D.1. Relationships with Employers and Employees

a. Role Definition.

Counselors define and describe for their employers and employees the parameters and levels of their professional roles.

b. Agreements.

Counselors establish working agreements with supervisors, colleagues, and subordinates regarding counseling or clinical relationships, confidentiality, adherence to professional standards, distinction between public and private material, maintenance and dissemination of recorded information, workload, and accountability. Working agreements in each instance are specified and made known to those concerned.

c. Negative Conditions.

Counselors alert their employers to conditions that may be potentially disruptive or damaging to the counselor's professional responsibilities or that may limit their effectiveness.

d. Evaluation.

Counselors submit regularly to professional review and evaluation by their supervisor or the appropriate representative of the employer.

e. In-Service.

Counselors are responsible for in-service development of self and staff.

f. Goals.

Counselors inform their staff of goals and programs.

g. Practices.

Counselors provide personnel and agency practices that respect and enhance the rights and welfare of each employee and recipient of agency services. Counselors strive to maintain the highest levels of professional services.

h. Personnel Selection and Assignment.

Counselors select competent staff and assign responsibilities compatible with their skills and experiences.

i. Discrimination.

Counselors, as either employers or employees, do not engage in or condone practices that are inhumane, illegal, or unjustifiable (such as considerations based on age, color, culture, disability, ethnic group, gender, race, religion, sexual orientation, or socioeconomic status) in hiring, promotion, or training. (See A.2.a. and C.5.b.)

j. Professional Conduct.

Counselors have a responsibility both to clients and to the agency or institution within which services are performed to maintain high standards of professional conduct.

k. Exploitive Relationships.

Counselors do not engage in exploitive relationships with individuals over whom they have supervisory, evaluative, or instructional control or authority.

l. Employer Policies.

The acceptance of employment in an agency or institution implies that counselors are in agreement with its general policies and principles. Counselors strive to reach agreement with employers as to acceptable standards of conduct that allow for changes in institutional policy conducive to the growth and development of clients.

D.2. Consultation (See B.6.)

a. Consultation as an Option.
Counselors may choose to consult with any other professionally competent persons about their clients. In choosing consultants, counselors avoid placing the consultant in a conflict of interest situation that would preclude the consultant being a proper party to the counselor's efforts to help the client. Should counselors be engaged in a work setting that compromises this consultation standard, they consult with other professionals whenever possible to consider justifiable alternatives.

b. Consultant Competency.
Counselors are reasonably certain that they have or the organization represented has the necessary competencies and resources for giving the kind of consulting services needed and that appropriate referral resources are available.

c. Understanding with Clients.
When providing consultation, counselors attempt to develop with their clients a clear understanding of problem definition, goals for change, and predicted consequences of interventions selected.

d. Consultant Goals.
The consulting relationship is one in which client adaptability and growth toward self-direction are consistently encouraged and cultivated. (See A.1.b.)

D.3. Fees for Referral

a. Accepting Fees from Agency Clients.
Counselors refuse a private fee or other remuneration for rendering services to persons who are entitled to such services through the counselor's employing agency or institution. The policies of a particular agency may make explicit provisions for agency clients to receive counseling services from members of its staff in private practice. In such instances, the clients must be informed of other options open to them should they seek private counseling services. (See A.10.a., A.11.b., and C.3.d.)

b. Referral Fees.
Counselors do not accept a referral fee from other professionals.

D.4. Subcontractor Arrangements

When counselors work as subcontractors for counseling services for a third party, they have a duty to inform clients of the limitations of confidentiality that the organization may place on counselors in providing counseling services to clients. The limits of such confidentiality ordinarily are discussed as part of the intake session. (See B.1.e. and B.1.f.)

Section E: Evaluation, Assessment, and Interpretation

E.1. General

a. Appraisal Techniques.
The primary purpose of educational and psychological assessment is to provide measures that are objective and interpretable in either comparative or absolute terms. Counselors recognize the need to interpret the statements in this section as applying to the whole range of appraisal techniques, including test and nontest data.

b. Client Welfare.
Counselors promote the welfare and best interests of the client in the development, publication, and utilization of educational and psychological assessment techniques. They do not misuse assessment results and interpretations and take reasonable steps to prevent others from misusing the information these techniques provide. They respect the client's right to know the results, the interpretations made, and the bases for their conclusions and recommendations.

E.2. Competence to Use and Interpret Tests

a. Limits of Competence.
Counselors recognize the limits of their competence and perform only those testing and assessment services for which they have been trained. They are familiar with reliability, validity, related standardization, error of measurement, and proper application of any technique utilized. Counselors using computer-based test interpretations are trained in the construct being measured and the specific instrument being used prior to using this type of computer application. Counselors take reasonable measures to ensure the proper use of psychological assessment techniques by persons under their supervision.

b. Appropriate Use.
Counselors are responsible for the appropriate application, scoring, interpretation, and use of assessment instruments, whether they score and interpret such tests themselves or use computerized or other services.

c. Decisions Based on Results.
Counselors responsible for decisions involving individuals or policies that are based on assessment results have a thorough understanding of educational and psychological measurement, including validation criteria, test research, and guidelines for test development and use.

d. Accurate Information.
Counselors provide accurate information and avoid false claims or misconceptions when making statements about assessment instruments or techniques. Special efforts are made to avoid unwarranted connotations of such terms as IQ and grade equivalent scores. (See C.5.c.)

E.3. Informed Consent

a. Explanation to Clients.
Prior to assessment, counselors explain the nature and purposes of assessment and the specific use of results in language the client (or other legally authorized person on behalf of the client) can understand, unless an explicit exception to this right has been agreed upon in advance. Regardless of whether scoring and interpretation are completed by counselors, by assistants, or by computer or other outside services, counselors take reasonable steps to ensure that appropriate explanations are given to the client.

b. Recipients of Results.
The examinee's welfare, explicit understanding, and prior agreement determine the recipients of test results. Counselors include accurate and appropriate interpretations with any release of individual or group test results. (See B.1.a. and C.5.c.)

E.4. Release of Information to Competent Professionals

a. Misuse of Results.
Counselors do not misuse assessment results, including test results, and interpretations, and take reasonable steps to prevent the misuse of such by others. (See C.5.c.)

b. Release of Raw Data.
Counselors ordinarily release data (e.g. protocols, counseling or interview notes, or questionnaires) in which the client is identified only with the consent of the client or the client's legal representative. Such data are usually released only to persons recognized by counselors as competent to interpret the data. (See B.1.a.)

E.5. Proper Diagnosis of Mental Disorders

a. Proper Diagnosis.
Counselors take special care to provide proper diagnosis of mental disorders. Assessment techniques (including personal interview) used to determine client care (e.g., locus of treatment, type of treatment, or recommended follow-up) are carefully selected and appropriately used. (See A.3.a. and C.5.c.)

b. Cultural Sensitivity.
Counselors recognize that culture affects the manner in which clients' problems are defined. Clients' socioeconomic and cultural experience is considered when diagnosing mental disorders.

E.6. Test Selection

a. Appropriateness of Instruments.
Counselors carefully consider the validity, reliability, psychometric limitations, and appropriateness of instruments when selecting tests for use in a given situation or with a particular client.

b. Culturally Diverse Populations.

Counselors are cautious when selecting tests for culturally diverse populations to avoid inappropriateness of testing that may be outside of socialized behavioral or cognitive patterns.

E.7. Conditions of Test Administration

a. Administration Conditions.

Counselors administer tests under the same conditions that were established in their standardization. When tests are not administered under standard conditions or when unusual behavior or irregularities occur during the testing session, those conditions are noted in interpretation, and the results may be designated as invalid or of questionable validity.

b. Computer Administration.

Counselors are responsible for ensuring that administration programs function properly to provide clients with accurate results when a computer or other electronic methods are used for test administration. (See A.12.b.)

c. Unsupervised Test-Taking.

Counselors do not permit unsupervised or inadequately supervised use of tests or assessments unless the tests or assessments are designed, intended, and validated for self administration and/or scoring.

d. Disclosure of Favorable Conditions.

Prior to test administration, conditions that produce most favorable test results are made known to the examinee.

E.8. Diversity in Testing

Counselors are cautious in using assessment techniques, making evaluations, and interpreting the performance of populations not represented in the norm group on which an instrument was standardized. They recognize the effects of age, color, culture, disability, ethnic group, gender, race, religion, sexual orientation, and socioeconomic status on test administration and interpretation and place test results in proper perspective with other relevant factors. (See A.2.a.)

E.9. Test Scoring and Interpretation

a. Reporting Reservations.

In reporting assessment results, counselors indicate any reservations that exist regarding validity or reliability because of the circumstances of the assessment or the inappropriateness of the norms for the person tested.

b. Research Instruments.

Counselors exercise caution when interpreting the results of research instruments possessing insufficient technical data to support respondent results. The specific purposes for the use of such instruments are stated explicitly to the examinee.

c. Testing Services.

Counselors who provide test scoring and test interpretation services to support the assessment process confirm the validity of such interpretations. They accurately describe the purpose, norms, validity, reliability, and applications of the procedures and any special qualifications applicable to their use. The public offering of an automated test interpretations service is considered a professional-to-professional consultation. The formal responsibility of the consultant is to the consultee, but the ultimate and overriding responsibility is to the client.

E.10. Test Security

Counselors maintain the integrity and security of tests and other assessment techniques consistent with legal and contractual obligations. Counselors do not appropriate, reproduce, or modify published tests or parts thereof without acknowledgment and permission from the publisher.

E.11. Obsolete Tests and Outdated Test Results

Counselors do not use data or test results that are obsolete or outdated for the current purpose. Counselors make every effort to prevent the misuse of obsolete measures and test data by others.

E.12. Test Construction

Counselors use established scientific procedures, relevant standards, and current professional knowledge for test design in the development, publication, and utilization of educational and psychological assessment techniques.

Section F: Teaching, Training, and Supervision

F. 1. Counselor Educators and Trainers

a. Educators as Teachers and Practitioners.

Counselors who are responsible for developing, implementing, and supervising educational programs are skilled as teachers and practitioners. They are knowledgeable regarding the ethical, legal, and regulatory aspects of the profession, are skilled in applying that knowledge, and make students and supervisees aware of their responsibilities. Counselors conduct counselor education and training programs in an ethical manner and serve as role models for professional behavior. Counselor educators should make an effort to infuse material related to human diversity into all courses and/or workshops that are designed to promote the development of professional counselors.

b. Relationship Boundaries with Students and Supervisees.

Counselors clearly define and maintain ethical, professional, and social relationship boundaries with their students and supervisees. They are aware of the differential in power that exists and the student's or supervisee's possible incomprehension of that power differential. Counselors explain to students and supervisees the potential for the relationship to become exploitive.

c. Sexual Relationships.
Counselors do not engage in sexual relationships with students or supervisees and do not subject them to sexual harassment. (See A.6. and C.5.b.)

d. Contributions to Research.
Counselors give credit to students or supervisees for their contributions to research and scholarly projects. Credit is given through coauthorship, acknowledgment, footnote statement, or other appropriate means, in accordance with such contributions. (See G.4.b. and G.4.c.)

e. Close Relatives.
Counselors do not accept close relatives as students or supervisees.

f. Supervision Preparation.
Counselors who offer clinical supervision services are adequately prepared in supervision methods and techniques. Counselors who are doctoral students serving as practicum or internship supervisors to master's level students are adequately prepared and supervised by the training program.

g. Responsibility for Services to Clients.
Counselors who supervise the counseling services of others take reasonable measures to ensure that counseling services provided to clients are professional.

h. Endorsement.
Counselors do not endorse students or supervisees for certification, licensure, employment, or completion of an academic or training program if they believe students or supervisees are not qualified for the endorsement. Counselors take reasonable steps to assist students or supervisees who are not qualified for endorsement to become qualified.

F.2. Counselor Education and Training Programs

a. Orientation.
Prior to admission, counselors orient prospective students to the counselor education or training program's expectations, including but not limited to the following: (1) the type and level of skill acquisition required for successful completion of the training, (2) subject matter to be covered, (3) basis for evaluation, (4) training components that encourage self-growth or self-disclosure as part of the training process, (5) the type of supervision settings and requirements of the sites for required clinical field experiences, (6) student and supervisee evaluation and dismissal policies and procedures, and (7) up-to-date employment prospects for graduates.

b. Integration of Study and Practice.
Counselors establish counselor education and training programs that integrate academic study and supervised practice.

c. Evaluation.

Counselors clearly state to students and supervisees, in advance of training, the levels of competency expected, appraisal methods, and timing of evaluations for both didactic and experiential components. Counselors provide students and supervisees with periodic performance appraisal and evaluation feedback throughout the training program.

d. Teaching Ethics.

Counselors make students and supervisees aware of the ethical responsibilities and standards of the profession and the students' and supervisees' ethical responsibilities to the profession. (See C.1. and F.3.e.)

e. Peer Relationships.

When students or supervisees are assigned to lead counseling groups or provide clinical supervision for their peers, counselors take steps to ensure that students and supervisees placed in these roles do not have personal or adverse relationships with peers and that they understand they have the same ethical obligations as counselor educators, trainers, and supervisors. Counselors make every effort to ensure that the rights of peers are not compromised when students or supervisees are assigned to lead counseling groups or provide clinical supervision.

f. Varied Theoretical Positions.

Counselors present varied theoretical positions so that students and supervisees may make comparisons and have opportunities to develop their own positions. Counselors provide information concerning the scientific bases of professional practice. (See C.6.a.)

g. Field Placements.

Counselors develop clear policies within their training program regarding field placement and other clinical experiences. Counselors provide clearly stated roles and responsibilities for the student or supervisee, the site supervisor, and the program supervisor. They confirm that site supervisors are qualified to provide supervision and are informed of their professional and ethical responsibilities in this role.

h. Dual Relationships as Supervisors.

Counselors avoid dual relationships such as performing the role of site supervisor and training program supervisor in the student's or supervisee's training program. Counselors do not accept any form of professional services, fees, commissions, reimbursement, or remuneration from a site for student or supervisee placement.

i. Diversity in Programs.

Counselors are responsive to their institution's and program's recruitment and retention needs for training program administrators, faculty, and students with diverse backgrounds and special needs. (See A.2.a.)

F.3. Students and Supervisees

a. Limitations.

Counselors, through ongoing evaluation and appraisal, are aware of the academic and personal limitations of students and supervisees that might impede performance. Counselors assist students and supervisees in securing remedial assistance when needed, and dismiss from the training program supervisees who are unable to provide competent service due to academic or personal limitations. Counselors seek professional consultation and document their decision to dismiss or refer students or supervisees for assistance. Counselors assure that students and supervisees have recourse to address decisions made, to require them to seek assistance, or to dismiss them.

b. Self-Growth Experiences.
Counselors use professional judgment when designing training experiences conducted by the counselors themselves that require student and supervisee self-growth or self-disclosure. Safeguards are provided so that students and supervisees are aware of the ramifications their self-disclosure may have on counselors whose primary role as teacher, trainer, or supervisor requires acting on ethical obligations to the profession. Evaluative components of experiential training experiences explicitly delineate predetermined academic standards that are separate and not dependent on the student's level of self-disclosure. (See A.6.)

c. Counseling for Students and Supervisees.
If students or supervisees request counseling, supervisors or counselor educators provide them with acceptable referrals. Supervisors or counselor educators do not serve as counselor to students or supervisees over whom they hold administrative, teaching, or evaluative roles unless this is a brief role associated with a training experience. (See A.6.b.)

d. Clients of Students and Supervisees.
Counselors make every effort to ensure that the clients at field placements are aware of the services rendered and the qualifications of the students and supervisees rendering those services. Clients receive professional disclosure information and are informed of the limits of confidentiality. Client permission is obtained in order for the students and supervisees to use any information concerning the counseling relationship in the training process. (See B.1.e.)

e. Standards for Students and Supervisees.
Students and supervisees preparing to become counselors adhere to the Code of Ethics and the Standards of Practice. Students and supervisees have the same obligations to clients as those required of counselors. (See H.1.)

Section G: Research and Publication

G .1. Research Responsibilities

a. Use of Human Subjects.
Counselors plan, design, conduct, and report research in a manner consistent with pertinent ethical principles, federal and state laws, host institutional regulations, and scientific standards governing research with human subjects. Counselors design and conduct research that reflects cultural sensitivity appropriateness.

b. Deviation from Standard Practices.
Counselors seek consultation and observe stringent safeguards to protect the rights of research participants when a research problem suggests a deviation from standard acceptable practices. (See B.6.)

c. Precautions to Avoid Injury.
Counselors who conduct research with human subjects are responsible for the subjects' welfare throughout the experiment and take reasonable precautions to avoid causing injurious psychological, physical, or social effects to their subjects.

d. Principal Researcher Responsibility.
The ultimate responsibility for ethical research practice lies with the principal researcher. All others involved in the research activities share ethical obligations and full responsibility for their own actions.

e. Minimal Interference.
Counselors take reasonable precautions to avoid causing disruptions in subjects' lives due to participation in research.

f. Diversity.
Counselors are sensitive to diversity and research issues with special populations. They seek consultation when appropriate. (See A.2.a. and B.6.)

G.2. Informed Consent

a. Topics Disclosed.
In obtaining informed consent for research, counselors use language that is understandable to research participants and that: (1) accurately explains the purpose and procedures to be followed; (2) identifies any procedures that are experimental or relatively untried; (3) describes the attendant discomforts and risks; (4) describes the benefits or changes in individuals or organizations that might be reasonably expected; (5) discloses appropriate alternative procedures that would be advantageous for subjects; (6) offers to answer any inquiries concerning the procedures; (7) describes any limitations on confidentiality; and (8) instructs that subjects are free to withdraw their consent and to discontinue participation in the project at any time. (See B.1.f.)

b. Deception.
Counselors do not conduct research involving deception unless alternative procedures are not feasible and the prospective value of the research justifies the deception. When the methodological requirements of a study necessitate concealment or deception, the investigator is required to explain clearly the reasons for this action as soon as possible.

c. Voluntary Participation.
Participation in research is typically voluntary and without any penalty for refusal to participate. Involuntary participation is appropriate only when it can be demonstrated that participation will have no harmful effects on subjects and is essential to the investigation.

d. Confidentiality of Information.
Information obtained about research participants during the course of an investigation is confidential. When the possibility exists that others may obtain access to such information, ethical research practice requires that the possibility, together with the plans for protecting confidentiality, be explained to participants as a part of the procedure for obtaining informed consent. (See B.1.e.)

e. Persons Incapable of Giving Informed Consent.
When a person is incapable of giving informed consent, counselors provide an appropriate explanation, obtain agreement for participation and obtain appropriate consent from a legally authorized person.

f. Commitments to Participants.
Counselors take reasonable measures to honor all commitments to research participants.

g. Explanations After Data Collection.
After data are collected, counselors provide participants with full clarification of the nature of the study to remove any misconceptions. Where scientific or human values justify delaying or withholding information, counselors take reasonable measures to avoid causing harm.

h. Agreements to Cooperate.
Counselors who agree to cooperate with another individual in research or publication incur an obligation to cooperate as promised in terms of punctuality of performance and with regard to the completeness and accuracy of the information required.

i. Informed Consent for Sponsors.
In the pursuit of research, counselors give sponsors, institutions, and publication channels the same respect and opportunity for giving informed consent that they accord to individual research participants. Counselors are aware of their obligation to future research workers and ensure that host institutions are given feedback information and proper acknowledgment.

G.3. Reporting Results

a. Information Affecting Outcome.
When reporting research results, counselors explicitly mention all variables and conditions known to the investigator that may have affected the outcome of a study or the interpretation of data.

b. Accurate Results.
Counselors plan, conduct, and report research accurately and in a manner that minimizes the possibility that results will be misleading. They provide thorough discussions of the limitations of their data and alternative hypotheses. Counselors do not engage in fraudulent research, distort data, misrepresent data, or deliberately bias their results.

c. Obligation to Report Unfavorable Results.
Counselors communicate to other counselors the results of any research judged to be of professional value. Results that reflect unfavorably on institutions, programs, services, prevailing opinions, or vested interests are not withheld.

d. Identity of Subjects.
Counselors who supply data, aid in the research of another person, report research results, or make original data available take due care to disguise the identity of respective subjects in the absence of specific authorization from the subjects to do otherwise. (See B.1.g. and B.5.a.)

e. Replication Studies.
Counselors are obligated to make available sufficient original research data to qualified professionals who may wish to replicate the study.

G.4. Publication

a. Recognition of Others.
When conducting and reporting research, counselors are familiar with and give recognition to previous work on the topic, observe copyright laws, and give full credit to those to whom credit is due. (See F.1.d. and G.4.c.)

b. Contributors.
Counselors give credit through joint authorship, acknowledgment, footnote statements, or other appropriate means to those who have contributed significantly to research or concept development in accordance with such contributions. The principal contributor is listed first and minor technical or professional contributions are acknowledged in notes or introductory statements.

c. Student Research.
For an article that is substantially based on a student's dissertation or thesis, the student is listed as the principal author. (See F.1.d. and G.4.a.)

d. Duplicate Submission.
Counselors submit manuscripts for consideration to only one journal at a time. Manuscripts that are published in whole or in substantial part in another journal or published work are not submitted for publication without acknowledgment and permission from the previous publication.

e. Professional Review.
Counselors who review material submitted for publication, research, or other scholarly purposes respect the confidentiality and proprietary rights of those who submitted it.

Section H: Resolving Ethical Issues

H.1. Knowledge of Standards

Counselors are familiar with the *Code of Ethics* and the *Standards of Practice* and other applicable ethics codes from other professional organizations of which they are members, or from certification and licensure bodies. Lack of knowledge or misunderstanding of an ethical responsibility is not a defense against a charge of unethical conduct. (See F.3.e.)

H.2. Suspected Violations

a. Ethical Behavior Expected.
Counselors expect professional associates to adhere to the *Code of Ethics*. When counselors possess reasonable cause that raises doubts as to whether a counselor is acting in an ethical manner, they take appropriate action. (See H.2.d. and H.2.e.)

b. Consultation.

When uncertain as to whether a particular situation or course of action may be in violation of the *Code of Ethics,* counselors consult with other counselors who are knowledgeable about ethics, with colleagues, or with appropriate authorities.

c. Organization Conflicts.

If the demands of an organization with which counselors are affiliated pose a conflict with the *Code of Ethics,* counselors specify the nature of such conflicts and express to their supervisors or other responsible officials their commitment to the *Code of Ethics.* When possible, counselors work toward change within the organization to allow full adherence to the *Code of Ethics.*

d. Informal Resolution.

When counselors have reasonable cause to believe that another counselor is violating an ethical standard, they attempt to first resolve the issue informally with the other counselor if feasible, providing that such action does not violate confidentiality rights that may be involved.

e. Reporting Suspected Violations.

When an informal resolution is not appropriate or feasible, counselors, upon reasonable cause, take action such as reporting the suspected ethical violation to state or national ethics committees, unless this action conflicts with confidentiality rights that cannot be resolved.

f. Unwarranted Complaints.

Counselors do not initiate, participate in, or encourage the filing of ethics complaints that are unwarranted or intend to harm a counselor rather than to protect clients or the public.

H.3. Cooperation with Ethics Committees

Counselors assist in the process of enforcing the *Code of Ethics.* Counselors cooperate with investigations, proceedings, and requirements of the ACA Ethics Committee or ethics committees of other duly constituted associations or boards having jurisdiction over those charged with a violation. Counselors are familiar with the ACA Policies and Procedures and use it as a reference in assisting the enforcement of the *Code of Ethics.*

Standards of Practice

All members of the American Counseling Association (ACA) are required to adhere to the *Standards of Practice* and the *Code of Ethics.* The *Standards of Practice* represent minimal behavioral statements of the *Code of Ethics.* Members should refer to the applicable section of the *Code of Ethics* for further interpretation and amplification of the applicable Standard of Practice.

Section A: The Counseling Relationship

Standard of Practice One (SP-1)
Nondiscrimination
Counselors respect diversity and must not discriminate against clients because of age, color, culture, disability, ethnic group, gender, race, religion, sexual orientation, marital status, or socioeconomic status. (See A.2.a.)

Standard of Practice Two (SP-2)
Disclosure to Clients
Counselors must adequately inform clients, preferably in writing, regarding the counseling process and counseling relationship at or before the time it begins and throughout the relationship. (See A.3.a.)

Standard of Practice Three (SP-3)
Dual Relationships
Counselors must make every effort to avoid dual relationships with clients that could impair their professional judgment or increase the risk of harm to clients. When a dual relationship cannot be avoided, counselors must take appropriate steps to ensure that judgment is not impaired and that no exploitation occurs. (See A.6.a. and A.6.b.)

Standard of Practice Four (SP-4)
Sexual Intimacies with Clients
Counselors must not engage in any type of sexual intimacies with current clients and must not engage in sexual intimacies with former clients within a minimum of two years after terminating the counseling relationship. Counselors who engage in such relationship after two years following termination have the responsibility to thoroughly examine and document that such relations did not have an exploitative nature.

Standard of Practice Five (SP-5)
Protecting Clients During Group Work
Counselors must take steps to protect clients from physical or psychological trauma resulting from interactions during group work. (See A.9.b.)

Standard of Practice Six (SP-6)
Advance Understanding of Fees
Counselors must explain to clients, prior to their entering the counseling relationship, financial arrangements related to professional services. (See A.10. a.–d. and A.11.c.)

Standard of Practice Seven (SP-7)
Termination
Counselors must assist in making appropriate arrangements for the continuation of treatment of clients, when necessary, following termination of counseling relationships. (See A.11.a.)

Standard of Practice Eight (SP-8)
Inability to Assist Clients
Counselors must avoid entering or immediately terminate a counseling relationship if it is determined that they are unable to be of professional assistance to a client. The counselor may assist in making an appropriate referral for the client. (See A.11.b.)

Section B: Confidentiality

Standard of Practice Nine (SP-9)
Confidentiality Requirement
Counselors must keep information related to counseling services confidential unless disclosure is in the best interest of clients, is required for the welfare of others, or is required by

law. When disclosure is required, only information that is essential is revealed and the client is informed of such disclosure. (See B.1. a.–f.)

Standard of Practice Ten (SP-10)
Confidentiality Requirements for Subordinates
Counselors must take measures to ensure that privacy and confidentiality of clients are maintained by subordinates. (See B.1.h.)

Standard of Practice Eleven (SP-11)
Confidentiality in Group Work
Counselors must clearly communicate to group members that confidentiality cannot be guaranteed in group work. (See B.2.a.)

Standard of Practice Twelve (SP-12)
Confidentiality in Family Counseling
Counselors must not disclose information about one family member in counseling to another family member without prior consent. (See B.2.b.)

Standard of Practice Thirteen (SP-13)
Confidentiality of Records
Counselors must maintain appropriate confidentiality in creating, storing, accessing, transferring, and disposing of counseling records. (See B.4.b.)

Standard of Practice Fourteen (SP-14)
Permission to Record or Observe
Counselors must obtain prior consent from clients in order to electronically record or observe sessions. (See B.4.c.)

Standard of Practice Fifteen (SP-15)
Counselors must obtain client consent to disclose or transfer records to third parties, unless exceptions listed in SP-9 exist. (See B.4.e.)

Standard of Practice Sixteen (SP-16)
Data Disguise Required
Counselors must disguise the identity of the client when using data for training, research, or publication. (See B.5.a.)

Section C: Professional Responsibility

Standard of Practice Seventeen (SP-17)
Boundaries of Competence
Counselors must practice only within the boundaries of their competence. (See C.2.a.)

Standard of Practice Eighteen (SP-18)
Continuing Education
Counselors must engage in continuing education to maintain their professional competence. (See C.2.f.)

Standard of Practice Nineteen (SP-19)
Impairment of Professionals
Counselors must refrain from offering professional services when their personal problems or conflicts may cause harm to a client or others. (See C.2.g.)

Standard of Practice Twenty (SP-20)
Accurate Advertising
Counselors must accurately represent their credentials and services when advertising. (See C.3.a.)

Standard of Practice Twenty-one (SP-21)
Recruiting Through Employment
Counselors must not use their place of employment or institutional affiliation to recruit clients for their private practices. (See C.3.d.)

Standard of Practice Twenty-two (SP-22)
Credentials Claimed
Counselors must claim or imply only professional credentials possessed and must correct any known misrepresentations of their credentials by others. (See C.4.a.)

Standard of Practice Twenty-three (SP-23)
Sexual Harassment
Counselors must not engage in sexual harassment. (See C.5.b.)

Standard of Practice Twenty-four (SP-24)
Unjustified Gains
Counselors must not use their professional positions to seek or receive unjustified personal gains, sexual favors, unfair advantage, or unearned goods or services. (See C.5.e.)

Standard of Practice Twenty-five (SP-25)
Clients Served by Others
With the consent of the client, counselors must inform other mental health professionals serving the same client that a counseling relationship between the counselor and client exists. (See C.6.c.)

Standard of Practice Twenty-six (SP-26)
Negative Employment Conditions
Counselors must alert their employers to institutional policy or conditions that may be potentially disruptive or damaging to the counselor's professional responsibilities, or that may limit their effectiveness or deny clients' rights. (See D.1.c.)

Standard of Practice Twenty-seven (SP-27)
Personnel Selection and Assignment
Counselors must select competent staff and must assign responsibilities compatible with staff skills and experiences. (See D.1.h.)

Standard of Practice Twenty-eight (SP-28)
Exploitive Relationships with Subordinates
Counselors must not engage in exploitive relationships with individuals over whom they have supervisory, evaluative, or instructional control or authority. (See D.1.k.)

Section D: Relationship with Other Professionals

Standard of Practice Twenty-nine (SP-29)
Accepting Fees from Agency Clients
Counselors must not accept fees or other remuneration for consultation with persons entitled to such services through the counselor's employing agency or institution. (See D.3.a.)

Standard of Practice Thirty (SP-30)
Referral Fees
Counselors must not accept referral fees. (See D.3.b.)

Section E: Evaluation, Assessment, and Interpretation

Standard of Practice Thirty-one (SP-31)
Limits of Competence
Counselors must perform only testing and assessment services for which they are competent. Counselors must not allow the use of psychological assessment techniques by unqualified persons under their supervision. (See E.2.a.)

Standard of Practice Thirty-two (SP-32)
Appropriate Use of Assessment Instruments
Counselors must use assessment instruments in the manner for which they were intended. (See E.2.b.)

Standard of Practice Thirty-three (SP-33)
Assessment Explanations to Clients
Counselors must provide explanations to clients prior to assessment about the nature and purposes of assessment and the specific uses of results. (See E.3.a.)

Standard of Practice Thirty-four (SP-34)
Recipients of Test Results
Counselors must ensure that accurate and appropriate interpretations accompany any release of testing and assessment information. (See E.3.b.)

Standard of Practice Thirty-five (SP-35)
Obsolete Tests and Outdated Test Results
Counselors must not base their assessment or intervention decisions or recommendations on data or test results that are obsolete or outdated for the current purpose. (See E.11.)

Section F: Teaching, Training, and Supervision

Standard of Practice Thirty-six (SP-36)
Sexual Relationships with Students or Supervisees
Counselors must not engage in sexual relationships with their students and supervisees. (See F.1.c.)

Standard of Practice Thirty-seven (SP-37)
Credit for Contributions to Research
Counselors must give credit to students or supervisees for their contributions to research and scholarly projects. (See F.1.d.)

Standard of Practice Thirty-eight (SP-38)
Supervision Preparation
Counselors who offer clinical supervision services must be trained and prepared in supervision methods and techniques. (See F.1.f.)

Standard of Practice Thirty-nine (SP-39)
Evaluation Information
Counselors must clearly state to students and supervisees in advance of training, the levels of competency expected, appraisal methods, and timing of evaluations. Counselors must provide students and supervisees with periodic performance appraisal and evaluation feedback throughout the training program. (See F.2.c.)

Standard of Practice Forty (SP-40)
Peer Relationships in Training
Counselors must make every effort to ensure that the rights of peers are not violated when students and supervisees are assigned to lead counseling groups or provide clinical supervision. (See F.2.e.)

Standard of Practice Forty-one (SP-41)
Limitations of Students and Supervisees
Counselors must assist students and supervisees in securing remedial assistance, when needed, and must dismiss from the training program students and supervisees who are unable to provide competent service due to academic or personal limitations. (See F.3.a.)

Standard of Practice Forty-two (SP-42)
Self-growth Experiences
Counselors who conduct experiences for students or supervisees that include self-growth or self-disclosure must inform participants of counselors' ethical obligations to the profession and must not grade participants based on their nonacademic performance. (See F.3.b.)

Standard of Practice Forty-three (SP-43)
Standards for Students and Supervisees
Students and supervisees preparing to become counselors must adhere to the *Code of Ethics* and the *Standards of Practice* of counselors. (See F.3.e.)

Section G: Research and Publication

Standard of Practice Forty-four (SP-44)
Precautions to Avoid Injury in Research
Counselors must avoid causing physical, social, or psychological harm or injury to subjects in research. (See G.1.c.)

Standard of Practice Forty-five (SP-45)
Confidentiality of Research Information
Counselors must keep confidential information obtained about research participants. (See G.2.d.)

Standard of Practice Forty-six (SP-46)
Information Affecting Research Outcome
Counselors must report all variables and conditions known to the investigator that may have affected research data or outcomes. (See G.3.a.)

Standard of Practice Forty-seven (SP-47)
Accurate Research Results
Counselors must not distort or misrepresent research data, nor fabricate or intentionally bias research results. (See G.3.b.)

Standard of Practice Forty-eight (SP-48)
Publication Contributors
Counselors must give appropriate credit to those who have contributed to research. (See G.4.a. and G.4.b.)

Section H: Resolving Ethical Issues

Standard of Practice Forty-nine (SP-49)
Ethical Behavior Expected
Counselors must take appropriate action when they possess reasonable cause that raises doubts as to whether counselors or other mental health professionals are acting in an ethical manner. (See H.2.a.)

Standard of Practice Fifty (SP-50)
Unwarranted Complaints
Counselors must not initiate, participate in, or encourage the filings of ethics complaints that are unwarranted or intended to harm a mental health professional rather than to protect clients or the public. (See H.2.f.)

Standard of Practice Fifty-one (SP-51)
Cooperation with Ethics Committees
Counselors must cooperate with investigations, proceedings, and requirements of the ACA Ethics Committee or ethics committees of other duly constituted associations or boards having jurisdiction over those charged with a violation. (See H.3.)

Appendix B

American Psychological Association, Ethical Principles of Psychologists and Code of Conduct

Introduction

The American Psychological Association's (APA's) Ethical Principles of Psychologists and Code of Conduct (hereinafter referred to as the Ethics Code) consists of an Introduction, a Preamble, six General Principles (A–F), and specific Ethical Standards. The Introduction discusses the intent, organization, procedural considerations, and scope of application of the Ethics Code. The Preamble and General Principles are aspirational goals to guide psychologists toward the highest ideals of psychology. Although the Preamble and General Principles are not themselves enforceable rules, they should be considered by psychologists in arriving at an ethical course of action and may be considered by ethics bodies in interpreting the Ethical Standards. The Ethical Standards set forth enforceable rules for conduct as psychologists. Most of the Ethical Standards are written broadly, in order to apply to psychologists in varied roles, although the application of an Ethical Standard may vary depending on the context. The Ethical Standards are not exhaustive. The fact that a given conduct is not specifically addressed by the Ethics Code does not mean that it is necessarily either ethical or unethical.

Professional materials that are most helpful in this regard are guidelines and standards that have been adopted or endorsed by professional psychological organizations. Such guidelines and standards, whether adopted by the American Psychological Association (APA) or its Divisions, are not enforceable as such by this Ethics Code, but are of educative value to psychologists, courts, and professional bodies. Such materials include, but are not limited to, the APA's General Guidelines for Providers of Psychological Services (1987), Specialty Guidelines for the Delivery of Services by Clinical Psychologists, Counseling Psychologists Industrial/Organizational Psychologists, and School Psychologists (1981), Guidelines for Computer Based Tests and Interpretations (1987), Standards for Educational and Psychological Testing (1985), Ethical Principles in the Conduct of Research With Human Participants (1982), Guidelines for Ethical Conduct in the Care and Use of Animals (1986), Guidelines for Providers of Psychological Services to Ethnic, Linguistic, and Culturally Diverse Populations (1990), and Publication Manual of the American Psychological Association (3rd ed., 1983). Materials not adopted by APA as a whole include the APA Division 41 (Forensic Psychology)/American Psychology-Law Society's Specialty Guidelines for Forensic Psychologists (1991).

Membership in the APA commits members to adhere to the APA Ethics Code and to the rules and procedures used to implement it. Psychologists and students, whether or not they are APA members, should be aware that the Ethics Code may be applied to them by state psychology boards, courts, or other public bodies.

This Ethics Code applies only to psychologists' work-related activities, that is, activities that are part of the psychologists' scientific and professional functions or that are psychological in nature. It includes the clinical or counseling practice of psychology, research, teaching, supervision of trainees, development of assessment instruments, conducting assessments, educational counseling, organizational consulting, social intervention, administration, and other activities as well. These work-related activities can be distinguished from the purely private conduct of a psychologist, which ordinarily is not within the purview of the Ethics Code.

The Ethics Code is intended to provide standards of professional conduct that can be applied by the APA and by other bodies that choose to adopt them. Whether or not a psychologist has violated the Ethics Code does not by itself determine whether he or she is legally liable in a court action, whether a contract is enforceable, or whether other legal consequences occur. These results are based on legal rather than ethical rules. However, compliance with or violation of the Ethics Code may be admissible as evidence in some legal proceedings, depending on the circumstances.

In the process of making decisions regarding their professional behavior, psychologists must consider this Ethics Code, in addition to applicable laws and psychology board regulations. If the Ethics Code establishes a higher standard of conduct than is required by law, psychologists must meet the higher ethical standard. If the Ethics Code standard appears to conflict with the requirements of law, then psychologists make known their commitment to the Ethics Code and take steps to resolve the conflict in a responsible manner. If neither law nor the Ethics Code resolves an issue, psychologists should consider other professional materials and the dictates of their own conscience, as well as seek consultation with others within the field when this is practical.

The procedures for filing, investigating, and resolving complaints of unethical conduct are described in the current Rules and Procedures of the APA Ethics Committee. The actions that APA may take for violations of the Ethics Code include actions such as reprimand, censure, termination of APA membership, and referral of the matter to other bodies. Complainants who seek remedies such as monetary damages in alleging ethical violations by psychologists must resort to private negotiations, administrative bodies, or the courts. Actions that violate the Ethics Code may lead to the imposition of sanctions on a psychologist by bodies other than APA, including state psychological associations, other professional groups, psychology boards, other state or federal agencies, and payors for health services. In addition to actions for violation of the Ethics Code, the APA Bylaws provide that APA may take action against a member after his or her conviction of a felony, expulsion or suspension from an affiliated state psychological association, or suspension or loss of licensure.

Preamble

Psychologists work to develop a valid and reliable body of scientific knowledge based on research. They may apply that knowledge to human behavior in a variety of contexts. In doing so, they perform many roles, such as researcher, educator, diagnostician, therapist, supervisor, consultant, administrator, social interventionist, and expert witness. Their goal is to broaden knowledge of behavior and, where appropriate, to apply it pragmatically to improve the condition of both the individual and society. Psychologists respect the central importance of freedom of inquiry and expression in research, teaching, and publication. They also strive to help the public in developing informed judgments and choices concerning human behavior. This Ethics Code provides a common set of values upon which psychologists build their professional and scientific work.

This Code is intended to provide both the general principles and the decision rules to cover most situations encountered by psychologists. It has as its primary goal the welfare and protection of the individuals and groups with whom psychologists work. It is the individual responsibility of each psychologist to aspire to the highest possible standards of conduct. Psychologists respect and protect human and civil rights, and do not knowingly participate in or condone unfair discriminatory practices.

The development of a dynamic set of ethical standards for a psychologist's work-related conduct requires a personal commitment to a lifelong effort to act ethically; to encourage ethical behavior by students, supervisees, employees, and colleagues, as appropriate; and to consult with others, as needed, concerning ethical problems. Each psychologist supplements, but does not violate, the Ethics Code's values and rules on the basis of guidance drawn from personal values, culture, and experience.

General Principles

Principle A: Competence

Psychologists strive to maintain high standards of competence in their work. They recognize the boundaries of their particular competencies and the limitations of their expertise. They provide only those services and use only those techniques for which they are qualified by education, training, or experience. Psychologists are cognizant of the fact that the competencies required in serving, teaching, and/or studying groups of people vary with the distinctive characteristics of those groups. In those areas in which recognized professional standards do not yet exist, psychologists exercise careful judgment and take appropriate precautions to protect the welfare of those with whom they work. They maintain knowledge of relevant scientific and professional information related to the services they render, and they recognize the need for ongoing education. Psychologists make appropriate use of scientific, professional, technical, and administrative resources.

Principle B: Integrity

Psychologists seek to promote integrity in the science, teaching, and practice of psychology. In these activities psychologists are honest, fair, and respectful of others. In describing or reporting their qualifications, services, products, fees, research, or teaching, they do not make statements that are false, misleading, or deceptive. Psychologists strive to be aware of their own belief systems, values, needs, and limitations and the effect of these on their work. To the extent feasible, they attempt to clarify for relevant parties the roles they are performing and to function appropriately in accordance with those roles. Psychologists avoid improper and potentially harmful dual relationships.

Principle C: Professional and Scientific Responsibility

Psychologists uphold professional standards of conduct, clarify their professional roles and obligations, accept appropriate responsibility for their behavior, and adapt their methods to the needs of different populations. Psychologists consult with, refer to, or cooperate with other professionals and institutions to the extent needed to serve the best interests of their patients, clients, or other recipients of their services. Psychologists' moral standards and conduct are personal matters to the same degree as is true for any other person, except as psychologists' conduct may compromise their professional responsibilities or reduce the public's trust in psychology and psychologists. Psychologists are concerned about the ethical compliance of their colleagues' scientific and professional conduct. When appropriate, they consult with colleagues in order to prevent or avoid unethical conduct.

Principle D: Respect for People's Rights and Dignity

Psychologists accord appropriate respect to the fundamental rights, dignity, and worth of all people. They respect the rights of individuals to privacy, confidentiality, self-determination, and autonomy, mindful that legal and other obligations may lead to inconsistency and conflict with the exercise of these rights. Psychologists are aware of cultural, individual, and role differences, including those due to age, gender, race, ethnicity, national origin, religion, sexual orientation, disability, language, and socioeconomic status. Psychologists try to eliminate the effect on their work of biases based on those factors, and they do not knowingly participate in or condone unfair discriminatory practices.

Principle E: Concern for Others' Welfare

Psychologists seek to contribute to the welfare of those with whom they interact professionally. In their professional actions, psychologists weigh the welfare and rights of their patients or clients, students, supervisees, human research participants, and other affected persons, and the welfare of animal subjects of research. When conflicts occur among psychologists' obligations or concerns, they attempt to resolve these conflicts and to perform their roles in a responsible fashion that avoids or minimizes harm. Psychologists are sensitive to real and ascribed differences in power between themselves and others, and they do not exploit or mislead other people during or after professional relationships.

Principle F: Social Responsibility

Psychologists are aware of their professional and scientific responsibilities to the community and the society in which they work and live. They apply and make public their knowledge of psychology in order to contribute to human welfare. Psychologists are concerned about and work to mitigate the causes of human suffering. When undertaking research, they strive to advance human welfare and the science of psychology. Psychologists try to avoid misuse of their work. Psychologists comply with the law and encourage the development of law and social policy that serve the interests of their patients and clients and the public. They are encouraged to contribute a portion of their professional time for little or no personal advantage.

Ethical Standards

1. General Standards

These General Standards are potentially applicable to the professional and scientific activities of all psychologists.

1.01 Applicability of the Ethics Code
The activity of a psychologist subject to the Ethics Code may be reviewed under these Ethical Standards only if the activity is part of his or her work-related functions or the activity is psychological in nature. Personal activities having no connection to or effect on psychological roles are not subject to the Ethics Code.

1.02 Relationship of Ethics and Law
If psychologists' eithical responsibilities conflict with law, make known their commitment to the Ethics Code and take steps to resolve the conflict in a responsible manner.

1.03 Professional and Scientific Relationship
Psychologists provide diagnostic, therapeutic, teaching, research, supervisory, consultative, or other psychological services only in the context of a defined professional or scientific relationship or role. (See also Standards 2.01, Evaluation, Diagnosis, and Interventions in Professional Context, and 7.02, Forensic Assessments.)

1.04 Boundaries of Competence
a. Psychologists provide services, teach, and conduct research only within the boundaries of their competence, based on their education, training, supervised experience, or appropriate professional experience.

b. Psychologists provide services, teach, or conduct research in new areas or involving new techniques only after first undertaking appropriate study, training, supervision, and/or consultation from persons who are competent in those areas or techniques.

c. In those emerging areas in which generally recognized standards for preparatory training do not yet exist, psychologists nevertheless take reasonable steps to ensure the competence of their work and to protect patients, clients, students, research participants, and others from harm.

1.05 Maintaining Expertise
Psychologists who engage in assessment, therapy, teaching, research, organizational consulting, or other professional activities maintain a reasonable level of awareness of current scientific and professional information in their fields of activity, and undertake ongoing efforts to maintain competence in the skills they use.

1.06 Basis for Scientific and Professional Judgments
Psychologists rely on scientifically and professionally derived knowledge when making scientific or professional judgments or when engaging in scholarly or professional endeavors.

1.07 Describing the Nature and Results of Psychological Services
a. When psychologists provide assessment, evaluation, treatment, counseling, supervision, teaching, consultation, research, or other psychological services to an individual, a group, or an organization, they provide, using language that is reasonably understandable to the recipi-

ent of those services, appropriate information beforehand about the nature of such services and appropriate information later about results and conclusions. (See also Standard 2.09, Explaining Assessment Results.)

b. If psychologists will be precluded by law or by organizational roles from providing such information to particular individuals or groups, they so inform those individuals or groups at the outset of the service.

1.08 Human Differences

Where differences of age, gender, race, ethnicity, national origin, religion, sexual orientation, disability, language, or socioeconomic status significantly affect psychologists' work concerning particular individuals or groups, psychologists obtain the training, experience, consultation, or supervision necessary to ensure the competence of their services, or they make appropriate referrals.

1.09 Respecting Others

In their work-related activities, psychologists respect the rights of others to hold values, attitudes, and opinions that differ from their own.

1.10 Nondiscrimination

In their work-related activities, psychologists do not engage in unfair discrimination based on age, gender, race, ethnicity, national origin, religion, sexual orientation, disability, socioeconomic status, or any basis proscribed by law.

1.11 Sexual Harassment

a. Psychologists do not engage in sexual harassment. Sexual harassment is sexual solicitation, physical advances, or verbal or nonverbal conduct that is sexual in nature, that occurs in connection with the psychologists' activities or roles as a psychologist, and that either: (1) is unwelcome, is offensive, or creates a hostile workplace environment, and the psychologist knows or is told this; or (2) is sufficiently severe or intense to be abusive to a reasonable person in the context. Sexual harassment can consist of a single intense or severe act or of multiple persistent or pervasive acts.

b. Psychologists accord sexual-harassment complainants and respondents dignity and respect. Psychologists do not participate in denying a person academic admittance or advancement, employment, tenure, or promotion, based solely upon their having made, or their being the subject of, sexual-harassment charges. This does not preclude taking action based upon the outcome of such proceedings or consideration of other appropriate information.

1.12 Other Harassment

Psychologists do not knowingly engage in behavior that is harassing or demeaning to persons with whom they interact in their work based on factors such as those persons' age, gender, race, ethnicity, national origin, religion, sexual orientation, disability, language, or socioeconomic status.

1.13 Personal Problems and Conflicts

a. Psychologists recognize that their personal problems and conflicts may interfere with their effectiveness. Accordingly, they refrain from undertaking an activity when they know or should know that their personal problems are likely to lead to harm to a patient, client, colleague, student, research participant, or other person to whom they may owe a professional or scientific obligation.

b. In addition, psychologists have an obligation to be alert to signs of, and to obtain assistance for, their personal problems at an early stage, in order to prevent significantly impaired performance.

c. When psychologists become aware of personal problems that may interfere with their performing work-related duties adequately, they take appropriate measures, such as obtaining professional consultation or assistance, and determine whether they should limit, suspend, or terminate their work-related duties.

1.14 Avoiding Harm
Psychologists take reasonable steps to avoid harming their patients or clients, research participants, students, and others with whom they work, and minimize harm where it is foreseeable and unavoidable.

1.15 Misuse of Psychologists' Influence
Because psychologists' scientific and professional judgments and actions may affect the lives of others, they are alert to and guard against personal, financial, social, organizational, or political factors that might lead to misuse of their influence.

1.16 Misuse of Psychologists' Work
a. Psychologists do not participate in activities in which it appears likely that their skills or data will be misused by others, unless corrective mechanisms are available. (See also Standard 7.04, Truthfulness and Candor.)

b. If psychologists learn of misuse or misrepresentation of their work, they take reasonable steps to correct or minimize the misuse or misrepresentation.

1.17 Multiple Relationships
a. In many communities and situations, it may not be feasible or reasonable for psychologists to avoid social or other nonprofessional contacts with persons such as patients, clients, students, supervisees, or research participants. Psychologists must always be sensitive to the potential harmful effects of other contacts on their work and on those persons with whom they deal. A psychologist refrains from entering into or promising another personal, scientific, professional, financial, or other relationship with such persons if it appears likely that such a relationship reasonably might impair the psychologist's objectivity or otherwise interfere with the psychologist's effectively performing his or her functions as a psychologist, or might harm or exploit the other party.

b. Likewise, whenever feasible, a psychologist refrains from taking on professional or scientific obligations when preexisting relationships would create a risk of such harm.

c. If a psychologist finds that, due to unforeseen factors, a potentially harmful multiple relationship has arisen, the psychologist attempts to resolve it with due regard for the best interests of the affected person and maximal compliance with the Ethics Code.

1.18 Barter (with Patients or Clients)
Psychologists ordinarily refrain from accepting goods, services, or other nonmonetary remuneration from patients or clients in return for psychological services because such arrange-

ments create inherent potential for conflicts, exploitation, and distortion of the professional relationship. A psychologist may participate in bartering only if (1) it is not clinically contraindicated, and (2) the relationship is not exploitative. (See also Standards 1.17, Multiple Relationships, and 1.25, Fees and Financial Arrangements.)

1.19 Exploitative Relationships

a. Psychologists do not exploit persons over whom they have supervisory, evaluative, or other authority such as students, supervisees, employees, research participants, and clients or patients. (See also Standards 4.05–4.07 regarding sexual involvement with clients or patients.)

b. Psychologists do not engage in sexual relationships with students or supervisees in training over whom the psychologist has evaluative or direct authority, because such relationships are so likely to impair judgment or be exploitative.

1.20 Consultations and Referrals

a. Psychologists arrange for appropriate consultations and referrals based principally on the best interests of their patients or clients, with appropriate consent, and subject to other relevant considerations, including applicable law and contractual obligations. (See also Standards 5.01, Discussing the Limits of Confidentiality, and 5.06, Consultations.)

b. When indicated and professionally appropriate, psychologists cooperate with other professionals in order to serve their patients or clients effectively and appropriately.

c. Psychologists' referral practices are consistent with law.

1.21 Third-Party Requests for Services

a. When a psychologist agrees to provide services to a person or entity at the request of a third party, the psychologist clarifies to the extent feasible, at the outset of the service, the nature of the relationship with each party. This clarification includes the role of the psychologist (such as therapist, organizational consultant, diagnostician, or expert witness), the probable uses of the services provided or the information obtained, and the fact that there may be limits to confidentiality.

b. If there is a foreseeable risk of the psychologist's being called upon to perform conflicting roles because of the involvement of a third party, the psychologist clarifies the nature and direction of his or her responsibilities, keeps all parties appropriately informed as matters develop, and resolves the situation in accordance with this Ethics Code.

1.22 Delegation to and Supervision of Subordinates

a. Psychologists delegate to their employees, supervisees, and research assistants only those responsibilities that such persons can reasonably be expected to perform competently, on the basis of their education, training, or experience, either independently or with the level of supervision being provided.

b. Psychologists provide proper training and supervision to their employees or supervisees and take reasonable steps to see that such persons perform services responsibly, competently, and ethically.

c. If institutional policies, procedures, or practices prevent fulfillment of this obligation, psychologists attempt to modify their role or to correct the situation to the extent feasible.

1.23 Documentation of Professional and Scientific Work

a. Psychologists appropriately document their professional and scientific work in order to facilitate provision of services later by them or by other professionals, to ensure accountability, and to meet other requirements of institutions or the law.

b. When psychologists have reason to believe that records of their professional services will be used in legal proceedings involving recipients of or participants in their work, they have a responsibility to create and maintain documentation in the kind of detail and quality that would be consistent with reasonable scrutiny in an adjudicative forum. (See also Standard 7.01, Professionalism, under Forensic Activities.)

1.24 Records and Data

Psychologists create, maintain, disseminate, store, retain, and dispose of records and data relating to their research, practice, and other work in accordance with law and in a manner that permits compliance with the requirements of this Ethics Code. (See also Standard 5.04, Maintenance of Records.)

1.25 Fees and Financial Arrangements

a. As early as is feasible in a professional or scientific relationship, the psychologist and the patient, client, or other appropriate recipient of psychological services reach an agreement specifying the compensation and the billing arrangements.

b. Psychologists do not exploit recipients of services or payors with respect to fees.

c. Psychologists' fee practices are consistent with law.

d. Psychologists do not misrepresent their fees.

e. If limitations to services can be anticipated because of limitations in financing, this is discussed with the patient, client, or other appropriate recipient of services as early as is feasible. (See also Standard 4.08, Interruption of Services.)

f. If the patient, client, or other recipient of services does not pay for services as agreed, and if the psychologist wishes to use collection agencies or legal measures to collect the fees, the psychologist first informs the person that such measures will be taken and provides that person an opportunity to make prompt payment. (See also Standard 5.11, Withholding Records for Nonpayment.)

1.26 Accuracy in Reports to Payors and Funding Sources

In their reports to payors for services or sources of research funding, psychologists accurately state the nature of the research or service provided, the fees or charges, and where applicable, the identity of the provider, the findings, and the diagnosis. (See also Standard 5.05, Disclosures.)

1.27 Referrals and Fees

When a psychologist pays, receives payment from, or divides fees with another professional other than in an employer-employee relationship, the payment to each is based on the services (clinical, consultative, administrative, or other) provided and is not based on the referral itself.

2. Evaluation, Assessment, or Intervention

2.01 Evaluation, Diagnosis, and Interventions in Professional Context

a. Psychologists perform evaluations, diagnostic services, or interventions only within the context of a defined professional relationship. (See also Standard 1.03, Professional and Scientific Relationship.)

b. Psychologists' assessments, recommendations, reports, and psychological diagnostic or evaluative statements are based on information and techniques (including personal interviews of the individual when appropriate) sufficient to provide appropriate substantiation for their findings. (See also Standard 7.02, Forensic Assessments.)

2.02 Competence and Appropriate Use of Assessments and Interventions

a. Psychologists who develop, administer, score, interpret, or use psychological assessment techniques, interviews, tests, or instruments do so in a manner and for purposes that are appropriate in light of the research on or evidence of the usefulness and proper application of the techniques.

b. Psychologists refrain from misuse of assessment techniques, interventions, results, and interpretations and take reasonable steps to prevent others from misusing the information these techniques provide. This includes refraining from releasing raw test results or raw data to persons, other than to patients or clients as appropriate, who are not qualified to use such information. (See also Standards 1.02, Relationship of Ethics and Law, and 1.04, Boundaries of Competence.)

2.03 Test Construction

Psychologists who develop and conduct research with tests and other assessment techniques use scientific procedures and current professional knowledge for test design, standardization, validation, reduction or elimination of bias, and recommendations for use.

2.04 Use of Assessment in General and with Special Populations

a. Psychologists who perform interventions or administer, score, interpret, or use assessment techniques are familiar with the reliability, validation, and related standardization or outcome studies of, and proper applications and uses of, the techniques they use.

b. Psychologists recognize limits to the certainty with which diagnoses, judgments, or predictions can be made about individuals.

c. Psychologists attempt to identify situations in which particular interventions or assessment techniques or norms may not be applicable or may require adjustment in administration or interpretation because of factors such as individuals' gender, age, race, ethnicity, national origin, religion, sexual orientation, disability, language, or socioeconomic status.

2.05 Interpreting Assessment Results

When interpreting assessment results, including automated interpretations, psychologists take into account the various test factors and characteristics of the person being assessed that might affect psychologists' judgments or reduce the accuracy of their interpretations. They indicate any significant reservations they have about the accuracy or limitations of their interpretations.

2.06 Unqualified Persons

Psychologists do not promote the use of psychological assessment techniques by unqualified persons. (See also Standard 1.22, Delegation to and Supervision of Subordinates.)

2.07 Obsolete Tests and Outdated Test Results

a. Psychologists do not base their assessment or intervention decisions or recommendations on data or test results that are outdated for the current purpose.

b. Similarly, psychologists do not base such decisions or recommendations on tests and measures that are obsolete and not useful for the current purpose.

2.08 Test Scoring and Interpretation Services

a. Psychologists who offer assessment or scoring procedures to other professionals accurately describe the purpose, norms, validity, reliability, and applications of the procedures and any special qualifications applicable to their use.

b. Psychologists select scoring and interpretation services (including automated services) on the basis of evidence of the validity of the program and procedures as well as on other appropriate considerations.

c. Psychologists retain appropriate responsibility for the appropriate application, interpretation, and use of assessment instruments, whether they score and interpret such tests themselves or use automated or other services.

2.09 Explaining Assessment Results

Unless the nature of the relationship is clearly explained to the person being assessed in advance and precludes provision of an explanation of results (such as in some organizational consulting, preemployment or security screenings, and forensic evaluations), psychologists ensure that an explanation of the results is provided using language that is reasonably understandable to the person assessed or to another legally authorized person on behalf of the client. Regardless of whether the scoring and interpretation are done by the psychologist, by assistants, or by automated or other outside services, psychologists take reasonable steps to ensure that appropriate explanations of results are given.

2.10 Maintaining Test Security

Psychologists make reasonable efforts to maintain the integrity and security of tests and other assessment techniques consistent with law, contractual obligations, and in a manner that permits compliance with the requirements of this Ethics Code. (See also Standard 1.02, Relationship of Ethics and Law.)

3. Advertising and Other Public Statements

3.01 Definition of Public Statements

Psychologists comply with this Ethics Code in public statements relating to their professional services, products, or publications or to the field of psychology. Public statements include but are not limited to paid or unpaid advertising, brochures, printed matter, directory listings, personal resumes or curricula vitae, interviews or comments for use in media, statements in legal proceedings, lectures and public oral presentations, and published materials.

3.02 Statements by Others

a. Psychologists who engage others to create or place public statements that promote their professional practice, products, or activities retain professional responsibility for such statements.

b. In addition, psychologists make reasonable efforts to prevent others whom they do not control (such as employers, publishers, sponsors, organizational clients, and representatives of the print or broadcast media) from making deceptive statements concerning psychologists' practice or professional or scientific activities.

c. If psychologists learn of deceptive statements about their work made by others, psychologists make reasonable efforts to correct such statements.

d. Psychologist do not compensate employees of press, radio, television, or other communication media in return for publicity in a news item.

e. A paid advertisement relating to the psychologist's activities must be identified as such, unless it is already apparent from the context.

3.03 Avoidance of False or Deceptive Statements

a. Psychologists do not make public statements that are false, deceptive, misleading, or fraudulent, either because of what they state, convey, or suggest or because of what they omit, concerning their research, practice, or other work activities or those of persons or organizations with which they are affiliated. As examples (and not in limitation) of this standard, psychologists do not make false or deceptive statements concerning (1) their training, experience, or competence; (2) their academic degrees; (3) their credentials; (4) their institutional or association affiliations; (5) their services; (6) the scientific or clinical basis for, or results or degree of success of, their services; (7) their fees; or (8) their publications or research findings. (See also Standards 6.15, Deception in Research, and 6.18, Providing Participants with Information About the Study.)

b. Psychologists claim as credentials for their psychological work, only degrees that (1) were earned from a regionally accredited educational institution or (2) were the basis for psychology licensure by the state in which they practice.

3.04 Media Presentations

When psychologists provide advice or comment by means of public lectures, demonstrations, radio or television programs, prerecorded tapes, printed articles, mailed material, or other media, they take reasonable precautions to ensure that (1) the statements are based on appropriate psychological literature and practice, (2) the statements are otherwise consistent with this Ethics Code, and (3) the recipients of the information are not encouraged to infer that a relationship has been established with them personally.

3.05 Testimonials

Psychologists do not solicit testimonials from current psychotherapy clients or patients or other persons who because of their particular circumstances are vulnerable to undue influence.

3.06 In-Person Solicitation

Psychologists do not engage, directly or through agents, in uninvited in-person solicitation of business from actual or potential psychotherapy patients or clients or other persons who because of their particular circumstances are vulnerable to undue influence. However, this does not preclude attempting to implement appropriate collateral contacts with significant others for the purpose of benefiting an already engaged therapy patient.

4. Therapy

4.01 Structuring the Relationship
a. Psychologists discuss with clients or patients as early as is feasible in the therapeutic relationship appropriate issues, such as the nature and anticipated course of therapy, fees, and confidentiality. (See also Standards 1.25, Fees and Financial Arrangements, and 5.01, Discussing the Limits of Confidentiality.)

b. When the psychologist's work with clients or patients will be supervised, the above discussion includes that fact, and the name of the supervisor, when the supervisor has legal responsibility for the case.

c. When the therapist is a student intern, the client or patient is informed of that fact.

d. Psychologists make reasonable efforts to answer patients' questions and to avoid apparent misunderstandings about therapy. Whenever possible, psychologists provide oral and/or written information, using language that is reasonably understandable to the patient or client.

4.02 Informed Consent to Therapy
a. Psychologists obtain appropriate informed consent to therapy or related procedures, using language that is reasonably understandable to participants. The content of informed consent will vary depending on many circumstances; however, informed consent generally implies that the person (1) has the capacity to consent, (2) has been informed of significant information concerning the procedure, (3) has freely and without undue influence expressed consent, and (4) consent has been appropriately documented.

b. When persons are legally incapable of giving informed consent, psychologists obtain informed permission from a legally authorized person, if such substitute consent is permitted by law.

c. In addition, psychologists (1) inform those persons who are legally incapable of giving informed consent about the proposed interventions in a manner commensurate with the persons' psychological capacities, (2) seek their assent to those interventions, and (3) consider such persons' preferences and best interests.

4.03 Couple and Family Relationships
a. When a psychologist agrees to provide services to several persons who have a relationship (such as husband and wife or parents and children), the psychologist attempts to clarify at the outset (1) which of the individuals are patients or clients and (2) the relationship the psychologist will have with each person. This clarification includes the role of the psychologist and the probable uses of the services provided or the information obtained. (See also Standard 5.01, Discussing the Limits of Confidentiality.)

b. As soon as it becomes apparent that the psychologist may be called on to perform potentially conflicting roles (such as marital counselor to husband and wife, and then witness for one party in a divorce proceeding), the psychologist attempts to clarify and adjust, or withdraw from, roles appropriately. (See also Standard 7.03, Clarification of Role, under Forensic Activities.)

4.04 Providing Mental Health Services to Those Served by Others

In deciding whether to offer or provide services to those already receiving mental health services elsewhere, psychologists carefully consider the treatment issues and the potential patient's or client's welfare. The psychologist discusses these issues with the patient or client, or another legally authorized person on behalf of the client, in order to minimize the risk of confusion and conflict, consults with the other service providers when appropriate, and proceeds with caution and sensitivity to the therapeutic issues.

4.05 Sexual Intimacies with Current Patients or Clients

Psychologists do not engage in sexual intimacies with current patients or clients.

4.06 Therapy with Former Sexual Partners

Psychologists do not accept as therapy patients or clients persons with whom they have engaged in sexual intimacies.

4.07 Sexual Intimacies with Former Therapy Patients

a. Psychologists do not engage in sexual intimacies with a former therapy patient or client for at least two years after cessation or termination of professional services.

b. Because sexual intimacies with a former therapy patient or client are so frequently harmful to the patient or client, and because such intimacies undermine public confidence in the psychology profession and thereby deter the public's use of needed services, psychologists do not engage in sexual intimacies with former therapy patients and clients even after a two-year interval except in the most unusual circumstances. The psychologist who engages in such activity after the two years following cessation or termination of treatment bears the burden of demonstrating that there has been no exploitation, in light of all relevant factors, including (1) the amount of time that has passed since therapy terminated, (2) the nature and duration of the therapy, (3) the circumstances of termination, (4) the patient's or client's personal history, (5) the patient's or client's current mental status, (6) the likelihood of adverse impact on the patient or client and others, and (7) any statements or actions made by the therapist during the course of therapy suggesting or inviting the possibility of a posttermination sexual or romantic relationship with the patient or client. (See also Standard 1.17, Multiple Relationships.)

4.08 Interruption of Services

a. Psychologists make reasonable efforts to plan for facilitating care in the event that psychological services are interrupted by factors such as the psychologist's illness, death, unavailability, or relocation or by the client's relocation or financial limitations. (See also Standard 5.09, Preserving Records and Data.)

b. When entering into employment or contractual relationships, psychologists provide for orderly and appropriate resolution of responsibility for patient or client care in the event that the employment or contractual relationship ends, with paramount consideration given to the welfare of the patient or client.

4.09 Terminating the Professional Relationship

a. Psychologists do not abandon patients or clients. (See also Standard 1.25e, under Fees and Financial Arrangements.)

b. Psychologists terminate a professional relationship when it becomes reasonably clear that the patient or client no longer needs the service, is not benefiting, or is being harmed by continued service.

c. Prior to termination for whatever reason, except where precluded by the patient's or client's conduct, the psychologist discusses the patient's or client's views and needs, provides appropriate pretermination counseling, suggests alternative service providers as appropriate, and takes other reasonable steps to facilitate transfer of responsibility to another provider if the patient or client needs one immediately.

5. Privacy and Confidentiality

These Standards are potentially applicable to the professional and scientific activities of all psychologists.

5.01 Discussing the Limits of Confidentiality
a. Psychologists discuss with persons and organizations with whom they establish a scientific or professional relationship (including, to the extent feasible, minors and their legal representatives) (1) the relevant limitations on confidentiality, including limitations where applicable in group, marital, and family therapy or in organizational consulting, and (2) the foreseeable uses of the information generated through their services.

b. Unless it is not feasible or is contraindicated, the discussion of confidentiality occurs at the outset of the relationship and thereafter as new circumstances may warrant.

c. Permission for electronic recording of interviews is secured from clients and patients.

5.02 Maintaining Confidentiality
Psychologists have a primary obligation and take reasonable precautions to respect the confidentiality rights of those with whom they work or consult, recognizing that confidentiality may be established by law, institutional rules, or professional or scientific relationships. (See also Standard 6.26, Professional Reviewers.)

5.03 Minimizing Intrusions on Privacy
a. In order to minimize intrusions on privacy, psychologists include in written and oral reports, consultations, and the like only information germane to the purpose for which the communication is made.

b. Psychologists discuss confidential information obtained in clinical or consulting relationships, or evaluative data concerning patients, individual or organizational clients, students, research participants, supervisees, and employees, only for appropriate scientific or professional purposes and only with persons clearly concerned with such matters.

5.04 Maintenance of Records
Psychologists maintain appropriate confidentiality in creating, storing, accessing, transferring, and disposing of records under their control, whether these are written, automated, or in any other medium. Psychologists maintain and dispose of records in accordance with law and in a manner that permits compliance with the requirements of this Ethics Code.

5.05 Disclosures
a. Psychologists disclose confidential information without the consent of the individual only as mandated by law, or where permitted by law for a valid purpose, such as (1) to provide needed professional services to the patient or the individual or organizational client, (2) to obtain appropriate professional consultations, (3) to protect the patient or client or others

from harm, or (4) to obtain payment for services, in which instance disclosure is limited to the minimum that is necessary to achieve the purpose.

b. Psychologists also may disclose confidential information with the appropriate consent of the patient or the individual or organizational client (or of another legally authorized person on behalf of the patient or client), unless prohibited by law.

5.06 Consultations

When consulting with colleagues, (1) psychologists do not share confidential information that reasonably could lead to the identification of a patient, client, research participant, or other person or organization with whom they have a confidential relationship unless they have obtained the prior consent of the person or organization or the disclosure cannot be avoided, and (2) they share information only to the extent necessary to achieve the purposes of the consultation. (See also Standard 5.02, Maintaining Confidentiality.)

5.07 Confidential Information in Databases

a. If confidential information concerning recipients of psychological services is to be entered into databases or systems of records available to persons whose access has not been consented to by the recipient, then psychologists use coding or other techniques to avoid the inclusion of personal identifiers.

b. If a research protocol approved by an institutional review board or similar body requires the inclusion of personal identifiers, such identifiers are deleted before the information is made accessible to persons other than those of whom the subject was advised.

c. If such deletion is not feasible, then before psychologists transfer such data to others or review such data collected by others, they take reasonable steps to determine that appropriate consent of personally identifiable individuals has been obtained.

5.08 Use of Confidential Information for Didactic or Other Purposes

a. Psychologists do not disclose in their writings, lectures, or other public media, confidential, personally identifiable information concerning their patients, individual or organizational clients, students, research participants, or other recipients of their services that they obtained during the course of their work, unless the person or organization has consented in writing or unless there is other ethical or legal authorization for doing so.

b. Ordinarily, in such scientific and professional presentations, psychologists disguise confidential information concerning such persons or organizations so that they are not individually identifiable to others and so that discussions do not cause harm to subjects who might identify themselves.

5.09 Preserving Records and Data

A psychologist makes plans in advance so that confidentiality of records and data is protected in the event of the psychologist's death, incapacity, or withdrawal from the position or practice.

5.10 Ownership of Records and Data

Recognizing that ownership of records and data is governed by legal principles, psychologists take reasonable and lawful steps so that records and data remain available to the extent needed to serve the best interests of patients, individual or organizational clients, research participants, or appropriate others.

5.11 Withholding Records for Nonpayment
Psychologists may not withhold records under their control that are requested and immi-
nently needed for a patient's or client's treatment solely because payment has not been received, except as otherwise provided by law.

6. Teaching, Training Supervision, Research, and Publishing

6.01 Design of Education and Training Programs
Psychologists who are responsible for education and training programs seek to ensure that the
programs are competently designed, provide the proper experiences, and meet the requirements for licensure, certification, or other goals for which claims are made by the program.

6.02 Descriptions of Education and Training Programs
a. Psychologists responsible for education and training programs seek to ensure that there is
a current and accurate description of the program content, training goals and objectives, and
requirements that must be met for satisfactory completion of the program. This information
must be made readily available to all interested parties.

b. Psychologists seek to ensure that statements concerning their course outlines are accurate
and not misleading, particularly regarding the subject matter to be covered, bases for evaluating progress, and the nature of course experiences. (See also Standard 3.03, Avoidance of
False or Deceptive Statements.)

c. To the degree to which they exercise control, psychologists responsible for announcements, catalogs, brochures, or advertisements describing workshops, seminars, or other non-
degree-granting educational programs ensure that they accurately describe the audience for
which the program is intended, the educational objectives, the presenters, and the fees involved.

6.03 Accuracy and Objectivity in Teaching
a. When engaged in teaching or training, psychologists present psychological information
accurately and with a reasonable degree of objectivity.

b. When engaged in teaching or training, psychologists recognize the power they hold over
students or supervisees and therefore make reasonable efforts to avoid engaging in conduct
that is personally demeaning to students or supervisees. (See also Standards 1.09, Respecting
Other, and 1.12, Other Harassment.

6.04 Limitation on Teaching
Psychologists do not teach the use of techniques or procedures that require specialized
training, licensure, or expertise, including but not limited to hypnosis, biofeedback, and pro-
jective techniques, to individuals who lack the prerequisite training, legal scope of practice,
or expertise.

6.05 Assessing Student and Supervisee Performance
a. In academic and supervisory relationships, psychologists establish an appropriate process
for providing feedback to students and supervisees.

b. Psychologists evaluate students and supervisees on the basis of their actual performance
on relevant and established program requirements.

6.06 Planning Research

a. Psychologists design, conduct, and report research in accordance with recognized standards of scientific competence and ethical research.

b. Psychologists plan their research so as to minimize the possibility that results will be misleading.

c. In planning research, psychologists consider its ethical acceptability under the Ethics Code. If an ethical issue is unclear, psychologists seek to resolve the issue through consultation with institutional review boards, animal care and use committees, peer consultations, or other proper mechanisms.

d. Psychologists take reasonable steps to implement appropriate protections for the rights and welfare of human participants, other persons affected by the research, and the welfare of animal subjects.

6.07 Responsibility

a. Psychologists conduct research competently and with due concern for the dignity and welfare of the participants.

b. Psychologists are responsible for the ethical conduct of research conducted by them or by others under their supervision or control.

c. Researchers and assistants are permitted to perform only those tasks for which they are appropriately trained and prepared.

d. As part of the process of development and implementation of research projects, psychologists consult those with expertise concerning any special population under investigation or most likely to be affected.

6.08 Compliance with Law and Standards

Psychologists plan and conduct research in a manner consistent with federal and state law and regulations, as well as professional standards governing the conduct of research, and particularly those standards governing research with human participants and animal subjects.

6.09 Institutional Approval

Psychologists obtain from host institutions or organizations appropriate approval prior to conducting research, and they provide accurate information about their research proposals. They conduct the research in accordance with the approved research protocol.

6.10 Research Responsibilities

Prior to conducting research (except research involving only anonymous surveys, naturalistic observations, or similar research), psychologists enter into an agreement with participants that clarifies the nature of the research and the responsibilities of each party.

6.11 Informed Consent to Research

a. Psychologists use language that is reasonably understandable to research participants in obtaining their appropriate informed consent (except as provided in Standard 6.12, Dispensing with Informed Consent). Such informed consent is appropriately documented.

b. Using language that is reasonably understandable to participants, psychologists inform participants of the nature of the research; they inform participants that they are free to participate or to decline to participate or to withdraw from the research; they explain the foreseeable consequences of declining or withdrawing; they inform participants of significant factors that may be expected to influence their willingness to participate (such as risks, discomfort, adverse effects, or limitations on confidentiality, except as provided in Standard 6.15, Deception in Research); and they explain other aspects about which the prospective participants inquire.

c. When psychologists conduct research with individuals such as students or subordinates, psychologists take special care to protect the prospective participants from adverse consequences of declining or withdrawing from participation.

d. When research participation is a course requirement or opportunity for extra credit, the prospective participant is given the choice of equitable alternative activities.

e. For persons who are legally incapable of giving informed consent, psychologists nevertheless (1) provide an appropriate explanation, (2) obtain the participant's assent, and (3) obtain appropriate permission from a legally authorized person, if such substitute consent is permitted by law.

6.12 Dispensing with Informed Consent

Before determining that planned research (such as research involving only anonymous questionnaires, naturalistic observations, or certain kinds of archival research) does not require the informed consent of research participants, psychologists consider applicable regulations and institutional review board requirements, and they consult with colleagues as appropriate.

6.13 Informed Consent in Research Filming or Recording

Psychologists obtain informed consent from research participants prior to filming or recording them in any form, unless the research involves simply naturalistic observations in public places and it is not anticipated that the recording will be used in a manner that could cause personal identification or harm.

6.14 Offering Inducements for Research Participants

a. In offering professional services as an inducement to obtain research participants, psychologists make clear the nature of the services, as well as the risks, obligations, and limitations. (See also Standard 1.18, Barter [with Patients or Clients].)

b. Psychologists do not offer excessive or inappropriate financial or other inducements to obtain research participants, particularly when it might tend to coerce participation.

6.15 Deception in Research

a. Psychologists do not conduct a study involving deception unless they have determined that the use of deceptive techniques is justified by the study's prospective scientific, educational, or applied value and that equally effective alternative procedures that do not use deception are not feasible.

b. Psychologists never deceive research participants about significant aspects that would affect their willingness to participate, such as physical risks, discomfort, or unpleasant emotional experiences.

c. Any other deception that is an integral feature of the design and conduct of an experiment must be explained to participants as early as is feasible, preferably at the conclusion of their participation, but no later than at the conclusion of the research. (See also Standard 6.18, Providing Participants with Information About the Study.)

6.16 Sharing and Utilizing Data
Psychologists inform research participants of their anticipated sharing or further use of personally identifiable research data and of the possibility of unanticipated future uses.

6.17 Minimizing Invasiveness
In conducting research, psychologists interfere with the participants or milieu from which data are collected only in a manner that is warranted by an appropriate research design and that is consistent with psychologists' roles as scientific investigators.

6.18 Providing Participants with Information About the Study
a. Psychologists provide a prompt opportunity for participants to obtain appropriate information about the nature, results, and conclusions of the research, and psychologists attempt to correct any misconceptions that participants may have.

b. If scientific or humane values justify delaying or withholding this information, psychologists take reasonable measures to reduce the risk of harm.

6.19 Honoring Commitments
Psychologists take reasonable measures to honor all commitments they have made to research participants.

6.20 Care and Use of Animals in Research
a. Psychologists who conduct research involving animals treat them humanely.

b. Psychologists acquire, care for, use, and dispose of animals in compliance with current federal, state, and local laws and regulations, and with professional standards.

c. Psychologists trained in research methods and experienced in the care of laboratory animals supervise all procedures involving animals and are responsible for ensuring appropriate consideration of their comfort, health, and humane treatment.

d. Psychologists ensure that all individuals using animals under their supervision have received instruction in research methods and in the care, maintenance, and handling of the species being used, to the extent appropriate to their role.

e. Responsibilities and activities of individuals assisting in a research project are consistent with their respective competencies.

f. Psychologists make reasonable efforts to minimize the discomfort, infection, illness, and pain of animal subjects.

g. A procedure subjecting animals to pain, stress, or privation is used only when an alternative procedure is unavailable and the goal is justified by its prospective scientific, educational, or applied value.

h. Surgical procedures are performed under appropriate anesthesia; techniques to avoid infection and minimize pain are followed during and after surgery.

i. When it is appropriate that the animal's life be terminated, it is done rapidly, with an effort to minimize pain, and in accordance with accepted procedures.

6.21 Reporting of Results
a. Psychologists do not fabricate data or falsify results in their publications.

b. If psychologists discover significant errors in their published data, they take reasonable steps to correct such errors in a correction, retraction, erratum, or other appropriate publication means.

6.22 Plagiarism

Psychologists do not present substantial portions or elements of another's work or data as their own, even if the other work or data source is cited occasionally.

6.23 Publication Credit

a. Psychologists take responsibility and credit, including authorship credit, only for work they have actually performed or to which they have contributed.

b. Principal authorship and other publication credits accurately reflect the relative scientific or professional contributions of the individuals involved, regardless of their relative status. Mere possession of an institutional position, such as Department Chair, does not justify authorship credit. Minor contributions to the research or to the writing for publications are appropriately acknowledged, such as in footnotes or in an introductory statement.

c. A student is usually listed as principal author on any multiple-authored article that is substantially based on the student's dissertation or thesis.

6.24 Duplicate Publication of Data

Psychologists do not publish, as original data, data that have been previously published. This does not preclude republishing data when they are accompanied by proper acknowledgment.

6.25 Sharing Data

After research results are published, psychologists do not withhold the data on which their conclusions are based from other competent professionals who seek to verify the substantive claims through reanalysis and who intend to use such data only for that purpose, provided that the confidentiality of the participants can be protected and unless legal rights concerning proprietary data preclude their release.

6.26 Professional Reviewers

Psychologists who review material submitted for publication, grant, or other research proposal review respect the confidentiality of and the proprietary rights in such information of those who submitted it.

7. Forensic Activities

7.01 Professionalism

Psychologists who perform forensic functions, such as assessments, interviews, consultations, reports, or expert testimony, must comply with all other provisions of this Ethics Code to the extent that they apply to such activities. In addition, psychologists base their forensic work on appropriate knowledge of and competence in the areas underlying such work, including specialized knowledge concerning special populations. (See also Standards 1.06, Basis for Scientific and Professional Judgments; 1.08, Human Differences; 1.15, Misuse of Psychologists' Influence; and 1.23, Documentation of Professional and Scientific Work.)

7.02 Forensic Assessments

a. Psychologists' forensic assessments, recommendations, and reports are based on information and techniques (including personal interviews of the individual, when appropriate) sufficient to provide appropriate substantiation for their findings. (See also Standards 1.03, Professional and Scientific Relationship; 1.23, Documentation of Professional and Scientific

Work; 2.01, Evaluation, Diagnosis, and Interventions in Professional Context; and 2.05, Interpreting Assessment Results.)

b. Except as noted in c, below, psychologists provide written or oral forensic reports or testimony of the psychological characteristics of an individual only after they have conducted an examination of the individual adequate to support their statements or conclusions.

c. When, despite reasonable efforts, such an examination is not feasible, psychologists clarify the impact of their limited information on the reliability and validity of their reports and testimony, and they appropriately limit the nature and extent of their conclusions or recommendations.

7.03 Clarification of Role
In most circumstances, psychologists avoid performing multiple and potentially conflicting roles in forensic matters. When psychologists may be called on to serve in more than one role in a legal proceeding—for example, as consultant or expert for one party or for the court and as a fact witness—they clarify role expectations and the extent of confidentiality in advance to the extent feasible, and thereafter as changes occur, in order to avoid compromising their professional judgment and objectivity and in order to avoid misleading others regarding their role.

7.04 Truthfulness and Candor
a. In forensic testimony and reports, psychologists testify truthfully, honestly, and candidly and, consistent with applicable legal procedures, describe fairly the bases for their testimony and conclusions.

b. Whenever necessary to avoid misleading, psychologists acknowledge the limits of their data or conclusions.

7.05 Prior Relationships
A prior professional relationship with a party does not preclude psychologists from testifying as fact witnesses or from testifying to their services to the extent permitted by applicable law. Psychologists appropriately take into account ways in which the prior relationship might affect their professional objectivity or opinions and disclose the potential conflict to the relevant parties.

7.06 Compliance with Law and Rules
In performing forensic roles, psychologists are reasonably familiar with the rules governing their roles. Psychologists are aware of the occasionally competing demands placed upon them by these principles and the requirements of the court system, and attempt to resolve these conflicts by making known their commitment to this Ethics Code and taking steps to resolve the conflict in a responsible manner. (See also Standard 1.02, Relationship of Ethics and Law.)

8. Resolving Ethical Issues

8.01 Familiarity with Ethics Code
Psychologists have an obligation to be familiar with this Ethics Code, other applicable ethics codes, and their application to psychologists' work. Lack of awareness or misunderstanding of an ethical standard is not itself a defense to a charge of unethical conduct.

8.02 Confronting Ethical Issues

When a psychologist is uncertain whether a particular situation or course of action would violate this Ethics Code, the psychologist ordinarily consults with other psychologists knowledgeable about ethical issues, with state or national psychology ethics committees, or with other appropriate authorities in order to choose a proper response.

8.03 Conflicts Between Ethics and Organizational Demands

If the demands of an organization with which psychologists are affiliated conflict with this Ethics Code, psychologists clarify the nature of the conflict, make known their commitment to the Ethics Code, and to the extent feasible, seek to resolve the conflict in a way that permits the fullest adherence to the Ethics Code.

8.04 Informal Resolution of Ethical Violations

When psychologists believe that there may have been an ethical violation by another psychologist, they attempt to resolve the issue by bringing it to the attention of that individual if an informal resolution appears appropriate and the intervention does not violate any confidentiality rights that may be involved.

8.05 Reporting Ethical Violations

If an apparent ethical violation is not appropriate for informal resolution under Standard 8.04 or is not resolved properly in that fashion, psychologists take further action appropriate to the situation, unless such action conflicts with confidentiality rights in ways that cannot be resolved. Such action might include referral to state or national committees on professional ethics or to state licensing boards.

8.06 Cooperating with Ethics Committees

Psychologists cooperate in ethics investigations, proceedings, and resulting requirements of the APA or any affiliated state psychological association to which they belong. In doing so, they make reasonable efforts to resolve any issues as to confidentiality. Failure to cooperate is itself an ethics violation.

8.07 Improper Complaints

Psychologists do not file or encourage the filing of ethics complaints that are frivolous and are intended to harm the respondent rather than to protect the public.

Appendix C

National Association of Social Workers, Code of Ethics

Overview

The National Association of Social Workers Code of Ethics is intended to serve as a guide to the everyday professional conduct of social workers. This code includes four sections. Section one, "Preamble," summarizes the social work profession's mission and core values. Section two, "Purpose of the Code of Ethics," provides an overview of the Code's main functions and a brief guide for dealing with ethical issues or dilemmas in social work practice. Section three, "Ethical Principles," presents broad ethical principles, based on social work's core values, that inform social work practice. The final section, "Ethical Standards," includes specific ethical standards to guide social workers' conduct and to provide a basis for adjudication.

Preamble

The primary mission of the social work profession is to enhance human well-being and help meet basic human needs of all people, with particular attention to the needs and empowerment of people who are vulnerable, oppressed, and living in poverty. An historic and defining feature of social work is the profession's focus on individual well-being in a social context and the well-being of society. Fundamental to social work is attention to the environmental forces that create, contribute to, and address problems in living.

Social workers promote social justice and social change with and on behalf of clients. "Clients" is used inclusively to refer to individuals, families, groups, organizations, and communities. Social workers are sensitive to cultural and ethnic diversity and strive to end discrimination, oppression, poverty, and other forms of social injustice. These activities may be in the form of direct practice, community organizing, supervision, consultation, administration, advocacy, social and political action, policy development and implementation, education, and research and evaluation. Social workers seek to enhance the capacity of people to address their own needs. Social workers also seek to promote the responsiveness of organizations, communities, and other social institutions to individuals' needs and social problems.

The mission of the social work profession is rooted in a set of core values. These core values, embraced by social workers throughout the profession's history, are the foundation of social work's unique purpose and perspective:

Service
Social justice
Dignity and worth of the person
Importance of human relationships
Integrity
Competence

The constellation of these core values reflect what is unique to the social work profession. Core values, and the principles which flow from them, must be balanced within the context and complexity of the human experience.

Purpose of the Code of Ethics

Professional ethics are at the core of social work. The profession has an obligation to articulate its basic values, ethical principles, and ethical standards. The NASW Code of Ethics sets forth values, principles, and standards to guide social workers' conduct. The code of ethics is relevant to all social workers and social work students, regardless of their professional functions, the settings in which they work, or the populations they serve.

This NASW Code of Ethics serves six purposes:

The code identifies core values on which social work's mission is based.

The code summarizes broad ethical principles that reflect the profession's core values and establishes a set of specific ethical standards that should be used to guide social work practice.

The code of ethics is designed to help social workers identify relevant considerations when professional obligations conflict or ethical uncertainties arise.

The code provides ethical standards to which the general public can hold the social work profession accountable.

The code socializes practitioners new to the field to social work's mission, values, ethical principles, and ethical standards.

The code articulates standards that the social work profession itself can use to assess whether social workers have engaged in unethical conduct. NASW has formal procedures to adjudicate ethics complaints filed against its members.[1] In subscribing to this code social workers are required to cooperate in its implementation, participate in NASW adjudication proceedings, and abide by any NASW disciplinary rulings or sanctions based on it.

This code offers a set of values, principles, and standards to guide decision making and conduct when ethical issues arise. It does not provide a set of rules that prescribe how social

[1]For information on NASW adjudication procedures, see NASW Procedures for the Adjudication of Grievances.

workers should act in all situations. Specific applications of the code must take into account the context in which it is being considered and the possibility of conflicts among the code's values, principles, and standards. Ethical responsibilities flow from all human relationships, from the personal and familial to the social and professional.

Further, the code of ethics does not specify which values, principles, and standards are most important and ought to outweigh others in instances when they conflict. Reasonable differences of opinion can and do exist among social workers with respect to the ways in which values, ethical principles, and ethical standards should be rank-ordered when they conflict. Ethical decision making in a given situation must apply the informed judgment of the individual social worker and should also consider how the issues would be judged in a peer review process where the ethical standards of the profession would be applied.

Ethical decision making is a process. There are many instances in social work where simple answers are not available to resolve complex ethical issues. Social workers should take into consideration all the values, principles, and standards in this code that are relevant to any situation in which ethical judgment is warranted. Social workers' decisions and actions should be consistent with the spirit as well as the letter of this code.

In addition to this code, there are many other sources of information about ethical thinking that may be useful. Social workers should consider ethical theory and principles generally, social work theory and research, laws, regulations, agency policies, and other relevant codes of ethics, recognizing that among codes of ethics social workers should consider the NASW Code of Ethics as their primary source. Social workers also should be aware of the impact on ethical decision making of their clients' and their own personal values, cultural and religious beliefs, and practices. They should be aware of any conflicts between personal and professional values and deal with them responsibly. For additional guidance social workers should consult relevant literature on professional ethics and ethical decision making, and seek appropriate consultation when faced with ethical dilemmas. This may involve consultation with an agency-based or social work organization's ethics committee, regulatory body, knowledgeable colleagues, supervisors, or legal counsel.

Instances may arise where social workers' ethical obligations conflict with agency policies, relevant laws or regulations. When such conflicts occur, social workers must make a responsible effort to resolve the conflict in a manner that is consistent with the values, principles, and standards expressed in this code. If a reasonable resolution of the conflict does not appear possible, social workers should seek proper consultation before making a decision.

This code of ethics is to be used by NASW and by other individuals, agencies, organizations, and bodies (such as licensing and regulatory boards, professional liability insurance providers, courts of law, agency boards of directors, government agencies, and other professional groups) that choose to adopt it or use it as a frame of reference. Violation of standards in this code does not automatically imply legal liability or violation of the law. Such determination can only be made in the context of legal and judicial proceedings. Alleged violations of the code would be subject to a peer review process. Such processes are generally separate from legal or administrative procedures and insulated from legal review or proceedings in order to allow the profession to counsel and/or discipline its own members.

A code of ethics cannot guarantee ethical behavior. Moreover, a code of ethics cannot resolve all ethical issues or disputes, or capture the richness and complexity involved in striving to make responsible choices within a moral community. Rather a code of ethics sets forth values, ethical principles and ethical standards to which professionals aspire and by which their actions can be judged. Socials workers' ethical behavior should result from their personal commitment to engage in ethical practice. This code reflects the commitment of all social workers to uphold the profession's values and to act ethically. Principles and standards must be applied by individuals of good character who discern moral questions and, in good faith, seek to make reliable ethical judgments.

Ethical Principles

The following broad ethical principles are based on social work's core values of: service, social justice, dignity and worth of the person, importance of human relationships, integrity, and competence. These principles set forth ideals to which all social workers should aspire.

Value: Service

Ethical Principle: Social workers' primary goal is to help people in need and to address social problems.
Social workers elevate service to others above self-interest. Social workers draw on their knowledge, values, and skills to help people in need and to address social problems. Social workers are encouraged to volunteer some portion of their professional skills with no expectation of significant financial return (pro bono service).

Value: Social Justice

Ethical Principle: Social workers challenge social injustice.
Social workers pursue social change, particularly with and on behalf of vulnerable and oppressed individuals and groups of people. Social workers' social change efforts are focused primarily on issues of poverty, unemployment, discrimination, and other forms of social injustice. These activities seek to promote sensitivity to and knowledge about oppression, and cultural and ethnic diversity. Social workers strive to ensure equality of opportunity, access to needed information, services, resources, and meaningful participation in decision making for all people.

Value: Dignity and Worth of the Person

Ethical Principle: Social workers respect the inherent dignity and worth of the person.
Social workers treat each person in a caring and respectful fashion, mindful of individual differences and cultural and ethnic diversity. Social workers promote clients' socially responsible self-determination. Social workers seek to enhance clients' capacity and opportunity to change and to address their own needs. Social workers are cognizant of their dual responsibility to clients and to the broader society. They seek to resolve conflicts between clients' and the broader society's interests in a socially responsible manner consistent with the values, ethical principles, and ethical standards of the profession.

Value: Importance of Human Relationships

Ethical Principle: Social workers recognize the central importance of human relationships. Social workers understand that relationships between and among people are an important vehicle for change. Social workers engage people as partners in the helping process. Social workers seek to strengthen relationships among people in a purposeful effort to promote, restore, maintain, and enhance the well-being of individuals, families, social groups, organizations, and communities.

Value: Integrity

Ethical Principle: Social workers behave in a trustworthy manner.
Social workers are continually aware of the profession's mission, values, ethical principles, and ethical standards, and practice in a manner consistent with them. Social workers act honestly and responsibly and promote ethical practices on the part of the organizations with which they are affiliated.

Value: Competence

Ethical Principle: Social workers practice within their areas of competence and develop and enhance their professional expertise.
Social workers continually strive to increase their professional knowledge and skills and to apply them in practice. Social workers should aspire to contribute to the knowledge base of the profession.

Ethical Standards

The following ethical standards are relevant to the professional activities of all social workers. These standards concern: (1) social workers' ethical responsibilities to clients, (2) social workers' ethical responsibilities to colleagues, (3) social workers' ethical responsibilities in practice settings, (4) social workers' ethical responsibilities as professionals, (5) social workers' ethical responsibilities to the profession, and (6) social workers' ethical responsibilities to the broader society.

Some of the standards that follow are enforceable guidelines for professional conduct and some are more aspirational in nature. The extent to which each standard is enforceable is a matter of professional judgment to be exercised by those responsible for reviewing alleged violations of ethical standards.

1. Social Workers' Ethical Responsibilities to Clients

1.01 Commitment to Clients
Social workers' primary responsibility is to promote well-being of clients. In general, clients' interests are primary. However, social workers' responsibility to the larger society or specific legal obligations may on limited occasions supercede the loyalty owed clients and clients

should be so advised. (Examples include when a social worker is required by law to report that a client has abused a child or has threatened to harm self or others.)

1.02 Self-Determination
Social workers respect and promote the right of clients to self-determination and assist clients in their efforts to identify and clarify their goals. Social workers may limit clients' right to self-determination when, in their professional judgment, clients' actions or potential actions pose a serious, foreseeable, and imminent risk to themselves or others.

1.03 Informed Consent
a. Social workers should provide services to clients only in the context of a professional relationship based, when appropriate, on valid informed consent. Social workers should use clear and understandable language to inform clients of the purpose of the service, risks related to the service, limits to service because of the requirements of a third-party payor, relevant costs, reasonable alternatives, clients' right to refuse or withdraw consent, and the time frame covered by the consent. Social workers should provide clients with an opportunity to ask questions.

b. In instances where clients are not literate or have difficulty understanding the primary language used in the practice setting, social workers should take steps to ensure clients' comprehension. This may include providing clients with a detailed verbal explanation or arranging for a qualified interpreter and/or translator whenever possible.

c. In instances where clients lack the capacity to provide informed consent, social workers should protect clients' interests by seeking permission from an appropriate third party, informing clients consistent with their level of understanding. In such instances social workers should seek to ensure that the third party acts in a manner consistent with clients' wishes and interests. Social workers should take reasonable steps to enhance such clients' ability to give informed consent.

d. In instances where clients are receiving services involuntarily, social workers should provide information about the nature and extent of services, and of the extent of clients' rights to refuse service.

e. Social workers who provide services via electronic mediums (such as computers, telephone, radio, and television) should inform recipients of the limitations and risks associated with such services.

f. Social workers should obtain clients' informed consent before audiotaping or videotaping clients, or permitting third party observation of clients who are receiving services.

1.04 Competence
a. Social workers should provide services and represent themselves as competent only within the boundaries of their education, training, license, certification, consultation received, supervised experience, or other relevant professional experience.

b. Social workers should provide services in substantive areas or use intervention techniques or approaches that are new to them only after engaging in appropriate study, training, consultation, and/or supervision from persons who are competent in those interventions or techniques.

c. When generally recognized standards do not exist with respect to an emerging area of practice, social workers should exercise careful judgment and take responsible steps—including appropriate education, research, training, consultation, and supervision—to ensure the competence of their work and to protect clients from harm.

1.05 Cultural Competence and Social Diversity

a. Social workers should understand culture and its function in human behavior and society, recognizing the strengths that exist in all cultures.

b. Social workers should have a knowledge base of their clients' cultures and be able to demonstrate competence in the provision of services that are sensitive to clients' cultures and to differences among people and cultural groups.

c. Social workers should obtain education about and seek to understand the nature of social diversity and oppression with respect to race, ethnicity, national origin, color, sex, sexual orientation, age, marital status, political belief, religion and mental or physical disability.

1.06 Conflicts of Interest

a. Social workers should be alert to and avoid conflicts of interest that interfere with the exercise of professional discretion and impartial judgment. Social workers should inform clients when a real or potential conflict of interest arises and take responsible steps to resolve the issue in a manner that makes the clients' interests primary and protects clients' interests to the greatest extent possible. In some cases, protecting clients' interests may require termination of the professional relationship with proper referral of the client.

b. Social workers should not take unfair advantage of any professional relationship or exploit others to further their personal, religious, political, or business interests.

c. Social workers should not engage in dual or multiple relationships with clients or former clients in which there is a risk of exploitation or potential harm to the client. In instances when dual or multiple relationships are unavoidable, social workers should take steps to protect clients and are responsible for setting clear, appropriate, and culturally sensitive boundaries. (Dual or multiple relationships occur when social workers relate to clients in more than one relationship, whether professional, social, or business. Dual or multiple relationships can occur simultaneously or consecutively.)

d. When social workers provide services to two or more persons who have a relationship with each other (for example, couples, family members), social workers should clarify with all parties which individuals will be considered clients and the nature of social workers' professional obligations to the various individuals who are receiving services. Social workers who anticipate a conflict of interest among the individuals receiving services, or who anticipate having to perform in potentially conflicting roles (for example, when a social worker is asked to testify in a child custody dispute or divorce proceedings involving clients), should clarify their role with the parties involved and take appropriate action to minimize any conflict of interest.

1.07 Privacy and Confidentiality

a. Social workers should respect clients' right to privacy. Social workers should not solicit private information from clients unless it is essential to providing service or conducting social work evaluation or research. Once private information is shared, standards of confidentiality apply.

b. Social workers may disclose confidential information when appropriate with a valid consent from a client, or a person legally authorized to consent on behalf of a client.

c. Social workers should protect the confidentiality of all information obtained in the course of professional service, except for compelling professional reasons. The general expectation that social workers will keep information confidential does not apply when disclosure is necessary to prevent serious, foreseeable, and imminent harm to a client or other identifiable person or when laws or regulations require disclosure without a client's consent. In all instances, social workers should disclose the least amount of confidential information necessary to achieve the desired purpose; only information that is directly relevant to the purpose for which the disclosure is made should be revealed.

d. Social workers should inform clients, to the extent possible, about the disclosure of confidential information and the potential consequences and, when feasible, before the disclosure is made. This applies whether social workers disclose confidential information as a result of a legal requirement or based on client consent.

e. Social workers should discuss with clients and other interested parties the nature of confidentiality and limitations of clients' right to confidentiality. Social workers should review with clients circumstances where confidential information may be requested and where disclosure of confidential information may be legally required. This discussion should occur as soon as possible in the social worker–client relationship and as needed throughout the course of the relationship.

f. When social workers provide counseling services to families, couples, or groups, social workers should seek agreement among the parties involved concerning each individual's right to confidentiality and obligation to preserve the confidentiality of information shared by others. Social workers should inform participants in family, couples, or group counseling that social workers cannot guarantee that all participants will honor such agreements.

g. Social workers should inform clients involved in family, couples, marital, or group counseling of the social worker's, employer's, and/or agency's policy concerning the social worker's disclosure of confidential information among the parties involved in the counseling.

h. Social workers should not discuss confidential information to third party payors, unless clients have authorized such disclosure.

i. Social workers should not disclose confidential information in any setting unless privacy can be assured. Social workers should not discuss confidential information in public or semi-public areas (such as hallways, waiting rooms, elevators, and restaurants).

j. Social workers should protect the confidentiality of clients during legal proceedings to the extent permitted by law. When a court of law or other legally authorized body orders social workers to disclose confidential or privileged information without a client's consent and such disclosure could cause harm to the client, social workers should request that the court withdraw or limit the order as narrowly as possible and/or maintain the records under seal, unavailable for public inspection.

k. Social workers should protect the confidentiality of clients when responding to requests from members of the media.

l. Social workers should protect the confidentiality of clients' written and electronic records and other sensitive information. Social workers should take reasonable steps to ensure that clients' records are stored in a secure location and that clients' records are not available to others who are not authorized to have access.

m. Social workers should take precautions to ensure and maintain the confidentiality of information transmitted to other parties through the use of computers, electronic mail, facsimile machines, telephones and telephone answering machines, and other electronic or computer technology. Disclosure of identifying information should be avoided whenever possible.

n. Social workers should transfer or dispose of clients' records in a manner that protects clients' confidentiality and is consistent with state statutes governing records and social work licensure.

o. Social workers should take reasonable precautions to protect client confidentiality in the event of the social worker's termination of practice, incapacitation, or death.

p. Social workers should not disclose identifying information when discussing clients for teaching or training purposes, unless the client has consented to disclosure of confidential information.

q. Social workers should not disclose identifying information when discussing clients with consultants, unless the client has consented to disclosure information or there is a compelling need for such disclosure.

r. Social workers should protect the confidentiality of deceased clients consistent with the preceding standards.

1.08 Access to Records
a. Social workers should provide clients with reasonable access to records concerning them. Social workers who are concerned that clients' access to their records could cause serious misunderstanding or harm to the client should provide assistance in interpreting the records and consultation with the client regarding the records. Social workers should limit client access to social work records, or portions of clients' records, only in exceptional circumstances when there is compelling evidence that such access would cause serious harm to the client. Both the client's request and the rationale for withholding some or all of the record should be documented in the client's file.

b. When providing clients with access to their records, social workers should take steps to protect the confidentiality of other individuals identified or discussed in such records.

1.09 Sexual Relationships
a. Social workers should under no circumstances engage in sexual activities or sexual contact with current clients, whether such contact is consensual or forced.

b. Social workers should not engage in sexual activities or sexual contact with clients' relatives or other individuals with whom clients maintain a close, personal relationship where there is a risk of exploitation or potential harm to the client. Sexual activity or sexual contact with clients' relatives or other individuals with whom clients maintain a personal relationship has the potential to be harmful to the client and may make it difficult for the social worker and client to maintain appropriate professional boundaries. Social workers—not their clients, their clients' relatives or other individuals with whom the client maintains a personal relationship—assume the full burden for setting clear, appropriate and culturally sensitive boundaries.

c. Social workers should not engage in sexual activities or sexual contact with former clients because of the potential for harm to the client. If social workers engage in conduct contrary to this prohibition or claim that an exception to this prohibition is warranted due to extraordinary circumstances, it is social workers—not their clients—who assume the full burden of demonstrating that the former client has not been exploited, coerced, or manipulated, intentionally or unintentionally.

d. Social workers should not provide clinical services to individuals with whom they have had a prior sexual relationship. Providing clinical services to a former sexual partner has the potential to be harmful to the individual and is likely to make it difficult for the social worker and individual to maintain appropriate professional boundaries.

1.10 Physical Contact
Social workers should not engage in physical contact with clients where there is a possibility of psychological harm to the client as a result of the contact (such as cradling or caressing clients). Social workers who engage in appropriate physical contact with clients are responsible for setting clear, appropriate, and culturally sensitive boundaries that govern such physical contact.

1.11 Sexual Harassment
Social workers should not sexually harass clients. Sexual harassment includes sexual advances, sexual solicitation, requests for sexual favors, and other verbal or physical conduct of a sexual nature.

1.12 Derogatory Language
Social workers should not use derogatory language in their written or verbal communications to or about clients. Social workers should use accurate and respectful language in all communications to and about clients.

1.13 Payment for Services
a. When setting fees, social workers should ensure that the fees are fair, reasonable, and commensurate with the service performed. Consideration should be given to the client's ability to pay.

b. Social workers should avoid accepting goods or services from clients as payment for professional services. Bartering arrangements, particularly involving services, create the potential for conflicts of interest, exploitation, and inappropriate boundaries in social workers' relationships with clients. Social workers should explore and may participate in bartering only in very limited circumstances where it can be demonstrated that such arrangements are an accepted practice among professionals in the local community, considered to be essential for the provision of service, negotiated without coercion and entered into at the client's initiative and with the client's informed consent. Social workers who accept goods or services from clients as payment for professional services assume the full burden of demonstrating that this arrangement will not be detrimental to the client or the professional relationship.

c. Social workers should not solicit a private fee or other remuneration for providing services to clients who are entitled to such available services through the social workers' employer or agency.

1.14 Clients Who Lack Decision-Making Capacity

When social workers act on behalf of clients who lack the capacity to make informed decisions, social workers should take reasonable steps to safeguard the interests and rights of those clients.

1.15 Interruption of Services

Social workers should make reasonable efforts to ensure continuity of services in the event that they are interrupted by factors such as unavailability, relocation, illness, disability, or death.

1.16 Termination of Services

a. Social workers should terminate services to clients, and professional relationships with them, when such services and relationships are no longer required or no longer serve the clients' needs or interests.

b. Social workers should take reasonable steps to avoid abandoning clients who are still in need of services. Social workers should withdraw services precipitously only under unusual circumstances, giving careful consideration to all factors in the situation and taking care to minimize possible adverse effects. Social workers should assist in making appropriate arrangements for continuation of services when necessary.

c. Social workers in fee-for-service settings may terminate services to clients who are not paying an overdue balance if the financial contractual arrangements have been made clear to the client, if the client does not pose an imminent danger to self or others, and if the clinical and other consequences of the current non-payment have been addressed and discussed with the client.

d. Social workers should not terminate services to pursue a social, financial, or sexual relationship with a client.

e. Social workers who anticipate the termination or interruption of services to clients should notify clients promptly and seek the transfer, referral, or continuation of services in relation to the clients' needs and preferences.

f. Social workers who are leaving an employment setting should inform clients of appropriate options for the continuation of service and their benefits and risks.

2. Social Workers' Ethical Responsibilities to Colleagues

2.01 Respect

a. Social workers should treat colleagues with respect, and represent accurately and fairly the qualifications, views, and obligations of colleagues.

b. Social workers should avoid unwarranted negative criticism of colleagues with clients or with other professionals. Unwarranted negative criticism may include demeaning comments that refer to colleagues' level of competence or to individuals' attributes such as race, ethnicity, national origin, color, age, religion, sex, sexual orientation, marital status, political belief, mental or physical disability, or any other preference, personal characteristic, or status.

c. Social workers should cooperate with social work colleagues and with colleagues of other professions when it serves the well-being of clients.

2.02 Confidentiality with Colleagues
Social workers should respect confidential information shared by colleagues in the course of their professional relationships and transactions. Social workers should ensure that such colleagues understand social workers' obligation to respect confidentiality and any exceptions related to it.

2.03 Interdisciplinary Collaboration
a. Social workers who are members of an interdisciplinary team should participate in and contribute to decisions that affect the well-being of clients by drawing on the perspectives, values, and experiences of the social work profession. Professional and ethical obligations of the interdisciplinary team as a whole and of its individual members should be clearly established.

b. Social workers for whom a team decision raises ethical concerns should attempt to resolve the disagreement through appropriate channels. If the disagreement cannot be resolved social workers should pursue other avenues to address their concerns, consistent with client well-being.

2.04 Disputes Involving Colleagues
a. Social workers should not take advantage of a dispute between a colleague and employer to obtain a position or otherwise advance the social worker's own interests.

b. Social workers should not exploit clients in a dispute with a colleague or engage clients in any inappropriate discussion of a social worker's conflict with a colleague.

2.05 Consultation
a. Social workers should seek advice and counsel of colleagues whenever such consultation is in the best interests of clients.

b. Social workers should keep informed of colleagues' areas of expertise and competencies. Social workers should seek consultation only from colleagues who have demonstrated knowledge, expertise and competence related to the subject of the consultation.

c. When consulting with colleagues about clients, social workers should disclose the least amount of information necessary to achieve the purposes of the consultation.

2.06 Referral for Services
a. Social workers should refer clients to other professionals when other professionals' specialized knowledge or expertise is needed to serve clients fully, or when social workers believe they are not being effective or making reasonable progress with clients and additional service is required.

b. Social workers who refer clients to other professionals should take appropriate steps to facilitate an orderly transfer of responsibility. Social workers who refer clients to other professionals should disclose, with clients' consent, all pertinent information to the new service providers.

c. Social workers are prohibited from giving or receiving payment for a referral when no professional service is provided by the referring social worker.

2.07 Sexual Relationships

a. Social workers who function as supervisors or educators should not engage in sexual activities or contact with supervisees, students, trainees, or other colleagues over whom they exercise professional authority.

b. Social workers should avoid engaging in sexual relationships with colleagues where there is potential for a conflict of interest. Social workers who become involved in, or anticipate becoming involved in, a sexual relationship with a colleague have a duty to transfer professional responsibilities when necessary, in order to avoid a conflict of interest.

2.08 Sexual Harassment

Social workers should not engage in any sexual harassment of supervisees, students, trainees, or colleagues. Sexual harassment includes sexual advances, sexual solicitation, requests for sexual favors, and other verbal or physical conduct of a sexual nature.

2.09 Impairment of Colleagues

a. Social workers who have direct knowledge of a social worker colleague's impairment which is due to personal problems, psychosocial distress, substance abuse, or mental health difficulties, and which interferes with practice effectiveness, should consult with that colleague when feasible and assist the colleague in taking remedial action.

b. Social workers who believe that a social work colleague's impairment interferes with practice effectiveness and that the colleague has not taken adequate steps to address the impairment should take action through appropriate channels established by employers, agencies, NASW, licensing and regulatory bodies, and other professional organizations.

2.10 Incompetence of Colleagues

a. Social workers who have direct knowledge of a social work colleague's incompetence should consult with that colleague when feasible and assist the colleague in taking remedial action.

b. Social workers who believe that a social work colleague is incompetent and has not taken adequate steps to address the incompetence should take action through appropriate channels established by employers, agencies, NASW, licensing and regulatory bodies, and other professional organizations.

2.11 Unethical Conduct of Colleagues

a. Social workers should take adequate measures to discourage, prevent, expose, and correct the unethical conduct of colleagues.

b. Social workers should be knowledgeable about established policies and procedures for handling concerns about colleagues' unethical behavior. Social workers should be familiar with national, state, and local procedures for handling ethics complaints. These include policies and procedures created by NASW, licensing and regulatory bodies, employers, agencies, and other professional organizations.

c. Social workers who believe that a colleague has acted unethically should seek resolution by discussing their concerns with the colleague when feasible and when such discussion is likely to be productive.

d. When necessary, social workers who believe that a colleague has acted unethically should take action through appropriate formal channels (such as contacting a state licensing board or regulatory body, NASW committee on inquiry, or other professional ethics committees).

e. Social workers should defend and assist colleagues who are unjustly charged with unethical conduct.

3. Social Workers' Ethical Responsibilities in Practice Settings

3.01 Supervision and Consultation

a. Social workers who provide supervision or consultation should have the necessary knowledge and skill to supervise or consult appropriately and should do so only within their areas of knowledge and competence.

b. Social workers who provide supervision or consultation are responsible for setting clear, appropriate, and culturally sensitive boundaries.

c. Social workers should not engage in any dual or multiple relationships with supervisees in which there is a risk of exploitation of or potential harm to the supervisee.

d. Social workers who provide supervision should evaluate supervisees' performance in a manner that is fair and respectful.

3.02 Education and Training

a. Social workers who function as educators, field instructors for students, or trainers should provide instruction only within their areas of knowledge and competence, and should provide instruction based on the most current information and knowledge available in the profession.

b. Social workers who function as educators or field instructors for students should evaluate students' performance in a manner that is fair and respectful.

c. Social workers who function as educators or field instructors for students should take reasonable steps to ensure that clients are routinely informed when services are being provided by students.

d. Social workers who function as educators or field instructors for students should not engage in any dual or multiple relationships with students in which there is a risk of exploitation or potential harm to the student. Social work educators and field instructors are responsible for setting clear, appropriate, and culturally sensitive boundaries.

3.03 Performance Evaluation

Social workers who have the responsibility for evaluating the performance of others should fulfill such responsibility in a fair and considerate manner, and on the basis of clearly stated criteria.

3.04 Client Records

a. Social workers should take reasonable steps to ensure that documentation in records is accurate and reflective of the services provided.

b. Social workers should include sufficient and timely documentation in records to facilitate the delivery of services and to ensure continuity of services provided to clients in the future.

c. Social workers' documentation should protect clients' privacy to the extent that is possible and appropriate, and should include only that information that is directly relevant to the delivery of services.

d. Social workers should store records following the termination of service to ensure reasonable future access. Records should be maintained for the number of years required by state statutes or relevant contracts.

3.05 Billing

Social workers should establish and maintain billing practices that accurately reflect the nature and extent of services provided, and by whom the service was provided in the practice setting.

3.06 Client Transfer

a. When an individual who is receiving services from another agency or colleague contacts a social worker for services, the social worker should carefully consider the client's needs before agreeing to provide services. In order to minimize possible confusion and conflict, social workers should discuss with potential clients the nature of their current relationship with other service providers and the implications, including possible benefits or risks, of entering into a relationship with a new service provider.

b. If a new client has been served by another agency or colleague, social workers should discuss with the client whether consultation with the previous service provider is in the client's best interest.

3.07 Administration

a. Social work administration should advocate within and outside of their agencies for adequate resources to meet clients' needs.

b. Social workers should advocate for resource allocation procedures that are open and fair. When not all clients' needs can be met, an allocation procedure should be developed that is nondiscriminatory and based on appropriate and consistently applied principles.

c. Social workers who are administrators should take reasonable steps to ensure that adequate agency or organizational resources are available to provide appropriate staff supervision.

d. Social work administrators should take reasonable steps to ensure that the working environment for which they are responsible is consistent with and encourages compliance with the NASW Code of Ethics. Social work administrators should take reasonable steps to eliminate any conditions in their organizations that violate, interfere with, or discourage compliance with the Code of Ethics.

3.08 Continuing Education and Staff Development

Social work administrators and supervisors should take reasonable steps to provide or arrange for continuing education and staff development for all staff for whom they are responsible. Continuing education and staff development should address current knowledge and emerging developments related to social work practice and ethics.

3.09 Commitments to Employers

a. Social workers generally should adhere to commitments made to employers and employing organizations.

b. Social workers should work to improve employing agencies' policies and procedures, and the efficiency and effectiveness of their services.

c. Social workers should take reasonable steps to ensure that employers are aware of social workers' ethical obligations as set forth in the NASW Code of Ethics and their implications for social work practice.

d. Social workers should not allow an employing organization's policies, procedures, regulations, or administrative orders to interfere with their ethical practice of social work. Social workers should take reasonable steps to ensure that their employing organizations' practices are consistent with the NASW Code of Ethics.

e. Social workers should act to prevent and eliminate discrimination in the employing organization's work assignments and in its employment policies and practices.

f. Social workers should accept employment or arrange student field placements only in organizations where fair personnel practices are exercised.

g. Social workers should be diligent stewards of the resources of their employing organizations, wisely conserving funds where appropriate, and never misappropriating funds or using them for unintended purposes.

3.10 Labor-Management Disputes

a. Social workers may engage in organized action, including the formation of and participation in labor unions, to improve services to clients and working conditions.

b. The actions of social workers who are involved in labor-management disputes, job actions, or labor strikes should be guided by the profession's values, ethical principles, and ethical standards. Reasonable differences of opinion exist among social workers concerning their primary obligation as professionals during an actual or threatened labor strike or job action. Social workers should carefully examine relevant issues and their possible impact on clients before deciding on a course of action.

4. Social Workers' Ethical Responsibilities as Professionals

4.01 Competence

a. Social workers should accept responsibility or employment only on the basis of existing competence or the intention to acquire the necessary competence.

b. Social workers should strive to become and remain proficient in professional practice and the performance of professional functions. Social workers should critically examine, and keep current with, emerging knowledge relevant to social work. Social workers should routinely review professional literature and participate in continuing education relevant to social work practice and social work ethics.

c. Social workers should base practice on recognized knowledge, including empirically based knowledge, relevant to social work and social work ethics.

4.02 Discrimination

Social workers should not practice, condone, facilitate, or collaborate with any form of discrimination on the basis of race, ethnicity, national origin, color, age, religion, sex, sexual orientation, marital status, political belief, or mental or physical disability.

4.03 Private Conduct
Social workers should not permit their private conduct to interfere with their ability to fulfill their professional responsibilities.

4.04 Dishonesty, Fraud, and Deception
Social workers should not participate in, condone, or be associated with dishonesty, fraud, or deception.

4.05 Impairment
a. Social workers should not allow their own personal problems, psychosocial distress, legal problems, substance abuse, or mental health difficulties to interfere with their professional judgment and performance or jeopardize the best interests of those for whom they have a professional responsibility.

b. Social workers whose personal problems, psychosocial distress, legal problems, substance abuse, or mental health difficulties interfere with their professional judgment and performance should immediately seek consultation and take appropriate remedial action by seeking professional help, making adjustments in workload, terminating practice, or taking any other steps necessary to protect clients and others.

4.06 Misrepresentation
a. Social workers should make clear distinctions between statements made and actions engaged in as a private individual and as a representative of the social work profession, a professional social work organization, or of the social worker's employing agency.

b. Social workers who speak on behalf of professional social work organizations should accurately represent the official and authorized positions of the organizations.

c. Social workers should ensure that their representations to clients, agencies, and the public of professional qualifications, credentials, education, competence, affiliations, services provided, or results to be achieved are accurate. Social workers should claim only those relevant professional credentials they actually possess and take steps to correct any inaccuracies or misrepresentations of their credentials by others.

4.07 Solicitations
a. Social workers should not engage in uninvited solicitation of potential clients who, because of their circumstances, are vulnerable to undue influence, manipulation, or coercion.

b. Social workers should not engage in solicitation of testimonial endorsements (including solicitation of consent to use a client's prior statement as a testimonial endorsement) from current clients or from other persons who, because of their particular circumstances, are vulnerable to undue influence.

4.08 Acknowledging Credit
a. Social workers should take responsibility and credit, including authorship credit, only for work they have actually performed and to which they have contributed.

b. Social workers should honestly acknowledge the work of and the contributions made by others.

5. Social Workers' Ethical Responsibilities to the Social Work Profession

5.01 Integrity of Profession

a. Social workers should work toward the maintenance and promotion of high standards of practice.

b. Social workers should uphold and advance the values, ethics, knowledge, and mission of the profession. Social workers should protect, enhance, and improve the integrity of the profession through appropriate study and research, active discussion, and responsible criticism of the profession.

c. Social workers should contribute time and professional expertise to activities that promote respect for the value, integrity, and competence of the social work profession. These activities may include teaching, research, consultation, service, legislative testimony, presentations in the community and participation in their professional organizations.

d. Social workers should contribute to the knowledge base of social work and share with colleagues their knowledge related to practice, research, and ethics. Social workers should seek to contribute to the profession's literature and to share their knowledge at professional meetings and conferences.

e. Social workers should act to prevent the unauthorized and unqualified practice of social work.

5.02 Evaluation Research

a. Social workers should monitor and evaluate policies, the implementation of programs, and practice interventions.

b. Social workers should promote and facilitate evaluation and research in order to contribute to the development of knowledge.

c. Social workers should critically examine and keep current with emerging knowledge relevant to social work and fully utilize evaluation and research evidence in their professional practice.

d. Social workers engaged in evaluation or research should consider carefully possible consequences and should follow guidelines developed for the protection of evaluation and research participants. Appropriate institutional review boards should be consulted.

e. Social workers engaged in evaluation or research should obtain voluntary and written informed consent from participants, when appropriate, without any implied or actual deprivation or penalty for refusal to participate, without undue inducement to participate, and with due regard for participants' well-being, privacy and dignity. Informed consent should include information about the nature, extent, and duration of the participation requested and disclosure of the risks and benefits of participation in the research.

f. When evaluation or research participants are incapable of giving informed consent, social workers should provide an appropriate explanation to them, obtain the participant's assent, and obtain consent from an appropriate proxy.

g. Social workers should never design or conduct evaluation or research that does not use consent procedures, such as certain forms of naturalistic observation and/or archival research, unless rigorous and responsible review of the research has found it to be justified because of its prospective scientific yield, educational, or applied value and unless equally effective alternative procedures that do not involve waiver of consent are not feasible.

h. Social workers should inform participants of their rights to withdraw from evaluation and research at any time without penalty.

i. Social workers should take appropriate steps to ensure that participants in evaluation and research have access to appropriate supportive services.

j. Social workers engaged in evaluation or research should protect participants from unwarranted physical or mental distress, harm, danger, or deprivation.

k. Social workers engaged in the evaluation of services should discuss collected information only for professional purposes and only with persons professionally concerned with this information.

l. Social workers engaged in evaluation or research should ensure the anonymity or confidentiality of participants and the data obtained from them. Social workers should inform participants of any limits of confidentiality, the measures that will be taken to ensure confidentiality, and when any records containing research data will be destroyed.

m. Social workers who report evaluation and research results should protect participants' confidentiality by omitting identifying information unless proper consent has been obtained authorizing disclosures.

n. Social workers should report evaluation and research findings accurately. They should not fabricate or falsify and should take steps to correct any errors later found in published data using standard publication methods.

o. Social workers engaged in evaluation or research should be alert to and avoid conflicts of interest and dual relationships with participants, should inform participants when a real or potential conflict of interest arises, and should take steps to resolve the issue in a manner that makes participants' interests primary.

p. Social workers should educate themselves, their students, and colleagues about responsible research practices.

6. Social Workers' Ethical Responsibilities to the Broader Society

6.01 Social Welfare
Social workers should promote the general welfare of society, from local to global levels, and the development of people, their communities, and their environment. Social workers should advocate for living conditions conducive to the fulfillment of basic human needs and promote social, economic, political, and cultural values and institutions that are compatible with the realization of social justice.

6.02 Public Participation
Social workers should facilitate informed participants by the public in shaping social policies and institutions.

6.03 Public Emergencies
Social workers should provide appropriate professional services in public emergencies, to the greatest extent possible.

6.04 Social and Political Action

a. Social workers should engage in social and political action that seeks to ensure that all persons have equal access to the resources, employment, services, and opportunities that they require in order to meet their basic human needs and to develop fully. Social workers should be aware of the impact of the political arena on practice, and should advocate for changes in policy and legislation to improve social conditions in order to meet basic human needs and promote social justice.

b. Social workers should act to expand choice and opportunity for all persons, with special regard for vulnerable, disadvantaged, oppressed, and exploited persons and groups.

c. Social workers should promote conditions that encourage respect for the diversity of cultures and social diversity within the United States and globally. Social workers should promote policies and practices that demonstrate respect for difference, support the expansion of cultural knowledge and resources, advocate for programs and institutions that demonstrate cultural competence, and promote policies that safeguard the rights of and confirm equity and social justice for all people.

d. Social workers should act to prevent and eliminate domination, exploitation, and discrimination against any person, group, or class on the basis of race, ethnicity, national origin, color, age, religion, sex, sexual orientation, marital status, political belief, mental or physical disability, or any other preference, personal characteristic, or status.

Appendix D

List of Specialized Ethics Codes and Guidelines in Mental Health Disciplines

American Association of Sex Educators, Counselors and Therapists. (1993). *1993 Code of Ethics.* Chicago: Author.

American Mental Health Counselors Association. (1987). *Code of ethics for mental health counselors.* Alexandria, VA: Author.

American Psychiatric Association. (1993). *Principles of medical ethics with annotations especially applicable to psychiatry.* Washington, DC: Author.

American Psychological Association (APA). (1981). *Specialty guidelines for the delivery of services: Clinical psychologists, counseling psychologists, organizational/industrial psychologists, school psychologists.* Washington, DC: Author.

American Psychological Association (APA). (1986). *Guidelines for computer-based tests and interpretations.* Washington, DC: Author.

American Psychological Association (APA). (1993a). *Guidelines for ethical conduct in the care and use of animals.* Washington, DC: Author.

American Psychological Association (APA). (1993b). *Guidelines for providers of psychological services to ethnic, linguistic and culturally diverse populations.* Washington, DC: Author.

American Psychological Association (APA). (1993c). *Record keeping guidelines.* Washington, DC: Author.

American Psychological Association (APA). (1994). Guidelines for child custody evaluations in divorce proceedings. *American Psychologist, 49,* 677–680.

American Psychological Association (APA), Committee on Legal Issues. (1996). Strategies for private practitioners coping with subpoenas or compelled testimony for client records or test data. *Professional Psychology: Research and Practice, 27,* 245–251.

American Psychological Association (APA), Committee on Professional Practice and Standards. (1995). Twenty-four questions (and answers) about professional practice in the area of child abuse. *Professional Psychology: Research and Practice, 26,* 377–383.

American Psychological Association (APA), Committee on Psychological Testing and Assessment. (1996). Statement on the disclosure of test data. *American Psychologist, 51,* 644–648.

American Psychological Association (APA), Committee on Women in Psychology. (1989). If sex enters into the psychotherapy relationship. *Professional Psychology: Research and Practice, 20,* 112–115.

American Rehabilitation Counseling Association. (1987). *Code of professional ethics for rehabilitation counselors.* Arlington Heights, IL: Author.

American School Counselor Association (ASCA). (1992). *Ethical standards for school counselors.* Alexandria, VA: Author.

Association for Counselor Education and Supervision (ACES). (1990). Standards for counseling supervisors. *Journal of Counseling and Development, 69,* 30–32.

Association for Counselor Education and Supervision (ACES). (1993). Ethical guidelines for counseling supervisors. *Counselor Education and Supervision, 34,* 270–276.

Association for Specialists in Group Work (ASGW), Executive Board. (1989). *Ethical guidelines for group counselors.* Alexandria, VA: American Counseling Association.

Association of State and Provincial Psychology Boards (ASPPB). (1991). *ASPPB code of conduct.* Montgomery, AL: Author.

Canadian Psychological Association. (1991). *Canadian code of ethics for psychologists. Revised.* Ottawa, ON: Author.

Committee on Ethical Guidelines for Forensic Psychologists. (1991). Specialty guidelines for forensic psychologists. *Law and Human Behavior, 15,* 655–665.

International Association of Marriage and Family Counselors (IAMFC). (1993). *Ethical code for the International Association for Marriage and Family Counselors.* Alexandria, VA: Author.

National Association of School Psychologists (NASP). (1992). *Principles for professional ethics.* Silver Spring, MD: Author.

National Board for Certified Counselors. (1989). *National Board for Certified Counselors: Code of Ethics.* Alexandria, VA: Author.

National Career Development Association. (1987). *National Career Development Association ethical standards.* Alexandria, VA: Author.

Appendix E

Association for Specialists in Group Work, Ethical Guidelines for Group Counselors

Preamble

One characteristic of any professional group is the possession of a body of knowledge, skills, and voluntarily, self-professed standards for ethical practice. A Code of Ethics consists of those standards that have been formally and publicly acknowledged by the members of a profession to serve as the guidelines for professional conduct, discharge of duties, and the resolution of moral dilemmas. By this document, the Association for Specialists in Group Work (ASGW) has identified the standards of conduct appropriate for ethical behavior among its members.

The Association for Specialists in Group Work recognizes the basic commitment of its members to the Ethical Standards of its parent organization, the American Association for Counseling and Development (AACD) and nothing in this document shall be construed to supplant that code. These standards are intended to complement the AACD standards in the area of group work by clarifying the nature of ethical responsibility of the counselor in the group setting and by stimulating a greater concern for competent group leadership.

The group counselor is expected to be a professional agent and to take the processes of ethical responsibility seriously. ASGW views *ethical process* as being integral to group work and views group counselors as *ethical agents*. Group counselors, by their very nature in being responsible and responsive to their group members, necessarily embrace a certain potential for ethical vulnerability. It is incumbent upon group counselors to give considerable attention to the intent and context of their actions because the attempts of counselors to influence human behavior through group work always have ethical implications.

The following ethical guidelines have been developed to encourage ethical behavior of group counselors. These guidelines are written for students and practitioners, and are meant to stimulate reflection, self-examination, and discussion of issues and practices. They address the group counselor's responsibility for providing information about group work to clients and the group counselor's responsibility for providing group counseling services to clients. A final section discusses the group counselor's responsibility for safe-guarding ethical practice and procedures for reporting unethical behavior. Group counselors are expected to make known these standards to group members.

Ethical Guidelines

1. Orientation and Providing Information: Group counselors adequately prepare prospective or new group members by providing as much information about the existing or proposed group as necessary. Minimally, information related to each of the following areas should be provided.

   a. Entrance procedures, time parameters of the group experience, group participation expectations, methods of payment (where appropriate), and termination procedures are explained by the group counselor as appropriate to the level of maturity of group members and the nature and purpose(s) of the group.

   b. Group counselors have available for distribution, a professional disclosure statement that includes information on the group counselor's qualifications and group services that can be provided, particularly as related to the nature and purpose(s) of the specific group.

   c. Group counselors communicate the role expectations, rights, and responsibilities of group members and group counselor(s).

   d. The group goals are stated as concisely as possible by the group counselor including *whose* goal it is (the group counselor's, the institution's, the parent's, the law's, society's, etc.) and the role of group members in influencing or determining the group's goal(s).

   e. Group counselors explore with group members the risks of potential life changes that may occur because of the group experience and help members explore their readiness to face these possibilities.

   f. Group members are informed by the group counselor of unusual or experimental procedures that might be expected in their group experience.

   g. Group counselors explain, as realistically as possible, what services can and cannot be provided within the particular group structure offered.

   h. Group counselors emphasize the need to promote full psychological functioning and presence among group members. They inquire from prospective group members whether they are using any kind of drug or medication that may affect functioning in the group. They do not permit any use of alcohol and/or illegal drugs during group sessions and they discourage the use of alcohol and/or drugs (legal or illegal) prior to group meetings which may affect the physical or emotional presence of the member or other group members.

   i. Group counselors inquire from prospective group members whether they have ever been a client in counseling or psychotherapy. If a prospective group member is already in a counseling relationship with another professional person, the group counselor advises the prospective group member to notify the other professional of their participation in the group.

   j. Group counselors clearly inform group members about the policies pertaining to the group counselor's willingness to consult with them between group sessions.

   k. In establishing fees for group counseling services, group counselors consider the financial status and the locality of prospective group members. Group members are not charged fees for group sessions where the group counselor is not present and the policy of charging for sessions missed by a group member is clearly communicated. Fees for participating as a group member are contracted between group counselor and group member for a specified period of time. Group counselors do not increase fees for group counseling services until the existing contracted fee structure has expired. In the event that the established fee structure is inappropriate for a prospective member, group counselors assist in finding comparable services of acceptable cost.

2. Screening of Members: The group counselor screens prospective group members (when appropriate to their theoretical orientation). Insofar as possible, the counselor selects group members whose needs and goals are compatible with the goals of the group, who will not impede the group process, and whose well-being will not be jeopardized by the group experience. An orientation to the group (i.e., ASGW Ethical Guideline #1), is included during the screening process. Screening may be accomplished in one or more ways, such as the following:
   a. Individual interview,
   b. Group interview of prospective group members,
   c. Interview as part of a team staffing, and,
   d. Completion of a written questionnaire by prospective group members.

3. Confidentiality: Group counselors protect members by defining clearly what confidentiality means, why it is important, and the difficulties involved in enforcement.
   a. Group counselors take steps to protect members by defining confidentiality and the limits of confidentiality (i.e., when a group member's condition indicates that there is clear and imminent danger to the member, others, or physical property, the group counselor takes reasonable personal action and/or informs responsible authorities).
   b. Group counselors stress the importance of confidentiality and set a norm of confidentiality regarding all group participants' disclosures. The importance of maintaining confidentiality is emphasized before the group begins and at various times in the group. The fact that confidentiality cannot be guaranteed is clearly stated.
   c. Members are made aware of the difficulties involved in enforcing and ensuring confidentiality in a group setting. The counselor provides examples of how confidentiality can nonmaliciously be broken to increase members' awareness, and help to lessen the likelihood that this breach of confidence will occur. Group counselors inform group members about the potential consequences of intentionally breaching confidentiality.
   d. Group counselors can only ensure confidentiality on their part and not on the part of the members.
   e. Group counselors video or audio tape a group session only with the prior consent, and the members' knowledge of how the tape will be used.
   f. When working with minors, the group counselor specifies the limits of confidentiality.
   g. Participants in a mandatory group are made aware of any reporting procedures required of the group counselor.
   h. Group counselors store or dispose of group member records (written, audio, video, etc.) in ways that maintain confidentiality.
   i. Instructors of group counseling courses maintain the anonymity of group members whenever discussing group counseling cases.

4. Voluntary/Involuntary Participation: Group counselors inform members whether participation is voluntary or involuntary.
   a. Group counselors take steps to ensure informed consent procedures in both voluntary and involuntary groups.
   b. When working with minors in a group, counselors are expected to follow the procedures specified by the institution in which they are practicing.
   c. With involuntary groups, every attempt is made to enlist the cooperation of the members and their continuance in the group on a voluntary basis.
   d. Group counselors do not certify that group treatment has been received by members who merely attend sessions, but did not meet the defined group expectations. Group members are informed about the consequences for failing to participate in a group.

5. Leaving a Group: Provisions are made to assist a group member to terminate in an effective way.
   a. Procedures to be followed for a group member who chooses to exit a group prematurely are discussed by the counselor with all group members either before the group begins, during a prescreening interview, or during the initial group session.
   b. In the case of legally mandated group counseling, group counselors inform members of the possible consequences for premature self-termination.
   c. Ideally, both the group counselor and the member can work cooperatively to determine the degree to which a group experience is productive or counterproductive for that individual.
   d. Members ultimately have a right to discontinue membership in the group, at a designated time, if the predetermined trial period proves to be unsatisfactory.
   e. Members have the right to exit a group, but it is important that they be made aware of the importance of informing the counselor and the group members prior to deciding to leave. The counselor discusses the possible risks of leaving the group prematurely with a member who is considering this option.
   f. Before leaving a group, the group counselor encourages members (if appropriate) to discuss their reasons for wanting to discontinue membership in the group. Counselors intervene if other members use undue pressure to force a member to remain in the group.

6. Coercion and Pressure: Group counselors protect member rights against physical threats, intimidation, coercion, and undue peer pressure insofar as is reasonably possible.
   a. It is essential to differentiate between *therapeutic pressure* that is part of any group and *undue pressure,* which is not therapeutic.
   b. The purpose of a group is to help participants find their own answer, not to pressure them into doing what the group thinks is appropriate.
   c. Counselors exert care not to coerce participants to change in directions which they clearly state they do not choose.
   d. Counselors have a responsibility to intervene when others use undue pressure or attempt to persuade members against their will.
   e. Counselors intervene when any member attempts to act out aggression in a physical way that might harm another member or themselves.
   f. Counselors intervene when a member is verbally abusive or inappropriately confrontive to another member.

7. Imposing Counselor Values: Group counselors develop an awareness of their own values and needs and the potential impact they have on the interventions likely to be made.
   a. Although group counselors take care to avoid imposing their values on members, it is appropriate that they expose their own beliefs, decisions, needs, and values, when concealing them would create problems for the members.
   b. There are values implicit in any group, and these are made clear to potential members before they join the group. (Examples of certain values include: expressing feelings, being direct and honest, sharing personal material with others, learning how to trust, improving interpersonal communication, and deciding for oneself.)
   c. Personal and professional needs of group counselors are not met at the members' expense.
   d. Group counselors avoid using the group for their own therapy.
   e. Group counselors are aware of their own values and assumptions and how these apply in a multicultural context.
   f. Group counselors take steps to increase their awareness of ways that their personal reactions to members might inhibit the group process and they monitor their countertransference. Through an awareness of the impact of stereotyping and discrimination (i.e., biases based on age, disability, ethnicity, gender, race, religion, or sexual preference), group counselors guard the individual rights and personal dignity of all group members.

8. Equitable Treatment: Group counselors make every reasonable effort to treat each member individually and equally.
   a. Group counselors recognize and respect differences (e.g., cultural, racial, religious, lifestyle, age, disability, gender) among group members.
   b. Group counselors maintain an awareness of their behavior toward individual group members and are alert to the potential detrimental effects of favoritism or partiality toward any particular group member to the exclusion or detriment of any other member(s). It is likely that group counselors will favor some members over others, yet all group members deserve to be treated equally.
   c. Group counselors ensure equitable use of group time for each member by inviting silent members to become involved, acknowledging nonverbal attempts to communicate, and discouraging rambling and monopolizing of time by members.
   d. If a large group is planned, counselors consider enlisting another qualified professional to serve as a co-leader for the group sessions.

9. Dual Relationships: Group counselors avoid dual relationships with group members that might impair their objectivity and professional judgment, as well as those which are likely to compromise a group member's ability to participate fully in the group.
   a. Group counselors do not misuse their professional role and power as group leader to advance personal or social contacts with members throughout the duration of the group.
   b. Group counselors do not use their professional relationship with group members to further their own interests either during the group or after the termination of the group.
   c. Sexual intimacies between group counselors and members are unethical.

     d. Group counselors do not barter (exchange) professional services with group members for services.

     e. Group counselors do not admit their own family members, relatives, employees, or personal friends as members to their groups.

     f. Group counselors discuss with group members the potential detrimental effects of group members engaging in intimate inter-member relationships outside of the group.

     g. Students who participate in a group as a partial course requirement for a group course are not evaluated for an academic grade based upon their degree of participation as a member in a group. Instructors of group counseling courses take steps to minimize the possible negative impact on students when they participate in a group course by separating course grades from participation in the group and by allowing students to decide what issues to explore and when to stop.

     h. It is inappropriate to solicit members from a class (or institutional affiliation) for one's private counseling or therapeutic groups.

10. Use of Techniques: Group counselors do not attempt any technique unless trained in its use or under supervision by a counselor familiar with the intervention.

     a. Group counselors are able to articulate a theoretical orientation that guides their practice, and they are able to provide a rationale for their interventions:

     b. Depending upon the type of an intervention, group counselors have training commensurate with the potential impact of a technique.

     c. Group counselors are aware of the necessity to modify their techniques to fit the unique needs of various cultural and ethnic groups.

     d. Group counselors assist members in translating in-group learnings to daily life.

11. Goal Development: Group counselors make every effort to assist members in developing their personal goals.

     a. Group counselors use their skills to assist members in making their goals specific so that others present in the group will understand the nature of the goals.

     b. Throughout the course of a group, group counselors assist members in assessing the degree to which personal goals are being met, and assist in revising any goals when it is appropriate.

     c. Group counselors help members clarify the degree to which the goals can be met within the context of a particular group.

12. Consultation: Group counselors develop and explain policies about between-session consultation to group members.

     a. Group counselors take care to make certain that members do not use between-session consultations to avoid dealing with issues pertaining to the group that would be dealt with best in the group.

     b. Group counselors urge members to bring the issues discussed during between-session consultations into the group if they pertain to the group.

     c. Group counselors seek out consultation and/or supervision regarding ethical concerns or when encountering difficulties which interfere with their effective functioning as group leaders.

    d. Group counselors seek appropriate professional assistance for their own personal problems or conflicts that are likely to impair their professional judgment and work performance.

    e. Group counselors discuss their group cases only for professional consultation and educational purposes.

    f. Group counselors inform members about policies regarding whether consultation will be held confidential.

13. Termination from the Group: Depending upon the purpose of participation in the group, counselors promote termination of members from the group in the most efficient period of time.

    a. Group counselors maintain a constant awareness of the progress made by each group member and periodically invite the group members to explore and reevaluate their experiences in the group. It is the responsibility of group counselors to help promote the independence of members from the group in a timely manner.

14. Evaluation and Follow-up: Group counselors make every attempt to engage in ongoing assessment and to design follow-up procedures for their groups.

    a. Group counselors recognize the importance of ongoing assessment of a group, and they assist members in evaluating their own progress.

    b. Group counselors conduct evaluation of the total group experience at the final meeting (or before termination), as well as ongoing evaluation.

    c. Group counselors monitor their own behavior and become aware of what they are modeling in the group.

    d. Follow-up procedures might take the form of personal contact, telephone contact, or written contact.

    e. Follow-up meetings might be with individuals, or groups, or both to determine the degree to which; (i) members have reached their goals, (ii) the group had a positive or negative effect on the participants, (iii) members could profit from some type of referral, and (iv) as information for possible modification of future groups. If there is no follow-up meeting, provisions are made available for individual follow-up meetings to any member who needs or requests such a contact.

15. Referrals: If the needs of a particular member cannot be met within the type of group being offered, the group counselor suggests other appropriate professional referrals.

    a. Group counselors are knowledgeable of local community resources for assisting group members regarding professional referrals.

    b. Group counselors help members seek further professional assistance, if needed.

16. Professional Development: Group counselors recognize that professional growth is a continuous, ongoing, developmental process throughout their career.

    a. Group counselors maintain and upgrade their knowledge and skill competencies through educational activities, clinical experiences, and participation in professional development activities.

    b. Group counselors keep abreast of research findings and new developments as applied to groups.

Appendix F

American Association for Marriage and Family Therapy, Code of Ethics

The Board of Directors of the American Association for Marriage and Family Therapy (AAMFT) hereby promulgates, pursuant to Article 2, Section 2.013 of the Association's By laws, the Revised AAMFT Code of Ethics, effective August 1, 1991.

The AAMFT Code of Ethics is binding on Members of AAMFT in all membership categories, AAMFT Approved Supervisors, and applicants for membership and the Approved Supervisor designation (hereafter, AAMFT Member).

If an AAMFT Member resigns in anticipation of, or during the course of an ethics investigation, the Ethics Committee will complete its investigation. Any publication of action taken by the Association will include the fact that the Member attempted to resign during the investigation.

Marriage and family therapists are strongly encouraged to report alleged unethical behavior of colleagues to appropriate professional associations and state regulatory bodies.

1. Responsibility to Clients

Marriage and family therapists advance the welfare of families and individuals. They respect the rights of those persons seeking their assistance, and make reasonable efforts to ensure that their services are used appropriately.

1.1 Marriage and family therapists do not discriminate against or refuse professional service to anyone on the basis of race, gender, religion, national origin, or sexual orientation.

1.2 Marriage and family therapists are aware of their influential position with respect to clients, and they avoid exploiting the trust and dependency of such persons. Therapists, therefore, make every effort to avoid dual relationships with clients that could impair professional judgment or increase the risk of exploitation. When a dual relationship cannot be avoided, therapists take appropriate professional precautions to ensure judgment is not impaired and no exploitation occurs. Examples of such dual relationships include, but are not limited to, business or close personal relationships with clients. Sexual intimacy with clients is prohibited. Sexual intimacy with former clients for two years following the termination of therapy is prohibited.

1.3 Marriage and family therapists do not use their professional relationships with clients to further their own interests.

1.4 Marriage and family therapists respect the right of clients to make decisions and help them to understand the consequences of these decisions. Therapists clearly advise a client that a decision on marital status is the responsibility of the client.

1.5 Marriage and family therapists continue therapeutic relationships only so long as it is reasonably clear that clients are benefiting from the relationship.

1.6 Marriage and family therapists assist persons in obtaining other therapeutic services if the therapist is unable or unwilling, for appropriate reasons, to provide professional help.

1.7 Marriage and family therapists do not abandon or neglect clients in treatment without making reasonable arrangements for the continuation of such treatment.

1.8 Marriage and family therapists obtain written informed consent from clients before videotaping, audiorecording, or permitting third party observation.

2. Confidentiality

Marriage and family therapists have unique confidentiality concerns because the client in a therapeutic relationship may be more than one person. Therapists respect and guard confidences of each individual client.

2.1 Marriage and family therapists may not disclose client confidences except: (a) as mandated by law; (b) to prevent a clear and immediate danger to a person or persons; (c) where the therapist is a defendant in a civil, criminal, or disciplinary action arising from the therapy (in which case client confidences may be disclosed only in the course of that action); or (d) if there is a waiver previously obtained in writing, and then such information may be revealed only in accordance with the terms of the waiver. In circumstances where more than one person in a family receives therapy, each such family member who is legally competent to execute a waiver must agree to the waiver required by subparagraph (d). Without such a waiver from each family member legally competent to execute a waiver, a therapist cannot disclose information received from any family member.

2.2 Marriage and family therapists use client and/or clinical materials in teaching, writing, and public presentations only if a written waiver has been obtained in accordance with Subprinciple 2.1(d), or when appropriate steps have been taken to protect client identity and confidentiality.

2.3 Marriage and family therapists store or dispose of client records in ways that maintain confidentiality.

3. Professional Competence and Integrity

Marriage and family therapists maintain high standards of professional competence and integrity.

3.1 Marriage and family therapists are in violation of this Code and subject to termination of membership or other appropriate action if they: (a) are convicted of any felony; (b) are convicted of a misdemeanor related to their qualifications or functions; (c) engage in conduct which could lead to conviction of a felony, or a misdemeanor related to their qualifications or functions; (d) are expelled from or disciplined by other professional organizations; (e) have their licenses or certificates suspended or revoked or are otherwise disciplined by regulatory bodies; (f) are no longer competent to practice marriage and family therapy because they are impaired due to physical or mental causes or the abuse of alcohol or other substances; or (g) fail to cooperate with the Association at any point from the inception of an ethical complaint through the completion of all proceedings regarding that complaint.

3.2 Marriage and family therapists seek appropriate professional assistance for their personal problems or conflicts that may impair work performance or clinical judgment.

3.3 Marriage and family therapists, as teachers, supervisors, and researchers, are dedicated to high standards of scholarship and present accurate information.

3.4 Marriage and family therapists remain abreast of new developments in family therapy knowledge and practice through educational activities.

3.5 Marriage and family therapists do not engage in sexual or other harassment or exploitation of clients, students, trainees, supervisees, employees, colleagues, research subjects, or actual or potential witnesses or complainants in investigations and ethical proceedings.

3.6 Marriage and family therapists do not diagnose, treat, or advise on problems outside the recognized boundaries of their competence.

3.7 Marriage and family therapists make efforts to prevent the distortion or misuse of their clinical and research findings.

3.8 Marriage and family therapists, because of their ability to influence and alter the lives of others, exercise special care when making public their professional recommendations and opinions through testimony or other public statements.

4. Responsibility to Students, Employees, and Supervisees

Marriage and family therapists do not exploit the trust and dependency of students, employees, and supervisees.

4.1 Marriage and family therapists are aware of their influential position with respect to students, employees, and supervisees, and they avoid exploiting the trust and dependency of such persons. Therapists, therefore, make every effort to avoid dual relationships that could impair professional judgment or increase the risk of exploitation. When a dual relationship cannot be avoided, therapists take appropriate professional precautions to ensure judgment is not impaired and no exploitation occurs. Examples of such dual relationships include, but are not limited to, business or close personal relationships with students, employees, or supervisees. Provision of therapy to students, employees, or supervisees is prohibited. Sexual intimacy with students or supervisees is prohibited.

4.2 Marriage and family therapists do not permit students, employees, or supervisees to perform or to hold themselves out as competent to perform professional services beyond their training, level of experience, and competence.

4.3 Marriage and family therapists do not disclose supervisee confidences except: (a) as mandated by law; (b) to prevent a clear and immediate danger to a person or persons; (c) where the therapist is a defendant in a civil, criminal, or disciplinary action arising from the supervision (in which case supervisee confidences may be disclosed only in the course of that action); (d) in educational or training settings where there are multiple supervisors, and then only to other professional colleagues who share responsibility for the training of the supervisee; or (e) if there is a waiver previously obtained in writing, and then such information may be revealed only in accordance with the terms of the waiver.

5. Responsibility to Research Participants

Investigators respect the dignity and protect the welfare of participants in research and are aware of federal and state laws and regulations and professional standards governing the conduct of research.

5.1 Investigators are responsible for making careful examinations of ethical acceptability in planning studies. To the extent that services to research participants may be compromised by participation in research, investigators seek the ethical advice of qualified professionals not directly involved in the investigation and observe safeguards to protect the rights of research participants.

5.2 Investigators requesting participants' involvement in research inform them of all aspects of the research that might reasonably be expected to influence willingness to participate. Investigators are especially sensitive to the possibility of diminished consent when participants are also receiving clinical services, have impairments which limit understanding and/or communication, or when participants are children.

5.3 Investigators respect participants' freedom to decline participation in or to withdraw from a research study at any time. This obligation requires special thought and consideration when investigators or other members of the research team are in positions of authority or influence over participants. Marriage and family therapists, therefore, make every effort to avoid dual relationships with research participants that could impair professional judgments or increase the risk of exploitation.

5.4 Information obtained about a research participant during the course of an investigation is confidential unless there is a waiver previously obtained in writing. When the possibility exists that others, including family members, may obtain access to such information, this possibility, together with the plan for protecting confidentiality, is explained as part of the procedure for obtaining informed consent.

6. Responsibility to the Profession

Marriage and family therapists respect the rights and responsibilities of professional colleagues and participate in activities which advance the goals of the profession.

6.1 Marriage and family therapists remain accountable to the standards of the profession when acting as members or employees of organizations.

6.2 Marriage and family therapists assign publication credit to those who have contributed to a publication in proportion to their contributions and in accordance with customary professional publication practices.

6.3 Marriage and family therapists who are the authors of books or other materials that are published or distributed cite persons to whom credit for original ideas is due.

6.4 Marriage and family therapists who are the authors of books or other materials published or distributed by an organization take reasonable precautions to ensure that the organization promotes and advertises the materials accurately and factually.

6.5 Marriage and family therapists participate in activities that contribute to a better community and society, including devoting a portion of their professional activity to services for which there is little or no financial return.

6.6 Marriage and family therapists are concerned with developing laws and regulations pertaining to marriage and family therapy that serve the public interest, and with altering such laws and regulations that are not in the public interest.

6.7 Marriage and family therapists encourage public participation in the design and delivery of professional services and in the regulation of practitioners.

7. Financial Arrangements

Marriage and family therapists make financial arrangements with clients, third party payors, and supervisees that are reasonably understandable and conform to accepted professional practices.

7.1 Marriage and family therapists do not offer or accept payment for referrals.

7.2 Marriage and family therapists do not charge excessive fees for services.

7.3 Marriage and family therapists disclose their fees to clients and supervisees at the beginning of services.

7.4 Marriage and family therapists represent facts truthfully to clients, third party payors, and supervisees regarding services rendered.

8. Advertising

Marriage and family therapists engage in appropriate informational activities, including those that enable laypersons to choose professional services on an informed basis.

General Advertising

8.1 Marriage and family therapists accurately represent their competence, education, training, and experience relevant to their practice of marriage and family therapy.

8.2 Marriage and family therapists assure that advertisements and publications in any media (such as directories, announcements, business cards, newspapers, radio, television, and facsimiles) convey information that is necessary for the public to make an appropriate selection of professional services. Information could include: (a) office information, such as name, address, telephone number, credit card acceptability, fees, languages spoken, and office hours; (b) appropriate degrees, state licensure and/or certification, and AAMFT Clinical Member status; and (c) description of practice. (For requirements for advertising under the AAMFT name, logo, and/or the abbreviated initials AAMFT, see Subprinciple 8.15, below.)

8.3 Marriage and family therapists do not use a name which could mislead the public concerning the identity, responsibility, source, and status of those practicing under that name and do not hold themselves out as being partners or associates of a firm if they are not.

8.4 Marriage and family therapists do not use any professional identification (such as a business card, office sign, letterhead, or telephone or association directory listing) if it includes a statement or claim that is false, fraudulent, misleading, or deceptive. A statement is false, fraudulent, misleading, or deceptive if it (a) contains a material misrepresentation of fact; (b) fails to state any material fact necessary to make the statement, in light of all circumstances, not misleading; or (c) is intended to or is likely to create an unjustified expectation.

8.5 Marriage and family therapists correct, wherever possible, false, misleading, or inaccurate information and representations made by others concerning the therapist's qualifications, services, or products.

8.6 Marriage and family therapists make certain that the qualifications of persons in their employ are represented in a manner that is not false, misleading, or deceptive.

8.7 Marriage and family therapists may represent themselves as specializing within a limited area of marriage and family therapy, but only if they have the education and supervised experience in settings which meet recognized professional standards to practice in that specialty area.

Advertising Using AAMFT Designations

8.8 The AAMFT designations of Clinical Member, Approved Supervisor, and Fellow may be used in public information or advertising materials only by persons holding such designations. Persons holding such designations may, for example, advertise in the following manner:

- Jane Doe, Ph.D., a Clinical Member of the American Association for Marriage and Family Therapy.

Alternately, the advertisement could read:

- Jane Doe, Ph.D., AAMFT Clinical Member.
- John Doe, Ph.D., an Approved Supervisor of the American Association for Marriage and Family Therapy.

Alternately, the advertisement could read:

- John Doe, Ph.D., AAMFT Approved Supervisor.
- Jane Doe, Ph.D., a Fellow of the American Association for Marriage and Family Therapy.

Alternately, the advertisement could read:

- Jane Doe, Ph.D., AAMFT Fellow.

More than one designation may be used if held by the AAMFT Member.

8.9   Marriage and family therapists who hold the AAMFT Approved Supervisor or the Fellow designation may not represent the designation as an advanced clinical status.

8.10   Student, Associate, and Affiliate Members may not use their AAMFT membership status in public information or advertising materials. Such listings on professional resumes are not considered advertisements.

8.11   Persons applying for AAMFT membership may not list their application status on any resume or advertisement.

8.12   In conjunction with the AAMFT membership, marriage and family therapists claim as evidence of educational qualifications only those degrees (a) from regionally accredited institutions or (b) from institutions recognized by states which license or certify marriage and family therapists, but only if such state regulation is recognized by AAMFT.

8.13   Marriage and family therapists may not use the initials AAMFT following their name in the manner of an academic degree.

8.14   Marriage and family therapists may not use the AAMFT name, logo, and/or the abbreviated initials AAMFT or make any other such representation which would imply that they speak for or represent the Association. The Association is the sole owner of its name, logo, and the abbreviated initials AAMFT. Its committees and divisions, operating as such, may use the name, logo, and/or the abbreviated initials AAMFT in accordance with AAMFT policies.

8.15   Authorized advertisements of Clinical Members under the AAMFT name, log, and/or the abbreviated initials AAMFT may include the following: the Clinical Member's name, degree, license or certificate held when required by state law, name of business, address, and telephone number. If a business is listed, it must follow, not precede the Clinical Member's name. Such listings may not include AAMFT offices held by the Clinical Member, nor any specializations, since such a listing under the AAMFT name, logo, and/or the abbreviated initials, AAMFT, would imply that this specialization has been credentialed by AAMFT.

8.16   Marriage and family therapists use their membership in AAMFT only in connection with their clinical and professional activities.

8.17   Only AAMFT divisions and programs accredited by the AAMFT Commission on Accreditation for Marriage and Family Therapy Education, not businesses nor organizations, may use any AAMFT-related designation or affiliation in public information or advertising materials, and then only in accordance with AAMFT policies.

8.18 Programs accredited by the AAMFT Commission on Accreditation for Marriage and Family Therapy Education may not use the AAMFT name, logo, and/or the abbreviated initials AAMFT. Instead, they may have printed on their stationery and other appropriate materials a statement such as:

The (name of program) of the (name of institution) is accredited by the AAMFT Commission on Accreditation for Marriage and Family Therapy Education.

8.19 Programs not accredited by the AAMFT Commission on Accreditation for Marriage and Family Therapy Education may not use the AAMFT name, logo, and/or the abbreviated initials AAMFT. They may not state in printed program materials, program advertisements, and student advisement that their courses and training opportunities are accepted by AAMFT to meet AAMFT membership requirements.

Appendix G

American School Counselor Association, Ethical Standards for School Counselors

Preamble

The American School Counselor Association is a professional organization whose members have a unique and distinctive preparation grounded in the behavioral sciences, with training in clinical skills adapted to the school setting. The counselor assists in the growth and development of each individual and uses his/her highly specialized skills to insure that the rights of the counselee are properly protected within the structure of the school program. School counselors subscribe to the following basic tenets of the counseling process from which professional responsibilities are derived:

1. Each person has the right to respect and dignity as a human being and to counseling services without prejudice as to person, character, belief or practice.
2. Each person has the right to self-direction and self-development.
3. Each person has the right of choice and the responsibility for decisions reached.
4. Each person has the right to privacy and thereby the right to expect the counselor-client relationship to comply with all laws, policies and ethical standards pertaining to confidentiality.

In this document the American School Counselor Association has specified the principles of ethical behavior necessary to maintain and regulate the high standards of integrity and leadership among its members. The Association recognizes the basic commitment of its members to the *Ethical Standards* of its parent organization, the American Association for Counseling and Development (AACD), and nothing in this document shall be construed to supplant that code. *The Ethical Standards for School Counselors* was developed to complement the AACD standards by clarifying the nature of ethical responsibilities of counselors in the school setting. The purposes of the document are to:

1. Serve as a guide for the ethical practices of all school counselors regardless of level, area, population served, or membership in this Association.
2. Provide benchmarks for both self-appraisal and peer evaluations regarding counselor responsibilities to students, parents, colleagues and professional associates, school and community, self, and the counseling profession.

3. Inform those served by the school counselor of acceptable counselor practices and expected professional deportment.

A. Responsibilities to Pupils

The school counselor:

1. Has a primary obligation and loyalty to the pupil who is to be treated with respect as a unique individual, whether assisted individually or in a group setting.
2. Is concerned with the total needs of the student (educational, vocational, personal, and social) and encourages the maximum growth and development of each counselee.
3. Informs the counselee of the purposes, goals, techniques and rules of procedure under which she/he may receive counseling assistance at or before the time when the counseling relationship is entered. Prior notice includes confidentiality issues such as the possible necessity for consulting with other professionals, privileged communication, and legal or authoritative restraints. The meaning and limits of confidentiality are clearly defined to counselees.
4. Refrains from consciously encouraging the counselee's acceptance of values, lifestyles, plans, decisions, and beliefs that represent only the counselor's personal orientation.
5. Is responsible for keeping abreast of laws relating to students and strives to ensure that the rights of students are adequately provided for and protected.
6. Avoids dual relationships which might impair his/her objectivity and/or increase the risk of harm to the client (e.g., counseling one's family members, close friends or associates). If a dual relationship is unavoidable, the counselor is responsible for taking action to eliminate or reduce the potential for harm. Such safeguards might include informed consent, consultation, supervision and documentation.
7. Makes appropriate referrals when professional assistance can no longer be adequately provided to the counselee. Appropriate referral necessitates knowledge of available resources.
8. Protects the confidentiality of student records and releases personal data only according to prescribed laws and school policies. Student information maintained through electronic data storage methods is treated with the same care as traditional student records.
9. Protects the confidentiality of information received in the counseling relationship as specified by law and ethical standards. Such information is only to be revealed to others with informed consent of the counselee and consistent with the obligation of the counselor as a professional person. In a group setting, the counselor sets a norm of confidentiality and stresses its importance, yet clearly states that confidentiality in group counseling cannot be guaranteed.
10. Informs the appropriate authorities when the counselee's condition indicates a clear and imminent danger to the counselee or others. This is to be done after careful deliberation and, where possible, after consultation with other professionals. The counselor informs the counselee of actions to be taken so as to minimize confusion and clarify expectations.
11. Screens prospective group members and maintains an awareness of participants' compatibility throughout the life of the group, especially when the group emphasis is on self-disclosure and self-understanding. The counselor takes reasonable precautions to

protect members from physical and/or psychological harm resulting from interaction within the group.

12. Provides explanations of the nature, purposes and results of tests in language that is understandable to the client(s).

13. Adheres to relevant standards regarding selection, administration, and interpretation of assessment techniques. The counselor recognizes that computer-based testing programs require specific training in administration, scoring and interpretation which may differ from that required in more traditional assessments.

14. Promotes the benefits of appropriate computer applications and clarifies the limitations of computer technology. The counselor ensures that (1) computer applications are appropriate for the individual needs of the counselee, (2) the counselee understands how to use the application, and (3) follow-up counseling assistance is provided. Members of underrepresented groups are assured of equal access to computer technologies and the absence of discriminatory information and values within computer applications.

15. Has unique responsibilities in working with peer programs. In general, the school counselor is responsible for the welfare of students participating in peer programs under his/her direction. School counselors who function in training and supervisory capacities are referred to the preparation and supervision standards of professional counselor associations.

B. Responsibilities to Parents

The school counselor:

1. Respects the inherent rights and responsibilities of parents for their children and endeavors to establish a cooperative relationship with parents to facilitate the maximum development of the counselee.

2. Informs parents of the counselor's role with emphasis on the confidential nature of the counseling relationship between the counselor and counselee.

3. Provides parents with accurate, comprehensive and relevant information in an objective and caring manner, as appropriate and consistent with ethical responsibilities to the counselee.

4. Treats information received from parents in a confidential and appropriate manner.

5. Shares information about a counselee only with those persons properly authorized to receive such information.

6. Adheres to laws and local guidelines when assisting parents experiencing family difficulties which interfere with the counselee's effectiveness and welfare.

7. Is sensitive to changes in the family and recognizes that all parents, custodial and non-custodial, are vested with certain rights and responsibilities for the welfare of their children by virtue of their position and according to law.

C. Responsibilities to Colleagues and Professional Associates

The school counselor:

1. Establishes and maintains a cooperative relationship with faculty, staff, and administration to facilitate the provision of optimum guidance and counseling services.

2. Promotes awareness and adherence to appropriate guidelines regarding confidentiality, the distinction between public and private information and staff consultation.
3. Treats colleagues with respect, courtesy, fairness, and good faith. The qualifications, views and findings of colleagues are represented accurately and fairly to enhance the image of competent professionals.
4. Provides professional personnel with accurate, objective, concise and meaningful data necessary to adequately evaluate, counsel, and assist the counselee.
5. Is aware of and fully utilizes related professions and organizations to whom the counselee may be referred.

D. Responsibilities to the School and Community

The school counselor:

1. Supports and protects the educational program against any infringement not in the best interest of students.
2. Informs appropriate officials of conditions that may be potentially disruptive or damaging to the school's mission, personnel and property.
3. Delineates and promotes the counselor's role and function in meeting the needs of those served. The counselor will notify appropriate officials of conditions which may limit or curtail their effectiveness in providing programs and services.
4. Assists in the development of (1) curricular and environmental conditions appropriate for the school and community, (2) educational procedures and programs to meet student needs, and (3) a systematic evaluation process for guidance and counseling programs, services, and personnel. The counselor is guided by the findings of the evaluation data in planning programs and services.
5. Actively cooperates and collaborates with agencies, organizations, and individuals in the school and community in the best interest of counselees and without regard to personal reward or remuneration.

E. Responsibilities to Self

The school counselor:

1. Functions within the boundaries of individual professional competence and accepts responsibility for the consequences of his/her actions.
2. Is aware of the potential effects of his/her own personal characteristics on services to clients.
3. Monitors personal functioning and effectiveness and refrains from any activity likely to lead to inadequate professional services or harm to a client.
4. Recognizes that differences in clients relating to age, gender, race, religion, sexual orientation, socioeconomic and ethnic backgrounds may require specific training to ensure competent services.
5. Strives through personal initiative to maintain professional competence and keep abreast of innovations and trends in the profession. Professional and personal growth is continuous and ongoing throughout the counselor's career.

F. Responsibilities to the Profession

The school counselor:

1. Conducts herself/himself in such a manner as to bring credit to self and the profession.
2. Conducts appropriate research and reports findings in a manner consistent with acceptable educational and psychological research practices. When using client data for research, statistical or program planning purposes, the counselor ensures protection of the identity of the individual client(s).
3. Actively participates in local, state and national associations which foster the development and improvement of school counseling.
4. Adhere to ethical standards of the profession, other official policy statements pertaining to counseling, and relevant statutes established by federal, state and local governments.
5. Clearly distinguishes between statements and actions made as a private individual and as a representative of the school counseling profession.
6. Contributes to the development of the profession through the sharing of skills, ideas and expertise with colleagues.

G. Maintenance of Standards

Ethical behavior among professional school counselors, Association members and nonmembers, is expected at all times. When there exists serious doubt as to the ethical behavior of colleagues, or if counselors are forced to work in situations or abide by policies which do not reflect the standards as outlined in these Ethical Standards for School Counselors or the ACA Ethical Standards, the counselor is obligated to take appropriate action to rectify the condition. The following procedure may serve as a guide:

1. If feasible, the counselor should consult with a professional colleague to confidentially discuss the nature of the complaint to see if he/she views the situation as an ethical violation.
2. Whenever possible, the counselor should directly approach the colleague whose behavior is in question to discuss the complaint and seek resolution.
3. If resolution is not forthcoming at the personal level, the counselor shall utilize the channels established within the school and/or school district. This may include both informal and formal procedures.
4. If the matter still remains unresolved, referral for review and appropriate action should be made to the Ethics Committees in the following sequence: local counselor association, state counselor association, national counselor association.
5. The ASCA Ethics Committee functions as an educative and consultative capacity and does not adjudicate complaints of ethical misconduct. Therefore, at the national level, complaints should be submitted in writing to the ACA Ethics Committee for review and appropriate action. The procedure for submitting complaints may be obtained by writing the ACA Ethics Committee, c/o The Executive Director, American Counseling Association, 5999 Stevenson Avenue, Alexandria, VA 22304.

H. Resources

School counselors are responsible for being aware of, and acting in accord with, the standards and positions of the counseling profession as represented in official documents such as those listed below:

Code of Ethics (1989). National Board for Certified Counselors. Alexandria, VA.

Code of Ethics for Peer Helping Professionals (1989). National Peer Helpers Association. Glendale, CA.

Ethical Guidelines for Group Counselors (1989). Association for Specialists in Group Work. Alexandria, VA.

Ethical Standards (1988). American Association for Counseling and Development. Alexandria, VA.

Position Statement: The School Counselor and Confidentiality (1986). American School Counselor Association. Alexandria, VA.

Position Statement: The School Counselor and Peer Facilitation (1984). American School Counselor Association. Alexandria, VA.

Position Statement: The School Counselor and Student Rights (1992). American School Counselor Association. Alexandria, VA.

Ethical Standards for School Counselors was adopted by the ASCA Delegate Assembly, March 19, 1984. This revision was approved by the ASCA Delegate Assembly, March 27, 1992.

As of July 1, 1992 the American Association for Counseling and Development (AACD) becomes the American Counseling Association (ACA).

Author Index

Subject Index